Europe in the 20th Century
Volume 2   1914-25

Readings in 20th Century History

General Editor: Dr. J. M. Roberts

Taplinger Publishing Company
New York

First Published in the United States in 1971 by
TAPLINGER PUBLISHING CO. INC.
New York, New York

Copyright © 1971 B.P.C. Publishing

International Standard Book Number
0-8008-2524-1

Library of Congress Catalog Card
Number 79-144351

Printed in Great Britain

Contents

Volume II · Part one
The Opening Moves

At the outbreak of the First World War it was almost universally assumed that this was to be a short-lived affair. Kitchener was one of few who foresaw a long struggle: both the French and German staffs looked forward to being back home 'before the leaves fall'. Such, after all, was then the pattern of modern war. This meant that much that was to turn out to be of crucial importance in deciding the eventual outcome of the war was not initially apparent: not only rapid mobilization and immediate firepower would count but also long-term economic and financial resources. As first months and then years went by, this was to become increasingly a struggle between whole societies organized for war-making. The concept of the 'nation under arms' was of course not new (indeed, in the German empire almost every fit man of military age belonged, in theory, to the army); but in 1914 it was a concept that aimed rather at putting the maximum number of men immediately into the field than at keeping them there indefinitely.

For Germany, General von Schlieffen, chief of the general staff from 1892 to 1905, had laid down the strategy for a war of movement against France: a German army, strengthened from the first with reserve divisions, was to sweep swiftly through Belgium and encircle Paris from the west. In the event, Moltke, chief of the general staff in 1914, had begun to meddle with the Schlieffen Plan even before his armies went into action. The right wing of Schlieffen's plan had already been weakened; Moltke continued to meddle as the campaign opened, reducing the immediate striking power of Germany in the west. Perhaps his worst blunder came on 25th August, when he detached two infantry corps from their key position on the German right wing, in response to a panic call from his eastern front. These two corps, which spent crucial days shunting through Germany towards a front where they were no longer needed, would have been sufficient to plug the famous 'gap' that opened up in the German advance on the Marne. As it was, the way was open for a French and British counter-attack. From having total victory within their grasp, the Germans were driven back into northernmost France.

The French were as determined as the Germans that this was to be a war of movement. They held as to an article of faith to the belief that attack, pressed home at whatever cost, was the key to success. *Elan* was all, and determination more important than tactics. And so the French infantry, bravely but swelteringly accoutred in their traditional uniforms of red and blue, marched out to employ tactics of attack similar to those with which the Napoleonic armies had failed against Wellington. The failure of Joffre's first offensive against the German centre put his left wing into an increasingly untenable position. By 23rd August it was in retreat. The British Expeditionary Force had been in action around Mons, plugging the gap between the French and the sea, and already had impressed the Germans with the speed and accuracy of their rifle-fire. When, unforewarned, they found the French were moving back they too had to retreat. From the consequences of this situation the French and British were saved by the German errors on the Marne—errors which, arguably, they in their turn failed to exploit to the full. On both sides the objectives of 1914 were unachieved. As for the doctrine of a war of movement, commanders who had been fervent in advocacy seemed less sure in execution. By the end of the year warfare on the Western Front had run itself into the ground.

Misguided though he may have been in diverting troops from the Western Front, Moltke had reason enough that August to be perturbed at happenings in the east. While Germany looked to her Austro-Hungarian allies to take the main initiative in the east, Russia was urged by the exhortations of France into making a swift assault upon East Prussia. With her population of 167,000,000, Russia looked a formidable adversary. Yet her weaknesses were swiftly apparent. Poor communications and a grudging treasury limited the immediate and the long-term effectiveness of her army. An economy excessively dependent on manual labour was excessively vulnerable to the siphoning off of manpower into the armed forces. Whereas Russian plans provided for the immediate deployment of thirty corps, containing some 2,700,000 men, three weeks after mobilization less than half of these had appeared, and what men there were in the field soon found themselves short of arms and supplies. Nevertheless the advance of two Russian armies into East Prussia seemed to paralyse the defences, and it took a change of German command to retrieve the situation. While the Russians prepared to execute a pincer movement, the newly-appointed General Paul von Hindenburg was able to exploit the internal communications that were the acknowledged defensive strength of East Prussia and deploy his army so as to fall with terrible effect on first one and then the other arm of the Russian pincers. At grievous cost the Russians struggled back eastwards; but they had at least performed for their allies the strategic service of preventing the Germans from fighting with full strength on the Western Front.

In Galicia, however, Russia was on the verge of triumph. There they confronted the putative might of the Austro-Hungarian Empire, whose forces rose on mobilization to some 3,000,000 men. That army, though for many it epitomized the ideal of a supra-national society, was as a fighting machine untested and cumbersome. Its command was wedded to the fashionable principles of attack, which its troops had neither the training nor the morale to put into effect. Faced with the Russians, the whole Austro-Hungarian front quaked and collapsed. Withdrawal became a rout and for Russia the path to Silesia — to Germany itself — lay open. Again, Hindenburg retrieved the situation for Germany. Fresh from his triumphs in East Prussia, he showed the same skills in striking back at the Russians in Galicia. Though he failed to achieve the conclusive victory that was his ambition, he effectively stifled the Russian offensive. With the onset of winter, fighting on this front too came to a standstill.

Equally disastrous for the Austro-Hungarians was their assault on Serbia. Full of confidence they crossed the river Sava on 11th August planning to destroy this 'nation of pig-breeders' with an enveloping movement from the west and north-west. Though fighting on their natural terrain and though inflicting terrifying losses on the Austrians, the Serbs were pushed back into the rain-swept Balkan mountains. By the end of November the Austrians believed it was all over; by 13th December what remained of their army was streaming in panic back across the Sava. Contrary to all reason and all the rules of the war, the little Serbian army, decimated, hungry and almost out of ammunition, had hurled itself back in a direct frontal assault on the Austrian lines — and routed them utterly.

For Germany 1914 was a disappointing introduction to the abilities of her comrades-in-arms. She was disappointed too in her initial expectation of another ally in the west. At the time war broke out, Italy had for thirty years been joined to Austria-Hungary and Germany by the Triple Alliance of 1882. But the war found Italy unprepared. Italian political parties were broadly divided into two blocks, of whom the establishment parties generally favoured the Central Powers, while the radicals were mostly against war on anyone's behalf. Indecision was followed by a declaration of neutrality, neutrality by a willingness to trade promises of alignment for promises of territorial concessions. This Britain and France were prepared to do, and on 24th May 1915, in response to the guarantees incorporated in the Treaty of London and in the expectation of a short and profitable war, Italy took up arms against Austria-Hungary.

The Adversaries

Major-General Moulton

George Stephenson and General Lazare Carnot could well be called the grandfathers, or perhaps the great grandfathers, of the European military system of 1914. From the French Revolution and from Carnot, who had built the armies Napoleon used, came the concept of the nation in arms – so-called, though it would be more accurate to call it the concept of 'the whole manpower of the nation in the army'. Under Napoleon this system had overwhelmed the armies of the old regime. To save themselves the other great continental powers had been forced to adopt it, but once peace was re-established, a military as well as a political reaction had set in, and armies had reverted to traditionalism and long-service professionalism.

In 1857 Prince Wilhelm, Regent of Prussia, appointed General Helmuth von Moltke chief of general staff of his army, and, in 1859, another reforming general, Albrecht von Roon, minister for war. Meeting bitter political opposition to army reform, Roon suggested the appointment of Bismarck as minister-president. Under these four, Wilhelm, soon King of Prussia, Bismarck, Moltke, and Roon, the nation in arms idea re-appeared in Prussia and there reached its prime. In 1866 the Prussians quickly and decisively defeated the old-style Austrian army, then, in 1870 at the head of the North German Confederation, overwhelmed the French.

Roon in 1870 put 1,183,400 officers and men into the field. Moltke had been a pupil of Clausewitz, but he could not have handled effectively and rapidly an army of this size if there had not been two vital technical advances. First, the development of agriculture and industry had provided the means to feed, arm, and equip great numbers, and indeed produced the larger populations from which they sprang. Second, railways could now assemble this massed manpower along frontiers, supply it, and effect further strategic movements as needed. Deeply impressed by the events of 1866 and 1870, the armies of continental Europe made haste to imitate the Prussian model.

The weapons of 1870 were a marked advance on those used in the Napoleonic Wars. By 1914 weapons had been further developed. Not at the pace to which we are accustomed today, but faster than at any previous time in history. The magazine rifle, the machine-gun, and the breech-loading quick-firing field gun, especially, had been perfected since 1870. But, partly because the internal combustion engine was still in its childhood, and much more because soldiers and statesmen in power are inherently prejudiced against change, no new military system had appeared. Strategy remained a strategy dependent on railways. Movement at the 15-20 mph of the troop train became movement at the age-old 15-20 miles a day, normal march for men and horsedrawn transport, as soon as contact with the enemy became likely. Tactical theory, recoiling from the ugly lessons of 1870 and of the American Civil War of 1861-65, had gone into reverse, and reflected ideas that had already started to be out of date in the days of muzzle-loaders.

The German Aufmarsch
The German empire, proclaimed in the Hall of Mirrors, Versailles in 1871, had in 1914 a population of over 65,000,000. In theory, except for the small number required by the navy, all fit men of military age belonged to the army. Called up each year, from the age of seventeen to twenty they were enrolled in the *Landsturm*, Class I. At twenty those who were fit joined the active army for two-years' service, or the cavalry and horse artillery for three. Afterwards they went into the Reserve for five years (in the case of the cavalry and horse artillery for four years). In practice, the active army could only take about half the annual call-up, and the surplus, together with those excused for other reasons, was enrolled in the *Ersatz* Reserve, receiving, at best, very limited training. From the age of twenty-seven to thirty-nine, all served

in the *Landwehr,* then from thirty-nine to forty-five in the *Landsturm,* Class II.

The active army of twenty-five and a half army corps — each of two divisions — and eleven cavalry divisions was maintained at fifty to sixty per cent war strength. In addition, there were thirty-two reserve, seven *Ersatz* reserve and the equivalent of sixteen *Landwehr* divisions.

Mobilization was a vast and critical operation, during which the army would be largely ineffective as a fighting machine. Nor did it end there, for the army must be deployed, which in 1914 meant deployment by rail. This operation, the *Aufmarsch,* was vital and planned with at least as much care as mobilization itself, for on it would hang the success of the opening campaign and, it was thought, of the war. Mobilization must be ordered in time so that the enemy could not establish a lead, and once ordered it led inevitably to the *Aufmarsch.* The armies could perhaps then be halted on the frontier, but the possibility was not seriously canvassed, and in 1914 mobilization spelled war.

Schlieffen's strategy

To this pattern, almost standard in Europe, the Germans had made two exceptions. Seeking to achieve crushing superiority for a quick victory against France in a war on two fronts, General von Schlieffen, chief of the general staff from 1892 to 1905, had planned to use reserve and *Ersatz* reserve divisions in the opening battles, relying on the well-trained regular and reserve officers and on strong cadres of regular non-commissioned officers to make good the reserves' deficiencies of training. Secondly, six infantry brigades with attached cavalry, artillery, and pioneers were maintained in peace at war strength and quartered close to the Belgian frontier, ready to seize the Liége forts and open the way through Belgium to northern France as soon as war was declared.

The peacetime strength of the army in 1914 was 856,000. On mobilization, trained reserves would bring it up to 3,800,000, but in emergency a maximum of 8,500,000 could be called to the colours. Against France seven armies would be deployed, totalling thirty-four army corps — of which eleven were reserve formations — and four cavalry corps. In the east, the VIII Army — four army corps of which one was a reserve corps with cavalry and some *Landwehr* — comprised some 200,000 and would hold off the Russians as best it could. There were other garrisons, depots, and reserves, and in Schleswig-Holstein a reserve army corps was held back in case the British attempted a landing.

Despite their defeat in 1870, the French had given the Germans more than one sharp lesson about the power of the breech-loading rifle against men in the open, and in their training afterwards the Germans took modern fire power seriously. When the machine-gun was perfected, the Germans took it up more seriously than other armies. Schlieffen's strategic plan to envelop the French armies by a massive advance through Belgium stemmed from his realization that frontal attack would be costly and indecisive. Watching the German manoeuvres of 1895, an expert British observer wrote that the soldiers '. . . act like intelligent beings, who thoroughly understand their duty, and the fact speaks volumes for the way in which even privates are taught to use their initiative'.

But as the years passed, memories of 1870 faded and traditionalism and arrogance asserted themselves. The Germans remained good soldiers, but of the manoeuvres of 1911, Colonel Repington of *The Times* wrote, 'there is insufficient test of the initiative of commanders of any units large or small . . . The infantry lack dash and display no knowledge of the ground . . . offer vulnerable targets at medium ranges . . . are not trained to understand the connection between fire and movement and seem totally unaware of the effect of modern fire'.

In theory the vain and unstable Wilhelm ·II would command in war, and as late as 1908 he frequently spoke of actually doing so. He lacked his grandfather's serious interest in military affairs, revelling in display rather than warlike efficiency. Schlieffen pandered to him with military spectacle, cavalry charges, and unrealistic victories in manoeuvres and war games. General von Moltke, nephew of the great Moltke and also a Helmuth, who became chief of general staff at the beginning of 1906, refused to do so. Artistic, doubting his own military ability, obsessed by fear of revolution, he had accepted the appointment in the belief that he would not be called upon to command in war. Lacking the conviction and force of character needed to carry through the Schlieffen Plan, he tampered with it, weakening the enveloping right wing, strengthening the holding left and the Eastern Front. In war games he accepted frontal offensives as practicable. In 1914 he was sixty-six, in poor health, past the work to which he had never been equal.

Below him came the army commanders: on the vital right wing, commanding the I, II and III Armies respectively, a trio of sixty-eight-year-olds, Generals von Kluck, von Bülow, and von Hausen, hard men, drivers—especially Kluck, brutal, a little brittle in crisis. Next came a trio of royals: the Duke of Württemberg commanding the IV Army; the Crown Prince, the V; Prince Rupprecht of Bavaria, the VI; then finally von Heeringen, sixty-four, ex-minister for war, the VII. In the Prussian tradition their chiefs of staff supported them with authority almost equal to theirs. Commanding the VIII Army in East Prussia was General von Prittwitz und Gaffron, sixty-six, fat, self-important, indolent, with connections so far proof against Moltke's wish to remove him. Major-General Ludendorff, forty-nine—his name was unadorned with the aristocratic von—was assistant chief of staff of the II Army, having lost the key post of head of the deployment section under Moltke for too much insistence on increasing the intake of the army.

The populations of France and the North German Confederation had in 1870 been approximately equal, but by 1914, while the population of the German empire had risen to over 65,000,000, that of France was still under 40,000,000. The disparity dominated French strategic thinking, and, with tragic irony, led in the end to a military creed savagely extravagant of human life.

France had astonished the world with the speed of her recovery after 1870. She had re-organized her army on the Prussian model with short service and a powerful general staff. Where the loss of Alsace and Lorraine had laid open her eastern frontier, she had built a strong fortified line stretching from Belfort to Verdun. At the turn of the century the army had been racked and discredited by the Dreyfus Affair. In 1905 military service had been cut down to two years. Confronted with the rising menace of Germany, the prestige of the army and willingness to serve in it re-covered, and in 1913 service was restored to three years. After that men served in the Reserve, the Territorial Army and the Territorial Reserve for varying periods up to the age of forty-eight.

In July 1914 the peace strength of the French army was 736,000. On mobilization it rose to 3,500,000, of which some 1,700,000 were in the field army of five armies, in all twenty-one army corps, plus two colonial, three independent, ten cavalry, and twenty-five reserve divisions, the rest in territorials, garrisons, and depots. The five armies stretched from the Swiss frontier, where the 1st Army had its right at Belfort, to a third of the way along the Belgian frontier, where the left of the 5th was near Hirson. Beyond that was a cavalry corps of three divisions. A German offensive from Metz would thus be covered, but one through Belgium would meet only a weak cavalry screen.

French élan

The French, however, had no intention of waiting for any offensive to develop, for the army had persuaded itself that the disasters of 1870 had been due to lack of offensive spirit on their side. Looking back to Napoleonic and even earlier battles, the army had become imbued with mystical faith in the attack, pressed home regardless of cost, as the answer to all military problems. To ensure its élan, when the Germans went sensibly into field grey, the French had retained the traditional long blue coats and bright red trousers of their infantry. More practical matters were neglected, and the French infantryman wore his long coat and heavy military underwear even in the heat of August, his boots were hard, and a load of sixty-six pounds was piled on him compared to the German's fifty-six.

For fire power, the French relied on the rifle and the 75-mm field gun, an outstanding weapon produced in large numbers. Machine-guns were neglected. As for tactics, 'Success depends,' said the manual of 1913, 'far more on forcefulness and tenacity than upon tactical skill.' Luckily the French soldier was not only brave but also adaptable and able to learn quickly, while the colonial empire, which during the war would supply 500,000 men, was available to replace some of the first shattering losses.

General Joffre, sixty-two, was vice-president of the war council, earmarked as commander-in-chief on an outbreak of war. He had been appointed in 1911, largely because the disciples of attack wished to get rid of his predecessor. Ponderous, very taciturn but a good listener, veteran of colonial service, he had no strong views on strategy or tactics, but was an engineer, and expert in military movement. He was to prove imperturbable and able in crisis, but did nothing before the war to check the ideas and plans that made crisis inevitable when war came. Galliéni, Joffre's superior in the colonies, more alert and realistic, had refused the appointment, and was now without military employment.

Of the army commanders, Lanrezac of the 5th Army, brilliant, pessimistic, impatient, and outspoken, was thought of by many as Joffre's eventual successor. Foch, responsible as commandant of the staff college for spreading the doctrine of attack, was a corps commander. Like Joffre he would be strong in crisis, and had in Weygand a chief of staff who could translate his wishes into clear orders. Pétain, out of favour for his realistic belief in fire power, commanded a division.

Neutral Belgians: British 'mercenaries'

Standing in the path of the main German thrust, Belgium deployed a field army of six infantry divisions totalling some 117,000 men, and three fortress garrisons, Antwerp, Liége, and Namur. Because Belgium was neutral, two infantry divisions faced France, one at Antwerp, Great Britain, one at Liége, Germany, with the rest in central reserve.

Relying on her neutrality, Belgium had neglected her army. Service in it was unpopular, training severely limited, morale poor, the officer corps seriously disunited. The fortresses were obsolete, improvements planned in 1882 were still incomplete and had by now been themselves overtaken by weapon development. There was one bright spot, however. King Albert, thirty-nine, was intelligent and brave, and he had great personal integrity. He did not control the army in peace, but when war came he was obliged by the constitution to command it.

The British, as is their habit, were in two minds about sending an army to the Continent at all. In 1908 Haldane had reorganized the British army, forming the units at home into an Expeditionary Force, six infantry and one cavalry division totalling some 160,000 men, capable of supporting either the garrisons of the empire or a Continental ally. In 1905 staff talks with the French had been authorized, but had languished until, early in 1911, the francophile Major-General Henry Wilson had come to the War Office as director of military operations. That August the Agadir Crisis had revealed an alarming divergence of war plans between the War Office, where Wilson had made detailed arrangements with the French for the deployment of the Expeditionary Force on the left of the 5th Army, and the Admiralty, which strongly opposed continental commitment of the army, though it did not have a properly worked out proposal to put in place of Henry Wilson's. The Council of Imperial Defence had deferred formal decision, but allowed the War Office to continue planning with the French.

When in 1914 war was declared, there were those who thought that the Expeditionary Force should remain in Great Britain, or should go direct to Belgium in fulfilment of the British guarantee of neutrality, but it was too late now to change, and on 6th August the cabinet decided that it should go to France as planned, but without two of its divisions which would for the present remain in Great Britain.

Although small, the British army was well-trained and equipped. On the South African veldt Boer bullets had taught it something of the reality of fire power. Now the marksmanship of the infantry was in an entirely different class from that of continental armies. The cavalry, too, were armed with a proper rifle, not the neglected carbine of continental cavalry, and knew how to use it, but there peacetime reaction was setting in and the glamorous, futile charge coming back into fashion.

Called by the Germans an army of mercenaries and, more flatteringly, a perfect thing apart, the British army was recruited from volunteers, who enlisted for seven years followed by five in the reserve. Each battalion at home found drafts for another in the overseas empire, so that its men were often raw and its numbers short. There were experienced men in the divisions that went to France, but to see them all as hardened professionals is a mistake;

some were young soldiers, others reservists grown soft in civil life.

Continuing an old tradition in modern shape, the Territorial Force and the Yeomanry had been organized by Haldane into a second-line army of fourteen divisions, far from fully trained or equipped, but a good deal more effective than many realized. Beyond that there were the older reservists and the militia for replacements, and the distant imperial garrisons and armies of India and the dominions.

Field Marshal Sir John French, commander-in-chief, British Expeditionary Force, had been a successful cavalry commander in South Africa, but at sixty-two was showing his age. Lieutenant-General Sir Douglas Haig, commanding the 1st Corps, French's chief-of-staff in South Africa and Haldane's assistant in the subsequent reforms, was able and ambitious, but inflexible and wedded to cavalry doctrine. Kitchener, now secretary of state for war, a tremendous national figure, had flashes of insight amounting almost to genius but little appreciation of staff organization or civilian control. In general, British officers were efficient and devoted but narrow in outlook. However, a far higher proportion of them than of officers in France and Germany had experienced the reality of war.

The armies in the East

With the main German strength committed in the west, the clash in the east would be between Austria-Hungary and Russia. Austria had been worsted by the French in 1859, and in 1866 trounced by Prussia. Since then the army had been reformed on the Prussian model, but not for forty-eight years tested in war.

The population, 50,000,000 in 1914, was a complex racial mixture. Germans were the ruling group in Austria, Magyars in Hungary; Poles in Austria and Croats in Hungary had special privileges; Ruthenes, Czechs, Slovaks, Slovenes, Serbs, Italians, and Rumanians were potentially disaffected. Languages, literacy, religions, and racial characteristics differed widely. Slav races formed two-thirds of the infantry, and the Germans in charge notoriously lacked the high martial seriousness of the Prussians. Yet, if the sottish chaos described by Jaroslav Hašek, a Czech writer, in *The Good Soldier Schweik,*

typified one side of the coin, there was another: to many the army stood for an ideal of the empire as a supra-national society.

At the beginning of 1914 the peace strength of the Austro-Hungarian army was some 450,000. On mobilization it rose to over 3,000,000, of which some 1,800,000 formed the field army of six armies, in all sixteen army corps—mostly of three divisions, some of them reserve divisions—and eleven cavalry divisions. In a war against Serbia, the III, V, and VI Armies would be deployed in the south, according to Plan B (Balkans); but in a war against Russia and Serbia, Plan R, the III Army would be deployed northeast with I, II, and IV in the Galician plain beyond the Carpathian mountains. By ordering partial mobilization on 25th July the army was committed to Plan B, until the III Army could be recalled from the Serbian front.

General Conrad von Hötzendorf, chief of general staff, sixty-two, a cavalryman, hard working, spartan, a writer on tactics and training, was, like Foch, a firm apostle of the offensive. His recipe for victory against Russia was an early attack before the vast manpower of the enemy could be brought into action, but that plan was now seriously compromised by partial mobilization. Conrad would command the northern armies, General Potiorek, another spartan, keen, vain, incompetent, with powerful court connections, responsible for the muddle that had given the Sarajevo assassins their chance, would command against Serbia.

Although Russia went to war to rescue Serbia, the Serbian army, under Marshal Putnik, 190,000 strong, organized in three armies each little stronger than an Austrian corps, was in grave danger of being overwhelmed before help could become effective. Leaving delaying detachments on the frontier, it assembled in north Serbia, ready to deploy wherever the attack came. It had fought in the Balkan Wars of 1912 and 1913. Its men were seasoned, inspired by fierce patriotism, and looked back undaunted on generations of relentless warfare. The prospect of engaging it in its native mountains might have given pause to better soldiers than Conrad and Potiorek.

The Russian masses

For Russia, whose population numbered 167,000,000, manpower seemed the least of her problems. Bad roads, scant railways, low industrial capacity, poor standards of education and literacy, and a grudging treasury limited the size and effectiveness of her army. Later it would appear that so much of the Russian economy depended on sheer manual labour, that it would suffer disproportionately from withdrawal of manpower. For the moment, the great distances and bad communications slowed mobilization. Officer and non-commissioned officer cadres were weak in numbers and education, weapons, and equipment were in short supply, ammunition reserves set low, manufacture severely restricted.

Russia had fought Japan in Manchuria in 1904-05 and had been worsted. Since then efforts had been made with the aid of large loans from France to modernize the army, but the combination of vast numbers and restricted resources had prevented it reaching the standard of Western armies of the day. In such choice as there was between quantity and quality, Russia had chosen quantity, instinctively believing that sheer numbers would bring victory. While a Russian division had sixteen battalions against a German division's twelve, its fighting power was only about half that of the German.

The peace strength of the Russian army was 1,423,000. On mobilization, three million men were called up at once, with 3,500,000 more to follow before the end of November. There were thirty-seven corps, mostly of two divisions, and in all seventy first-line divisions, nineteen independent brigades, thirty-five reserve divisions, twenty-four cavalry and Cossack divisions with twelve reserve.

It was planned to deploy thirty corps — ninety-five infantry and thirty-seven cavalry divisions, some 2,700,000 men — against Germany and Austria, but of these only fifty-two divisions could appear by the twenty-third day of mobilization (22nd August). Two armies, the 1st and 2nd, would face East Prussia; three, the 5th, 3rd and 8th, Austria. Another, the 4th, would deploy against Germany (Plan G), if the main German strength came east, or against Austria (Plan A), if it struck west against France. Two more armies watched the Baltic and Caucasian flanks. General mobilization was ordered on 29th July, and on 6th August, deployment on Plan A.

General Sukhomlinov, minister for war since 1909, had been an energetic reorganizer, backed by the Tsar; he was corrupt, possibly pro-German, and a military reactionary, boasting that he had not read a manual for twenty-five years. Grand Duke Nicholas, commander-in-chief, fifty-eight, an imposing figure six-foot-six tall, was a champion of reform and opposed by Sukhomlinov. The jealousy of his nephew, the Tsar, had kept him from the Russo-Japanese War, depriving him of the chance to prove his worth as a commander, but also keeping him free of blame for the defeat. General Zhilinsky, commanding against East Prussia, had visited France in 1912 when chief of general staff, and had absorbed Foch's military beliefs, while also becoming personally committed to Russia's undertaking for an early advance against Germany.

Almost from the moment of declaration of war, France began to urge Russia to make this advance quickly and in strength. Russia responded gallantly, sacrificing her chance of massive deployment before action. Perhaps it need hardly be added that in Russia, as elsewhere, progressives and reactionaries were agreed on one thing, their faith in the offensive.

The Battle for Northern France

Brigadier Peter Young

At the outbreak of the First World War both the German and the French general staffs looked forward to a quick war – 'home before the leaves fall'. After all, the last two major European wars, the Austro-Prussian (1866) and the Franco-Prussian (1870-71), had been quick, decisive wars of 'movement'. Few foretold anything different on 3rd August 1914. And, indeed, the opening phase of the war, the struggle for northern France, began in traditional style. For Germany a knock-out blow, as prescribed by the Schlieffen Plan, was essential if she were to avoid a two-front war against France and Russia. The French hoped that the pattern of offensives called for by Plan 17 would bring a quick recovery of the lost provinces, Alsace and Lorraine.

The French plan

But the battle did not proceed according to plan. That was hardly surprising in so far as France was concerned, since Plan 17, based on wishful thinking, made assumptions which were wholly unjustifiable. It was considered that even should the Germans violate Belgian neutrality, they would not be able to extend their offensive dispositions north of Luxembourg. This deduction led the French to concentrate their five armies between Belfort and Mézières, leaving a gap of 125 miles between their left and the sea. Nor can this be excused by saying that they counted on the British Expeditionary Force and the Belgians to hold this gap, for no arrangements could be made with neutral Belgium, while the BEF was to arrive in France in total ignorance of its allies' intentions. In defence of Plan 17 it should be pointed out that a move westward to the Sambre, about eighty-five

miles from the sea, was envisaged in the plan – and anyway, a concentration of forces on the Belgian frontier would have looked very curious in peacetime. Even so, at the tactical level, the French doctrine was thoroughly unsound. The *'offensive à outrance'* – all-out attack with the bayonet – was the ideal, but it was a system which had not even worked in the days when Wellington's line used to shatter Napoleon's column by its concentrated fire. There had been no war with Germany for forty-four years and it is understandable that training should have become unrealistic. Still, a careful study of the South African and Russo-Japanese Wars might have saved the lives of many of the 300,000 Frenchmen who fell in August 1914. But whatever their disadvantages, the French had one great asset: the monumental calm of their phlegmatic commander, General Joffre. (This quality was to compensate for his manifest faults.)

The German plan

The German plan, calling for a great enveloping movement round the French left wing, seemed far from being unrealistic. By including twelve reserve corps in their order of battle the Germans were able to deceive the French as to their numbers, and had the younger Moltke, the chief of the general staff, had anything of the genius for war displayed by his uncle, the victor of 1866 and 1870, the campaign of 1914 might well have ended in the fall of Paris and the rout of the French armies. The unprincipled decision to invade Belgium added the BEF and the Belgian army to Joffre's order of battle and went some way towards redressing the balance of numbers. But these reinforcements were far from being sufficient to turn the tide against the Germans. In truth, they had no worse enemy than their elderly commander, who besides continually tinkering with the Schlieffen Plan, never had that firm control of the battle which is the hallmark of military greatness. It may also be that the Germans paid insufficient attention to the problem of supplying their strong right wing.

At the tactical level the Germans were certainly superior to the French, handling their machine-guns and heavy artillery to much better effect. Their infantry were rather inclined to bunch, a fault which had not been sufficiently checked at manoeuvres, and therefore paid a heavy price for their advances.

Army commanders on both sides, except for the princes among them, were rather elderly by modern standards, and two at least — Moltke, and French, in command of the BEF, who had suffered a mild stroke — should never have passed the doctor.

The strategic moves of both sides were governed by their relative slowness once they were beyond the railways. When a corps could make only fifteen to twenty miles in a day, and had no motor transport to lift it, it behoved the staff to see that they really marched them to the right place. False moves were paid for by the exhaustion of the men, and a decline in morale. To many the *pavé* roads of northern France were far more terrible than a brisk skirmish.

Few military plans survive the opening phases of a battle, since commanders have to improvise as their opponents' moves interfere with their cherished combinations. In 1914 the Germans managed to adhere to their plan for considerably longer than their enemies, for the French plan came unstuck in about five days.

The Germans were first off the mark. On 5th August Kluck's I Army attacked the Belgian fortress of Liége, whose reduction was a necessary preliminary to the deployment south and south-west across Belgium of the two northernmost German armies. The Belgian garrison under Lieutenant-General Leman put up a spirited resistance. Unfortunately, however, the forts, built twenty years earlier, had not been connected by a trench system as planned by their constructor, the famous engineer, Brialmont. As a result the Germans penetrated the line by a night attack and took the city. This daring exploit very nearly went wrong, but General Ludendorff took command of a lost brigade and seized the citadel on 7th August. The forts had still to be reduced, but they were smashed by the huge Austrian 42-cm. Skoda howitzers — and by 14th August the German columns were pouring through the city. The last fort fell on the 16th.

The French wings had begun to probe forward as early as 6th August. On the left General Sordet's cavalry corps got within nine miles of Liége, but did little

to dispel the fog of war, because the area explored was as yet unoccupied by the Germans. On the extreme right a detachment of Dubail's army made a brief foray into Alsace.

By 16th August it was clear at Joffre's headquarters that seven or eight German corps and four cavalry divisions were pushing westwards between Givet and Brussels 'and even beyond these points'. It was thought that there were six or seven corps and two or three cavalry divisions between Bastogne and Thionville. South of Metz the Germans appeared to be acting on the defensive. While this intelligence was not inaccurate the presence of reserve corps had not yet been discovered.

Joffre's offensive fails
Joffre now planned to take the offensive, intending to break the German centre, and then to fall upon their advanced right wing. His plan was decidedly optimistic. He had no reason to suppose that his centre outnumbered Moltke's and, therefore, he should not have counted on a break-through.

The French offensive opened in the south where for several days Prince Rupprecht of Bavaria fell back according to plan, until early on the 20th he counter-attacked in the battles of Sarrebourg and Morhange. The French 2nd Army was driven back and the 1st conformed to its movement, though it struck back on the 25th and checked the pursuit. Eventually the front became stabilized just inside the French frontier.

The ill success of his right wing was not enough to alert Joffre, whose early service had been in the engineers, to the shortcomings of French infantry training. On 21st August the 3rd and 4th Armies crossed the frontier and after an advance of some ten or fifteen miles the heads of their columns ran broadside on into the German armies of the Crown Prince and the Duke of Württemberg in slightly superior force, which were crossing their front. In the actions at Virton, Tintigny, Rossignol, and Neufchateau they were defeated with heavy loss especially in officers – it was a point of honour with the latest 'promotion' from St Cyr to wear white gloves and their full-dress shakos for their 'baptism of fire'. It is understandable that, caught in the narrow wooded defiles of the Ardennes, the French had been unable to employ their artillery to much purpose. They fell back to the Meuse. Joffre's bid to break the German centre had collapsed.

The real trouble was that the infantry ignored the basic tactical principle known as 'fire and movement', by which, even in those distant days, sub-units helped each other forward, engaging the enemy with aimed fire. Here the unreasoning belief in the bayonet took its toll of French manhood. Had it not been for a premature attempt at an enveloping movement by the Crown Prince the disaster to the French might have been still worse. German casualties were also heavy, especially when their columns exposed themselves to the fire of the 75s.

BEF goes into action

On 21st August the BEF, which had begun to mobilize on the 5th and had crossed the Channel without the least interruption from the German navy, was approaching the Mons-Condé Canal. By this time the situation was that the Belgian field army had been driven back into the fortress of Antwerp, though not before inflicting considerable delay on the Germans, notably in the action at Haelen on 18th August, a check which may account for the undue caution of the German cavalry in the fighting that followed.

Of the Allied armies only those under Lanrezac and French had so far escaped a mauling. The Allies' strategic situation was hardly brilliant at the moment when the BEF stepped upon the stage. The Schlieffen Plan was unrolling itself with something like clockwork precision. The only real hitch had been the failure to drive the Belgian field army away from Antwerp. This had compelled them to employ two corps in investing that city. Victory was within Moltke's grasp. Without the four divisions of the BEF which lay that night (21st August) with its outposts overlooking Marlborough's old battlefield of Malplaquet (1709) Joffre, for all his iron nerve and relentless will, could never have turned the tide which was running so strongly against him.

The BEF was in action next day. From the first, British musketry asserted its superiority. In a skirmish that same afternoon the Scots Greys inflicted thirty or forty casualties for the loss of one officer wounded. This superiority was to be a factor of prime importance until the campaign died out in the damp November woods round Ypres.

While the BEF was moving up French had on 17th August visited Lanrezac to confer as to their future co-operation. Neither understood the other's language, Lanrezac, tense with anxiety, was needlessly rude, and the interview, so far from doing good left the two army commanders in a state of profound mutual distrust. Lanrezac told Joffre that the British would not be ready until the 24th at the earliest, that their cavalry were to be employed as mounted infantry and could be counted upon for no other purpose. More significant still, he raised the question of possible confusion if the British used the same roads 'in the event of retirement'. It was a considerable shock to Joffre to find that Lanrezac, who, in peacetime had been 'a veritable lion', not only had made no attempt to join in the great French advance, but was now thinking of withdrawal.

On 23rd August the long-awaited storm broke over Lanrezac's army when Bülow attacked him with four corps on the line of the Sambre. 'It rained shells,' was all that one French soldier could remember of that day's fighting. An Algerian battalion, 1,030 strong, charged a German battery, bayonetted the gunners, and returned, it is said, with only two men unhit! Everywhere the French suffered terrible losses especially in officers. One corps was compelled to fall back.

During the night Hausen brought four corps, supported by 340 guns against Lanrezac's line on the Meuse, gaining bridgeheads west of the river. Here they were up against a great soldier General Franchet d'Esperey ('desperate Frankie' to his British allies), the commander of 1st Corps. D'Esperey had actually made his men dig in, but this was simple prudence not over-caution. His corps counterattacked and pitched the Saxons back across the river.

Through the long day Lanrezac remained at his headquarters, Philippeville, a 'prey to extreme anxiety'. Well he might be. He received no guidance from Joffre, merely demands for his opinion of the situation. At noon came the well-nigh incredible news that the Belgians were evacuating Namur, the great fortress hinge of the Sambre-Meuse line. He received no information from Langle on his right, but on his left French, while declining to attack Bülow's right, guaranteed to hold the Mons Canal for twenty-four hours.

While Lanrezac watched the endless column of Belgian refugees drifting through the square at Philippeville, his staff opportuned him with vain demands for a counter-attack. Lanrezac ordered no such thing. Perhaps he was pusillanimous as his critics assert: he was certainly correct. Late in the day came news of Langle's retreat, which left the Meuse unguarded between Lanrezac's right and Sedan, where the French had met with disaster in 1870, as they were to do again in 1940. The day ended with another splendid counter-attack on d'Esperey's front, when General Mangin's brigade drove the Saxons out of their bridgehead at Onhaye. But this did not alter the fact that Lanrezac's position was untenable. At the risk of being taken for a 'catastro-phard' he ordered a general retreat. To one of his staff he remarked 'We have been beaten but the evil is reparable. As long as the 5th Army lives, France is not lost.'

Mons and the retreat

This was the situation when on 23rd August the BEF fought its first serious action in the coalfields round Mons, on a line about nine miles northward of Lanrezac's main position and with both flanks in the air. For a loss of about 1,600 casualties and two guns the 2nd Corps, under General Smith-Dorrien, delayed Kluck's advance for a whole day and inflicted very severe losses on three of his corps (III, IV, and IX). A German account frankly describes the fighting: 'Well entrenched and completely hidden, the enemy opened a murderous fire . . . the casualties increased . . . the rushes became shorter, and finally the whole advance stopped . . . with bloody losses, the attack gradually came to an end.' The XII Brandenburg Grenadiers (III Corps) attacking the 1st Battalion Royal West Kent lost twenty-five officers and over 500 men. The 75th Bremen Regiment (IX Corps) lost five officers and 376 men in one attack. Frontal attack was worse than useless against British troops dug in in such a position. Only a flanking movement could turn them out and this — belatedly — Kluck realized. Lanrezac neither consulted nor warned

French before retreating, and it was not until 11 pm on the 23rd that Sir John was told of it by his liaison officer, Lieutenant Spears. With the BEF left in the air its temperamental commander was beset with gloom, and in a letter to Kitchener next day hinted that he was contemplating departure, 'I think immediate attention should be directed to the defence of Havre.'

By this time the BEF, to the astonishment of the Brandenburger captain, Bloem, who had seen his men slaughtered the previous day, was in full retreat. By the 24th even the placid Joffre recognized that his army was 'condemned to a defensive posture' and must hold out, making use of its fortified lines, wear down the enemy, and await the favourable moment for a counter-attack. The lack of success so far he attributed not to any fault of his own, but to 'grave shortcomings on the part of commanders'. That some had broken cannot be denied. During the Ardennes battle one divisional commander had actually committed suicide. Joffre sacked the weaklings ruthlessly. There was some recognition of French tactical failings and on the 24th Joffre issued a training instruction emphasizing the need for collaboration between infantry and artillery in the capture of 'points d'appui' ('strongpoints'): 'Every time that the infantry has been launched to the attack from too great a distance before the artillery has made its effect felt, the infantry has fallen under the fire of machine-guns and suffered losses which might have been avoided.

'When a point d'appui has been captured it must be organized immediately, the troops must entrench, and artillery must be brought up.'

'Reign of terror'

Joffre's lesson on tactics would have seemed pretty elementary stuff to the officers of the BEF — or to the Germans for that matter. But they, too, had their troubles. The British after long marches up the pavé in the August sun, had won a victory, and were now, incomprehensibly, invited to march back the way they had come. They felt they were being 'messed about'. The Germans had a special nightmare of their own: the franc tireur (guerrilla). Captain Bloem records that on a day when his company marched twenty-eight miles not a man fell out: 'the thought of falling into the hands of the Walloons was worse than sore feet.'

To orderly German minds the thought of civilians intervening as snipers, albeit for hearth and home, was utterly repugnant. Princess Blücher was told that there were thirty German officers in hospital at Aachen, their eyes gouged out by Belgian women and children. Atrocities, even imaginary ones, breed reprisals, and *Shrecklichkeit* (Frightfulness) was a matter of deliberate policy with the German high command which did not mean to detach strong forces to guard the lines of communication. Had not the great Clausewitz laid it down that terror was the proper way to shorten war? Only by making the civilian population feel its effects could the leaders be made to change their minds, and sue for peace. In Belgium the first important massacre was at Andenne where Bülow had 211 people shot on 20th and 21st August. At Tamines, sacked on the 21st, 400 were executed in the main square. The Saxons pillaged and burnt Dinant on the 23rd, leaving their aged commander, Hausen, 'profoundly moved', but indignant against the Belgian government which 'approved this perfidious street fighting contrary to international law'. The sack of Louvain — sparked off, apparently by German soldiers firing on each other in panic after a Belgian sortie from Antwerp — was the worst episode of this reign of terror. If anything these atrocities served to stiffen the resolution of the Belgians and their allies.

The retreat continued, but with five German armies carving their way into France, Joffre never despaired of resuming the offensive. By this time he had realized that the forces of his left wing were insufficient to stop the German onrush. On 25th August he ordered the formation of a new French army, the 6th under Maunoury. Its divisions were to be found from the now static front in Lorraine, and it was to take its position on the left of the BEF.

Moltke's fatal error

On the 25th Moltke also was taking men from the Western Front, not, however, from Lorraine where they could perhaps have been spared, but from his right wing! And this at a time when Kluck was detaching one of his corps to invest Maubeuge. Moltke was worried by the Russian threat to East Prussia and determined to reinforce the latter with two corps, though, ironically enough, they were not to arrive until the Germans had won their decisive victory at Tannenberg. Beyond question this was fatal alteration to the Schlieffen Plan at a moment when decisive victory lay within his grasp. The trouble was that by the 24th the Germans thought that they only had beaten men before them. That this was not so was forcibly demonstrated by the BEF at Le Cateau on the following day.

Late on the night of the 25th Smith-Dorrien (2nd Corps) realized that, with some of his units only just coming in, and with many scattered and exhausted, it was not possible to carry out French's orders to continue the retreat. He decided to stand and fight.

Battle of Le Cateau

Kluck had nine divisions within reach of the battlefield at dawn, but only managed to bring two of them, with three cavalry divisions, into action against Smith-Dorrien's three. Kluck had, however, a tremendous concentration of artillery, and it was really this which made the British stand difficult. The German infantry came on in bunches, firing from the hip, and suffered severely. Kluck's strong right wing (two corps) allowed itself to be engaged by Sordet's cavalry corps and a French territorial division. The corps on his left, marching and counter-marching, covered eleven miles without intervening in the fight. In consequence Smith-Dorrien managed to extricate himself with a loss of some 8,000 men and thirty-eight guns. Mons and Le Cateau left Kluck with a profound respect for the BEF — 'it was an incomparable army', he told British officers after the war. Its rapid rifle fire had convinced many Germans that the BEF had twenty-eight machine-guns per battalion when in fact they had two.

While the battle of Le Cateau was in progress Joffre held a conference with French and Lanrezac at St Quentin in order to explain his latest plans. General Order No. 2 had reached GHQ the previous night, but there had not yet been time to study it. Joffre was shocked by French's excited complaints. He was threatened with envelopment by superior numbers and his right had been left in the air by Lanrezac's sudden withdrawal. His men were too tired to go over to the offensive.

After this uncomfortable meeting Joffre departed, suspecting that the BEF had lost its cohesion. The truth was that GHQ had lost touch with the army it was supposed to control, and things were not as gloomy as French thought. Kluck for his part saw things in much the same light as Sir John. On the 27th he hoped to 'cut off the British who were in full flight westwards'. With Namur in his hands and Bülow pressing Lanrezac's broken troops Moltke was feeling the 'universal sense of victory' that now pervaded the German army. But already things were going wrong. In three days furious fighting (24th-27th August) Rupprecht's twenty-six divisions had been hurled back from Toul, Nancy, and Epinal by Castelnau and Dubail. On the Meuse Langle held up the Duke of Württemberg from the 26th to the 28th.

On the 29th Bülow's army, astride the river Oise, blundered head-on into Lanrezac's columns, which were crossing their front, and suffered a severe check. In the battles of Guise and St Quentin Lanrezac was counter-attacking, most reluctantly, on direct orders from Joffre, who stayed with him and watched him for three hours of the battle. Had French permitted Haig's corps, which was still practically intact, to co-operate, the Germans might have suffered a severe defeat. Once more a counter-attack by d'Esperey's corps sustained the right wing at the moment of crisis. It was a magnificent spectacle. Bands playing, colours flying, the French infantry, covered by the fire of the 75s, swept eagerly forward and the Germans gave way. That night the 5th Army withdrew unimpeded.

The pursuit continued, though thanks to the absence of five corps – practically the equivalent of an army – awkward gaps were beginning to appear in the German right wing. On 31st August Kluck abandoned his pursuit of the British who had disappeared south of Compiègne, and wheeled south to strike at Lanrezac. On 1st September he crossed the Oise reaching Crépy-en-Valois and Villers-Cotterets, a bare thirty miles from Paris. The same day a stormy interview took place in the British embassy in Paris, when Kitchener, in his field-marshal's uniform, made it clear to the sulking French that he was to keep the BEF in the line and conform to the movements of his allies.

'We must strike'

Moltke was now attracted by the idea of driving the French south-east and thus cutting them off from Paris. He ordered Kluck to cover this movement in the direction of Paris, 'remaining in the rear of the Second Army'. The independent-minded Kluck, whose army was the farthest forward and the best placed to attack the French 5th Army, did not see this. Nor did he anticipate any danger from Paris. On the evening of the 2nd he gave orders to cross the Marne next day, leaving only one weak corps as a flank guard. That night the French government left Paris for Bordeaux. Next morning General Galliéni, the governor, still thought the Germans were marching on the capital. When at noon an airman reported their columns moving east towards the south-east, Maunoury's staff refused to credit it, but at 7 pm it was confirmed. 'We must strike!' cried Galliéni, and having given warning orders, asked Joffre's permission. At 8 am on the 4th one of his officers reached Joffre's headquarters at Bar-sur-Aube, and the intelligence staff traced Kluck's latest moves on the wall map. 'But we have them,' they exclaimed. 'We must stop the retreat and seize our heaven-sent chance at once.'

Joffre himself appeared. 'A remarkable situation,' was his comment. 'The Paris army and the British are in a good position to deliver a flank attack on the Germans as they are marching on the Marne.' It remained to convince Sir John French.

D'Esperey, who had replaced Lanrezac, was ready with proposals for an attack on the 6th. These he had drawn up in concert with Major-General Wilson, French's deputy chief-of-staff. Galliéni pointed out that by the 7th the Germans would have scented the danger threatening them from the direction of Paris.

Meanwhile, Moltke's mood of elation was deteriorating through a period of deepening panic towards complete nervous breakdown. Despite the pictures painted by his generals, there were still no masses of prisoners, no parks of captured guns. The French and British had refused to admit defeat, Kluck was following his own devices, and French reinforcements were approaching Paris from the east. At 6 pm on the 4th he sent out the following order by wireless: 'I and II Armies will remain facing Paris, I Army between Oise and Marne, II Army between Marne and Seine.' This order did not reach Kluck until next day, by which time he had crossed the Marne. He gave the order to advance towards the Seine on the 5th, leaving only one corps behind the Marne.

On the afternoon of the 5th Joffre visited French's headquarters at Melun in order to ensure British co-operation. Later he wrote: 'I put my whole soul into convincing French that the decisive hour had come and that an English abstention would be severely judged by history. Finally, striking the table with my fist, I cried: *"Monsieur le Maréchal*. The honour of England is at stake!"* French blushed, and murmured with emotion, "I will do all that is possible", and for me that was the equivalent of an oath.'

The battle of the Marne

The battle of the Marne was in effect a series of disjointed combats. It began on the afternoon of the 5th when the French 6th Army moving up to its start line on the river Ourcq unexpectedly ran into Kluck's flank guard, IV Reserve Corps, in the hills north of Meaux.

During the evening an emissary from Moltke, who was still running the campaign by remote control from Luxembourg, arrived at Kluck's HQ. This was Lieutenant-Colonel Hentsch, chief of intelligence branch, whose mission was to explain the real situation and in effect to bring him to heel. Kluck resigned himself to a withdrawal, but as yet unaware of the action on the Ourcq, contented himself with a leisurely retrograde move which left most of his army south of the Marne.

The three armies on the Allied left made a little progress on the 6th. Until the previous day the BEF and the 5th Army had continued the retreat, and the sudden change left them in cautious mood. The 6th Army was held up some six miles short of the Ourcq. The River Marne and a gap of eight miles separated its right from the

BEF. In the south the 1st and 2nd French Armies successfully resisted the German VII and VI under Rupprecht, and on the 8th Moltke finally abandoned the unprofitable Lorraine offensive. The 3rd French Army, now under General Sarrail, and the 4th Army held their own well against the German V and IV Armies. But where Hausen's Saxons threatened Foch's much weaker 9th Army there was serious cause for disquiet.

On the 7th, Gronau reinforced by two more of Kluck's corps recalled from farther south, had little difficulty in holding Maunoury west of the Ourcq. The aggressive Kluck now conceived the notion of attacking the 6th Army from the north, hoping to drive it back on Paris and enter the capital on its heels. For this masterstroke he switched his two remaining corps with astonishing speed from south of the Marne to his northern wing. By so doing he opened a gap of some twenty miles between himself and Bülow, a gap which was masked by a fairly strong screen of nine infantry battalions (eight being *Jäger*) and two cavalry corps on the Petit Morin.

German retreat

If the British were slow to exploit this advantage the fault lay with GHQ rather than the men, who were in good spirits now that they were going forward once more. D'Esperey's progress on the 7th was comparable with that of the BEF, but by this time Foch, under severe pressure, was being driven south from the marshes of Saint-Gond. It was on the 8th that he sent the legendary report to Joffre: 'My centre is yielding, my right wing is giving way. An excellent situation. I attack tomorrow.' But the Germans no longer hoped for a break-through; rather it was their aim to extricate Bülow and close the gap. Shortly before 9 am on the 9th an aviator reported to Bülow that there were five British columns with their heads on or across the Marne. Another had already reported that there were no German troops in the path of the BEF's advance. Warning Kluck of his intention, Bülow issued orders for a retirement. Almost simultaneously Kluck also gave orders for a withdrawal in the general direction of Soissons. It was about 5.30 pm before it became evider⊥ to the British that the

Germans were abandoning the battlefield. Their success had not been particularly costly; between 6th and 10th September the BEF's casualties numbered no more than 1,701.

The battle of the Marne, in which, it has been calculated, some fifty-seven Allied divisions (eight cavalry) turned back fifty-three German (seven cavalry) was over, and with it died the famous Schlieffen Plan. Tactically its results were disappointing, for it was not fought to the bitter end. Strategically it was of profound importance, for it meant that all hope of a swift knockout blow was over. As in 1940 the Germans counted on a swift *blitzkrieg* to defeat their semi-mobilized enemies and win the war. Could they have won? The two corps sent to East Prussia would have been more than sufficient to close that famous gap.

Joffre is not generally numbered among the great captains, but he had won one of the strategically decisive battles of all time.

By the morning of the 10th the Germans had vanished, Kluck retiring to the Aisne at Soissons and Bülow to the Vesle at Rheims. In general it cannot be said that the pursuit was vigorous, though much transport, some forty guns and about 14,000 prisoners were taken. Bad weather prevented air reconnaissance and the French, whose men and horses were tired, could only average six or seven miles a day. There was still a gap between the German I and II Armies, but this was not evident to the Allies. On the 13th the VII reserve corps, released by the fall of Maubeuge, arrived in the nick of time to close the gap. By a forced march of forty miles in twenty-four hours it just succeeded in forestalling Haig's corps.

The offensive had left one-tenth of France, with much of her coal and iron, in German hands. The failure of the Schlieffen Plan had brought Moltke's secret replacement by General Erich von Falkenhayn, the minister of war, who at fifty-three was a mere boy compared to most of the army commanders on the Western Front. Neither he nor Joffre quite despaired of a speedy decision in a war of movement. When the battle of the Aisne began to crystallize into the trench warfare of the next four years, both improvised plans to outflank the other's northern

flank, between the Oise and the sea. With the Belgian field army, 65,000 strong, ensconced in Antwerp, the Allies had some hopes of a success in Flanders. Winston Churchill, the First Lord of the Admiralty, did his best to stiffen the garrison with a naval division, 12,000 strong (30th October), but two-thirds of these men were neither well-trained nor properly equipped. The Germans began to bombard the city on the 7th and General Deguise, the fortress commander made no attempt to hold out to the last. The north-eastern forts were tamely surrendered without bombardment or attack, but the field army escaped westwards to the River Yser.

Meanwhile, Joffre had agreed that the six British divisions on the Aisne should be transferred to Flanders and they began to detrain near Abbeville on 9th October. On the same day the 7th Division landed at Ostend, and, since Antwerp had fallen, became part of the BEF.

First battle of Ypres

With Antwerp in his hands Falkenhayn had a fleeting chance of a break-through, for he had five reserve corps available for instant action. They were not the best troops in the world for 'the men were too young and the officers too old', but they showed the most determined bravery in the first battle of Ypres, which raged between Arras and the sea in that autumn (12th October to 11th November).

The fighting opened well enough for the Allies but by 21st October the Germans had won the initiative, and battered away at the Allied line for the next three weeks. The Kaiser himself appeared in the battle area to witness the break-through. The climax of the battle came on the 31st when the Germans broke into the British line at Gheluvelt.

In an astonishing counter-attack, inspired by Brigadier-General Fitzclarence, the 368 survivors of the 2/Worcestershires threw them out. Eventually, the storm died out with the repulse of the Prussian Guard on 11th November.

The BEF had, it is estimated, lost over 50,000 men, and the Germans at least twice as many, including about half the infantry engaged.

The Western Front now ran from Switzerland to the sea, following the line of the Vosges, the Moselle, the Meuse hills, the Argonne, the Chemin des Dames, the Aisne, until by way of Armentières and Ypres it reached Dixmude. There were still those who believed that with the spring would come the return of open warfare. But the line was not to move more than ten miles either way for the next three years.

The Eastern Front

John Erickson

Within a week of the German invasion of Belgium, 800 miles to the east the battle lines of the 'Eastern Front', running from the gloomy East Prussian marches in the north to the high Carpathians in the south, were already drawn up and the several armies swarming on them, the Russian, the Austro-Hungarian and the German, were on the point of being set in full motion. The Russians, though mobilization had so far brought only one-third of their available manpower into the field, were intent on breaking into East Prussia: the Germans concentrated to defend it. In southern Poland and Galicia the Austro-Hungarians, their army a multi-national patchwork stitched out of Germans, Slavs, and Magyars, prepared to strike at the Russians, while the Russians proposed to launch their main attack against Austria-Hungary. The result was soon a whirlpool of battles which sucked in whole armies to destruction, crippling the Austrians, battering the Russians, and straining the Germans. Wild as the fighting was, with the masses of Austrian and Russian peasant soldiers lumbering about, the Eastern Front impinged directly on operations in the west when, at a crucial stage in the flailing German offensive against 'the Franco-English Army', the German command drew off men and speeded them eastwards to hold sacred German soil, the sanctum of Prussia, against the Slav intruder, the historical image of whose 'frightfulness' fevered the German mind. The rival armies in the east each played their special supporting parts: Russia marched on East Prussia at France's urgent request, Austria-Hungary, battling with Serbia, lunged across the Russian frontiers at Germany's prompting. For Germany, the two-front war had materialized, not in military mathematics, but as gunfire on its own frontiers.

The armies which rolled upon each other in the east did so in accordance with the war plans upon which the respective general staffs had prepared long before the actual clash. German planners wrestled with the intractabilities of a two-front war; early planning variants (relying on the lengthy period which they presumed Russian mobilization would take) stripped East Prussia of men, but subsequent signs of waxing Russian strength caused a revision; according to the new plan the VIII Army was to be stationed in East Prussia, its role essentially defensive. Austria-Hungary nurtured two war plans. The first, Plan B, envisaged war against Serbia only, against whom three armies would be committed while the other three held Galicia against the Russians; the second, Plan R, related to war with Serbia and Russia: two armies would march on Serbia and four against Russia. Russia, meanwhile, developed two war plans of its own, one defensive, Plan G, the other offensive, Plan A. Plan G assumed a primary German effort against Russia, in which contingency the North-Western and South-Western Army Groups would first retire, and then the Russians would make a counteroffensive. Plan A prescribed an offensive when the German blow was directed against France: Russian armies would strike at East Prussia and Galicia, the bulk of Russian strength (four armies) falling on the Austrians, with two driving into East Prussia.

This military calculus was based, not only upon guesses about what would happen, but also upon the possibilities (and the restrictions) of the supposed 'front'. Overshadowing all else was the giant Russian salient—Russian Poland—which jutted out to the west, its tip not 200 miles from Berlin. The salient was both a springboard and a trap for the Russians; from it they could leap into Silesia, but they could be militarily entombed if German troops from East Prussia and Austrian troops from Galicia struck from north and south to crumple the salient. East Prussia was unmistakably exposed but, thanks to German attention to interior communications, eminently defensible. In terms of plans, Germany determined to hold East Prussia: Russia, at France's insistence, opted for Plan A: Austria-Hungary, having first set in motion Plan B, suddenly switched to Plan R (which meant pulling the whole II Army back from Serbia).

The Russians take the field

At daylight on 12th August 1914, under a calm morning sky, the first units from Rennenkampf's 1st Army – cavalry squadrons and a rifle regiment – crossed the frontier into East Prussia. The Russian invasion had begun, a converging attack mounted with two armies of General Zhilinsky's North-Western Group: Rennenkampf's 1st Army was to strike from the east, Samsonov's 2nd Army from the southeast, two claws digging into East Prussia to crumple and destroy it. On the German side, Lieutenant-General von Prittwitz had already begun to deploy the four corps of the VIII Army assigned to defend East Prussia: to block the Russian drive from the east, three corps took positions along the line of the river Angerapp and a fourth was deployed to the south, amid the lakes and forests of Tannenberg, barring the way to the Russian army moving from the south-east. Deliberately, taking advantage of excellent internal communications – and with substantial knowledge of Russian movements, thanks to an appalling carelessness shown by the Russians in transmitting orders *en clair* for much of the time – Prittwitz drew up his corps and made his plans: he would deal with one Russian army at a time, striking first at Rennenkampf and then at Samsonov. Though the alarm bells were beginning to ring through Prussia, there seemed to be a margin of time and therefore an assurance of safety.

Certainly the Imperial Russian Army was – at France's entreaty – rushing into the attack; as a consequence it was incompletely mobilized. Yet this was not its basic weakness. The real defects lay deeper. To shortcomings in organization, training, equipment, and supply were added the fatal flaws of a corrupt, ruinously inefficient society where no institution could respond to 'the concentrated demands of wartime'. In addition, the Russian army was fearfully short of fire-power: even where the guns did exist, the available ammunition often ran out. The Russian Plan A nevertheless went into operation, and the attack on East Prussia slowly ground into gear. On 17th August Rennen-

kampf's 1st Army moving from the east, its columns separated and its northern flank dangerously bare, crossed the frontier in force. Samsonov in the south-east was not due to move off for another five days.

Meanwhile, farther south, Austro-Hungarian troops had crossed the Russian frontier on 10th August. Following the dictates of Plan R, Field-Marshal Conrad von Hötzendorf launched the Austro-Hungarian armies from Austrian Poland (Galicia) towards the north to engage the main Russian forces, which he assumed lay in this direction. The field-marshal's assumption proved to be totally wrong; Russian strength lay in yet another direction, to the south-east, and this again was due to the mistaken anticipation by the Russian command of Austrian intentions. General Ivanov, South-Western Group commander, expected the Austrians to strike from the direction of Lemberg (Lwów) and it was here that he proposed to make his own maximum effort. These initial misconceptions, therefore, played a major role in producing a lop-sided battlefront, with the Austrians flailing away in the north and the Russians loosing a massive attack in the south.

At first, Austrian and Russian armies blundered into each other along the Austrian line of advance to the north (in the direction of Lublin-Kholm, though after 23rd August heavy fighting developed. Vastly encouraged by the first results, Conrad reinforced his left flank and ordered the III Army into the attack east of Lemberg – where the Russians were ready and waiting: and having switched from Plan B to Plan R, Conrad brought II Army shuttling up from Serbia. On 26th August Ivanov opened his own offensive with two armies (3rd and 8th) which smashed into the depleted, struggling Austrian III Army: the III Army fell back in disorder on Lemberg. Late in August Conrad was facing a confused though by no means desperate situation – the gleam of success in the north, the spurt of danger in the south. The field-marshal decided to fight for his Lemberg front, not of itself a disastrous decision, but the manner in which he implemented it finally provided Ivanov with the opportunity to rip the whole Austrian front wide open.

The Russians are trapped

Though Russian armies were on the verge of a vast triumph in Galicia, the invasion of East Prussia had come to terrible grief. From its first set-piece arrangement, the battle for East Prussia rapidly developed into a rolling, lurching, savage affair, pitching into violent motion when the impetuous commander of the German I Corps, General François, brought Rennenkampf to battle ahead of the line chosen by Prittwitz. But the undiscerning Rennenkampf ploughed on, thereby helping to restore reality to German plans. On 20th August Samsonov began his advance from the south-east, a signal for Rennenkampf to halt calmly so that Samsonov might catch up in time and space. Prittwitz determined to act, proposing to launch a counterblow at Rennenkampf, much to the disgust of his chief operations officer, Max Hoffmann, for it meant unravelling the German line. General François once again led the I Corps against Rennenkampf and other corps engaged in the 'battle of Gumbinnen', a wild, swirling encounter in which the German XVII Corps was badly mauled. News of this, intelligence of Samsonov's advance, and panic that the Russians might burst through the Insterburg Gap, splitting the VIII Army apart, caused Prittwitz to lose what little nerve he possessed. He decided on precipitate retreat to the Vistula, to the consternation of his commanders. Adamant about withdrawal, Prittwitz proceeded to petrify the high command with the details of disaster he retailed by telephone to Helmuth von Moltke (the German chief of general staff) at Coblenz—the Vistula it had to be, and Prittwitz doubted that he could hold this line without reinforcement.

This wailing from the east cut across the gigantic battle raging in the west. Moltke wasted no time: he despatched Major-General Erich Ludendorff as chief-of-staff and General Paul von Hindenburg (hitherto on the retired list) as the new commander of the VIII Army. Prittwitz was brushed aside. The idea of hasty withdrawal had already been abandoned in the east and Hoffmann devised a plan to draw off troops facing Rennenkampf to pit them against Samsonov. Rennenkampf failed to follow through after Gumbinnen; he hung poised in the north, an undoubted threat but a stationary one. Samsonov inched his way long, arguing all the way with Zhilinsky. The VIII Army command faced one crucial question: was there time to knock out Samsonov before Rennenkampf came down from the north? On the morning of 25th August that problem received swift, if startling resolution; uncloaked by code, Rennenkampf broadcast his line of advance and its distance. The Russian 1st Army would not, on this evidence, strike into the rear of the VIII Army. As for Samsonov, imagining himself to be pursuing a broken enemy, he proposed to rest his troops on 25th August. It seemed as if the Russians were inviting their own destruction. Further news from their own command, however, brought disquiet to the Germans; at Coblenz, Moltke had decided to pull out three corps and a division from the Western Front—where every unit was needed—as reinforcement for the east. Two corps and a cavalry division were already detached on 26th August, an action Moltke justified by arguing that 'the decision' in the west had already been gained. Yet three corps, loaded as they were on troop trains and trundling over Germany, could not 'save' East Prussia and remained lost to the German right wing on the Western Front.

Meanwhile the VIII Army, speeded along internal railway lines, shifted its weight to the south. The Russian 'pincers' waved in the air: at the *Stavka* (Russian GHQ) concern mounted at Rennenkampf's dawdling. Zhilinsky did nothing to urge Rennenkampf to close with Samsonov, whom he thought to be in no danger. On 26th August Samsonov's 2nd Army resumed its advance, the Russian centre moving all unsuspecting into a German trap ringed with four corps: the full weight of VIII Army —all but one division, which was holding Rennenkampf in the north—crashed on Samsonov's hungry, ill-clad men. The 'battle of Tannenberg', running its course for three agonizing days, snared three Russian corps (13th, 15th, and 23rd) in the German net: German guns lashed the Russian divisions, the Russians broke and the fight continued in the woods and across the marshes. On 29th August Samsonov knew the extent of the catastrophe; that evening he spent huddled in a clearing in the forest. Shortly after midnight he drew aside and shot himself. The Germans took over 100,000 prisoners and large quantities of guns. Two Russian corps (13th and 15th) were obliterated, another (23rd) drastically thinned, and the two flank corps reduced to the strength of mere divisions.

With the defeat of Samsonov, the killing was but half done. Rennenkampf in the north was now marked down for destruction and the VIII Army, coiling across East Prussia like a spring and strengthened by reinforcement arriving from the west, regrouped to attack once more. On 5th September the German drive on Rennenkampf's left flank opened, and 'the battle of the Masurian Lakes' began; at the centre Rennenkampf held off the German assault, but in so doing weakened the whole of the 1st Army. On 9th September Rennenkampf ordered a general withdrawal to pull the 1st Army out of the trap closing on it, and also launched one stabbing attack with two divisions—enough to slow down the German right wing. The Russian infantrymen trudged eastwards: Rennenkampf made the journey in the comfort of his car, back to and over the Russian frontier. His army did escape, but had suffered a grievous mauling, with 100,000 men lost. The invasion of Prussia, which cost the Russians almost a quarter of a million men, had failed. Zhilinsky tried—unsuccessfully—to unload the blame on Rennenkampf: Rennenkampf (whose conduct incurred suspicions of treason) stayed and Zhilinsky was dismissed.

The rout of the Austrians

9th September 1914: the Germans had failed on the Marne: Samsonov was dead, Rennenkampf in retreat: the Russians were defeated in East Prussia, and almost triumphant in Galicia. Conrad, in trying to cover himself at Lemberg, opened a gap in the north and the Russian 5th Army came bursting through. To escape encirclement, the Austrian command ordered a general withdrawal, and withdrawal degenerated into pell-mell flight. The whole Austro-Hungarian front quivered and collapsed, caving in to a depth of a hundred miles and immolating over 300,000 men in the Galician catastrophe. Russian troops took Lemberg and swept on to cut off the great fortress of Przemyśl, bottling up 100,000 more men. In this whole *débâcle,* the Austro-Hungarian armies suffered a loss not even suggested by numbers, for many of the cadre 'Austrian' officers,

the hard core of the army, were lost or captured. The rout of the Austrians in Galicia, for it was nothing short of that, brought fresh dangers to Germany: the Russians were already opening a pathway into Silesia. The situation called for German troops, but Erich von Falkenhayn (who replaced Moltke after the first battle of the Marne) would let none go from the Western Front. Hindenburg therefore stripped East Prussia of four of its six corps to form a new German army in the east, the IX, which began to deploy at Czestochowa late in September, closing with the Austrian I Army. Both sides—Russian and German—were at this stage planning to attack and a phase of fierce, formidable battles in the east was about to begin. The Russians found themselves once more under pressure from the French to mount a major attack, this time in the direction of the German industrial base in Silesia; the Russian threat to Cracow did itself involve the security of Silesia—and Hindenburg had hurried to close the most staring gap—but an offensive along the Warsaw-Posen axis by Russian armies would mean great and growing danger for Germany. Towards the end of September, Russian armies were regrouping for this new offensive.

Hindenburg, however, struck first, using his new IX Army and aiming straight at the huge Russian base of Warsaw, the attack for which the Austrians had pleaded at the end of August. For the first time the Russians learned of the existence of the IX Army and rushed every available man to the Vistula to hold off the German advance: Austrian troops also started an attack towards the line of the river San. Late in September the IX Army rolled forward and by 9th October Hindenburg was on the Vistula. Three days later German troops began their advance on Warsaw. To hold the city the Russian command speeded up the movement of Siberian regiments from the Far East, troops released for service in European Russia at the end of August when Japan entered the war against Germany and Russia had no further fear of a clash with Japan. At the end of a month's journey, the Far Eastern regiments detrained in Warsaw and went straight into action, fighting savage bouts with the bayonet under the walls of the city.

By mid-October, with two Russian armies (1st and 2nd) piling up on his northern flank, Hindenburg deemed it prudent to withdraw; the IX Army began to fall back, the Austrians were floundering to the south and by the end of the month German and Austrian troops were back in the positions they had occupied towards the close of September. It was now the turn of the Russian command to take the offensive, to launch an invasion of Silesia with four armies while a fifth (1st Army, still under the command of Rennenkampf) protected the Russian northern flank from its positions on the Vistula. Once again, with staggering negligence, the Russians blared their movements over the air and once again the Russian command failed to take speedy German redeployment into account. The German IX Army, formidable and efficient, was already on the move, speeding along good rail communications to its new concentration area, a blocking position between Posen and Thorn; the place of IX Army in the German-Austrian line was taken by the Austrian II Army which had been moved up from the Carpathians.

The scene was almost set for the fiercest round fought so far, without the grand tragedy of East Prussia or the massive confusion of Galicia, but a test of arms of a very decisive nature, itself connected with a subtle but profound change which was overtaking the war in the east — at least from the German side. Hindenburg and Ludendorff now assumed over-all command of German troops in the east. They were already the inseparable martial pair, twinned by the triumphs of East Prussia and set upon that rise which took them finally to supreme military control of Germany's destiny. In the east the German army fought a war of mobility and also in the east Ludendorff sought to realize Schlieffen's idea of victory — not attained in the west — that true victory must be wholly and utterly decisive. Ludendorff was therefore embarked on his search for 'a decision' in the east, which inevitably brought a clash over the claims of the west: it meant conflict with Falkenhayn, and it required reinforcements, the addition of strength to mobility.

To fend off the Russians, the German command determined to pre-empt their attack. With the IX Army drawn up in its new operational area, now under General von Mackensen's command, the German plan envisaged an operation timed for 11th November and designed to crumple the Russian drive into Silesia by driving between the 1st and 2nd Russian Armies. On the Western Front Falkenhayn was fighting the last great battle of 1914 at Ypres, and having broken through the British lines to the south-east, he espied eventual victory: no men could be spared for the east. Hindenburg and Ludendorff, however, could not afford to wait, being persuaded — correctly — of the gravity of the Russian threat. On 11th November, as planned, the IX Army attacked on a front west and north-west of Łódź, closing on the 1st and 2nd Russian armies. This did not prevent the Russians from loosing their armies in a westerly drive towards Silesia three days later, but within forty-eight hours the Russian offensive was brought to an abrupt halt. The German IX Army had crashed straight into the junction of 1st and 2nd Armies — and the fault this time lay unambiguously with Rennenkampf in charge of the 1st Army. On 16th November the enormity of the situation finally broke over the Russian command, who had been waiting for the IX Army to be crushed between the two Russian armies — a Russian Tannenberg where the IX Army would march to its doom. But Mackensen tossed Rennenkampf's corps aside — badly strung out as they were — and then ripped into the right flank of the Russian 2nd Army, which the Germans intended to encircle, the second time that this unfortunate army was to be done to death.

With the grip of winter tightening each day, the fight for Łódź and for the life or death of the 2nd Army lasted until early in December. Furious fighting flared as the Germans closed in and as the Russians beat them off. The Russian 5th Army was ordered to close with the 2nd: two Russian corps, driven along in forced marches, managed to press the right flank of the IX Army back. The left flank of the IX Army lapped right round to the south-east of Łódź, giving the Russians the chance to spring a trap of their own, though late in November the German corps fought its way out. In the end neither the German nor the Russian trap had closed fully, but early in December Russian troops began withdrawing from Łódź, whereupon German troops immediately entered the city in their wake. After his showing in these battles, Rennenkampf was finally dragged out of his command of the 1st Army; the new commander, General Litvinov, quickly ordered a withdrawal to the Bzura and Rawka river lines where the army wintered. The battle of Łódź, even if it enjoyed none of the fame of Tannenberg, nevertheless had a decisiveness all its own: frustrated though they were in their tactical designs, Hindenburg and Ludendorff had throttled completely the Russian offensive aimed at Germany.

Russia licks her wounds

For the rest of December the Eastern Front remained quiet. Four months of fighting, however, had wrought some fearful changes. Russian armies had been dreadfully mauled in East Prussia: Austria-Hungary suffered calamitous losses in Galicia and a motley army lost much of its irreplaceable 'Austrian' cadre. The Russian triumph in Galicia could momentarily blot out disaster in East Prussia, but Tannenberg inflicted a deep and terrible wound: worse, it stood as a sinister portent. The Russian infantryman, ill-equipped and under-fed, performed prodigies of endurance and raw, unflinching courage, but manpower could not continually match a murderous enemy firepower: German superiority in artillery mangled the Imperial Russian Army. Within a month of the opening of the war Russian armies were chronically starved of ammunition and the gun-batteries, insufficient as they were, remained all but bereft of shells. The war minister, Sukhomlinov, 'an empty and slovenly man', bore most of the responsibility for this disgraceful state of affairs, but it was the regime itself which allowed men like Sukhomlinov to grow fat on inefficiency and to flourish on calamity. The Russian high command showed mostly its ineptitudes: the Imperial Army took the field inadequately trained, indifferently and incompetently led, badly supplied—and for all this the peasant soldier had to pay in blood. His back proved broad, but not unbreakable.

At the end of 1914, though Russian losses were already grievous—shocking enough to promote feelings that a settlement with Germany would be the best course, or that again Russia was shouldering an unfairly heavy burden—Russian armies still cover-

ed Warsaw, the front was advantageously shortened in western Poland and much of Galicia was in Russian hands. The Russian command had plunged from the outset into the offensive in fulfilment of their agreement with the French, even though only a third of the Imperial Army was mobilized and deployed: Tannenberg and then the disaster at the Masurian Lakes had followed. 'The first days of war were the first days of disgrace,' branding a sense of helplessness, of ineradicable inferiority into Russian consciousness in the face of a German war-machine which clicked, whirred, and roared to command. The German success in the east was huge and enlarged by the developing myth of Hindenburg-Ludendorff; the German command waged a relentless, fierce war, applying the principle of mobility and maximum concentration against the weakest point with devastating effect.

It was also a brutal war: if 'the flames of Louvain' blazed in the west, so did 'the flames of Kalisz' crackle in the east. For a moment, when the fat, trembling Prittwitz had the telephone to Moltke in his hand, disaster seemed to loom, but massed German guns, the speeding German trains, the tactical ingenuity of the command swept this away. Yet, almost ironically, the very magnitude of German successes in the east conjured up problems of a singular order for the military leaders; the critical issue was not that some German formations had moved from west to east during a particular battle, but that the idea burgeoned of winning the war by actions in the east. German victory in this theatre itself contributed directly to sustaining hopes for speedy, 'total' victory—and the prospect of knocking an enfeebled, bumbling Russia out of the war seemed glittering. General Falkenhayn was not so very greatly impressed (nor, for the moment, was Russia's military prospect utterly critical); Falkenhayn, committed to guarding the gains in the west and launching limited offensives to tear at the enemy, was firmly of the opinion that 'no decision in the east . . . could spare us from fighting to a conclusion in the west'. Hindenburg and Ludendorff perforce argued that Germany could not afford—if for no other reason because of the need to hold up a tottering Austria-Hungary—to defer or avoid seeking a decision in the east.

Serbia Fights Back

Alan Palmer

As the Germans thrust towards Paris and the Russians blundered into disaster at Tannenberg, the world press tended to forget that the initial dispute in 1914 had been between the small Balkan kingdom of Serbia and her mighty neighbour, Austria-Hungary. Yet the opening shots of the First World War were fired, not by advancing infantry on the Eastern Front or massed artillery on Germany's borders, but by Austrian naval gunners manning their weapons more than seven hundred miles from the sea. For on 29th July 1914, five days before war came to the west, two monitors of the Danubian flotilla slipped downstream from their moorings at the Austro-Hungarian frontier-town of Zemun, lobbed some salvoes into Belgrade and turned back up river as the Serbian guns on the heights above the city began to return their fire.

Militarily, this isolated and indecisive duel was unimportant since it was followed by long days of unbroken calm along the Danube; but it emphasized what the map showed all too clearly – Belgrade was the only capital in Europe on an international frontier. Small wonder that the Serbian general staff assumed that the first objective of Austro-Hungarian policy must be the occupation of the city. They had made every preparation for the expected assault. Even before war was declared, the royal court and the government were evacuated to Niš and the limestone hills around Belgrade were filled with troops and guns. Marshal Radomir Putnik, the sixty-seven year old Serbian chief-of-staff, was ready to defend the city street by street. But he knew that the blow might fall elsewhere along the 250-mile frontier with Austria-Hungary. Determined to take no chances, he concentrated his reserve divisions south of Belgrade, where they would have greater freedom of movement. It was as well that he did so.

The Austrian war-plan against Serbia – Plan B – had been devised by General Conrad von Hötzendorf, the fire-eating chief-of-staff who had pressed for a punitive campaign in Serbia ever since the Bosnia Crisis of 1908. The plan was strategically far more subtle than the Serbian general staff believed. For Conrad proposed to destroy 'this kingdom of pig-breeders' not by a frontal assault on Belgrade, but by an enveloping movement from the west and north-west which would strike deep into the Balkan lands. Three Austrian Armies were to be concentrated along the River Sava and its tributary, the Drina. The V Army would bridge the Drina and thrust twenty-five miles inland to the small town of Valjevo, supported by the II Army crossing the Sava in the north and the VI Army advancing from Bosnia in the south-west. This invading force, comprising 400,000 men, would establish a line from Belgrade through Valjevo to Užice and then march on Niš and the Bulgarian frontier – an advance which would not only cut Serbia in half, but have the incidental effect of occupying the one Serbian munitions factory, at Kragujevac. Within fourteen days Conrad reckoned that Serbia would be destroyed as a national unit.

The Austrians appeared to have all the advantages. Their troops were fresh, for whereas the Serbs had fought two campaigns in as many years, it was nearly half a century since Austrian guns had been tested in battle. The Serbs were short of rifles, machine-guns, and heavy artillery, and were cut off from their western allies. Only by calling up reservists in their sixties and seventies could the Serbs equal in size the enemy force concentrated along their western frontier – and they had to keep a wary eye to the east in case Bulgaria might seek revenge for her defeat in the Second Balkan War. Serbian morale was high, while some of the Slav regiments of Austria-Hungary, particularly the Czechs, were unwilling to fight and eager to desert; but no one could be certain how the Serbian peasants would react if ordered to abandon their homes to an invader.

To chastise the Serbs

Conrad was so confident of an easy victory that he left Balkan operations in the hands of a subordinate and set off for headquarters in Galicia, where the Russian threat posed more pressing problems. At the same time he placed restrictions on the use of the II Army, for he needed its 75,000 men at an early stage for operations against the Russians: they might make a demonstration against the Serbs but not run the risk of heavy casualties. The man to whom Conrad entrusted Plan B was the governor of Bosnia, General Oskar Potiorek, an officer with an intense personal desire to chastise the Serbs, for he had been sitting in front of Archduke Franz Ferdinand on that fateful June day in Sarajevo when Princip's shots broke the peace of Europe.

At first all went well. The II Army crossed the Sava during the night of 11th August and took the Serbian town of Šabac without difficulty. At dawn on 12th August, forty miles to the south, the V Army crossed the Drina at a point where it was more than a hundred yards wide but where small islands gave some cover to the assault troops. But once the V Army reached the far bank it came under heavy fire from two Serbian divisions, fighting in their own home districts, along the valley of the small river Jadar. The gradually ascending terrain favoured the defenders, who were securely entrenched along the ridge of hills. With the temperature in the eighties, the Austrians found that they could make only painfully slow progress. On the second day the offensive ground to a halt, twenty miles short of its objective, Valjevo. It was clear that the Austrians would have to prise the Serbs from their hill positions before continuing the advance.

Putnik hurriedly sent four fresh divisions to assist his troops along the Jadar, with some hardy veterans marching sixty miles in forty-eight hours despite the heat. The Serbs were in their natural element among the rocky clefts of Mount Cer, where a fortress originally built by the Roman Emperor Trajan crowned a crest 2,250 feet high. The Austrian losses were terrifying, but for four days they pushed forward through undergrowth into woods and eventually to the bare face of the rock. Desperate telegrams from Potiorek

to Conrad secured permission for the II Army to move forward into the mountains south of Šabac; but soon it too was halted by the natural bastions of rock. With the VI Army still waiting for the order to advance, Potiorek's nerve began to fail; and, as the Serbs launched a counterattack on 19th August, he pulled his troops back across the river. By 24th August he had completely withdrawn from Serbian territory.

Potiorek's influential connexions with the court in Vienna saved him from disgrace. He insisted that he had made a strategic withdrawal in order to re-group his forces for a second attack. And, indeed, a fortnight later—on 7th September—the Austrians duly launched another offensive across the Drina. The II Army had by now been transferred to Galicia and Potiorek relied on a powerful thrust by the combined V and VI Armies, making full use of the Austrian superiority in artillery. This time the Serbs suffered heavy casualties, for one of their divisions had penetrated into Hungarian territory and was caught by Potiorek's guns as it sought to re-cross the Sava, losing nearly five thousand men in a few hours. But the Austrians could make no more progress against the fastness of the Cer than they had in August. Moreover, finding that Potiorek had left the approaches to Bosnia lightly defended, Putnik daringly ordered two Serbian divisions to seek to turn the Austrian flank and march on Sarajevo. It was a most successful counterthrust, for Potiorek immediately broke off the battle on the lower Drina and for seven weeks pursued the elusive Serbian force through the woods of Bosnia so as to ensure the safety of Sarajevo. Once again the Austrians were halted in their tracks.

Rain, ice, and snow

Time was, however, on the side of the Austrians: they had the men and material, and the Serbs did not. As rain and ice swept down on the Balkan mountains, turning the Serbian supply-lines into a quagmire, Potiorek prepared for a third thrust across the Drina. In the first week of November a thunderous bombardment echoed down the Jadar valley as the Austrian artillery sought to wipe the Serbian defences off the map and reduce

the end of the 19th century the Italian irredentists had seen Slav pressure grow, politically, economically, socially, and culturally. They could not disregard it. They wanted to become part of Italy; but they were, nevertheless, also willing to fight a war for the Triple Alliance.

When it became certain that there would be a European war the Nationalists, therefore, had few doubts. They wanted Italy to enter the war on the side of Austria-Hungary and Germany. They admired Germany and considered the Habsburg empire a great bulwark against the Slav advance. And they were concerned more about the Mediterranean and the colonies than about the Balkans. The real enemy for them was Italy's 'Latin sister', France, who had usurped the position of a great power, while she was becoming ever weaker on account of her democratic misgovernment.

The Liberals supported the Triple Alliance for rather different reasons. The Liberals, who still considered themselves the true 'governing party', prided themselves on being cautious and realistic, and for that very reason were unwilling to break old ties. One could see this simply by reading their mass-circulation newspapers, whether Giolittian or anti-Giolittian, northern or southern. *La Stampa, La Tribuna, Il Giornale d'Italia, Il Mattino,* and *Il Resto del Carlino,* all predicted, or at least admitted, that Italy would intervene on the side of the Central powers. They may have been frightened at the prospect of Great Britain entering the war, but what they feared more was isolation. They regarded the Triple Alliance as a means by which Italy could assert itself. There were some exceptions, but even Luigi Albertini, editor of the *Corriere della Sera,* who regretted the Austrian ultimatum and its result, did not exclude the possibility of Italy entering the war on the side of her ancient allies.

Then there were the Catholics who, for the most part, made the arguments of the Liberals their own. They felt a special sympathy with Austria, the great Catholic state and bulwark against the Orthodox Christian Slavs. Everyone—Nationalists, Liberals, Catholics, at any rate—severely judged the popular parties which, at a moment's notice, organized meetings and demonstrations against the war. The government alone had the right to the last say: the state must be strong and disciplined. Memories of the 'Red Week' lingered on, aggravating the differences between the parties.

The view of the popular parties

Even among the popular parties there were some who, like Arturo Labriola, the tireless spokesman of revolutionary syndicalism, were in favour of Italy's intervention on the side of the Central powers. Some influential Radical parliamentarians were of the same opinion but, on the whole, the popular parties were against war. They revived their past preoccupations: opposition to the Triple Alliance, sympathy for France, distrust for the monarchy, the antimilitarism which had been growing since 1911, internationalism and pacifism. They organized demonstrations and took up again their traditional catchphrases 'against Austrian militarism which had erected gallows and gibbets in Italy'. 'No blood, no money, no complicity with the Habsburgs'. 'Let governments of all Europe set light to the fuse; the explosion will blow them up and them only'. But events took the popular parties by surprise and their various moves were badly coordinated. News from beyond the Alps of the international proletariat's trial of strength (to prevent war) was dishearteningly bad. Moreover, there was bad blood between revolutionaries, Social Reformists, and Radicals. The popular parties, while seeking a decision in favour of neutrality, were already showing their weaknesses.

These party divisions gave the government a fairly free hand, but it did not find it easy to orientate itself. The right-wing Liberal-Conservative, Antonio Salandra, had replaced Giolitti as prime minister in March. Giolitti cabled from Paris in favour of neutrality, but Sidney Sonnino, the old political friend of Salandra, the real leader of the Liberal-Conservative wing, insisted on fighting with Italy's allies. And for his part the chief of general staff, General Cadorna, had on 29th July already taken military measures to strengthen defences against France. Two days later he even suggested to the King that half the Italian army should be transferred to the Rhine to help the Germans. Nevertheless, the government was increasingly favouring the course of neutrality and on 2nd August the Italian government declared itself neutral. Nothing in the Triple Alliance compelled Italy to mobilize, and Austria-Hungary was opposed to any discussion on the 'compensations' foreseen by the treaty. The Italian government therefore reasserted its freedom of action. But there were many alternatives. San Giuliano, the foreign minister, was soon to consider war against Austria, though without excluding other eventualities: 'it suits us to make every effort to maintain good relations for after the war with the allies', he wrote to Salandra on 4th August. Later he confided to his friends, 'The ideal for us would be for Austria to be defeated on one side and France on the other'. Despite everything, the legacy of the Triple Alliance was still strong. And it is here that we have the key to our understanding of the events.

Only a few days after the declaration of neutrality the Nationalists made a *volte face*. They now argued that Italy should enter the war against Austria-Hungary. The leap was certainly enormous. Nevertheless, the Nationalists did not try to disclaim the attitude they had held earlier. They still wanted Italy to become a really great power. But the Central powers, they argued, had left Italy in the lurch, and the Triple Alliance no longer served any purpose. It was better, therefore, to gain supremacy in the Adriatic. Italy had to wage 'her own war', the 'Italian War', and conquer Trento, Trieste, and Dalmatia. Italy had no interests in common with France, Great Britain, or Russia. Her natural alliances were not with these powers; and once the war was over she would have to reconstruct them. Austria-Hungary, the Nationalists thought, should be reduced but should not disappear, Germany would be conquered but still powerful. Some time in the future, Italy would march again hand in hand with the Central powers for the great conflict, which would take place in the Mediterranean.

For the Nationalists in particular, an alliance between Italy and Germany, nations who had come recently into being as unified states at the same time inspired by the same national enthusiasm, obeyed the laws of history.

The Nationalists (Corradini, Federzoni, Rocco, and others) were few in number, and had only three representatives in parliament (ten if one includes their allies). But they spoke a great deal and got themselves talked about even more. They had the sympathy of many Liberal-Conservatives and Catholics. In order to strengthen their position, they were prepared to come to an agreement even with the interventionists from the popular parties. The Nationalists intended to use them, not to serve them. The war, they thought, would mark the triumph of the authority of true values: tradition, hierarchy, discipline, 'in place of the three false ideals – innovation, equality, and liberty'. The Nationalists, in fact, wanted as always to drag in the other parties of order, and, unfortunately, they met no insuperable obstacles.

The Liberal reaction

The Liberals remained the largest party, but now they seemed unequal to the gravity of the situation. They were split into neutralists and interventionists. Perhaps it was not so much this that mattered but rather that they no longer shared the ideas of the Nationalists, without managing to find any realistic alternatives. Whether neutralists or interventionists, it was on the whole difficult for them to go beyond their programme: to negotiate with Austria-Hungary (for Trentino and part of Venezia-Giulia) or to declare 'our war'.

The Liberals were also deeply reluctant to abandon completely the July 1914 position. Those who tended to favour war wanted first to discover whether Vienna would concede any of the Italian districts in Austrian possession. Those inclined towards neutrality wanted to be sure that it would not imperil Italy's position. They would stay neutral, but only at a price – which they were prepared to make Austria-Hungary pay. In other words, they were prepared for a purely 'Italian War', one that would not involve them too much with the Entente powers and would not, if possible, mean an irreparable break with Germany. They had their own views undoubtedly; but it was almost impossible to stand in the way of the Nationalists.

Giolitti, 'the old wizard' of Italian politics, was for once in danger of failing to produce the magic formula to calm the tempest. He was still the head of the majority party, but he brushed aside the advice of friends to bring down the Salandra government. He preferred to influence affairs from the outside. Salandra, prime minister mainly because of Giolitti's support, was a Liberal-Conservative, and an old enemy; but the Liberal-Conservatives in fact were hesitating, inclined towards neutrality, but neutrality 'with profit and with honour'. This almost coincided with Giolitti's policy. With his experience, with his hidden but deep faith in the liberal state, Giolitti tried to study the problem deeply, but he did not this time manage to find a clear-cut solution. All too often he measured events with a pre-war yardstick. He thought, in spite of everything, that the real friction was between Great Britain and Russia in the Dardanelles and in Asia, and that in any case the Entente between Great Britain, France, and Russia was not stable. In Giolitti's opinion, everything was still in a state of flux.

In the spring of 1915 *La Stampa,* the great Giolittian newspaper, let it be understood that Italy's real hope for the future would consist in an Anglo-German-Italian agreement. Italy, as long as she could, would have to move between Great Britain and Germany.

Certainly, for the moment at least, it was hard to separate Germany from Austria-Hungary. Giolitti felt that hostility against Austria-Hungary would automatically mean hostility against Germany, and this seemed to him a very strong argument in favour of neutrality. But at moments Giolitti appeared to share the idea that Germany would leave Austria at her hour of need to her own destiny and that Italy could declare war against Austria with Germany's agreement or connivance. Just as in May 1915, one of his followers was later to reveal, Giolitti still hoped that some secret factor would be found which could justify the government's decision — that secret factor being an agreement with Germany at Austria-Hungary's expense. Giolitti considered that Italy was still too weak, and that one had to weigh things carefully before exposing her to war.

In January 1915 Giolitti published a famous letter, in which he declared himself in favour of negotiations with Vienna. Giolitti, as usual, was thinking of Trentino, of part of Venezia-Giulia, of Trieste Free City — all territories he seriously wanted to obtain. 'If the war ends without our gaining any advantage there will be trouble. Even present neutralists will throw stones,' he confided to his friends.

Giolitti was a relative neutralist; and so, in the main, were the business community and the organized Catholics. So too was the Holy See, which took it for granted that Italy should obtain part of the unredeemed territory from Austria — otherwise intervention was inevitable. Such was the predominant mood in Italy.

The popular parties and intervention

No serious guarantee of neutrality was possible. The PSI, a number of Syndicalists, and Anarchists tried to ensure it, but in vain. The masses, in particular the large peasant masses, were calm. As many Prefects reported, they were quite resigned. In the event of intervention against Austria-Hungary, there would be no serious disorders.

The defence of neutrality did not allow any effective political initiative. Many revolutionaries (Socialists, Republicans, Anarchists, and Syndicalists) were soon convinced of this. Benito Mussolini, editor of the Socialist newspaper *Avanti!,* was one of these.

Those of the revolutionaries who favoured intervention on the side of the Entente powers considered that, from the beginning, the government's position of neutrality had been equivocal. The parties of order, they thought, were beating about the bush, were still aiming at some kind of compromise with the feudal authoritarian Central powers. The revolutionary interventionists felt that the war was a 'revolution of the people' — against the establishment, against the old ruling class, against the monarchy, and for a revolutionary cause and for international democracy. They wanted to bring to a happy end the *Risorgimento* (the 19th-century wars in which Italy threw off the Austrian yoke), and secure the triumph of a vague 'proletarian nationalism'.

In reality there was a great deal of confusion in these ideas. Popular leaders like Bissolati, Salvemini, and Battisti tried to clarify the situation. They were the leaders of another form of interventionism, which was openly democratic. They wanted to see the disappearance of Austria-Hungary and the triumph of the principle of 'nationality'. Intervention, participation in the 'democratic war', had, they thought, become a duty as well as a necessity. But they failed to convince even all their own followers; and they succeeded even less in convincing the parties of order.

In fact, as when Italy declared herself neutral, in August, the final word was again left to the government, which had to resolve the dilemma: negotiations with Austria or an 'Italian war'.

Giolitti was in agreement; but this time he had committed two errors: he had not taken into account Austria-Hungary's habit of always arriving 'an hour late' at the appointments of history. Furthermore, he had not fully realized what leaving a free hand to the government in power, principally to the key men, might involve—particularly when the key men were men like Salandra and Sonnino, who became foreign minister in November 1914, after San Giuliano's death. The consequences of these two errors, when added to one another, were irreparable. Salandra and Sonnino, of course, started serious negotiations in Vienna, and also in Rome with Bülow, the former German chancellor. But when Austria hesitated and procrastinated about considering territorial concessions, Salandra and Sonnino, much more readily than Giolitti, embraced the idea of war. Salandra and Sonnino were not warmongers; they suppressed mass demonstrations of the interventionists. But as good Liberal-Conservatives they reasoned differently from Giolitti. In Italy they thought there was a need to reinforce the authority of the state, to strengthen traditional institutions, to improve the prestige of both crown and army. A victorious war— which, as many thought at the time, would last six months or a year at the most— could be just what was needed.

At the beginning of March they opened negotiations with the Entente powers; on 26th April 1915 they signed the Treaty of London. Sonnino, who in 1914 had so decisively supported intervention on the side of Austria-Hungary and Germany, had now taken the plunge. But he did not abandon all his ideas. By the treaty Italy was to obtain south Tyrol (Trentino), Trieste, Venezia-Giulia, and northern Dalmatia together with several islands, in order to guarantee Italian supremacy in the Adriatic against the Slavs. In short, the treaty corresponded to the 'Italian War' concept. Moreover, the treaty did not say in so many words that relations with Germany would irreparably be broken off. At least

that is what Salandra and Sonnino relied on. And it was not to be until the middle of 1916 that Italy declared war against Germany.

Nevertheless, there was more than enough in this treaty to trouble Giolitti and the majority of Liberals and Catholics. When the news broke there were also several Liberal-Conservatives who thought that Salandra and Sonnino had jumped the gun. Giolitti returned to Rome, and soon afterwards, on 13th May, the ministry resigned.

It was the last but one act of the drama. Salandra and Sonnino were really quite willing to cede power or to accept Giolitti's advice: to re-open negotiations with Vienna. They interpreted the Treaty of London as an agreement between governments and not between states, especially as military plans were still unsettled. And the recent Austro-German victory at Gorlice-Tarnów (2nd May) caused anxiety. But it was now too late to reappraise the situation.

Passions had been roused little by little; interventionists, once united, organized demonstration after demonstration at which d'Annunzio made his inspiring calls to rebellion, to war, and to violence; the neutralists, uncertain and passive, were as usual not keeping up with events. Giolitti himself did not want to take back the reins of power. The situation was getting too hot to handle, and the risk of failure after having advised resumption of negotiations, was too great.

Italy declares war

The King had, meanwhile, refused to accept the resignation of the Salandra ministry. On the 24th May 1915 Italy entered the war against Austria-Hungary, Salandra invoking what he called *sacro egoismo*—the sacred demands of self-interest—to justify this action. But the situation was by no means clear. The old ruling class was by now split. The interventionists once again started squabbling among themselves. The Socialists had lost the initiative. Economic preparations were inadequate, and were arranged from day to day. Moreover, the country in a large measure was passive. This assuredly was not a good start for the terrible ordeal to come.

Foreign policy encountered far more serious difficulties. During the negotiations with Austria-Hungary, and during those which led up to the Treaty of London, the aims of national unity for the 'unredeemed territories' had certainly established the directive throughout. But between *real-politik* and nationalism the liberal aim of the 19th century had now dispersed itself. In 1914-15 the myth of the 'last war of the *Risorgimento*' was still alive, but had little or at least only indirect, influence on the ruling classes.

What is more, with Italy's intervention, the problem created by the Habsburgs' rule over many widely differing nationalities had been put into the 'melting pot'. But Italy, under the Treaty of London, could not co-operate with the other oppressed nationalities of the Habsburg empire. The possibilities of a happy solution were more remote than ever.

The army was also in difficulties. Much money had been spent on it, but military preparations had followed old-fashioned methods. Moreover — it is the only conclusion which could be deduced from the fighting which had already taken place in the war — tactical and strategic plans were based on the theory that frontal attack on the enemy troops would be the best method of fighting. The battles and the massacres of the Isonzo were not far off. That the chief of staff, the army commander in the war, should be the very same Cadorna who in July 1914 had suggested that half the Italian army should be mobilized on the Rhine against France, seemed at the moment only an ironical symbol of the troubled thinking which led Italy into the war. *(Translation)*

Part two · Central Powers Ascendant

For the Allies, 1915 was stained with disasters. They entered it with high hopes and with the majority of their leaders, both military and political, believing that within twelve months the war would be won. Those months went by and the demands made by the war became bigger than ever, without either side seemingly being able to produce a decision. When they looked back on it they saw that on balance things had gone better for the Central Powers than for themselves. The entry of Italy into the war had been offset by the loss of Serbia; a German offensive had sent Russia reeling backwards; and, whatever conclusions were to be drawn about the course of the war on the Western Front, there had been undeniable British failure in the Dardanelles.

The Gallipoli adventure sparked controversy which has remained lively to this day. It was launched in response to a Russian plea to her allies for a 'demonstration' against Turkey, whose troops were entering the Caucasus. Underlying it too was a sound strategic insight—that the Western Front might yield less decisive results in proportion to the force expended there than would 'sideshow' attacks on Germany's allies. Churchill had already, in late 1914, proposed a naval attack on the Dardanelles. Now he resurrected and enlarged upon the plan, and his persuasiveness overrode the ineffectualities of the War Council and the open alarm of Admiralty colleagues. From a naval point of view, he underestimated the hazards of the Dardanelles currents and the effectiveness of the Turkish inner defences: the British fleet suffered humiliating losses. Militarily, the affair was a chaos of non-communication, which nevertheless came near to success. Indeed the road to success was left open by the inept

way in which the German commander disposed his defences. He was saved by British mismanagement, by good luck, and by the courage of the Turkish troops, hitherto the despair of their German officers. The subsidence of the Gallipoli fronts into trench warfare made the decision to withdraw only a matter of time.

On the Western Front the Allied leaders believed that the key to success lay in a reversion to open warfare. The enemy had eluded them by digging in after the Marne: drive him from his holes, force him into 'real' battle, and victory would follow. They derived encouragement for this view from the east, where a combination of space, limited firepower, and great bodies of cavalry gave the campaign an appearance altogether different from the closely-fought positional battles of the west. The Germans, for their part, were encouraged by their eastern successes of 1914 to believe that a decisive result against Russia could be obtained by a comparatively modest increase in the strength of their forces there. The Western Front, meanwhile, would necessarily be defensive, but not seriously depleted.

Of the several Allied attempts to drive the war out into the open, the first, Haig's assault at Neuve-Chapelle, could have been exploited to the point of success. In several places the attackers broke right through into open country—a feat they were not to repeat for two and a half years. Enfeebled by hesitant leadership and poor communications, they merely milled about until the Germans had time to throw together an improvised but adequate second line. (Ironically the Germans in turn created, and failed to grasp, the same opportunity for themselves at Ypres when their use of poison gas for the first time, against French colonial troops, resulted in the immediate collapse of the Allied line.) The lessons of Neuve-Chapelle were learnt by the Germans but not by the British. The Germans acknowledged that they had underestimated the potential of the British artillery and hastily began to dig deeper and more heavily reinforced defences. The British concluded that 'by means of careful preparation' a section of the enemy's front line could be captured with little loss. In the face of the terrible defensive power of the machine gun, direct frontal assaults were to go on. From the ensuing bloody debacles little was learnt, though the increasing reliance on preparation by bombardment was to make revolutionary demands on industry for guns and ammunition (indeed the British shortage of shells at the front became a domestic scandal).

News from the east brought no comfort for the Allies. In the early summer the long delayed German offensive burst upon the Russian right flank. One by one all the towns whose fall had cheered the Allies at the end of 1914 were abandoned by the Tsarist armies as the Germans cut great swathes into their defences and took hundreds of thousands of prisoners. In the west, the Allies decided that a massive attack was necessary — massive enough to draw back the bulk of the German army across Poland and give relief to the failing Russians. Ironically, by the time the attack was launched, orders had already been given for the German offensive in the east to be halted, and the divisions transferred to France. The place, selected by Joffre, was Loos, the result another bloodbath and miserable defeat. For the British, perhaps the most significant effect was the dismissal of Sir John French. Haig's promotion, and the transfer of Robertson to London as chief of the imperial general staff. This created a military duumvirate which was to dominate British strategic thinking for the remainder of the war.

The Germans had a secondary objective in the east: in August 1915 they determined to eliminate Serbia from the war. Although the Serbs had thrown back the Austro-Hungarians in 1914, their army, now depleted by casualties and ravaged by typhus, was in no position to withstand a substantial assault unaided. Such aid as the Allies did send, a scratch force of 13,000 diverted from Gallipoli, was too little and arrived too late. With not only the armies of Germany and Austria-Hungary, but those of Bulgaria also, pressing down upon them from the north and east, the Serbs withdrew into the south-west. In November, not just an army, but virtually the whole Serbian nation was on the march towards the hoped-for safety of the Adriatic coast. Tens of thousands of them, men, women, and children, died in the passage through the frozen mountains of Albania.

The Dardanelles Campaign

Robert Rhodes James

It is doubtful whether any single campaign of either of the two World Wars has aroused more attention and controversy than the ill-fated venture to force the Dardanelles in 1915. 'Nothing so distorted perspective, disturbed impartial judgement, and impaired the sense of strategic values as the operations on Gallipoli,' Sir Edward Grey has written. Lord Slim — who fought at Gallipoli, and was seriously wounded — has described the Gallipoli commanders in scathing terms as the worst since the Crimean War. The defenders of the enterprise — notably Winston Churchill, Sir Roger Keyes, and General Sir Ian Hamilton — have been no less vehement and there have been other commentators who have thrown a romantic pall over the campaign. 'The drama of the Gallipoli campaign,' wrote the British official historian, 'by reason of the beauty of its setting, the grandeur of its theme, and the unhappiness of its ending, will always rank amongst the world's classic tragedies.' He then went on to quote Aeschylus's words: 'What need to repine at fortune's frowns? The gain hath the advantage, and the loss does not bear down the scale.'

Today, more than fifty years later, the Gallipoli controversies still rumble sulphurously, and the passions that the campaign aroused have not yet been stilled.

Amateurs in council

Few major campaigns have been initiated under stranger circumstances. The opening months of the war had imposed a strain upon the Liberal government from which it never really recovered. Asquith's leadership at the outbreak of war had been firm and decisive, but subsequently — whether from ill-health, as has been recently suggested by Lord Salter, or from other causes

is immaterial in this narrative — his influence had been flaccid and irresolute. The creation of a War Council in November had not met the essential problem; the council met irregularly, its Service members were silent, and its manner of doing business was amateurish and unimpressive. As Winston Churchill commented in a memorandum circulated in July 1915: 'The governing instrument here has been unable to make up its mind except by very lengthy processes of argument and exhaustion, and that the divisions of opinion to be overcome, and the number of persons of consequence to be convinced, caused delays and compromises. We have always sent two-thirds of what was necessary a month too late.'

The military situation itself played a crucial part in what developed. The first fury of the war had been spent, and the opposing lines writhed from the Channel to the Swiss frontier; Russia had reeled back from her advance on East Prussia; everywhere, the belligerents had failed to secure their primary objectives. Already, the character of the battle on the Western Front had become grimly evident, and by the end of 1914 Churchill (first lord of the Admiralty), Lord Fisher (first sea lord), Lloyd George (chancellor of the exchequer), and Sir Maurice Hankey (secretary to the War Council) were thinking in terms of using British force — and particularly sea power — in another sphere.

It was Churchill who emerged with the most attractive proposal. Since the early weeks of the war his restlessness had been unconcealed, and he had already proposed, at the first meeting of the War Council on 25th November, a naval attack on the Dardanelles, with the ultimate object of destroying the German warships, *Goeben* and *Breslau,* whose escape from British squadrons in the Mediterranean in August had been a decisive factor in bringing Turkey into the war at the beginning of November on the German side. The suggestion had been shelved, but the idea had been put forward, and Hankey is not alone in stressing the significance of this first airing of the plan.

Impatience with the lack of progress on the Western Front was now buttressed by an appeal from Russia for a 'demonstration' against Turkey, after a large Turkish army had advanced into the Caucasus. (By the time the appeal was received, the Turks had been defeated, but this was not known for some time in London.) Churchill at once revived the idea of an assault on the Dardanelles, and telegraphed to the British admiral — Carden — in command of the squadron standing off the western entrance of the Dardanelles about the possibilities of a purely naval assault. Admiral Carden replied cautiously to the effect that a gradual attack might succeed; Churchill pushed the issue, and Carden was instructed to submit his detailed plans; when these arrived, Churchill put the matter before the War Council.

The extent to which Churchill's service colleagues at the Admiralty were alarmed at this speed was not communicated to the ministers on the council, a fact which to a large degree absolves them from their collective responsibility. Churchill's account was brilliant and exciting, and on 15th January the War Council agreed that 'the Admiralty should prepare for a naval expedition in February to bombard and take the Gallipoli peninsula, with Constantinople as its object'. Churchill took this as a definite decision; Asquith, however, considered that it was 'merely provisional, to prepare, but nothing more'; Admiral Sir Arthur Wilson, a member of the council, subsequently said that 'it was not my business. I was not in any way connected with the question, and it had never in any way officially been put before me'. Churchill's naval secretary considered that the naval members of the council 'only agreed to a purely naval operation on the understanding that we could always draw back — that there should be no question of what is known as forcing the Dardanelles'. Fisher, by this stage, was very alarmed indeed.

Quite apart from the matter of whether the navy had sufficient reserve of men and ships — even old ships, which was a major part of Churchill's scheme — to afford such an operation, the forcing of the Dardanelles had for long been regarded with apprehension by the navy, and Churchill himself had written in 1911 that 'it should be remembered that it is no longer possible to force the Dardanelles, and nobody would expose a modern fleet to such peril'. But Churchill — as his evidence to the Dardanelles Commission, only recently available for examination, clearly reveals — had been profoundly impressed by the effects of

German artillery bombardments on the Belgian forts, and it was evident that the Turkish batteries were conspicuously sited, exposed, and equipped with obsolete equipment. And Churchill was not alone in rating Turkish military competence low. The admirals' doubts were put aside, Fisher swallowed his misgivings, and Carden prepared for the assault.

All this represented a considerable achievement for Churchill. There is no doubt that he forced the pace, that the initiative was solely his, and that his subsequent account in *The World Crisis* must be approached with great caution. A case in point is his version of the negotiations to persuade Lord Kitchener (secretary of state for war) to release the Regular 29th Division for the Eastern Mediterranean. The recently revealed minutes of the War Council make it plain that Churchill had no intention of using the troops for the attack on the Dardanelles, but to employ them subsequently 'to reinforce our diplomacy' and garrison Constantinople. It was not surprising that Kitchener did not agree to send the division until March 10th.

The plans for the naval attack continued, and the British and Dominion (Australian and New Zealand) troops in Egypt were put on the alert. Carden opened his attack on 19th February, and had no difficulty in suppressing the outer forts at Sedd-el-Bahr and Kum Kale. The difficulties really began when the warships entered the Straits.

The intermediate and inner defences consisted of gun emplacements on the Gallipoli and Asiatic shores. These were supplemented by batteries capable of causing damage only to lightly armoured ships, and by mobile batteries. The Straits had been mined since the beginning of the war, but it was only in February and March that the lines of mines represented a serious menace. The attempts of the British minesweepers — East Coast fishing trawlers manned by civilian crews and commanded by a naval officer with no experience whatever of minesweeping — ended in complete failure. Marines went ashore at Kum Kale and Sedd-el-Bahr on several occasions, but early in March the resistance to these operations increased sharply.

Bad weather made the tasks of the warships and the hapless trawlers — barely able to make headway against the fierce Dardanelles current, operating under fire in wholly unfamiliar circumstances—even more difficult. Carden was an ailing man. The warships—with the exception of the brand-new battleship *Queen Elizabeth*—were old and in many cases in need of a refit. The standard of the officers was mixed. The Turkish resistance was more strenuous with every day that passed. The momentum of the advance faltered.

Urged on by Churchill, Carden decided to reverse his tactics; the fleet would silence the guns to allow the sweepers to clear the minefields. On the eve of the attack Carden collapsed and was replaced by Rear-Admiral Robeck.

By now, the soldiers were on the scene. Lieutenant-General Birdwood, a former military secretary to Kitchener now commanding the Anzacs in Egypt, had been sent by Kitchener to the Dardanelles to report on the situation. His reports were to the effect that military support was essential. Slowly a military force was gathered together, and General Sir Ian Hamilton was appointed commander-in-chief of what was called the Mediterranean Expeditionary Force, and which consisted at that moment of some 70,000 British, Dominion, and French troops. Hamilton was informed of his new appointment on 12th March; he left the next day—Friday, 13th March—with a scratch staff hastily gathered together, a series of instructions from Kitchener, and some meagre scraps of information about the area and the Turks. He arrived just in time for the *débâcle* of 18th March. Robeck lost three battleships sunk, and three crippled, out of nine; the minefields had not been touched.

Much ink has subsequently been spilled on the subject of what Robeck ought to have done. He did not know, of course, that the Turkish lack of heavy shells made their situation desperate. Even if he had, the fact remained that it was the mobile and minor batteries that were holding up the minesweepers. Roger Keyes's plan of using destroyers as minesweepers and storming the minefields was the only one that had a real chance of success, and it would have taken some time to prepare them.

The soldiers, however, were very willing to take over. On 22nd March Hamilton and Robeck agreed on a combined operation, and Hamilton sailed off to Alexandria to re-organize his scattered forces. 'No formal decision to make a land attack was even noted in the records of the Cabinet or the War Council,' as Churchill has written. '. . . This silent plunge into this vast military venture must be regarded as an extraordinary episode.' It was, however, no more extraordinary than the events that had preceded the crucial conference of 22nd March. Attempts by Hankey to obtain better information and an agreed assessment of the situation made no progress. 'The military operation appears, therefore, to be to a certain extent a gamble upon the supposed shortage of supplies and inferior fighting qualities of the Turkish armies,' he wrote in one of a series of prescient memoranda. But the War Council did not meet from the middle of March until two months later.

What subsequently happened was the direct result of the manner in which the British drifted haphazardly into a highly difficult amphibious operation. No calculation had been made of whether the British had the resources to undertake this operation. As Hankey wrote at the end of March: 'Up to the present time . . . no attempt has been made to estimate what force is required. We have merely said that so many troops are available and that they ought to be enough.' The state of affairs was subsequently well summarized by Sir William Robertson: 'The Secretary of State for War was aiming for decisive results on the Western Front. The First Lord of the Admiralty was advocating a military expedition to the Dardanelles. The Secretary of State for India was devoting his attention to a campaign in Mesopotamia. The Secretary of State for the Colonies was occupying himself with several small wars in Africa. And the Chancellor of the Exchequer was attempting to secure the removal of a large part of the British army from France to some Eastern Mediterranean theatre.'

One can sympathize with the cry of the GOC Egypt, Sir John Maxwell: 'Who is co-ordinating and directing this great combine?'

Furthermore, there was divided command in the eastern Mediterranean. Maxwell was in command in Egypt; Hamilton had his army; Robeck his ships. Before the campaign ended, there were further complications. Each commander fought for his own force and his own projects, and the limited supplies of men and material were distributed on an *ad hoc* and unco-ordinated basis.

To all these difficulties, Hamilton added some of his own. His refusal to bring his administrative staff into the initial planning—and, indeed, into anything at all so long as he was commander-in-chief—had some easily foreseeable results. Security was non-existent. 'The attack was heralded as few have ever been,' the Australian military historian has written. 'No condition designed to proclaim it seems to have been omitted.' This was not Hamilton's fault, yet his protests were wholly ineffective.

His plan for landing on Gallipoli—Asia he ruled out entirely, over the strong arguments of Birdwood and Hunter-Weston, commanding the 29th Division—was imaginative and daring. The 29th Division was to land at five small beaches at the southern end of the peninsula; the Anzacs were to land farther to the north on the western shore, just above the jutting promontory of Gaba Tepe, and then to push overland to the eminence of Mal Tepe, overlooking the narrows. There were to be feint landings at Bulair, at the 'neck' of the peninsula, and (by the French) at Besika Bay, opposite the island of Tenedos. The French were also to make a real, but temporary, landing at Kum Kale, to protect the landing of the 29th Division.

Meanwhile, the Turks had been having their own problems. Until March the Turkish forces in the area had been scattered and few in number. In spite of the urgency of the situation, the Turks acted lethargically. When, on the morning of 26th March, General Liman von Sanders arrived to take command of the troops at the Dardanelles, the situation that faced him was grim indeed. In short, his task was to defend a coast-line of some 150 miles with a total force of 84,000 men, but an actual fighting strength of only about 62,000. His army had no aircraft, and was seriously deficient in artillery and equipment. The men themselves, for so long used to defeat, were the despair of the German officers, and it would have been difficult to see in these poorly equipped and ragged formations the army that was to rise to such heights of valour and resource.

Sanders has been fortunate to have been treated at his own valuation by the majority of British commentators. In fact, he committed several major errors which might have been fatal. He placed two divisions at the neck of the peninsula, two on the Asiatic shore, one to defend the entire southern Gallipoli peninsula, and a final division in reserve near Mal Tepe. The entire area south of the bald, dominant height of Achi Baba was defended by one regiment and one field battery, with the reserves placed several hours' marching away to the north. To the dismay of the Turkish officers, Sanders drew his forces back from the beaches and concentrated them inland. This, the Turks argued, overlooked the fact that on the whole of the peninsula there were barely half a dozen beaches on which the British could land; Sanders, like Hamilton, over-estimated the effects of naval bombardment on well dug-in troops. He was saved by the epic courage of the Turkish troops, good luck, and mismanagement by the enemy from losing the entire campaign on the first day.

It is impossible, even now, to contemplate the events of 25th April 1915, without emotion. The British and Dominion troops sailed from Mudros Harbour, in the island of Lemnos, in a blaze of excitement and ardour. 'Courage our youth will always have,' Lord Slim has written, 'but those young men had a vision strangely medieval, never, I think, to be renewed.' It was the baptism of fire for the Anzacs. It was also, in a real sense, the day on which Turkey began her emergence as a modern nation.

Three of the British landings at Helles were virtually unopposed. One was resisted, but the enemy defeated. But the fifth, at Sedd-el-Bahr, was a catastrophe. As the British came ashore, a torrent of fire was poured upon them as they waded through the water or sat helplessly jammed in open boats; others who attempted to land from a converted collier, the *River Clyde,* fared no better. In this crisis Hunter-Weston did not show himself to advantage. He was in a cruiser, barely five minutes' sailing from the disastrous beach, yet it was not until the day was well advanced that he was aware of what had occurred. The day ended with the British, exhausted and shaken, clinging to their positions.

The Anzacs had had a day of very mixed fortunes. They had been landed over a mile to the north of their intended position, in some confusion, to be faced with precipitous cliffs and plunging, scrub-covered gorges. As the first men moved inland, congestion built up at the tiny beach – Anzac Cove – which had to cope with all reinforcements and supplies. Only one battery of field artillery was landed all day, and units became hopelessly intermingled. As in the south, the maps were dangerously inaccurate. By mid-morning the Turks had begun to counter-attack and, spurred on by the then unknown Colonel Mustapha Kemal, these attacks developed in fury throughout the day. By evening, the Anzacs were pushed back to a firing-line which extended only a thousand yards inland at the farthest point; casualties had been heavy, and Birdwood's divisional commanders advised evacuation. In the event, although Birdwood reluctantly agreed, Hamilton ordered him to hang on. This was virtually the only initiative taken by Hamilton – on board the *Queen Elizabeth* – throughout the day. As Birdwood wrote – some months later, 'he should have taken much more personal charge and *insisted* on things being done and really taken command, which he has never yet done'. Thus began the epic defence of Anzac, a fragment of cliff and gorge, overlooked by the enemy.

Hamilton pressed on at Helles, but although a limited advance was made, it was apparent by 8th May that the initial effort of his troops was spent. Casualties had been horrific – over 20,000 (of whom over 6,000 had been killed) out of a total force of 70,000 – and the medical and supply arrangements had completely collapsed under the wholly unexpected demands. The arrival of a German submarine and the sinking of three battleships – one by a Turkish torpedo-boat attack – deprived the army of the physical and psychological support of the guns of the fleet. Thus ended the first phase of the Gallipoli Campaign.

A week later the Liberal government fell, the first major casualty of the campaign, although there were other important contributory causes. Asquith formed a new coalition government in which Balfour, the former Conservative leader, replaced Churchill as first lord of the Admiralty. An inner cabinet, from 7th June called the Dardanelles Committee, took over the conduct of operations, and a ministry of munitions was established. The new government resolved to support

Hamilton, and more troops were dispatched. Hamilton continued to batter away at Helles throughout May and July until, in the memorable words of a British corporal, the battlefield 'looked like a midden and smelt like an opened cemetery'. Achi Baba still stood defiantly uncaptured, and the army was incapable of further sustained effort. To the shelling, the heat, and the harsh life of the trenches was now added the scourge of dysentery.

Hamilton now swung his assault north. A daring scheme for capturing the commanding heights of the Sari Bair range had been worked out at Anzac. Unfortunately, as in April, other schemes were added to this basic project, until it developed into a joint operation as complex and dangerous as the first. The Anzacs, with British and Indian reinforcements, would break out of the Anzac position to the north, and scale the incredibly tangled gullies and ridges to the summit of the Sari Bair range by night after diversionary attacks at the south of the Anzac position and at Helles. At dawn on 6th August, a new Army Corps would be landed in Suvla Bay, which was thought to be sparsely defended and which lay to the north of Anzac, and, at first light, the Turkish positions at Anzac would be assaulted from front and rear. Some 63,000 Allied troops would be attacking an area defended by well under 30,000 Turks.

This time, the veil of secrecy that descended on the operation was so complete that senior commanders were not informed until very late. Sir Frederick Stopford, the commander of the 9th Corps, which was to land at Suvla, was allowed to amend his instructions so that his task was merely to get ashore and capture the bay. There was no co-ordination between General Stopford and Birdwood at Anzac, either before or during the action. Hamilton stayed at his headquarters for two vital days.

In the circumstances, the marvel was that the operation came so close to success. Sanders, once again, was outwitted by Hamilton. The night march from Anzac was a chaotic and frightening business, but by dawn on August 7th the New Zealanders were within a fraction of seizing the vital summit. The Suvla landing, although opposed by small units and something of a shambles in other respects, was successful. By the morning of August 7th the Turkish situation at Sari Bair was desperate, but the heat, the exhaustion and inexperience of the British, and dilatoriness by their commanders, saved Sanders; the Turks, as always, fought with frenzy and unheeding valour. It developed into a weird, ghastly battle. At Suvla, 9th Corps remained glued to the shore, and advanced only with timidity. At Anzac, the failures in advance planning and command meant that everything depended on the courage and initiative of the troops and their immediate officers; neither were lacking, and the fighting was intensely bitter, even by Gallipoli standards; but they were insufficient. Sanders gave command of the entire area to Kemal, who checked the British at Suvla just as they were making a positive forward movement on the urgent commands of Hamilton, and at Sari Bair he launched a desperate attack at first light on August 10th that swept the Allies from the positions that had been won and held at a severely high cost. One British officer, commanding men of the 1/6th Gurkhas, had a glimpse of the Dardanelles.

The rest was aftermath. Hamilton launched one last abortive attack at Suvla which was in terms of numbers the biggest battle of the campaign, but the issue had already been decided. At home, the many opponents of the venture became more vociferous and urgent; a new army was sent to Salonika; the Gallipoli fronts subsided into trench warfare; the weather got colder, and the decision of Bulgaria to enter the war meant that Austrian guns began to shell the exposed British lines with a new accuracy. In October Hamilton was recalled. His successor was Sir Charles Monro, a man of a very different stamp, who recommended evacuation. Bluntly faced with the grim implications, the government became irresolute again. Kitchener went out to investigate, and was eventually persuaded of the necessity of withdrawal. Birdwood was in charge of the evacuation of Suvla and Anzac, which was brilliantly conducted, without a single casualty, on 19th-20th December.

The evacuation of Helles was now inevitable, and this was accomplished on 8th-9th January, again without loss of men, although that of stores and equipment was extensive. Thus, the campaign ended with a substantial triumph, an indication of what might have been achieved earlier.

The casualties were substantial. The first was the Asquith government, and, in particular, Churchill, whose removal from the Admiralty in May was a *sine qua non* for Conservative participation in the new coalition; it was many years before the shadow of Gallipoli was lifted from his reputation. Asquith's own prestige and position were badly shaken, as were those of Kitchener. The dream of a Balkan alliance against Germany was shattered, and Italy was the only Mediterranean nation that — in mid-May — joined the Allied cause. The British had acquired another vast commitment in Salonika. The Russian warm-sea outlet was irretrievably blocked. Compared with this last strategical disaster, the actual losses in battle or through disease — which are difficult to calculate on the Allied side but which were certainly over 200,000 (the Turkish are unknown, but must have been considerably greater, with a higher proportion of dead) — were perhaps of lesser significance. But, at the time, these loomed largest of all, and what appeared to many to be the futility of such sacrifice when the real battle was being fought almost within sight of the shores of Great Britain had an enduring effect. On 28th December the cabinet formally resolved that the Western Front would be the decisive theatre of the war. The stage was set for the vast killing-matches to come.

Had it all been loss? The enterprise came near to success on several occasions, but it is questionable whether even the capture of Gallipoli and the Straits would have had the decisive effects that appeared at the time. The entire operation grimly justified words written by Loyd George before it had even been seriously considered: 'Expeditions which are decided upon and organised with insufficient care generally end disastrously.'

1915: Disaster for the Allies

Alan Clark

A majority of the Allied leaders, both military and political, suffered in the opening months of 1915 from the delusion that the war would be won that year.

The generals, British and French, believed that this victory would follow from a reversion to 'open' warfare. They had seen their enemy elude them (as it appeared) by 'digging in' after the battle of the Marne. If the key could be found to unlock this barrier the character of the fighting would alter, and the Allies would have the advantage.

The first of these propositions is incontestable, the second highly dubious. The science of military analysis was not much heeded by the French generals, still less by the British, both preferring the doctrine of their own infallibility — which was good for morale. It seems that they interpreted the German adoption of trench warfare as an admission of weakness, a form of cowardice it could be said, by an enemy who feared the outcome of a 'real' battle. It is probable also that they drew encouragement from the east, where a combination of space, limited firepower, and enormous bodies of cavalry endowed the campaign with the appearance of something in a different epoch from that of the close-fought positional battles in the west.

But if the setting was different, the principles of grand strategy were immutable, and in due course the Russians had been caught by their application. The bloody defeat of Samsonov's army at Tannenberg stopped the Russian steam-roller short, and eliminated the threat to East Prussia. Furthermore, it showed to Falkenhayn, the chief of the German general staff, that although the Schlieffen plan had failed its purpose might still be attained because the scale of forces needed

to defeat the Tsar was not — on account of the tactical clumsiness and ineptitude of the Russian commanders — irreconcilable with an active, though necessarily defensive, Western Front.

Accordingly, in his appreciation for 1915, Falkenhayn recommended a defensive posture in France and concentration of strength in the east. After some vacillation the Kaiser had agreed and the necessary redeployment (which also entailed taking divisions from Hindenburg and Ludendorff in Silesia) was put in motion. Headquarters, and the imperial train, moved to the east, carrying the German centre of gravity with it.

All this took time, and during those weeks the southern wing of the Russian armies continued to batter away at the Austro-Hungarians, taking the famous fortress town of Przemyśl in March. Friction began to develop between the German commanders. Ludendorff had his own, more radical scheme for defeating the Russians by a wide outflanking stroke from the north, and resented being held in check while Falkenhayn concentrated for a direct approach on the Galician front.

The battle of Neuve-Chapelle
To the Allies, therefore, appearance augured better than reality. The Germans appeared to be standing on the defensive in France from fear of their opponent, while in the east they were still in retreat. Considerations of grand strategy vied with those of national — and personal — prestige to make a Western contribution to this giant 'pincer' urgently desirable.

Joffre was intending to mount the French offensive in May. But there were private reasons which made the British commanders in the field keen to stage a 'demonstration' at a much earlier date. Lord Kitchener, the secretary of state (who enjoyed poor relations with the commander of the British Expeditionary Force, Sir John French), favoured using the new units which had been formed during the winter for an amphibious assault on Ostend and Zeebrugge in Belgium. Both Sir John, and Douglas Haig, his subordinate, saw that this would entail restricting the size and resources of the BEF — perhaps indefinitely — in favour of a new army which would come under the command of Kitchener or his nominee. Accordingly they planned to attack the enemy themselves as soon as weather permitted.

The area selected was the German salient which protruded around the village of Neuve-Chapelle. It was lightly defended, by some six companies who disposed of twelve machine-guns between them, set out in a line of shallow sand-bag breast-works (the ground was too waterlogged for a proper trench system). Against this 'position' – in effect little more than a screen – Haig threw no fewer than forty-eight battalions supported by sixty batteries of field artillery, and a hundred and twenty heavy siege pieces. In several places the attackers broke right through, into open country – a feat which they were not to repeat for two and a half years. But the expected 'open' warfare never materialized. To hesitant leadership, at every level, was added poor communications and a cumbersome chain of command.

During the night the troops who had broken through milled about aimlessly on the edge of certain natural barriers that were very lightly held by scratch groups of enemy infantry, in the belief that it was the German 'second line'. In fact, the Germans had no second line, but they energetically improvised one, with two companies of bicycle-mounted sharpshooters, during the early hours of the morning. On the second day less than a dozen machine-guns held up the whole British army, whose artillery had practically no ammunition left to deal with them. However, the British numerical superiority was still more than seven to one and Haig, the army commander, ordered that 'attacks are to be pressed regardless of loss'. Loss, not surprisingly, was the only result.

The battle of Neuve-Chapelle exemplifies the way in which the relation of attack to defence remained constant – though the degree of force applied on either side was to escalate violently throughout the war. Ammunition shortage had lulled the Germans into underestimating the power of the British artillery, hence their feeble, lightly-manned defence works. If the British had disposed of the firepower which the French enjoyed they might well have broken through at their second attempt; if the German line had included the deep concrete *Wohngraben* shelters which they began hastily to dig after digesting the shock of the Neuve-Chapelle attack, the British would never have got across no man's land – as was to be painfully demonstrated in the Aubers offensive two months later. In point of fact the two forces remained in balance (which meant of course that the defence prevailed) all the way up to the ten-day barrages and concrete pillbox chains of Passchendaele in November of 1917.

Both sides drew their conclusions from the failure to exploit the initial breakthrough at Neuve-Chapelle. Falkenhayn expressed the view that 'the English troops, in spite of undeniable bravery and endurance on the part of the men, have proved so clumsy in action that they offer no prospect of accomplishing anything decisive against the German Army in the immediate future'.

But the British staff took a different view. A GHQ memorandum, dated the 18th April, concludes the 'lessons' of Neuve-Chapelle with the assertion that '. . . by means of careful preparation as regards details it appears that a section of the enemy's front line can be captured with comparatively little loss'.

And this was a judgement which Joffre regarded as needlessly conservative. Of his own prospects, he confided to Sir Henry Wilson (the liaison officer at French HQ) that 'he was bringing up even more troops and really thought he would break the line past mending, and that it might be, and ought to be, the beginning of the end'.

Poison gas

Meanwhile, time was running out for the Russian armies in south Poland, as Falkenhayn gradually accumulated fresh German divisions behind the depleted Austrian line in readiness for his counter-offensive. The Germans planned to reinforce their local numerical superiority (fourteen divisions against two) by tactical surprise (the use of a new weapon – poison gas). However, the commanders responsible for mounting the gas attack had insisted that the new weapon should first be tried under actual battle conditions, and it was decided to stage the dress rehearsal in the west.

The area selected was a quiet four-mile stretch of front at the northern corner of the Ypres salient. The line was held by French colonial troops whose erratic tactics and discipline had been a source of friction between the British and French commanders for some weeks. Ill-fitted to resist a determined conventional attack, they collapsed immediately under the impact of this new and frightening weapon. This time it was the Germans who broke right through the trench line (they, too, would have to wait almost three years before they could repeat the performance) and it was their turn to be surprised by the opportunity which offered. The gas had been used without any particular objective, even at tactical level, in mind. The German Corps commander quickly tried to improvise an operation which might pinch out the whole Ypres salient from the north, but he was frustrated by his own meagre resources and by the extraordinary heroism of small detachments of Canadian and British troops who placed themselves across his advance.

Once the German impetus had died away Sir John French staged a series of ill-managed and extravagant counter-attacks against the new enemy positions (the British troops were told to protect themselves against gas by dipping their handkerchiefs in a solution of water and Boric acid, and tying them across their mouths). These achieved little except the destruction of two brigades of the Indian army and the dismissal of Sir Horace Smith-Dorrien, the first — and last — senior commander to protest against the cost in casualties of repetitive frontal attacks.

The experience of 'Second Ypres' (as the April battles in the salient were called) confirmed the lesson that the fighting soldier was fatally vulnerable to accurate — but remote — artillery and isolated machine-gunners under conditions of 'open' warfare. In fact, his only defence was to dig, as fast and as deep as he could. But the senior Allied commanders continued to regard a break-up of the trench system as their goal, and held the view that this could be attained by the application of the same formula; though in heavier and heavier concentrations. In any case it was now too late to alter the plans for the next British offensive, to be launched against the Aubers ridge on the 9th May, timed to coincide with Joffre's own, delayed, attack farther to the south.

This time the British artillery was weaker than at Neuve-Chapelle, the German defences stronger. As the first wave went over the top the Germans were amazed to see that '. . . there could never before in war have been a more perfect target than this solid wall of khaki men side-by-side. There was only one possible order to give — "Fire! Until the barrels burst!"' The attack was stopped dead. But the men who had been moved up to 'exploit' it now congested the forward trenches, and they too were ordered to attack — in exactly the same place, and with the same result. There could be no thought of working round the enemy flank. It was a point of honour to advance directly on to his guns. Two days later there were no shells left, and very few men. In some gloom (and unusual candour) an officer at Haig's headquarters wrote that '. . . Our attack has failed, and failed badly, and with heavy casualties. That is the bald and most unpleasant fact.'

Soon after the failure at Aubers news began to seep back to the western capitals of a terrible disaster in Poland. Falkenhayn's long delayed offensive had burst upon the Russian right flank, and four German Army Corps were pouring through the gap. Within a week they had advanced seventy miles; a fortnight passed and the San, the great river barrier in the Russian rear, had been forced at Jaroslaw; a month, and Przemyśl had been recaptured – all those fortress towns whose fall had cheered the Allied press in the winter months of 1914 were now abandoned by the fleeing Tsarist armies.

The Russian collapse

There was much to distract the British public – the Dardanelles. the 'Shells Scandal' (the British lack of shells was fiercely attacked in the press), the cabinet changes. But the hard facts remained. While the Allies licked their wounds impotently on the Western Front the Russian collapse became daily more serious. If she should be forced out of the war, the German strategic purpose – the original motive of the Schlieffen plan – would be achieved and the whole weight of the German army could be shifted to France.

How was it that the front, on either side, could so often be broken in the east, so seldom in the west? Why was it that gains in Poland were measured in hundreds of miles, in France in yards?

The force-to-space ratio (force being an

amalgam of numbers and firepower) was widely different between the two theatres. In France the ratio was very high and steadily increasing. But in Russia the front was four times as long, the number of men engaged little higher than in the west, their scale of armament very much lower. Wheeling cavalry formations encountering the odd machine-gun could simply gallop off into the steppe, out of range. The Russians were short even of rifles, and those equipped with them seldom had more than twenty rounds per man. Many of the Austrian rifles were not even magazine-fed.

Across this sprawling, under-manned battlefield the well-led, well-equipped Germans cut a deep swathe: following his victory at Gorlice-Tarnów on 2nd May, Falkenhayn at last allowed the impatient Ludendorff to debouch from East Prussia and seize the vital rail junction of Bialystok in July. Under this double threat the Russian armies, plagued by desperate munition shortages, stumbled back to the shelter of the Dvina and the Pripet. By the middle of August they had lost 750,000 prisoners.

Now the Allied motives swung right round; so far indeed, that the solution, seen from the opposite pole, seemed identical. Massive attacks in the west were urgently necessary, no longer as part of a victorious pincer movement but as succour for the failing Russian strength, a desperate attempt to draw the bulk of the German army back across Poland to the west.

Joffre, as always, was optimistic; his British colleagues less so. The French were to attack in Champagne, the British at Loos. The British did not yet have enough artillery to support the whole of their attack frontage and Haig decided to use gas on a large scale. This immediately put his men at a disadvantage as gas depends for its effectiveness on a favourable prevailing wind (which could not, naturally, be guaranteed at H-hour) nor, by itself, will it cut barbed wire. In addition, the British and French sections were too far apart to give mutual support. For some weeks the British procrastinated and all the time the news from the east got worse. Finally, the date was fixed, for 25th September – ironically, a week after Falkenhayn had ordered that offensive

operations in the east were to be halted, and the divisions transferred to France.

No one had much confidence in the prospects. The ground had been selected, not by the British themselves, but by Joffre. As the hour approached Sir John French's nerve began to fail and he sent a message (effectively calling the whole operation off) that he '. . . would assist according to ammunition'. There was uproar at French HQ. 'Sir John had better walk warily,' growled Henry Wilson into his diary. Joffre himself complained to Kitchener, darkly hinting that he had been made personally responsible for securing English co-operation and that if he should be sacked the politicians might make a separate peace. Haig, meanwhile, had recovered his own confidence and believed that the attack would be successful. Under this double pressure, from above and below, Sir John could do nothing but go along with the plan. All that could be hoped was that by committing everything, including two raw volunteer divisions that had just arrived in France, something might be achieved – even if it was only to impress our Allies with our 'sincerity'.

Winston Churchill has described how, back in London, '. . . The Private Secretary informed me that Lord Kitchener wished to see me. He ('K') looked at me sideways with a very odd expression on his face. I saw he had some disclosure of importance to make, and waited. After appreciable hesitation he told me that he had agreed with the French to a great offensive in France. I said at once that there was no chance of success. He said that the scale would restore everything, including of course the Dardanelles. He had an air of suppressed excitement, like a man who has taken a great decision of terrible uncertainty, and is about to put it into execution'.

In the event, the battle of Loos was a miserable defeat. Like Neuve-Chapelle in its clumsy repetition of frontal attacks and disdain for the indirect approach, it differed when the attackers came to the enemy second line. This time they were ordered straight at it, without any preparation, artillery or reconnaissance or even – in the case of the two fresh volunteer divisions – being given a meal. A German Regimental war diary records how: 'Ten columns of extended line could clearly be distinguished, each one estimated at more than a thousand men, and offering such a target as had never been seen before, or even thought possible. Never had the machine-gunners such straightforward work to do nor done it so effectively. They traversed to and fro along the enemy's ranks unceasingly. As the entire field of fire was covered with the enemy's infantry the effect was devastating . . .'

Nothing, at either strategic or tactical level, was achieved by the Loos offensive. Nor can anything be said to have been learned from it. But its effects were highly important. Sir John French was dismissed; Haig was promoted; Robertson, a close personal associate of Haig's, was transferred to London where, as chief of the imperial general staff, he controlled the strategic direction of the war.

Kitchener, whose deep Imperial vision and gloomy assessment of the Western Front obstructed all those commanders whose ambition resided there, was left without real power and henceforth the strategic decisions were taken by the Haig-Robertson duumvirate, a combination irrevocably committed to the continental strategy, the massive land force on the Western Front, and to a rejection of the imperial strategic principles of William Pitt, which had stood inviolate for a hundred and fifty years.

Serbia Overrun

Alan Palmer

Throughout the spring and summer of 1915, while the great guns scarred the Gallipoli peninsula and gas-clouds drifted over the Flanders trenches, the war along the Danube seemed to hang fire, remote and curiously irrelevant to the issues being decided on other fronts. In December 1914 the Serbs had ejected the Austro-Hungarian invaders from their kingdom and liberated their capital, Belgrade, and there had been talk in London and Paris of sending aid to Serbia through neutral Greece. But the inexorable demands of the commanders in the west and the frustrations of Gallipoli soon pushed all strategic diversions to the back of men's minds; and for ten months the Serbs and Austrians faced each other over the broad river, reluctant to resume a conflict for which neither side had men or material. The only assistance to reach Serbia was a small naval force (which converted Danube launches into improvised torpedo-boats) and seven surgical hospital units sent to combat the scourge of typhus which was carrying off a thousand victims a day in the overcrowded towns of Niš, Kragujevac, and Skoplje. The cumulative effect of this epidemic and the casualties in the earlier battles was that, after a year of war, the Serbs could put into the field rather less than 200,000 combatants, only half as many as they mobilized in the previous summer.

The decision to eliminate Serbia as a military unit was taken by General Falkenhayn at German headquarters in Pless at the start of August 1915. His prime strategic motive was to strengthen the bonds between the Central powers and their Turkish partner: only by sweeping aside the Serbian obstacle from the middle Danube would it be possible for German troops and supplies to move freely along the trans-European railways, so as to make Turkey an effective ally. The assault on the Serbian positions was to be undertaken by German and Austrian units which would cross the Danube and the Sava under the command of General Mackensen. Within a week this force would receive assistance from two Bulgarian armies advancing from the east, on Nis and Skoplje respectively, so as to cut the links between central Serbia and Salonika along the Morava-Vardar valleys. As a reward for participation in the campaign Bulgaria would secure the areas in Macedonia which she had sought in vain during the Balkan Wars. It was assumed that, before the coming of the full rigours of a Balkan winter, the Serbs would be trapped at the foot of the savage mountains and destroyed by a force that outnumbered them by more than two to one.

The Serbs discovered that the Germans had made overtures to Bulgaria for a military alliance in the middle of September. Immediately Pašič, the Serbian prime minister, telegraphed to Paris an appeal for 150,000 Allied soldiers to be sent to Salonika so as to safeguard the vital railway up the Vardar. The British and French found Venizelos, the prime minister of Greece, not unsympathetic to the landing of Allied troops on Greek soil, but they could not raise so large an army as Pašic had requested. By diverting units from Gallipoli they gathered together a scratch force of 13,000 men, who disembarked at Salonika on 5th October. This Allied response to Serbia's appeal was, however, both too slight and too late. That very day King Constantine of Greece, the Kaiser's brother-in-law, forced Venizelos to resign and installed a new Greek government which was strictly neutralist, if not pro-German. Fifteen hours later, nearly three hundred miles to the north of Salonika, Mackensen's guns opened up on Belgrade and the German and Austrian troops moved through mist and rain to their advanced positions. With the Greek authorities sullenly unco-operative and with three ranges of mountains separating the defenders of Belgrade from the Salonika force, it seemed unlikely that the Allies could bring effective succour to the Serbs.

The initial stages of Mackensen's offensive were a masterpiece of strategic planning, conceived in secrecy and executed with meticulous precision. Falkenhayn had issued a directive that the troops should have 'practically nothing to do but march up and proceed instantly with the crossing'. Concentrated artillery fire ensured that Falkenhayn's orders were carried out to the letter. Within two days Belgrade had fallen, even though the Serbs defended it street by street. Despite a treacherous wind, a bridge was soon thrown across the Danube so that a quarter of a million men were able to begin an advance on Kragujevac within ten days of the start of operations. The Bulgarians duly declared war on 14th October and despatched the I Army in the general direction of Niš, the temporary capital of Serbia and a vital railway-junction only forty-five miles from the Bulgarian frontier.

Mackensen's plan was to break the Serbian army somewhere along the seventy miles which separated Niš from Kragujevac. Putnik, the Serbian chief-of-staff, knew that conditions were desperate but hoped to delay the enemy advance long enough for aid to reach him from the Franco-British force which General Maurice Sarrail was concentrating in Salonika. On 22nd October news reached Putnik that French infantry had thrown back a Bulgarian column near Strumica. The skirmish had taken place more than two hundred miles south of Kragujevac, but it heartened the Serbs. In Niš the citizens decorated the streets with bunting so as to welcome the French force. The bedraggled flags were still flying mournfully in the rain when the Bulgarians entered the town on 5th November.

The Germans and Austrians failed to trap the Serbs at Kragujevac. The constant rain delayed their advance while the Bulgarians, to the south-east, were held up by the stubborn defenders of the small fortress of Pirot. But the loss of Kragujevac on 31st October was a hard blow for the Serbs. If they were to fall back towards the mountains they had to abandon their stores and supplies. As Mackensen's troops entered the town, flames shot high into the sky and a roar of explosions marked the destruction of Serbia's arsenal.

For another fortnight Putnik's men continued to retreat into the mountainous plateau bordering Albania. Once, and once only, there seemed a chance that Sarrail's army might break through to the Serbs. The French pressed up the Vardar to Negotin, within twenty-five miles of the Serbian outposts at Veles. But at Negotin the French were delayed by an unforeseen obstacle, a bridge left unrepaired from the time of the Balkan Wars. By the time they had crossed the river, Veles had fallen to the Bulgarians and, although they were able to harry the Bulgarian flank, they could not prevent Mackensen tightening his noose around the retreating Serbs.

A nation on the march

By the middle of November the remnants of the Serbian army were on the plateau of Kosovo, where the medieval Serbian kingdom had fought its final valiant battle against the Turks in 1389. With three of the four escape routes in enemy hands and with a blizzard sweeping in from the east, Putnik decided to make one last bid for safety. Ordering the remaining trucks and guns to be destroyed, he split his force into four columns which were to force their way through the Albanian mountains so as to reach the Adriatic, where it was hoped that Allied naval vessels would be at hand to evacuate the survivors. On 23rd November the Serbian horde—for it could hardly now be termed an army—took to the mountains.

The Serbian retreat across Albania is an epic of courage and tragedy unique in the chronicle of the First World War. No one knows for certain how many refugees perished in the narrow defiles between the mountain peaks, famished and frozen, as Napoleon's Grand Army had been as it stumbled from the Berezina to the Niemen in 1812. In one contingent alone twenty thousand men and women died during the three weeks which they were forced to spend in the mountains; most were killed by the terrible conditions, but typhus continued to claim its victims and some were butchered by Albanian tribesmen. This was the march of a nation, rather than the withdrawal of a fighting unit from battle. There were men over seventy and boys of twelve and thirteen in the long columns which wound their way slowly towards the coast. King Peter, aged seventy-one, had first fought the Turks in these wild mountains half a century ago; now he trudged along beside his peasant soldiers until, too sick to continue the march, they bore him with them down to the plain. Prince-Regent Alexander, his son and the eventual King of Yugoslavia, was only twenty-seven, but throughout the march he suffered agonies from a stomach ulcer and underwent an operation before reaching the Adriatic. Putnik, the veteran chief-of-staff, was also a sick man; he was carried across the mountains, barely conscious, in an improvised sedan-chair. Among those on the retreat were Austrian prisoners, captured in the previous campaign, and a group of British nurses – mostly Scottish – who had come to Serbia with the medical units earlier in the year under the auspices of the Women's Suffrage Federation.

For three weeks after the withdrawal from Kosovo there was hardly any news of the Serbs. The enemy was not so rash as to pursue them through the snow, although the Bulgarian VIII Division advanced cautiously into eastern Albania in the middle of December. Sarrail's troops and the British 10th Division (which had been caught by the blizzard along the Bulgaro-Greek frontier) fell back on Salonika where work started on the construction of a fortified camp. The Bulgarians, for the moment, halted on the border of Greece and Serbia.

On 15th December the first Serbian units reached the plain around Scutari, at the northernmost tip of Albania. Many men had trudged for over a hundred miles through the mountains. At Scutari they seemed momentarily safe, protected from the Austrian enemy by their Montenegrin allies to the north. During the following fortnight other groups struggled down from the mountains. But, in reality, the Serbs were still far from safety. At the beginning of January, 1916, the Austrian forces launched an offensive from their Dalmatian bases on Montenegro and forced the Montenegrins, too, to seek refuge in flight.

Scutari soon became untenable and fell to the Austrians on 22nd January. Once more the Serbs were on the move. This time they found shelter at Durazzo, fifty miles to the south and within the Italian sphere of influence in Albania. There the older men were taken off by sea to Italy or to recuperate in Bizerta. But Durazzo was no resting place. The Austrians approached so rapidly that it was impossible, with such inadequate harbour facilities, to get all the Serbian troops embarked; and, after one last skirmish with the Austrians, the Serbian survivors resumed their southward trek on 10th February down the coast to Valona, the best port in Albania, 130 miles away. Ships of the Royal Navy escorted fifteen Italian and fourteen French transports from Valona down the ninety-mile channel to Corfu which, although a Greek island, had been occupied by the French in January 1916, despite loud protests from King Constantine in Athens.

That spring hundreds of Serbs lay for weeks in hospital tents on Corfu, recuperating from the rigours of the retreat and the long march south. Perhaps as many as 10,000 died in Corfu or on the small islands off its coast. But others recovered quickly under the warm Ionian sun. Their country was in enemy hands but their spirit remained unbroken. At Salonika, Sarrail was gathering a cosmopolitan force which, by the end of May 1916, was to number more than 300,000 men. More than a third of this 'Army of the Orient' consisted of veterans from Serbia, re-equipped by the French and transported in convoys from Corfu through the submarine-infested waters around the Cyclades so as to resume the fight. And by the end of November 1916 they were again on Serbian soil, with the town of Monastir in their hands and the confidence that, in time, they would sweep the invaders back to the Danube and beyond.

Part three · Attrition

In 1916 each of the main combatant nations made great efforts to achieve a decisive victory. On the Western Front these efforts centred round the two battles which more than any other came to symbolize the First World War for the post-war generation — Verdun and the Somme. At Verdun, Germany for once abandoned her strategy of standing on the defensive in the west: the aim was to cripple the French army by luring it to the defence of an indefensible position. France was to be bled white, while for Germany the outlay of men would be almost trivial though a massive use of artillery would be required. The assault on 21st February found the garrisons of Verdun underequipped and undermanned. Within a few days the outer defences and one of the great forts, Douaumont, were in German hands. But then the advance bogged down. The crisis appointment of Petain to hold Verdun 'at whatever cost' led to a stabilization of the French front: German losses were already greater than anticipated; on both sides the deadly process of escalation had begun. It was a battle in which the acknowledged casualties were to exceed 700,000, a battle of non-stop bombardments under which most men fell without ever having seen their enemy, a battle which perpetuated its own existence long after the original strategic objectives had passed out of sight.

Even before Verdun began the Western Allies had laid plans for a great offensive that summer, centred on a Franco-British push astride the Somme. By May Joffre was insisting that the date for the offensive must be brought forward: if the Germans were not distracted from Verdun the French army would cease to exist. Yet although Haig finally agreed to bring the date forward to 1st July, it was not this offensive which first brought relief to the defenders of Verdun, but news from the Eastern Front. Here forty Russian divisions under Brusilov struck at the heavily entrenched Austro-Hungarian lines. Aided by thorough artillery preparation, surprise, and a certain lack of military dedication among his opponents, the first thrust of Brusilov's offensive was wildly successful: indeed he subsequently claimed that had he been properly supported he could have won the war for the Allies in that year. As it was, he at least saved the Allies from the probability of defeat. Austrian troops had to abandon their successful campaigning in Italy and rush north; and Germany transferred no fewer than thirty-five divisions from France to the Eastern Front. The Russian advance, already prodigal in men, had lost its impetus when in mid-August Rumania entered the war on the Allied side. The prompt collapse of the Rumanian army turned this new alliance into a terrible liability for the Russians. Before long a quarter of the Russian army was committed to Rumania, an extension of the front which stretched resources and morale to breaking. For the Germans, on the other hand, Rumania's entry into the war seemed a blessing. They now occupied the Rumanian oilfields and wheatlands and enjoyed better communications with their Turkish allies.

Duly, on 1st July, the Allied push on the Somme began. It was a section of the front which offered no particularly compelling strategic objective. Joffre had fixed upon it largely because here French and British were manning the trenches side by side and he felt he could be most assured of British co-operation if British troops went over the top 'arm in arm' with French. But because of Verdun, the French contribution had been drastically reduced: now and henceforward Great Britain was to shoulder the main burdens on the Western Front. The offensive followed a dreadfully familiar pattern. In the course of the battle it was only when they departed from the conventional that the British came close to real success—in Rawlinson's night attack on 14th July and in the success achieved by tanks, in use for the first time, at Flers on 15th September. On both occasions poor communications again lost the Allies their opportunity to exploit success. Haig, to do him justice, had initially advocated a change in tactics, but he had been won over back to the established idea of a long artillery preparation followed by direct frontal assault. The five-day bombardment served only to tell the Germans what to expect next. As soon as the shelling stopped they scrambled up virtually unscathed from the deep security of their dugouts to train their machine guns on the lines of British troops, who were seen advancing 'at a steady easy pace as if expecting to find nothing alive in our front trenches'— an expectation swiftly and bloodily dispelled. The bombardment had also failed to destroy the German wire through which the assault waves had to advance. The troops themselves were not trusted by their commanders to attempt the techniques of indirect attack and infiltration which both French and Germans had developed at Verdun. It was to be frontal assault at whatever cost, and the cost was terrible. By the time the 'Big Push' bogged down in the winter rains the British had lost some 420,000, the Germans probably as many, and the French about 200,000. And nothing of any strategic value had been attained.

The Territorials and the men of Kitchener's 'New Armies' who made up the bulk of the British assault troops on the Somme were still volunteers. However the volunteer system was causing problems. War production suffered when skilled men did their patriotic duty and joined the colours; moreover it was becoming clear that volunteering alone was not going to provide enough men. Despite the opposition of Kitchener and others, conscription was introduced in 1916. Not only the system of sustaining the strength of the army was seen to be inadequate. The Defence of the Realm Act of 1914 had given the government wide powers over both persons and property, and much had already been achieved in the reorganization of industry (bringing, incidentally, greater status for women in proportion to their increasing contribution to munitions and other war industry). Even so Asquith's government had not properly co-ordinated the national war effort. His virtues seemed not to be the appropriate ones for a time of crisis. Under him the War Council was notably ineffectual. Splits in the coalition government at the end of 1916 enabled Lloyd George to realize his ambitions and attain the premiership. Already, as minister of munitions and as war secretary he had grappled with the problems of arms production and transport services. Now he set about reorganizing the entire government for total war.

The repercussions of total war were felt in the Empire also, and had their effect in politics throughout the dominions. Though the war created comparatively few domestic problems for New Zealand, and indeed raised the level of agricultural prosperity, in Australia the issue of conscription caused a political crisis. The Canadian war effort was achieved only at the cost of deepening the antagonisms within her mixed population, and in South Africa there existed a substantial segment of the population which actively sought a German victory. Although Botha and Smuts achieved a great contribution to the Allied effort, not only in campaigns against the Germans in Africa itself but also by sending troops to the Middle East and the Western Front, that contribution was bought at the expense of deepening rifts in South African loyalties. Through the Dominions generally the cost of involvement in Great Britain's war would not be forgotten.

Verdun and the Somme

Alistair Horne

The year 1916 was the watershed of the First World War. Beyond it all rivers ran in changed directions. It was the year that saw German hopes of outright victory vanish, and the Allied prospects of winning the war with their existing tactics and resources – without the United States – disappear. It was the last year in which Russia would be a powerful military force, and by the end of it Great Britain would have assumed the principal burden on the Western Front. It was also the last year in which the 'Old World' of pre-1914 still had a chance of surviving by means of a negotiated, 'stalemate' peace; it would have been as good a year as any to have ended the war. Finally, 1916 was the year of heavy guns, and – with the exception of the cataclysm of 1918 – the year that brought the highest casualty lists.

On land in 1916 there were two battles which more than any others came to symbolize the First World War for the post-war generation: Verdun and the Somme. Verdun was the occasion of Germany's only deviation – between 1915 and 1918 – from her profitable strategy of standing on the defensive in the west and letting the Allies waste themselves against an almost impregnable line at unimaginable cost.

By the end of 1915 deadlock had been reached along a static front stretching from Switzerland to the Channel. The Germans had failed, at the Marne, to win the war by one sledge-hammer blow against their numerically superior enemies, while suffering three-quarters of a million casualties. In attempting to repulse them from her soil, France had lost 300,000 killed and another 600,000 wounded, captured, and missing. Great Britain's naval might had proved impotent to wrest the Dardanelles from Turkey.

Isolated Russia staggered on from defeat to defeat, yet still the Central powers could not bring the war to a decision in the limitless spaces of the east.

But on neither side had these early losses and disillusions impaired the will to fight on. Civilian resolution matched military morale. The opposing troops of France and Germany were no longer the green enthusiasts of 1914, nor yet the battle-weary veterans of 1917-18; they represented the best the war was to produce. In the munitions industries of both sides, artillery programmes had also reached a peak. In Great Britain Kitchener's army of conscripts was about to replace the lost 'First Hundred Thousand'.

On 2nd December, 1915, Joffre, the 'victor of the Marne', was appointed supreme commander of French military forces throughout the world. A sixty-three year-old engineer with little experience of handling infantry, he was now incomparably the most powerful figure on the Allied side and his new ascendancy enabled him to concentrate everything on the Western Front. Four days later Joffre held an historic conference of the Allied commanders at his HQ in Chantilly. From it sprang plans for a co-ordinated offensive by all the allies the following summer. By then, for the first time, there would be an abundance of men, heavy guns, and ammunition. The principal component of this offensive would be a Franco-British 'push' astride the river Somme. Forty French and twenty-five British divisions would be involved. There were no strategic objectives behind this sector of the front; Joffre's principal reason for selecting it was his instinct that he could be most assured of full British participation if they went over the top arm in arm with the French – *'bras dessus bras dessous'*.

Sir Douglas Haig, who had also just taken over command of the British forces in France from General French, would have preferred to attack in Flanders (a preference which was to reassert itself with disastrous consequences a year later). However, after a meeting with Joffre on 29th December, he allowed himself to be won over to the Somme strategy. But on the other side of the lines, the chief of the German general staff, General Erich von Falkenhayn – a strange compound of ruthlessness and indecision – had his own plans. The Germans were to beat the Allies to the draw.

To bleed France white

Prospects would never again seem so bright for German arms as at the close of 1915. In mid-December Falkenhayn prepared a lengthy memorandum for the Kaiser in which he argued that the only way to achieve victory was to cripple the Allies' main instrument, the French army, by luring it into the defence of an indefensible position. Verdun, perched precariously at the tip of a long salient, about 130 air miles south-east of where Joffre intended to attack on the Somme and just 150 miles due east of Paris, fulfilled all of Falkenhayn's requirements.

Verdun's history as a fortified camp stretched back to Roman times, when Attila had found it worth burning. In the 17th century Louis XIV's great engineer, Vauban, had made Verdun the most powerful fortress in his cordon protecting France; in the Franco-Prussian War of 1870 it had been the last of the great French strongholds to fall, surviving Sedan, Metz, and Strasbourg. After 1870 it had become the key bastion in the chain of fortresses guarding France's frontier with Germany. In 1914, Verdun had provided an unshakable pivot for the French line, and without it Joffre might not have been able to stand on the Marne and save Paris.

From his knowledge both of her history and character, Falkenhayn calculated that France would be forced to defend this semi-sacred citadel to the last man. By menacing Verdun with a modest outlay of only nine divisions, he expected to draw the main weight of the French army into the salient, where German heavy artillery would grind it to pieces from three sides.

In Falkenhayn's own words, France was thus to be 'bled white'. It was a conception totally novel to the history of war and one that, in its very imagery, was symptomatic of that Great War where, in their callousness, leaders could regard human lives as mere corpuscles.

The V Army, commanded by the Kaiser's heir, the Crown Prince, was appointed to conduct the victorious operation. Day and night the great cannon and their copious munition trains now began to flow toward the V Army from all other German fronts. Aided by the railways behind their front and the national genius for organization, preparations moved with astonishing speed and secrecy. By the beginning of February 1916 more than 1,200 guns were in position – for an assault frontage of barely eight miles. More than 500 were 'heavies', including 13 of the 420mm 'Big Bertha mortars', the 'secret weapon' of 1914 which had shattered the supposedly impregnable Belgian forts. Never before had such a concentration of artillery been seen.

Verdun lay less than ten miles up the tortuous Meuse from the German lines. Most of its 15,000 inhabitants had departed when the war reached its gates in 1914, and its streets were now filled with troops, but this was nothing new for a city which had long been a garrison town.

In notable contrast to the featureless open country of Flanders and the Somme, Verdun was surrounded by interlocking patterns of steep hills and ridges which provided immensely strong natural lines of defence. The key heights were studded with three concentric rings of mighty underground forts, totalling no less than twenty major and forty intermediary works.

Each was superbly sited so that its guns could dislodge any enemy infantry appearing on the superstructure of its neighbour. With concrete carapaces eight feet thick, staunch enough to resist even the German 'Big Berthas', some of the major forts – such as Douaumont – were equipped with heavy artillery and machine-guns firing from retractable steel turrets. Outlying blockhouses linked by subterranean passages made them able to repel an attack from whatever direction it might come, and in their shell-proof cellars each could house as much as a battalion of infantry.

These forts lay between five and ten miles from Verdun itself. Between them and no man's land stretched a protective network of trenches, redoubts, and barbed wire such as was to be found throughout the whole length of the Western Front. Verdun deserved its reputation as the world's most powerful fortress. In theory.

In fact – despite, or perhaps because of, its reputation – by February 1916, Verdun's defences were in a lamentable state. The fate of the Belgian forts had persuaded Joffre to evacuate the infantry garrisons from the Verdun forts, and remove many of their guns. The troops themselves had become slack, lulled by many months spent in so quiet and 'safe' a sector, whose deceptive calm was deepened by the influence of one of the nastiest, rainiest, foggiest, and most enervating climates in France. The French soldier has never been renowned for his ardour for digging in, and the forward lines of trenches at Verdun compared poorly with the immensely deep earthworks the Germans had constructed at their key points on the Western Front. And, in contrast to the seventy-two battalions of elite storm troops, the Crown Prince held ready for the attack, the French trenches were manned by only thirty-four battalions, some of which were second-class units.

One outstanding French officer, Lieutenant Colonel Emile Driant, who commanded two battalions of *chasseurs* in the very tip of the salient, actually warned the French high command of the impending attack and the bad state of the Verdun defences. For this impertinence, his knuckles were severely rapped; the imperturbable Joffre paid little attention.

'Sauve qui peut!'

After a nine-day delay caused by bad weather (the first serious setback to German plans), the bombardment began at dawn on 21st February. For nine appalling hours it continued. Even on the shell-saturated Western Front nothing like it had ever been experienced. The poorly prepared French trenches were obliterated, many of their defenders buried alive. Among the units to bear the brunt of the shelling were Driant's *chasseurs*.

At 4 that afternoon the bombardment lifted and the first German assault troops moved forward out of their concealed positions. This was, in fact, but a strong patrol action, testing like a dentist's probe for the weakest areas of the French front. In most places it held. The next morning, the brutal bombardment began again. It seemed impossible that any human being could have survived in that methodically worked-over soil. Yet some had, and, with a heroic tenacity that was to immortalize the French defence during the long months ahead, they continued to face the unseen enemy from what remained of their trenches.

On the afternoon of 22nd February the Germans' first main infantry wave went in. The defenders' front line buckled. Driant was shot through the head while withdrawing the remnants of his *chasseurs*. Of these two battalions, 1,200 strong, a handful of officers and about 500 men, many of them wounded, were all that eventually straggled back to the rear. But the French resistance once again caused the German storm troops to be pulled back, to await a third softening-up bombardment the following morning.

On 23rd February, there were signs of mounting confusion and alarm at the various HQs before Verdun. Telephone lines were cut by the shelling; runners were not getting through; whole units were disappearing from the sight of their commanders. Order and counter-order were followed by the inevitable consequence. One by one the French batteries were falling silent, while others shelled their own positions, in the belief that these had already been abandoned to the enemy.

24th February was the day the dam burst. A fresh division, flung in piecemeal, broke under the bombardment, and the whole of the second line of the French defences fell within a matter of hours. During that disastrous day, German gains equalled those of the first three days put together. By the evening it looked as if the war had again become one of movement – for the first time since the Marne.

Between the attackers and Verdun, however, there still lay the lines of the forts – above all, Douaumont, the strongest of them all, a solid bulwark of comfort behind the backs of the retreating *poilus*. Then, on 25th February, the Germans pulled off – almost in a fit of absentmindedness – one of their greatest coups of the entire war. Acting on their own initiative, several small packets of the 24th Brandenburg Regiment, headed by a twenty-four-year-old lieutenant, Eugen Radtke (who, though seriously wounded later on, still lives in Berlin today), worked their way into Douaumont without losing a man. To their astonishment, they discovered the world's most powerful fort to be virtually undefended.

In Germany church bells rang throughout the country to acclaim the capture of Douaumont. In France its surrender was rightly regarded as a national disaster of the first magnitude (later reckoned to have cost France the equivalent of 100,000 men). Through the streets of Verdun itself survivors of broken units ran shouting, '*Sauve qui peut!*'

At his headquarters in Chantilly even Joffre had at last become impressed by the urgency of events. To take over the imminently threatened sector, he dispatched Henri Philippe Pétain, France's outstanding expert in the art of the defensive. No general possessed the confidence of the *poilu* more than Pétain. Now – in tragic irony – this uniquely humanitarian leader was called upon to subject his men to what was becoming the most inhuman conflict of the whole war. Pétain's orders were to hold Verdun, 'whatever the cost'.

But the German attack was beginning to bog down. Losses had already been far heavier than Falkenhayn had anticipated, many of them inflicted by flanking fire from French guns across the Meuse. The German lines looped across the river to the north of Verdun, and, from the very first, the Crown Prince had urged that his V Army be allowed to attack along both banks simultaneously. But Falkenhayn – determined to keep his own outlay of infantry in the 'bleeding white' strategy down to the barest minimum – had refused, restricting operations to the right bank. Now, to clear the menace of the French artillery, Falkenhayn reluctantly agreed to extend the offensive across to the left bank, releasing for this purpose another army corps from his tightly hoarded reserves. The deadly escalation of Verdun was under way.

Mission of sacrifice
The lull before the next phase of the German offensive enabled Pétain to stabilize the front to an almost miraculous extent. He established a road artery to Verdun, later known as the Voie Sacrée, along which the whole lifeblood of France was to pour, to reinforce the threatened city; during the critical first week of March alone 190,000 men marched up it.

The Crown Prince now launched a new all-out attack along the left bank toward a small ridge called the Mort-Homme, which, with its sinister name, acquired from some long-forgotten tragedy of another age, was to be the centre of the most bitter, see-saw fighting for the better part of the next three months. On this one tiny sector a monotonous, deadly pattern was establishing that continued almost without let-up. It typified the whole battle of Verdun. After hours of saturating bombardment, the German assault troops would surge forward to carry what remained of the French front line. There were no longer any trenches; what the Germans occupied were for the most part clusters of shell-holes, where isolated groups of men lived and slept and died defending their 'position' with grenade and pick helve.

'You have a mission of sacrifice', ran the typical orders that one French colonel gave to his men. 'Here is a post of honour where they want to attack. Every day you will have casualties . . . On the day they want to, they will massacre you to the last man, and it is your duty to fall.'

At Verdun most fell without ever having seen the enemy, under the murderous nonstop artillery bombardment, which came to characterize this battle perhaps more than any other. 'Verdun is terrible,' wrote French Sergeant-Major César Méléra, who was killed a fortnight before the armistice, 'because man is fighting against material, with the sensation of striking out at empty air . . .' Describing the effects of a bombardment, Paul Dubrulle, a thirty-four-year-old Jesuit serving as an infantry sergeant (also later killed), said: 'The most solid nerves cannot resist for long; the moment arrives where the blood mounts to the head; where fever burns the body and where the nerves, exhausted, become incapable of reacting . . . finally one abandons oneself to it, one has no longer even the strength to cover oneself with one's pack as protection against splinters, and one scarcely still has left the strength to pray to God.'

Despite the heroic sacrifices of Pétain's men, each day brought the sea of *Feldgrau* a few yards closer to Verdun. By the end of March, French losses totalled 89,000; but the attackers had also lost nearly 82,000 men. Even once they had taken the Mort-Homme, the Germans found themselves hamstrung by French guns on the Côte 304, another ridge still farther out on the flank. Like a surgeon treating galloping cancer, Falkenhayn's knife was enticed ever farther from the original point of application. More fresh German divisions were hurled into the battle—this time to seize Côte 304.

Not until May was the German 'clearing' operation on the left bank of the Meuse at last completed. The final push towards Verdun could begin. But the Crown Prince was now for calling off the offensive, and even Falkenhayn's enthusiasm was waning. The strategic significance of Verdun had long since passed out of sight; yet the battle had somehow achieved a demonic existence of its own, far beyond the control of generals of either nation. Honour had become involved to an extent which made disengagement impossible. On the French side, Pétain—affected (too deeply, according to Joffre) by the horrors he had witnessed—was promoted and replaced by two more ferocious figures: General Robert Nivelle and General Charles Mangin, nicknamed 'The Butcher'.

By now men had become almost conditioned to death at Verdun. 'One eats, one drinks beside the dead, one sleeps in the midst of the dying, one laughs and sings in the company of corpses,' wrote Georges Duhamel, the poet and dramatist, who was serving as a French army doctor. The highly compressed area of the battlefield itself had become a reeking open cemetery where 'you found the dead embedded in the walls of the trenches; heads, legs and half-bodies, just as they had been shovelled out of the way by the picks and shovels of the working party'. Conditions were no longer much better for the attacking Germans; as one soldier wrote home in April under the French counterbombardment: 'Many would rather endure starvation than make dangerous expeditions for food.'

On 26th May a 'very excited' Joffre visited Haig at his HQ and appealed to him to advance the date of the Somme offensive. When Haig spoke of 15th August, Joffre shouted that 'The French Army would cease to exist if we did nothing by then.' Haig finally agreed to help by attacking on 1st July instead. Although Haig entertained vague hopes of a breakthrough to be exploited by cavalry, neither he nor Rawlinson—whose 4th Army were to fight the battle—had yet arrived at any higher strategic purpose than that of relieving Verdun and 'to kill as many Germans as possible' (Rawlinson).

Meanwhile, at Verdun the beginning of a torrid June brought the deadliest phase in the three-and-a-half-month battle, with the Germans throwing in a weight of attack comparable to that of February—but this time concentrated along a front only three, instead of eight, miles wide. The fighting reached Vaux, the second of the great forts, where 600 men under Major Sylvain Eugène Raynal in an epic defence held up the main thrust of the German V Army for a whole week until thirst forced them to surrender.

The Suicide Club

Then, just as Vaux was falling, the first of the Allied summer offensives was unleashed. In the east, General Brusilov struck at the Austro-Hungarians with forty divisions, achieving a spectacular initial success. Falkenhayn was forced to transfer troops badly needed at Verdun to bolster up his sagging ally. Verdun was reprieved; although in fact it was not until 23rd June that the actual crisis was reached. On that day, using a deadly new gas called phosgene, the Crown Prince (reluctantly) attacked towards Fort Souville, astride the last ridge before Verdun. At one moment, machine-gun bullets were striking the city streets. Still the French held but there were ominous signs that morale was cracking. Just how much could a nation stand?

Two days later, however, the rumble of heavy British guns was heard in Verdun. Haig's five-day preliminary bombardment on the Somme had begun.

Because of her crippling losses at Verdun, the French contribution on the Somme had shrunk from forty to sixteen divisions, of which only five actually attacked on 1st July, compared with fourteen British divisions. Thus, for the first time, Great Britain was shouldering the main weight in a Western Front offensive. Of the British first-wave divisions, eleven were either Territorials or from Kitchener's 'New Armies'. Typical of the latter force was one battalion which had only three 'trained officers', including one who was stone deaf, another who suffered from a badly broken leg, and a sixty-three-year-old commanding officer who had retired before the Boer War. These new amateur units of 'civvies' had been trained to advance in rigid parade-ground formations that would have served well at Dettingen—straight lines two to three paces between each man, one hundred yards between each rank in the assault waves. In their rawness, their leaders did not trust them to attempt any of the more sophisticated tactics of infiltration such as the Germans and French had evolved at Verdun — despite a recommendation by Haig himself. French farmers were reluctant to allow their fields to be used for badly needed extra infantry training. But what 'K's' men lacked in expertise, they more than made up for in zeal and courage.

The Somme meanders through a flat, wide, and marshy valley. In the areas where the battle was to be fought, there are few geographical features of any note, except the high ground running south-east from Thiepval to Guillemont. This lay in German hands, and was the principal tactical objective for Rawlinson's 4th Army. The British, therefore, would everywhere be fighting uphill; whereas opposite General Fayolle's 6th Army, the French faced more or less level ground. The Germans had superb observation points gazing down on the British lines, their excellence matched only by the depth of their fortifications.

In the nearly two years that they had sat on the Somme, they had excavated dugouts and vast dormitories out of the chalk as deep as forty feet below ground, comfortably safe from all but the heaviest British shell. Ironically, the British, by their policy of continual 'strafing' (in contrast to the prevalent German and French philosophy of 'live and let live'), had provoked the defenders to dig even deeper. When captured, the German dugouts astonished everybody by their depth and complexity. The German line on the Somme was, claims Churchill, 'undoubtedly the strongest and most perfectly defended position in the world'.

British security surrounding the Somme offensive was by no means perfect. Among other indiscretions, the press reported a speech made by a member of the government, Arthur Henderson, requesting workers in a munitions factory not to question why the Whitsun Bank Holiday was being suspended. In his diary for 10th June, Crown Prince Rupprecht, the German army group commander, wrote: '. . . This fact should speak volumes. It certainly does so speak, it contains the surest proof

that there will be a great British offensive before long. . . .' Abundantly aware of just where the 'Big Push' was coming, for several weeks previously the German defenders had industriously practised rushing their machine-guns up from the dugouts. This had been perfected to a three-minute drill, which would give the Germans an ample margin on 'Z-day' between the lifting of the British barrage and the arrival of the attacking infantry.

For five days Rawlinson's artillery preparation blasted away without let-up (Haig would have preferred a short preliminary bombardment) — thereby dissipating what little element of surprise there still remained. By British standards of the day, it was a bombardment of unprecedented weight. Yet on their much wider front they could mount not nearly half as many heavy guns as the French; and they had nothing to compare with the French 240mm mortars and 400 'super-heavies' with which Foch (French northern army group commander) had equipped Fayolle. A depressing quantity of the British shells turned out to be dud; while defective American ammunition caused so many premature explosions that some of the 4.5 howitzer gun crews nicknamed themselves 'the Suicide Club'. The fire-plan also suffered from the same inflexibility which characterized the training of the new infantry. Through sheer weight of metal, large sections of the German front-line trenches were indeed obliterated, their skeleton outposts killed. But down below in the secure depths of the dugouts, the main body of the German defenders sat playing *Skat* while the shelling raged above.

The worst shortcoming of the five-day bombardment, however, was that it failed in its essential task of breaking up the barbed wire through which the British assault waves were to advance. Divisional commanders appear to have known this, but to have kept the knowledge to themselves. On the eve of the 'Big Push', Haig wrote in his diary with the misguided optimism that was to be found at almost every level prior to 1st July: 'The wire has never been so well cut, nor the Artillery preparation so thorough. I have seen personally all the Corps commanders and one and all are full of confidence. . . .'

At 0245 hours on 1st July a German listening post picked up a message from

Rawlinson wishing his 4th Army 'Good Luck'. A little less than five hours later there was suddenly a strange silence as the British bombardment ended. Somewhere near a hundred thousand men left their trenches at this moment and moved forward at a steady walk. On their backs they carried their personal kit – including a spare pair of socks – water bottles, a day's rations, two gas masks, mess tins and field dressings, as well as rifle, bayonet, 220 rounds of ammunition, and an entrenching tool. Some also carried hand grenades or bombs for a trench mortar. The minimum load was 66lb; some men were laden with as much as 85 to 90lb. It was about to become a broiling hot day.

'. . . They got going without delay,' wrote the commanding officer of a battalion of the Royal Inniskilling Fusiliers;

'No fuss, no shouting, no running, everything solid and thorough – just like the men themselves. Here and there a boy would wave his hand to me as I shouted good luck to them through my megaphone. And all had a cheery face . . . Fancy advancing against heavy fire with a big roll of barbed wire on your shoulders! . . .'

Seen from the defenders' point of view, a German recorded that the moment the bombardment lifted:

'. . . Our men at once clambered up the steep shafts leading from the dug-outs to daylight and ran for the nearest shell craters. The machine-guns were pulled out of the dug-outs and hurriedly placed into position, their crews dragging the heavy ammunition boxes up the steps and out to the guns. A rough firing line was thus rapidly established. As soon as in position, a series of extended lines of British infantry were seen moving forward from the British trenches. The first line appeared to continue without end to right and left. It was quickly followed by a second line, then a third and fourth. They came on at a steady easy pace as if expecting to find nothing alive in our front trenches. . . .'

Reading from left to right along the line, the British forces involved in the principal offensive were the 8th, 10th, 3rd, 15th, and 13th Corps, while below them on the river Somme itself came the French 20th and 35th Corps. General Hunter-Weston's 8th Corps had the most difficult task of all – the terrain was particularly difficult – and, because of its inexperience, it was the corps about which Haig had entertained the most doubts. With the 31st Division holding its left flank, the Yorks and Lancs were encouraged to see ahead of them numerous gaps in the wire opened up by the shelling. But at the moment of reaching them, they were scythed down by devastating machine-gun fire from the weapons which the Germans had rushed up from their dug-outs. It was an experience that was to be repeated innumerable times that day. By early afternoon the 31st Division had lost 3,600 officers and men, of whom only eight were prisoners.

Next to it, the 29th Division, recently returned from Gallipoli, had the task of rushing the 'Hawthorn Redoubt' after an immense mine had been detonated under it. But the mine had been timed to go off ten minutes before zero hour; giving the German machine-gunners plenty of time to reoccupy the crater. Moving across no man's land the Royal Fusiliers could see ahead of them the bodies of their first waves festooning the uncut wire; all that came back from this one battalion was 120 men. The divisional commander, in a supreme understatement, noted that his men had been 'temporarily held up by some machine-guns', and pushed up another brigade; one battalion found itself so obstructed by the dead and the endless lines of wounded that it physically could not get forward. Attacking unsuccessfully but with fantastic courage at Beaumont-Hamel, the Newfoundlanders won their greatest battle honour: in a matter of minutes 710 men fell.

Also at Beaumont-Hamel, troops that had captured the Heidenkopf position were tragically shot down by the second wave, unaware that the German strong-point was already in British hands.

By nightfall, the 8th Corps alone had lost 14,000 officers and men without even broaching the main objective. It had taken only twenty-two prisoners. For the 10th, the 3rd, and part of 15th Corps the story of bloody failure was much the same:

'I get up from the ground and whistle,' recalled an officer commanding an Irish battalion in the second wave. 'The others rise. We move off with steady pace. I see rows upon rows of British soldiers lying dead, dying or wounded in no man's land. Here and there I see the hands thrown up and then a body flops on the ground. The bursting shells and smoke make visibility poor. We proceed. Again I look southward from a different angle and perceive heaped up masses of British corpses suspended on the German wire, while live men rush forward in orderly procession to swell the weight of numbers in the spider's web. . . .'

The Highland Light Infantry went into battle behind their pipers. Swiftly their leading companies invested the German trenches, but while they were still exulting at their success, hidden German machine-guns opened fire. Within little more than an hour of the beginning of the attack, half the HLI were killed or wounded, bringing the assault to a sudden halt.

Opposite Thiepval, the 36th (Ulster) Division came tantalizingly, tragically close to achieving success. Better trained than most of Rawlinson's units, the Inniskillings managed to advance a mile in the first hour of the attack, attaining the top of the ridge and capturing the Schwaben Redoubt, an important strongpoint in the German first-line. But, following the experiences of 1915 when so many field officers had been killed off, it was Haig's orders that no battalion commanding officers or second-in-commands should go in with their men in the first wave. Thus there was no one senior enough to consolidate the Ulstermen's fine success. Communications with the rear were appalling. Runners sent back for fresh orders never returned. Precious time was thrown away, while the Germans recovered their balance. When finally a reserve brigade was sent up to reinforce the Inniskillings, it too had no senior officers with it; with the result it advanced too fast, running into its own artillery barrage, where it lost something like two-thirds of its soldiers. That evening, of the 10th Corps' 9,000 losses, over half came from the Ulster Division—a fact which was long to cause bitterness against the neighbouring English units. The division was left clinging precariously to the German front line.

On the 3rd Corps' front, the 8th Division was another unit to suffer appalling casualties in return for very little progress. It lost a shocking total of 1,927 officers and men killed; one of its battalions, the 2nd Middlesex, lost 22 officers and 601 men, another—the 8th Yorks and Lancs—21 and 576 respectively, out of an average of 27-30 officers and roughly 700 men to a battalion.

Over the whole British front, only Congreve's 13th Corps, next door to the French, registered any notable success that day. Attacking through Montauban, it captured the entire HQ of the German 62nd Regiment; making a total bag of 1,882 prisoners (compared with the 8th Corps' 22). At Montauban, the cellars were found to be filled with German dead; apparently killed by the French heavy mortars.

Fighting in hell

Indeed, for all the incredible fortitude of Kitchener's men, it was the French who won the laurels on 1st July. The terrain opposite them was admittedly much more favourable, the defences weaker; they had more and heavier guns, which had smashed up even some of the deepest enemy dugouts; their infantry moved with greater skill and flexibility; and they had the advantage of a certain degree of surprise. After the losses inflicted at Verdun, German intelligence could not believe that the French were capable of making a serious contribution on the Somme. To reinforce this belief, Foch cleverly delayed the French attack until several hours after the British.

By early afternoon, Fayolle's troops had taken 6,000 prisoners, destroyed the whole of the German 121st Division's artillery, and come close to making a breakthrough. Péronne itself was threatened. General Balfourier, commanding the 'Iron' (20th) Corps which had saved Verdun in February, urged Congreve on his left to join him in continuing the advance. But Congreve would budge no farther. Above him, Rawlinson was bent more on consolidation than exploitation. Thus Balfourier, with his left flank hanging in the air, was unable to advance either. It was not until 10 o'clock that night that Rawlinson made any attempt to push reserves up to the areas of least resistance. What prospect there had been of capitalizing on any success gained during the 1st July was swiftly lost; the Germans were soon replacing the machine-guns destroyed that day.

When the casualties were counted, the British figures came to 60,000, of which the dead numbered 20,000. Most of the slaughter had been accomplished by perhaps a hundred German machine-gun teams. 1st July was one of the blackest days in British history. Even at Verdun, the total French casualty list for the worst month barely exceeded what Great Britain had lost on that one day. Fayolle lost fewer men than the defending Germans.

Haig had no idea of the full extent of the British losses until 3rd July and neither he nor Rawlinson quite knew why some efforts had succeeded and others failed. On the 3rd Haig ordered Rawlinson to attack again; this time rightly trying to follow up the good results achieved on his southern sector. But the guns were now short of ammunition, and the losses on 1st July greatly reduced the strength of the new blows. That night it rained, and the next day 'walking, let alone fighting, became hellish'.

On 14th July, Rawlinson—chastened by the terrible casualties his army had suffered—decided to try something new. He would attack by night. Describing it caustically as 'an attack organized for amateurs by amateurs', the French predicted disaster. Haig, equally dubious, caused the attack to be postponed twenty-four hours—a delay that diminished the chances of success. Nevertheless, throwing in six brigades which totalled some 22,000 men, Rawlinson after a short hurricane bombardment punched out a salient four miles wide and a thousand yards deep, breaching the Germans' second line—and thereby briefly restoring the element of surprise to the Western Front. A French liaison officer telephoned the sceptical Balfourier: *'Ils ont osé. Ils ont réussi!'*

Once again, however, the fruits of victory were thrown away by poor communications and the painful slowness to react of the British command. As at Gallipoli, there was a horrifying absence of any sense of urgency. The cavalry were waiting in the wings, but too far back to be available to exploit any gains, and not until mid-afternoon that day was it decided to push up the already battle-weary 7th Infantry Division. Thus nine valuable hours were wasted, and darkness was falling when at last the British cavalry and infantry reserves attacked. By then the shaken Germans had rallied.

Deeply disappointed, Haig now settled for a long-protracted 'battle of attrition'. Writing to the government, he declared his intention 'to maintain a steady pressure on Somme battle . . . proceeding thus, I expect to be able to maintain the offensive well

into the Autumn. . . .' All through August and into September the bloody slogging match continued. As seen by the Australian official history, Haig's new technique 'merely appeared to be that of applying a battering-ram ten or fifteen times against the same part of the enemy's battle-front with the intention of penetrating for a mile, or possibly two . . . the claim that it was economic is entirely unjustified'. By the end of the summer, one level-headed Australian officer was writing '. . . we have just come out of a place so terrible that . . . a raving lunatic could never imagine the horror the last thirteen days. . . .'

Meanwhile, however, Verdun had been finally and definitively relieved by the dreadful British sacrifices on the Somme. On 11th July, one last desperate effort was mounted against Verdun, and a handful of Germans momentarily reached a height whence they could actually gaze down on Verdun's citadel. It was the high-water mark of the battle, and—though not apparent at the time—was perhaps the turning point, the Gettysburg of the First World War. Rapidly the tide now receded at Verdun, with Falkenhayn ordering the German army to assume the defensive all along the Western Front.

At the end of August Falkenhayn was replaced by the formidable combination of Hindenburg and Ludendorff.

Visiting the Somme, Ludendorff criticized the inflexibility of the defence there; '. . . Without doubt they fought too doggedly, clinging too resolutely to the mere holding of ground, with the result that the losses were heavy. . . . The Field Marshal and I could for the moment only ask that the front line should be held more lightly. . . .' It was a prelude to the strategic withdrawal to the 'Hindenburg Line' in the following spring.

'A pretty mechanical toy'

On the Somme, 15th September was to become a red-letter day in the history of warfare. Haig decided to throw into a third major attack the first fifty newly invented tanks. Rejected by Kitchener as 'a pretty mechanical toy but of very limited military value', the tank had been developed under the greatest secrecy and crews trained with similar security behind a vast secret enclosure near Thetford in Norfolk. Even the name 'tank' was intended to deceive the enemy. Its inventors begged the army not to employ the first machines, however, until they were technically more reliable; while even Asquith visiting the front on 6th September thought it: '... a mistake to put them into the battle of the Somme. They were built for the purpose of breaking an ordinary trench system with a normal artillery fire only, whereas on the Somme they will have to penetrate a terrific artillery barrage, and will have to operate in a broken country full of shell-craters ...'

But Haig was determined. Historians will long continue to argue whether he was right or not; on Haig's side, the Cambrai raid the following year tends to prove that the surprise value of the tank had not entirely been thrown away, and undoubtedly, sooner or later, it would have had to be tried out under battle conditions.

On the day of the attack, only thirty-two of the original fifty tanks reached the assembly area in working order; twenty-four actually went into battle, and most of these broke down, became bogged, or were knocked out. At Flers the tank showed what it could do, and the infantry advanced cheering down the main street of the village behind four solitary machines. But once again poor communications between front and rear gave the Germans a chance to reorganize before success could be exploited. By the evening of the 15th all the tanks were either scattered or destroyed. With them vanished the last of Haig's three opportunities on the Somme; Montauban on 1st July, Rawlinson's night attack on the 14th, and Flers on 15th September.

Now the equinoctial rains turned the battlefield into a slippery bog. But, pressed by Joffre, Haig stuck out his Celtic jaw and soldiered on, in the mystic belief that — somehow, somewhere — an exhausted foe might suddenly break. The British army was equally exhausted. Conditions became even more appalling. In November, a soldier wrote: '... Whoever it is we are relieving, they have already gone. The trench is empty ... Corpses lie along the parados, rotting in the wet; every now and then a booted foot appears jutting over the trench. The mud makes it all but impassable, and now, sunk in it up to the knees, I have the momentary terror of never being able to pull myself out ... This is the very limit of endurance. ...'

In a last attack on 13th November, shat-

tered Beaumont-Hamel was finally captured. Having won the bloodily disputed high ground, the British were now fighting their way down into the valley beyond — condemning themselves to spend a winter in flooded trenches. Nothing of any strategic value had been attained. The 'Big Push' was over.

At Verdun in the autumn, Nivelle and Mangin recaptured forts Douaumont and Vaux in a series of brilliant counter-strokes — plus much of the territory gained so painfully by the Crown Prince's men. By Christmas 1916 both battles were finished. After ten terrible months Verdun had been saved. But at what a cost! Half the houses in the city itself had been destroyed by the long-range German guns, and nine of its neighbouring villages had vanished off the face of the earth. When the human casualties came to be added up, the French admitted to having lost 377,231 men, of whom 162,308 were listed as dead or missing. German losses amounted to no less than 337,000. But, in fact, combined casualties may easily have totalled much more than 800,000.

What caused this imprecision about the slaughter at Verdun, as well as giving the battle its particularly atrocious character, was the fact that it all took place in so concentrated an area – little larger than the London parks. Many of the dead were never found, or are still being discovered to this day. One combatant recalled how 'the shells disinterred the bodies, then reinterred them, chopped them to pieces, played with them as a cat plays with a mouse'. Inside the great sombre *Ossuaire* at Verdun lie the bones of more than 100,000 unknown warriors.

On the Somme, the British had lost some 420,000 men; the French about 200,000 and the Germans probably about 450,000 — although a miasma of mendacity and error still surrounds the exact figures. On the battlefields of Verdun and the Somme, there also expired the last flickers of idealism; yet the war would go on.

The casualties of the two battles included among them the highest warlords on both sides. Falkenhayn had fallen; then Joffre, to be replaced (disastrously) by Nivelle, and Asquith by Lloyd George; a few months later Premier Briand's head would also topple. Because of the appalling extent to which Verdun had 'bled white' his own army, Falkenhayn's grim experiment had failed. Yet, in its longer-range effects, it contained an element of success. As Raymond Jubert, a young French ensign, wrote in prophetic despair before he was killed at Verdun: 'They will not be able to make us do it again another day; that would be to misconstrue the price of our effort. . . .' The excessive sacrifices of the French army at Verdun germinated the seeds of the mutinies that were to sprout in the summer of 1917, thereby making it finally plain that the war could no longer be won without American troops.

In many ways Verdun and Somme were the First World War in microcosm, with all its heroism and futility, its glorious and unspeakable horrors. They were indecisive battles in an indecisive war. Of the two, Verdun undoubtedly had the greater historical significance. Years after the 1918 Armistice this Pyrrhic victory of the 20th century continued to haunt the French nation. From the role the forts at Verdun had played, France's military leaders (headed by Pétain) drew the wrong conclusions, and the Maginot Line — with all its disastrous strategic consequences in 1940 — was born.

Spiritually, perhaps, the damage was even greater. More than three-quarters of the whole French army passed through the hell of Verdun — almost an entire generation of Frenchmen. Nobody knew this better than Pétain who, years after the war, remarked that at Verdun 'the constant vision of death had penetrated him (the French soldier) with a resignation which bordered on fatalism'.

For a symbol of what Verdun did to France, one need hardly search beyond the tragic figure of Pétain, the warrior-hero of 1916, the resigned defeatist of 1940.

The Brusilov Offensive

J. N. Westwood

After its great retreat of autumn 1915 the Russian army, which had withdrawn in good order though with great losses, settled down on a new line. This ran from north to south for over 500 miles, from Riga on the Baltic through the Pinsk marshes to the Rumanian frontier. In the north it faced the Germans under Ludendorff, in the south the Austrians under Archduke Frederick. The line was divided into three fronts (army groups). The northernmost of these was the North-West Front, commanded by the same Kuropatkin who in the Russo-Japanese War had specialized in the tactic of the mis-timed retreat. The next sector was the West Front commanded by General Evert, who was also to manifest a dislike for offensive actions. Finally there was the South-West Front commanded by another master of timidity, General Ivanov.

Major-General Alekseyev who, as chief of staff to the commander-in-chief (Tsar Nicholas), was responsible for the Russian operations, was one of the better generals of the First World War—but his front commanders certainly were not. That men of their outlook held such responsible positions was, on the one hand, an indictment of the Russian political situation: with the Tsar, weak-willed in any case, out of touch at the front, the conduct of affairs at Petrograd (as St Petersburg was now called) was dependent more and more on the intrigues of the Tsarina and her favourites, and this circle tended to oppose the appointment of men of strong character and intellectual energy. On the other hand, there was another reason why so many Russian officers were unaggressive: the victory of 1812 over Napoleon had by now, aided by Tolstoy's dramatic and erroneous interpretation in *War and Peace,* entered the Russian tradition as a victory won by a great general called Kutuzov who had deliberately retreated in order to win the war. Thus there existed a concept—conscious and subconscious—of victory through retreat, which is why so many Russian generals seemed reluctant and over-anxious in attack.

During the winter of 1915-16 the Russian army was slowly restored to fighting condition. The deficiencies in 1915, the lack of rifles, of ammunition, of boots, and of properly-trained soldiers, would not be repeated in 1916. In early 1916 rifles were being produced at the rate of 10,000 per month; most front-line units had their full complement of field and machine-guns; ammunition, except perhaps for the heaviest guns, was being delivered fast enough to build up stocks for a full summer campaign; the quiet winter months had given time for proper training of recruits—although the shortage of good experienced officers could not be remedied so easily. The Red Cross detachments organized by local civilians were doing much to maintain front-line morale, not least because they made it their business to provide for many of the physical and recreational needs which the war ministry had so obviously neglected.

The last battle of 1915 had been a minor Russian offensive in the south, aimed at helping the Serbian army, which had been driven into retreat when Bulgaria declared war. In the winter an inter-Allied military conference held at Chantilly in France laid plans for the 1916 summer campaign. Russia was to play a relatively small part in these plans, because of the heavy losses she had sustained in 1915: the main Allied offensive was to be on the Somme, and was to be preceded by a small diversionary attack made by the Russian army. However, the Germans disturbed this scheme by their massive attack on Verdun in February: not for the first time—nor the last—Russia was called upon to save her western allies by mounting a hastily-planned offensive to draw German divisions from the west to the east. In March and April a Russian army of the West Front, with artillery support whose intensity surprised the Germans, attacked through the mud of the spring thaw and overcame the German advanced lines. Ludendorff brought up reinforcements, for some reason the Russian GHQ withdrew its heavy artillery and aircraft from the sector, and the Russian soldiers were left almost defenceless in shallow marsh trenches, without gas masks. Unable to withstand the prolonged barrage of gas and high-explosive shells, and sustaining great losses, the Russians, still singing their hymns, were driven back to their start line in one day.

This disaster – the battle of Lake Naroch – was a relatively minor action, and the Russians were already planning bigger things, both to honour their pledge to the Allies (for the Somme operation was still scheduled) and to take pressure off the French, who were bearing heavy losses and in a desperate situation at Verdun. On 14th April the Tsar had presided at a meeting of the front commanders at GHQ. By this time the pessimistic Ivanov had been replaced by General Alexey Brusilov, who as an army commander had distinguished himself in the 1915 retreat even though he was a champion of an offensive strategy.

Brusilov risks his reputation

At the 14th April meeting the idea of attacking on the West (Evert's) Front was discussed. Both Evert and Kuropatkin declared that they preferred to stay on the defensive, alleging that there was not enough heavy artillery and shells to start an offensive. Brusilov disagreed, and recommended attacks on all fronts. This latter proposal was made in view of the superior rail communications on the German side of the line. By quickly shifting troops from a quiet sector the German command could easily reinforce that part of its line under threat: if the Russian attack came not at one point but at several this would be more difficult, especially as it would be hard to divine which of the attacks was intended to develop into the main thrust.

It was finally agreed that an offensive would be launched at the end of May, and that Brusilov's South-West Front would make the first move but that the main thrust would in fact start soon afterwards on Evert's West Front and be directed towards Wilno.

As he left this meeting Brusilov was told by a colleague that he had been unwise to risk his reputation by offering to launch an offensive. Unperturbed by this pessimism, he returned to his South-West Front to make the most of his six-week preparation time. He decided not to concentrate his forces but to ask each of the generals commanding his four armies to prepare an attack; with preparations being made at four places on his 200-mile sector of the line the enemy would be unable to anticipate where the main blow would fall. In previous actions, as Brusilov was well aware, both the place and the time of an attack had seemed to produce no surprise, so, in addition to avoiding troop concentrations, he took the precaution of dismissing newspaper correspondents. Also, since he suspected that the Tsarina was a careless talker, he avoided telling her the details of his plan.

The Austro-Hungarian line which Brusilov was preparing to break through was strongly fortified, consisting in most parts of three defensive belts one behind the other at intervals of one or two miles. Each belt had at least three lines of full-depth trenches, with fifty to sixty yards between each trench. There were well-built dugouts, machine-gun nests, sniper hideouts, and as many communication trenches as were needed. Before each belt there was a barbed wire barrier, consisting of about twenty rows of posts to which were attached swathes of barbed wire, some of which was very thick and some electrified or mined. Brusilov's aircraft had made good photographs of these defences and the information was transferred to large-scale maps so that, as was shown later, the Russian officers had as good maps of the opposing line as had the Austrians. Moreover, although during the preparation period most of the soldiers were kept well behind the line, the officers spent much time in advanced positions studying the terrain over which they would fight. Meanwhile, with odd sighting shots the gunners were able to get the range of their prescribed targets, and shell stocks were building up. Trenches to serve as assembly and jumping-off points were dug near to the front-line Austrian trenches, in some places getting as close as one hundred or even seventy-five yards. Because this was to be a widely dispersed effort and not a conventional hammer-blow attack, no reserves were assembled.

While his four army commanders were

each planning the details of their respective attacks, Brusilov was in touch — frequently acrimonious touch — with GHQ on the question of timing. On the one hand, Evert was declaring that his West Front attack, for which Brusilov's was only a preliminary diversion, needed more preparation time. On the other hand, to the urgent situation at Verdun was now added the rout of the Italian army by the Austrians at Trentino: unless Russia could do something to relieve the pressure Italy would be driven out of the war and the Central powers would be able to bring even greater strength against Verdun. In the end, 'Brusilov's Offensive', as it was later called (it was the only victory during the First World War named after a commander) was launched on 4th June.

The Archduke's birthday party

Three of Brusilov's four armies broke through at once, aided by thorough artillery preparation, surprise, and the alacrity with which the Czech elements of the Austro-Hungarian army offered themselves as grateful prisoners of war. Brusilov's main thrust was towards Lutsk and Kovel. The former was taken on the 8th: the Archduke Josef Ferdinand was forced by Russian shells to abandon his birthday party which he was celebrating there. With three deep and wide gaps in their line the Austrians were soon in full and fast retreat. However, the ever-reluctant Evert was still unwilling to start his own attack and on 9th June Brusilov learned that this attack would be postponed until the 18th. By this time Ludendorff was desperately trying to organize a counter-attack, and scraping together German units which he sent south to stiffen the demoralized Austrians. Fortunately for Austria, Brusilov's main thrust, confused by unclear instructions from GHQ, advanced in two directions at once, and thus lost the chance of capturing Kovel.

On 18th June Evert's promised attack towards Wilno did not materialize. Instead, that general made a minor, ill-prepared, and unsuccessful advance farther south at Baranowicze. By now it was clear that GHQ would do what Brusilov had always opposed: instead of attacking on the West Front it would send Evert's troops to Brusilov, believing that the latter with these reinforcements would be able to exploit his success fully. As Brusilov expected, as soon as the Germans noticed these Russian troop movements they felt able to transfer their own troops southwards and, because they had better railways, got there first. In this way the German command was able to make the best possible use of its scanty resources. Despite a renewed push at the end of July, Brusilov made less and less headway as he found more and more German units opposing him. In general, the Brusilov Offensive came to an end about 10th August, by which time the Austrians had lost not only vast areas of territory but also 375,000 prisoners of war, not to speak of killed and wounded. But Russian casualties already exceeded half a million.

Brusilov later claimed that if his wildly successful offensive had been properly exploited, Russia could have won the war for the Allies. It does seem very possible that if Evert had carried out the main attack as planned (thus occupying those German troops which in fact were sent to help the Austrians) Brusilov would have been able to drive Austria out of the war — which almost certainly would have entailed the surrender of Germany before the end of 1916. In any case, Brusilov's Offensive achieved all the aims which it had been set, and more: Austrian troops in Italy had to abandon their victories and rush north to fight the Russians, and the Germans were forced to end the Verdun operation and transfer no less than thirty-five divisions from France to the Eastern Front. Even if Brusilov had not won the war, he probably stopped the Allies losing it.

Persuading Rumania

In mid-August, just as Brusilov's Offensive was slowing down, it was brought to a definite end by the decision of Rumania to abandon her neutrality and join the Allies, her first step in this direction being to sign a military alliance.

Right from the beginning of the war Allied diplomacy had been busy in Rumania. The Russian effort in this respect was two-pronged and, in view of the Tsar's habit of acting independently of his ministers, it is possible that neither prong knew what the other was doing.

The conventional weapon in this diplomatic campaign was the Russian ambassador in Bucharest, who enjoyed a certain influence in Rumanian political circles. But his talents were well matched by the Rumanian statesman Brătianu, who was long able to postpone a decision. Rumania at this time had well-balanced ties with both Russia and the Central powers, and public opinion was more or less equally split between those who favoured the Allies and those who supported Germany and Austria. It seems likely that most Rumanians were behind Brătianu in his efforts to delay a decision until the bandwagon of ultimate victory had moved unmistakably in one direction or another.

Russia's second agent in Bucharest was less correct than the ambassador, but may have been more effective in the long run. This was Rear-Admiral Veselkin, who from his miniature flagship *Rus* commanded the Danube Flotilla of the Russian Imperial Navy. This flotilla, directly controlled by GHQ, had been formed in 1914 by arming Danubian steamers and adding a few gunboats from the Black Sea Fleet. Its purpose had been to keep Serbia supplied, but after that nation was overrun it had little to do, apart from engaging in intrigues to push Rumania into war on Russia's side.

Veselkin was a witty, open-hearted, and eloquent officer, popular with his colleagues and, more important, a favourite of the Tsar. Whether he dabbled in genuine cloak-and-dagger activities is doubtful: the mysterious packages which he entrusted to transient Russians for strictly personal delivery to the Tsar contained not secret documents but merely Nicholas's favourite kind of Rumanian smoked sausage. But certainly he devoted all his spare time to the persuasion of the Rumanians. He had been entrusted with two million roubles' worth of jewellery which he distributed as 'gifts' to influential Rumanians and their wives. However, this was little compared to the wealth at the disposal of the German agents (who admittedly needed large sums to bribe railwaymen to turn a blind eye on the thinly-disguised war materials passing through on their way from Germany to Turkey). In mid-1916 it seemed that the pro-German party in Rumania was still strong enough to thwart Russian efforts.

In any case, some influential Russians believed that a neutral Rumania was more advantageous than an allied Rumania. Both the Russian naval and military attachés were sending mournful accounts of Rumania's unpreparedness for any serious war, and other Russian officials had the foresight to realize that an Allied Rumania would ask for help which Russia could not spare. However, a change of Russian foreign ministers was followed by what was virtually an ultimatum setting Rumania a time limit in which to make up her mind: the success of Brusilov's Offensive—then in progress—had encouraged this Russian move while at the same time providing an extra inducement for Rumania to choose the side of the Allies.

Rumania at war

Thus it came about that on 17th August Rumania signed the military alliance which had been pressed upon her, and then immediately began to disprove the belief —still current among the great powers fifty years later—that an ally is inevitably better than a neutral. The Allies had hoped that the more than half-a-million-strong Rumanian army would be sent south against Bulgaria, and then perhaps join up with their own forces at Salonika. However, Rumanian appetites in the direction of Bulgaria had already been satisfied by the Treaty of Bucharest of 1913 which had ended the Balkan War. On the other hand, Rumania still had desires (termed 'national aspirations') for Austrian Transylvania. So, on 27th August, to the consternation of friends and enemies alike, Rumania struck north.

Germany, which had been hoping that the Rumanian government would procrastinate just a little longer, was ill-placed to meet this new threat: help had already been sent to Austria to stop Brusilov, the western Allies were starting their Somme offensive at the same time as their forces at Salonika were becoming more active. So at first the Rumanian army carried all before it, capturing the capital of Transylvania in early September. However, by tight organization and by taking great risks in scraping together reinforcements from quiet sectors of other fronts, the German high command did just manage to master the situation. Falkenhayn attacked the Rumanians in Transylvania, while Mackensen went through Bulgaria and attacked the new enemy from the south, forcing the Rumanians to relinquish their Dobrudja territory. It now became evident that the Rumanian army was even worse trained and worse equipped than the pessimists had claimed, and in any case the easy-going Rumanian officers were ill-adapted to modern warfare. The Rumanians called for Russian help, and it was Russian troops which inflicted a temporary check on Mackensen in mid-September. Before the end of the month, despite Russian diversionary pressure farther north, the two German armies were threatening the heart of Rumania. In the south Mackensen drove his enemy over the Danube, while the Rumanian forces which had so cheerfully invaded Transylvania a month previously, were now in full retreat. On 23rd October Mackensen captured the key Black Sea port of Constanta, and in early December Bucharest fell. The Rumanian army was now finished for the time being: it occupied a small part of Rumanian territory around Jassy and was being reorganized by a French general in the hope of better days to come.

By this time two Russian armies were involved in Rumania, and it was not long before a quarter of the Russian army was devoted to this area. The Russian front had now, in effect, been extended to the Black Sea: no longer was there a safely neutral Russo-Rumanian frontier, so that for Petrograd at least the Rumanian alliance had proved to be of negative value. For Germany, once the immediate crisis was over, the entry of Rumania was a blessing: she now occupied the wheatlands and oilfields of that country and had better communications with her ally Turkey. Moreover, rightly or wrongly, the German high command had been anticipating the entry into the war of Holland and Denmark on the Allied side, and the rout of Rumania convinced it that these two countries were now unlikely to risk the same fate.

The Rumanian opportunists did the best they could to retrieve their country's fortunes: they declared peace in May 1918 but rejoined the Allies on the eve of their final victory.

Britain Organizes for Total War

C. L. Mowat

'We are going to lose this war', Lloyd George told Colonel Maurice Hankey, the all-important but unobtrusive secretary of the cabinet's War Committee, some time in November 1916. And indeed 'this war' was going very badly, and no end, let alone victory, seemed in sight after more than two years of fighting.

Herbert Asquith, the Liberal prime minister, seemed to many to be unsuited for his task. His virtues, equanimity, patience, a certain lack of imagination, a readiness to wait for the right moment to decide and to act, had served well in the 'constitutional crisis' of 1909-11, less well during the Ulster rebellion of 1912-14. Now they seemed irrelevant: '. . . with the war going badly, the Prime Minister appeared positively wooden . . . the passive spectator of events, fundamentally unwilling . . . to alter the course of the juggernaut he had helped set in motion', a later commentator wrote. Asquith had retained the cabinet of twenty-one members and had resorted to improvised bodies, a war council, then the Dardanelles Committee, then a War Committee, to deal with wartime administration and policy; but he had not given these committees the necessary authority. The final decisions, after another round of argument, still rested with the cabinet. There was no one to direct and co-ordinate the general management of the war. Kitchener, 'an ageing ignorant man armed only with a giant's reputation', was put in as secretary of war and left both to direct strategy and to organize his voluntary armies without informed criticism from outside; and Asquith's failure to demand information and to co-ordinate the plans of the War Office and Admiralty had contributed to the Dardanelles disaster. The system of 'business as usual', applied to munitions and supplies, helped to bring about the 'shell scandal' of May 1915. The coalition government which Asquith had formed at that time had brought in Conservatives and Labour MPs to share responsibility; and in fact problems of war production and administration were tackled much more effectively when this had been done. There remained, or seemed to remain (and in war, psychology is a vital factor), a lack of drive and grasp of purpose.

With the main parties already within the government, change could come only from within. Lloyd George alone 'had a passion to win the war', and as minister of munitions (May 1915-June 1916), and then, after Kitchener's death, as war secretary, he had grappled with the production of arms and the transport services, and was ready, indeed desperately anxious, to have a wider scope for initiative. But as Asquith wrote to Bonar Law, the Conservative leader, 'he lacks the one thing needful—he does not inspire trust'. No change of direction could be made without the support of the Conservatives and they, in particular, distrusted Lloyd George. But there were notable exceptions: Bonar Law, the cautious, melancholy leader, aware of his precarious authority within his own party, and adventurers like Carson, the Ulster leader, Milner, the rabid imperialist, and Northcliffe, the overweening press lord, who saw in Lloyd George a kindred spirit. What was needed was a go-between, to bring together those who, acting together, could produce a change of direction. And one was at hand: Max Aitken (later Lord Beaverbrook). It was at Aitken's country house, Cherkley (near Leatherhead), that Bonar Law and Lloyd George met after Kitchener's death; Bonar Law's support persuaded Asquith to appoint Lloyd George to the War Office—a portent for the future.

Lloyd George takes over

The political crisis which brought Lloyd George to the premiership on 7th December 1916 occurred inside a week—or rather a week-end—but it had really begun early in November when Carson quarrelled with Bonar Law over some trivial matter and was followed by almost half the Conservatives. Aitken went into action to save his friend Bonar Law: a series of meetings, calls, dinners followed. Lloyd George had his own reasons for wanting a change (and had been in touch with Carson and Milner): his authority at the War Office was limited by the independent position of the chief of the general staff, Sir William Robertson, who worked against Lloyd George and leaked information to the press. Lloyd George wanted a small and effective war cabinet for the direction of the war, with himself as the working chairman, though Asquith as prime minister would be the formal head. On 25th November Bonar Law, Lloyd George, Carson, and Aitken met at Bonar Law's London house, Pembroke Lodge, and agreed to put forward to Asquith the plan for a war cabinet. Asquith's reply on the 27th was a polite rejection.

Lloyd George, confident of Bonar Law's support, though of little else, now acted. On 1st December he wrote to Asquith, again proposing a war cabinet. Asquith declined. Bonar Law, dining with Aitken at the Hyde Park Hotel, decided that he must see Lloyd George that evening. 'I had the means of finding Lloyd George at that time at any hour of the day or night, and I knew he was dining at the Berkeley Hotel,' wrote Aitken in his long and fascinating story of the crisis. They hauled Lloyd George out of his dinner party. Bonar Law decided that night to hold firm in supporting Lloyd George. Next day the *Daily Express* and the *Daily Chronicle* came out in criticism of the government and called for a 'war council': for this Aitken was responsible, though not for other newspaper comment favourable to Lloyd George. Similar comment in the Sunday papers increased the annoyance of Bonar Law's Conservative colleagues, and they came to a meeting at Pembroke Lodge, on Sunday 3rd December, in an angry mood. They believed that Asquith was indispensable as prime minister and preserver of national unity, and wanted to turn Lloyd George out. They passed a resolution calling on Asquith to resign because 'in our opinion the publicity given to Mr Lloyd George's intentions makes reconstruction from within no longer possible', and declared that they would themselves resign if Asquith refused. The intention was to enable him to form a new government with or without Lloyd George. However, when Bonar Law

told him of the resolution that afternoon, Asquith took fright at the word 'resignation'. He decided to compromise with Lloyd George over his plans and that night published a notice that the government was being reconstructed.

On Monday 4th December, Asquith changed his mind. Several Liberal ministers advised him to stand firm, and Lord Curzon and other Conservative ministers promised him support, Curzon pledging himself not to take office under either Lloyd George or Bonar Law. Asquith was also annoyed by an editorial in that morning's *Times,* which he wrongly attributed to Lloyd George. He sent Lloyd George a note that evening again rejecting his plan. Lloyd George resigned. After discouraging advice from both Liberal and Conservative ministers, Asquith also resigned. Bonar Law saw Lloyd George a little later; again, they agreed to act together, each to support the other in forming a government.

At the Palace that night (5th December) the King asked Bonar Law to form a government. For this Asquith's support was essential. Asquith refused, and Bonar Law resigned the commission. Lloyd George was given the task next day, and succeeded. He had the support of Bonar Law, of course, and the other Conservatives (Curzon forgot his pledge). Balfour, the ex-prime minister, who had been ill during the crisis, agreed at once to join. So did many Liberals, whose support was canvassed by Dr Christopher Addison. And Lloyd George won round the Labour leaders, promising the party a larger share in the government.

These events had important consequences, and not only in the direction of the war. The Liberals were split, a large number following Asquith into opposition. The decline of the Liberal Party has been attributed to this division and blamed on Lloyd George's conspiracy and seizure of power. Four points must be made. There is such a thing as legitimate ambition. Lloyd George was convinced that he could save his country and win the war; stalemate, the reckless, hopeless outpouring of life, seemed the alternative. If he split with Asquith, Asquith equally split with him; by refusing to join a new government Asquith perpetuated the split — whether because, as he said, he could serve the country more effectively in opposition, or because he believed that Lloyd George would fail and he would be recalled to office untrammelled, makes no difference. There are many reasons, besides those of personalities, which underlie the Liberal decline. And, lastly, Lloyd George would never have gained office without the support of the Conservatives, and particularly of Bonar Law—but equally, he could not have succeeded without the support of the press and the public—which believed, without necessarily liking or admiring him, that he had the vision and power which the country needed.

The War Cabinet

Lloyd George at once formed his proposed War Cabinet. Carson (who became first lord of the Admiralty) was not a member; instead, Lloyd George chose Curzon and Milner, men of great ability who represented important sides of the Conservative party, Bonar Law and Arthur Henderson (Labour). None of these except Bonar Law, who was chancellor of the exchequer, had departmental responsibilities. The War Cabinet met almost daily (200 days in the first 235), devoting itself to over-all problems of strategy and administration. For three periods in 1917 and 1918 it was reinforced by the prime ministers of the Dominions, becoming the Imperial War Cabinet. This was a large and imaginative development, though it did not survive the war.

Lloyd George's reorganization of the government for total war was a combination of drive, information, and co-ordination. At the top was the War Cabinet, with its own secretary (Hankey) and secretariat, its agenda and minutes; hitherto, the cabinet had had no secretariat, no official records (the system survived the war and peacetime cabinets continued to keep minutes). Much of the work of the War Cabinet was done by committees of which one or other of its members was in charge. At the other end came the regular government departments, reinforced by new ministries (Labour, Food, Shipping, Pensions) and innumerable departments and committees. The essential link between the two ends was provided partly by committees, partly by the prime minister's enlarged number of secretaries. These bright young men, often called the 'garden suburb' (because of the huts they were

housed in) and disliked as interfering and superior persons, were Lloyd George's 'leg men', co-ordinating the work of the War Cabinet with the other layers of government. Many of them came from Milner's old 'Kindergarten' which had helped to reorganize South Africa after the Boer War: Lionel Curtis, Philip Kerr (later Lord Lothian), Leopold Amery, Waldorf Astor. Among their many functions was the gathering of precise information and statistics, information either lacking altogether or buried in departments isolated from each other. Thus one secretary was Joseph Davies, a statistician from the South Wales coal trade, whose work on the statistics of ship sinkings and farm production was of the highest value. Only in the co-ordination of political and military strategy did the system fail to achieve full success, largely because of the mutual distrust of Lloyd George and the generals—a difficulty Churchill overcame in the Second World War.

War and welfare

Before looking at the effects of these new arrangements we should notice that much had already been done, piecemeal, to gear the nation for total war. By the Defence of the Realm Act ('Dora'), passed on 8th August 1914, the government had taken powers to make regulations of the widest scope over persons and property. Almost everything was subject to government regulations from the internment of aliens and the taking over of factories to street lighting or the whistling for cabs. An early problem was trade union opposition to the replacement ('dilution') of skilled labour in engineering works and shipyards by the employment of less skilled men and of women. An agreement was made between the employers and the unions in November 1914 (the Crayford Agreement), but difficulties continued until the 'Treasury Agreement' was made at a conference in March 1915 presided over by Lloyd George (then chancellor of the exchequer). Dilution was accepted but with certain safeguards, and on condition that after the war working conditions would return to normal; disputes were to be arbitrated, strikes outlawed. Plenty of room remained for friction, and the unions, by supporting government measures, were accused of deserting the workers and were challenged by a shop stewards' movement. The worst troubles were in the engineering works and shipyards on the Clyde, and culminated in the arrest and deportation (to Edinburgh) of David Kirkwood and other leaders of the Clyde Workers' Committee in March 1916. Industrial conscription, though talked of, was never introduced; but there were regulations controlling the employment and discharge of workmen – in particular a system of leaving certificates by which, if withheld, his employer could prevent a worker from moving to another job. Wage increases and bonuses averted many disputes, but there were some strikes – for example, a coal strike in South Wales in July 1915. The railways were taken under government control at the start of the war and put under an executive committee of the leading managers. Shipping and the ports were progressively controlled under a system of requisitions and licensing. The South Wales coalfield was put under government control on 1st December 1916. Government purchases built up stocks of sugar, wheat, meat, and hides; for example, the government took over the entire meat exports of Australia and New Zealand in 1915. Drunkenness and absenteeism led the government into controlling licensing hours through the Central Control Board (Liquor Traffic) created in June 1915; early in 1916 the board took over all licensed premises in three districts, Enfield Lock, Carlisle and Gretna, and Invergordon. Government control of the public's drinking habits, through licensing laws, is one of the so far permanent legacies of the First World War.

The most spectacular advance was in munitions manufacture. The War Office and Admiralty were slow to expand the channels through which they traditionally procured equipment. Lloyd George early took up the question, and Asquith appointed a special committee in October 1914, but its work was thwarted by Kitchener. The 'shell scandal' of May 1915 followed newspaper reports from the front of the shortage of ammunition. When, soon afterwards, Asquith formed his Coalition government, Lloyd George took over a new Ministry of Munitions. Within a year he had built up a department whose headquarters staff alone numbered 25,000. Businessmen, engineers, and economists were drawn in, a network of local commit-

tees created; huge orders were placed at home and abroad, often in anticipation of far greater demands than the service chiefs recognized; firms were persuaded to change over to munitions production. New 'national factories' were built, 73 in 1915, 218 by the end of the war.

Three inter-related consequences followed. In munitions work, as in industry and transport generally, women were employed in place of men; the status of women was raised, and their emancipation advanced by the war. Equally, the new field of industrial welfare developed. Building factories in new areas and transferring workers, particularly women, to them brought the need for amenities hitherto thought unnecessary: canteens, nurseries, rest rooms, hostels, billeting arrangements. Lloyd George created a welfare section of the ministry of munitions and put in charge of it Seebohm Rowntree, a pioneer in new methods of management. And to protect war workers in the future, unemployment insurance which had been started in a small way in the National Insurance Act of 1911 was extended in 1916 to all workers in munitions and a wide range of related industries. War and the welfare state were as closely linked between 1914 and 1918 as they were between 1939 and 1945.

Conscription for military service was the other side of the coin. The pre-war army and the Territorials were recruited from volunteers. Kitchener continued to raise volunteer armies, and enlisting became a patriotic duty. War production suffered when skilled men joined the colours, though a system of badges encouraged many to stay at work without stigma to their patriotism. The toll of life in the campaigns of 1915 soon made it clear that volunteering, besides being wasteful and undiscriminating, would fail to keep up the strength of the army. Kitchener resisted conscription, however, and so did many Liberals, so that the demand for it, pushed by the Conservatives, nearly split Asquith's government. Asquith first bought time by getting Lord Derby to head a recruiting scheme (October 1915) under which men would 'attest' their willingness to serve, and if rejected on personal grounds, or because they were needed on the Home Front, would be issued with khaki armbands. No married men were to be called up until the unmarried had been taken. When it was clear that many unmarried men had not attested, a conscription bill was introduced in January 1916, imposing service on unmarried men not subject to exemption. This, too, proved inadequate, and a second act in May 1916 applied conscription to all men between the ages of eighteen and forty-one. As an afterthought some provisions were added for conscientious objectors; many were allowed to do civilian work of national importance, many others served prison sentences, including a hard core of 985 'absolutists'.

Leviathan

All this organization for war, widely ramified by the end of 1915, was extended and knit together under Lloyd George's government in 1917. Industrialists like Lord Inverforth, Lord Leverhulme, Lord Rhondda, Albert Stanley (Lord Ashfield), and Sir Joseph Maclay were brought in to head new ministries or offices. Rationing of meat, sugar, butter, eggs was introduced in 1918, more because of queues and hoarding than because of actual shortages of supply. Flour mills were taken over in April 1918. Agricultural production was encouraged by the new Food Production Department (created 1st January 1917) under the Board of Agriculture. The government empowered itself to seize and cultivate unoccupied or badly farmed land. Guaranteed prices were offered, and agricultural wages raised under local wages boards. Some two million acres of grassland were ploughed up for grain crops. All coal mines were put under the Coal Controller in March 1917 (sequel to control in South Wales). By the end of the war the nation was at full stretch, and no sphere of life was outside the rule of war.

The wartime controls and organization were swept away within three years. Other effects remained. Lack of price control, rising prices, matched more or less by increased wages, produced inflation: in December 1918 the index of retail food prices stood at 229 (1913=100). Many new fortunes had been made, but there were also the 'new poor' who lived on fixed incomes or slowly rising salaries; working men, and particularly unskilled and semi-skilled workers, were better off unless unemployment overtook them. At the same time taxation took a much larger share of the national income, eighteen per cent after the war compared to seven and a half per cent before. The budget, which in 1913 was under £200 millions, allowed for expenditure of £2,579 millions in 1918. Income tax had been raised from 1s. 8d. in the £ to 6s.; surtax had been raised, and the exemption limit lowered from £5,000 to £2,000; and excess profits were taxed at eighty per cent. Here, as in the extent of the government's powers, the scale of its operations and the number of its civil servants and workers, Leviathan big government, had taken over, never to retreat.

The Dominions at War

C. Falkus

The Great War was a world war from the moment of Great Britain's entry on 4th August 1914. For she declared war not only on behalf of the 45,000,000 inhabitants of the British Isles, but also of the 400,000,000 members of a far-flung empire which was near the zenith of its extent and self-confidence. Within that empire the self-governing dominions could, if they chose, decline active support. But none did choose, and soon troops were on their way from remote corners of the world to battlefields many thousands of miles from home. Canadians, Australians, New Zealanders, and South Africans, representing the dominions, took their places in the trenches beside their European allies, as did the Sikhs, Gurkhas Mussalmans and many more from the Indian sub-continent.

The participation of the British empire involved all the non-European continents in the war, and in time the entry of Japan and the United States would transform it into a global conflict on a grand scale. Inevitably such a war brought a whole series of problems. In countries far from the Western Front it was sometimes difficult to promote that sense of urgency needed for supreme effort. The vagaries of colonization had left some countries, like South Africa and Canada, with ethnic divisions which threatened grave crises under the stresses of war. In India growing nationalism foreshadowed a transformation in the character of the empire, while for all 'emerging' nations the question was raised of the part they were to play in the post-war world.

This article will deal with the effect of war on the political developments and ambitions of the dominions of the British empire which, geographically, were among the numerous countries on the perimeter of the conflict. A full list of participants – active and passive – would include not only the dominions and colonies of Great Britain but also the colonies of other European powers as well as numerous South and Central American countries who declared war in the wake of the United States. These were Cuba, Panama, Brazil, Guatemala, Nicaragua, Costa Rica, Haiti, and Honduras, while Siam, Liberia, and China also declared war on the Central powers. The contributions of the dominions considered here, while statistically smaller than those of the leading nations, were nevertheless of great significance, and emphasize the merging of European history into that of a widening world.

Australia

More than most other countries of the empire, Australia was able to boast that she entered the war a united people. The majority of her 5,000,000 inhabitants were bound by strong ties of race and sentiment to the mother country, and the major political parties vied with each other in expressions of support for Great Britain's policy. Joseph Cook, the Liberal leader, said: 'Whatever happens, Australia is part of the Empire right to the full. When the Empire is at war, so is Australia at war. All our resources are in the Empire and for the preservation and security of the Empire.' His Labour opponent, Andrew Fisher, declared that 'should the worst happen, after everything has been done that honour will permit, Australia will stand behind the mother country to help and defend her to our last man and our last shilling'. Such statements echoed the country's eager, even exuberant, mood. The governor-general cabled that there was 'indescribable enthusiasm and entire unanimity throughout Australia in support of all that tends to provide for the security of the Empire in war'.

The outbreak of war coincided with an election which resulted in a decisive Labour victory. Fisher was thus called upon to preside over the early stages of a war effort which involved measures quite out of keeping with Australian experiences and traditions. Sweeping powers over aliens, settlers of enemy origin or recent ancestry, censorship of the press, and control of publications were acquired by such measures as the War Precautions Act which gave the government authority to impose virtually a military regime. Inevitably the exercise of such authority in a country proud of its democratic way of life caused problems. Overzealous censorship, for example, caused friction between the government and press, while at times the rights of states seemed threatened by the powers of the federal government. When the Queensland premier, T.J.Ryan, spoke against conscription the federal government forbade publication of the speech and seized numerous copies. Ryan thereupon initiated action against the government for alleged violation of the rights of his sovereign state and found himself summoned before a Brisbane police court on charges of having prejudiced the public interest. The charges and counter-charges were allowed to drop, but Ryan's speech was nevertheless printed in the Parliamentary Debates with the 'censored' extracts appearing in heavy type.

Dealing with aliens was no great problem for Australia and only in the later stages of the war was there much prejudice shown against Germans in matters of employment and other forms of discrimination. South Australia, and other states to a lesser extent, assisted the war effort by appointing committees to replace traditional Germanic place-names with neutral or patriotic substitutes like Mount Kitchener in place of Kaiserstuhl.

These were trivial matters, however, compared with the great crisis of Australia's war effort, the struggle over conscription. As the first enthusiasm faded, and as the Western Front added to the toll of Gallipoli, Australia was faced with a man-power shortage which had become acute by the end of 1916. Recruiting figures dropped so rapidly that, whereas in June 1915, for example, recruits had numbered over 12,000, a year later the figure was little more than half that. To one man, at least, it was clear that something would have to be done: that man was William Morris Hughes, the former attorney-general, who became prime minister in October 1915.

Hughes was one of the most colourful, as well as capable, statesmen in Australian history. Born into a poor Welsh family, at an early age he emigrated to Australia, where he studied law, entered politics, and with the aid of administrative gifts and

fervent oratory rose to the highest position at a critical time. In more ways than one his career resembled that of his great contemporary, Lloyd George, though even the latter would probably have been incapable of Hughes's characteristic effrontery when, at the post-war peace conference, he was rebuked by no less a figure than President Wilson for his insistence on retaining New Guinea. Wilson said: 'Mr Prime Minister of Australia, do I understand your attitude aright? If I do, it is this, that the opinion of the whole civilized world is to be set at naught. This conference, fraught with such infinite consequences to mankind for good or evil, is to break up with results which may well be disastrous to the future happiness of 18 hundred millions of the human race, in order to satisfy the whim of 5 million people in this remote southern continent whom you claim to represent.' Hughes smartly replied: 'Very well put, Mr President, you have guessed it. That's just so.'

In March 1916 Hughes visited Great Britain for four months, a visit which, with the passage of time, has taken on the qualities of legend. His aggressive, uncompromising speeches made him a figure of international fame and the Australian press rejoiced in the triumphs of their leader. He spoke of 'the happy privilege of Australians now in France to fight alongside the men of my native country'. He declared that 'we must win! We are fighting for a deathless principle. And though we walk for a time through the valley of the shadow of death, yet our cause is right and it shall prevail'. Such words hit the right note when Great Britain herself was searching for resolute leadership, and the *Evening Standard* asked 'who are the two men amongst us today wielding the biggest sway over the minds and the hearts of the British people? Surely Mr Lloyd George and Mr W.M.Hughes, the Australian prime minister. Both are Welshmen of fervid imagination who appeal by their eloquence, their fire, their patriotism'.

But on his return Hughes was to embark on a policy which split, not only his party, but the nation, and threatened seriously to jeopardize the Australian war effort. This policy, to extend compulsory service to overseas duty, met with a humiliating rebuff in a national referendum held in October 1916. The Australian people rejected his proposals by a majority of over 72,000, though for reasons which are not easy to discover. Hughes enjoyed the support of the press and of most prominent figures which, together with his own Herculean labours, indicated a 'Yes' majority. But the combination of war-weariness, remoteness from the main areas of conflict, a developing and perhaps healthy national tradition of defeating the government on referenda, all combined to defeat the forecasts. In addition there was the remorseless figure of Dr Mannix, Roman Catholic coadjutor archbishop of Melbourne, campaigning tirelessly against conscription. He did not scruple to play on Irish feelings in the aftermath of the Easter Rising, or to suggest that Australia had already done more than her fair share in the war.

The referendum divided party and nation. Anti-conscriptionists resigned from the government; Hughes left the Labour party. He was able to carry on only with the support of the Liberals, and when his government shortly became a Nationalist coalition, headed by himself but maintained by his political opponents, his position was indeed strangely similar to that of the prime minister of Great Britain.

Hughes's Nationalists won an overwhelming victory in the 1917 election, which encouraged him to appeal once more for powers to enforce conscription. By this time recruiting figures had dropped to below half the figure of 7,000 a month considered necessary. The prime minister said bluntly: 'I tell you plainly that the government must have this power. It cannot govern the country without it, and will not attempt to do so.' Yet again he was disappointed, this time by an even larger adverse vote. He resigned as he had promised, but, with no alternative government possible, came back on the following day with the identical cabinet which had resigned with him. Compulsion was now impossible, and the government tried to make the best of things with a vigorous recruiting campaign. But they were hampered by growing opposition, particularly from trades unionists and a militant body called International Workers of the World, which demanded immediate peace through negotiation. It is probable that a serious division within Australian society on the war issue was averted only by the unexpected collapse of the German armies in the autumn of 1918.

Australia's political crisis was to remain significant long after the conclusion of the war. But despite these troubles her contribution to the final victory was remarkable. Her proportion of troops in the field and of casualties sustained compared favourably with those of other dominions and of Great Britain herself. Moreover in the 'Anzac spirit' she discovered, in conjunction with the New Zealanders, a sense of national identity as well as of national pride.

New Zealand

The First World War presented fewer problems in New Zealand than in the other dominions. Her political life was not disrupted by minority problems, social cleavages, or conscription debates. The country as a whole vigorously supported the war, and compulsory overseas service was adopted in 1916 not because of any lack of recruits but out of a sense of 'fair play'. The coalition government which had been created the previous year reflected no crisis, as in Great Britain and Australia, but rather the desire for national unity at a time of national effort.

By 1914, New Zealand politics were undergoing a process of transition. Until recently the Liberal party had reigned supreme under the impetus given by the extraordinary Richard Seddon — gross, uncultivated, far from high-principled, yet firmly entrenched prime minister from 1893 to 1906. His successor, Joseph Ward, continued to enjoy a success which had been built on strong support from the farmers, and it was a right-wing defection among the farmers which allowed the recently created Reform Party to form its first government in 1912.

The prime minister, William Ferguson Massey, was in many ways an uninspiring figure. He continued the 'Seddon tradition' of lack of refinement and intellectualism, but was without Seddon's overpowering personality. Narrow, bigoted, but resolute and energetic, Massey managed to remain prime minister continuously for thirteen years, though it is probable that Ward, his coalition partner and treasurer, exercised a greater control in wartime.

New Zealand entered the war with alacrity. Her traditions, recent though they were, were decidedly imperialistic.

She had urged Great Britain to pursue a more active policy in the Pacific and her adoption of compulsory military service for home defence in 1909 involved calling up all males over the age of 12. She took pride in being the first dominion to offer troops, and throughout the war maintained a 'pro-British' sentiment which has become part of her national characteristic. She is regarded as considerably more 'British' than her Australian neighbour.

There was little social unrest to hamper her war effort. In the years preceding 1914 there had been, it is true, some violent incidents when Massey ruthlessly crushed a series of strikes. But the Labour movement, which would one day destroy the Liberals, was in its infancy; only half a dozen Labour members formed a party in opposition to the war. On the whole the war was a period of prosperity for New Zealand's agriculture. Her promise to feed Great Britain was profitable to both sides of the agreement, and her exportable wool, meat, and dairy produce was commandeered by the government to be sold at guaranteed high prices. The military effort was, for a country with such a small population, astonishing.

Altogether about 120,000 New Zealanders saw active service, of whom 17,000 were killed – a vast number of young men whose loss was severely felt in the difficult inter-war years. The Maoris, at first understandably reluctant to enlist, served with distinction, whether as volunteers or conscripts. Despite the smallness of her population and her distance from Europe, New Zealand's contribution to the Allied victory was far from negligible.

New Zealanders were proud of their effort in the war. The performance of their troops at Gallipoli, their occupation of German Samoa, their voice in the counsels of the empire and in the League of Nations all assisted that growth of identity so important in the evolution of a colony into a nation.

Canada

As in Australia and New Zealand, in Canada both major political parties were outspoken in their support for the war. The Conservative prime minister, Sir Robert Borden, said that 'as to our duty, we are all agreed: we stand shoulder to shoulder with Britain and the other British Dominions in this quarrel, and that duty we shall not fail to fulfil as the honour of Canada demands'. Sir Wilfrid Laurier, leader of the Liberals and spokesman for the majority of French Canadians, claimed that 'this war is for as noble a cause as ever impelled a nation to risk her all upon the arbitrament of the sword'.

Such assertions hid a fundamental division in Canadian society which was to loom larger as the war progressed. The so-called Anglo-Canadians, together with British-born immigrants, had a vastly different outlook from that of the insular, tightly-knit community of French-speaking *Canadiens*. Naturally enough the French-speaking settlers felt less attachment to the British empire than their countrymen. Less obviously, but equally important, the French community retained fewer ties with their own 'mother country' and their support for the war was, on the whole, passive rather than overtly enthusiastic. This situation was not helped by the attitude of the administration. The minister of militia, Sam Hughes, made no pretence of his disgust at the low recruiting figures from the French-speaking provinces. Efforts to create specifically *Canadien* forces were usually obstructed; English was uniformly adopted as the language of command; and *Canadien* recruits seemed to suffer almost insuperable difficulties when it came to promotion.

These problems lay in the future, however, when Canada, in common with the rest of the empire, embarked on her struggle of unprecedented magnitude. Borden's greatest tasks, as he saw them, were two-fold. First he had to mobilize the nation for war, second, to ensure that his country participated in the direction of the effort to which he committed so many of his country's resources. Raising sufficient troops was far from easy. Canadian traditions were non-military and her pre-war permanent army numbered a mere 3,000. No doubt a feeling of security due to the nearness of her powerful neighbour with its protective Monroe Doctrine played its part in this lack of preparedness, but it meant that Canada felt the war-time dislocation even more severely than other countries.

In view of her traditions Canada's achievements were formidable. Though the target of 500,000 troops had become evidently unattainable by 1917, Canada played her full share in the war effort. Lloyd George's verdict on the quality of the Canadian troops after their exploits on the Somme in 1916 was that they 'played a part of such distinction that thenceforward they were marked out as storm troops; for the remainder of the war they were brought along to head the assault in one great battle after another. Whenever the Germans found the Canadian Corps coming into the line, they prepared for the worst'.

With his country performing such feats, Borden considered that he should play some part in formulating the policies for which his troops were committed. When told by Bonar Law, the colonial secretary, that his schemes were impractical he retorted that 'it can hardly be expected that we shall put 400,000 or 500,000 men in the field and willingly accept the position of having no more voice and receiving no more consideration than if we were toy automata. Any person cherishing such an expectation harbours an unfortunate and even dangerous delusion. Is this war being waged by the United Kingdom alone, or is it a war waged by the whole Empire?' Such language had its effect, and after Lloyd George became prime minister in December 1916 the dominions found themselves consulted to a much greater extent. An Imperial War Cabinet was set up in March 1917, the same month for which an Imperial War Conference was summoned. It was Borden, appropriately enough, who moved the famous resolution at the conference, claiming for the dominions a 'right to an adequate voice in foreign policy and in foreign relations'. After the war, Borden led the dominions' demands for representation at the peace conference and for their individual membership of the League of Nations.

But while Sir Robert was demanding more influence for Canada, his country was being torn by a grave crisis over conscription in 1917. The enormous losses sustained in Europe during the previous year made man-power shortages general throughout all belligerent countries. Recruiting figures, high in the early months of the war, fell alarmingly until they were less, month by month, than the casualties. By 1917 not only was conscription an urgent problem, but party politics had been renewed in a way which lent considerable bitterness to the struggle

The growing opposition of the *Canadiens*, which was fostered by the treatment of their recruits, long-standing grievances over the exclusive use of English in schools in Ontario, and a series of frauds at governmental level all helped to create a dangerous political climate. Moreover, Laurier was determined to maintain the separate identity and different ideals of the French-Canadians, and these seemed threatened, not only by conscription, but by the coalition government advocated by the prime minister. So the Liberal leader fought the Military Service Act every inch of the way until it became law in August 1917; but the issue split his party and Borden was able to form his coalition in October with the help of Liberal defections. Moreover in the December elections, fought, like the parliamentary battle, over conscription, along racial lines, Laurier was heavily defeated by the government. Quebec, however, solidly supported him with 62 out of 65 seats. There is much truth in the accusation that the election was at least partly influenced by 'shameless manipulation'. For example, special legislation enfranchised those who were most committed to the war and therefore likely to be conscriptionist, but disenfranchised others who would be expected to vote the other way. In addition the soldiers' vote, which was solidly conscriptionist, was distributed in those provinces where it was most likely to show the best results for the government.

Perhaps the worst feature of the conscription crisis was that the political victory committed the country to a goal it was unable to achieve. Mass pleas for exemption, together with evasion and desertion cut the projected figure of 100,000 by nearly forty per cent, and most of those were too late to reach Europe anyway. Quebec was, of course, the most recalcitrant province, but farmers and trades unionists were to be found objecting in all parts of Canada.

So Canada's war effort was achieved at the cost of a deepening antagonism within her mixed population. But she had at least managed to sustain that effort without major disunity on the issue of the war itself. This no doubt had its effect on bringing the insular *Canadiens* to a fuller realization of the part they were compelled to play in world events. And that part had significantly grown when, in these years, Canada took the lead in asserting that the daughters of the mother country had come of age.

South Africa

South Africa's role in the war was dominated by two factors peculiar to her among the dominions. She alone had a military front line bordering her territory; and she alone had a large minority of settlers not only opposed to war but actively seeking a German victory as a means of throwing off the British connexion.

Causes of unrest in South Africa are not hard to discover. Memories of the Jameson raid and the Boer War (p. 13) remained strong, particularly among the Dutch farmers of Transvaal and the Orange Free State. All their lives these men had learned to regard the British as their chief enemies, and it was too much to expect that the grant of dominion status in the Union of 1910 would at once dispel the antagonism of generations. That despite these cleavages the Union remained intact under the stresses of war was due in large measure to the loyalty of two men. Louis Botha and Jan Smuts, South Africa's greatest soldier-statesmen, both pursued a policy of uniting their country within the framework of empire. The extent of their success must rank both men in the forefront of the world's leaders of the 20th century.

The existence of a strategically important German colony in South West Africa made any prospect of South African neutrality impossible. On the contrary, Great Britain immediately asked South Africa to undertake the conquest of the neighbouring territory, and Botha, the prime minister, was quick to agree. But his initial plans were scarcely completed when operations had to be suspended. For a serious rebellion among anti-British and pro-German elements threatened to undermine the war effort and perhaps to topple the government itself. The rebels included soldiers of the calibre of Colonel Maritz, commander of the frontier forces, General Beyers, and General de Wet. Suppressing this revolt was thus South Africa's first major achievement of the war, though the personal anguish of Botha, as he relentlessly pursued those who had formerly

been comrades-in-arms against the British, can only be imagined. Smuts, the minister of defence, who directed from headquarters this destruction of former colleagues, said that 'few know what Botha went through in the rebellion. He lost friendships of a lifetime, friendships he valued perhaps more than anything in life. But Botha's line remained absolutely consistent. No one else in South Africa could have stuck it out. You wanted a man for that . . .'

Botha's statesmanship was never more clearly revealed than by his measures after the surrender of the rebels in February 1915. He was so lenient that only one man was executed — surely a record for a large-scale revolt in wartime. Meanwhile, he was able personally to conduct a campaign against German South West Africa, which has been called 'one of the neatest and most successful campaigns of the Great War'. Troops were also sent under Smuts to co-operate with British and Indian troops in German East Africa against the redoubtable Lettow Vorbeck, a campaign which was virtually over when Smuts left for London to represent his country at the Imperial War Conference.

Arriving in March 1917, Smuts originally intended to stay only a few weeks. He remained in Europe for two-and-a-half years, proving himself both militarily and politically among the ablest and most visionary of the British government's advisers. He was consulted by Lloyd George on tactics and strategy in Europe, spoke on imperial affairs so effectively that he was dubbed 'Orator for the Empire', recommended the creation of an independent command for the RAF, and was even used to end a strike of Welsh miners at Tonypandy. On that famous occasion he quietened the tumult by asking the miners to sing. They returned the compliment by returning to work. Lloyd George paid tribute to him as a man of 'rare and fine gifts of mind and heart', and that 'of his practical contributions to our councils during these trying years it is difficult to speak too highly'.

Besides serving on their own continent, South Africans also saw duty in the Middle East and on the Western Front where they enjoyed some notable triumphs. In all, some 136,000 white South Africans saw active service in a greater variety of conditions than the troops of any of the other dominions. But while the troops were winning distinction, and Smuts was earning unique prestige as an imperial statesman, Botha was severely troubled at home. Republicans, hostile to the empire, kept up constant pressure. Their party, the Nationalists, led by J.B.M.Hertzog, continually tried to obstruct the prosecution of the war, even to the extent of opposing, in 1918, Botha's motion hoping that God would grant victory to Great Britain.

South Africa's war effort had very mixed results. On the one hand the Union remained intact, South African prestige grew with the magnitude of her efforts, and her statesmen demonstrated the calibre which could be brought to British councils from distant parts of the empire. But numbers of her population remained unreconciled to the imperial connexion, and many who sought to protect the Afrikaner against the British extended this policy to seek greater protection for the white South African against the black. The war deepened rifts in South African loyalties and foreshadowed later internal developments which were to have important consequences for the nation's future.

Part four · The War at Sea

The first months of the war on land had shown that almost all the assumptions on which the generals had based their plans were false. At sea, there was to be almost as great a gap between expectation and fact; it was not as immediate but just as far-reaching and vital.

Before 1914, the strategy of a future naval war between Great Britain and Germany had been widely discussed, and growing naval rivalry had been a major cause in increasing hostility between the two powers. Until the early 1890s, the Royal Navy had had no serious rivals, and its ships were scattered across the globe to guard the Imperial trade routes. When Kaiser Wilhelm II gave his support to a major increase in German naval power his admirals were faced with a fundamental choice which would dictate their building programme and foreshadow the type of naval confrontation which might occur when war broke out. Were they to concentrate on building fast, well-armed cruisers with which to attack the sea routes of their only major naval rival or were they to build up a battle fleet which could directly threaten the British Isles?

At first, intent on the acquisition of a growing colonial empire, the Germans chose to build cruisers, but after Tirpitz became secretary of state for naval affairs in 1895 a determined start was made on building up a major battle fleet. However, cruisers were not forgotten, and a balanced strategy seemed to be the aim with a battle fleet to threaten the British Isles and force the Royal Navy to concentrate its strength at home to meet the direct challenge while swift raiders fell on the under-protected trade routes.

The threat which Germany's new naval power would pose did not immediately become a major issue in Britain; warnings were issued from time to time in the press, but it was not until after the Boer War when the openly hostile German reaction had inflamed public opinion that the naval question became a major issue. The Royal Navy reacted predictably: under the leadership of Fisher, the building programme was increased and the main strength of the fleet was concentrated at home. Protection of the trade routes would be left largely to the navies of the dominions and to Britain's new ally, Japan. In 1906 Britain launched the revolutionary battleship *Dreadnought* and from that date until 1914 both powers were engaged in a race to build up their battle fleets while popular opinion and the press urged politicians and admirals to greater and greater expenditure.

Thus, when war did break out, the great fleets were in everyone's mind, and it was expected that the first major actions would be between them. But it was further afield that the first blows were struck, for German cruisers scattered across the South Atlantic, Indian, and Pacific Oceans moved in on largely unprotected merchant shipping and wreaked havoc. It might have seemed that the basic German strategy which had been overshadowed by the naval race was working well. In November the East Asia Squadron annihilated a British force at the battle of Coronel inflicting its first major defeat for more than a century on the Royal Navy. But the German admiralty failed to give adequate support to the raiders, and the British were at last forced into decisive action. Two battle-cruisers were detached from the Grand Fleet and in December the German squadron was destroyed. By the end of the year only one raider was still at large, and this was soon to be tracked down and destroyed.

The war of movement had taken both sides by surprise, for the effectiveness of the raiders had not been foreseen. But the early months of the war also demonstrated one fact—that the surface raiders had only a limited life if the Royal Navy was left free to track them down without any distractions. The Germans would have to find other methods if they were to mount a really effective assault against Britain's lifeline.

The German battle fleet had never been intended to match the full force of the Royal Navy. From the opening days of the war it had been the Germans' aim to try and lure a part of the Grand Fleet into a position where it could be annihilated piecemeal, while the British had been content to cover the German bases and avoid any unnecessary activity. It was not until May 1916 that the long-awaited confrontation of the two fleets took place, and then it produced a stalemate, a draw or a victory according to the basis of assessment. The German fleet never came out in force again and the focus of the naval war swung back to a far less glamorous area which was proving far more vital.

Commerce was to be the crucial theme of naval activity during the First World War, and throughout the Germans were on the strategic defensive, forced to react ever more desperately to the success of the British in imposing and sustaining a blockade of their shores. Despite its slowness over the raiders, the Royal Navy had swiftly cut off the bulk of Germany's overseas trade except through neutral vessels, and successive British measures effectively reduced trade through neutrals. The blockade quickly proved harmful to the German economy, and her leaders were forced to turn to a hitherto untested weapon—the submarine—in an attempt to find an effective reply. In February 1915 they declared that the whole of the area around the British Isles was a war zone in which any vessel might be sunk without warning. Six months later, despite the sinking of a considerable tonnage of British shipping, the increasing protests from neutrals, particularly the United States, forced them to abandon the campaign.

The British too had had to face neutral protests, but they had been able to produce precedents for their activities, and their stopping of neutral vessels and confiscation of suspect cargoes was in no way as provocative or as dangerous as the German submarine warfare.

However, the lull in the use of U-boats could not last long, for it had been far too successful and as conditions at home became progressively worse both the German public and their leaders came to see the submarine as the one really effective way in which British resistance could be broken and the war ended. Early in 1916 the British blockade was further intensified by putting certain neutral firms on a 'Black List' and forbidding all transactions with them. In reply the Germans again resorted to unrestricted U-boat warfare. Neutral protests soon brought a lull, but in September 1916 there was a further burst of activity. On both occasions the U-boats were highly successful, sinking a large number of ships while the British admiralty, strangely reluctant to use convoys, was unable to find any adequate response.

Towards the end of the year there was another lull, the German leaders who favoured unrestricted use of submarines regardless of the consequences were still controlled by the politicians who feared the wider implications. But the implications of the year's activities at sea were ominous for both sides. The Allies were faced with the prospect of renewed and steadily increasing losses to an enemy which they could not control, while the Germans were faced with the terrible dilemma as to whether to risk the intervention of the United States by allowing the U-boats to finish the job of crippling Britain's trade or risk losing the war through exhaustion at home. If the U-boats were to be successful not only must they be effective, but they must be quick, otherwise Germany would find herself hopelessly outnumbered.

At last the decision was taken and the U-boats unleashed and, as expected, the United States came quickly into the war. But the U-boats were unable to meet their deadline, for British countermeasures, chiefly convoys and mines, proved too effective.

Jutland

Captain Donald Macintyre and Vice-Admiral Friedrich Ruge

British view/Captain Donald Macintyre
With the arrival of spring 1916, the First World War was eighteen months old. On land a decision had eluded the opposing armies; they had settled into a war of attrition bleeding both sides white. At sea the two most powerful fleets the world had ever seen faced each other across the North Sea, each eager to engage the other, but neither able to bring about an encounter on terms favourable to itself.

The British Grand Fleet, under Admiral Sir John Jellicoe, was concentrated at Scapa Flow, in the Orkneys, whence, it was calculated, the northern exit from the North Sea could be closed to the enemy, while the German fleet could still be intercepted and brought to battle should it threaten the British coasts. The British ability to read German coded radio messages enabled them to obtain warning of any impending moves.

The German High Seas Fleet, numerically much inferior to its opponent, could contemplate battle with only a portion of the British Grand Fleet. From almost the beginning of the war its strategy had been aimed at forcing the British to divide their strength so that this might be brought about. Raids by the German battle-cruiser force, commanded by Rear-Admiral Hipper, on English east coast towns had been mounted. The failure of the Grand .Fleet to intercept these had resulted in the Grand Fleet's battle-cruiser force, under Vice-Admiral Sir David Beatty, being based at Rosyth; and when Hipper again sortied in January 1915 he had been intercepted. In the battle of Dogger Bank which had followed, the German armoured cruiser *Blücher* had been sunk and the battle-cruiser *Seydlitz* had narrowly escaped destruction when a shell penetrated her

after turret, starting a conflagration among the ammunition. Only flooding the magazine had saved her.

Further adventures by the High Seas Fleet had been forbidden by the Kaiser and the Germans had launched their first unrestricted U-boat campaign against Allied merchant shipping. For the rest of 1915 the High Seas Fleet had languished in port, chafing against its inaction.

But in January 1916, its command had been taken over by Admiral Reinhard Scheer who had at once set about reanimating it. Raids on the English coast were resumed. As before, the Grand Fleet, in spite of the warnings received through radio interception, had been unable to reach the scene from Scapa Flow in time to interfere. Jellicoe was forced to agree to his 5th Battle Squadron – the fast and powerful Queen Elizabeth-class ships – joining Beatty's Battle-cruiser Fleet at Rosyth.

When in May 1916, the U-boat campaign was called off at the threat of American intervention on the Allied side and the submarines recalled, Scheer had the conditions necessary for his ambition to bring about a fleet action on favourable terms by bringing the three arms of the fleet simultaneously into play. His surface forces were to sortie for a bombardment of Sunderland and lure the enemy to sea where his U-boats could ambush them, while his Zeppelin airships would scout far afield and so enable him to avoid any confrontation with a superior enemy concentration.

Plans were drawn up for the latter part of May; the actual date, to be decided at the last moment, would depend upon when the fleet was brought up to full strength by the return of the battle-cruiser *Seydlitz* from repairs caused by mine damage during a previous sortie, and upon suitable weather for the airships to reconnoitre efficiently. Meanwhile the U-boats, sixteen in number, sailed on 17th May for their stations off Scapa, Cromarty, and the Firth of Forth. Their endurance made the 30th the latest possible date. The *Seydlitz* did not rejoin until the 28th, however, and then a period of hazy weather set in, unsuitable for air reconnaissance.

Against such a development, an alternative plan had been prepared. Hipper's battle-cruiser force was to go north from the Heligoland Bight and 'trail its shirt' off the Norwegian coast where it would be duly reported to the British. Beatty's battle-cruiser fleet from Rosyth would come racing eastwards to fall into the trap of the High Seas Fleet battle squadrons, waiting some forty miles to the southward of Hipper, before the Grand Fleet from Scapa could intervene.

The trap is set
Such a plan—assuming an unlikely credulity on the part of the British—was naïve, to say the least, even allowing for the fact that the British ability to read German wireless signals was not realized. Nevertheless, when the thick weather persisted throughout the 28th and 29th, it was decided to employ it. On the afternoon of 30th May, the brief signal went out to the High Seas Fleet assembled in the Schillig Roads— 31GG2490, which signified 'Carry out Secret Instruction 2490 on 31st May'.

This was duly picked up by the Admiralty's monitoring stations and though its meaning was not known, it was clear from various indications that some major operation by the German fleet was impending. At once the organization for getting the Grand Fleet to sea swung into action; the main body under the commander-in-chief, with his flag in the *Iron Duke,* including the three battle-cruisers of the 3rd Battle-Cruiser Squadron, who had been detached there from Rosyth for gunnery practice, sailed from Scapa Flow; from the Cromarty Firth sailed the 2nd Battle Squadron, the 1st Cruiser Squadron, and a flotilla of destroyers. These two forces were to rendezvous the following morning (31st) in a position some ninety miles west of Norway's southerly point. When joined, they would comprise a force of no less than 24 dreadnought battleships, 3 battle-cruisers, 8 armoured cruisers, 12 light cruisers, and 51 destroyers. Beatty's Battle-Cruiser Fleet—6 battle-cruisers, the four 15-inch-gun, fast Queen Elizabeth-class battleships, 12 light cruisers, 28 destroyers, and a seaplane carrier—was to steer from the Firth of Forth directly to reach a position some 120 miles west of the Jutland Bank at 1400 on the 31st, which would place him sixty-nine miles ahead of the Grand Fleet as it steered towards the Heligoland Bight. If Beatty had sighted no enemy by that time, he was to turn north to meet Jellicoe.

Thus, long before the first moves of

Scheer's plan to lure Beatty out had been made, the whole vast strength of the British fleet was at sea. The schemer was liable to have the tables turned on him. The first aim of Scheer's project had already been missed. His U-boats had failed to deliver any successful attacks on the British squadrons as they sortied; furthermore their reports of what they had seen added up only to various isolated squadrons at sea and gave no warning that the Grand Fleet was at sea in strength.

At 0100 on 31st May, therefore, the first ships of Hipper's force—five battle-cruisers of the 1st Scouting Group (*Lützow* (flagship), *Derfflinger, Seydlitz, Moltke, Von der Tann*), four light cruisers of the 2nd Scouting Group, and 33 destroyers led by another light cruiser—weighed anchor and steered north past Heligoland and through the swept channels, leaving the Horn Reef light vessel to the eastward of them. They were followed, fifty miles astern, by Scheer, his flag in the *Friedrich der Grosse,* leading 16 dreadnought battleships, 6 pre-dreadnoughts, and accompanied by 5 light cruisers of the 4th Scouting Group and 39 destroyers led by a light cruiser.

By 1400 Hipper was abreast the Jutland Bank off the Danish coast—his scouting light cruisers spread on an arc extending from ahead to either beam, some seven to ten miles from the battle-cruisers. It was a clear, calm, summer day with visibility extreme but likely to become hazy as the afternoon wore on. Unknown to Hipper and equally ignorant of his presence, Beatty was fifty miles to the north-westward, zig-zagging at 19 knots on a mean course of east and approaching the eastward limit set for his advance, with his light cruisers scouting ahead in pairs. The signal to turn north was made at 1415 and was obeyed by all except the light cruiser *Galatea* which held on to investigate smoke on the eastern horizon. This came from a Danish merchantman and was simultaneously being investigated by the western-most of Hipper's light cruisers, the *Elbing.* The two warships thus came in sight of one another, reported, and fired the opening shots of the battle of Jutland.

The two battle-cruiser admirals turned at once towards the sound of the guns which soon brought them in sight of one another on opposite courses, when Hipper altered course to the southward to lead his opponents towards the advancing German battle squadrons. That these were at sea was still unknown to either Beatty or Jellicoe. The British radio monitoring stations had been led to believe that the High Seas Fleet was still in harbour, misled by an arrangement on the part of Scheer's staff which transferred the flagship's call-sign to a shore station so that the commander-in-chief would not be distracted by administrative matters.

The battle-cruisers open fire

The *Lion,* leading *Princess Royal, Queen Mary, Tiger, New Zealand* and *Indefatigable* (in that order), turned on a parallel course and at 1548 each side opened fire. Hipper was outnumbered, six ships to five. He would have been even more, perhaps disastrously, inferior, but for Beatty's impetuosity in racing at full speed into action without waiting for the 5th Battle Squadron, which was not only initially six miles farther from the enemy but, owing to signal confusion, failed to conform at once to Beatty's movements. By the time it did so, it was ten miles astern, and it was not until twenty-seven minutes after action had been joined that the 15-inch guns of the British battleships could open fire.

In the interval much had happened. Hipper's ships had quickly displayed a gunnery superiority over their opponents who were very slow to find the range. The *Lion, Princess Royal,* and *Tiger* had all been heavily hit before a single German ship had suffered; though the *Seydlitz, Derfflinger,* and *Lützow* were then each hit hard, the advantage had continued to lie with Hipper's ships and at 1600 Beatty's rear ship, *Indefatigable,* had blown up and sunk as shells plunged through into her magazines. Almost simultaneously the *Lion* had been only saved from a similar fate by flooding the magazine of her mid-ship turret when it was penetrated by a shell from the *Lützow.*

But now, at last, the 5th Battle Squadron (*Barham, Valiant, Warspite, Malaya,* lying in that order) was able to get into action. Their gunnery was magnificent. The two rear ships of Hipper's line were quickly hit. Disaster must have overwhelmed him but for a defect of the British shells, some of which broke up on impact instead of penetrating the armour. Nevertheless, it seemed impossible Hipper could

survive long enough for Scheer's battle-squadrons, still over the horizon, to come to his rescue. In spite of this the German battle-cruisers continued to shoot with deadly accuracy and at 1626 the *Queen Mary,* betrayed, like the *Indefatigable,* by her inadequate armour, blew up.

Meanwhile, a destroyer battle had been raging between the lines, the flotillas on each side moving out to attack with torpedoes and meeting to fight it out with guns. Of all the torpedoes fired, one only, from the British *Petard,* found a billet in the *Seydlitz,* but did not damage her enough to put her out of action. Two British destroyers were sunk.

The fast-moving battle had left the majority of Beatty's scouting cruisers behind, except for Commodore Goodenough's 2nd Light Cruiser Squadron which by 1633 had succeeded in getting two miles ahead of the *Lion.* At that moment to Goodenough's astonished gaze the top masts of a long line of battleships hove in sight. In the radio rooms of the ships of the British fleet, the message, which all had almost despaired of ever hearing, was taken in: 'Have sighted enemy battle fleet, bearing SE. Enemy's course North.'

Hipper had been saved in the nick of time, and his task of luring Beatty brilliantly achieved. Goodenough's timely warning, however, enabled the latter to escape the trap. Before the enemy battle fleet came within range, Beatty reversed course to the northward. The 5th Battle Squadron held on for a while to cover the damaged battle-cruisers' retreat. By the time they turned back themselves they came under heavy fire from the German battle squadrons and *Malaya,* in particular, received damaging hits. In reply they did heavy damage to the *Lützow, Derfflinger,* and *Seydlitz,* as well as hitting the leading German battleships.

The situation had now been reversed, with Beatty drawing the enemy after him towards a superior force the latter knew nothing of—the Grand Fleet, pressing southwards at its best speed of 20 knots. Jellicoe's twenty-four battleships were in the compact cruising formation of six columns abeam of each other, with the fleet flagship leading the more easterly of the two centre columns. Before encountering the enemy they would have to be deployed into a single battle line to allow all ships to bring their guns to bear. If deployment was delayed too long, the consequences could be disastrous. To make a deployment by the right method, it was essential that the admiral should know the bearing on which the approaching enemy would appear.

For various reasons—discrepancy between the calculated positions of the two portions of the fleet and communication failures—this was just what Jellicoe did not know. And, meanwhile, the two fleets were racing towards each other at a combined speed of nearly 40 knots. Even though Beatty's light cruisers had made visual contact with Jellicoe's advanced screen of armoured cruisers at 1630, though the thunder of distant gun-fire had been audible for some time before the *Marlborough,* leading the starboard column of the Grand Fleet battleships, sighted gun-flashes through the gathering haze and funnel smoke ahead at 1750, and six minutes later Beatty's battle-cruisers were sighted from the *Iron Duke* racing across the line of Jellicoe's advance—and incidentally spreading a further pall of black smoke—it was not until nearly 1815 that at last, in the nick of time, the vital piece of information reached the commander-in-chief from the *Lion:* 'Enemy battle fleet bearing south-west.'

Jellicoe's vital decision
During the next minute or so, through the mind of Jellicoe as he stood gazing at the compass in its binnacle on the bridge of the *Iron Duke,* sped the many considerations on the accurate interpretation of which, at this moment of supreme crisis, the correct deployment and all chances of victory depended. The decision Jellicoe made—to deploy on his port wing column on a course south-east by east—has been damned and lauded by opposing critics in the controversy that was later to develop.

To the appalled Scheer, as out of the smoke and haze ahead of him, between him and retreat to his base, loomed an interminable line of dim grey shapes from which rippled the flash of heavy gunfire, and a storm of shell splashes began to fall round the leading ships of his line, there was no doubt. His 'T' had been crossed— the worst situation possible in a fleet action. Fortunately for him a counter to such a calamity, a simultaneous 'about

turn' by every ship of the battle columns— a manoeuvre not lightly undertaken by a mass of the unwieldy battleships of the day—had been practised and perfected by the High Seas Fleet. He ordered it now, and so, behind a smoke screen laid by his destroyers extricated himself from the trap so brilliantly sprung by Jellicoe.

His escape was only temporary, nevertheless. Between him and his base was a force whose full strength he had been unable as yet to determine, which he must either fight or somehow evade.

While the trap was thus being sprung on Scheer, some final spectacular successes had been achieved by the Germans. Of the 5th Battle Squadron, the *Warspite,* with her helm jammed, had charged towards Scheer's battle line and before she could be got under control again, had been severely damaged and forced out of action. Jellicoe's advanced screen of armoured cruisers had been caught at short range by Hipper's battle-cruisers and the leading German battleships as they emerged from the smoke haze. The *Defence* had been overwhelmed and blown up, the *Warrior* so heavily damaged that she staggered out of action to sink on her way back to harbour. Then the German battle-cruisers had encountered the three battle-cruisers attached to the Grand Fleet. In a brief gun duel at short range, the Germans had suffered many hits and further damage; but in reply had sunk the *Invincible* whose magazine was penetrated in the same way as in the *Indefatigable* and *Queen Mary.*

This was the last major success for the Germans, however. They had fought magnificently and, with the aid of superior ship design and ammunition, had had much the better of the exchanges, though the *Lützow* was by now fatally crippled, limping painfully off the scene, and only the stout construction and well-designed compartmentation of the other battle-cruisers was saving them from a similar state. But Scheer was now desperately on the defensive, though he had not yet realized that it was the whole Grand Fleet he had encountered. As soon as his initial retreat brought relief from the concentration of fire on his van, he reversed course once again in the hope of being able to cut through astern of the enemy to gain a clear escape route to the Horn Reef lightship and safety behind his own minefields. Once again he ran up against the immense line of dreadnoughts of which all he could see in the poor visibility to the eastward was the flickering orange light of their broadsides. Once again he had hastily to retire or be annihilated.

While he was extricating himself he launched his much-tried battle-cruisers on a rearguard thrust and his destroyer flotillas to deliver a massed torpedo attack. The former miraculously survived a further hammering before being recalled. The latter launched a total of twenty-eight torpedoes at the British line. More than any other single factor they were to save the High Seas Fleet from disaster, robbing Jellicoe of the fruits of the strategic masterpiece he had brought about.

The counter to the massed torpedo attack by destroyers, which could be backed by long-range torpedo fire from retreating battleships, had been carefully studied. There were several alternatives; the only one sufficiently effective in Jellicoe's opinion, was a simultaneous turn away by his own battle line. This was promptly carried out—a turn of 45 degrees.

Contact lost

The two battle fleets were now on widely diverging courses and rapidly ran out of range and sight of one another. By the time the twenty-eight torpedoes had been avoided—not one scored a hit—and the British battle line turned back to regain contact, more than fifteen miles separated Jellicoe and Scheer. Sunset was barely half an hour away. Yet there was time in the long summer twilight ahead for the battle to be renewed on greatly advantageous terms for Jellicoe if he turned at once to an interception course. That he did not do so until too late for various reasons, not the least of which was the failure of his scouting forces to keep him informed of the enemy's position and movements, was to be the central feature of much criticism.

The van of the German battle fleet came, in fact, briefly into view from the nearest British battleship division at the moment that Jellicoe, who was not willing to accept the uncertain fortunes of a night action, ordered a turn away and the adoption of a compact night cruising disposition. The opportunity was let slip, never to return.

Nevertheless, at this stage, as night settled down over a calm sea, the outlook for Scheer was bleak, indeed. Between him and his base was an overwhelming enemy force. Unless he could get past it during the night, the battle must be resumed at daybreak and, with a long summer day ahead, it could only spell annihilation for him. He decided his only hope was to try to bludgeon his way through, regardless of consequences. To his fleet he signalled the course for the Horn Reef Light at a speed of 16 knots, adding the instruction that this course was to be maintained at all costs.

Jellicoe, having formed his night disposition and ordered his flotillas (many of whom had not yet been in action) to the rear, was steering a course slightly converging with that of Scheer but at a knot faster. From Jellicoe's point of view, Scheer had the choice of two routes—to the entrance of the channels which began at the Horn Reef Light or southward into the German Bight before turning eastward round the mined areas. The extra knot would keep the Grand Fleet between Scheer and the latter. If he chose the former he must pass astern of Jellicoe's battle squadrons, where he would encounter the massed British flotillas which could be counted on to inflict severe losses and to keep Jellicoe informed.

In the event the British flotillas failed to do either of these things. The pre-dreadnought battleship *Pommern* and a light cruiser were their sole victims in a series of night encounters, and they passed no information of the position and course of the enemy. On the other hand Scheer's message to his fleet was intercepted by the Admiralty and was passed to Jellicoe, though a further message in which Scheer asked for airship reconnaissance of the Horn Reef area at dawn which would have clinched the matter, was withheld.

In the absence of certain knowledge of the enemy's movements, Jellicoe held on through the night. Scheer crossed astern of him and by daylight was safe, a development which seemed little short of miraculous to the German admiral.

The battle of Jutland was over. Controversy as to its outcome was to rage for decades. The bald facts, of which German publicity made the most in claiming a great victory, while the British Admiralty's communiqué did nothing to explain or qualify them, showed that a superior British force had lost three capital ships, three cruisers, and a number of destroyers against one battle-cruiser, a pre-dreadnought battleship, four cruisers, and some destroyers sunk on the German side.

Even to-day more than fifty years since the battle, it is not easy to strike a balance sheet of victory and defeat. British losses were largely the result of inferior armour protection in their battle-cruisers, which had been accepted in favour of mounting bigger guns, the advantage of which had been lost through faulty design of armour-piercing shells. Even so, one of the surviving German battle-cruisers only reached harbour in a sinking condition, another was a hideous shambles with 200 casualties, bearing witness to the pounding they had received even from defective shells.

The High Seas Fleet was no longer fit for battle on the morning of the 1st June 1916 and could only make for harbour and repairs, fortunately close at hand. The Grand Fleet was largely intact and ready to renew the fight. Jellicoe may be said, perhaps, to have lost the battle of Jutland. Scheer can hardly be judged to have won anything but an escape from annihilation.

So much for the immediate results of the encounter. They do not add up to a victory for either side. In the larger context of the war at sea as a whole, it is no easier to weigh the results. When Scheer led the High Seas Fleet out once again in August 1916 (except for *Seydlitz* and *Derfflinger*, still under repair), he narrowly escaped being caught in a second Jutland trap, with no safe base under his lee this time, in spite of Zeppelin reconnaissance aloft. Both Scheer and the Kaiser's general headquarters were finally convinced that the risks to be faced in attempting to bring about a sea fight were unacceptable. The High Seas Fleet, built at such cost to challenge Great Britain's seapower, was ordered back on to the defensive. The fatal decision was taken to revert to the unrestricted submarine warfare which was to bring America into the war.

It is true, of course, that the High Seas Fleet kept 'in being', forced the continued maintenance of the huge Grand Fleet, absorbing many thousands of trained seamen and a hundred destroyers which could have been more profitably employed combating the U-boats. On the other hand, that same High Seas Fleet, its ships lying idle in harbour, the morale of its crews sinking, degenerated into a centre of discontent and revolution. In August 1917 Scheer had to quell an open mutiny. A year later, when ordered to sea by its new commander, Hipper, it flared into revolt and led the disintegration of the Kaiser's Germany. This, too, can be accounted one of the consequences of Jutland—perhaps the most important when reviewing the whole war.

German view /
Vice-Admiral Friedrich Ruge
Jutland was the last of many naval battles fought by long lines of closely spaced big ships with heavy guns. Its tactical details are well-known, for each ship kept a log. Its results were inconclusive. It was the climax of the Anglo-German naval rivalry, with the scuttling of the German fleet at Scapa Flow three years later as the anticlimax.

This rivalry, which cost both nations dearly, was at least partly caused by the fact that the Germans did not fully realize the implications of seapower. In their difficult position in central Europe they needed a navy of some strength to balance the fleets of the Franco-Russian alliance. But from their inferior strategic position in the south-eastern corner of the North Sea they could neither protect their overseas trade nor attack the sea routes vital to Great Britain. When war broke out in 1914 the Royal Navy was not compelled to attack the German bases but could content itself on the whole with a distant blockade from Scapa Flow.

In the first two years of the war there were a number of operations and clashes in the North Sea which did not change the situation, since neither side wanted to give battle too far from their own bases. In 1916 this changed to some extent. Admiral Reinhard Scheer, the new commander-in-chief of the German High Seas Fleet, was more aggressive than his predecessors. On the Allied side, the Russians felt the blockade heavily and clamoured for the British to force the Baltic so that they might receive ammunition and raw materials which they needed desperately. An operation of that kind had no prospects of success, however, as long as the High Seas Fleet was intact. Therefore it was decided that stronger efforts should be made to bring it to battle. The Grand Fleet under Admiral Sir John Jellicoe had been considerably reinforced by new ships. In spring 1916 it was almost twice as strong as the German fleet.

Early in March, the German fleet made a sortie into the southern North Sea and came within sixty miles of Lowestoft. On 25th March British light forces operated south of Horn Reef, and aircraft from a sea-plane-carrier tried to bombard airship sheds. Bad weather prevented contact of the heavy ships. On 25th April German battle-cruisers bombarded Lowestoft. Early in May the British repeated the attempt to attack airship sheds. Both fleets were at sea, but no contact was established.

For the second half of May, Admiral Scheer planned an operation with all his forces. The battle-cruisers were to bombard Sunderland, and twelve submarines were stationed off the British bases to attack the squadrons of the Grand Fleet when they put to sea. Scouting by airships was necessary for the German fleet to avoid being cut off by superior forces. When the time ran out for his submarines after two weeks at sea and the weather remained unfavourable, Scheer compromised on a sweep of his light forces through the Skagerrak backed up by the battle fleet. Shortly after midnight of 30th to 31st May 1916 the German scouting forces (5 battle-cruisers, 5 light cruisers, and 30 destroyers under Rear-Admiral Hipper) left Schillig Roads near Wilhelmshaven, soon followed by the battle fleet (16 new and 6 old battleships, 6 light cruisers, and 33 destroyers).

The Grand Fleet at sea

At that time the Grand Fleet was already at sea, course set for the Skagerrak, too. The bombardment of Lowestoft had roused public opinion, the situation of the Russians had deteriorated, and Jellicoe now planned to set a trap for the German fleet. Light cruisers were to sweep through the Skagerrak deep into the Kattegat; in the meantime the main forces would take up position near Horn Reef to meet the Germans who were sure to come out in order to intercept the British cruisers operating in the Kattegat.

In the early afternoon of 31st May occurred the first of the incidents which greatly changed the course of the events. The British battle-cruiser fleet, under Vice-Admiral Sir David Beatty in *Lion*, changed course from east to north to rendezvous with the battle fleet under Admiral Jellicoe in *Iron Duke*. At 1430 *Lützow*, flying Admiral Hipper's flag, was only forty-five miles east of *Lion* steering a slightly converging course. Contact would have been made considerably later but for a small Danish steamer plodding along between the two forces. Two German destroyers and a British light cruiser were dispatched to examine her. Soon the first salvoes were fired; the first hit (a dud) was made by *Elbing* on *Galatea*.

Within minutes wireless messages informed the admirals of the situation. Signals went up, Hipper swung his force round, and Beatty soon followed suit. The crews were alerted by bugles sounding action stations, guns and powder rooms were manned, steam was raised in reserve boilers, and damage parties assembled deep down in the ships. The gunnery officers climbed to their elevated positions, received ready reports from turrets, range-finders, and fire-control-stations, and then reported their batteries ready for action to their captains. Now a hush of expectancy fell over the great ships while the distance decreased by nearly a mile a minute.

At first, sight was obscured by the smoke of the cruisers. Then these fell back on their battle-cruisers, and the huge shapes of the adversaries came into each other's sight, but only for the few men whose duty was to watch the enemy. Almost all the technical personnel and most of the sailors fought without seeing an enemy ship.

Hipper faced heavy odds, ten ships with heavier guns against his five. His plan was simple: to draw the enemy to Scheer's battle fleet, which was following at a distance of fifty miles. His smaller calibres (11- and 12-inch as against 12-, 13-, and 15-inch in the British ships) made it imperative for him to get comparatively close before opening fire. He offered battle on a north-westerly course, reversed course when Beatty tried to cut his force off, and with a few terse signals coolly manoeuvred his fine ships through the danger zone. At 1548 they were at the right distance (16,500 yards) and in perfect order. The *Lützow* opened fire.

Beatty's ships started answering quickly but they were not yet in formation to use all their guns. Because of delays in signalling, the four powerful and fast battleships of the Queen Elizabeth-class had fallen astern and were out of range. Conditions for a gunnery duel were perfect: visibility was good, especially to the west, and there was hardly any seaway.

First blood to the Germans

The first salvoes all appear to have fallen wide, perhaps because the range-takers were more interested in the details of their foes than in measuring the distance exactly. After three minutes the Germans obtained hits on *Lion, Princess Royal,* and *Tiger.* Because the first target in sight had been light cruisers, the gunnery officer of *Lützow* had given orders to load shells detonating on impact. For reasons of ballistics he did not change over to armour-piercing shells. *Lion* was hit twelve times and suffered heavy casualties, but minor injuries only, except for one shell which penetrated the roof of a turret, killed the gun crews, and ignited powder-bags. The turret-commander, Major Harvey of the Royal Marines, was fatally wounded but before he died he ordered the magazines to be flooded and thus saved the ship.

Now disaster struck the rear of the British line. Here *Indefatigable* and *Von der Tann* fought an even match. At 1604, *Indefatigable,* hit by two salvoes in quick succession, erupted in a violent explosion, turned over to port and disappeared in the waves. *Von der Tann* had fired fifty-two 11-inch shells in all. Twenty minutes later a similar fate overtook *Queen Mary* who had come under the concentrated fire of *Derfflinger* and *Seydlitz.* After vehement detonations she capsized and went down with her propellers still turning. *Tiger,* the next astern, barely avoided crashing into the wreck.

In spite of these losses the situation now eased for the British. The magnificent 5th Battle Squadron, ably handled by Rear-Admiral Evan-Thomas, came up and took the rear ships of the German line under fire. When one of the projectiles, weighing almost a ton, struck *Von der Tann* far aft, the whole ship vibrated like a gigantic tuning-fork. Hipper increased speed and distance and sent his destroyers to the attack. They were met by British destroyers, and in the ensuing mêlée *Nomad* and two Germans were sunk. At the same time 1630 the 2nd Light Cruiser Squadron under Commodore Goodenough sighted smoke to the south-east and, soon after, a seemingly endless column of heavy ships surrounded by light cruisers and destroyers.

Now the tables were turned. Under heavy fire Beatty reversed course and steered to the north to draw the High Seas Fleet to the British Battle Fleet. *Barham* and *Malaya* received several hits which did not, however, impair their speed, but, *Nestor,* attacking the German van with some other destroyers, was sunk. When her boatswain was rescued with other survivors he was mainly disgusted at the smallness and squalor of the coal-burning torpedo-boat which had picked him up.

All through these events the British Battle Fleet had been steadily drawing nearer, in cruising formation with its twenty-four battleships in six divisions, these in line abreast, screened by armoured and light cruisers and destroyers. The 3rd Battle-Cruiser Squadron, under Rear-Admiral Hood in *Invincible,* was twenty-five miles ahead and far to the east of its calculated position. Jellicoe, 'the only man who could lose the war in an afternoon', was now faced with the decision on which course to form his divisions into single line ahead. In all war games and exercises the rule had been 'towards Heligoland'. Yet the reports he received were incomplete and contradictory, it was impossible to get a clear picture of the situation. At the last moment, when Beatty's battle-cruisers came in sight, Jellicoe ordered his division to turn together to port to the north-east. In this way he gained a favourable position for crossing the enemy's T. He was unintentionally assisted by the 3rd Battle-Cruiser Squadron, which almost missed the Germans, but now closed in from the east and brought the German van between two fires. The light cruiser *Wiesbaden* soon lay dead in the water. For hours the battle raged around her, she was fired upon by many British ships, but did not sink until 0200 on 1st June. Only one survivor was picked up, two days later.

The delay in forming the line of battle put part of the screen and the 5th Battle Squadron in a difficult situation at what was later called 'Windy Corner'. Making room for Beatty's battle-cruisers to go to the van of the line, some armoured cruisers came into range of the German battleships. *Defence* blew up in view of both fleets; *Warrior* was saved a similar fate by the chance intervention of *Warspite*. The 5th Battle Squadron was forced to counter-march and came under the fire of several battleships. After a hit *Warspite*'s rudder jammed; she turned towards the German line, thus masking *Warrior*, who was able to creep away, but sank on the next morning. *Warspite* almost collided with *Valiant* and made two full circles at high speed before her rudder was in working order again. Heavily damaged she was ordered home and reached Rosyth after evading the attack of a German submarine.

Visibility was now generally decreasing and greatly varying as a result of masses of funnel and artificial smoke. For the commanders-in-chief it was most difficult to gain a reliable picture of the actual situation from their own limited observations (radar was not yet invented) and the reports of their subordinates. For a few moments Scheer toyed with the idea of splitting his line to take Windy Corner under two fires. However, there was no battle signal for this promising but unusual procedure, his van was evidently hard pressed, and so he continued with his battleships in line ahead. With the loss of the destroyer *Shark* the 3rd Battle-Cruiser Squadron had inflicted heavy damage on the Germans and now took up station at the head of the British line followed by Beatty's battle-cruisers.

For more than half an hour the German ships could see no more than the flashes of the enemy guns. Then at 1830 visibility suddenly improved, *Lützow* and *Derfflinger* sighted *Invincible,* the leading ship, at a distance of 9,500 yards and sank her in a few minutes. There were only six survivors, among them the gunnery officer who, as he said, 'merely stepped from the foretop into the water'.

At that time Scheer ordered a battle turn reversing course to get his ships out of the overwhelming enemy fire. Beginning from the rear the heavy ships had to turn to starboard in quick succession until single line ahead was formed on the opposite course. Light cruiser squadrons and destroyer flotillas had to conform. This manoeuvre was all the more difficult because the fleet was now disposed almost in a semi-circle, but it was successful, sup-ported by a destroyer attack on the centre of the British line. The fleets drew apart, and the fire slackened and then ceased altogether. A German destroyer was crippled and sank later, and the battleship *Marlborough* received a torpedo-hit which reduced her speed.

The German fleet now steamed to the west south-west, and the British fleet slowly hauled round to the south. With its higher speed it had a good chance of cutting off the Germans from their bases. Scheer sensed this even though contact had been lost completely. Therefore he ordered another battle turn to the old course with the express intention to deal the enemy a heavy blow, to surprise and confuse him, to bring the destroyers to the attack, to facilitate disengaging for the night, and, if possible, to rescue the crew of the *Wiesbaden*. The execution of this plan has been criticized but there is no doubt that Scheer succeeded in getting his fleet out of a difficult situation although his van suffered heavily.

The German thrust was directed against the British centre. The attacking ships soon came under heavy fire without being able to reply effectively because visibility was better to the west and favoured the British gunnery. Scheer saw his fleet rush into a wide arc of gun flashes and decided to support the destroyer attack by the battle-cruisers while the battle fleet executed its third battle turn. To the battle-cruisers he made the well-known signal, 'Ran' ('At them'), which meant charging regardless of consequences. *Lützow* could not take part because after twenty-three hits she was far down by the bow and could steam no more than 15 knots. So *Derfflinger* led that death ride. Her captain transmitted Scheer's signal to all battle stations and was answered by a thundering roar, gun crews shouting, stokers banging their shovels against bulk-heads. The destroyers went in, fired torpedoes, and retreated, the battle-cruisers then turned after receiving numerous hits. Not a single torpedo reached a target, for Jellicoe turned away. Contact ceased again and a lull in the battle followed. Both fleets hauled round to the south until their courses converged. The Germans proceeded in inversed order and in several columns, the British in single line ahead, sixteen miles long.

At sunset (2020) the terribly mauled battle-cruisers again came under the fire of the leading British battleships, the old ships of the II Battle Squadron under that of the British battle-cruisers. The Germans were silhouetted against the western horizon, their opponents were hardly visible to them. As a British officer later wrote: 'I sighted an obsolete German battleship firing in a desultory way at apparently nothing.' All the German columns turned to the west; the British did not follow but took up night-cruising order, the battleships in divisions abreast, destroyer flotillas following in their wake, course south-east, speed 17 knots. Jellicoe intended to put himself between the Germans and their bases and to renew the battle at daylight. Scheer collected his units practically on the same course which took some time, and at 2300 headed south-east for Horn Reef, speed 16 knots. Because of the heavy odds against him, he wanted to fight a renewed battle nearer to his bases. It was another whim of fate that, as a consequence, the German main body crashed through the British flotillas which were not looking for the enemy but were waiting for the day battle. In contrast the German destroyers searched in vain for the heavy ships of the enemy.

The night actions

During the short northern summer night there were numerous clashes. They started with a furious fight between light cruisers at short distance. *Dublin* and *Southampton* suffered heavy damage and casualties; the obsolete *Frauenlob* was hit by a torpedo and sank with most of her crew. Next the 4th Destroyer Flotilla, led by *Tipperary*, converged upon the German van, came under the fire of half a dozen battleships, and turned away in disorder firing torpedoes and leaving *Tipperary*, burning fiercely, behind. When the battleships turned to starboard to avoid the torpedoes, the light cruiser *Elbing* was rammed and remained stopped with flooded engine-rooms. The battleship *Nassau* tried to ram the destroyer *Spitfire*: they collided on nearly opposite courses, and the destroyer bounced off the side armour of her robust opponent leaving part of her bridge behind. With her forecastle a shambles, *Spitfire* succeeded in limping home.

Both sides resumed course and soon met again. In the intense fire *Broke,* and immediately afterwards *Contest,* rammed *Sparrowhawk,* which kept afloat to the morning. This time a torpedo crippled the light cruiser *Rostock.* Half an hour later, shortly after midnight, the unlucky 4th Flotilla encountered the same ships for the third time and lost *Fortune* and *Ardent.* Most of the other destroyers were damaged, it was no more a fighting unit.

A short time later a large ship approached the centre of the German line from port. It was the armoured cruiser *Black Prince.* She had probably been damaged when *Defence* blew up, and had tried to follow the battle fleet. Too late she turned away, and in minutes was a blazing pyre. Without firing a single shot she disintegrated.

These clashes saved the 6th Battle Squadron from an encounter with German battleships. It lagged behind because torpedo damage prevented *Marlborough,* the flagship, from keeping up 17 knots. As it were the German van passed no more than three miles astern at around 0100. A little later it hit the rear of a line of thirteen destroyers belonging to four flotillas. *Turbulent* was sunk, others damaged, the Germans carried on. At early dawn, after a calm of an hour, they were sighted and attacked by the 12th Flotilla. The German ships succeeded in evading a great number of torpedoes but the old battleship *Pommern* was hit and broke in two after several detonations.

The great battle was over. At 0300 the Germans were approaching Horn Reef, the British battle fleet, thirty miles to the south-west, reversed course, neither commander-in-chief was inclined to renew the fight. Jellicoe went north to look for German stragglers. However, *Lützow, Elbing,* and *Rostock* had already been scuttled after German destroyers had taken their crews off. Both fleets steered for their bases. The *Ostfriesland* struck a mine in a field laid a few hours earlier by *Abdiel* but reached port without assistance.

The battle changed neither the ratio of strength between the two fleets nor the strategic situation. The British blockade continued, and Russia remained cut off from the supplies she needed urgently. The tactical advantage was with the Germans: they had inflicted about double their own losses on a greatly superior opponent. The fleet was proud of this achievement, and Scheer was willing to go on baiting the British. On 19th August 1916 both fleets were again in the North Sea but missed each other by thirty miles. However, it was evident — and Scheer said so in his reports — that the war could not be decided by this strategy. The situation on the fronts deteriorated after Allied offensives, and lack of food was painfully felt at home. Therefore the German government declared unrestricted submarine warfare two weeks before the Russian revolution broke out. The submarines did great havoc to Allied shipping, but brought the United States into the war.

As to the High Seas Fleet it did not remain inactive in port as has been alleged. In April 1918 it made its last sweep to the latitude of Bergen/Shetlands. But its main duty was now to support the submarine war by protecting the minesweepers and by giving its best young officers and ratings to the submarine arm. Other reasons for the sudden break-up of this efficient fighting force in November 1918 were psychological mistakes, malnutrition, and subversion, aggravated by the hopeless political and military situation of Germany.

Blockade

Captain S. W. Roskill

Warring states have from the earliest times endeavoured to deprive their enemies of seaborne supplies. But blockade in its modern form dates only from the beginning of the 17th century when Hugo Grotius, the famous Dutch jurist, put forward the claim for 'Mare Liberum'—the Freedom of the Seas. This meant that ships flying the flag of a neutral nation, and the goods they carried, should be exempt from seizure by belligerents. The British reply was that he who commanded the sea automatically acquired the right to control all traffic passing over it, regardless of nationality. Thus was born the claim to 'Belligerent Rights', which remained a cardinal feature of British maritime policy for more than two centuries, but was always very unpopular with neutral nations.

In 1856 the Declaration of Paris, an appendage to the treaty ending the Crimean War, was signed. It abolished privateering, from which Great Britain had suffered serious losses in earlier wars; but as it exempted the property of a belligerent state from capture, except in the case of contraband, it went a long way towards accepting Grotius's doctrine. The situation remained unchanged until the winter of 1908-09 when, shortly after the conclusion of the second Hague conference, the principal naval powers met in London and formulated the Declaration of London. This document attempted to define contraband of war by dividing commodities into three classes—absolute contraband, conditional contraband, and free goods. Though it accepted that foodstuffs carried in neutral ships might be declared contraband, such commodities as oil, raw cotton, and rubber were classed as free goods.

Though the Bill giving the Declaration of London the force of law was passed by the Liberal majority in the House of Commons it was thrown out by the House of Lords. Nonetheless, shortly after the outbreak of war in 1914, the Asquith government announced its intention of adhering to its terms. This seemingly short-sighted and gratuitous acceptance of a self-imposed handicap probably arose from the desire to placate opinion in neutral countries, and especially the USA. But it is also true to say that no nation realized at the time that in total war between industrialized countries economic pressure would prove an extremely powerful, perhaps decisive weapon.

There are two types of blockade—usually described as naval blockade and commercial (or economic) blockade. The two types, however, nearly always overlap—that is to say a naval blockade also has commercial implications, and vice versa. A naval blockade is enforced by stationing warships off an enemy port with the object of preventing his warships coming out, or of engaging them if they do try to escape. This form of blockade was brought to a fine art by the Royal Navy in the Napoleonic War, and contributed greatly to the defeat of imperial France.

A commercial blockade, on the other hand, aims to cripple the enemy's economy and starve his people into submission by seizing all goods destined to him, even if they are consigned to a neutral nation in the first place, and regardless of the ownership of the ship carrying the goods. The procedure followed begins with the recognized right of a belligerent to 'visit and search' a ship on the high seas, continues with the detention of the cargo if it is believed to be contraband, and ends with the condemnation of the cargo, and possibly of the ship as well, before a nationally constituted Prize Court.

Prior to the Agadir crisis of 1911 the Asquith government, preoccupied as it was by a far-reaching programme for social and electoral reform, paid comparatively little attention to defence policy or to the strategy to be employed should the threat of war with Germany and her allies (Austria-Hungary and Italy) materialize. But shortly after the crisis, Winston Churchill became first lord of the Admiralty, and under his vigorous direction naval policy and plans became a live issue. The Committee of

Imperial Defence (CID), an advisory body of which the prime minister was chairman, began to meet more frequently, and one of its sub-committees reviewed the susceptibility of the Central European powers to the economic pressure of a blockade, and the means required to apply such pressure.

At about the same time, the Admiralty considered the strategy to be employed against the powerful German High Seas Fleet, based in the southern North Sea, and the detached squadrons of cruisers which the German navy had stationed overseas — especially in the Mediterranean and the Pacific. Although the 1908 War Orders had reaffirmed the ancient principle that the Royal Navy's primary function was 'to bring the main German fleet to decisive action', and so secure command of all the seas and oceans, the Admiralty recognized that the High Seas Fleet might well not fall in with such a purpose. Therefore that fleet must be neutralized by a naval blockade of its home bases. The same principle applied to the much less well developed bases used by the detached cruisers, such as Tsingtao on the north east coast of China and the Austrian bases in the Adriatic.

By the early years of the 20th century technical progress, and especially the development of the mine, the submarine, the torpedo, and aircraft had obviously made the old concept of close blockade on the Napoleonic War model totally obsolete. Nonetheless, there was in British naval circles a good deal of hesitation about abandoning what was regarded as a well-tried and provenly effective strategy. Not until the middle of 1912 was close blockade replaced by what was called an 'observational blockade' of the Heligoland Bight. This was to be enforced by a line of cruisers and destroyers patrolling the North Sea from the south-west coast of Norway to the Dutch coast, with heavy squadrons from the main fleet in support to the north and west. But this idea proved short-lived, since it was plainly impossible to patrol a 300-mile-long line effectively, by night and day, in winter and summer.

The blockade plan laid down
A month before the outbreak of war the observational blockade was therefore abandoned in favour of a 'distant block- ade' designed to control the exits from the North Sea. This was made possible by the geographical chance which has placed the British Isles like a breakwater across the passages leading from the outer oceans to the German seaports and naval bases on their North Sea and Baltic coasts. The British plan was that the Channel Fleet, based chiefly on the Thames estuary ports, Dover, and Portsmouth, would close the Straits of Dover, while the much more powerful Grand Fleet would be based on Scapa Flow in the Orkneys and would throw out a line of cruisers or armed merchant cruisers (called the Northern Patrol) to watch the remote and stormy waters between the Shetland Islands, Norway, and Iceland. Such was, in brief outline, the final naval blockade plan which was brought into force in August 1914.

But recent technical developments had a much wider influence than merely to render the concept of close blockade obsolete. They all, but especially the mine, proved potent instruments of blockade in their own right, and both sides laid large numbers of mines, and disposed submarines in the approaches to the other side's ports and bases for this purpose. Unfortunately, the early British mines, like their torpedoes, were extremely inefficient, and it was not until 1917, when an exact copy of the German mine was produced in quantity, that the Royal Navy was provided with an efficient mine.

The Admiralty always expected that the enemy's reply to the British blockade would, as in all earlier wars, take the form of an attack on commerce by cruisers and armed merchantmen. This was a perfectly legal form of warfare, subject to the regulations incorporated in the Hague Conventions regarding the safety of the crews of captured merchant ships; and the German surface raiders in fact showed humanity in their observance of those regulations. Before the war the CID reviewed the measures necessary to keep shipping moving despite the possibility of capture, and recommended that the State should receive eighty per cent of the insurance premiums required to cover war risks on merchant ships and stand eighty per cent of the losses. The Treasury, however, was not at first willing to accept such an intrusion into the field of private enterprise, and the War Risks

Insurance scheme did not actually come into force until the outbreak of war.

By July 1915 all the German raiders which had been at sea at the beginning of the war had been destroyed. Allied (mainly British) seapower so dominated the outer seas and oceans that German trade had been brought to an almost complete halt immediately war broke out –except in the Baltic. Many German merchant ships sought refuge in neutral ports, and the transfer of cargoes destined for Germany to neutral ships began at once. Freight rates rose very sharply, and the neutral nations began to reap enormous profits. These developments stimulated British concern over the emasculation of Belligerent Rights by the Declarations of Paris and London. The first step taken to restore the earlier state of affairs was to issue Orders in Council transferring various commodities from the 'free goods' to the contraband list, and in 1915 the distinction between conditional and absolute contraband was all but wiped out.

On 20th November 1914 a small British merchant ship was sunk by a German submarine in the North Sea and the crew left in the boats – contrary to the Hague Conventions. Other sinkings by submarines soon followed, and thus was ushered in an entirely new element in the German attack on trade – and one for which the Royal Navy was almost totally unprepared. Plainly the implications were very serious. On 11th March 1915 the British government issued an Order in Council, generally referred to as the 'Reprisals Order', since it was made in reprisal for the illegal use of submarines. It declared that goods which could be shown to be destined for Germany were liable to seizure, even though the vessel carrying them was bound for a neutral port.

This led to strong protests from the neutrals, and especially from the USA, regarding interference with what they regarded as legitimate – and of course highly profitable – trade. The USA never moved from the position that the Reprisals Order was illegal – until they themselves were at war. But the real reason for the issue of the order was that the British government was aware that the Scandinavian countries and Holland were importing vastly greater quantities of goods which were on the British contraband list than they had taken before the war. Obviously the surplus was being passed direct to Germany, and the shipping services of the neutral nations were thus replacing the immobilized German merchant fleet. The leak through the blockade via Italy was never serious, and when she entered the war on the Allied side in May 1915 it stopped altogether. But with the Scandinavian countries and Holland the leak was very large indeed, and it did not prove easy to stop it.

In home waters the British blockade was operated through contraband control stations in the Orkneys and the Downs (the anchorage in the Channel between the Goodwin Sands and the coast), and ships intercepted were sent into one or other unless their cargoes were above suspicion. In 1915 the Northern Patrol cruisers intercepted 3,098 ships, and in the following year 3,388. Those sent in for examination totalled 743 and 889 respectively. Many neutral ships called voluntarily at the examination stations, and they were given priority for clearance; but there were always some to whom the prospect of high profits outweighed the risks involved in not conforming with the British regulations. When flagrant cases came to light a series of seizures in prize would probably be organized. For example the very high shipments of lard from USA to Scandinavia were stopped by the seizure of four cargoes in rapid succession in October and November 1914.

Ruffled neutral feathers

On the outbreak of war the CID set up a 'Trading with the Enemy Committee' to control imports through neutral countries; but its procedure proved too slow and cumbrous, and its functions were therefore taken over in March 1915 by the War Trade Intelligence Department, which collected evidence regarding consignees, studied the scale of neutral imports of all commodities and generally 'acted as a clearing house for the collection, analysis, and dissemination of economic data relating to enemy and neutral trade'. The Exports Control Committee under the Intelligence Department was responsible for issuing import and export licences to shippers, and ruffled neutral feathers were often smoothed by purchasing detained cargoes instead of seizing them in prize.

Nonetheless, difficulties with neutral nations sometimes became acute. Intercepted ships were often subject to long delays, and sometimes they were sunk while being taken into port under British armed guard. After the war the British government paid full value plus five per cent accrued interest on all ships sunk in such circumstances. Because of neutral susceptibilities the British government had to move with caution and moderation, especially in dealings with the USA, where the anti-British lobby was powerful and vociferous. The process of keeping American public opinion sweet was, however, aided by German ruthlessness—notably over the sinking of the great Cunard liner *Lusitania* on 7th May 1915 with a heavy loss of civilian lives including 128 Americans.

The German reply to the tightening British blockade was to declare on 4th February 1915 the whole of the waters around the British Isles a 'War Zone' in which any ship might be sunk without warning. Thus began the first unrestricted submarine campaign. It lasted until August, when the rising tide of neutral protests caused the German government to order a return to less flagrantly illegal methods. However, the substantial tonnage sunk by submarines in that phase (748,914 tons in the whole of 1915) caused great anxiety in Allied circles, and should have provided an opportunity to find the proper antidote—namely convoy. Such, however, was not the case, since the Admiralty remained stubbornly opposed to convoy.

The winter of 1915-16 saw a revival of German surface ship raiders; but this time disguised merchantmen instead of warships were employed. Altogether five such ships were sent out, and one of them (the *Möwe*) made two cruises and sank 122,000 tons of shipping. Two were caught right at the beginning of their careers, but the others proved skilful and elusive enemies. Like their predecessors of the cruiser period they caused considerable delay and dislocation to shipping, and the last of them was not eliminated until early in 1918.

Despite the success achieved by the first unrestricted submarine campaign, the situation as regards the blockade and counterblockade at the end of 1915 was not unfavourable to the Allies. This was the more fortunate because in all theatres of military operations that year was one of unmitigated defeat and disaster for their cause. True, there was a shortage of shipping, caused partly by excessive requisitioning by the service departments; but the flow of supplies of all kinds had been kept up, and losses of merchant ships, which had totalled 855,721 tons during the year, had been replaced by newly built and captured vessels.

With complete deadlock prevailing on the Western Front, the commercial blockade of Germany had obviously gained in importance. Accordingly in February 1916 the British government set up a new Ministry of Blockade under Lord Robert Cecil to co-ordinate the political and administrative measures necessary to cripple the Central powers' resources. The new ministry, working closely with the War Trade Intelligence Department, gradually built up world-wide control over the movement of all merchant ships and the shipment of cargoes. Consular shipping control officers were installed in all important ports, and they transmitted to London a stream of information regarding the true shippers and consignees of cargoes. With this knowledge in hand the ministry was able to compile a list of firms known to be trading with the enemy, and great ingenuity was shown in exerting pressure to curb their activities. Because bunkering facilities in many overseas ports were British-controlled it was possible to deprive ships of coal and other essential supplies when they called. The location of the greater part of the world's banking and insurance business in London enabled credit and insurance cover to be refused to firms whose activities were not above suspicion. And British control over most of the world's wireless and cable communications made it improbable that such activities would long remain uncovered. Finally, if a ship did sail with an illicit cargo, the Admiralty would be asked to take special steps to intercept it; and if that succeeded condemnation in prize was virtually certain.

But the Ministry of Blockade did not only work to prevent shipment of contraband cargoes. Neutral nations' imports were rationed with increasing stringency at a figure no greater than they had taken before the war; and goods which were particularly vital to the enemy war effort, such as the special minerals (wolfram and tungsten, for example) used in weapon and armour plate manufacture, were controlled by the pre-emptive purchase of the whole available supply.

One of the first actions of the Ministry of Blockade was to issue (29th February 1916) a 'Statutory Black List' of firms in neutral countries with whom all transactions were forbidden. This aroused strong American protests – since a number of the firms were American. In the following month a system known as 'Letters of Assurance' for approved shippers was introduced. These were always referred to as 'Navicerts' (from the code word used in cables referring to them), and possession of such a letter ensured a ship unhindered passage through the blockade. Encouragement was given to shippers to arrange with London for advance booking of cargoes, which would then be approved or disapproved by the Contraband Committee.

Neutral shipowners were also given every encouragement to order their ships to call in voluntarily for examination at Scapa Flow and the Downs or at Halifax, Alexandria, and Gibraltar where additional stations were set up. In 1916 no less than 1,878 neutral vessels called in voluntarily, 950 were intercepted and sent in, and only 155 (some five per cent of the total) successfully ran the blockade. New Orders in Council were issued to increase the stringency of the blockade – notably that of 7th July 1916 which repealed the Declaration of London Order in Council of August 1914. Throughout 1916 the effectiveness of the Allied machinery of commercial blockade steadily increased.

The Germans did not, of course, take this escalation of Allied blockade measures lying down. In March 1916 they renewed the unrestricted submarine campaign, and again quickly achieved a fairly high rate of sinkings – 126,000 tons in April. However, they once again caused the loss of American lives, and the resultant protests produced a temporary lull. In September they tried again, and despite the wide variety of measures introduced by the Admiralty to combat the submarine menace – minefields, nets, surface patrols, and the much advertised 'mystery' or 'Q-ships' – German submarines sank nearly 147,000 tons of shipping in October. The implications were plainly very serious, since if the upward trend continued the loss to be anticipated in 1917 would exceed 2,000,000 tons. Furthermore the total Allied shipping losses in 1916 amounted to 1,237,634 tons, which was nearly fifty per cent higher than in the previous year; and, finally, the rate of sinking of U-boats had not been satisfactory in relation to the speed at which new ones were built. From the beginning of the war to the end of 1916 only forty-six had been sunk.

But if the closing months of 1916 brought little comfort to those responsible for maintaining the flow of Allied supplies, to the German people the implication of that year's developments were far more threatening. Though their armed forces had not yet suffered appreciably, since they were given priority for all available supplies, the condition of the civilian population was beginning to deteriorate seriously. The 1915 and 1916 harvests had been bad, due chiefly to lack of imported fertilizers, the conquered territories in eastern Europe had failed to replace supplies from overseas, home producers of foodstuffs were withholding their produce or selling it on the extensive black market, the calorific value of the civilian ration was falling steadily, and the shortage of clothing was becoming increasingly acute. With the winter of 1916-17 approaching – it was to be remembered in Germany as the 'Turnip Winter' – the outlook was grim indeed.

Such was the state of affairs that led the German government to adopt the desperate expedient of renewed submarine warfare on merchant shipping in February 1917; and that led to the entry of the USA into the war, and so to the utter defeat of the Central powers.

The Fatal Decision

Wolfgang Steglich

At long last, on 9th January 1917, Bethmann Hollweg, the German chancellor, at a conference at GHQ, Pless in Upper Silesia, signified his concurrence with the resolution in favour of unrestricted submarine warfare, that is he agreed to the torpedoing of enemy and neutral merchant and passenger ships without warning. His feelings were similar to those which had burdened him during the crisis of July 1914. For him the Pless decision was a leap in the dark, like the action of Austria-Hungary against Serbia in July 1914. On that occasion he realized that any attempt to overthrow Serbia might well lead to a European war. Now he was tormented by anxiety lest the reckless use of the U-boats result in war with the United States. And on both occasions his fears were justified.

In 1914 it was the growing consolidation of the Triple Entente, the increasing strength of Russia, and the critical situation in the Balkans which drove the German government to approve and guarantee the Austro-Hungarian attack on Serbia regardless of the risk of a European war. In 1917 the German government was impelled by the hopelessness of the land war to agree to unrestricted submarine warfare and thereby to run the risk of a conflict with the USA. In 1917, as in 1914, Bethmann Hollweg yielded to the military demands through a mixture of fatalism and a hope that the general situation might be changed by violent action. Bethmann Hollweg's two shattering decisions resembled each other in that each was based on a collapse of political leadership and an excessive regard for the military standpoint.

The arguments about U-boat warfare among the military and political leaders of the German empire had begun as far

back as late 1914. The first impulse was given by the unsatisfactory progress of the naval war. At enormous cost a German battle fleet had been built up in sharp rivalry with Great Britain. On the outbreak of war, however, any large-scale naval enterprise was discouraged by the government, which needed to maintain the German fleet intact as a political instrument. It was not until 1916 that the naval commanders ventured to engage the Royal Navy, and the battle of Jutland showed that Germany had not enough naval power to defeat the great British fleet in a battle on the high seas. The pretensions of the German naval leaders were badly injured because of the limited effectiveness of the fleet since 1914, and Germany was driven more and more to rely on submarine warfare against British seaborne commerce. The aim was to destroy the economic life and supply lines of Great Britain and thus force it to sue for peace. But this strategical switch was by no means due solely to the German navy's ambition to play some part in the war. It was forced on the naval leaders by the grim fact that in a few months Great Britain had won complete command of the world's seas and was trying to cut off Germany's overseas imports by a distant blockade. It seemed essential not to accept this gigantic British success meekly but to find some counterstroke in reply. In the first months of the war German U-boats had destroyed several large British warships by underwater torpedo attacks, and these brilliant successes led to an over-estimation of the U-boat weapon, which in fact was still comparatively undeveloped. The chief of the naval staff, Admiral von Pohl, pressed for a blockade of the British coasts as early as the beginning of November 1914. And a little later Admiral von Tirpitz, state secretary of the imperial navy office, gave an interview to Karl von Wiegand, a representative of the American press, in which he drew the world's attention to the possibility of a German blockade of Great Britain by submarines. Among the German people an impression grew that the U-boats were an infallible weapon in the war with Great Britain. The result was a violent public agitation concerning U-boats.

Commercial warfare by U-boat actually began as far back as February 1915 and was consistently carried on in various forms for two years, until January 1917. During this period the German government had time and again to justify the employment of a novel method of warfare in face of the vehement complaints of the European neutrals and, especially, of the United States. Yielding to such opposition, it set its face, until 9th January 1917, against the unrestricted use of the U-boat weapon demanded by the naval authorities. But at the same time, in internal debates, it repeatedly asserted that its negative attitude was not due to consideration for international law but was purely for military and political reasons. When, in January 1917, the ruthless exploitation of U-boat warfare was finally decided upon, Bethmann Hollweg expressly declared that he had never opposed it on principle, but had always been governed by the general situation and the respective strengths of U-boat weapons. In the various deliberations it was the Kaiser Wilhelm II alone who expressed humanitarian scruples. For him 'the drowning of innocent passengers was 'a frightful thought'.

As the U-boat was a new weapon, there were in 1914 no international rules regarding its use in commercial warfare. The German government should have striven to obtain international recognition for the new weapon, for both the present and any future war. But instead, the Germans admitted the illegality of U-boat commerce war from the first by describing it as a reprisal measure against the illegal methods adopted by the British in their commercial blockade. For Great Britain, like Germany, had been forced by the advance of weapon technique to break the traditional international rules dealing with blockades. Because of the danger to its naval forces it could not carry on a close blockade of the German coasts—hitherto the only permissible method—but had to engage in a distant blockade directed at neutral as well as German ports. For this purpose the British declared the whole of the North Sea to be a war zone and prescribed for neutral shipping fixed navigational routes which could be supervised by British naval vessels. Moreover, Great Britain extended the regulations about war contraband and the confiscation of cargoes in neutral vessels. Liable to seizure were not only goods useful for the arming and

supply of enemy forces, but all foodstuffs and raw materials intended for the Central powers. It was immaterial whether the cargoes were being carried direct to enemy ports or through neutral countries.

The new British contraband regulations initiated an economic and hunger blockade which was aimed at the enemy's civilian population. The German reprisal measure, commercial war by U-boat, was similarly directed against the civilian population. It might therefore be considered as merely a similar measure, by way of reprisal. But in fact there was one great difference. The British blockade was merely a confiscation of material goods, but the German submarine attacks endangered the lives of crews and passengers. When an underwater torpedo was fired without warning, it was impossible to take any steps to save the lives of those on board. And if the ship was attacked from the surface the crew and passengers taking to the lifeboats were exposed to the perils of wind and wave on the open seas, for the U-boat was in no position to pick them up and bring them to a place of safety.

The most difficult thing to justify was the effect of commercial war by U-boat on the neutrals, in whose case there was, of course, no question of reprisal. Instead, the German government demanded that the neutrals submit to submarine warfare as they had submitted to the British blockade of the North Sea. But there was only partial justification for this demand. True, neutral shipping used the prescribed routes through the English Channel and submitted to examination of cargoes in British ports. Nevertheless, the European neutrals, in spite of the British blockade, had delivered large food cargoes to Germany down to 1916. On the German side there was no desire to suppress neutral shipping by submarine warfare, but only to drive it out of certain sea areas. In the proclamation of 4th February 1915, which initiated submarine warfare, the waters around Great Britain and Ireland, including the whole of the English Channel, were declared a war zone. Every enemy merchant ship encountered in the war zone would be destroyed. Neutral ships were advised to avoid it, as attacks on enemy ships might, in the uncertainties of naval warfare, well affect neutral ships also. It was hoped that this warning might frighten neutral shipping off trade with Great Britain. Admiral von Pohl wanted to emphasize this warning by ordering all ships within the war zone to be sunk without distinction, a step which meant unrestricted submarine warfare. He actually wanted a few neutral ships to be sunk without warning at the outset of the U-boat operations so that there should be general uncertainty and neutral trade with Great Britain stopped as soon as possible. In subsequent deliberations the deterrent effect on neutral shipping was an important factor.

At the beginning of 1915, and again at the beginning of 1916, such intimidation seemed especially necessary, for Germany at those times was far from possessing enough U-boats to carry on a successful economic war with Great Britain. In February 1915 there were only twenty-one U-boats available for watching the shipping lanes to Great Britain. As the voyage to the war zone, the return journey, and the overhaul afterwards, took a considerable time, there were never more than three or four boats operating at any one time on the coasts of Great Britain. Obviously there were not enough of them to inflict any considerable damage to Great Britain's trade by direct action. Thus it was very important to keep neutral ships, and as many enemy ships as possible out of the war zone. But the Germans had no success. Even before the announced U-boat commerce war started on 18th February, very firmly worded notes of protest reached Berlin from the neutral maritime powers affected. Most serious of all, the American government held the German government strictly accountable for all measures that might involve the destruction of any merchant vessel belonging to the United States or for the death of any American subject. The war situation of the Central powers in February 1915 was much too strained to risk complications with powerful neutral states. The chancellor therefore persuaded the Kaiser to order the U-boats to spare neutral ships, especially those belonging to the United States or Italy. The U-boat commerce war began four days late, on 22nd February 1915, in this modified form. In March 1915, out of 5,000 vessels entering and leaving British ports only twenty-one were sunk. Neutral shipping soon resumed trade with Great Britain.

The Lusitania incident

In spite of precautions taken during the period of restricted submarine warfare, a grave incident occurred on 7th May 1915, when a German U-boat sank the British ocean liner *Lusitania* with an underwater torpedo. Among the drowned were 128 American citizens. The sinking of the *Lusitania* aroused intense indignation in the United States, and a sharp exchange of notes between the American and German governments ensued. President Wilson had no desire to precipitate an armed conflict with Germany by his *Lusitania* notes, but he feared that a continuation of the U-boat war would one day leave him no other choice. He tried repeatedly to persuade Great Britain to allow food imports into Germany through neutral countries. At the same time he took a firm stand against the contempt for humane principles shown in the kind of warfare used by the U-boats. The first *Lusitania* note of the American government on 15th May 1915 denied the legality in international law of any form of U-boat commerce war, inasmuch as in neither an underwater nor a surface attack could the safety of passengers and crew be guaranteed. In the third *Lusitania* note of 23rd July 1915 Wilson conceded that submarines were a novelty in naval warfare and that no provision could have been made for them in the international regulations. At the same time it was admitted that the German submarine operations of the last two months had complied with the customs of war and had demonstrated the possibility of eliminating the chief causes of offence. This remarkable concession on the part of the Americans was based on the fact that since May 1915 the U-boats had been fitted with deck guns and, owing to the uncertainty of hitting the target with torpedoes, had carried on the commerce war in 'cruiser' style, according to the rules laid down for the taking of prizes. The U-boat came to the surface when attacking a ship and before sinking it allowed the persons on board to take to the boats. All enemy vessels were sunk without exception, but neutral ships were sunk only when they were carrying contraband.

Although this was the actual method of operation during the *Lusitania* crisis, the German naval authorities obstinately opposed any restriction being placed on submarine warfare and especially any attempt to confine U-boats to the rules of 'cruiser' warfare. They maintained that such methods were an intolerable danger to the submarine and its crew. They named as the chief dangers attempts of the merchant ships to ram the submarine, concealed guns on the ships, the use of a neutral flag by British ships, and attacks by enemy warships during the necessarily lengthy searches. The German government was not informed by the navy that in the period May-July 1915 eighty-six per cent of the merchant vessels that were sunk were dealt with according to the cruiser warfare rules, and that from February to July 1915 250 merchant ships carrying a neutral flag were examined and only on three occasions was any misuse of the flag discovered. By its policy of secrecy the navy apparently wanted to avoid being permanently restricted to 'cruiser' warfare and losing for ever the chance of unrestricted submarine warfare. On 6th June 1915 the Kaiser ordered that all large passenger liners, whether enemy or neutral, must be spared. Nevertheless, on 19th August, the British liner, *Arabic,* was sunk without warning, two more American citizens losing their lives. The Kaiser then ordered that no passenger liner was to be sunk until it had been warned and the passengers and crew given a chance to escape. During the arguments about U-boat methods in the summer of 1915 Tirpitz, in order to put pressure on the Kaiser, twice offered his resignation. His offers were abruptly refused. Yet the Kaiser changed his chief of naval staff at the beginning of September. Vice-Admiral Bachmann, a Tirpitz adherent who had held the office since February 1915, was replaced by Admiral von Holtzendorff, who was more amenable to the political views of the chancellor. On 18th September 1915 Holtzendorff gave orders that the U-boat commerce war on the west coast of Great Britain and in the Channel should be carried out on the 'cruiser' system. The naval commanders were not ready for this step and brought the U-boat war around Great Britain to a standstill. Thus ended the first phase of the U-boat war. The *Arabic* case was settled on 6th October by German compliance. The German government did not defend the action of the U-boat commander, which infringed the

order of 6th June. The *Lusitania* case remained unsettled. The German government refused to admit that the U-boat attack on the *Lusitania* was contrary to international law, for if it did so future unrestricted submarine warfare would be impossible.

In 1915 several U-boats, large and small, were sent to the Austro-Hungarian naval base of Pola, and also to Constantinople. These carried on trade war in the Mediterranean and the Black Sea with great success, limiting their actions to the 'cruiser' rules. They restricted the flow of supplies to the Anglo-French forces in the Dardanelles and Salonika. But at the beginning of 1916 U-boat activities were severely handicapped by the progressive arming of the enemy's merchant vessels. The U-boat flotilla at Pola therefore asked the naval staff for permission to sink any armed merchant ship without warning. Holtzendorff granted the request, but with the proviso that passenger ships should continue to be exempt. At the same time he re-opened the trade war around Great Britain by issuing the same orders. A new phase in the submarine war was begun on 29th February 1916 and was termed 'intensified' U-boat war.

The high-ranking officers of the German navy looked on the new measures as a mere transitional phase. Since the beginning of the year the prospects for unrestricted submarine war had considerably improved, for General von Falkenhayn, chief of the army general staff, was now expressly demanding it. Since the autumn of 1914 the German armies, in co-operation with those of Austria-Hungary, Turkey, and Bulgaria, had created firm front lines on enemy territory; they had driven the Russians far back to the east, and by the occupation of Serbia had opened the way to Constantinople. Falkenhayn was at the peak of his military successes. In February 1916 he intended to deliver an all-out offensive on the Western Front, starting with a holding attack on Verdun. In the summer and autumn of 1915 he had firmly advised against the ruthless use of the U-boat weapon because he thought that a break with the United States might produce unfavourable reactions from the European neutrals and in particular might make Bulgarian assistance in the campaign against Serbia doubtful. In 1916, on the other hand, when the Balkan situation had been stabilized, such considerations were no longer valid. He believed that unrestricted submarine warfare directed against Great Britain would help his offensive on the Western Front. The U-boat action was timed to start in the middle of March. Almost the whole of the German press advocated ruthless use of the U-boats. The alliance between Falkenhayn and the navy on this point put Bethmann Hollweg in a very difficult position, and he spent the first weeks of the New Year in a very worried state. He feared that the adoption of unrestricted submarine warfare 'might result in condemnation by the whole civilized world and a sort of crusade against Germany'.

The Charleville conference

In the decisive conference with the Kaiser on 4th March 1916 at GHQ, Charleville, Falkenhayn declared that, in view of the dwindling resistance of the German allies and the German civil population, the war must be brought to an end before the year was out. The only means of achieving this was by unrestricted submarine warfare. On his part Bethmann Hollweg argued that Germany could stand another winter campaign. He would rather have a compromise peace than risk prolonging the war indefinitely by challenging America. In his opinion there were still insufficient U-boats. In the middle of March 1916 there were only fourteen large submarines capable of carrying on a commerce war in British waters.

On 4th March 1916 the Kaiser, unable to make up his mind, postponed his final decision until the beginning of April and then indefinitely. Nevertheless, with the agreement of the chancellor, a further tightening of the U-boat blockade was ordered on 13th March 1916. In the war zone both armed and unarmed merchant ships were to be destroyed without warning. Outside the war zone the previous orders remained in force. Tirpitz, who had not been called to the Charleville conference, reported sick to the Kaiser in protest and on 15th March he agreed to resign. One of Bethmann Hollweg's chief opponents had left the scene.

Whereas the instruction for the sinking of armed merchant ships was made public, the new order of 13th March was kept secret. Its effects, however, were viewed by the neutrals with growing alarm. Washington suspected that Germany had already started unrestricted submarine warfare. A new incident soon gave rise to another German-American crisis. On 24th March 1916 two Americans were injured when the cross-Channel passenger steamer, Sussex, was torpedoed without warning. In the erroneous belief that American citizens had lost their lives in the sinking President Wilson sent a note on 18th April threatening to break off diplomatic relations with Germany if it did not abandon its current methods of submarine warfare. Under pressure from this ultimatum the Kaiser gave orders, at Bethmann Hollweg's request, cancelling the tightened-up rules for submarine warfare in the combat zone around Great Britain. The rules of the 'cruiser' system were to be observed until further notice. The commanding officers on the naval front declared that such a procedure was unworkable, because of the danger to the U-boats, and they brought the submarine war in British waters to a complete standstill. In the Mediterranean the U-boats continued the campaign according to the new rules.

At the end of April 1916, when the reply to the American note had to be drafted, Falkenhayn again tried to persuade the Kaiser to agree to unrestricted submarine warfare. He asserted that he would have to forego action against Verdun if the U-boat war was suspended. Bethmann Hollweg indignantly rejected such an alternative and after a bitter dispute he once again convinced the Kaiser. In a note dated 4th May 1916 the German government agreed to the demands of the American government and informed it that the German naval forces had been instructed to observe the canons of international law with regard to the stopping, searching, and destruction of merchant vessels. At the same time it expressed its expectation that the United States would now induce the British government to abandon as soon as possible such of its methods of waging naval war as were contrary to international law. The German government reserved its complete freedom to alter its decision if this were not done. Wilson at once protested against the German claim to make respect for the rights of American citizens on the high seas dependent on the behaviour of the British government. Responsibility in such matters was individual not joint, absolute not relative. The two opposing standpoints were thus definitely laid down. If Germany again intensified the submarine war, it was to be expected that the United States would promptly enter the war.

It was but a few months after the settlement of the *Sussex* case that the problem of unrestricted submarine warfare once again became acute. During the summer of 1916 the war situation was completely transformed. The Central powers, who had held the initiative for a whole year, were now forced into defensive battles lasting for months by the persistent offensive of the Russians in Volhynia and eastern Galicia and of the British and French on the Somme, which could only be withstood by enormous efforts and casualties. Falkenhayn had to break off the battle for Verdun, which was bleeding not only France but also Germany to death. His prestige was shattered, and when Rumania entered the war against the Central powers on 27th August 1916 he was replaced by Hindenburg and Ludendorff. Hindenburg, who was the most popular of the German military leaders, became chief of the general staff. Bethmann Hollweg had worked for Hindenburg's appointment to this post during the critical summer months of 1916 because he thought that a moderate peace could be made acceptable to the German people, so misled by exaggerated hopes, only if it were covered by the name of Hindenburg. In other words, Bethmann Hollweg hoped to use the great authority of the field marshal in his efforts towards a peace of understanding. But Hindenburg's authority was fatal to Bethmann Hollweg's policy. Hindenburg and Ludendorff were advocates of unrestricted submarine warfare. After they had been summoned to take up the highest posts in the army they pleaded for a temporary postponement of this war measure only with respect to the difficult military situation. For at the moment great danger threatened from Rumania, and sufficient troops had to be made available as security against the European neutrals, who might regard unrestricted submarine warfare as a challenge. By the end of December 1916 the Rumanian army was defeated and in the following months military deployments against European neutrals could be initiated.

Bethmann Hollweg had previously been able to stifle the arguments of Falkenhayn and the naval authorities in favour of unrestricted submarine warfare because the war situation in the spring of 1916 did not make such a risky measure absolutely essential. By the summer, however, the war was threatening to become one of attrition of man power and exhaustion of resources. Germany would not be strong enough in 1917 to undertake a large-scale offensive with the land forces available. A weapon that might well win the war was offered by the U-boats.

In these circumstances Bethmann Hollweg, in the latter part of 1916, tried to avoid the necessity of unrestricted submarine warfare by bringing about an early peace of compromise. President Wilson was working for the same end, because he wanted to keep America out of the war. On 12th December 1916 the Central powers made a peace offer to the Allies. On the 21st President Wilson invited the belligerents to state their war aims and announced his willingness to take part in the discussions. Hindenburg and Ludendorff had notified their concurrence with the peace offer of the Central powers, but as soon as the first negative reports began to arrive from the camp of the Allies they demanded, at the end of December 1916, speedy and energetic action at sea.

The prospects for unrestricted submarine warfare at the beginning of 1917 were much better than they had been a year before. Germany now had 105 U-boats, of which 46 large and 23 small vessels were available for the campaign in British waters. In view of the bad world harvests of 1916 unrestricted submarine warfare, if started before the chief overseas transport season began in early February, would foreseeably have a grave effect on Great Britain's grain supplies. Since 6th October 1916 the U-boats had carried on the commerce war in British waters on the 'cruiser' rules. Total sinkings were reckoned at 400,000 tons a month (in actual fact the figure was round about 325,000). By the removal of restrictions one expected an increase to 600,000 tons. The navy estimated that such a figure, enhanced by the consideration that neutral shipping would be frightened away, would in five months reduce the trade with Great Britain by thirty-nine per cent. This would force Great Britain to sue for peace. About the results of an American intervention in the war there was wide difference of opinion. The army thought that any great increase in the supply of American war material to the Allies was impossible, nor did it expect the arrival in Europe of large numbers of American troops. The politicians, however, thought that the American entry would encourage the Allied nations to hold out, would put large financial resources at their disposal, and would bring many American volunteers to join the Allies in Europe.

On the question of U-boat warfare Hindenburg and Ludendorff found their views supported by the vast majority of the German people. The largest party in the Reichstag, the Centre Party, passed a resolution on 7th October 1916 saying that the decision of the chancellor regarding submarine warfare must be based on the views of the supreme army command. As the Conservatives and National Liberals were in any case outright champions of unrestricted submarine warfare, Bethmann Hollweg knew that if he refused to make use of the U-boat weapon in opposition to Hindenburg and Ludendorff he could no longer count on a majority in the Reichstag. The feeling of the people was summed up by Bethmann Hollweg in his memoirs: 'No nation will stand for not winning a war when it is convinced that it can win.' He himself, in spite of his constant resistance to unrestricted submarine warfare, seems at times to have wondered whether, after all, the use of this extreme weapon might not achieve a turn for the better.

For the moment Bethmann Hollweg left the problem unsolved. When on 9th January 1917 he went to Pless to discuss the ever more pressing problem, he found the naval staff and the supreme army command united against him and they had already won over the Kaiser to their side. Hindenburg and Ludendorff saw no possibility of bringing the war to a victorious end unless the U-boats were used without restrictions. They declared themselves ready to shoulder all responsibility for any results caused by this war measure. The chief of the naval staff guaranteed that he

could force Great Britain to its knees before the next harvest. Once again Bethmann Hollweg produced all his objections, but after the failure of the Central powers' peace move all hopes for a peace of understanding seemed to have vanished. Bethmann Hollweg could no longer maintain his opposition to the demands of the military and he told the Kaiser that he could not recommend him to oppose the vote of his military advisers. He felt he must refrain from offering his resignation, so as not to expose the inner dissensions in the German leadership to all the world. Until the last moment, however, he continued to doubt the wisdom of the decision of 9th January 1917. When towards the end of the month the prospects for a successful outcome of Wilson's peace efforts seemed more favourable, he tried to secure a postponement of unrestricted submarine warfare, but the naval staff assured him that most of the U-boats had already been despatched.

The beginning of unrestricted submarine warfare on 1st February 1917 was at first countered by Wilson with the rupture of diplomatic relations, whereby he hoped to bring Germany to its senses. The political tension between the two countries was increased at the beginning of March by the publication of a German offer of alliance to Mexico (intercepted by the British intelligence service) should the United States enter the war because of the submarine war. The sinking of seven American merchant ships by U-boats by 21st March finally obliged Wilson to summon Congress, which on 4th and 6th April approved a declaration of war.

At first the figures of sinkings by the U-boats surpassed the forecasts and expectations of the German naval authorities, reaching its maximum in April 1917. But when in the course of the summer merchant ships sailing for Great Britain were assembled in convoys and protected by destroyers the number of successes dwindled. Nevertheless, unrestricted submarine warfare brought Great Britain difficulties which led the British government to begin to take an interest in political solutions. But on the whole the strong urge towards peace that was expected from the U-boat menace failed to materialize. Looking back, it is clear that the German military leaders and politicians regarded the unrestricted submarine warfare as a failure. For from March 1917 onwards the Central powers were relieved of a great burden by the Russian Revolution. Russia dropped out of the war in the winter of 1917-18, and negotiations for a general peace of understanding might have been possible had not the Allies been encouraged to hold on by the prospect of American armed assistance. But the principal effect of unrestricted submarine warfare was on America itself, for it caused the abandonment of America's policy of isolation and its entry into world politics. *(Translation)*

The U-boats Overcome

Captain S. W. Roskill

Whereas in 1915-16 the German naval and military 'Hawks' had been subdued by the political 'Doves' over the prosecution of unrestricted U-boat warfare, at the beginning of 1917 the renewed tussle in Berlin ended in success for the 'Hawks'. They guaranteed victory within six months — despite the likelihood of the USA entering the war on the Allied side. Accordingly orders were issued to resume unrestricted warfare on 1st February; and three days later President Wilson broke off diplomatic relations. Meanwhile, on 16th January, the German foreign minister had sent via Washington to the ambassador in Mexico City the message still known as the 'Zimmermann Telegram'. It promised to Mexico that in return for alliance with Germany the 'former lost territory' of the southern states of the USA would be restored to her. This astonishing *gaucherie* was intercepted and deciphered in London, and was passed to the American ambassador, Walter Page, at a carefully chosen moment. The indignation it aroused in America made active intervention certain, and on 6th April the USA declared war on Germany.

In actual fact, the claims put forward by the German 'Hawks' were by no means as fantastic as they may now appear, and for the first four months it seemed quite likely that they would be fulfilled. In 1916 the U-boat fleet had more than doubled (from 54 to 133) and only twenty-two had been sunk. Allied and neutral shipping losses rocketed from 386,000 tons in January 1917 to the colossal total of 881,000 tons in April — a figure which, if maintained for a few more months, would have brought a German victory. The chief burden of countering the U-boat campaign naturally fell on the British navy, and as the many and varied antidotes adopted had failed to prove effective the dispute over whether convoy should be introduced grew hotter. The Admiralty, supported by a good deal of Merchant Navy opinion, considered that the disadvantages, such as lengthened 'turn-round' of ships, outweighed the possible advantages. But the Ministry of Shipping was confident that such arguments, which were in fact supported by wholly misleading Admiralty statistics regarding the relation between losses and safe arrivals of ships, were false. Lloyd George, the prime minister, took the same view. At the end of April he forced the Admiralty to try convoy, and the recommendations of the Atlantic Convoy Committee, which was set up in May and produced a comprehensive scheme early in the following month, were at once adopted. Admiral W.S.Sims, commander of the US Naval Forces in Europe, was also a strong supporter of convoy, and with the help of the American destroyers, which soon began to operate from Queenstown (now Cobh) in southern Ireland, the experiment proved wholly successful. Not only did shipping losses decline sharply after April, but sinkings of U-boats increased from twenty in the first half of the year to forty-three in the second half. However, the confrontation between Lloyd George and the Admiralty caused a considerable loss of confidence in the Board on the part of the political leaders. In July therefore Lloyd George appointed Sir Eric Geddes first lord in place of Sir Edward Carson, who had consistently supported the sea lords' views on the convoy issue; and in December Geddes abruptly dismissed Admiral Sir John Jellicoe, the first sea lord.

A barrage of mines

Though the introduction of convoy was without doubt the most important factor in surmounting the crisis, it would be misleading to ascribe it entirely to that measure. The conflict between minelayer and minesweeper was now at its height, and in the autumn the British at last had available an efficient mine — copied from the Germans. The Straits of Dover were the crucial area, since unless both the long-range High Seas Fleet U-boats working from the German North Sea bases and the smaller boats based on Zeebrugge and Ostend could pass through the English Channel they would be forced to take the much longer route round the north of Scotland to reach their operational areas in the western approaches to the British Isles. In consequence the British concentrated a great effort on creating an impenetrable barrage of mines and nets, with surface vessels patrolling constantly overhead, in the Dover Straits. Though these measures gradually took effect, in 1917 U-boats made no less than 250 successful transits through the English Channel, mostly at night and on the surface. Not until the end of the year, by which time the barrage had been provided with night illumination, did it become really dangerous for U-boats to attempt the short passage. Nor was minelaying confined to the narrow waters of the Channel. The British discovered, from deciphered messages, the routes used by the U-boats to pass in and out of the Heligoland Bight, and hundreds of mines were laid to catch them at the beginning or end of their patrols. The Germans did not, of course, take the strengthening of the Dover Barrage and the obstruction of the U-boat routes lying down. Their minesweeping service struggled hard to keep the channels to and from the North Sea bases clear, while their surface ships several times attacked the vessels patrolling the Dover minefields. But although the British patrols sometimes suffered quite heavy losses, the Germans could not reverse the current trend, which showed all too plainly that the passage of the Straits was becoming unacceptably hazardous.

Of all the many anti-submarine measures adopted in 1917 the mine, with twenty U-boats sunk, was by far the most successful U-boat killer. Surface ship or submarine patrols sank sixteen enemies, convoy escorts and Q-ships (decoys) each sank six, and about a dozen were lost through accidents of one sort or another. Yet although the total sinkings in 1917 (sixty-three) were nearly three times greater than in the previous year, new construction more than kept pace with losses. At the end of the year the U-boat fleet of 142 was actually greater by nine than it had been twelve months earlier; and many of the new boats were of improved types. Plainly, then, the battle was as yet far from won by the Allies.

Blocking the blockaders

To turn back to the German scene, the entry of the USA into the war enabled the Allied naval-economic blockade to be tightened to a stranglehold. German merchant ships which had long sheltered in American ports were seized; and – more important still – there was no longer any question of American firms trying to send contraband goods to Germany, or of American merchant ships running the British blockade to reach Scandinavia or Dutch ports with such cargoes. Almost overnight on 6th April 1917 Allied control of seaborne traffic became worldwide and complete. To make matters worse for Germany the 1917 harvest was again bad, largely because of the lack of imported fertilizers; and civilian food rations were cut to a level at which it was no longer possible to remain in good health. Furthermore, there was now an acute shortage of many metals, and in consequence the equipment of the armed forces began to suffer. The renowned discipline of the German people had not yet weakened seriously, but by the end of 1917 it was becoming plain that unless the shortages of every kind, and sheer hunger, were alleviated in the fairly near future a collapse was likely on the home front.

By the beginning of 1918 some 5,000 mines had been laid in the Dover Barrage, but U-boat transits none the less continued – in March there were twenty-nine. The British were especially anxious to put the Flanders U-boat bases out of action – if the army could not capture them. Indeed the terribly costly prolongation of the 3rd battle of Ypres into the autumn of 1917 must be ascribed partly to Admiralty pressure to capture Ostend and Zeebrugge. When that offensive had plainly failed the earlier idea of a blocking operation was resurrected, and after several false starts it was carried out on the night of 22nd-23rd April. Although at the time the British believed that Zeebrugge had been effectively blocked, it is now clear that this was not so. Despite the great gallantry with which the attack was carried out (no less than eleven Victoria Crosses were awarded to participants) by early May the U-boats could work their way round the blockships. And the attack on Ostend, though repeated on 10th May, was a total failure on both occasions.

Germany feels the pinch

With the U-boats forced increasingly to use the long route round the north of Scotland the possibility of laying a gigantic minefield between the Orkneys and the Norwegian coast was raised. As the distance was some 250 miles, and the depth of water was in places far greater than the Straits of Dover, this was an undertaking of a very different order from the blocking of the twenty-mile-wide Straits. In July 1917 a new American mine was ready for mass production, and the decision was taken to go ahead. The US Navy carried out the lion's share of the laying, often in very bad weather. By the end of the war 56,000 American and 13,000 British mines had been laid in this Northern Barrage. Unfortunately, many of the American mines exploded prematurely, and there was always a gap at the eastern end in Norwegian territorial waters — which the U-boats were not slow to exploit. Though this barrage probably did make U-boat passages to their operational areas slower and more dangerous, the results achieved (three U-boats possibly sunk and another three damaged) were hardly commensurate with the effort involved.

The Mediterranean had until 1918 been a happy hunting ground for U-boats, which had sunk merchant ships with almost complete impunity. The Austrian submarine fleet totalled twenty-seven boats, most of them ex-German, and they were reinforced by German boats sent out periodically through the Straits of Gibraltar to work from Cattaro (now Kotor) or Pola. Hence arose the attempt to construct yet another barrage — across the Straits of Otranto — to block the routes to and from the Adriatic bases. Once again mines, nets, and surface and air patrols were all used; but with very little success. It was without doubt the introduction of convoy which defeated the Mediterranean U-boats. Of the ten sunk in those waters in 1918 at least half can be attributed to convoy escorts. One of the most interesting of these successes was the capture of Karl Dönitz from UB.68 on 4th October 1918, since he was to command Germany's U-boat fleet in the Second World War.

In July 1918 the Germans made a last desperate attempt to pass U-boats down-Channel to attack the troopships which were bringing an ever increasing flood of American soldiers to the Western Front. Of the six boats sent out only three returned home, and two of them were severely damaged. The last west-bound transit took place in August, and at the end of that month the Germans accepted that only the long northern route remained open to them. Meanwhile, a mine barrage had been laid off the east coast of England, where U-boats had previously achieved considerable successes; and more mines were laid in the Heligoland Bight. It was at this time that the British laid the first magnetic mines, off the Flanders bases, which were now virtually useless to the Germans. Also in August a heavy attack was made on the morale of the U-boat crews by publishing the names of 150 officers, most of them captains of boats, known to have been killed or captured. Recent analysis of this list shows how well-informed were the Admiralty's anti-submarine and intelligence departments.

Submarine death toll

On 25th October Admiral Reinhard Scheer, commander of the High Seas Fleet, recalled all U-boats from the sea routes with a view to their taking part in a final sortie by his fleet. There were twenty-three at sea at the time. Nine days later all possibility of carrying out that desperate plan was eliminated by widespread mutinies among Scheer's major warships; but the U-boat crews remained loyal to the end. A condition of the armistice terms signed at Compiègne on 11th November was that all surviving U-boats should be surrendered.

There is no doubt at all that in 1918 Allied anti-submarine forces inflicted a heavy defeat on the U-boats. Though seventy new ones had been built, sixty-nine were sunk, and total strength declined from 142 to 134. The convoy escorts and surface ship patrols between them accounted for thirty-four enemies; but mines, with eighteen U-boats destroyed, again proved very effective. Air escorts and patrols sank few, if any, enemies; but they played an increasingly important part by reporting U-boats' positions and forcing them to remain submerged. Of all the varied weapons in the armoury of the Allied anti-submarine forces the mine was, taking the war as a whole, much the most effective, with forty-eight successes to its credit. The depth charge with thirty came second, the torpedo with twenty third, and the ram with nineteen fourth. But the sinkings achieved by the U-boats totalled the immense figure of 11,153,506 tons out of total losses by all nations from all causes of 12,850,814 tons. The British Merchant Navy was by far the heaviest sufferer, and the 7,759,090 tons lost was no less than thirty-seven per cent of its pre-war total tonnage. The loss of 178 U-boats was perhaps a small price to pay for the amount of shipping destroyed.

As to the Allied blockade of the Central powers, by August 1918 the civilian ration in Germany was reduced below 2,000 calories daily, resistance to disease had been much lowered by malnutrition, and the death rate was rising very sharply. Perhaps the best indication of the effect of the blockade on the German people is the fact that during the four years 1915-18 civilian deaths exceeded by 760,000 the number which pre-war statistics indicated as probable. Though the German armies were as thoroughly defeated on land as their U-boats were at sea, and the so-called 'stab in the back' by the civil population's collapse is a fiction of German militaristic imagination, it is nonetheless true that the blockade inflicted great suffering on the German and Austrian people. In Great Britain and France, though rationing of food was made increasingly stringent after 1916, there was no comparable degree of suffering; nor did the war industries of the Allied nations suffer difficulties such as the shortage of raw materials caused in Germany. Thus there is a good deal of truth in the saying that the Allied victory of 1918 was achieved through 'the triumph of unarmed forces', as well as by the successes of the fighting services on land, at sea, and in the air.

Part five · Russia's Collapse

For two years, Tsarist Russia had been one of the Allies' greatest assets. Even when inactive, the threat which she posed on the Eastern Front had tied down a considerable proportion of the German forces which might have been decisive in the west. And Allied leaders had come to assume that, despite their obvious weaknesses, the Russian forces could be called upon to make periodic massive assaults which could further force the Germans to reduce their pressure in the west. This touching belief in the apparently endless staying power of the Russian giant was still widespread at the end of 1916, even though there was growing evidence of strains which could shatter the whole machinery of the Russian state.

The inefficiency of the Tsarist regime had been apparent for so long that the rest of the world had seemed to accept that although incurable it would in no way affect Russian power. Yet when the country was called upon to face its first major challenge for over fifty years, the war with Japan in 1904, it was humiliated by a succession of defeats on land and sea. Dissatisfaction with the regime welled up into strikes, rioting, and demands for a democratic constitution. The Tsar gave way, setting up a representative assembly and promising other reforms. But as so often in the past, all attempts to alter or reinvigorate the traditional institutions proved ineffective, and in 1914 Russia remained a vast country with huge resources, but with a antiquated regime which was manifestly incapable of coping with the problems which increasingly rapid industrialization was posing.

The traditional revolutionary force in Russia had been attempts by disgruntled upper-class intellectuals to arouse the vast, discontented, but incohesive peasant class. But industrialization had brought into being a small industrial middle-class which was profoundly critical of the inefficiency of the government and its own exclusion from power, but unwilling to ally itself with the new and equally restless industrial proletariat and take any positive action to reform the government.

The first months of the war saw a serious defeat for the Russians at Tannenberg in East Prussia, but compensatory successes in the south where an Austrian invasion had been effectively repulsed. On a purely military balance, her allies could be reasonably satisfied. Russia had attacked, and despite great losses had shown that the Germans could not afford to be complacent about their Eastern Front.

It was, however, in the economic and social sectors that there were far more serious signs, for the economy had shown itself unable to satisfy the demands imposed on it by war and the government was showing itself incapable of inspiring the country or even of organizing it adequately. At the front the huge new conscript armies were woefully underequipped, while at home production was dropping and a fuel crisis forced many factories to a halt. The disastrous summer campaign of 1915 and growing loss of confidence at home forced the Tsar to act. Some unpopular ministers were dismissed and the government attempted to find some compromise by which it could gain the support of the bourgeois liberal opposition parties. But in September 1915 Nicholas brushed aside any suggestion of a compromise and announced that he was taking personal command of the armed forces.

The Tsar had correctly seen that there was a growing gap between the people and the monarchy. But his solution had increased the possibility of disaster rather than lessened it. The prestige of the imperial family was now directly involved; in future all defeats and failures would be blamed directly on the Tsar and not solely on his ministers. Also, the Tsar increasingly cut himself off from such advisory institutions as did exist and relied more and more on the advice of a small court clique which centred around the dubious figure of Rasputin. The middle classes were now completely alienated from the government.

The year 1916 opened with strikes and unrest. During the summer, the Brusilov offensive seemed to bring some respite; apparent military success calmed the tension in other fields. But this could not last long, and by the end of 1916 almost complete economic collapse had brought a severe food crisis and a wave of strikes. The Tsar and his family were now personally discredited at all levels of society, and talk of forcing abdication began to turn into active planning.

At the end of the year, Rasputin was murdered by a group of ardent monarchists who saw in him the source of all the Tsar's problems. But his death did nothing to improve the situation. Food shortages continued to keep tempers high and there were continual strikes in the major industrial centres. It was obvious that government control was collapsing at all levels of society. Finally, at the end of February, there was general rioting in Petrograd. The military commanders proved helpless as their troops began to desert and finally, after the Tsar had attempted to dissolve the Duma, the Duma elected a Provisional Committee which was to become the Provisional Government when Nicholas abdicated in March.

Composed of representatives of all the major parties in the Duma except the Bolsheviks, the Provisional Government was dedicated to the aim of giving Russia a democratic regime and staying in the war. But it was a middle-class body, out of touch with the deepest aspirations of the people and determined to uphold Russia's place as a major power and to continue to play a major part in the war. Ominously, on the same day as the Provisional Committee had been set up, another body had come into existence—the Petrograd Soviet of Workers, heir to the Soviet which had led the revolt in 1905. This body was in no way dedicated to the continuation of the war and in a rough and ready way represented the wishes and longings of the ordinary people of Russia.

The story of the next eight months is the struggle of these two bodies for control of the central government, and the key to this struggle was the question of war or peace. Over this the Provisional Government forfeited any support which it might have had from the majority of the people.

Russia's allies had watched events during the spring with growing anxiety, for it was essential that whatever government gained power it should continue the war. In June 1917 it looked as if all was well, for Kerensky, the prime minister of the Provisional Government, was determined to launch another great offensive. But it was a disaster, not simply militarily, but because the army disintegrated and it became obvious that whichever party could satisfy the massive demand for peace and provide the possibility of an equitable land policy would gain the support of the bulk of the population. This the Provisional Government was unable to do, and when its attempts to suppress the mutiny and subsequent unrest failed, the way was open for the Bolsheviks as the only cohesive party which had not been completely discredited to move in and seize absolute power.

Russia at War

Alexander Grunt

For Russia 1st August 1914 was the last day of peace. At about seven o'clock in the evening of that day the car of the German ambassador, Count Pourtales, drew up outside the building of the Russian ministry of foreign affairs on Palace Square in St Petersburg. The ambassador entered the building, where he was received by S.D. Sazonov, the minister of foreign affairs, to whom he handed a statement to the effect that Germany considered herself in a state of war with Russia. A day later Germany declared war on France. At dawn on 5th August the British ambassador in St Petersburg, Sir George Buchanan, received a telegram from his government which read: 'War with Germany – take action.'

It had turned out to be impossible to resolve the tangle of conflicting interests, which had emerged at many different points of the globe, without resorting to war; and so began the most painful and bloody war of any that mankind had known. For the majority of people with little interest in politics the war came as a surprise. After all, what could the illiterate Russian peasant or factory worker know of the actual plans and aims of his own or of other governments? On the face of it one thing was clear: the German Kaiser had attacked Russia, and Russia must be defended. And it never occurred to those who were closer to the centre of affairs and understood what was happening to try and explain the real significance of events to the ordinary people. At a ceremonial session of the State Duma everybody, from the monarchists to the representatives of the liberals and of the petit-bourgeois *Trudoviki*, who inclined towards the Socialist Revolutionaries and had until then been in opposition to the government, declared their full support for its actions, thus demonstrating the 'patriotic unity' of the Tsar with the people and of the people with the Tsar. The war suited them, because it promised the acquisition of new territories, markets for their goods, sources of raw materials, and huge profits. The sober voice of a Social Democratic deputy, who protested in the name of the working people against the fratricidal slaughter, was drowned in the general chorus of loyal speeches. The Social Democrats' refusal to vote for the military budget did not alter the situation. It was passed by an overwhelming majority. That is why in the first days of the war the country was swept by a wave of patriotic demonstrations in which the ordinary people also took part.

Only in time and after much suffering did the millions of ordinary people come to feel and understand how utterly unnecessary and senseless was the bloody slaughter into which they had been led by their rulers, that it was not for their native land but for the achievement of entirely selfish ends.

Meanwhile, the news from the front brought little consolation. An attempt by the Russian armies to drive deep into East Prussia ended in failure. They were forced to retreat, having lost 20,000 men dead and 60,000 prisoners. The situation was somewhat better on the south-western section of the front. The Russians had taken Galicia and thus threatened German Silesia, where a considerable part of German industry was concentrated. But they did not succeed in inflicting a final defeat on the Austro-Hungarian army. Towards the end of the year the exhausted troops on both sides went over to the defence. The front also became stabilized in the west, where the Germans had failed to inflict a decisive defeat on France. Hopes of a quick victory on one side or the other turned out to be illusory. All the warring countries found themselves faced with the necessity of waging a long and exhausting war which would require gigantic efforts of every kind.

Russia had entered the war without sufficient preparation. Though a great power, with a population of over 150,000,000 and inexhaustible natural resources, she lagged considerably behind the foremost countries of western Europe in terms of economic and political development. The basic reason for this backwardness was the fact that the country's economic and political system had retained features handed down from the feudal past. The preservation of the inequitable form of land ownership was the principal economic survival of this nature. About 300,000 square miles of land belonged to 30,000 landowners. And a similar area of land was divided among 10,000,000 peasant holdings.

Survivals from the days of serfdom in the agrarian system acted as a brake on the development not only of agriculture but of industry as well. On the eve of the war, in 1913, Russia produced less than 4,000,000 tons of coal, and 9,000,000 tons of oil. Russia continued to be an agrarian country: eighty-six per cent of the total population of the empire was employed on the land, and agricultural output accounted for sixty per cent of the total national product.

The strain of war

Russia had remained an autocratic monarchy. The establishment of the State Duma, which the Tsar had been forced to accept during the first Russian revolution of 1905-07, had turned out to be no more than the semblance of a parliament. Even the bourgeoisie, let alone the working people in the population, were debarred from taking part in 'high politics'. The real power in the state was in the hands of the monarchy, which represented primarily the interests of the small and politically conservative class of courtiers and landowners. Civil rights were practically non-existent. All this naturally acted as a brake on the country's advancement and had a negative effect on all aspects of its life. The industrial bourgeoisie, though they disliked the situation in which they found themselves and could not come to terms with the 'extremes' of reactionary policy, still lacked the resolution to enter into open battle with the monarchy, fearing a violent upheaval by the masses, who had already demonstrated their strength in the first Russian revolution. The activity of the bourgeois parties did not go farther than modest parliamentary opposition in the Duma.

The first months of war had already shown that the Russian economy was not capable of satisfying the demands placed on it by the war. It was immediately affected by the call-up into the army which in the course of the war snatched 15,000,000 able-bodied men out of industry and agriculture. The stocks of arms and ammunition in the war department's stores were quickly used up, and industry could not make good the losses. Attempts on the part of the government to introduce controls over the economy and to mobilize industry for war production brought no substantial results and served in the end only to speed the collapse of the economic structure.

The exhaustion and gradual running down of the economy soon became apparent. Businesses were closed down one after the other. In 1915 alone 573 factories and mills stopped work. Only half the total number of plants were operating throughout the war. Production began to drop in the most important branches of the economy. By 1916 36 of the 151 blast-furnaces which the Russian iron and steel industry had at the beginning of the war had been shut down. The whole of the output of the iron and steel industry went to meet war needs, and this had a disastrous effect on those branches of industry which were not connected with the war. The country began to experience a fuel crisis, and a considerable proportion of the country's industrial plants came to a standstill through lack of fuel.

Transport, that most important element in the economy, was in a state of paralysis. At the beginning of 1916 there were 150,000 truck-loads of goods waiting to be moved on the railways. Five hundred and seventy-five railway stations were no longer capable of handling any goods at all. In the port at Archangel, through which communications were maintained with the Allies, the crates of goods literally sank into the ground under the weight of the fresh deliveries of various kinds of machinery and equipment piled on top of them. As a result of the disorganization of transport, there were food shortages in the towns of central Russia as early as 1915, while at the same time thousands of tons of grain, meat, and butter were rotting away at railway stations in Siberia. Following the February Revolution the former chairman of the council of ministers, B.V.Stürmer, said in his evidence before the special commission of investigation: 'There were so many trucks blocking the lines that we had to tip some of them down the embankments to move the ones that arrived later.'

The country's financial system was also disorganized. The conduct of the war involved enormous expenditure, which the normal pre-war budget was quite unable to cover. Increased taxes and the launching of domestic loans did not make up for the losses. The government had to resort to foreign loans and to increasing the circulation of paper money without adequate gold backing. This soon led to a fall in the value of the rouble, the disorganization of the whole financial system, and to an exceptional rise in the cost of living.

The war also had a very bad effect on agriculture. Large-scale mobilization left the countryside without man-power, while the requisitioning of horses deprived it of draught animals. Even before the war the manufacture of agricultural machinery had not been a very flourishing branch of industry. Now it came to a complete standstill, as did the production of chemical fertilizers. The result of all this was a sharp fall in the output of every kind of agricultural produce. The threat of famine hung over the country.

Rumblings of discontent

As is always the case, it was not the propertied classes but the labouring sections of the population who felt the burden and the deprivations of war soonest and most harshly.

As early as December 1914 prices of manufactured goods had risen by twenty-five per cent compared with 1913, while prices of consumer goods were up by eleven per cent. In 1915 prices of manufactured goods rose by 145 per cent and food prices rose by 122 per cent. Wage increases lagged far behind the catastrophic rise in the cost of living. Between 1914 and 1916 the working man's earnings rose on the average by 100 per cent, while prices of foodstuffs and consumer goods increased by from 300 per cent to 500 per cent.

Millions of ordinary people were bound sooner or later to ask themselves the purpose of all their suffering, the end to which they were sacrificing their lives and their health. They saw, and they knew from their own experience, that the war would bring them nothing but misfortune and privation. The first burst of patriotic excitement

quickly passed, to be replaced among the masses of the people by a smouldering discontent with the war and the whole policy of Tsarism. This elemental discontent and ferment among the masses sought an outlet, and it could not fail ultimately to take the form of open revolt against the existing order. The police prepared alarming reports about the growth of the strike movement, which had practically ceased in the first months of the war. A particularly serious wave of strikes swept the country in June 1915, when 80,000 workers downed tools. A strike of textile workers in Kostroma in the same month ended in a bloody clash with the police. In August the blood of the working people was again flowing, when troops fired at a demonstration of textile workers in Ivanovo-Voznesensk. These repressive actions on the part of the authorities evoked indignation among the workers in many towns throughout the country. In September 200,000 working people were on strike.

The Russian revolutionary movement, which had gained great experience in the struggle against Tsarism during the years 1905-07, began once again, after a brief lull, to gather strength and to become a major factor in public life.

The growth of anti-war feeling was further encouraged by Russia's experiences in the war itself. Russian troops ended the campaign of 1914 in a state of extreme exhaustion. They had suffered great losses. The army had lost half a million men, and the situation with regard to the supply of arms and ammunition was bad. Reinforcements arriving at the fronts remained in their transports because there were no rifles to arm them with. The situation was just as bad when it came to providing the army with uniforms and food. 'We go about in ragged uniforms, and without boots. I have to go practically barefoot, just in my socks,' one soldier wrote home. 'Our infantry is so poor, they march in home-made boots', wrote another. This sort of thing could not fail to have its effect on the army's fighting qualities. Cases of desertion became more frequent; there was a sharp increase in the number of soldiers who deliberately inflicted wounds on themselves so as to avoid military service; and on every side could be heard comments on the futility of the war in which Russia's foolish rulers had involved the country.

Meanwhile, having failed to achieve a victory in the 1914 campaign, the German high command decided to concentrate its efforts on the Russian front, to inflict a defeat on Russia, put her out of the war, and then turn all its forces against Great Britain and France. In the first days of May 1915 German and Austrian troops succeeded in making a breach in the Russian front in Galicia, forced the Russians to withdraw from Galicia and Poland, and seized part of Russian territory. Altogether in the summer campaign of 1915 the Germans achieved several major successes, while the Russians suffered enormous losses, which now totalled, since the beginning of the war, no less than 3,400,000 men. Of these 300,000 were killed and 1,500,000 officers and men were taken prisoner.

Patriotic alarm

These defeats at the front brought about a sudden change in the relations between the bourgeois circles, for which the State Duma provided a platform, and the ruling group at the top. Hopes that the monarchy would be able to organize a victorious war, put an end to revolutionary ferment and, finally, involve the bourgeoisie in the business of governing the country were not borne out. 'Patriotic enthusiasm' gave way to 'patriotic alarm'.

The military machine turned out to be incapable of carrying out the tasks which faced it. Ominous signs of popular revolt became ever more evident. Efforts on the part of bourgeois circles to put their relations with the authorities on a proper business-like footing met with no success.

As they acquired a steadily increasing importance in the country's economy, the Russian bourgeoisie tried to find a place for themselves at the centre of the country's administration and to influence policy in the way they wanted it to go. In the first days of June 1915 a conference was held in Petrograd, as St Petersburg was now called in deference to anti-German feelings, of representatives of trade and industry to consider questions connected with the adaptation of industry to wartime needs. The conference decided to set up war industry committees which were to become one of the political centres of the bourgeoisie, in the same way as had the unions of the zemstvos and town councils which

had been set up in the summer of 1914. From the very beginning these unions tried to interfere in the business of running the country's economy, but all their efforts were brought to nothing by the government, and were limited to rendering help to the sick and wounded. The leader of the central war industry committee was the energetic and determined A.I.Guchkov, the recognized leader of the upper bourgeoisie and one of the organizers of the Octobrist Party (the party of rich bourgeoisie and landowners formed in October 1905 which supported the Tsardom).

One of the principal demands put forward by the bourgeois community at the Petrograd conference was that the State Duma should be called into session. Since the beginning of the war the Duma had met on only two occasions – in August 1914, in connection with the outbreak of war, and in February 1915, for the formal approval of the budget. This did not suit the bourgeoisie in the least, because it regarded the Duma as the one institution able to exert pressure on the government. 'The State Duma,' said P.N.Milyukov, leader of the Kadet Party (Constitutional Democrats), at one of its meetings, 'is the only organizational centre of the national mind and will, the only institution which is capable of standing up to the bureaucracy.'

Insistent demands that the Duma should be summoned went along with a further demand that the government itself should be re-formed. The liberal bourgeoisie, in the form of the Kadet Party, was not prepared at that time to announce as part of its programme the demand for a 'responsible ministry', since it considered it possible to make do with changes in the membership of the council of ministers. After all, to enter into open battle with the authorities would have meant appealing to the masses and giving rein to the forces of revolution, which the bourgeoisie feared no less than reaction. The frequent introduction of new people into the cabinet, 'to ensure the correct organization of the home front, the maintenance of internal peace in the country, and close collaboration between the government and the public', was put forward as a condition for summoning the Duma and one that would ensure that it worked effectively.

Defeats at the front and the growth of bourgeois opposition forced Nicholas II to make certain concessions. A group of people was formed within the council of ministers itself who considered it necessary to pay more attention to 'public opinion' and to adopt a more moderate policy towards the 'public'. It became ever more clear that the council of ministers could not, in its original composition, meet the Duma without coming into sharp conflict with it.

N.A.Maklakov, the minister for internal affairs, was the first to be dismissed. He was succeeded by Prince N.V.Shcherbatov, a member of the State Council, whom the liberal press described as 'a conservative in the European sense of the word', who respected the law and was opposed to any 'extremes'. However restrained were the opinions of the new minister, the departure of Maklakov gave great satisfaction to the middle classes who considered him, together with the war minister V.A.Sukhomlinov, one of the men principally responsible for all the troubles and misfortunes besetting Russia. Sukhomlinov, who had been in charge of the war department since 1909, was next to go after Maklakov. He was replaced by General A.A.Polivanov.

The campaign against Sukhomlinov had begun in the spring of 1915 when Russian troops were swept out of Galicia. His opponents dug up everything they could find against the minister: his compromising marriage with the wife of a Kiev landowner, Butovich, his close relations with a very doubtful character called Altschuller, and his connection with the German spy Myasoyedov, who was hanged in the winter of 1915. The word 'treachery' was heard ever more frequently in connection with the war minister. One way or another Sukhomlinov had to be got rid of. As for Polivanov, it would have been difficult to think of a better sop to throw to the Duma. Even when he had been assistant to the war minister, from 1908 to 1912, Polivanov had won popularity for himself in the Duma through his ability to get along with the bourgeoisie, and had earned the reputation of being a 'leftist' in bureaucratic circles. The Tsar had no special liking for the man, but force of circumstances obliged him to agree to his appointment.

Two others to be dismissed were I.G. Shcheglovitov, the minister of justice, and V.K.Sabler, chief procurator of the Holy Synod (head of the church council). The former was replaced by A.A.Khvostov and the latter by A.D.Samarin, both completely conservative in their views but lacking the regard of the empress Alexandra Fedorovna and Rasputin, which was in itself an excellent recommendation in the eyes of the bourgeoisie. These appointments were the only changes which were made in the composition of the government on the eve of the new session of the Duma. The council of ministers was still headed by the very elderly I.L.Goremykin, who had long since earned himself the reputation of being an extreme reactionary and a persecutor of any kind of liberalism. The danger of a conflict between the 're-formed' government and the bourgeoisie had not been removed. This was fully confirmed by the events which followed.

The Duma meets again

It was on 1st August 1915, the first anniversary of the outbreak of war, that the State Duma met again. And, while the right-wing groups, representing the landowners, continued as before to give the government their unconditional support, the bourgeois section of the Duma made no attempt to conceal its dissatisfaction. The bourgeoisie was not interested in bringing about a radical change in the policy of the Tsarist regime. Their only concern was to introduce into the government people enjoying the unquestioned confidence of the middle classes, and able to represent their interests in it. A substantial majority of the factions in the Duma united around the slogan of 'a ministry of confidence'. The liberal Moscow newspaper *Morning Russia* even published a commentary under the heading 'A Cabinet of Defence' in which it gave the possible composition of a government which would suit the bourgeoisie. M.V.Rodzyanko, the Octobrist and chairman of the Duma, was named as premier, another Octobrist, A.I.Guchkov, was named as minister for internal affairs, and the Kadet P.N.Milyukov was named as minister for foreign affairs.

On 22nd August negotiations between the leaders of the factions in the Duma concluded, with the signature of a formal agreement among them. In this way a

'Progressive Bloc' came into being in the Duma–an organization which was fated to become the political centre of the whole bourgeois opposition. Many of the twenty-five members of its bureau– P.N.Milyukov, A.I.Shingarev, N.V.Nekrasov, V.N. Lvov, I.V.Godnev, and others later became members of the Provisional Government. Six of the factions in the Duma, from the Kadets to the 'progressive' nationalists– 236 of the 442 deputies– entered the Bloc. Those who remained outside it were, on the right, the extreme right wing and the nationalists, and, on the left, the Social Democrats and the Mensheviks, and the Socialist Revolutionaries. The Socialist Revolutionaries, though they did not formally enter the Bloc, always voted with it and supported its policies.

As for the Bloc's programme, its central point was the demand for the formation of a 'government of confidence'. The remaining points in it were very modest: changes in the personnel of local administration, a partial amnesty for religious and political offences, some initial steps towards removing the restrictions placed on Jews, the revival of trade-union activities, and so forth. There was nothing in it likely to undermine the power of the Tsar. The programme was not aimed at bringing about a breach with Tsarism, but at achieving agreement with it on the basis of liberal reforms and the organization of a victorious war with Germany. The central idea in the minds of the leaders of the Bloc was to bring about such a state of affairs in the country as would exclude the very possibility of a revolutionary outburst, which appeared to them as equivalent to utter chaos and anarchy. But even this extremely modest programme was too much for the monarchy. The formation in the Duma of a stable majority in opposition would put an end to any possibility of manoeuvring between the extreme flanks of the bourgeois landowning parties as the ruling group at the top had done since the first Russian revolution. Less than a month passed before the Tsar signed a decree dissolving the Duma. 'They brushed aside the hand that was offered them,' P.N.Milyukov recalled later. 'The conflict between the monarchy on the one hand and the representatives of the people and society on the other became an open breach.'

The leader of the opposition was obviously exaggerating when he said that what happened in September marked the end of efforts to find a compromise solution. Even before the final breach came about the bourgeoisie had more than once offered its hand to the government in the hope of arriving at a solution acceptable to both sides. But so far the monarchy had been quite unyielding. The sudden swing of policy away from partial concessions to reaction was not limited simply to the dissolution of the Duma. Before that Nicholas II had dismissed the Grand Duke Nikolay Nikolayevich from the post of supreme commander-in-chief and put himself in his place. It was quite clear that this change was in no way dictated by military considerations. Nicholas was not a military man and could be no more than a decorative figurehead. His assumption of the post of 'supremo' was unquestionably a political move, inspired by the Empress and Rasputin. Neither the objections of his ministers nor protests from members of the Tsar's family could make him alter his decision. The pro-German group led by the Empress Alexandra Fedorovna did its best to divert Nicholas's attention from domestic affairs, to put an end to the insignificant concessions being made to society, and to set course towards a separate peace with Germany.

This time it turned out to be not so difficult to deal with the bourgeois opposition. The concluding session of the Duma lasted just three minutes. The deputies listened in deathly silence to the words of the imperial decree pronouncing their dissolution, shouted a loyal 'hurrah', and dispersed without a single word of protest. They had too great a fear of the 'street', of any movement on the part of the masses, to embark on any open opposition to the whole system of government which had led the country to disaster.

Months passed. There were no signs of an end to the war, and the situation in the country became ever more tense. At the beginning of 1916 the strike movement flared up again on an even greater scale. Every year the working people of Russia went on strike in memory of those who died in the 'Bloody Sunday' of 22nd January 1905. On this occasion the traditional January strike assumed enormous proportions. In Petrograd alone at least 100,000 people went on strike. Neither police arrests nor the use of the army to guard the largest factories brought the movement to an end. The ferment of revolution spread even into the army. The people of the villages, crushed by the excessive requisitions, also began to raise their voice. An enormous quantity of inflammatory material was piling up, ready to burst into flame at any moment. The landowners and farmers began to be haunted by the memory of the things that had happened to them in 1905.

Government of tumblers

The Tsar and his government were helpless in the face of the approaching catastrophe. They were unable to avert either the economic crisis or the advance of the revolutionary movement. In their search for a solution the Tsar and those close to him had recourse to the dismissal of persons holding major posts in the government, and this only threw into relief the crisis among the men at the top, who had lost the capacity to assess the situation in a realistic and sober manner.

I.L.Goremykin, the prime minister, that faithful defender of the foundations of the monarchy, was the first to lose his seat in the government. It was the same story as in the summer of 1915. There was no question of any real change of policy in the direction of 'liberalization' but only of giving the Duma an opportunity to work off its anger on those who were dismissed. Goremykin's place was taken by the sixty-eight-year-old B.V.Stürmer, whose political reputation left no doubt that there was no reason to expect any changes for the better. Moreover, Stürmer's pro-German sentiments were widely known, which made it seem not unreasonable to regard his appointment as evidence of the Tsar's desire to start negotiations for a separate peace with Germany. The news was received with unconcealed alarm by the French and British ambassadors. Sir George Buchanan wrote: 'Possessed of only a second-class mind, having no experience of statesmanship, concerned exclusively with his own personal interests, and distinguished by his capacity to flatter and his extreme ambition, he owed his new appointment to the fact that he was a friend of Rasputin and enjoyed the support of the crowd of intriguers around the empress.'

There is a vast literature in existence about Rasputin. Innumerable legends have grown up around the name of that semi-literate peasant from Tobolsk who became the uncrowned ruler of Russia. Maybe not everything in them is true, but there can be no question about the tremendous influence which 'our friend', as the Tsarina called him, exerted on the country's policy. There can also be no doubt but that the emergence of Rasputin and all that Rasputin meant became possible only at a time when the whole system of autocracy was in decline and in a state of decomposition and decay.

Goremykin's replacement by Stürmer was not the end of the business. Sazonov, the minister for foreign affairs, and Polivanov, the war minister, were retired soon afterwards – both men with whom the bourgeoisie had had great hopes of collaborating. A real game of 'ministerial leap-frog' now began. Ministers were replaced one after the other. Two and a half years of war saw the removal of four prime ministers, six ministers of internal affairs, three war ministers, and three foreign ministers, among others. No wonder the council of ministers came to be known as the 'government of tumblers'.

The summer of 1916 appeared to bring some easing of the situation. There was some improvement in the way things were going at the front. Thanks to the energetic measures taken by General A. A. Brusilov, the talented commander of the south-western front, Russian troops had not only succeeded in breaching the Austro-German front in the Lutsk region, but also in turning the break-through into a strategic advance which led to the rout of the Austro-Hungarian army. The advance on the south-western front forced the Germans to transfer dozens of reserve divisions to the east and halt their attacks on Verdun. The Austrians were obliged, in their turn, to bring their advance in Italy to a halt. But, in the absence of support from the other fronts, the Russian advance did not affect the outcome of the war. Towards the end of the summer the armies had reverted again to trench warfare.

The tension within the country also appeared to have relaxed. There was some reduction in the wave of strikes by the proletariat, which raised hopes that the revolutionary movement would be suppressed. It is true that a spontaneous uprising broke out in the south-eastern regions of the country—in Kazakhstan and Central Asia—among the local population, which had been reduced to a state of desperation, but the government did not at first attach serious importance to it. The bourgeois opposition also appeared to have quietened down. In any case the so-called 'voluntary' organizations set up to manage wartime supplies and industry, who had formed the core of bourgeois opposition, now worked hard to establish contact with government circles.

Disaster strikes

But all this was no more than a passing, and to a large extent illusory, period of calm. By the end of 1916 the catastrophic situation in which Russia found herself became fully apparent. Disaster struck every single branch of the economy. Industry, transport, finance, and agriculture were all in a state of complete collapse. One of the signs of the general economic disorganization was the severe food crisis which broke out in the autumn of 1916.

The grave economic situation, the severe shortage of foodstuffs, and the government's repressive measures led the workers to embark on a new wave of strikes on a larger scale than anything that had gone before.

In September 1916 the strike movement had not involved more than 50,000 working people. But in October 1916 nearly 200,000 people were on strike. No less than 1,542 strikes were recorded in the course of 1916, involving more than 1,000,000 workers— that is, roughly twice as many as in the previous year, 1915. The strikes assumed an ever larger scale and the strikers' demands became ever more insistent, with workers being drawn into the movement from the remoter districts as well as from the industrial centres. It was not, however, simply that the strike movement became a real mass movement, embracing the whole country; in the final months of 1916 it took on a clearly defined political colouring. What had been a struggle for the satisfaction of limited economic demands became a struggle against the existing system

of monarchic rule, against the war and those who had brought it on the people.

The Bolshevik section of the Russian Social Democratic Party played a great part in giving this spontaneous movement an organized and purposeful character. The Bolshevik party had close links with the more advanced, most intelligent, and most active part of the working class, and it was in effect the only one of the socialist parties to have fought consistently and uncompromisingly against the war and against Tsarism. It regarded revolution and a complete break with the domestic and foreign policy of Tsarism as the only way to save the country from ruin.

But the party had to work in unbelievably difficult conditions. As far back as November 1914 the five Bolshevik deputies to the State Duma had been arrested and exiled to Siberia, and this meant the loss of a most important legal centre and platform from which the party could put forward its views. It therefore had to operate in conditions of complete secrecy. But despite all the difficulties and dangers besetting the Bolsheviks at every step, their revolutionary anti-war activity was not halted. It is sufficient to say that, from the beginning of the war and up to the February Revolution, local branches of the party put out more than 600 leaflets totalling around 2,000,000 copies. They were published in eighty towns and distributed throughout the country. In Petrograd, Moscow, Riga, Kharkov, and several other towns the Bolsheviks even succeeded in publishing illegal newspapers, and although these publications were usually soon shut down by the police, they did their job of educating the people and exposing the truth about the war. Bolshevik slogans became steadily more popular with the masses who were exhausted by the intolerable burden of war.

Despite the obstacles to communication put up by the censor, news of the tense situation at home, and of the growth of the revolutionary mood and revolutionary ferment got through to the front. Indignation grew in the army at the actions of the government and the Tsar in bringing the country to disaster. Instead of being an instrument for pacifying and suppressing the emancipation movement, the army became a part of the revolutionary people, ready for an assault on a regime which had outlived its day.

'We shall be crushed'

The ruling and owning classes found themselves faced with an inexorably approaching revolutionary explosion. Both the supporters of the Tsarist system and the opposition-minded bourgeoisie started feverishly to look for a way out of the crisis. The state in which the ruling group at the top found themselves towards the end of 1916 can be described in one word — isolation. They were isolated even from those classes and social groups whose interests they had represented and defended for many long years. Even the landowners, that most conservative of all the classes in Russian society, backed away from the group of intriguers around the throne who were all heavily under the baleful influence of Rasputin. Significantly, even V.M.Purishkevich, one of the most violent reactionaries and an opponent of any kind of freedom, who hated the liberals hardly less than he did the revolutionaries, appealed publicly for the Tsar's attention to be drawn to the 'terrible reality' and for Russia to be 'rid of Rasputin and supporters of Rasputin, both big and small'. The landowners wanted to preserve the monarchy, but not in the person of the indecisive and weak-willed Nicholas II, who was surrounded by rogues and careerists and who 'decided' on policies at the dictation of his wife and the black-bearded 'monk' Rasputin. In such circumstances there remained only one thing for the intriguers at the court to do: to carry the policy of repression to the very extreme and at the same time to conclude a separate peace with Germany as quickly as possible and, with the help of their old friend 'Willy', Wilhelm II of Germany, to put an end once and for all to both the 'revolutionary infection' and the liberals. This is the path on which the clique at the court decided. From autumn 1916 efforts to get talks going with the German government were transferred to the realm of practical politics.

The possibility of such a solution to the situation in no way suited the Russian bourgeoisie, for it would only prevent them from achieving the objectives at which they were aiming in the war, and they feared the political consequences of such a step for the country's internal order. The class which dominated the country economically could not, and certainly did not want to, find itself cut off from the centre of power. On this issue the bourgeoisie had a large and very important account to settle with the monarchy, and to achieve this long-cherished aim they were ready to resort to anything — anything, that is, except an appeal to the masses.

Fear of the masses, the fear of revolution, pushed the bourgeois opposition into making sharp attacks on a government which was incapable of dealing with revolution. But that same fear forced them at the same time to refuse to enter into conflict with the government. They feared that harsh words spoken in the State Duma might serve as a spark to start the conflagration which would destroy the throne, the government, and the bourgeoisie itself. It was V.V. Shulgin, one of the leaders of the Progressive Bloc, who put the situation remarkably neatly when he said: 'The crowd is pushing us in the back. . . . We are being pushed and we have to move, though we resist as far as the strength lies in us, but all the same we must move. . . . If we stop moving we shall be crushed, the crowd will break through and rush for that thing which we are trying to preserve — to preserve, despite all our protests, complaints, and reproaches — and that thing is power.'

The hopelessness of the situation became more apparent every day. Nicholas remained deaf to appeals by members of the Duma and the more reasonable of his officials. Neither he nor the clique of maniacs grouped so tightly around him would retreat a single step from the reactionary course they had set in domestic affairs and insisted on working for the conclusion of a separate peace with Germany. But outside the palace, in the working-class districts, the tide of popular discontent was rising and was ready at any moment to reach the flood. It was in these conditions that the bourgeoisie, having lost faith in the possibility of 'persuading' the monarchy to make concessions, embarked on the preparation of a palace revolution. The idea of such a step had been broached some time previously. One evening in the autumn of 1915 when one of the usual attempts to come to an agreement with the government had failed, a member of the Bloc said 'I am relying on 23rd March'. More than one hundred years before, on 23rd March 1801, conspirators had murdered Paul I and enthroned a new emperor. This was the recollection of men who could not and would not fight the Tsarist regime together with and at the head of the people. But at that time it was just talk.

In the autumn of 1916, however, such a solution turned out to be the only one possible. Leaders of the Progressive Bloc and of the bourgeois voluntary organizations joined the circle of conspirators. Generals Krymov, Denikin, Ruzsky, and others were also drawn into the affair. According to A.I.Guchkov, one of the active participants in the plot, it was proposed to seize the imperial train between GHQ and Tsarskoye Selo with the help of reliable guards' units, to force Nicholas to abdicate, then with the same forces to arrest the government in Petrograd, and then to announce what had taken place. If the Tsar refused to sign the abdication, his 'physical removal' would have to be carried out, as Denikin wrote later. Those were the plans and the immediate future would show how practicable they were.

The murder of Rasputin

On the frosty night of 30th December one more event occurred which was an interesting and not insignificant page in the historical drama which unfolded towards the end of 1916. On that night Grigory Rasputin was murdered in Prince Felix Yusupov's private residence in Petrograd by a small group of conspirators, Yusupov himself, Grand Duke Dmitry Pavlovich, and the deputy V.M.Purishkevich. Although the direct participants in the murder were few, behind them stood a wide circle of men interested in the elimination of the all-powerful favourite of the imperial couple. The idea of removing Rasputin and the Empress from affairs had been debated in aristocratic circles from the beginning of 1916, and towards the autumn of 1916 the idea began to assume its final form.

After Rasputin's murder the wife of the chairman of the Duma, Rodzyanko, wrote to Princess Yusupova: 'I am told that there are 106 persons under suspicion . . .' It was not, however, only the aristocracy, but members of the Duma too who were drawn into the conspiracy against the 'monk'. Quite apart from Purishkevich, a direct part

was played in the preparations for the murder by V.A.Maklakov, a prominent member of the Kadet Party and brother of the former minister for internal affairs. It was he who gave the conspirators the potassium cynanide which they put in the food and into the madeira with which Rasputin was to be 'entertained'. It was he also who gave Felix Yusupov 'just in case' a rubber truncheon, which, incidentally, came in useful. A few days before the murder Purishkevich told his friend V.V.Shulgin about what was being planned. Other members of the Duma must also have known about it.

The drama which took place in the Yusupov mansion became public knowledge on the following day, when the body was hauled out of the Moyka into which it had been thrown. The Empress was beside herself and demanded severe punishment for the murderers. But Nicholas did not care to go very far, since it was found that members of the imperial household were involved in the affair. The Grand Duke Dmitry Pavlovich was exiled to Persia. Felix Yusupov was banished to his own estate in the Kursk *guberniya,* and Purishkevich, without any let or hindrance, got into his own hospital train and set off for the front. The Grand Duke Nikolay Mikhaylovich, who was also exiled as one of the people mixed up in the affair, wrote in his diary: 'Alexandra Fedorovna is triumphant, but I wonder if the wretched woman will remain in power very long.'

The murder of Rasputin, which was part of the general conspiracy against Nicholas II, was an attempt to save the monarchy in the 'old Russian way', and, as V.Shulgin very shrewdly pointed out, it was a 'profoundly monarchistic act'. But in itself it could change nothing and save nothing. The whole Rasputin affair had sunk roots deep into every part of the organism of the state. As though in reply to the murder, there followed a further series of reshuffles in the government. The position of chairman of the council of ministers was taken by the last premier of a Tsarist government, the weak-willed and decrepit Prince N.D.Golitsyn. The Romanov empire was rushing headlong downhill. It was the beginning of 1917, a year of revolution. *(Translation)*

Overthrow of the Tsar

David Floyd

The murder of Rasputin did nothing to restore the fortunes of the monarchy or increase popular respect for the Tsar. If the removal of her 'friend' lessened the influence of the Tsarina on the nation's affairs, Nicholas showed no inclination to listen to the advice of the more liberal-minded of his ministers; on the contrary, he turned his back on both the government and the Duma and relied on his own imagined authority, exercised primarily through his minister of the interior, Protopopov, who dominated the administration.

Throughout January 1917 the storm of discontent gathered as the war continued to take its toll on the economy. Food shortages and a rapidly rising cost of living resulted in widespread unrest among the industrial workers, particularly in Petrograd and Moscow. There were as many strikes in the first six weeks of 1917 as in the whole of the previous year. But discontent with the monarchy and the conduct of affairs extended far beyond the working-class and the peasantry, into the ranks of the middle class, the progressive deputies to the Duma, the military leaders, and even the Grand Dukes themselves.

In January the Grand Duke Alexander wrote to Nicholas to persuade him to set up a government capable of inspiring confidence in the people. 'The Tsar alone cannot govern a country like Russia', he wrote. Rodzyanko, the chairman of the Duma, warned the Tsar on 20th January that 'very serious outbreaks' were to be expected. Russia wanted a change of government because, he said, 'there is not one honest man left in your entourage; all the decent people have either been dismissed or have left.' But such warnings had no effect on the obstinate and auto-cratic Tsar. His only reaction to the increasing threat of trouble in the capital was, on 19th February, to place the city under the command of General Khabalov, who was made directly responsible to the Tsar alone for the maintenance of order. The Petrograd garrison was reinforced and equipped with artillery and machine guns. For the first fortnight of February an uneasy peace reigned in the capital; the police and the military appeared to have the situation in hand.

But Rodzyanko knew that the situation was deteriorating, and on 23rd February he told the Tsar he thought a revolution was possible. Nicholas brushed the warning aside and told Rodzyanko that, if the deputies did not watch their words, the Duma would be dissolved. It met, nevertheless, in the Tauride Palace on 27th February, and the government, expecting trouble during the session, stiffened the censorship, arrested all potential trouble-makers and braced itself against the popular wrath. Tension in the capital rose. A week later, on 7th March, the Tsar decided to leave Petrograd for the army GHQ in Mogilev.

Next day disorders broke out in the capital which were to lead only a week later to the overthrow of the monarchy. Apparently without any central direction, and initially without any clear political aims, the workers of several large factories in Petrograd came out on strike. Their action was mainly a protest at the breakdown in food supplies, but the nervous reaction of the authorities soon turned industrial and economic unrest into political protest.

Troops were sent immediately to back up the police in the working-class districts of the city, with the result that next day, 9th March, the disturbances spread to the whole city, and protests against the continuation of the war were added to the demand for bread. The central Nevsky Prospect became a mass of marching people, some of whom were now shouting 'Down with the autocracy!'. By the third day, a Saturday, 10th March, a quarter of a million workers were on strike, the city's transport was at a standstill, and the authorities were desperate.

But for Nicholas the situation presented no problem. From the remoteness of Mogilev he cabled Khabalov: 'I order that the disorders in the capital shall be ended tomorrow; they are quite inadmissible at this grave moment of war with Germany and Austria'. But Khabalov, faced with the whole population in revolt, was no longer in a position to carry out his monarch's orders.

It was not that he had scruples about using force to suppress the revolt. The fact was that he could no longer be sure he had the necessary force at his disposal, and that what he had was rapidly slipping out of his control. The normally trustworthy and brutal Cossacks he had sent into action against the crowds had simply been lost among the demonstrators. The police had started to fire on the crowds, only to incense them still further and make them bolder in their resistance to brutality. The wave of arrests had continued, but the protest movement had no obvious outstanding leaders, and Khabalov could not arrest the whole population.

An affair of the capital

What ultimately decided the outcome of the revolt and the collapse of the regime, however, was the defection of the soldiery to the side of the revolution. It began with isolated cases of 'fraternization' between soldiers and demonstrators on the Sunday of 11th March and then spread like wildfire throughout the Petrograd garrison, so that by the Monday evening the whole force of 150,000 men had disintegrated. And when, in despair, Khabalov formed a special detachment of a thousand picked men and sent them into action, they too disappeared among the crowds. Whole regiments revolted, shot their officers, and threw in their lot with the working people, taking their weapons with them. On the Monday evening the workers seized the arsenal, where they found 40,000 rifles which were quickly distributed round the city.

The government was helpless. A decision to have Khabalov declare a state of siege was rendered ineffective by the fact that the authorities no longer controlled a printing press on which the declaration could be produced. The Duma was equally incapable of taking effective action. When Rodzyanko, its chairman, sent the Tsar a message saying that the fate of both the country and the monarchy was in the balance, and that urgent steps must be taken,

Nicholas replied on 11th March with an order dissolving the Duma. Though it feared to defy the Tsar outright, the Duma remained in informal session and on 12th March elected a 'Provisional Committee' of twelve members, including representatives of the Progressive Bloc, with Alexander Kerensky, the Socialist Revolutionary, and Chkheidze, the Social Democrat. The Committee assumed the impossible task of 'restoring order'.

On the same day and in the same place — the Tauride Palace — another new body came into existence. It was the Petrograd Soviet (Council) of Workers' and Soldiers' Deputies, representing in a rough and ready way the interests of the rebelling factory workers, soldiers, and 'democratic and socialist parties and groups'. Such real power as could be said to exist in the capital — and in the country as a whole — was now vested in these two *ad hoc* bodies; the central government and the administration of the country had already collapsed. On the morning of Tuesday, 13th March, the Soviet issued a news sheet — *Izvestya* (News) — bearing a proclamation announcing its existence and calling on the people everywhere to take the conduct of affairs into their own hands. 'We shall fight to wipe out the old system completely and to summon a constituent assembly elected on the basis of universal, equal, secret, and direct suffrage.'

Rodzyanko kept the Tsar informed of the disastrous course events had taken, urging him first to institute reforms and then, when the situation worsened, to abdicate in the interests of the monarchy as an institution. Isolated and deprived of friends and supporters, Nicholas made his decision with surprising speed and lack of emotion. He left Mogilev to return to his capital on 13th March, but was diverted by the revolutionaries to Pskov. There, still in his royal train, on 15th March, he signed a document abdicating the throne in favour of his son Alexey and nominating his brother, the Grand Duke Michael, as regent. But before the two delegates from the Duma could reach Pskov Nicholas had changed his mind and finally handed them a document which said: 'We hereby transmit our succession to our brother, the Grand Duke Michael, and give him our blessing for his accession to the throne of the Russian empire'.

But, after some thought, Michael refused, and with that the Russian monarchy was at an end. It had been overthrown by the ordinary people of the capital with extraordinary little loss of life. Total casualties were estimated at less than 1,500, with less than 200 people killed. As Trotsky later pointed out, the revolution was almost exclusively an affair of the capital. 'The rest of the country simply followed its lead. Nowhere in the country were there any popular groups, parties, institutions, or military units prepared to defend the old regime. Neither at the front nor in the rear was there to be found a brigade or a regiment ready to fight for Nicholas II.'

The same day as Nicholas signed his act of abdication a Provisional Government was set up in Petrograd. But it had to share power with the Soviet, and the conflict between the two bodies was to occupy the next eight months of 1917.

Kerensky's Summer

George Katkov

On 15th March 1917 a large crowd of dishevelled soldiers, enthusiastic intellectuals and students, and glum-looking workers – a typical cross-section of the people who had been demonstrating in the streets of the capital since 8th March – milled around in the large Catherine Hall of the Tauride Palace in Petrograd. They knew that after the prorogation of the Duma by the Tsar on 11th March, a committee of its members had replaced the Tsarist government, which had ceased to exist after failing to control street rioting and the mutiny of a part of the Petrograd garrison.

The leader of the influential liberal Kadets (Constitutional Democrats), and of the parliamentary opposition to the autocratic regime, P.N.Milyukov, addressed the crowd, announcing that a Provisional Government had been set up and giving the names of its members. He was warmly applauded when he said that A.F.Kerensky (the head of the socialist, though non-Marxist, Labour faction of the Duma) had agreed to become minister of justice. Names of other ministers were greeted with surprise and disappointment in the crowd, and Milyukov was asked 'who appointed you?'. He answered that the Government had been appointed 'by the Revolution itself'. The crowd's suspicions were not allayed, and Milyukov was asked what was to become of the dynasty. When he disclosed the plan – which never materialized – to proclaim the infant Alexey Tsar under the regency of his uncle, indignant cries rose from the audience and Milyukov was at pains to point out the necessity of a gradual and orderly transition to a democratic regime. As soon as things were settled, he said, the people would elect a Constituent

Assembly by universal suffrage, and it would decide on the future of Russia. Democratic freedoms would be introduced immediately. This assurance restored the original delirious enthusiasm of the crowd and Milyukov was given an ovation and carried shoulder high from the hall.

Some eight months later, after a turbulent history in which the Provisional Government underwent at least four major reconstructions, only three of its original members remained in office. But the convocation of a Constituent Assembly, to secure a democratic regime for Russia, was still the aim of the government and the polling date was fixed for 28th November.

The footsteps of fate

Yet on 7th November 1917, on the eve of the elections to the Assembly, which could be expected to endorse its policy, the Provisional Government was reduced to a dozen distraught men, huddled in a room of the Winter Palace, with nothing but a group of cadet officers and a women's battalion to defend them from an assault of Red Guards and rebellious sailors led by Bolsheviks. As the approaching steps of the invaders rang through the endless corridors of the Winter Palace, the Provisional Government was asked whether the officer cadets should fight to prevent its falling into the hands of the rebels. The answer was that the Provisional Government would rather yield to force than have blood shed in its defence. And so the ministers were arrested and led off to prison in the Peter and Paul Fortress. The premier, Kerensky, was not among them; a few hours earlier he had left the capital to rally troops to fight the Bolshevik rebellion.

We may well ask what happened in these eight months to reduce the Provisional Government by the beginning of November to this sorry state of isolation and impotence. The Provisional Government was still vested with powers far exceeding those of the last Tsar; it still had under its orders a rudimentary administrative apparatus inherited from the old regime; Kerensky, the prime minister, was supreme commander of all Russian armed forces, at least in name. All political parties, except the monarchists and the Bolsheviks, were in some way represented in the government. And yet the people, whose will and aspirations the Provisional Government claimed to champion, made no move to support it in its hour of trial and Kerensky could not muster the few hundred soldiers needed to suppress the weak and poorly organized Bolshevik rising.

The government which was formed under the wavering and diffident leadership of Prince Lvov in March 1917, combined the highest executive power with full legislative powers; and it soon arrogated to itself the right to interfere with the judiciary. Its claim that it was entitled to act as head of state, replacing the monarch and assuming all his prerogatives, soon brought it into conflict with Finland and other national minorities of the Russian empire.

This concentration of power, the government claimed, was necessary for introducing reforms — such as putting an end to national and religious discrimination — without which no democratic election to the Constituent Assembly was possible. In fact there was more to it than that: the collapse of the monarchy and the promise of every kind of democratic liberty brought about spontaneous changes and threatened a general landslide in the social and legal structures of the country. In order to stem and canalize this revolutionary flood the Provisional Government sought to give a legal form to what were then known as 'the conquests of the Revolution'. But the former revolutionary parties which surfaced from the underground after the Revolution now insisted on 'taking it farther' by destroying every vestige of the 'accursed past' in the shape of state and public institutions, all privileges and prerogatives, and social and army discipline. The popular appeal of these parties, known as the 'revolutionary democracy', was considerable; they dominated the soviets (councils) of workers', soldiers', and peasants' deputies, as well as the trade unions and other rapidly proliferating professional organizations; and they infiltrated the newly formed soldiers' and officers' committees of army units, both at the front and in the rear. Their demands went beyond what the Provisional Government could concede if it was to maintain the fighting capacity of the army and guarantee freedom of decision to the future Constituent Assembly.

It soon became obvious that a certain amount of coercion was necessary to prevent anarchy. For this, however, the Provisional Government lacked both the will and the means of enforcement. The Provisional Government admitted its reluctance to resort to force when, in mid-March, it received the first news of agrarian disorders in the countryside. The government instructed its commissars that force could not be used against looting and rioting peasants: agrarian anarchy was to be prevented by local land committees who were instructed to prepare for the nationalization of land and exhort the peasants to be patient and await the decision of the Constituent Assembly on land reform. Similarly, when told that a mob of soldiers, whose train had been delayed at a station for half an hour, had beaten the station-master to death, the Provisional Government ordered the railway authorities to explain to the soldiers that delays were sometimes necessary to prevent collisions and loss of life to passengers. At the same time, the Provisional Government, though it had forbidden them, acquiesced in the unauthorized arrests of former Tsarist officials and army officers; some of them were kept for months in inhuman conditions in the naval fortress of Kronstadt in defiance of government orders.

Disorder in the army

Even if the government had been willing to use force in order to prevent 'revolutionary democracy' from interfering with its administration, it would have found itself without the proper means of doing so. One of the first actions of the Provisional Government had been to disband the police and gendarmerie — bodies which had been guilty of persecuting revolutionaries in the past. Local authorities were told to organize a 'people's militia' for the maintenance of order; but, lacking experience and training, this militia proved to be unequal to the task. There remained the army, but the Provisional Government was unlucky in its relations with the armed forces right from the beginning. In Petrograd, which had a garrison of just under 200,000, the Provisional Government pledged itself in its first proclamation not to transfer any of the units stationed in the capital. This was done to reassure those soldiers who had rebelled against the Tsar and had even killed some of their officers, and who were, therefore, afraid of possible reprisals if they were sent to the front.

The Provisional Government's control

over the army was further weakened by the publication on 15th March of the notorious Order No. I of the Petrograd Soviet. This introduced elected soldiers' committees in all units and boldly stated that orders of the Duma Committee were only to be obeyed when they conformed to the instructions of the Petrograd Soviet. Although addressed only to the troops in the capital, Order No. I soon set the pattern for 'revolutionizing' other garrisons and front-line units. It also put the armed forces in the capital virtually under the command of the Soviet, strengthening it against the Provisional Government.

Nor was the Provisional Government successful in its efforts to control the army in the field or in establishing good working relations with the successive supreme commanders whom it appointed. The 'revolutionary democracy' suspected the army, which had played no part in the February Revolution, of a lukewarm attitude to it, and was bent on 'revolutionizing' the rank and file. These efforts, made on the eve of a general offensive agreed upon with the Allies, met with resistance both from GHQ and from officers at the front. A horde of propagandists from Petrograd and other revolutionary centres in the rear descended on the troops at the front where they undermined discipline and relations between officers and men.

The first minister of war of the Provisional Government, Guchkov, did nothing to remedy this situation. He himself had fomented discontent and organized sedition against the Tsar before the Revolution, and now, on becoming minister of war, he started a purge of the officers' corps without consideration for the stability so necessary for an army in the field. Dismissed officers crowded GHQ, where they were joined by others who had lost their commands on the insistence of soldiers' committees infiltrated by Bolsheviks. They were resentful and bitter men looking for leadership in order to stop the process of 'deepening' the Revolution.

The Petrograd Soviet had issued at the end of March an appeal to all warring nations to conclude an early peace renouncing any aggressive war aims. The Provisional Government endorsed this in principle, at the same time assuring the Allies, through the minister of foreign affairs, Milyukov, that Russia would stand by its international obligations. Out of this hardly explicit discrepancy a conflict arose between Milyukov and Kerensky—who felt himself the representative of the Soviet attitude—and this led at the beginning of May to open demonstrations, some demanding and some opposing the resignation of the ministers of foreign affairs and war, Milyukov and Guchkov. Units of the Petrograd garrison took part in one of the demonstrations demanding their resignation. General Kornilov, whom the government had appointed commander-in-chief in Petrograd, had not authorized the demonstration and asked the government to support him and stop the Petrograd Soviet interfering with the troops under his command. Having failed to get satisfaction he resigned his post and returned to the army at the front. His departure coincided with the first ministerial crisis of the Provisional Government. Guchkov and Milyukov resigned, less as a concession to popular clamour than as a result of profound dissensions and divided loyalties inside the government itself. Party ties between Kadet and other liberal ministers proved less binding than the allegiance of some of them to the political masonic organization to which they belonged. Milyukov found himself 'betrayed' by his former deputy party chairman, Nekrasov, who like other Russian masons supported Kerensky in his conflict with Milyukov. His and Guchkov's departure opened the way to the entry of socialists into the cabinet and Kerensky emerged as the initiator of the first coalition government, in which he became minister of war.

Kerensky decided to instil into the army a new revolutionary spirit and a new faith in the justice of the cause for which it was fighting. The supreme commander, General Alexeyev, was dismissed without further ceremony and replaced by General Brusilov, known for his famous offensive in 1916. Kerensky instituted government commissars attached to various headquarters of the army, who would assist officers in all political matters, including contacts with soldiers' committees, and keep the government informed of the state of the army. The main weapon in Kerensky's arsenal was direct contact with the soldiers at army delegates' conferences and meetings of army units. Mesmerizing them by his eloquence, he impressed on his listeners that they had now become the army of a new-born world. With the proclamation of a 'just peace without annexations or indemnities' by the Revolutionary Democracy of Russia the war, he said, had changed its purpose and had obtained a new historical significance. The soldiers had always readily sacrificed their lives under the knout wielded by the tyrannical, autocratic regime. With how much more enthusiasm would they do so now, Kerensky claimed, as free citizens of a liberated Russia which would lead the world towards a new and happier era. Kerensky's exhortations flattered the other ranks who greeted him with ovations. The officers naturally resented being accused of having used cruel methods in the past to force their men to fight for the unworthy cause of the Rasputin clique: but they were willing to put up with anything which might raise the morale of the army.

When, however, the order for the offensive was given on 26th June, Bolshevik propaganda, supported by a fraternization campaign cleverly carried on by the German high command, proved stronger than Kerensky's oratory; soldiers' committees units at company, regiment, or even divisional level discussed battle orders and questioned their commanders' decisions to take the offensive in a war which supposedly had no aggressive aim. After an initial success, mainly due to patriotic volunteer detachments, the offensive collapsed ignominiously through the defection of whole units. The entire 11th Army deserted the front, lynching its officers, disrupting communications, looting, raping, and burning down whole villages. General Kornilov, who had been transferred from Petrograd to the south-western front, demanded that the government should call off the offensive and reintroduce the death penalty at the front as an emergency measure. In this he was supported by the government commissars attached to the units under his command, in particular by Savinkov, a Socialist Revolutionary (like Kerensky), and a former leading terrorist. In view of the desperate situation the Provisional Government not only met all Kornilov's demands but appointed him supreme commander-in-chief.

The need for a return to sanity in the army was forcefully impressed on the Provisional Government by the Bolshevik attempt to seize power on 16th July, which coincided with the German break-through in Galicia. The Bolsheviks organized a so-called 'spontaneous' peaceful, armed demonstration under the slogan 'All power to the soviets'. The Soviet and the Provisional Government, unable to rely on the capital's garrison, were faced with a rebellion of armed workers organized as Red Guards and Kronstadt sailors who had invaded the capital at the call of the Bolsheviks. The position of the Provisional Government, however, was quickly restored by the arrival of a few reliable troops from the front. But it had been a narrow escape, and the first coalition government never recovered from the shock.

The abortive Bolshevik coup sharpened the internal dissensions in the government between those who, like Prince Lvov and the Kadets, wanted to strengthen the authority of the government and those who, like Kerensky and the representatives of 'revolutionary democracy', sought to increase the government's popularity by initiating further revolutionary changes. On 20th July Prince Lvov and the Kadet ministers resigned, leaving Kerensky with the task of reconstructing the cabinet. After trying unsuccessfully for a whole fortnight to bridge the differences between the liberal and socialist camps, Kerensky himself resigned on 3rd August, leaving the country virtually without leadership. That same night his deputy, Nekrasov, summoned a memorable joint session of the cabinet and the party leaders in the Malachite Hall of the Winter Palace. After a torrent of speeches it was decided to accept and support a cabinet of Kerensky's choice. He was left free to define his programme, and the ministers were to be free of all control by their party committees and the Soviet.

Except for some changes of personnel, of which the departure of the 'defensist' Menshevik, Tsereteli, was the most important, the second coalition government differed little from the first. Premier Kerensky remained minister of war, but appointed Savinkov, the commissar at Kornilov's headquarters, to be his deputy in charge of the ministry. In practice, delicate political questions were dealt with by an unofficial 'inner cabinet', consisting of Kerensky, the minister of foreign affairs, Tereshchenko, and Nekrasov.

Kornilov himself, on accepting his appointment from a shaky and divided government, demanded that there should be no interference with his choice of commanding officers and claimed that as supreme commander he would be responsible only to his conscience and to the nation as a whole. He then urged the government to take the measures which he claimed were indispensable for restoring order in the country and the fighting capacity of the army. These measures, including the death penalty for sedition in the rear, spelled a curtailment of democratic freedoms – for instance freedom of propaganda, which was one of the 'conquests of the revolution' – which were deemed essential by the soviets for free elections. Kerensky hesitated, in spite of pressure from Savinkov who mediated between him and the supreme commander. Kerensky hoped to overcome the split in public opinion between supporters of Kornilov and those of the soviets at a monster debating rally, the Moscow State Conference, in late August. The conference only showed the chasm, presaging the possibility of civil war.

The Kornilov affair

After the failure of the conference, Kerensky decided, without consulting his cabinet, to approach Kornilov through Savinkov, asking for his loyal co-operation in fighting anarchy. He agreed to meet Kornilov's demands. If the publication of the new laws embodying them caused an outbreak of civil disobedience in Petrograd, it was to be suppressed by troops which Kornilov was to send to the capital and put at the disposal of the Provisional Government. A cavalry army corps was concentrated at the approaches to Petrograd on 9th September. Kerensky had not yet, however, put Kornilov's demands before the cabinet, despite Savinkov's urging. On 8th September he promised to do so that night, when the cabinet was to meet. Shortly before the meeting was due to start, Vladimir Lvov, a former member of the first two Provisional Government cabinets, an unbalanced, excitable, and totally irresponsible character, came to see Kerensky. Lvov had been acting as a self-appointed go-between posing both to Kerensky and Kornilov as a secret emissary of the other. From Lvov's confused and mendacious statement, Kerensky understood that Kornilov was now demanding the resignation of the government and the surrender of all power to him. The idea of a 'Kornilov ultimatum' henceforth dominated all Kerensky's actions at the helm of his foundering government, and was to be the major theme of everything he wrote during the next fifty years. When the cabinet met the same night, Kerensky denounced Kornilov's 'plot' and ultimatum and asked for a free hand to deal with the insubordination of the supreme commander. The ministers who had been given no information of the preceding developments, agreed, but, horrified by the new ordeal threatening Russia, handed in their resignations. Just before the meeting, Kerensky had been communicating with Kornilov by teleprinter, but failed to ascertain whether what he understood Lvov to have reported was correct: he feigned, however, to be in full agreement with Kornilov and promised to join him at GHQ the next day. Instead, after the cabinet meeting, he sent a curt informal telegram dismissing Kornilov from his post and summoning him to Petrograd. Indignantly Kornilov refused to submit and was backed by the overwhelming majority of his senior officers. The conflict had still not been made public and might have been settled, had not a proclamation of the Provisional Government denouncing Kornilov been released to the press prematurely. Kornilov appealed to the country, calling Kerensky's account a complete lie.

Neither Kornilov nor Kerensky disposed of sufficient forces to escalate their exchange of insults into a real trial of strength. The troops sent by Kornilov to Petrograd believed that they were going to support the Provisional Government and were shocked by the announcement of Kornilov's alleged mutiny: they refused to obey marching orders and broke up in confusion. Kerensky was not effectively in control of the capital's garrison; this and the Kronstadt sailors' detachments, ostensibly under the orders of the Soviet, were in fact controlled by the Bolsheviks.

The Kornilov affair petered out ingloriously. Kornilov called the whole thing off and allowed himself to be put under arrest. Kerensky appointed himself supreme commander. A committee of lawyers set up to investigate the alleged mutiny was appalled by the double-crossing and the lack of dignity on all sides, but was unable to complete its work before the collapse of the Provisional Government.

Kerensky is right in referring to the Kornilov affair as the 'prelude to Bolshevism'. But the return of the Bolsheviks to active politics and their final victory in November were made possible not by Kornilov's pressure on the Provisional Government to strengthen its authority, nor by his military measures to back up that pressure, nor even by his angry gesture of insubordination on being suddenly without warning denounced as a mutineer. These actions of Kornilov, who was widely supported by public opinion outside Soviet circles — even by socialists, such as Plekhanov and Argunov — were all brought about by the indecision and procrastination of Kerensky and his closest friends in the cabinet. While conceding in secret negotiations the urgency of the measures demanded by Kornilov, Kerensky seems never to have wanted to implement them and was relieved when he could interpret V.Lvov's incoherent innuendoes as an insolent and arrogant ultimatum by Kornilov, which released him from the promise he had just made to Savinkov to comply with the supreme commander's demands. Kerensky has only himself to blame that both his contemporaries and historians have shown so little sympathy with his behaviour at that critical moment. For after it he was considered by the officers' corps and the Kadets as one who had provoked Kornilov to rise in open rebellion and by the 'revolutionary democracy' as one who had had secret dealings with counter-revolutionary conspirators. Not even the ties binding Nekrasov, Kerensky, and Tereshchenko survived the Kornilov episode, and Nekrasov had to leave the government.

Kerensky's assumption of the highest functions of the state could not restore his popularity nor strengthen his authority. His attempt at establishing a kind of pre-parliament, from appointed representatives of various party and public organizations, led to a final humiliation: when Kerensky demanded full powers from the pre-parliament to deal with the incipient Bolshevik rising, he was rebuffed and told by the representatives of 'revolutionary democracy' that the Bolsheviks could best be fought by the acceptance of a government programme of immediate revolutionary reforms — reforms of a kind which were supposed to be decided by the future Constituent Assembly. Two days after his defeat in the pre-parliament, Kerensky was in flight from the Bolsheviks and the members of his government were incarcerated in the Peter and Paul Fortress.

Part six · 1917: The Allies' Worst Year

1916 had been a terrible year for Great Britain and France, yet 1917 was to be even blacker. On the Western Front the massive battles around Verdun and the Somme had decimated the manhood of all the contestants and caused desperate weariness and disillusion among soldiers and civilians alike. In the east the Brusilov offensive had ended uselessly after a promising start; in Italy successive attacks on the Isonzo had proved fruitless; and at sea the U-boats had given a foretaste of the havoc which they might wreak if once allowed to operate completely without check. There was some relief that the winter had not brought fighting of quite the same scale and intensity which had developed in the early days of Verdun and the Somme, but the scars left by these struggles had not healed before the Entente had fresh strains to bear while it was still enfeebled by the disasters of 1916.

None of the Allied leaders on the Western Front were able to think of any way of ending the apparently endless stalemate except by using the same methods which already proved totally ineffective. Joffre was replaced by the aggressive and self-confident Nivelle who was convinced that he had the formula for success – yet another massive assault, but this time with the French bearing the brunt of the fighting on a relatively narrow front.

The offensive was ill-conceived and foolhardy, taking place over difficult terrain against a well-prepared enemy. It failed disastrously and in its wake the French soldier suddenly turned against his leaders. For six months in the spring of 1917 much of the French army was in a state of mutiny and the Allied front in a state of disarray. Fortunately, swift action to impose total secrecy prevented the Germans from dis-

covering the extent of the disorder, and firm action by Pétain, the hero of Verdun, succeeded in nursing the morale of his soldiers back into shape.

Much was later made of the part which the mutinies played in influencing British strategy in 1917, but the main plan of the attacks on the Western Front had been decided well before the seriousness of the French army mutinies had become clear. After the failure of Nivelle's offensive and the collapse of Russia there was general agreement that offensive operations must continue to pin down the German forces. Most leaders felt that all that could be achieved was the continual wearing down and gradual exhaustion of the enemy, but Haig was still convinced that he could break through in the Ypres area and totally defeat the German army.

Despite increasing evidence of the collapse of the French army, and the scepticism of most of his colleagues, Haig launched his grandiose offensive with aims no less sweeping than all the previous assaults that had failed so completely. He had been convinced by his Intelligence that the Germans were so near to collapse that a high level of fighting would finally shatter them. For months the British army struggled forward in a series of ghastly battles which are usually known collectively as 'Passchendaele'. Little was achieved except massive slaughter. Haig had been misled as to the strength of German powers of resistance, and his later insistence that the attacks were continued to shield the French is difficult to uphold on available evidence and does not excuse the scale of assaults which were obviously achieving little except the deaths of thousands of Allied troops.

This grim struggle on the Western Front

has to be seen against a wider background of events, all of which were deeply depressing for the Allied leaders. The entry of the United States into the war as a result of the unrestricted U-boat campaign had brought a brief moment of exaltation, but this was soon forgotten in the long weary wait for the American armies to arrive in France. In the East, Russia became more and more obviously a spent force. During the winter of 1916, strikes and unrest showed that the home front was collapsing. In March the Tsar abdicated and a provisional government was set up. In June an attempt by the coalition government under Kerensky to launch another major offensive failed hopelessly because the troops deserted en masse, and finally in November another revolution gave all power to the Bolshevik party with its avowed intention of taking Russia out of the war as swiftly as possible.

In the Balkans, Rumania had been overrun, and the Allied army in Salonika seemed to be incapable of taking any sort of decisive action which might relieve pressure elsewhere.

Finally, in Italy, there came the final great military disaster of the year. Conrad, commander of the Austro-Hungarian forces, had long been obsessed with the need to launch a massive offensive which would eliminate the Italian front. For two years he had been held back by the reluctance of Germany to give any support to the assault, while the Italians battered away hopelessly with their morale sinking as each successive battle of the Isonzo brought no apparent gains. However, their persistence did force the Austrians and their ally to accept that they could not go on endlessly waiting to be attacked and that the best way to gain a breathing space would be to mount a major offensive. This they did at Caporetto. Aided by major errors of judgement on the Italian side, they swiftly punched a hole in the Italian front. As they did so the Italian army collapsed and nearly 500,000 soldiers just walked away from the battle with the unhurried determination that their war was over. When at last the retreat ended, the Italians had fallen back more than fifty miles, and their country, which had once been courted by all sides, now became a liability to her allies, needing the diversion of men and materials to keep her on her feet.

In many ways 1917 ended with apparent major gains for the Germans: they had succeeded in effectively ending their war on two fronts, and the troops which had been holding the Russians at bay for more than three years could now be brought back to reinforce the Western Front. Yet, despite appearances, the Allies could put something on the other side of the balance: the German home front was far more pressed by the blockade than the British, and the U-boats had failed to achieve the outright victory which had been essential. Now, with the United States firmly on the Allied side, the war could only end in a German defeat unless the German army attacked and won the war in the west before American numbers could begin to tell. The great offensive must come in the spring of 1918, and it must gain the decision which three and a half years of bitter fighting had failed to bring.

The French Army Mutinies

Douglas Johnson

These mutinies have been surrounded by the greatest mystery. For obvious reasons details were not made known at the time, and the suppression of information probably encouraged a number of wild rumours. The normal French tradition of not allowing archives to be consulted until fifty years have elapsed, together with certain unusual circumstances (such as the subsequent career of Marshal Pétain) meant that these mutinies could not be studied in any objective way, and the legend grew that here was one of the great mysteries of the war which would never be resolved because the story was too terrible to be revealed. However, the archives have now been made available and the whole affair has been examined with great objectivity by Guy Pedroncini, a French historian.

It should be remembered that the year of 1917 had opened with a number of promising peace proposals, such as that from President Wilson and that from Pope Benedict XV, which had come to nothing. But the most important event was the Russian revolution of March. Although the new government promised to continue the Russian war effort, it seemed likely that these events would strengthen the German position and the American declaration of war on 2nd April 1917 did not promise any immediate contribution to Allied strength. So far as the French were concerned little seemed to have been achieved. Battle after battle had failed to break the stalemate at the front; the heroism shown at the siege of Verdun or in the offensive on the Somme seemed to have yielded no results at all. Something approaching one and a half million Frenchmen were killed, missing, or captured, and the problem of replacing these losses was becoming acute. There was constant criticism of the military commanders by the politicians; and the generals were not alone in their anxiety concerning the unrest that was visible on the domestic front, much of which they attributed to the activities of socialists and pacifists.

One obvious way out of the impasse in which French strategy found itself was by a change of command. The commander-in-chief, Joffre, had lost the confidence of most. He was promoted to the rank of Marshal and was succeeded by Nivelle, an officer who had gained renown at the battle of Verdun. He was a supremely confident and articulate man, who believed that he had found a method of attack which would break the deadlock, by a combination of artillery power with infantry attack in depth and at speed. The fact that he was a Protestant and that he spoke good English were additional reasons to recommend his rapid promotion. He built up considerable forces and on 16th April 1917 the attack was launched on the Aisne. Many people, including the generals commanding the armies concerned, and the minister for war, Painlevé, had expressed doubts about the wisdom of this offensive. Nivelle had even offered his resignation, but it had not seemed possible to accept this and to cancel an important attack which was widely expected in the French army, especially in the atmosphere of Nivelle's self-confidence.

But everything that could go wrong did so. The Germans had already withdrawn to a strong defensive position, which put Nivelle's plan out of joint and which gave them large strategic reserves. Nivelle had circulated information about his plans, and important documents were captured by the enemy; German machine-gun fire decimated the advancing French; Nivelle found that his artillery was not as effective as he had expected; his tanks suffered heavy casualties; the medical services proved incapable of dealing with the vast numbers of wounded; the weather was bad; and above all, his collaborators quickly lost faith in the plan.

The first instance of mutiny appears to have taken place on the first day of the offensive, 16th April, when five soldiers and a corporal abandoned their position in the face of the enemy (five of them were subsequently sentenced to death but were reprieved). Another incident took place the next day when seventeen men abandoned their position and failed to take part in the attack (twelve of them were condemned to death and then reprieved). These were followed by a whole series of incidents which shook the French army and which Pétain and others were to describe as causing them the most anxious moments of the whole war. It did not appear impossible that the whole French army might collapse. These mutinies continued for some time, and although Pétain was to claim that they were over by October 1917 (by his victory at La Malmaison on 23rd October to be precise), a number of units continued to experience serious disciplinary troubles until January 1918. In all, according to the most recent calculations based on official records, it seems that there were some 250 incidents. About one fifth of the entire army was seriously affected; perhaps one third of the army does not seem to have known any form of mutiny at all; and the remainder varies between those units where there were some repeated instances of unrest and those where incidents were sparse and isolated. At first the mutinies were concentrated in the area of Nivelle's offensive, that is to say between Soissons and Aubérive, in the region of the Aisne. To the west of this region, where there was little fighting, everything was calm, and to the east, the incidents tended to be sporadic. As time went by the geographical distribution seems to have spread, and incidents are reported farther afield. But they are invariably associated with the offensive on the Aisne; they either affected troops who were being brought in to the area for the first time, or units which had been withdrawn from the fighting, and which, in some cases, were expecting to be sent back to the front.

The Internationale is sung

Obviously it is impossible to give an account of all these mutinies. Many have been described but there has been a great deal of inaccuracy in the descriptions. Often people have written from hearsay, or from their imaginations. If one wishes to give some sort of a representative account of the sort of incidents which occurred then a number of examples could be quoted. The incident on the 29th April at Mourmelon-le-Grand was one of the earliest. 200 men of an infantry regiment dispersed into the wood and were not present when their companies were sent off on renewed attacks against Téton. Most of these men appear to have returned spontaneously to their unit. But a number deserted and others hid. Only fifteen were tried for refusing to obey orders and of these six were condemned to death, although the sentences were never carried out.

One of the most famous incidents occurred a month later at Villers-sur-Fère. An infantry regiment (the 18th) which had been heavily engaged at the beginning of May, losing twenty officers and eight hundred and twenty-four men and having merited six hundred citations for bravery, was withdrawn from the front and rested. Because it had distinguished itself leave was promised on a large scale, but the promise was not, in fact, kept. 1,000 new men were drafted into the regiment, including a number of inexperienced officers. On 27th May, which was Whit Sunday, men from a neighbouring regiment came round and there was a good deal of drinking. During these celebrations the visitors, who came from a unit which had already had some disturbances, explained that there was a unit which had been due to move up to the front and which had refused. They suggested that the 18th Infantry Regiment would have to return because of this. That evening, the order was given for the 18th to prepare to return to the front. Several companies of men from the first and second battalions gathered together and discussed things excitedly, but they obeyed their officers when told to disperse. A short time later, however, they came together again and they explained to their colonel that they did not want to go back to the front, that they did not consider it was their turn. They claimed to have nothing against the colonel, and they even shouted 'Vive le colonel!' but they refused to obey his orders and some of them began to wander around the locality. There were some scuffles, some shots were fired, property was damaged and the Internationale was sung. Most of these men seem to have been from the second battalion since, shortly before midnight, the third battalion moved off, and after some trouble the first battalion followed. At 5 a.m. the next morning a detachment of gendarmes arrived at Villers-sur-Fère, and were confronted with eighty soldiers who refused to move and who threatened the gendarmes with their rifles. Only one shot was fired. Twenty soldiers then broke away from the others and said that they were ready to obey orders. The remaining sixty moved off to a small neighbouring town, escorted by the gendarmes. They claimed that they would take a train to Paris and they fired their rifles in the air. But at 7.30 a.m. they agreed to obey orders and they got into the waiting trucks. As a result of this, twelve soldiers and two corporals were court-martialled, on the charge of mutiny. A large number of witnesses were called, and although the contrary has often been maintained, it does seem as if the trial was careful and regular. Five soldiers were condemned to death, and although several officers put in pleas for all of them, only one was pardoned. Three were executed. The remaining prisoner, Corporal Moulia, who had earned two citations for bravery on the 5th May preceeding these incidents, escaped and was never recaptured. Quite recently it was claimed that he was still alive and living in France (although it had earlier been rumoured that he had made his way to South America). Two sentries were accused of negligence in allowing Moulia to escape and one of them was found guilty.

'Down with the war!'

There were further developments in a mutiny which took place at Coeuvres, a small town to the south-west of Soissons. This was used as a rest-camp for a number of units. At the end of May there were a number of demonstrations in the neighbourhood, and the commanding officer thought it wise to move one of the units, the 370th Infantry Regiment, out of Coeuvres. On the 2nd June the order to move was given at mid-day and it was accepted. But by 3 p.m. it was reported that two companies were refusing to obey the order. The men were respectful to their colonel, but obstinate. They claimed that there were too many shirkers who got out of joining up. They repeated rumours that the Americans were coming to France and were going to take jobs in the factories so that more French workers would be sent to the front and killed. They had heard too that women workers in the cities were being badly treated. Eventually about 600 men set off for Villers-Cotterets, saying that they were going to join up with some 15,000 men who were waiting for them somewhere in the forest and that they would then march on Paris. A good many fell away, and when the roll was called at Coeuvres it was discovered that 407 soldiers were absent. Without these men, on 3rd June the 370th Infantry Regiment moved off without any further difficulty. The mutineers seem to have wandered about in a state of some confusion, hoping to find some larger group to whom they could attach themselves. But they were not violent; they were worried about what would happen to them and repeatedly asked for promises that they would not be punished. But it was not until 4 a.m. on 8th June that they surrendered. Thirty-one were court-martialled, seventeen were condemned to death though only one was executed.

Sometimes the mutiny was both short and violent. In June, for example, at Beuvardes, one man in the 70th Chasseurs-à-Pied began to shout 'Down with the war! Long live the revolution! Down with the clergy!' He was rapidly joined by others, led by a corporal, and the cry of 'Long live Russia' was heard. Officers were unable to make themselves heard, and after breaking windows, setting fire to a hut and shooting at those who were trying to put the fire out, some 150 soldiers ran wildly about the town, and tried, unsuccessfully, to incite others to do likewise. But the next morning they came on parade and obeyed orders. Sometimes the mutiny was very particular, as with a battalion of the 308th Infantry Regiment, which refused to relieve another battalion because they would not be in their own section of the line. Some 250 men were involved. When a general came to speak to them they stood to attention, but explained their reasons. After six hours they accepted and obeyed orders. In this manifestation there was no disorder, no violence, and no shouting. On the other hand the countless incidents which took place in railway stations were often confined to the singing of the Internationale, the pulling of the communication cord, uncoupling the coaches, and the shouting of slogans in favour of peace, the Russians, even the Kaiser.

Pétain restores morale

A number of questions have to be answered concerning these mutinies. Firstly, is it possible to see any similarity amongst those mutineers who appeared before the courts? The answer here is quite straightforward. The men in question came from different parts of France, they included both young and old, married and unmarried, they had many different professions in their civilian existences. It is quite impossible to suggest that they came from any particular class. Secondly, is there any sign of these mutinies being organized, or at least inspired, by any political or social tendency? As is usually the case with any popular movement, such organization was alleged at the time, and often by the generals. They believed that pacifist literature was circulating amongst the troops and that when they had been in contact with civilians they were often under bad influences. It is certainly true that news of the strikes, and echoes of pacifist movements against the war, could well have had some effect. The suggestion that the authorities were being violent with female workers who went on strike seems to have influenced some of the mutineers. But it is noticeable that when there was a mutiny it was not accompanied by any fundamental pacifist or socialist action. Most frequently the authority of the officers and the needs of the war continued to be respected, except on one point: and that was invariably the refusal to go to a certain part of the front. To this must be added other considerations which were far from doctrinal, such as dissatisfaction about leave, or disappointment that certain promises about length of rest periods had not been kept. Thirdly, was there any real danger that the whole of the French army might have been affected? This is difficult to answer, but two features remain outstanding: that in units where incidents took place, there were always large numbers of men who were not affected; secondly, that the disaffection was often short-lived. In many cases the units concerned went on to take part in the battle. Sometimes all the excitement seems to have arisen from the most temporary of reasons: the men had been drinking.

The most likely overall explanation for these mutinies was that they were spontaneous protestations against a method of warfare. The terrible failure of Nivelle's offensive brought about a collective refusal to continue fighting in a manner which held out no hope of victory and which would only lead to a high rate of casualties. This was understood by Pétain who replaced Nivelle on 15th May 1917. The mutinies were not brought to an end by a bloody repression. Although over 400 were sentenced to death it is probable that not many more than twenty or thirty were actually executed. However, nearly 1,400 men were given sentences of more than five years' imprisonment. The only real way of ensuring that the mutinies did not recur was by proving that a successful offensive could be organized. And that was Pétain's achievement.

Passchendaele

Brian Bond

The name 'Passchendaele' applies, strictly speaking, to the last phase of the 3rd Ypres campaign of July-November 1917. But it is far more usual to find it used as a damning synonym for prolonged battles of attrition in the Flanders mud during the First World War. Half a century later, people are still arguing passionately about whether the offensive should ever have been undertaken in the first place, why it was allowed to go on for so long, and what effect it had on the course of the war as a whole.

On 15th November 1916 General Joseph Joffre, the French commander-in-chief, assembled a conference of the Entente military representatives at Chantilly to determine Anglo-French strategy for the coming year. He and Sir Douglas Haig, the British commander-in-chief, agreed that the attrition battles of the Somme and Verdun in 1916 had left the German army on the Western Front near to breaking point. Joffre feared that the French army could undertake only one more major offensive, but he hoped this would be decisive. He proposed a concerted offensive on all fronts in the spring of 1917 with the British cast for the leading role in the west. In December, however, General Joffre was replaced by the most junior of the French army commanders, General Robert Nivelle, who had persuaded both the French prime minister Aristide Briand and the British prime minister David Lloyd George that he could achieve a complete break-through in under forty-eight hours – a feat which had eluded both sides since September 1914. In Nivelle's plan the French were to strike the major blow on the Aisne sector, while Haig launched diversionary attacks near Arras and took over part of the French line south of the Somme.

Nivelle fails

In February and March 1917 the effective German director of strategy, General Erich Ludendorff, forestalled Nivelle's planned offensive for the spring by withdrawing between fifteen and twenty-two miles on a front of about seventy miles to a strong defensive position known – after the nominal commander – as the Hindenburg Line. Nivelle was reluctant to adjust his aims and – oblivious of the need for surprise – made no secret of his highly ambitious plan. The French offensive began on April 16th in an atmosphere of political and military mistrust between the Allies and lasted until May 7th. It penetrated up to four miles on a sixteen mile front, but this limited success contrasted too sharply with Nivelle's personal promises. Frustrated by failure, the French armies began to disintegrate. Long-festering grievances came to a head in mutinies that broke out in May and June in nearly half the units in the French army. General Henri-Philippe Pétain, the hero of Verdun, who replaced Nivelle on 15th May, quickly restored order, but also dropped strong hints that the French would have to remain largely on the defensive for the rest of the year until they could be backed up by American divisions and more tanks and heavy artillery. Meanwhile, after prolonging the gruelling battle at Arras to shield the French during their offensive on the Aisne, the British had to take a fresh look at the projected Flanders offensive in the light of conditions very different from those that had applied when the Allies had planned their strategy earlier in the year.

On May 4th, the French and British civilian war leaders and their military advisers met at Paris to revise their strategy after Nivelle's failure and the Russian February Revolution. The military chiefs agreed unanimously that offensive operations must be continued on the Western Front. Allied attacks, they believed, had already exhausted a large proportion of Germany's reserves and she must be prevented from throwing her full weight against either Russia or Italy. But, in the words of the chief of the imperial general staff, Sir William Robertson: 'It is no longer a question of aiming at breaking through the enemy's front and aiming at distant objectives. It is now a question of wearing down and exhausting the enemy's resistance. . . . We are all of the opinion that our object can be obtained by relentlessly attacking with limited objectives, while making the fullest use of our artillery. By this means we hope to gain our ends and with the minimum loss possible.' Both the British and French governments gave their approval to these recommendations. Before the seriousness of the French army mutinies began to be revealed to him early in June, the British commander-in-chief, Sir Douglas Haig, was already contemplating a bold stroke in Flanders very different in spirit from the cautious policy outlined above. The British government had laid down in November 1916 that the clearing of German submarine bases from the Flanders coast was a strategic objective of the first importance. Haig believed that such a break-through could be achieved from the Ypres salient, assisted by a supporting advance along the coast and an amphibious landing near Ostend. This aim rested on a very optimistic view of weakening German morale and reserves. It also assumed full French co-operation in supporting offensives, and this Pétain – who had just replaced Nivelle – promised on May 18th.

French support crumbles

But on 1st June the picture changed. General Debeney brought Haig a message from Pétain which mentioned euphemistically that 'the French army was in a bad state of discipline' and would not be able to fulfil the promise to attack in support of the opening of the British offensive at Ypres. A week later Pétain himself revealed in more detail the gravity of the situation but added that things were improving – as indeed they were. Thereafter, though hopes of really active French participation faded, Haig remained confident that the British army (assisted by six French divisions) could gain a major victory in Flanders. Lloyd George who, incidentally, knew even less about the breakdown of French discipline than Haig, grew increasingly sceptical about French co-operation. By 13th June he was harrying Robertson with a plan to remove twelve divisions from Haig's command 'to settle the war in Italy'. Robertson, a firm 'Westerner' who usually saw eye to eye with Haig, nevertheless cautioned him against 'large

and costly attacks without full co-operation by the French'; and on 13th June he wrote: 'Don't argue that you can finish the war this year, or that the German is already beaten. Argue that your plan [the concentration of all available troops and material on the Western Front] is the best plan – as it is – that no other would be *safe* let alone decisive, and then leave them to reject your advice and mine. They dare not do that'.

Why in these unpropitious circumstances, with even the loyal Robertson urging caution, did Haig decide to launch the Ypres offensive? It had long been apparent to the British commander-in-chief that the French war effort was flagging, so that the collapse of morale after Nivelle's abortive offensive came as no surprise to him. Judging from his diary entries Haig's motives were mixed: he wished to shield and encourage the French, but was also eager to gain a great victory for the British army which had now, at last, become the predominant partner. What needs to be stressed, however, is that the senior French commanders had no enthusiasm for a major offensive in Flanders designed to clear the Channel coast. Pétain, in fact, was opposed to any major offensive on the Western Front in 1917, and on 19th May he told Sir Henry Wilson – who had been attached to Nivelle's headquarters – that Haig's projected advance towards Ostend was certain to fail. General Ferdinand Foch, chief of the French general staff, was, if possible, even less encouraging and sarcastically referred to the campaign as 'a duck's march'.

Jellicoe's bombshell

The crucial incident, as far as the indecisive British war cabinet committee was concerned, occurred at a meeting on 19th June; namely 'Jellicoe's bombshell'. Not a single member of the committee, consisting of David Lloyd George, Andrew Bonar Law, Sir Alfred Milner, Lord Curzon, and General J.C.Smuts, favoured a major offensive on the Western Front in 1917, but the first sea lord shattered their assumption that time was on their side by declaring that German submarines were taking such a toll of merchant shipping that it would be impossible for Great Britain to continue the war into 1918. The Royal Navy would be in grave difficulty unless the Belgian coast could be cleared by the Army. Although this alarmist prediction suited Haig's own military views, it is very doubtful if he took Jellicoe's warning as seriously as is often supposed. As recently as 7th May Haig had described Jellicoe in a letter to his wife as 'an old woman', and after the meeting on 19th June he noted: 'No one present shared Jellicoe's view, and all seemed satisfied that the food reserves in Great Britain are adequate'. Even more revealingly General Charteris, Haig's chief of intelligence, recorded in his diary on 28th June: 'No one believed this [Jellicoe's] rather amazing view, but it had sufficient weight to make the Cabinet agree to our attack going on.'

The fundamental reason for Haig's determination to launch the Flanders offensive was, it seems clear, neither the necessity to shield the French nor to clear the Channel coast of enemy submarine bases. It was rather his conviction that the Germans were so near to collapse that six months of fighting at the present intensity on the Western Front could end the war that year. His confidence was increased by the auspicious beginning of operations on 7th June, when General Sir Herbert Plumer's 2nd Army – assisted by the explosion of nineteen enormous mines under the German front line – was brilliantly successful in carrying out a limited advance to seize the Messines Ridge and so straighten out the salient south of Ypres.

The interval of fifty-three days which then occurred between this successful preliminary advance and the opening of the main offensive on 31st July was to prove fatal. Haig's plans were not finally approved until 25th July and then only after the desirability of reinforcing the Italian Front in preference to Flanders had been endlessly debated by the war cabinet. Haig certainly had grounds for the bitter remark that he would have liked such confidence and support as the prime minister had recently given to Nivelle. More importantly however, as Haig's most recent biographer, John Terraine, has pointed out, Haig had intended even in the preliminary planning stage that there would be a delay of some six weeks between Messines and the main attack. Moreover, as the same author has written, Haig made his 'gravest and most fatal error' in 1917 of entrusting

the main role in the Flanders battle to the 5th Army commanded by General Sir Hubert Gough. It could be argued that Gough was the obvious choice for the bold strategy envisaged. He was, at forty-seven, the youngest army commander (whereas Plumer at sixty was by far the eldest); he was a cavalryman and a 'thruster' whereas Plumer – rather like Pétain – was noted for his cautious approach to planning and tactics, and his great concern to minimize casualties. Yet, quite apart from criticisms levelled at Gough and his staff for revising and mishandling Haig's plans, the transfer of command at such a time was bound to cause administrative complications and delays, particularly as the French contingent (General Anthoine's 1st Army) had to be fitted in on Gough's left between the 5th Army and Rawlinson's 4th Army on the coast.

Third Ypres opens

Like so many campaigns of the First World War, the actual operations of Third Ypres – which at last began on 31st July after a fortnight's preparatory bombardment and several postponements at the request of the army and corps commanders – soon ceased to bear much resemblance to the original plan. Essentially Haig had assumed that after eight days the 5th Army would have advanced fifteen miles and would have got control of the Ypres-Roulers-Thourout railway. Only when this was done would the 4th Army begin to attack along the coast, assisted by amphibious landings and, with Gough's support, would turn the German defences. Meanwhile the 2nd Army, after playing only a minor supporting role in the opening days, would advance to the north-east to secure the whole Passchendaele ridge.

This schedule proved to be far too optimistic. The campaign degenerated into a struggle for control of a plateau some sixty metres high. The operation fell into three distinct phases each containing three major actions. In the first phase Gough's 5th Army played the major role, and fought the battles of Pilckem Ridge (31st July), Gheluvelt Plateau (10th August) and Langemarck (16th August). The British had deliberately thrown away the chance of a surprise attack and they were hampered by driving rain. But despite this the first day, unlike the opening of the Somme battle on 1st July 1916, was far from being a disaster. The main assault was made by fourteen British and two French divisions supported by over 2,000 guns and howitzers on a very wide front of nearly twenty miles. The troops in the centre and to the left managed to reach the third and farthest target lines, and the only real check was suffered on the right of 5th Army's front-age. Here, from the Gheluvelt Plateau, specially trained German divisions made a fierce counter-attack, while the strength of the enemy's counter-bombardment during the battle as a whole showed how little real damage the British army's 'softening-up process' had done. Yet even if GHQ's initial assessment of British casualties at 15,000 was too low, it still compared very favourably with nearly 60,000 on the first day of the Somme.

Unfortunately atrocious weather had already begun to hamper further advance. On the first day the weather had completely prevented the British from using their superior air force for artillery reconnaissance. Far worse, as Colonel Fuller noted at Tank Corps headquarters: 'By July 31st from the Polygone de Zonnebeke through St Julien and northwards past Langemarck the Steenbeck had become a wide moat of liquid mud.' The British were unlucky in that the weather broke on the very first day. But meteorological reports for the previous eighty years could have showed GHQ that Flanders was notoriously wet in August. Rapidly, the swamp expanded, greatly assisted by the bombardment which had effectively destroyed the already precarious drainage system. Tank Corps headquarters daily sent a 'swamp map' to GHQ until instructed not to send any more. It seems unlikely that Haig ever saw these maps, and neither he nor Gough at this stage grasped the full significance of the appalling ground conditions. As early as 4th August General Charteris noted: 'All my fears about the weather have been realised. It has killed this attack. Every day's delay tells against us. We lose, hour by hour, the advantage of attack. . . . Even if the weather were to clear now, it will take days for the ground to harden, if indeed it ever can before the winter frost. . . . I went up to the front line this morning. Every brook is swollen and the ground is a quagmire. . . .'

Although there were some fine days in August, the weather and the terrain dictated the course of operations: Gough's second and third attempts to press forward (on 10th and 16th August) were thrown back by fierce counter-attacks. In his book *The Fifth Army*, Gough wrote that after 16th August he 'informed the Commander-in-Chief that tactical success was not possible, or would be too costly under such conditions, and advised that the attack should now be abandoned'. This advice was consistent with Lloyd George's prior condition that the attack should be discontinued if casualties were incommensurate with the amount of ground gained. In ignoring this condition and advice, Haig may still have been concerned to assist the French, but another explanation seems more likely. To call off the offensive at this stage would have entailed surrender to Lloyd George's nagging pressure to divert large forces to Italy. Haig and Robertson were fully agreed that such a move might result in losing the war on the Western Front.

Plumer plans carefully

At the end of August Haig transferred the main role in further operations from Gough to Plumer. This signified a return to a more cautious approach based on concentrating overwhelming artillery cover for each short infantry advance. Contrary to the caricature presented by his extreme critics, Haig did not favour remorseless tactical attrition once the initial attempt at a breakthrough had lost its impetus. Indeed he criticized Gough for ordering too many small attacks on isolated farmhouses and strong points since they were seldom effective and were too costly in lives and ammunition. It was ironic that although September was to be generally dry, in sharp contrast to August, Plumer spent the first three weeks of it meticulously preparing the next short step forward. The main sector of the offensive was limited to 4,000 yards with four divisions packed into the front line. The depth of the advance was restricted to 1,500 yards when a halt would be made to hold off counter-attacks and to await the ponderous advance of the huge mass of artillery. Plumer, and his chief of staff General Sir Charles Harington, calculated that the Passchendaele-Staden ridge could be cleared by four such limited attacks.

Anzac advance

The first of the three battles of the second phase—that of the Menin Road Ridge on 20th September—resulted in a clear victory. This was essentially an artillery triumph. General Birdwood, who commanded the 1st Anzac Corps in the battle, recalled that it was quite the best artillery barrage the Australians had ever seen. 'Creeping forward exactly according to plan, the barrage won the ground, while the infantry followed behind and occupied all the important points with a minimum of resistance.' The attack began at 5.40 am, and by mid-day the final objectives had been reached. The Germans were unable to counter-attack before 3.15 pm and were successfully beaten off. In bright sunshine British aircraft were able to report nearly four hundred objectives to the artillery. Ludendorff recorded: 'Another terrible assault was made on our lines on September 20th.... The enemy's onslaught was successful, which proved the superiority of the attack over the defence....'

Plumer's second offensive—at Polygon Wood on 26th September—closely resembled the Menin Road battle both in its careful preparation and encouraging results. It too was fought in good weather. Prince Rupprecht of Bavaria, commanding the German forces in Flanders, now began to worry about his defensive tactics and the scarcity of reserves. General Charteris, whose optimistic reports fed and fortified the convictions of his chief, noted that the situation at the end of September closely resembled that on the Somme the previous year. 'Now, as then, we had worn down the German resistance to very near breaking point; then as now the weather went against us. It is a race with time and a fight with the weather. One thing is certain, no other army but ours could fight on as we are fighting. D.H. is asking for the last ounce from it and getting a wonderful response.' Encouraged by Plumer's gains and Charteris's assessment of German exhaustion, Haig on 28th September revived the idea that the next advance should be immediately exploited. 'I am of the opinion that the enemy is tottering, and that a good vigorous blow might lead to decisive results. If we could destroy, or interrupt for 48 hours, the railway at Roulers there would probably be a débâcle, because the enemy would then have to rely on only one railway line for the supply of his troops between Ghent and the sea. . . .'

Plumer's third attack, the battle of Broodseinde on 4th October, followed the same pattern as the previous two: it was a heartening tactical victory but showed no signs of yielding those 'decisive results' which Haig had mentioned to his army commanders. It also marked the zenith of the artillery's contribution to the Third Ypres campaign before casualties, loss of guns, and the sheer impossibility of movement reduced its effectiveness. The Germans suffered particularly heavy casualties in this battle because the British barrage fell on five divisions just as they themselves were forming up to attack. This battle at last afforded the 2nd Army a foothold on the Passchendaele ridge. But a decision now had to be quickly made as to whether to halt the advance, particularly as the amphibious operations against Ostend had by now been abandoned and with them any real hope of reaching the Channel coast that year.

The day after Broodseinde Haig conferred with his army commanders. Charteris noted: 'We are far enough on now to stop for the winter, and there is much to be said for that. Unless we get fine weather for all this month, there is now no chance of clearing the coast. If we could be sure that the Germans would attack us here, it would be far better to stand fast. But they would probably be now only too glad to remain quiet here and try elsewhere. . . . Most of those at the conference, though willing to go on, would welcome a stop.'

Passchendaele—a 'porridge of mud'

The final phase of the campaign from 4th October to 6th November was fought for the almost obliterated village of Passchendaele, and as John Terraine rightly stresses, it 'bore throughout the characteristics which have generally been associated with the whole of it'. After the respite in September rain fell almost unceasingly through October and, with the continuing barrage, destroyed the few remaining signs of roads and tracks. By this time the whole area had reverted to a 'porridge of mud': mules and horses were known to have sunk beneath it with their loads; guns could find no solid ground to fire from; and it took sixteen bearers instead of two to carry each stretcher case the 4,000 yards to the field dressing stations. These conditions characterized the battle of Poelcapelle (9th October), the two battles for Passchendaele (12th and 26th October) and the eventual capture of the village by the Canadians on 6th November. For the troops it was, in Terraine's succinct phrase 'a month of dire misery and absolute frustration'. The Germans, as the defenders, at least had fewer problems of movement, but conditions were not much better for them. Ludendorff did not exaggerate when he wrote: 'It was no longer life at all. It was mere unspeakable suffering.'

Had Haig decided to halt after Brood-seinde it is unlikely that even the abominable conditions which characterized much of the fighting in August would have given the campaign its terrible reputation. Even Haig's warmest defenders have been obliged to look beyond the borders of Flanders in order to justify the Passchendaele battles. Thus Charteris wrote on 7th November: 'We have now got to where, with good weather, we should have been in early September, and with two months in front of us to carry on the operation and clear the coast. Now, from the purely local point of view, it is rather a barren victory, and if the home people decide on a defensive next year, it will be almost lives and labour thrown away.' The campaign had pushed out the Ypres salient to a maximum depth of seven miles and ended without capturing the whole Passchendaele-Staden ridge—which had been the first objective. Had Jellicoe's prediction—that Great Britain's ability to continue the war depended on the army clearing the Belgian coast—been well-founded the war would have been lost. Nor did the German IV Army voluntarily retire, as after the Somme campaign, to give the attackers the illusion of victory. Instead the Allies were obliged to defend the Ypres salient through yet another winter while the Germans were reinforced from the Eastern Front. The campaign had failed to realize Haig's hope of inflicting a decisive defeat on the German army.

Defending the disaster

There is a deep-rooted belief that Haig continued to fight at Passchendaele 'to save the French'. Haig's diaries contain several references in the summer to the need to 'encourage the French to keep fighting', and to give the Germans no opportunity to exploit their weakness. That the Germans were not actually planning to attack the French is no reflection on Haig's sincerity, though it was a surprising misjudgement by so experienced a staff officer. For the later phases however, Haig's own diaries reveal that his assessment of French capabilities changed. Thus on 1st September he noted: 'The result of our pressure at Ypres is shown by the slackening of German efforts on the Chemin des Dames, and the comparatively weak resistance which they have made to the French attack at Verdun. The French army has consequently had the quiet time desired by General Pétain in which to recover from the Nivelle offensive.' Moreover after Pétain had proved reluctant to attack in support of the British in September, Haig wrote to Robertson (on 8th October): 'Though the French cannot be expected to admit it officially, we know that the state of their armies and of the reserve manpower behind the armies is such that neither the French government nor the military authorities will venture to call on their troops for any further great and sustained offensive effort, at any rate before it becomes evident that the enemy's strength has been definitely and finally broken. Though they are staunch in defence and will carry out useful local offensives against limited objectives, the French armies would not respond to a call for more than that, and the authorities are well aware of it.'

Ten years after the campaign Haig asserted that Pétain had repeatedly urged him to attack 'on account of the awful state of the French troops'. But Haig meticulously recorded meetings with all important soldiers and statesmen and there is no suggestion that in his four meetings with Pétain *during the campaign* such a request was even hinted at. Pétain denied the post-war rumour, while Haig never mentioned this crucial piece of intelligence to the British government. Possibly Haig was confusing French requests during the Arras operations in April and May with later events in Flanders.

Counting the cost

It does not seem likely that by prolonging the Flanders offensive Haig gave indirect help to the Allies on other fronts. The Passchendaele phase prevented neither the final collapse of the Russian armies during the autumn of 1917 nor the rout of the Italians at Caporetto towards the end of October. Indeed Ludendorff was actually able to detach several divisions from the Western Front during the British offensive. There is plentiful evidence, including the war memoirs of Prince Rupprecht and Ludendorff, to support Haig's conviction that the Flanders attrition was having a serious effect on the IV Army's morale. But the Allies also suffered severely. Indeed, since the Germans were for the most part defending, and for much of the campaign adopted economical tactics of defence in depth from dispersed strong points, it would not be surprising if the attackers' morale was the more severely strained of the two. Moreover, Haig and his staff (though not Robertson) seem to have underrated the tonic effect on morale of Germany's tremendous victory over Russia which became ever more certain as the Flanders fighting dragged on inconclusively. Victory in the east gave the Germans vastly increased numbers—forty divisions were transferred to the Western Front from Russia and Rumania between 1st November and the middle of March and more followed later. And it gave them renewed hope—for a decisive blow in the spring of 1918.

Confusion and controversy over casualty statistics spring not only from gaps in the reliable first-hand sources against which differing estimates can be checked, but also from the different methods used by the belligerents in reckoning their losses. The British total of 245,000 killed and wounded given by the *British Official History* has been widely accepted as approximately correct, though in August 1918 the general staff gave the war cabinet an estimated total of just over 265,000, and Sir Basil Liddell Hart puts it as high as 300,000. The higher of the two German estimates (in their *Official History*) for their IV Army between 1st July and mid-November —covering a much wider front than the Ypres sector— is 202,000 including missing. The *German Medical History,* however, puts the total as low as 175,000. Even if the *British Official History* is accurate for British losses, and the higher German total is on the low side, it would still be impossible to argue that in the gruesome computation of casualties the third battle of Ypres had resulted in a clear gain for the British and French.

Haig misjudges Germany

Although at the time the gradual effects of attrition on enemy numbers and morale was regarded by GHQ as a valid reason for prolonging the battle, Haig himself appears to have been motivated chiefly by his persistent belief that Germany was near to total collapse. The baneful influence of General Charteris in sustaining this illusion has been widely recognized. 'In retrospect,' as one careful historian has written, 'we can say with certainty that General Charteris's estimates of enemy strength and morale were almost criminally optimistic, and that Haig was badly misled in basing his plans upon them.' Well-founded though this criticism is, it would be unjust to make the chief of intelligence a scapegoat for the commander-in-chief. Haig's extremely powerful and self-confident personality could be a source of a weakness as well as of strength: once his mind was made up on a subject he was not easily swayed. In his book *At G.H.Q.,* Charteris, without seeking to denigrate his former commander, cites more than one instance of Haig going well beyond his (already over-optimistic) intelligence reports and predictions. Haig's published papers, while they show clearly the size of the problems he faced also show that he just did not have the critical intelligence needed to judge objectively the enemy's capacity to go on fighting.

Civil-military relations, and Allied cooperation were strikingly defective during the campaign. Lloyd George and the war cabinet committee had little faith in Haig or his plan yet they neither felt able to replace him nor gave him their full support. In turn the commander-in-chief had no confidence in the prime minister and consequently appears to have withheld information about the French mutinies lest it should provide justification for weakening the Western Front. The French war minister and later prime minister, Paul Painlevé, gave Lloyd George stronger assurance than was proper that the French armies could and would give full support to Haig's offensive, and the commander-in-chief, Pétain, similarly made promises which he was reluctant to fulfil. Robertson was perhaps in the least enviable position, for in trying to restrain Lloyd George in his obsession with the Italian front and at the same time caution Haig against attempting too much in Flanders, he earned the former's hostility and the latter's suspicion. Haig did nothing to prevent his removal from office early in 1918.

Tragic waste
In legend, the battles of the Third Ypres campaign appear as nothing but ill-prepared bloodbaths. But they were more than this. Where conditions permitted they were carefully planned and skilfully executed. In particular Plumer's set-piece advances in June and September, and Pétain's operations on the Verdun sector, showed what could be achieved if objectives were strictly limited and superior artillery cover could be concentrated. Yet the Ypres salient was particularly unsuitable for an attempted break-through because of the precarious drainage system, the climate, and the terrain. Indeed, the faint possibility of a break-through to the Channel coast probably depended not only on the complete success of Gough's opening offensive, but also on the simultaneous launching of amphibious operations. Although the latter were carefully planned, the obstacles remained so formidable that it was probably a wise decision to cancel the operation when the land advance failed to make good progress.

The 1914-18 War still retains much of its terrible reputation because, on reflection, so much waste and suffering seem to have been exacted for no sufficient cause. Three years of indecisive slaughter, and the frailty of human judgements combined to produce the tragedy of the Third Ypres campaign in which the heroic endeavour of the troops appeared to yield only negligible results. No one, however, can be certain that the lives lost in Flanders were sacrificed in vain. Also, in changed circumstances – and because he had grown wiser from experience – Haig showed in 1918 that he could fight a more mobile and less costly campaign, culminating in the final victory which he had falsely anticipated in 1916 and 1917. 'Passchendaele', however, transcended the historical reality of an inconclusive campaign and became a potent historical myth. As such its influence reached far beyond 1918. Statesmen and soldiers are activated by such historical myths as well as by present realities. In 1939-45 Churchill and many of his generals had the memory of Passchendaele vividly before them: never again, they were resolved, should British troops be subjected to such a battle of attrition for anything short of national survival.

Caporetto

Ronald Seth

General Conrad von Hotzendorff, while chief of the Austrian general staff, had an obsession. He was firmly convinced that an all-out offensive against Italy, if properly equipped and timed, would be so effective that she would have to withdraw from the war. He had held this view long before Italy had joined the Allies, and time and again he had urged the old Emperor Franz Josef to let him launch such an attack on Italy. He argued that if she were reduced to military impotence she would more easily resist the temptation to jettison her neutrality in favour of the Allies. Franz Josef, who still believed that the rules governing the conduct of nations must be observed, and that a nation's neutrality must be respected unless she wantonly provoked retaliation, had refused to pander to his chief of staff's whim.

After Italy's entry into the war, Conrad had become more convinced than ever that his plan for a really massive attack on Italy was the only way in which the Italian Front could be eliminated. There is little doubt that if he had had sufficient forces to mount such an offensive without withdrawing the Austro-Hungarian troops on the Eastern Front opposite the Russians, and if he had not had to bow always to the will of the German high command, he would have acted as he proposed. But he had not enough forces; the Germans would not agree to his withdrawing his units on the Eastern Front; and every time he brought the matter up, they persistently maintained that they had no divisions to spare to give him the numbers which he needed.

But the longer the war went on, the more obsessed Conrad became. He flatly refused to believe that the unrestricted U-boat campaign which the Germans were planning, would end the war, as they were insisting it would; and he became such an embarrassment to his colleagues that a month after he last broached the subject—on 23rd January 1917—the new young Emperor Karl, who had succeeded when Franz Josef died in November 1916, replaced him with General Arz von Straussenburg, a much younger man.

Karl did not, however, retire Conrad; he sent him to command the western (Trentino) sector of the Austro-Italian Front.

The Italian Front

The Italian Front stretched from the Swiss-Italian borders in the west to the eastern frontier between Italy and Austria, via the line of the Alps. The eastern frontier more or less followed the course of the River Isonzo. The Isonzo enters the Adriatic Sea west of Trieste, and to get there from its source in the Julian Alps, winds along the eastern edge of the Friulian plain.

Except for about fifteen miles at its southern end, the Isonzo front was guarded by a spur of the main Alpine chain the Julian Alps, which, as it sweeps southwards, broadens out into plateaux and limestone hills. Running more or less parallel with this spur for half its length, the Isonzo cuts its way through a deep and rocky valley, which is separated from the Julian Alps by limestone uplands. Though the slope of these uplands is a fairly gentle gradient, they are deeply incised by a network of valleys and ridges.

South of the town of Tolmino, and rising out of the spur, is what the Italians call the Bainsizza plateau. The word plateau usually describes a flat mountain-top; but the Bainsizza is not flat; it is crossed and recrossed by ridges which rise steeply above the average level.

To the south of the Bainsizza is the Carso plateau, which has been described as 'a howling wilderness of stones, sharp as knives'. Between these two plateaux, but lying to the east, is the Selva di Ternova plateau, which is not so high as the other two, but is densely wooded.

Along the whole length of the front, the Austrians held the high ground and looked down on to the Friulian plain. This meant that unless the Italians attacked only on the fifteen mile coastal strip in the direction of Trieste, everywhere else they would be attacking uphill.

Eleven battles for seven miles

When the Italians came into the war in May 1915, General Cadorna had thirty-five divisions. This was a respectable force, as far as man-power went, but it was sadly short of artillery. In contrast, the Austro-Hungarians had ten divisions fewer; but were vastly superior in artillery.

Between the two sectors of the front where fighting was possible – at the western end north of Verona, and at the eastern end on the Isonzo – Cadorna deployed his forces. While the 1st and 4th Armies guarded the Venetian plain in the west, the 2nd and 3rd Armies took up positions on the Isonzo, together with the Carnia Group, comprising nineteen battalions of Alpine troops, at the very northern end of the front.

Cadorna decided to make his main effort on the Isonzo front. There were historical as well as military reasons for this. The Austrian provinces east of the Isonzo had once belonged to Italy, and since Italy had been transformed into a united kingdom in 1870, she had been asking for them to be restored to her; while on the military side, Italian pressure here would relieve Austrian pressure on Serbia.

Cadorna's general strategy on the Isonzo was to go forward in a series of what he called offensive bounds. He would attack the Austrians with limited objectives, pause to consolidate and re-form, and then leap forward again.

The plan, however, did not succeed. Between 23rd June 1915, when he launched his first offensive bound, and 29th August 1917, the Italian armies attacked the Austrians eleven times – the first to eleventh battles of the Isonzo – and by the end of the eleventh battle had gained a maximum of seven miles.

The reasons for so small a return for so great an effort were many and various. Discipline among the higher echelons of officers was faulty, chiefly because Cadorna ruthlessly eliminated any commander who failed to obtain the objectives set him. In the nineteen months before Caporetto he dismissed 217 generals, 255 colonels and 335 battalion commanders. The effect of this was to engender in his senior officers such a sense of insecurity

that they became over-cautious, and in their caution failed their commander-in-chief. At the same time it created a lack of contact between the supreme command and the field commanders which had the result of imprisoning Cadorna in an ivory tower by which he was denied all knowledge of the reactions of both officers and men to the war in general and their own problems in particular.

Equally serious, however, was the lack of equipment, and especially of artillery and heavy ammunition. At the vital moment there were not enough guns to press home the advantage, or ammunition supplies would fail.

This situation was partly due to the fact that the switch-over of Italian industry from peace-time to war-time production was difficult and slow; and partly due, particularly as the war developed, to sabotage of the military war-effort by extreme socialists, who were opposed to the war.

In addition, in the pauses between battles, the morale of the soldiers deteriorated. Until after Caporetto, absolutely nothing was done for the leisure entertainment of the troops. The men passed all their time in their dug-outs or tents, with nothing to divert them, and this situation was a breeding-ground for the wildest rumours purporting to describe what was going on behind the fronts. The Italian, with his tremendous attachment to family, grew fearful about his family's welfare, now that he was not there to protect it.

On the other hand, things were not much better on the Austrian side. The lack of a decisive victory and the extremely hard conditions imposed by the terrain and the weather conditions, particularly in the winter campaigns, had their effect on the morale of the Austrian soldier.

This was especially true after the Italian success, limited though it was, on the Bainsizza sector in the eleventh Isonzo battle of August 1917. After the conclusion of that battle, the Austrian military commanders seriously doubted whether their armies would be able to withstand a twelfth Isonzo battle, should Cadorna decide that the Italian army should launch one.

It was at this point that they recalled the old military adage that the best form of defence is attack. It also came back to them that Conrad had had a plan; and someone remembered that when he had last outlined his plan in detail he had suggested that the Caporetto sector of the Isonzo front should receive the main weight of the Austrian attack, since the Italian line was weakest there. A little elementary intelligence showed that this sector was still the weak link in the Italian Isonzo chain.

However, German help would still be needed, so on 25th August General Waldstatten was despatched to German general headquarters with instructions to use all his efforts to obtain German approval of and the required assistance for an offensive on the Isonzo.

The German Kaiser informed the Austrian Emperor that he could count on the whole of Germany to crush Italy. His high command had other ideas, but after some argument it was agreed that if Lieutenant-General Krafft von Dellmensingen, an expert in mountain warfare, having inspected the Isonzo at Caporetto, thought such a plan could succeed, then serious German consideration would be given to the proposals.

Dellmensingen went to the Isonzo, looked and reported. 'In view of the prevailing difficulties,' he wrote, 'success lies only just on the border of possibility.' This was sufficient for the Germans and practical plans were put in hand.

As it happened, Cadorna had no plans for launching a twelfth battle on the Isonzo. On 20th September he surprised the British and French military missions by telling them that he had abandoned his plans to renew his offensive and was going on to the defensive on the Isonzo— at least for the time being. He gave as his reason the necessity to conserve his supplies of ammunition.

In response to Cadorna's earlier pleas for artillery, the British and French had just sent a few heavy batteries to Italy 'on loan for the sole purpose of offensive operations'. When they heard that Cadorna intended to abandon the offensive, Lloyd George and his French opposite number Painlevé, in a fit of pique, accused Cadorna of getting the guns under false pretences and ordered them to be withdrawn. All the French batteries were recalled and two out of the three British batteries.

In his memoirs Cadorna explains what caused his decision. The intelligence he had received showed that the Austrians were going to make a tremendous effort to put Italy out of the war, and that they were going to make this effort soon, and not in the spring of 1918, as German agents in Switzerland were putting it about.

By 6th October forty-three enemy divisions had been identified on the Isonzo front. After this date the intelligence gradually became more precise. There were many troops on the Bainsizza sector and German troops were assembling in the Sava valley, sixty miles east of Caporetto.

On 9th October, the intelligence bulletin said that 'the last week of October might be accepted as the most probable date for the beginning of the enemy offensive'.

On 14th October General Capello, commander-in-chief of the Italian 2nd Army, on whose sector Caporetto was situated, was ordered to Padua by his doctors for a change of air and rest. This was a blow of the first order, for Capello had the total confidence of his troops, and his absence at a time when they were receiving the full force of the enemy attack could easily place the whole Isonzo front in jeopardy.

A week later Cadorna informed the British director of military operations: 'The attack is coming, but I am confident of being able to meet it. Owing to the very difficult country on the Tolmino sector, I am of opinion that an attack there can be checked without difficulty and I am consequently holding that sector lightly.' (Caporetto is north of Tolmino.)

In making this fatal decision, Cadorna had made serious errors of appreciation. He had accepted at face value the information given by a Czech deserter that the main attack would be made at Tolmino, and allowed this to colour his appreciation of more detailed information given by Austrian deserters. He had also allowed his knowledge of the Tolmino terrain to underestimate the probable weight of the enemy attack. Most serious of all, because of his confidence, he had failed to send out scouts to the area north of Tolmino—that is, in the neighbourhood of Caporetto—and so did not know that four Austro-German divisions were assembled, one behind the other, in the valley running northward of Plezzo.

The Austrians break through

Cadorna and Capello were two very different characters, and had had several differences of opinion throughout the war. Now they differed again about the plans for countering the enemy attack. Cadorna issued instructions for a defensive attitude with local counter-attacks; Capello favoured an offensive-defensive action, with a large-scale counter-attack, north-west from the Bainsizza.

Disregarding his supreme commander's instructions, Capello deployed his troops in readiness to carry out his own plan, with his three second-line corps *south* of Caporetto.

Though still in a high fever, Capello insisted on returning to his headquarters on the evening of 23rd October, but he grew worse. After dictating orders, he had to retire again. He had been gone only an hour or two, when, at 2 am on 24th October, the artillery of the Austro-German XIV Army on the Tolmino-Plezzo sector, opened fire with gas-shells on the Italian batteries and forward trenches. After two hours there was a two-hour pause. The Italian artillery replied, but after an initial fierceness it weakened and did little harm to the opposing infantry.

Soon after the bombardment began, light rain started to fall. Within a short time it changed to a heavy downpour, while on the heights there were snow-storms, and in the bottoms of the valleys thick mist. By dawn visibility everywhere was low.

At 6.30 am the bombardment was resumed with high explosive. From Plezzo down the whole length of the front to the sea, guns of every calibre opened up. Never before on the Isonzo had there been such an intense bombardment, and in a very short time the Italian defences had been reduced to rubble, while men's lungs were seized with a cruel agony which paralyzed their thoughts and actions as their gas-masks let through copious draughts of German poison gas.

And—calamity of calamities at such a time—all communications between commands and advance lines were destroyed.

At 8 am the firing of two giant mines gave the German XIV Army the signal to advance from Plezzo and Tolmino. To his surprise, General Krauss, at Plezzo, met no resistance from the Italians. By 9.30 am the front of the Italian 4th Corps had been pierced.

Meantime, General Stein, just north of Tolmino, had advanced with his divisions. He had been opposite the weakest spot in the Italian front.

In his pre-battle orders, Cadorna had instructed General Badoglio, who was to become famous in the Second World War as Marshal Badoglio, and who was commander of the 18th Corps covering the line from Plezzo to Tolmino, to withdraw his troops to the west bank of the Isonzo. For some reason never subsequently clarified, Badoglio deferred carrying out this order until shortly before the battle began, with the result that only a small force met Stein, and the remainder of the corps was cut off on the east bank.

Stein obliterated this small Italian force, and by doing so opened up a way across the river. By 4 pm he had occupied the village of Caporetto.

Thus, by mid-afternoon a fifteen-mile gap had been punched in the Italian line; and now, on the very first day, in the very sector where Cadorna had not expected an attack, the rot began.

The bogeyman comes

Up to this time the Italians had encountered only Austrians of whom they had no great opinion. In contrast, the reputation of the Germans as fighters was immense. Italian commanders had been wont to use it as a bogeyman to frighten recalcitrant troops into obedience.

Now the Germans were actually here!

When the truth dawned on the Italian troops, their morale, such as it was, snapped completely. In this they were matched by their junior commanders who did not know how to deal with tactics they had not been taught to counter.

The four divisions of General Cavaciocchi's 4th Corps melted away in flight, carrying with them Badoglio's 19th Division. Most of these troops fell prisoner in the next few days.

By nightfall, Krauss was making for Monte Stol, northwest of Caporetto and Stein had the greater part of his divisions on the west bank of the Isonzo. Only south of Tolmino had the Italian forces under

General Caviglia held; and as soon as Cadorna heard of the disaster in the north, he ordered them to fall back, too. At the same time he ordered the Duke of Aosta, commanding the 3rd Army, and General Capello to put the defences of the line of the Tagliamento river into a state of readiness with civilian labour, and 'with the utmost speed and maximum secrecy'. He explained that in order to save the 3rd Army and the remainder of the 2nd Army that had held firm, they might have to fall back on that line.

The next morning broke bright and clear, and the sun came out. The situation could be seen a little more clearly now, and Capello, who had returned to take command when the battle began, was forced to inform Cadorna that all positions on 2nd Army's front east of the Isonzo had been lost.

Cadorna ordered the Duke of Aosta to send back the less mobile of the 3rd Army's heavy and medium artillery to the River Piave, in the rear of the Tagliamento line. With the remainder he was to withdraw west of the Carso valley and prepare a line there to cover a general retreat.

At noon, Capello arrived at Cadorna's headquarters at Udine to discuss the situation. He was desperately ill and on the point of collapse. He told Cadorna that in his opinion all contact with the enemy should be broken off and a withdrawal made to the Tagliamento without delay. For once the two men agreed. But Cadorna did not issue the orders for the retreat for another twenty-four hours.

There have been many descriptions given of the flight of the Italian 6th and 27th Corps from Caporetto. Even put baldly and briefly it presents an almost unbelievable situation.

In his *History of the Great War,* C.R.M.F. Cruttwell has written: '400,000 soldiers were going home, with the determination that for them at least the war was ended. The reports of their behaviour are most curious. Having broken contact with the enemy, they were in no hurry; they stopped to eat and drink and pillage. One observer notes their air of "tranquil indifference", another that while they had all thrown away their arms, they kept their gas-masks; nearly as many civilians were fleeing, more wildly, from the face of the enemy, blocking what remained of the road space with their carts and household goods.'

Soldiers and civilians crowded down the valleys, using the only roads by which supplies and reinforcements could have reached them. They held up troops moving over to new lines. They had no thought for honour or country, they who had fought with amazing courage in the eleven battles of the Isonzo.

Yet there was something peculiarly Italian in this mass defection. General Raffaele Cadorna has told the author that his father related that there was no attempt to threaten officers, only a refusal to obey; and that when he himself rode among them, no one lifted a finger against him; on the contrary, as soon as they recognized him they stiffened and saluted.

Vengeance

The retreat, when ordered, took the 3rd Army commanders by surprise. It took the Austrian commander opposite equally by surprise, and he made no attempt to pursue. This was just as well, for there was a certain amount of initial disorder which could have been made worse had the rearguard had to fight.

The retreat of the 2nd Army, however, was extremely chaotic. This was scarcely to be wondered at, in view of the previous headlong flight of half that Army, and the fact that the German commander Berrer did pursue. He succeeded in splitting the 2nd Army irreparably in two.

On the other hand, all was not well with the Austro-Germans. The speed of their advance took them unprepared, and there were no orders which allowed for the full exploitation of the situation. As a result, orders were issued, then changed, and this gave rise to friction which bad staff work did not help to eradicate. In addition, army commanders and divisional commanders began to issue their own orders, and soon, they, too, were in a hopeless confusion.

This helped Cadorna considerably, and by 31st October, he had all his forces, except for the quarter million lost as prisoners, across the Tagliamento, and the Germans were still so mixed up that he was able to pause and take breath.

With the broad torrent of the river between them and the enemy, the Italian soldiers also took breath—for the first time for a week–and looked about them. What they saw seems to have brought them up short, and soon it was apparent to all observers that a new spirit was beginning to move them. Within a few days an amazing transformation was visible; military order and discipline were being quickly restored.

But the Germans also recovered, and when they made a large hole in the Tagliamento line, Cadorna decided to withdraw to the line of the River Piave. This further retreat was not without difficulties, but on 9th November all Italian armies stood in good order behind the Piave.

On that same day Cadorna was dismissed and was succeeded by General Diaz.

Throughout the remainder of the winter and the spring of the next year, Diaz re-grouped, reinforced, resupplied, and retrained his armies. The lessons of Caporetto were studied and heeded. New tactics were devised, designed to remove the weaknesses of the old which had been responsible for the heavy losses of men and had made Caporetto inevitable.

In June the Germans reopened their offensive. Eight days later it ended in complete victory for the Italians.

In October, Diaz went over to the offensive, and exactly a year to the day from Caporetto, he launched the battle of Vittorio Veneto and inflicted on the Austrians a far worse disgrace than they had inflicted on the Italians on the Isonzo.

Caporetto had been avenged.

Part seven · Bolshevik Revolution

In the autumn of 1917 the Russian people had reached a pitch of war-weariness and land-hunger that could no longer brook the machinations of Kerensky's Provisional Government. Their expectations, raised by revolutionary ideas and the ousting of the Tsarist dictatorship in March, were mocked by the ineffectual and half-hearted social measures of the new regime. The army was mutinous, the workers were on strike, the peasants were rebellious. Only Lenin's Bolshevik party promised the people what they wanted: land and peace, and only the Bolshevik party had the hard-core organization to canalize the revolutionary feelings of the people.

In the absence of a clear directive from the Provisional Government the peasants of their own accord set about dismantling the large estates of the landowners. As a result, by March 1919 virtually all the usable land had transferred to the peasants. This was the ground-swell of the revolution – a movement not specifically socialist in origin but crucial to the victory of Bolshevism.

So, too, with the centres of political activity. For the first time in three centuries Russia was without a Tsar. The resulting power vacuum was filled not by the increasingly remote Provisional Government but by the Petrograd Soviet of Workers' and Soldiers' Deputies. Similar soviets (or councils) had sprung up in Moscow and the provincial towns, and also in the countryside. Their members were elected on the factory floor and in the barracks.

In May 1917 Lenin had won acceptance at the Bolshevik party conference for his 'April Theses' calling for non-co-operation with the Provisional Government, for peace and for the end of the parliamentary republic and the transference of power to the soviets once these were dominated by the Bolsheviks. The socialist phase of the revolution was at hand, its slogan – 'All power to the soviets.'

Only the timing of the revolution remained to be decided. Open insurrections in Petrograd, sparked off by the effects of continuing war and increasing food shortages, encouraged Kerensky to take dictatorial measures. The Bolsheviks were suppressed as defeatists and agents of the Germans, and Lenin fled to Finland. What revived their fortunes was the failure of the military putsch in September by General Kornilov, the newly appointed commander-in-chief. His march on Petrograd was effectively destroyed long before it reached the capital: the Bolsheviks joined the Mensheviks and the Social Revolutionaries in a massive propaganda onslaught on the troops' wavering loyalty.

The Kornilov incident brought a sudden upsurge of strength into the Bolshevik camp. Within a week the Party had majorities in the soviets of Petrograd and Moscow. Revolution was imminent. 'History will not forgive us,' said Lenin, 'if we do not seize power now.'

On 23rd October at a meeting of the Central Committee of the Bolshevik Party the time was declared fully ripe to prepare for an armed insurrection. Lenin had emerged from hiding to take part in the debate and the resolution was passed by a majority of ten to two. On 29th October the Petrograd Soviet established a Military-Revolutionary Committee under the chairmanship of Trotsky to prepare and execute the subsequent coup. This was the beginning of 'the ten days that shook the world'.

The date for the uprising was fixed for 6th-7th November (24th-25th October by the old-style Julian Calendar: hence its generally known title the 'October Revolution'). On 3rd November the Petrograd garrison acknowledged the Petrograd Soviet as sole power, and on the 5th the Peter and Paul Fortress, with its arsenal of 100,000 rifles, went over to the soviet. On the night of the 6th-7th the Military-Revolutionary Committee, dominated by Bolsheviks and meeting at the Smolny Institute, gave the go-ahead.

Early in the morning of the 7th the coup was effected with scarcely any resistance. The keypoints of Petrograd were swiftly occupied, Lenin announced the victory of the socialist revolution, Kerensky fled in a car lent by the US Embassy, and Trotsky's posters hailing the overthrow of the Provisional Government appeared in the streets. This last claim was not as yet quite accurate. The Winter Palace was still occupied by those ministers who had chosen to remain, in the hope that Kerensky would still save the day by mustering a loyal army from the front.

The Palace was defended by a few hundred officer cadets and a women's battalion. Infiltrated by Red Guards, it capitulated late in the evening of the 7th. The coup was over; such blood as the revolution spilt would be shed later when the Bolsheviks sought to stabilize their power. That the present now belonged to the Bolsheviks was confirmed in the second All-Russian Congress of Soviets meeting on the 8th. Menshevik denunciations of the coup were stilled as the revolution swept the country.

Lenin, installed as President of the newly-formed Council of People's Commissars (as the Bolshevik Government was named), wasted no time in satisfying popular demand. The Decree on Land nationalized all private property—whether belonging to individual landowners, the Crown, or the Church—and distributed it into the custody of local land committees and peasant soviets.

Lenin's second decree concerned the settling of the war issue and invited 'all the belligerent peoples and their governments to open immediate negotiations for an honest democratic peace', i.e. a just peace without annexations or indemnities. The Decree on Peace initially met with silence from the Central Powers and hostility from the Allies. Concerned with the need to tie down German divisions on the Eastern Front the Allies threatened grave consequences if the Russians violated the treaty of 5th September 1914. Trotsky in turn denounced this as an intrusion in Russia's domestic affairs.

Meanwhile the Germans, threatened by economic exhaustion and a dangerous anti-war mood at home, agreed to negotiate on their own harsh terms. A Russo-German armistice was signed on 17th December 1917, and final ratification of the Treaty of Brest Litovsk by the Fourth Congress of Soviets followed on 16th March 1918. In the intervening months Trotsky's hopes for an internal revolution that would cripple Germany and Austria proved illusory: a wave of strikes and industrial unrest was no substitute for a revolutionary situation. His delaying tactics shown to be finally fruitless, and bereft of Allied support, the soviets were compelled to accept a humiliating 'dictated' peace. This entailed the forfeiting of Estonia, Latvia, Lithuania, and Russian Poland to Germany and Austria, the recognition of the Ukraine, Georgia, and Finland as independent states, and the evacuation of parts of Transcaucasia in favour of Turkey. By the Treaty of Brest Litovsk Russia lost a third of her agricultural land and her population, and more than four-fifths of her coal-mines.

Not surprisingly the rigour of the peace terms had split the Bolshevik Party. To accusations that the Treaty represented 'a betrayal of the international proletariat' Lenin repeated both his total disbelief in the Russian will to fight and his firm conviction in the need for a breathing space.

It was a policy of *reculer pour mieux sauter*. To continue to fight was to endanger the revolution; to play for time would enable consolidation of the home base—essential in the forthcoming ideological struggle for the world which Lenin foresaw. In the short term Germany won the Peace, but Russia won time: and ultimately, who can say that Lenin was wrong?

Eight months later an over-extended Germany, her Russian objectives nullified (though still dormant and shortly to be revived by the Nazis), capitulated to the Western Allies. The Treaty of Brest Litovsk was cancelled in November. The future seemed to be with Moscow: the arrival of a proletarian party at the head of the Russian state was to redefine the course of world history and—for a time at least—to polarize the world into two hostile camps.

The Bolshevik Revolution

Y. N. Gorodetsky

The overthrow of the autocratic Tsarist regime in March (February by the Julian Calender) 1917 was a great victory for the peoples of Russia. In alliance with the army, the working class of Russia fought for and won political freedom. The whole country was covered by a network of 'soviets' (councils) and of committees of soldiers and peasants. Power in the country was divided, but as early as June the Provisional Government had established a dictatorship with the help of the Mensheviks and Socialist Revolutionaries (SRs). Not a single one of the social aims of the revolution had been met. Neither the government of Prince Lvov nor Kerensky's government which followed it gave land to the peasants or rid them of their servitude to the landowners. Workers in the mills and factories continued to be cruelly exploited, their standard of living declined sharply, their wages were cut, and there was hunger in the towns. A country which had been exhausted by the First World War was now thirsting for peace, yet the Provisional Government's policy was to continue the war.

Russia was torn by violent contradictions. The progress of agriculture was held back by the fact that enormous areas remained in the hands of the landowners. At the same time modern industry was developing in the country, with a high level of concentration of production and manpower. The urban working class which amounted to about 20,000,000 of the country's population of over 150,000,000, was organized into trade unions and had learned a great deal about political struggle in the first Russian revolution of 1905.

The Bolshevik Party
The Bolshevik Party, led by Vladimir Ilyich Lenin, directed the struggle of the working class towards the acquisition of power, the solution of the land question, bringing the war to an end, establishing workers' control over production, and nationalizing banks and the more important branches of industry. But this struggle on the part of the workers and peasants came up against bitter resistance from representatives of the ruling classes.

In September 1917 the party of the Russian bourgeoisie, the Constitutional Democrats (Kadets), and the reactionary military circles led by General Kornilov tried to carry out a counter-revolutionary *putsch* and to set up a military dictatorship. This plot evoked general opposition among the people and rallied the revolutionary forces to the Bolshevik Party. At the beginning of September the Petrograd and Moscow soviets of workers' and peasants' deputies passed resolutions proposed by the Bolsheviks. The Moscow Soviet was led by one of the oldest members of the Bolshevik Party, V. P. Nogin, while L. D. Trotsky, who had only recently joined the Party, was elected chairman of the Petrograd Soviet.

The influence of the Bolsheviks in the soviets throughout the country spread rapidly in September and October. The Bolsheviks became the leading element in the soviets almost everywhere.

In the autumn of 1917 the revolution in Russia entered on its decisive stage.

All classes and all social groups in Russian society were drawn into the most far-reaching revolutionary crisis. It was a crisis affecting the whole nation, because it became apparent in all spheres of the nation's life, involving the working people, the ruling classes, and the political parties. With merciless precision Lenin revealed the inevitability of the collapse of a Russian economy dominated by the bourgeoisie and landowners and of the economic policy of the Provisional Government. It was not individual mistakes that brought the government to the brink of disaster. At a time when there was a tremendous growth in the revolutionary activity of the masses all efforts on the part of the Provisional Government to regulate economic life by reactionary bureaucratic means were doomed to failure. The government's whole policy was leading to famine and the disorganization of production, the destruction of economic contacts, and the creation of a state of chaos in the country. To carry out genuinely democratic measures for regulating the economy, to nationalize the banks and syndicates, and control production and demand would have meant taking a step forward – to socialism.

The collapse of the Provisional Government's food policy had an especially serious effect on the condition of the mass of ordinary people. Memories of the March days of 1917, which had started with food riots, were still very fresh in the people's minds. On the eve of the October Revolution the country's food situation worsened considerably as a result of the policy of the Kerensky government which paid no attention to the needs of the people.

The collapse of the Provisional Government's economic policy was seen in its most concentrated form in the breakdown of transport. This was the bloodstream sustaining the country's whole economic life and binding it together into a single organism, and it collapsed with tremendous speed. Towards the end of October 1917 the minister of transport, A.V.Liverovsky, admitted that the transport situation 'threatened to bring to a halt the major railroads which supplied the country with essential services'.

One very clear sign of the nationwide crisis was the break-up of the ruling parties of Socialist Revolutionaries (SRs) and the Social Democrats (Mensheviks). The formation of left-wing groups among the SRs and Mensheviks, the sharp intensification of conflicts between the leadership of these parties and the rank and file of their members and between the party headquarters and their local organizations, and the enforced rejection by the local committees of SRs and Mensheviks of the slogan of coalition with the bourgeoisie was the direct result of the collapse of those parties' reformist policy. On 4th November the soldiers' section of the All-Russian Central Executive Committee, led by SRs and Mensheviks, demanded peace and the transfer of land to the peasants, but proposed that power should be handed over to 'the democratic majority in the pre-parliament' – that spurious, representative body set up by the Provisional Goverment.

Traitors to the revolution

From the middle of October 1917 open warfare on the part of all the working people against the Provisional Government became a daily occurrence in the nation's life. The workers everywhere were arming themselves, the number of workers' armed detachments – the Red Guards – increased rapidly, and they developed their contacts and their plans for common action with the garrisons in the major towns. The workers had a tremendously revolutionizing effect on the troops at the fronts, especially on the Western and Northern Fronts. Sailors of the Baltic Fleet declared the Kerensky government to be a government of betrayal of the revolution. Councils of workers' and soldiers' deputies, regimental and divisional committees, and peasants' organizations proclaimed at the numerous conferences they held that none of the tasks of the revolution could be solved without the overthrow of the Provisional Government and the transfer of power to the soviets. A resolution passed at a congress of soviets of the Vladimir province on 29th October declared the Provisional Government and all the parties which supported it to be traitors to the cause of revolution and all the soviets in the province to be in a state of open and determined warfare with the Provisional Government. This was only one of the moves in this general process of decisive and ruthless warfare between the people and the government. The same resolution was supported by the soviets in Moscow, Ivanovo-Voznesensk, Aleksandrov, Kovrov, Ryazan, and other towns. When a congress of soviets in the Ryazan province decided to hand power over to the soviets immediately, Nikitin, the minister of the interior, demanded that armed force should be used against the people of Ryazan. On 31st October the minister cabled the commander of the Moscow military region: 'Impossible to take counteraction with resources of the civil authority.' But the military commander was also unable to render any assistance, because he had no dependable troops at his disposal. The soviet of the Moscow province proposed that all the soviets in the province should ignore the orders issued by the Provisional Government. The Vladivostok Soviet, some 6,000 miles from Moscow, issued instructions to the effect that failure to obey the soviet's orders would be regarded as a counter-revolutionary act. Soviets in the Urals declared that the main task was to overthrow the Provisional Government.

It was the industrial working class and its party which took the lead in this popular movement. Factory committees sprang up everywhere and quickly gathered strength, and they were everywhere dominated by the Bolsheviks. In Petrograd on 30th October - 4th November there took place the first All-Russian Conference of Factory Committees. Ninety-six of the 167 delegates belonged to the Bolsheviks.

Strikes and peasant revolt

The strike movement in the autumn of 1917 was closely connected with the soviets' struggle for power. There were strikes of metal-workers and woodworkers, of chemist-shop assistants and railway workers, of textile workers and miners. A general strike of 300,000 textile workers in the central industrial region (Moscow), which began on 3rd November, affected every branch of life in the region. The workers took control of the plants, occupied the telephone exchange, mounted guard over the warehouses and offices. It was more than a strike: the workers not only faced up directly to the problem of assuming power, they began to solve it. But in 1917 the strike was only one of many weapons used by the proletariat in its struggle. The Red Guards and the workers' militia, the establishment of factory guards and workers' control, the factory committees and the bold acts of intervention in the management of industrial plants – all these forms of organization and means of struggle gave the working class tremendous possibilities for influencing the course of events and leading them on a nationwide scale.

The strength of the working-class movement was multiplied by virtue of the fact that the industrial workers exercised a tremendous influence over the peasantry and themselves received in return support in the form of a spreading peasant war against the landowners. In September and October 1917 there were something like 2,000 cases in which the peasants took political action, killing the landlords and seizing the land.

'If, in a country of peasants, after seven months of a democratic republic, things could come to the point of a peasant revolt, this demonstrates . unquestionably the nationwide collapse of the revolution, the crisis it is in, which has reached unprecedented proportions, and the fact that the counter-revolutionary forces are reaching the limit of their resources,' Lenin wrote in mid-October 1917.

But the peasantry's official representative at the time was the All-Russian Council of Peasants' Deputies, which had been elected at the peasants' congress back in May and had long since lost any right to represent anybody. The executive committee of the All-Russian Council of Peasants' Deputies sanctioned punitive expeditions against the peasants, and supported the policy of hostility to the peasantry pursued by the government (in which the prime minister was the SR Kerensky and the minister of agriculture the SR Maslov). The peasant masses who had risen in revolt against the landowners took decisive action. In the main centres of peasant uprisings the struggle against the landowners acquired, under the influence of the industrial workers, both organization and a clear purpose. The 332 delegates to a peasant congress in the Tver province took a unanimous decision to hand over the land immediately to the management of land committees. The local land committees in the Tambov province seized land belonging to the Church and the landowners and rented it out to peasants who had very little or no land. Similar acts were repeated throughout the country.

Government force

How did the Provisional Government reply to these demands by the peasants? It organized punitive expeditions and drew up various legislative proposals providing for eventual reforms, the aim of which was to 'pacify' the peasants and certainly not to satisfy their demand that the land should be handed over to them.

The forces at the disposal of the Provisional Government for undertaking such punitive expeditions were limited, consisting mainly of Cossack and cavalry units. The actions undertaken by the peasants forced the Provisional Government to split up its troops between numerous areas in which there had been uprisings: in the Ryazan, Kursk, Tambov, Kiev, Tula, Saratov, Samara, Minsk, Kazan, Podolsk, Volhynia, and other provinces. Squadrons of Cossacks and cavalry detachments which were dispatched to particular districts became submerged in the vast sea of peasant revolt. Meanwhile, the provincial commissars of the Provisional Government demanded that soldiers be sent to *all* districts to suppress peasant disorders.

But even the local authorities soon realized the futility of using force against the peasantry. In the course of the peasant uprising even those land committees which supported the government's policy were forced to take over the property of the landowners and distribute it among the poorer peasants. The Kadets, the SRs, and the Mensheviks tried in every way to minimize the importance of the peasants' struggle, making out that it was just 'wild anarchy' and talking about 'pogroms' and 'disorders'. This falsification of the truth is disproved by the facts: in the main centres of the uprising the peasants transferred the land to the poor peasants in an organized manner. In those places where the SR party obstructed the work of the peasant committees the movement did indeed assume anarchistic forms. But the peasants had thoroughly learned the lessons of the first Russian revolution of 1905. The more advanced forms of peasant protest and revolt (the seizure of arable land and landowners' property) were three or four times as widespread in 1917 as they had been in 1905-07. In the autumn of 1917 between sixty and ninety per cent of all peasant actions included the seizure of land.

As for the proposed reforms, their essence is apparent from the final bill put forward by S.L.Maslov, the minister of agriculture. According to this bill, which was the most 'left-wing' for the Provisional Government, the landowners were to retain the right to own the land. The 'land-lease fund' to be set up under this bill was to take over only 'land not being cultivated by the resources of the owners'. The rent to be paid by the peasants was to go to the landowner.

The whole experience of the eight months during which the Provisional Government was in power demonstrated that without a further revolution the peasantry would not receive any land or rid itself of oppression by the landowners. It was this experience which pushed the peasantry to carry out an uprising which, when linked with the struggle of the industrial workers, created the most favourable conditions for the victory of the socialist revolution.

The revolutionary structure

By November 1917 the Bolshevik Party had about 350,000 members. But its strength was to be measured rather by its influence over the many millions of people embraced by the soviets, the trade unions, the factory committees, and the soldiers' and peasants' committees. At a time when an armed revolt was developing on a nationwide scale the task of Lenin's revolutionary party was to take care of the political and military organization of the forces of revolt. At the centre of this preparatory work stood the working class. The Red Guards were acquiring fighting experience, were learning the tactics of street fighting, and were establishing and strengthening their contacts with the revolutionary units in the army. In the districts inhabited by other nationalities the Bolsheviks gained the support of the oppressed peoples, who saw in the victory of a socialist revolution a guarantee of national and social emancipation. Major centres of revolutionary struggle were set up in all these districts and they linked the national liberation movement with the workers' and peasants' movement, bringing Petrograd and Moscow together with the outlying regions in a single revolutionary front. One such centre in central Asia was Tashkent, which as early as September 1917 raised the banner of struggle against the Kerensky government. In the Trans-Caucasus the centre was the industrial city of Baku; in the Ukraine Kharkov and the Donbass; in the Western territories of the country it was Minsk. The Bolsheviks were clearly the dominant force in the decisive places in the country: in the capital, in the industrial centres, on the Western and Northern Fronts, and in the major garrison towns in the interior. The seventy-five Bolshevik newspapers and periodicals which were published in all these regions were a very important organizing force.

The decision to work for an uprising, which was taken at the Sixth Congress of the Bolshevik Party in August 1917, was put consistently into practice. At a meeting on 23rd October, in which Lenin took part, the Central Committee of the Bolsheviks passed a resolution concerning the uprising. This decision did not set a date for the uprising, but it did stress that 'an armed uprising is inevitable and the time for it is fully ripe'. The Central Committee advised all the branches of the party to be guided by this fact and to consider and decide all practical issues with this in mind. The resolution was passed with Zinovyev and Kamenev voting against it. A week later Kamenev wrote an article opposing the decision in the Menshevik paper *Novaya Zhizn* (New Life). L.D. Trotsky voted in favour of the resolution on the uprising, but his later position amounted to delaying the beginning of the revolt until the All-Russian Congress of Soviets, which was to deal with the question of power. This attitude of Trotsky's was subjected to severe criticism by Lenin, who emphasized that to postpone the uprising until the Congress of Soviets would be to give the counter-revolutionary forces an opportunity of organizing themselves and dispersing the soviets.

On 29th October an enlarged session of the Central Committee of the Bolsheviks, attended by representatives of the Petrograd committee, the Bolsheviks' military organization, factory committees, and trade unions, approved the decision to organize an armed uprising and appointed from its number a Military-Revolutionary Centre composed of A.S.Bubnov, F.E. Dzerzhinsky, Y.M.Sverdlov, I.V.Stalin, and S.M.Uritsky. The leading spirit and organizer of the work of the Military-Revolutionary Committee was Yakov Sverdlov, a thirty-two-year-old Bolshevik who already had behind him seventeen years of revolutionary activity, prison, penal servitude, and seven escapes from deportation. This centre consisting of five men formed part of the Soviet's legal headquarters for the armed uprising—the Military-Revolutionary Committee of the Petrograd Soviet. A major part in the Committee was played by Bolsheviks N.I. Podvoysky and V.A.Antonov-Ovseyenko, and by the left-wing SR, P.E.Lazimir.

In late October provincial and district conferences and congresses of soviets, factory committees, and army and frontline committees took place throughout the country. History had never before seen such a mass mobilization of popular forces around the working class for a decisive attack on the capitalist system.

Meanwhile, the Provisional Government was trying to regain the initiative. On 1st November it dispersed the soviet in Kaluga, encircled Moscow and Minsk with Cossack troops, and tried to remove the revolutionary units of the capital's garrison from Petrograd. The only effect of these actions was that the revolutionary forces became even more active.

The Military-Revolutionary Committee appointed its own commissars to all units of the Petrograd garrison and to all the more important offices. The revolutionary troops and the Red Guards were brought to a state of readiness for battle. On 6th November the avalanche of popular wrath descended on the government which had betrayed the revolution. On that day the Central Committee of the Bolsheviks organized an alternative headquarters in the Peter and Paul Fortress and took decisions concerning the control of the postal and telegraph services, of the rail junction, and of the food supplies to the capital. The Petrograd garrison and the Red Guards went over to direct military action to bring about the immediate overthrow of the Provisional Government.

The Bolsheviks seize power

The city of Petrograd is situated on a number of islands, joined together by bridges. Hence the great strategic importance of the bridges. During the day of 6th November units of the Red Guards seized practically all the bridges and defeated efforts on the part of the officer cadets to cut the working-class districts off from the centre. Revolutionary troops occupied the central telegraph office, the central news agency, and the Baltic (Finland) station. Ships of the Baltic Fleet put out from Helsingfors and Kronstadt to come to the help of revolutionary Petrograd.

On the evening of 6th November Lenin left his secret hiding place and arrived at the headquarters of the armed uprising, and under his leadership the uprising developed at much greater speed. Troops of the Military-Revolutionary Committee occupied, on the night of 6th-7th November and the following morning, the telephone exchange, a number of railway stations, and the State Bank. The capital of Russia was in the hands of a people in revolt.

On the morning of 7th November Lenin wrote his appeal *To the Citizens of Russia,* which announced the transfer of power in the state into the hands of the Military-Revolutionary Committee. This, the first document to emerge from the victorious revolution, was immediately printed and posted up in the streets of Petrograd.

At two thirty-five on the afternoon of the same day the Petrograd Soviet went into session. There Lenin proclaimed the victory of the socialist revolution. In a short, moving speech he defined the main tasks of the revolution: the setting up of a Soviet government, the dismantling of the old state administration and the organization of new, Soviet administration, the ending of the war, a just and immediate peace, the confiscation of the property of the landowners, and genuine workers' control over industrial production.

Throughout the day of 7th November meetings of the party factions from the Congress of Soviets were taking place in the Smolny Institute. Details of the party composition of the second All-Russian Congress of Soviets bear witness to the depth and the extent of the process of Bolshevization among the ordinary people. At the first Congress the Bolsheviks had accounted for only ten per cent of the delegates, but at the second Congress they embraced fifty-two per cent of the delegates. The Bolsheviks carried with them a large group of left-wing SRs – more than fifteen per cent of the delegates, whereas there had been no left-wing SRs at all at the first All-Russian Congress of Soviets. Mensheviks and right-wing SRs of all shades of opinion, who had unquestionably dominated the first Congress of Soviets (eighty-four per cent of the delegates), accounted for only twenty-six per cent of the delegates at the second Congress.

There is no need to produce any more precise evidence to demonstrate the extent to which the *petit-bourgeois* parties had disintegrated; the decline from eighty-four per cent in June 1917 to twenty-six per cent in October is sufficiently clear. All the same, the Bolsheviks did not try to antagonize or isolate the other parties which formed part of the soviets.

The first session of the second All-Russian Congress of Soviets began at 10.40 pm on 7th November and came to an end just after five next morning.

The white-pillared hall of the Smolny Institute was seething with people. Within its walls were to be found representatives of the whole of Russia, of her industrial centres and farming regions, national territories, Cossack regions, and of all the war fronts and garrisons in the interior. It was a representative assembly from the whole of Russia, which had to decide the future course of the revolution.

Sitting on the platform were the downcast leaders of the old Central Executive Committee – Bogdanov, Gots, Dan, Filippovsky – but this was their last appearance as leaders of the supreme organ of the soviets. It was, at the same time, an admission of defeat for their policy of resistance to the popular will and an admission of the legitimacy of the Congress, to which, by the very fact of the official opening, the old Executive Committee was handing over its very reduced authority.

The Congress elected a presidium from among the Bolsheviks and the left-wing SRs, and Dan and his friends departed. Then the work of the Congress began.

There was, in the long stream of speeches, in the heated dispute about the revolution which had taken place, and in the sharp conflict between the political parties, a certain strict logic and system which reflected the relationship of social forces in the vast country stretching out beyond the confines of the Smolny Institute.

The Provisional Government, meeting in the Winter Palace in the centre of Petrograd, was utterly isolated from the country. The palace was defended by detachments of officer cadets, Cossacks, and women's battalions. As the ring of rebel forces drew closer round the Winter Palace, and as the reports from the war fronts grew ever more hopeless, so the speeches of the more conciliatory statesmen became more nervous and their actions became more devoid of logic. By continually walking out of the congress and then coming back to it the Mensheviks and the right-wing SRs tried to disorganize its work. The result of their efforts was very painful for them.

After some noisy demonstrations and much hysterical shouting and appeals the right-wing SRs and Mensheviks succeeded in taking with them out of the congress an insignificant group of people – about fifty of the delegates. At the same time there took place a significant regrouping of forces at the congress. The number of SRs was reduced by seven, but the group of left-wing SRs increased to eighty-one. The Mensheviks disappeared altogether, but the group of Menshevik-internationalists rose to twenty-one. This means that many members of the faction of Mensheviks and SRs did not obey the decision of their leaders to leave the congress, but preferred to switch over to the left-wing groups.

At about ten in the evening of 7th November the revolutionary troops surrounding the Winter Palace went over to the attack for which the signal was a shot fired by the cruiser *Aurora*. The Winter Palace was taken. Antonov-Ovseyenko arrested the members of the Provisional Government and put them in charge of the Red Guards to be taken to the Peter and Paul Fortress.

Pleading

Meanwhile, the forces of the counterrevolution – the Mensheviks, and rightwing SRs, pinned their hopes on the units at the front. During 6th and 7th November General Dukhonin from the General HQ and a representative of the war ministry, Tolstoy, sent messages from Petrograd demanding, begging, and pleading with the commanders of the fronts to send troops as quickly as possible to Petrograd to put down the uprising. The commanders of the South-Western and Rumanian Fronts, where the influence of the conciliators and nationalists seemed to be especially strong, declared that there were no units to be found which were suitable for the job of 'pacifying' Petrograd. And those regiments which they had succeeded by a trick in moving towards Petrograd were held up on the way by the railwaymen, the workers, and revolutionary soldiers. A strict revolutionary control was set up in Orsha, so that no trains were allowed through to Petrograd. The armoured trains which were sent off for Moscow were held up in Minsk. Vyazma and Gomel not only refused to let troops through but even held up telegrams from the staff of the Western Front.

Contrary to the hopes of the forces of counter-revolution, the soldiers on all fronts came out in defence of the soviets.

At 5.17 am N.V.Krylenko, an officer and a Bolshevik, representing the revolutionary forces of the Northern Front, went up on to the platform of the congress to speak; he was staggering from fatigue. He was soon to be made supreme commander-in-chief of the Russian army. The congress listened with enthusiasm to his statement that a Military-Revolutionary Committee

had been set up on the Northern Front, which had taken over the command and intended to prevent the movement of trainloads of counter-revolutionary troops in the direction of Petrograd. Delegations were continually arriving from the trains sent to Petrograd and declaring their support for the Petrograd garrison.

The first official state document of the socialist revolution – the *Appeal to the Workers, Soldiers, and Peasants* – was drawn up by Lenin. It proclaimed that the Congress of Soviets was taking power into its own hands and that all power throughout the country was passing into the hands of the soviets of workers', soldiers', and peasants' deputies. This was how the main question of the revolution was resolved in legislative terms – the power of the soviets was established.

The most difficult problems, around which a bitter struggle had been fought throughout the eight months of the revolution – the questions of peace, land, workers' control, the self-determination of nations, the democratization of the army – were posed and decided openly and straightforwardly in that document.

The *Appeal to the Workers, Soldiers, and Peasants* was approved with only two opposing votes and twelve abstentions. This represented a complete victory for Lenin's idea of transferring all power to the soviets.

The first decree approved by the second All-Russian Congress of Soviets was the decree concerning the peace.

Peace

Certain critics were later to assert, quite unfairly, that Russia could have had peace even without the Bolshevik Revolution, and that if it did not come about it was only because of mistakes committed by the governments of the Entente powers and the Provisional Government who did not succeed in seizing the initiative in deciding the question of war or peace.

There can be no question but that the Provisional Government committed plenty of 'mistakes' of every kind. But it was by no means a matter of the weakness of certain individuals or of their personal mistakes. Those mistakes were dictated by the class nature of the policy of the Provisional Government, its loathing of the revolutionary movement and its fear in the face of that movement, and its dependence on the governments of the Entente powers. The growth of this dependence led even to the expulsion from the government of the war minister, A.I.Verkhovsky, who suggested a negotiated peace with the German bloc so as to concentrate forces against the revolution.

At 9 pm on 8th November the second session of the Congress of Soviets opened. Lenin went up·on to the platform. 'Next Lenin, gripping the edge of the reading stand, letting his little winking eyes travel over the crowd as he stood there waiting, apparently oblivious to the long-rolling ovation, which lasted several minutes'—recalls the American journalist John Reed, who was an eye-witness of the events and a participant in them.

'The question of peace is the burning question, the most pressing question of the present time,' Lenin began. The proletarian revolution was not decked out in the flamboyant clothes of beautiful words, nor was it concealed behind noisy manifestoes and impossible promises. It got down in a businesslike way to the great and difficult job of liberating the peoples of Russia and of the whole world from bloody slaughter. There was a note of confidence and firmness in the words of Lenin's decree, which proposed that all the warring peoples and their governments should enter immediately into talks concerning a just peace, without annexations or indemnities.

The Decree on Peace gave legislative form to new principles of foreign policy—the principles of equality and respect for the sovereignty of all peoples, the abandonment of secret diplomacy, and the co-existence of different social systems. The decree was addressed not only to the governments but also to the peoples of the warring nations.

The diplomatic representatives of the Entente powers tried to ignore the Decree on Peace and pretend that the document 'did not exist'. But the decree became the property of hundreds of millions of working people. Evidence of this is to be found in the strikes and demonstrations which swept through many countries of the world at the end of 1917 and in 1918.

The Decree on Peace was approved unanimously by the congress.

The congress turned immediately to the second question: the immediate abolition of landlord property rights. The yearnings of the people, their century-long dreams of being free from the oppression of the landlords were expressed in the Decree on Land.

'Landlord property rights are abolished, immediately and without any compensation,' the decree said. All land was declared to be the property of the whole people. It was made the duty of the local soviets to draw up an accurate account of all property and to organize the strictest revolutionary protection for everything that was handed over to the national economy. There was a special point which proclaimed that the land of the ordinary peasants and Cossacks would not be confiscated. Part of the decree consisted of the peasants' demands, drawn up on the basis of 242 local peasant demands.

The Decree on Land was approved by a general vote of the delegates, with only one delegate voting against and eight abstaining. Thus the Bolsheviks won a complete victory on this cardinal question of the revolution as well. The peasantry received land from the hands of the victorious urban working class. This turned the alliance between the proletariat and the peasantry into a tremendous force promoting the further progress of the revolution. What the proletariat had failed to achieve in 1905—to unite its struggle for socialism with the democratic movement of the peasantry for land—was achieved triumphantly in November 1917.

Since it was by its nature an expression of revolutionary democracy, the Decree on Land was put into practice by methods which were both revolutionary and socialist. This is to say, it rid the land of the survivals of serfdom more resolutely and thoroughly than any bourgeois revolution had yet done. By abolishing the private ownership of land the Decree on Land took the first step towards the liquidation of capitalist ownership of banks, industrial undertakings, transport, and so on.

As a result of the agrarian reforms carried out on the basis of the Decree on Land and the subsequent legislation the poor and middle peasants received 540,000,000 acres of land. The big landowners, the royal family and the Church lost all their land—400,000,000 acres—and the rich peasants (kulaks) lost 135,000,000 of the 216,000,000 they had owned in 1914.

This revolutionary redistribution of land

served as the basis for further reforms in agriculture and for the development of a socialist farming system.

Bolshevik government

Since it enjoyed an overwhelming majority, it was natural that Lenin's party should form the new government. During the Congress the Central Committee of the Bolshevik Party had carried on intensive negotiations with the left-wing SRs about their participation in the government. The left-wing SRs had been members of the Military-Revolutionary Committee and they had — though, it is true, not without some hesitation — taken part in the armed uprising and supported the principal decisions taken by the Congress. But the left-wing SRs were too closely connected with their right-wing colleagues in the party and were too dependent on them in an ideological and organizational sense to be able to make up their minds immediately to join the Soviet government. It was a month later that they took this step.

At this point the Bolsheviks assumed the responsibility for forming a new government. 'We wanted a Soviet coalition government,' Lenin said. 'We did not exclude anyone from the Soviet. If they (the SRs and Mensheviks) did not wish to work together with us, so much the worse for them. The masses of the soldiers and peasants will not follow the Mensheviks and SRs.'

The decree which the Congress passed concerning the formation of a workers' and peasants' government headed by V.I.Lenin became in effect a constitutional document. It determined the name of the new government: the Soviet (Council) of People's Commissars, a name which reflected the fact that the new government was closely linked with the people and had developed out of the soviets. The decree laid down in general terms that the new government was subject to the control of the All-Russian Congress of Soviets and its Central Executive Committee. Thus the decree set out the constitutional principle regarding the responsibility of the workers' and peasants' government to the supreme bodies of the Soviet regime: the Congress of Soviets and the All-Russian Central Executive Committee, which had the right to remove people's commissars.

Once it had proved victorious in Petrograd the revolution spread quickly throughout the country. Immediately after Petrograd, the soviets were victorious in Moscow, where the battles for power were very violent and lasted for five days, ending on 16th November 1917 with the complete victory of the soviets.

In the course of three months the socialist revolution was victorious throughout the vast country. From the line of the Western Front to the shores of the Pacific Ocean and from the White Sea to the Black Sea. The ways in which the revolutionary power of the soviets was established varied greatly from place to place. In Smolensk, Voronezh, Kazan, Chernigov, Zhitomir, and Kiev the workers and peasants took power only after armed struggle with the counter-revolutionaries. In Minsk, Yaroslavl, Nizhny Novgorod, Samara, Kursk, and Perm the soviets came to power by peaceful means.

At the very beginning of its course the socialist revolution in Russia succeeded in doing what the Paris Commune tried but failed to do. The workers, peasants, and soldiers of Russia set up a new administration, formed their own government at the All-Russian Congress of Soviets, uniting millions of working people, resolved the questions of peace and land, and offered all the peoples of Russia the possibility of national independence.

Such was the victory of the Bolshevik Revolution, which changed the face of the world and had a decisive influence on the fate of mankind. *(Translation)*

The Treaty of Brest Litovsk

Jaroslav Valenta

No more than eight months separated the victorious peace settlement imposed on Russia by Kaiser Wilhelm's Germany at Brest Litovsk from Germany's capitulation at Compiègne. For eight months her rulers could dream that at last a decisive turning point had been reached in the war and that the most far-ranging aspirations would now be fulfilled – plans for establishing a ruling position for Germany throughout the world. The great power on Germany's eastern border, Russia, had been abased and compelled to sign a separate peace and her vast territory, seized by revolution and debilitated by civil war, appeared to be an easy prey.

The Peace of Brest Litovsk had wider implications than its effect on German-Russian relations. On 3rd March when Sokolnikov signed the treaty as Soviet representative it seemed that more had happened than the mere winning of the first round in the war; most contemporaries thought the balance had definitely shifted in favour of Germany and the Central powers. It looked as if willingness to risk a fight on two fronts had paid off. It seemed to have justified those military circles that favoured expansion and adventure.

The fanfares of triumph in Berlin and Vienna inevitably caused serious alarm among the Allies. Wheat from the Ukraine would make the sea blockade of the Central powers impotent, and there was reason to fear the transfer of huge contingents from the German and Austro-Hungarian armies to the French and Italian theatres before the American Expeditionary Force could arrive. In some Allied countries voices were again raised, suggesting that it would be better to reach a compromise than face a long drawn out war. The spokesmen for the national liberation movements among the suppressed peoples of Austria-Hungary were worried, and with reason.

The road from the ceasefire signed in December 1917 to the Treaty of Brest Litovsk was neither short nor easy. Each side needed time to analyse the actions of the other in order to clarify its expectations of what peace might bring. The Central powers, and in particular their economies, were on the verge of complete exhaustion. Ludendorff admits in his memoirs that he was waiting for a 'miracle', for a revolution in Russia to eliminate from the war an enemy whose endless territory had been swallowing up division after division. The problem of making peace on the Eastern Front was a double-edged one. As good a balance as possible had to be struck between the expansionist ambitions of some circles, particularly military ones, and more realistic intentions to bite off only as much as the Central powers could chew. Russia's withdrawal from the war had helped to spark off a highly unwelcome surge of discontent and revolutionary unrest in Austria-Hungary and Germany, which would be fanned by the conclusion of a palpably annexationist treaty.

Among the foremost exponents of a relatively realistic line were Richard von Kühlmann, first secretary in the German foreign office, and the Austrian foreign minister, Count Czernin. It would be wrong of course to imagine that there was any idyllic measure of agreement between Berlin and Vienna about the approach to peace with Russia. Early in December Czernin threatened to sign a separate treaty if necessary, regardless of Berlin's policy. This he hoped would eliminate the influence of extremist circles in Germany whose exaggerated demands were likely to prevent any peace settlement with Russia — a settlement which the Danubian monarchy needed even more urgently than its ally. Czernin seems to have realized that the insatiability of the German imperialists outran their real capabilities. This does not mean, however, that he was prepared to abandon all plans of annexation; he agreed with Kühlmann that Poland, Lithuania, Courland, and the greater part of Livonia should stay in the hands of the Central powers.

In Petrograd, similarly, the views of the

Soviet government about the peace problem were slowly changing. The Bolsheviks had gone into the revolution with the slogan of 'peace without annexations or indemnities', a policy of dissociation from both sides in the war and rejection of the aims of both great power alliances. Refusing to fight on, the Soviet government 'declared war on war'. It nevertheless made intensive efforts to avoid being identified in its peace offers with either side in the battle and proposed terms to all the contestants. Even after signing a ceasefire with the Central powers – who in view of their military, economic, and domestic political plight were in no position to reject any proposals out of hand – the revolutionary government in Petrograd continued to urge the Allies to join in the negotiations. It was reluctant to embark on a separate peace and its spokesmen went so far as to get the German negotiators to undertake that there would be no transfers of troops from the Russian to the Western Front. Indeed, even after the Brest negotiations had been broken off in February 1918 and the German offensive had started, the Bolsheviks appealed for help to the Allied missions in Russia.

Revolutionary hopes

Not even the Bolshevik Party was untouched by disagreements about the whole complex of issues involved in making peace with the Central powers. One wing of the party, and similarly one wing of the coalition partners in the government and in the Central Executive Committee of Soviets, was sharply opposed to the conclusion of the Brest Litovsk Treaty. Bukharin, as leader of the Left Communists, declared that the first proletarian state in the world must not sign an agreement which would betray the revolutionary movement in the other countries and repress the rising wave of revolutionary action. Similar arguments were used by the Left Socialist Revolutionaries, who were anti-German and pro-Allied in their sympathies. Without a close familiarity with the political theories then prevailing in Soviet Russia it is hard to understand how these ideas of a 'revolutionary war' could have been used in protest against the Brest negotiations – especially since the Russian army had virtually disintegrated.

It must be admitted that there were many illusions and unrealistic, though revolutionarily optimistic, assessments of the situation on the Soviet side. One illusion was that the curtain was about to go up on a pan-European, if not worldwide, revolution arising from the extraordinary intensification of political, class, and social antagonisms and conflicts brought about by the war. Even before the victorious October Revolution in Russia, Lenin had formulated his theory of the 'prologue', the theory that the Russian events would be a spark setting fire to a revolutionary conflagration throughout the main industrial countries of Europe – all of which were involved in the war – and above all in Germany. The spate of demonstrations and manifestations that followed the opening of negotiations in Brest Litovsk, both in Germany and still more in Austria-Hungary, seemed to bear out this expectation, and this was bound to influence decision-making quarters in Soviet Russia.

The first few weeks of negotiation, in December 1917 and January 1918, gave no indication of the slightest approximation of views between the two sides. On the contrary it became ever more clear that the real dictator at the conference was not Kühlmann, the titular head of the German delegation, but the brutal Prussian general Max Hoffmann, a spokesman of the most extreme imperialist and militarist circles in Germany. His *extempore* outbursts, culminating in the famous moment when he banged the table with his fist and demanded that the remaining Baltic territories should be evacuated by the Russians and taken under German 'protection', caused a crisis in the negotiations.

From January 1918 the Soviet peace delegation was headed by Trotsky, who shared Lenin's view that from a purely military standpoint Soviet Russia had no chance at all in a conflict with the Central powers. He agreed that a treaty must be signed as soon as Germany presented an ultimatum, and before leaving for Brest he assured Lenin that he had no intention of putting over a doctrine of 'revolutionary war'. But at the same time Trotsky considered that the radical mood of the population had made the home front of the Central powers so unstable that their armies would be incapable of launching an effective anti-Soviet offensive. It was therefore his policy to postpone the conclusion of an agreement until it might appear plain that the Central powers were not only determined, but actually able, to start large-scale military operations against Russia. When the German ultimatum was delivered, then, he declared the standpoint of the Soviet government to be 'neither peace nor war'; with that, the Soviet delegation went back to Petrograd.

The subsequent course of events fully bore out Lenin's attitude, which had previously failed to win majority support. The German and Austrian armies of intervention advanced without meeting serious obstacles, and the assumption that there would be a revolutionary upheaval inside Germany proved false. Soviet historians have recently considered the question of the magnitude of the opposition put up by improvised Red Army units and some at least now take the view that the much-vaunted victories of Narva and Pskov were isolated phenomena compared with the general abandonment of positions by the army. At the Seventh Congress of the Bolshevik Party Lenin ruefully described the capture by the enemy of railway stations which no one attempted to defend. 'Yes, we shall live to see worldwide revolution,' he remarked. 'But so far it is only a pretty fairy-tale, a most attractive fairy-tale.' Not that Lenin had ceased to believe in the forthcoming world revolution, but he recognized that revolution in Europe was not probable at that moment.

During the night of 23rd-24th February 1918 the Central Executive Committee of the Congress of Soviets ended a lively debate by voting 116 to 84 in approval of the earlier decision of the Bolshevik Party's Central Committee to accept the German peace ultimatum. A telegram in these terms was immediately despatched to the German headquarters, where meanwhile fresh and still stiffer conditions had been drafted. For Trotsky's previous reply had caused consternation among the German politicians. At the meeting of the Imperial Council called to seek a way out of the unexpected situation ('Are we to go running after the Russians, pen in hand?' Kühlmann had exclaimed) the state secretary had proposed taking note of Trotsky's declaration and awaiting further developments. Kühlmann felt obliged to take account of domestic reaction and to avoid needless exacerbation of the anti-war mood

of the masses by any aggressive prolongation of the war. But as usual in such moments of decision, it was the intransigent, expansionist, and annexationist views of the general staff that won the day, demanding the formal signature of a treaty incorporating further annexations. The same quarters were even playing with the idea of continuing the war, overthrowing the Bolsheviks, and setting up a new 'national' government of supporters of the monarchy to guarantee pro-German policies for the future — for the whole German offensive had virtually become a technical problem of organization rather than one of military strategy. German military circles were well aware that the Soviet government was 'inwardly hostile' to them.

After making a declaration that he was signing the document not as a negotiated peace treaty but as a *Diktat* under the pressure of *force majeure,* the Soviet representative put his name to the list of demands presented by the Central powers and by Germany in particular. The hostilities between the Central powers and Soviet Russia were formally at an end. For the temporary victors, the booty was enormous. Russia gave up so-called Congress Poland, Lithuania, Courland, Riga, and part of Belorussia pending a decision by the Central powers about the fate of these lands; in the Caucasus Kars, Ardahan, and Batum fell to Turkey; some million square kilometres with a pre-war population of forty-six million was ceded. Reparations totalling three thousand million roubles in gold were imposed on Russia.

The Treaty of Brest Litovsk had an immediate effect, of course, on the course of the war elsewhere. So far events had not been dominated by revolution, but by the war itself, whose general course determined the pattern and outcome of happenings that seemed to be only marginally connected with it. It is not surprising, then, that so many voices were raised immediately after the signing of the treaty, especially in the Allied countries, accusing the Soviet government of being a lackey to Germany. The dictated settlement was quoted as evidence that Lenin and his Bolsheviks, far from being a defeated party obliged by circumstances to swallow humiliating peace terms, were in fact the instrument and partner of

Germany and of its general staff in their fight for world domination. Even in Soviet Russia itself, indeed, not everyone saw the force of Lenin's argument that Russia had to sign the Treaty of Brest Litovsk because she had at this point to give way before superior force since she lacked the military strength to defend herself.

Bread at bayonet point

It soon became apparent, however, that the Brest Litovsk Treaty involved deep and insuperable contradictions which made co-operation between the parties impossible. The contrast in attitudes toward the peace, toward its short-term and long-term aims alike, condemned the agreement to failure before the signatures were even dry. Representatives of two social systems, one imperial and nationalist, the other proletarian and internationalist, based their attitudes on doctrines which promised ultimate results on an international scale. Germany, the undoubted leader of the Central powers, had a rapacious and undisguised desire to become the leader of Europe and so lay the foundations of world domination. The Soviet government, on the other hand, sought to be a beacon for pan-European, if not worldwide, revolutionary upheavals. Both aims were at the time unrealistic. Germany failed to foresee all kinds of developments latent in the situation of the moment, Russia paid no attention to anything except that its partner in the newly signed peace treaty would not be its partner for long. A relationship founded on such a basis was practically doomed to be short-lived and could not even furnish a practicable *modus vivendi* for forces which, however antagonistic to each other, continued to recognize to some extent a certain appreciation of the realities of power and the basic purposes of the other side. So the Treaty of Brest Litovsk could not outlast the First World War.

It was the Central powers, and especially Germany, who were the first to realize (and that very speedily) that the optimism they had invested in the treaty, loudly proclaimed on the home front as the *Brotfrieden* or Bread Peace, was built upon sand. The only hopes that were fulfilled were those associated with the freeing of part of their troops. By June 1918 there were over 200 divisions on the Western Front and only 40 on the Eastern. This transfer made possible the Germans' spring offensive, which the Allies required the utmost effort to withstand; for the Allies victory and peace now seemed distant indeed, a prospect for 1919 at the earliest.

The German hope that failed most completely was that of turning Russia, particularly the Ukraine, into an economic hinterland for the supply of food and raw materials to the Central powers, so that the catastrophic effects of the Allied blockade would be removed. Germany made a secret agreement with the Viennese government about economic policy in the eastern areas previously belonging to Russia. Since December a special office had also been set up under the former state secretary Helfferich not only to do the preparatory work, particularly on the economic and financial side, for the impending peace treaty, but in the long run to lay the ground for the complete domination of Russia's food and raw material supplies by German industry. The meeting of 16th May 1918 held between leaders of German economic and industrial life, showed that the permanent influence of Germany in Russia was to rest, above all, on the bayonets of the German army and the assistance of the entire military machine. But Germany's ruling circles had overestimated her strength and they mistook a temporary pattern of power for a valid foundation of long-term policy. The idea of basing economic exploitation on a military apparatus proved quite ineffective even during the course of 1918; the classic instance of this was the experience that befell the Austro-Hungarian occupying forces in the Ukraine.

The Ukrainian Central Council led by Hetman Skoropadsky had induced the Central powers without any difficulty to sign a separate peace recognizing its independent status, and the Brest Litovsk Treaty incorporated a commitment on the part of the Soviet government to come to terms with the Central Council too. But who was there to make peace with? The German politicians were well aware that they were treating with a fictitious government fully justifying Trotsky's sarcastic remark that the only territory the Central Council ruled over was the suite its delegates occupied in the Brest Litovsk hotel. In fact on the day before the signature of the separate peace with the Ukraine the entire Central Council had to flee from Kiev. The treaty was nevertheless signed, such was the beguiling effect of the delegates' 'personal guarantee' to deliver 'at least one million bushels of grain' to the Central powers.

Military requisitioning of grain in the countryside took too many soldiers and was ineffective anyway, while for normal trade relations there were not the most elementary economic conditions. The occupying power was unable to carry out any commercial acquisition of grain because its own militarized industry was incapable of furnishing capital or consumer goods in exchange, and had too few roubles for ordinary purchases in the villages.

Between the German and Austrian purchasing organizations there arose with increasing frequency not merely rivalry but mutual deception and fraud. In Kiev the German representatives were forever complaining that their Austrian colleagues were unfairly outbidding them, in violation of their agreement. The Austrians, moreover, exploited the more favourable communications between their own country and the Ukraine in order to seize the lion's share of the grain purchases, such as they were. In mid-May 1918 the German military inspectors reported that a mere 4,000 tons of grain had been exported to Germany to date, whereas Austria had procured 25,000 tons from the Ukraine. In all, the German and Austro-Hungarian conquerors were only able to squeeze out of the Ukraine about a fifth of the expected quantities of foodstuffs and agricultural products. In absolute terms the procurements were pretty sizeable, but they looked small in comparison with the conquerors' requirements and, indeed, with the hopes invested in the conquest of the Ukraine's 'black earth' belt. German officers and diplomats based on Kiev came gradually to the conclusion that the Central Council's authority was 'not to be taken seriously', for it showed itself incapable of organizing even the foundations of a viable economy. Ironically enough, one of the major problems of implementing the *Brotfrieden* in the Ukraine was rail transport. Although the Central powers had acquired among other things the whole hard-coal minefield of the Donets, they had to import 80,000 tons of coal month by month from Germany to keep transport going.

Hopes of economic profit from Soviet Russian deliveries likewise fell far short of expectations. The commercial attaché in Moscow, Lista, found that the Soviet government was putting a number of obstacles in the way of trade with Germany. In the summer of 1918 a practical barter operation was started up, but it remained small in scope and had no serious effect on Germany's food and raw material shortages. Nor did the forced surrender of part of Russia's gold reserve demanded by the Protocol of 27th August 1918, which supplemented the Brest Litovsk Treaty with provisions concerning reparation for German property nationalized or confiscated in Soviet Russia.

German political plans for Russia's future also underwent an interesting development after the Brest Litovsk Treaty, under the influence of extreme annexationist views, especially those represented by the military clique around General Ludendorff. To be fair, these views were not shared by some of the more sober civilian politicians like Kühlmann who (it has been said), when it came to argument over eastern policy, 'must always have felt doomed to defeat in any dispute with Ludendorff'.

Foretaste of Nazism

In recent years the attention of historians has been drawn not only to the nature of German aims at the beginning of the First World War, but also to a detailed examination of German objectives in the east after the signing of the Brest Litovsk Treaty. The subject is all the more important because of the number of similarities, in scope and strategy, between the annexationist aims of that period and those of Nazi Germany formulated a quarter of a century later at the zenith of the *Wehrmacht*'s successes. In both periods we find the same limitless and overweening rapacity, together with the crudest contempt for the basic rules of international life: the respect for treaties and for the rights of other countries. The appetite of the German high command ranged from Finland and the Baltic to Murmansk, from the Ukraine and the Crimea to the Caucasus, Georgia, and Baku. These ideas were fully supported by the still decisive influence of the court in the First World War: Wilhelm II was delighted by the *élan* of his generals. Objections raised against such flagrant violation of the recently concluded peace settlement were imperiously dismissed as 'fear politics', on the grounds that 'peace with Russia can only last as long as they are afraid of us'. In the spring of 1918, pursuing this strategy of fear, German troops crossed the arbitrarily fixed frontiers and entered the central Russian districts of Voronezh and Kursk, lending aid in money and arms to the Cossack leader Krasnov on the Don. Ludendorff even toyed with the idea of setting up a 'South-Eastern League', covering the whole area between the Don and the Caucasus, under German surveillance.

The policies of Ludendorff and the high command in the Crimea, after the peninsula had been occupied in the summer of 1918 by German troops from the Ukraine, were the very prototype of Nazi ambitions to establish a German enclave there. The original plan was to assign a certain influence on the Crimea to Germany's ally Turkey, as her Pan-Ottoman enthusiasts, remembering the former glories of the Ottoman empire, wished; but this plan soon collapsed. Instead, the Kaiser's headquarters started to think about a 'State of Crimea and Tauris', perhaps in federation with the Ukraine; under this plan the Crimea, of course, was to be settled mainly by German colonists from the Caucasus, the Volga basin, Bessarabia, and so on. Germany would be given sole use of the port of Simferopol and exercise a dominating economic influence over this whole artificial entity. The purpose of this fantastic plan was evidently to guard the Ukraine from the rear and ensure its obedience to German orders. This is clear, for example, from Ludendorff's argument that it was in the interests of the *Reich* 'that there should exist on the Black Sea a state under chiefly German influence to serve as a buttress to our significant economic interests in the East'.

These wide-ranging militarist plans for the east were of course quite out of proportion to Germany's military means at the time and merely put further strains upon them as the situation developed. They were in the strictest sense 'boundless', as leading officials of the *Wilhelmstrasse* described them. In order to 'secure' existing territorial gains and hopes of further spheres of influence, these plans always required involvement in more and more distant regions. In the case of the Caucasus they even led to a conflict of interests within the camp, between Germany and Turkey. For in addition to her immediate territorial gains under the Brest Litovsk settlement Turkey was already trying, exactly in German style, to enlarge her own sphere of influence at Russian expense to the north of the Caucasus, where she proposed to set up a chain of vassal buffer-states. Berlin, however, did not intend to make way for these ambitions. For Germany regarded Transcaucasia as a bridge for further penetration into Central Asia; she wanted to 'use an opportunity which occurs perhaps once in many centuries'. Ludendorff was personally disposed at the beginning to leave the Turks a free hand in the Caucasus. But he soon swung round to the opposite policy, in its extreme form as usual, and proposed sending 'small forces' into Transcaucasia. These he described as mere 'training units' for a future Georgian army, yet in the same breath he defined their role as similar to that of the German expeditionary force in Finland – a force which took on a decisive role in the civil war there.

In June 1918 Ludendorff explained Germany's expansionist aims in the Caucasus quite pragmatically. He stressed the importance of securing rich mineral deposits and supplies for Germany's war economy. He hoped it would be possible to form a native army to fight side by side with Germany against Russia and to create another 'Caucasian Bloc', possibly in alliance with the above-mentioned 'South-Eastern League' and with various Cossack and other states to the south-east of Russia. The German militarists gave willing support, especially in arms, to the most dubious local and tribal leaders who now converged on Berlin with offers of collaboration (a 'Kalmuk Prince' amongst them); they were to accept German protection after their artificial states had been set up with the help of German bayonets. This fully accorded with Wilhelm's idea of breaking up the Russian state into four tsardoms–the Ukraine, Transcaucasia and the whole south-east, Great Russia (Muscovy), and Siberia. Such a programme of course, if ever attempted, would mean further protracted warfare with Russia.

The real loser—Germany

The real victor to emerge from the Peace of Brest Litovsk was not Germany, who had dictated its brutal conditions, but Soviet Russia, who had accepted them with all the humiliation they involved. Lenin's tactics of prevarication and temporary retreat brought their expected reward. They gave Soviet Russia the necessary time for consolidation at a critical stage. The economic gain the Central powers had anticipated from a separate peace remained, despite the best efforts of the occupying powers to purchase or requisition goods, far below the expected levels. The 35,000 waggons of corn and other foodstuffs and raw materials sent out of the occupied area, mainly the Ukraine, in the course of six months' exploitation, were not enough to make any appreciable difference to the war economies of Germany and Austria-Hungary.

The treaty also spelt defeat for the Central powers in another and equally sensitive field. Multitudes of prisoners returned to Germany and Austria-Hungary after experiencing the revolution in Russia; they returned with very different scales of values and concepts than those they had had when they put on uniform in 1914. They were glad to be back home, of course—but not to get back into uniform and resume fighting. They became a source of infection in the army and doubtless accelerated its collapse as the Russian revolution itself and the dissemination of the politics and ideology, especially peace propaganda, that went with it undoubtedly did. The Austro-Hungarian army, like the state it served, broke up into its national components. In November 1918 German regiments started to set up military councils which took part in the revolutionary movements on German soil.

In November, too, the Soviet government denounced the Treaty of Brest Litovsk and Germany undertook to cancel it by signing peace terms at Compiegne. The time when she could enforce the conditions of a dictated peace had passed. The Soviet government no longer had to fear the possibility of German intervention. And official Berlin could no longer hope to maintain its hold in Russia with bayonets; it could not even maintain relations with the Soviet government when, under the impact of revolution at home, the very German soil was shaking under its feet.

The surprise and anxiety caused in the Allied countries by the signature of a separate peace in 1918 had a kind of epilogue in the fears aroused among some of the new post-war states of central Europe at the thought of a possible German-Soviet *rapprochement*. But these fears were groundless at the time when they occurred. The Brest Litovsk Treaty had left too sour a taste behind it to serve as a suitable psychological model for future policy. Besides, external circumstances had changed too much. When the November revolution broke out in Germany it seemed as if the moment which the Bolsheviks had prophesied, the moment of pan-European revolution, was finally approaching. Only gradually was it seen with sufficient clarity that none of the revolutionary outbursts in the rest of Europe had been powerful enough to overturn the existing structure of society. No link in Europe's social chain had been as weak as Tsarist Russia. The German-Soviet treaty later signed at Rapallo, some aspects of which were anticipated as early as 1920, was in no way a continuation of the Brest Litovsk pattern; it was not a *Diktat* but a treaty between equal partners. It implied a new approach to international problems and it signalled the creation of a new and more permanent constellation of forces. (*Translation*)

Part eight · The Beginning of the End

By 1918 war had become a way of life for the combatant nations. Like some hideous Moloch it demanded non-stop sacrifice — bloodshed on the battlefields, slaughter in the trenches, privations on the home front. As long as firm belief in the possibility of decisive victory continued, just so long would the killing last. 1917 was the year of shortages, the great year of war weariness, the year also of social discontent fanning into mutiny. Paradoxically, the prospect of the irreparable breakdown of society beneath the rigours of war did not discomfort the nations' rulers. What they did fear was revolution resulting from national defeat. The spectre of Bolshevism came to haunt Europe in the closing stages of the war, but in practice it served only to inspire the belligerents to yet greater violence.

So the juggernaut of war continued to roll over the endless battlefields of Europe. The search for the quick checkmate seemed as useless as ever. But in the last two years of the war two fresh considerations lent urgency to the military situation. German policy was affected by new developments on both Eastern and Western Fronts. On the Eastern Front the elimination of Russia from the war appeared imminent as 1917 drew to a close. The overthrow of the Tsar in March of that year was followed by a period of popular hostility to the Kerensky Government. In the wings Lenin bided his time. His Bolshevik Party promised a programme of peace. If Germany could disengage her divisions from the Eastern Front and switch them dramatically to the Western, she could still stun the enemy.

And daily the need to achieve this became more critical. On the western horizon a new factor had come into being — the impending arrival of an inexhaustible supply of American troops to swell the Allied ranks and boost Allied morale. It was an alarming prospect for the German High Command, and it was to forestall this dangerous imbalance that Ludendorff, quartermaster-general of the German forces, prepared to launch his offensive in March 1918.

It was a race against time. America had entered the war on the side of the Allies in April 1917. Her motives, as defined by Woodrow Wilson, were marked by much the same curious blend of high-minded idealism and naked self-interest that continues to baffle and enrage the world so today. To Wilson this *was* the war to end all wars. He was not interested in victory for the sake of victory but only as a means to ending the crude and intolerable balance-of-power system that had caused the war and would continue to threaten international havoc. He wished to replace anarchy with community, 'organized rivalries' with 'an organized common peace'. He came to see that the total military defeat of Imperial Germany was a necessary precondition for the peaceful reordering of world affairs. Only then — through the agency of the League of Nations and the peace-making mission of America — could his vision of 'pastures of quietness and peace' be realized.

The entry of the United States into the Great War was to have far-reaching implications on the course of 20th-century history. Wilson's declaration of war was a recognition — long overdue — of America's implicit status as a Great Power. While her interests in the Pacific were to become increasingly paramount, for the present it was her military impact on the Western Front that was crucial. Before 1917 she had acted as a mighty 'arsenal'. Now her soldiers brought the promise of victory to the discouraged Allied armies.

Hence the urgency of Ludendorff's plan of attack. He gambled everything on a single great offensive that would break the deadlock in the west and knock the British and French out of the war before American reinforcements could arrive in large numbers. His last fling, preceded by a massive artillery barrage, opened on 21st March 1918. It was the ultimate failure of this gamble that led the Central Powers to make serious peace overtures with — at last — a genuine view to ending the war.

It is a remarkable fact of the war that the hardships and privations of civilians and soldiers were only transformed into soul-destroying war-weariness once belief in victory had faded. Confidence was all-important. Thus the voices raised for peace in the first years of the war represented no more than light skirmishing. Between the belligerent powers there was no common ground. When Bethmann Hollweg, the German chancellor, issued his Peace Note on 12th December 1916, he was merely indicating Germany's vague willingness to negotiate. No terms were proposed. It was clear that he was more interested in victory than peace, and so long as Germany continued to include control of Belgium among her demands, so long would Allied response be unenthusiastic.

1917 witnessed in many ways and many countries a full-blown crisis of confidence, yet by the end of the year — with the exception of Russia — the political rulers had weathered the storm. War permeated every aspect and level of society. The national economies, locked together in deadly rivalry, were warped by the war effort and diverted along unfamiliar channels. Startling changes took place in both economic and social life. The gigantic conscript armies required enormous industrial support to equip and clothe them. It was estimated that at least three civilian workers were needed for every fighting soldier. In England the idea of government responsibility for directing the economy can be traced back to the First World War. In Germany Walther Rathenau brought the principal industries under government control.

1917 was for most of the participating countries 'the year of privations'. The new concept of total war justified the attacks on the civilian population. On 1st February Germany launched her unrestricted submarine campaign against Great Britain. Deprived of many of her basic imports Britain looked at first like foundering. Food queues appeared, and rationing was introduced. By Easter German U-Boats were destroying one out of every four ships sailing out of British ports, and it was only the last-minute adoption of the convoy system that eased the situation. In France hardship and social strains were more intense. Together with the slaughter at the battle of Verdun the previous year these threatened a complete collapse of French morale. At one time there were fifty-four divisions in a state of mutiny. Coal supplies had given out in the winter of 1916-17 and the cost of living had gone up by at least 80 per cent since 1914.

While Russia was shaken by revolution, industrial unrest spread in Great Britain and France. In France there were seven times as many strikes in 1917 as in the previous year. In Great Britain the 'May strikes' briefly threatened to dislocate war production. Spiralling food prices and war profiteering were common grievances.

Germany too was feeling the pinch of the British blockade. Food imports from neutral countries came to a halt, and by the severe winter of 1916-17 the German people were probably suffering more hardships than anything endured in England and France. Total German consumption of meat in 1917 was a quarter of what it had been in pre-war years. By late 1917 milk was practically unobtainable.

It is surprising that, amidst so much grimness, the year 1917 was to end on a note of hope for all the contestants. National enthusiasm revived. In France the accession of Clemenceau as prime minister in November promised a return of leadership and stability. Great Britain waited for the arrival of the Americans. Germany looked to the forthcoming treaty with Russia to release her eastern divisions. Savaged by strikes, she nevertheless succeeded in containing the forces of opposition — largely because Ludendorff's spring and summer offensives of 1918 once again reawakened the prospect of victory. The Social Democratic Party was bitterly divided within itself between the aims of class struggle and defence of the fatherland. Most people felt that the end was in sight, but few would have cared to predict the precise form that end would take.

America Redresses the Balance

Hugh Brogan

During the first years of the 20th Century the United States played the part of the Great Absentee. Some of her leaders—most notably Theodore Roosevelt—perceived that she could not long continue to do so, that one day the defence of her essential interests would require the assumption of conventional international responsibilities; but by far the largest part of her people, reposing on a century's isolationist tradition defied augury and insisted on abstention from all meaningful diplomatic commitment. Thus it was impossible for any American statesman to do anything to avert the coming of the Great War, although that war was to affect the United States so disastrously as to compel, in the end, her participation.

Participation, when it came, changed everything, reluctant though Americans were to believe it, and hard though they tried, in the 'twenties and 'thirties, to believe otherwise. Their country's power had been vastly enhanced between 1914 and 1918. Inevitably, it could never again enjoy the restful irresponsibility of freedom from international entanglements. America's decisions—whether they were economic, military, or diplomatic, whether to act or not to act—would now have crucial influence on the history of other nations, whose fate would in turn shortly determine America's, so close had involvement become. Since 1914 American diplomacy has been more important than at any other time since the earliest days of the Republic.

Thus it may be said that in the history of the United States, as well as in that of Europe, the Great War was of epochal significance, as Woodrow Wilson perceived at the time. 'We are participants', he said in 1916, 'whether we would or not, in the life of the world. The interests of all nations are our own also. We are partners with the rest. What affects mankind is inevitably our affair as well as the affair of the nations of Europe and of Asia.' The declaration of war on Germany had an even larger significance than its message of doom to the German cause. It was the first of the great decisions by which the United States has so radically affected the course of twentieth-century history. It showed that, in the language of *1066 And All That,* America had become Top Nation. It is in this sense, and not merely as an episode in military history, that it must be understood.

Not that its military impact was unimportant. It is true that, as Corelli Barnett says, 'American help *before* her entry into the war was more vital than many recognize; and American help *after* her entry less vital, at least for some fifteen months.' The United States was the great 'arsenal of democracy', and as such indispensable to the Allies, chiefly *before* 1917: when her armies were at length deployed in France they were largely dependent on British and French resources for artillery, ammunition, tanks, machine-guns, and planes. Compared to American potential, American achievements in the field—Château-Thierry, St Mihiel, Meuse-Argonne—though honourable, were of the second order of importance. It was America's vast strength that was of the first order, undermining the will of the Germans to continue fighting. They saw their enemies, smashed in the East and losing in the West, suddenly recruited by an endless flow of soldiers who were, as one German general said, 'fresh, well-fed, and with strong nerves that had known no strain'. No wonder morale cracked. The Allies were correspondingly encouraged. President Wilson's generous language hastened the surrender. Thus the Americans accelerated the coming of peace as well as victory. A notable feat, easy to state and to understand. Unhappily, if considered only in the military context, it is also easy to misunderstand.

The man who took America into the war, of course, ran no risk of such misunderstanding. Wilson eventually abandoned his slogan of 'peace without victory' and came to see the complete military defeat of Imperial Germany as good and necessary. But it was never, to him, an end in itself. He was not interested merely in redressing the balance of military power in Europe; indeed the very concept of the balance of power was repugnant to him. The image embodied a notion of international relations that was abhorrent to him; it reflected the international anarchy which had brought about the war. Plainly it could not be trusted to prevent another such struggle. As his insistence on America's status as an associated, not an allied, power shows, he was not just throwing America's strength behind the Entente cause. He was looking for a permanent end to mankind's worst problem. 'There must be,' he said, 'not a balance of power, but a community of power; not organized rivalries, but an organized common peace.' Wilson would have wished his actions to be judged; not merely by their contribution to the defeat of Germany, but by their contribution to the creation of a stable world society. This was his ambition; peace was his dream; the League of Nations was his chosen instrument. In the last desperate days before his collapse in 1919 he strained all his powers to enlist his countrymen in the cause, holding out a vision of 'pastures of quietness and peace such as the world never dreamed of before'. Otherwise, he warned, 'in another generation or two we must have another and far more disastrous war'.

Unfortunately, by Wilsonian standards, Wilson was a failure. For the second, more disastrous war occurred. The Treaty of Versailles, reflecting as it faithfully does the armistice which preceded it, makes some sort of sense as an attempt (however ill-advised) to solve the problem of German power by tilting the balance permanently in favour of the Entente states. It makes none at all as an attempt to found a new world order. The League of Nations was a hopeful experiment, to be sure, but no more. It did not offer the certainty which Wilson craved for. Even the hope proved misplaced, and as the world knows, Wilson fell, the hero of a poignant tragedy. Only his words and example remain to encourage the renewal of his quest. Living, he could not impose his vision on his times. The prophet went without honour.

He was not, however, a prophet only. As he remarked years before his presidency,

'The ear of the leader must ring with the voices of the people. He cannot be of the school of the prophets; he must be of the number of those who studiously serve the slow-paced daily need.' Wilson was an assiduous student. His career was marked by many judicious changes of course, yieldings and compromises, as well as by bold initiatives and brilliant obstinacy. The Treaty of Versailles reflects this side of his character.

Wilson approached its making anxiously, with forebodings of disappointment, but also with the confidence born of a clear programme of action based on a concrete analysis of world problems and needs. By 1918 a new age of ideological conflict was clearly dawning: the events which brought Wilson to the fore also brought Lenin. So clear was the President about this that he had deeply coloured America's intervention in the war with ideology — or with idealism, as he would have had it. He assumed the role of the great ideologue, challenging Bolshevism with a vision of his country's historic mission: 'America . . . was born, she said, to show mankind the way to liberty. She was born to make this great gift a common gift. She was born to show men the way of experience by which they might realize this gift and maintain it.' Wilson would be her interpreter. At the conference he was the best-informed of the great leaders, the hardest-working and most disinterested. He had long been preparing for peace-making, and had successfully maximized American influence over the Allies during the War. So enormous and essential had been the United States contribution to the Western cause that its leader met comparatively little difficulty in establishing a personal ascendency over the alliance, and in his long succession of public statements — the Fourteen Points, the Four Principles, and so on — he seemed to have gained general agreement to his programme. This was summed up in the phrase, 'the New Diplomacy'. His dislike of the European state system which had brought about the terrible war had nerved him to attempt its replacement. When America was at peace, he had been prepared to use his country's economic power to force the Allies to the conference-table; and not long after America went to war he showed even greater faith in that weapon. 'When the war is over we can force them to our way of thinking, because by that time they will, among other things, be financially in our hands.'

Unfortunately Herbert Hoover had been nearer the mark when he suggested that large armed forces in being would be the most useful assets at a peace conference. The United States disarmed with astonishing rapidity, and in the event Wilson, sensibly, could not bring himself to attempt financial blackmail of his associates. Lacking the means to impose his will on them he was obliged to compromise, and the result was a treaty which was inadequate—but which would have been far worse without his participation. The calamity of America's refusal to sign arose not because the treaty was a bad one but because Wilson, nearing the end of his tether, refused to practise, in negotiations with the United States Senate, the ratifying body, the arts of compromise that he had employed with Clemenceau and Lloyd George.

The whole of this tale of high ideals forced by reality into distasteful, unstable, almost ruinous, yet, in the end, forgivable and necessary compromise, epitomizes the story of American statesmanship since 1917. The people of the United States find it extremely difficult either to realize their ideals or to do without them. Wilson's moralizing strain, that so irritated the Europeans ('I never knew anyone to talk more like Jesus Christ and act more like Lloyd George,' said Clemenceau) has persisted in his successors, though the nature of the moralism has changed, slowly becoming more and more negative: Wilson's confidence in liberal democracy was buoyant enough to make him the only Western leader prepared to deal unhysterically and unafraid with the Bolshevik problem; 'to try to stop a revolutionary movement by massed armies is to use a broom to stop a great tide', he said. Today panicky anti-Communism regularly hampers American diplomacy. America's intractability as an ally—her instinctive unilateralism—which is still so marked a trait of her diplomatic personality, was shown in the skill and persistence with which Wilson, during the War, defended his own conceptions against all Allied pressure. To use the Russian example again, he sabotaged the Anglo-Franco-Japanese schemes for intervention after the Bolshevik Revolution because they threatened to jeopardize his preferred

strategy and his dream of a just peace based on self-determination. Similarly, Pershing's obstinate refusal to amalgamate American forces with the Allies armies, though amply justified by events, reflected a temperamental American bias which still persists. It was not Pershing, but the much more popular General Bliss who remarked of amalgamation: 'I do not believe our people would stand for it.' Pershing summed the matter up: '. . . the sticking point of the thing is service under another flag. If human beings were pawns it would be different, but they are our own men and we should therefore study very carefully our own national sentiment and the attitude of our army and the people toward the proposition. Generally speaking the army would be opposed to it.' The Allies would have to like or lump this natural pride, and the choice has confronted them ever since.

Nor should it be overlooked here that by 1919 the US government (not to mention Wall Street) had made huge loans to the Allied governments—nine and a half billion dollars in all. The creation of this vast debt had helped to win the war: inability to handle it and the linked reparations question were to play a large part in bringing on the 1929 Crash and the Great Depression of the 'thirties. For good and for ill, America's economic primacy was making itself felt politically throughout the world.

The events attending America's entry upon the First World War, then, show up clearly the nature of the United States as a Great Power and the necessity for ceaseless adjustment if it and others are to live and work together. They demonstrate American power, and the limits that events impose upon its use, and those permanent characteristics which non-American states have to reckon with. They show America redressing the balance of power in Europe, America bringing freedom from the worst effects of European nationalism. Unfortunately they also show, distantly but clearly, certain other, less creditable, equally significant aspects of the transatlantic connexion. America entered the war because she was an Atlantic power. She was unencumbered with the secret treaties and imperialist ambitions that complicated the policies of the Old World. But she was also a Pacific power, and as such behaved much like the other Pacific powers, France, Holland and England, which still enjoyed large empires in Asia. Time was to prove them only less evanescent than American rule in the Philippines. But, unlike the European nations, the United States has still not disentangled itself from the Far East. And its embarrassments, in Japan, Korea, Formosa, Laos, and Vietnam, to name only a few, still threaten to involve Europe in new emergencies. This is redressing the balance with a vengeance. It is now the turn of the Europeans to fear 'entangling alliances'. Even this most long-term development was foreshadowed in the diplomacy of the Great War. Page, the American ambassador in London, urged sympathy for the Allied cause because of the possible effect of its defeat on Japanese aggressive designs; Wilson feared that American involvement in Europe would give Japan too free a hand in the Far East, and at the peace conference exerted himself, with what his biographer calls 'almost incredible effrontery', to oust the Japanese from the Shantung province of northern China, where they had replaced the Germans as concessionaires. This was the road that led to Pearl Harbour, to the Korean and Vietnamese wars: along its length America was to lose most of its Wilsonian reputation; and it is hard to say that, even so early as 1919, American Far Eastern policy was really based on high-minded considerations. At best, what was idealism in Europe looked like hypocrisy in Asia.

Such, then, was the complex nature of the giant who so unexpectedly, yet so inevitably, crossed the horizon into Europe in 1917. Uncle Sam began to meddle in the Old World: he is at it still. The Old World on the whole approved of his efforts, but there has always been a current of doubt and distrust. So complicating and overwhelming is the American presence that this is not surprising. The process of digesting such an influence is necessarily a long one, something must be rejected, even though much is accepted; and the meal is not over yet. These are the truths of which 1917 should never cease to remind us.

The Meaning of Total War

Colin Cross

On 5th September 1917 Miss Barbara Adam, a twenty-year-old student at Cambridge University, married Captain Jack Wootton, aged twenty-six. According to the conventions of their era and class, neither was yet ready for marriage. It was simply because of the war that their families gave consent.

They had a twenty-four-hour honeymoon in the country and then a night at the Rubens Hotel, London, before Captain Wootton set off from Victoria Station to join his regiment at the front. Five weeks later, without his wife ever having seen him again, he died of wounds. The army sent his blood-stained kit to Mrs Wootton and she resumed her studies at Cambridge. She went on to make a considerable public career, ending as one of the first women to become a member of the House of Lords. She married again. Yet, describing her brief first marriage in her autobiography half a century later, she wrote that she still avoided any occasion for entering the Rubens Hotel.

In ordinary times, such a story would stand out as being especially tragic. But during the First World War it was routine; something of the kind happened to tens of thousands of couples. The most direct and most devastating result of the war was the wholesale killing of young men. Great Britain lost 680,000, France lost 1,300,000 and Germany lost 1,700,000. The point is not that the total numbers were particularly large — the warfare of the 1939-45 period accounted for many more deaths — but that the casualties were almost all of the same kind. It was as if some Pied Piper had travelled across Europe carrying off the young men.

There were so many widows and bereaved parents that, in Great Britain, a movement was started to make white the colour for mourning, lest the streets appear too gloomy. This did not catch on and the old mourning rituals were curtailed to a simple armband or dropped altogether. They never really returned. The Germans were rather more traditional. 'For weeks past the town [Berlin] seems to have been enveloped in an impenetrable veil of sadness, grey in grey, which no golden ray of sunlight seems to pierce, and which forms a fit setting for the white-faced, black-robed women who glide so sadly through the streets,' wrote Countess Evelyn Blücher, in her diary for 27th December 1915.

It would be false, however, to suppose that the mood in the combatant countries was one entirely of gloom. By 1916 the expectation cherished at the beginning by both sides, that the war would be a short one, had faded. But each side, convinced that it was fighting in self-defence against an evil enemy, was confident of ultimate victory. The roistering energies which over the previous period had revolutionized the European way of life were now turned inwards, to destruction. The war was not so much the end of 19th-century Europe as its consequence.

Land of Hope and Glory

The deepest impact was upon Great Britain where the war acted as an accelerator and distorter of social changes which had already begun in the unstable Edwardian period.

The key decision, from which every other change derived, was the novel one of creating a mass British army on a scale comparable to the gigantic conscript forces on the mainland of Europe. That army was intended to end the war by overwhelming Germany on the Western Front. (Unfortunately neither its training nor its higher leadership matched the enthusiasm of its recruits.)

During the first two years of the war the whole resources of public propaganda were used to recruit the army. The country was saturated with patriotic appeals. 'Land of Hope and Glory' became a second national anthem. 'God Save the King' was introduced as a customary item in theatre and cinema performances, a custom which still survives. Kitchener's poster 'Your King and Country Need YOU', with its pointed finger, can still be counted as the most memorable piece of outdoor advertising ever designed. Every locality had its own recruiting committee. There were private-enterprise recruiters, notably the outrageous Horatio Bottomley. Some clergymen preached sermons urging young men to join the army. Music-hall stars ended performances with patriotic tableaux and appeals for recruits. Military bands paraded the streets and young men fell in behind them to march to the recruiting sergeant. 'We don't want to lose you, but we think you ought to go' became an important popular song. The basic pay was a shilling a day, and many recruits did their first drills in public parks, with civilian spectators proudly looking on.

It became embarrassing to be a male civilian of military age. An admiral in Folkestone started a movement organizing girls to present white feathers to young men they saw in the streets in civilian dress. In one case, it was said, a winner of the VC got one while on leave. Some women went a stage farther. The romantic novelist, Baroness Orczy, founded the 'Women of England's Active Service League', every member of which pledged herself to have nothing to do with any man eligible to join up who had not done so. She aimed at 100,000 members; she actually achieved 10,000, and sent the names of all of them to the King.

The flaw, which by 1916 had become glaringly apparent, was that an army on such a scale required enormous industrial support to equip and clothe it. At least three civilian workers were required for every fighting soldier. By 1915 the shortage of artillery shells had become a national scandal and even so elementary a thing as soldiers' boots was presenting problems. Thousands of skilled workers had followed the band into the army and they were hard to replace.

The government takes over

So, on a makeshift and temporary basis, began the characteristically 20th-century phenomenon of wholesale government direction of industry, Lloyd George as minister of munitions directing the initial stages. Until the war the condition of the economy had been considered hardly more the responsibility of the government than the weather. Even socialists had thought more about distributing wealth and re-sources than about managing them. Although after the war most of the controls were to be removed, the idea remained that the government was ultimately responsible for the economy.

To an increasing extent party politics and elections were to centre around economic questions. Unemployment between the wars was to become a political issue on a scale which would previously have been impossible. Recruitment propaganda also had some influence in this direction. It was hinted, without any precise explanation of how it was to come about, that the military defeat of Germany would raise British living standards. The soldiers who came back tended to look to the politicians to raise them.

The aim in 1915 and 1916 was to create a tri-partnership of government, trade unions, and employers in which output, wages, and profits would be settled by negotiation instead of by the free play of the market. This had the incidental effect of increasing the size, status, and power of the unions. Instead of being pressure groups in the class war, they tended to become a recognized organ of the community, with rights and responsibilities to the whole nation as well as to their own members. Their membership rose dramatically, from 4,100,000 in 1914 to 6,500,000 in 1918; and when the soldiers returned it shot up to over 8,000,000. The effect was permanent (although numbers were to fall later) and it was one factor in the post-war displacement of the Liberal Party by the Labour Party.

By 1916 the war had become a way of life. The streets were curiously silent; the German bands and itinerant salesmen who in 1914 had enlivened them were now gone. There were short skirts and widows and multitudes of young men in uniform. For an army officer in uniform to have appeared in a tram or bus would in 1914 have been unknown; by 1916 it was commonplace for subalterns with their toothbrush moustaches to be handing their fares to girl conductors. Every issue of every newspaper carried lists of names of men who had been killed. Soldiers on leave sought to enjoy themselves before they died and nightclubs, previously furtive, almost unmentionable places, had become prominent features of the London scene. There were said to be 150 in Soho alone; in them the customers danced to the new jazz music which had just crossed the Atlantic. The older institution, the public house, had begun to decline; under emergency legislation the government had regulated the hours at which they could serve liquor and the phrase 'Time, gentlemen, please' had entered the language. The daytime thoughts of the nation were of the permanent battle which was being waged from trenches in France; sometimes in southern England the actual sound of the guns could be heard as a distant thunder.

Deadlock and disappointment

France and Germany, unlike Great Britain, had long prepared for the war in the sense that they had for generations run a system of universal military service and could, without improvisation, immediately mobilize a mass army. Neither, however, had reckoned on a long war. The German aim was a quick knock-out of France and then a switch of forces to the east to defeat the armies of archaic Tsarist Russia. The French, equally, had looked forward to dashing victories and the reconquest of the provinces of Alsace and Lorraine which they had lost to Germany forty-four years earlier. The outcome, a deadlock in France, was a disappointment to both sides.

The fighting on the Western Front was on French (and Belgian) soil, so that the French, unlike the Germans and the British, were on their home ground. Much of the industrial north-east of France was under German occupation. The result was that the French became less idealistic about the war than the British and Germans; they saw it as a plague rather than as an adventure. It was not until late 1917 that they found in Clemenceau an apt warlike leader. The French were drearily conscious of having been defeated in the initial battles of 1914, and by 1916 they feared that they were bleeding to death. The following year large segments of the French army were to mutiny in favour of a negotiated peace. German propaganda to the effect that Great Britain was willing to fight to the last Frenchman had its effect; the Germans actually subsidized the leading French left-wing paper, the *Bonnet Rouge*.

There was in France a special wartime drabness, save among the minority of industrial workers and their employers who made more money than ever before. In Paris the politicians quarrelled and at the front the soldiers died in thousands. Unlike the British and Germans, the French felt a widespread distrust of both politicians and generals, a distrust justified by some of the facts. There was no proper attempt at financial or industrial management. Since the richest industrial area was under German occupation, France had to rely upon imports from Great Britain, the United States, and Japan for the sinews of war and these were paid for by contracting debts. The internal debt also grew — in 1915 French revenue from taxes was actually lower than the ordinary peacetime level — and more and more paper money was printed. A crudely inefficient method was adopted by the government to finance munitions production. It lent capital, interest-free, to entrepreneurs; this, naturally, gave them enormous profits at the public expense. Few proper accounts were kept and by 1916 there was virtually no reliable information on the state of the public finances.

The mass French army consisted largely of peasants conscripted from their smallholdings and sent to the front. The women left behind continued to work the holdings, but the total food output, in peacetime sufficient to meet French needs, fell sharply. By 1916 sugar had become a luxury, there were two meatless days a week, and restaurants were restricted to serving three courses. According to historic practice, the government concentrated on controlling the supply and price of bread, and success in this was the civil population's great palliative; no matter what other hardships existed, there was bread for all. Other matters of price control and rationing were left to the departmental prefects, with the result that what supplies were available oscillated around France to the *départements* which momentarily allowed the highest prices. The Paris municipality incurred huge losses through trading in food; they were written off as 'insurance against public disorder'.

Paris in the early 20th century was at its peak as the international capital for the arts, culture, and the amenities of luxurious living. Every cultivated European and American regarded Paris as in some way his spiritual home. The war, if anything, increased this prestige. Although the street lights were extinguished and the city was on the edge of the war zone, Paris acquired extra glamour as an international city. By an odd compromise, the *Opéra* was allowed to stage performances on condition that the audiences did not wear evening dress.

The war struck deeply into French family and social life. The depreciation in money – by 1916 the cost of living had risen by forty per cent – was beginning to wreck the *rentier* class which, by tradition, had its savings in fixed interest bonds. Secure employment as a public official had, until 1914, been the most respectable thing to which a Frenchman could aspire. By 1916 the officials were losing their social prestige and being overtaken by businessmen, a process which was to continue.

French war-weariness, which was already apparent in 1916, seemed to sap the spirit of the nation. In the occupied sector the people were cowed by strict German administration; there was no attempt at a resistance movement. Although eventually France emerged as a nominal victor, and got back her lost provinces, there remained a loss of national confidence and a deep-rooted distrust of war. The seeds of the disaster of 1940 were being sown.

Ersatz *coffee and 'means-test' clothes*

In Germany in 1916 something still remained of the elation caused by the great victories of 1914. With the United States not yet in the war and the Russian empire obviously crumbling, it was reasonable for Germans to expect victory. The strategy was to be defensive in the west until forces could be brought from the Russian front to overwhelm the French and the British.

The main effect of the war on the national life was, apart from the enormous casualties, the shortages caused by the British blockade. Bread rationing had started as early as January 1915, and there was an agonizing dilemma, whether to use scarce nitrates to fertilize agricultural land or to make explosives. Generally the claims of the explosives got priority and so agricultural production, which in any case was insufficient for the nation's needs, declined. Further difficulty came because of bad weather – the winter of 1916-17 was known as the 'turnip winter' because early frosts had spoiled the potato harvest.

German ingenuity concentrated on producing substitute – '*ersatz*' – foods and some, although they sound dreadful, were quite palatable. It was possible to make an eatable cake from clover meal and chestnut flour. '*Ersatz*' coffee, made from roasted barley, rye, chicory, and figs, became a national drink. Schoolchildren were lectured on the need for thorough mastication to prevent the substitutes from harming their digestions.

The virtual dictator of the German economy was the Jewish industrialist, Walther Rathenau, a brilliant administrator brought in by the war office to organize supplies for the army. Step by step Rathenau brought the principal industries under government control and set up an elaborate bureaucracy to run them. As in Great Britain, this was public control without public ownership, but Rathenau's methods were more thorough than those of the British; government 'kommissars' participated in the actual management of companies, and the plan allotted everyone his place. In 1916 the Rathenau machine had reached the peak of its efficiency and the whole of Germany was organized for fighting the war.

To accompany Rathenau's economic planning there were elaborate rationing schemes, with everyone ticketed and docketed for what he was entitled to receive. Clothes were distributed in part on a 'means-test' system – a customer had to prove to an official that he needed a new suit.

The political effect of the war was still, in 1916, to reinforce confidence in the German imperial system. Germany consisted of twenty-five states, each with its ruling dynasty, the whole under the dominance of the largest state, Prussia, of which the Kaiser was King. It was an authoritarian and hierarchical system with a strong infusion of democracy – the imperial parliament was elected on universal manhood suffrage. (In Great Britain only fifty-eight per cent of adult males had the right to vote.) Although a strong Social Democrat opposition existed in parliament, the imperial and hierarchical system worked because the average German worker trusted his social superiors and was willing to vote for them.

Even the Social Democrat deputies had voted in favour of war credits. The military

victories had engendered further confidence in the system and war weariness
had hardly begun. Shortages, hardships,
and even casualty lists were tolerable as
the price of a certain German victory.

Of course the vast self-confidence of 1916
turned out to be a mistake. Within two
years the Kaiser and the authorities under
him were simply to vanish from German
politics. German success and German
power proved to have been a delusion. The
psychological shock was to be enormous and
lasting and it helped to cause the strange
and national mood in which so eccentric a
figure as Hitler was able to rise to power.

Debts and death

All the combatant countries financed the
war by loans rather than by taxation. In
Great Britain, for example, the highest
wartime rate of income tax reached only
6s. in the pound. The theory was to lay
the cost of the war upon the future generations it was being fought to protect. What
it really meant was that, instead of being
taxed outright, people subscribed to war
loans and so received the right to an annual
payment of interest.

After the war, France was to lessen the
burden of debt by allowing the franc to
depreciate in value. Germany got rid of it
altogether in the great inflation of 1923.
In Great Britain, however, where the value
of money remained stable or even increased, the war debt was a continuing
burden which contributed towards a sense
of national ill-being and inability to afford
costly projects, either for military defence
or for the promotion of living standards.

But the greatest single effect of the war,
clearly apparent in 1916, was the killing
of young men. Public imaginations exaggerated the effect of the casualties far
beyond statistical realities. In Great
Britain and Germany, particularly, appeared a cult of youth which has continued
ever since. There was impatience and even
contempt for the past. Jeremy Bentham's
plea that we should look to our ancestors,
not for their wisdom, but for their follies
became the fashionable mode of thought,
and even half a century later it is still
continuing.

Blockade Bites Deep

Arthur Marwick

None of the great powers was really prepared or equipped to wage a protracted war in which the rival blockades would increasingly impose siege conditions on the domestic populations. France, though industrially under-developed, came nearest in 1914 to self-sufficiency, with forty-two per cent of her active population still employed in agriculture; but the balance was totally distorted by the German invasion which involved a loss to France of almost ten per cent of her territory and fourteen per cent of her industrial potential. What France thus lost had to be supplied from outside. As the war dragged on into 1917 the situation became more and more critical. There was little scope for bringing more land under cultivation, and agricultural productivity steadily declined as the soil grew tired and the men who once had worked it were slaughtered on the field of battle.

Great Britain had been prodigal in her neglect of agriculture in the pre-war years, so that she had to depend on imports for four-fifths of her wheat and forty per cent of her meat, and relied on Austria and Germany for almost all of her beet sugar. For the island nation more than any other, trade was life: the unrestricted submarine campaign launched by Germany on 1st February 1917 threw the whole Allied war effort into dire jeopardy.

Submarine warfare
Before the war Germany had efficiently developed her agricultural and industrial resources and in 1914 was producing two-thirds of her own food and fodder requirements. Through scientific inventiveness and the use of *Ersatz* ('substitute') materials she was able to overcome many immediate shortages. The

initial advantage was Germany's, but as the war continued that advantage slowly, implacably, wasted away. It was as vital to Germany that her submarine campaign should achieve a quick kill as it was to the Allies to ward off that fate.

By Easter 1917 German submarines were doing such deadly business that one out of every four ships sailing out of British ports was doomed to destruction. Disruption in basic imports meant scarcity, high prices, profiteering, and austerity. Life in Great Britain and France took on the hue of battleship grey: 'Paris is no longer Paris,' a contemporary lamented; *l'année des privations* ('the year of privations'), was how another described 1917. Day and night were reversed. Once the streets had been filled, during the day, with breathless bustle; now they were deserted — for everyone had work to do, whether in a munitions factory or the local forces canteen. At night there was now complete darkness where once there had been a constellation of lights, and the sounds of steam-hammers and factory machinery where once there had been total silence. And the night was full of the noise of rumbling convoys and the long, ominous-looking trains that carried munitions or delivered the shattered bodies of soldiers straight to the sidings at the military hospitals.

Although the strain on civilian morale was severe, the crisis point in Great Britain was limited to a few anxious weeks in the summer of 1917 when it seemed likely that the entire war effort might founder. Then the last-minute adoption of the convoy system eased the situation. But in France hardship and social strains were more intense, and these, added to the terrible slaughter at the battle of Verdun, the previous year, created a condition in which a complete collapse of morale was always a possibility — a collapse which would have struck the foundations of the whole Allied effort.

Shortages everywhere
The first real shortages, and first queues appeared in Great Britain in the early months of 1917. The press described the kind of scene which became common everywhere: at Wrexham a farm-wagon laden with potatoes 'was surrounded by hundreds of clamouring people, chiefly women, who scrambled on to the vehicle in the

eagerness to buy. Several women fainted in the struggle and the police were sent for to restore order'.

In December 1916 David Lloyd George took over the government. He appointed a food controller who established himself amid the splendour of Grosvenor House where the suggestive flesh of the famous Rubens paintings was covered up to protect the morals of the girls recruited as typists for the new ministry. A scheme of voluntary rationing, whereby each citizen was to restrict himself to four pounds of bread, two-and-a-half pounds of meat, and three-quarters of a pound of sugar a week was announced on 3rd February–two days, it may be noted, after the start of unrestricted submarine warfare. At the beginning of May a Royal Proclamation on the saving of grain was read on successive Sundays in churches and chapels throughout the land, and a special food economy campaign was mounted. Some shops and local authorities established their own rationing schemes and these were reinforced by statutory food control committees formed throughout the country. Margarine, fats, milk, and bacon became very scarce. Sugar and butter were practically unobtainable. Even 'Government Control Tea'–often likened to sweepings off the floor – was very hard to get. Towards the end of the year there was a 'meat famine', followed by meat rationing early in the new year. Upper and middle-class families turned to substitute dishes. To them shepherd's pie still seemed something of an outrage: 'but mummy, it's a particularly nasty piece of shepherd', lamented a little boy in one of the many cartoons which concentrated on the food situation. For working-class families the biggest hardship was the steep rise in the price of bread: to make matters worse bread was 'Government Bread' whose various strange ingredients tended to go bad in warm weather.

Bombs, strikes and scandals

To ram home the consequence of their submarine blockade the Germans unleashed the heaviest civilian bombing raids of the entire war: the underfed, war-weary citizens of London took to the tubes for shelter. Across the Channel there was little bombing in 1917 but in other respects France did not fare so well.

During the harsh winter of 1916-17 coal supplies gave out. This was the topic upon which French cartoons concentrated: in one a lackey is depicted bowing obsequiously before the coalman–'Coal,' he says, indicating a richly carpeted stairway, 'take it up by the main staircase'. In various parts of the country coal wagons were forcibly commandeered by members of the public. *Pâtisseries* were closed, and restaurant menus subject to severe restriction. Because of flagrant profiteering, the government encouraged the founding of co-operative and civic restaurants and industrial canteens with *prix fixe* ('fixed price') menus. The cost of living had gone up by at least eighty per cent since 1914, causing special hardship to the million or so refugees from the German-occupied areas scattered throughout the main centres of population.

Farmers and many small tradesmen were able to do well for themselves (American troops became a particularly good source of quick profit) but many bakers, adversely affected by government price control, went bankrupt. The salaried middle class suffered severely from the rising cost of living. While sections of the working classes, protected by government minimum wage laws, did not do too badly, the real brunt of the war was borne by the peasantry, and their bitterness against their urban compatriots introduced a new and dangerous social tension.

The February and October revolutions in Russia, by which eventually a major country was lost to the Allied cause, spread a tremor of excitement throughout the working-class movement in Great Britain and France, though war weariness and the high cost of living were probably sufficient to account for the great outbreak of industrial unrest which characterized 1917. In France there were 689 strikes involving 293,810 strikers (compared with only 98 strikes and 9,344 strikers in 1916). In Great Britain the 'May strikes', breaking out on the 10th of the month and lasting for a fortnight, caused such dislocation of war production that on 13th June the government appointed commissions of enquiry into industrial unrest. The commissioners for the north-east declared that 'the high price of staple commodities have undoubtedly laid a severe strain upon the majority of the working classes, and in some instances have resulted in hardship and actual privation'.

Other commissions noted food prices and profiteering as the main grievances. In Great Britain the political structure, re-activated by Lloyd George, just managed to survive the test, though there were bitter struggles between politicians and military leaders. In France there was a succession of political scandals, some dangerously tainted with defeatism. By the end of the year three prime ministers had resigned: Aristide Briand in March, Alexandre Ribot in September, and Paul Painlevé in November. Only the accession on 15th November of the seventy-six-year-old Clemenceau gave promise of any restoration of leadership and stability.

The razor and the noose
In her use of submarine warfare Germany just failed to slash open the jugular vein of the Allied powers. But if the German weapon against the Allies was the razor, the Allies weapon against the Germans was the noose – and it was already applying slow strangulation. There were no blood-stains but the life was being squeezed from the German nation. As the war continued, so Germany's initial advantage disappeared: food imports from neutral countries came to a halt, and whatever requisitions Germany might make from conquered territories these fell far short of redressing the balance. By the winter of 1916-17 the German people were already suffering hardships beyond anything endured in Great Britain or France. Yet, while the Allied press did occasionally carry stories of shortages and hunger in Berlin, they more usually concentrated on praising the thoroughness of Teutonic organization, setting it up as an example for the Allies to follow. In fact, even since August 1916 when the dominion of General Erich Ludendorff (the new quartermaster general) and General Paul von Hindenburg (the new chief-of-staff) had been established, Teutonic organization was not doing too well against the vested interests which were stronger in the loose confederation known as the German empire than in more homogeneous countries like Great Britain and France. Part cause, more symptom, of Germany's troubles was the bad harvest of 1916: for all the pre-war advances farming was now in decay because of a shortage of

farm workers and, thanks to the blockade, of a shortage of fertilizers and farm implements.

No men, no trains
The problem upon which the new military rulers concentrated was that of Germany's manpower shortage, staggeringly revealed in a census of 1916 which showed that although there were a million more women and thousands more children in employment, total numbers in productive employment were three-and-a-half million less than before the war. The 'Hindenburg Programme' of December 1916 was basically intended to surmount the manpower problem. Under the terms of a law of 5th December every male German citizen aged between seventeen and sixty not on active service, was to be drafted into 'Patriotic Auxiliary Service'. Because of the resistance of employers, who were as reluctant to employ women as they were to release their skilled men, and because there were many routes through which wealthier citizens could escape their obligations (by, for instance, joining some voluntary wartime committee), the law was not very successful. The early months of 1917 revealed the 'Hindenburg Programme' to be falling far short of its targets. Manpower was the topic of the moment, rather as coal was in France and austerity food in Great Britain: one German cartoon pictured two ageing spinsters lamenting, 'If only compulsory female service would come – then perhaps the marriageable age would also be extended to fifty years.'

Undue attention to manpower concealed the chaos which was developing in German transport. Before the war German imports had come inland from the North Sea ports by river and canal: now, with these ports blockaded, the main transport burden lay on the rail connections to the Ruhr and Silesian coalfields, to the iron deposits of occupied France, and to the food-stores of the east. Trains simply began to go missing as the various state and local authorities raided them for the provisions they needed. Close on the heels of the transport crisis there followed a widespread coal deficiency.

Poor German production figures – thirty to forty per cent less than before the war by 1917 – revealed not so much inefficient leadership as the weariness of an underfed people. Etched deep into the German consciousness was the bitter 'Turnip Winter' of 1916-17 when in place of potatoes the people ate fodder beets – and there was not always a lot else to eat. For Germans it was not a question of the imposition of rationing – for two years they had had cards for bread, fats, milk, meat, and butter – but a question of whether the ration to which they were officially entitled would in fact be obtainable. At the beginning of 1917 men were subsisting on a basic ration of a quarter of a loaf of bread (200 grams) per day, and less than a quarter of a pound of fats per week; the procurement of other commodities was difficult and sporadic. Total German consumption of meat in 1917 was one quarter of what it had been in pre-war years, and what was available was most inequitably distributed.

Throughout the year schoolchildren and women's organizations collected kitchen waste, coffee-grounds, hawthorn fruits, kernels of fruit, acorns and chestnuts, stinging nettles, pine cones, green leaves (as fodder), paper waste, rubber waste, cork and cork waste, tin waste, metals, parts of bulbs, bones, bottles, celluloid, rags and tatters, photographic silver residues, platinum (from discarded sets of teeth, or from jewellery), gramophone records, women's hair. Most notorious example of all of German thoroughness was the conversion of dead horses into soap. This prompted the Allied atrocity story that Germany was building 'corpse-conversion factories' to make soap from dead soldiers.

To the pains of hunger and squalor was added anger over profiteering and black marketeering. Price control, in the hands of over a thousand separate agencies, was totally inadequate. 'The black market,' said a speaker in the Reichstag, 'has become the one really successful organization in our food supply system'. The famous memorandum from the Neukölln municipal council to the war food department, pirated in the left-wing press, revealed clearly what was happening. Big firms, using their economic power, or access to desirable commodities, were directly cornering food for their own employees; occasionally municipalities were able to do likewise, creating conditions of bitter local rivalry, and a complete breakdown of any pretence at food distribution. The memorandum

predicted that from 'shortage and famine' the country would go to 'catastrophe'.

Even those allowed extra rations by virtue of their heavy manual work were getting less than half the necessary intake of calories. By late 1917 milk was practically unobtainable. Scarcity of soap brought a new menace: lice. The toll in disease and premature death was heavy. Death among those under five increased by fifty per cent in 1917; deaths from tuberculosis doubled. On 16th April the government had planned a reduction in the meagre bread ration. Working-class opinion was not mollified by announcements in various localities that such extras as sauerkraut, barley groats or smoked herring (one quarter of a herring per week) would be made available, and the proposed cut was met by the first wave in what, as in France and Great Britain, was to prove a year of strikes. Altogether nearly two million working days were lost, compared with less than a quarter of a million in 1916 and 42,000 in 1915. In the German navy, bottled up in its own ports, frustration, privation, and bitterness were at boiling point. Sailors, as well as workmen and food rioters, participated in the second wave of strikes which broke out in June.

German morale crumbles

Social and industrial troubles, naturally, bubbled over into politics. The political crisis of July began with various vague promises of reform: if the workers had no bread, then they must have political rights – that was the argument of politicians. It ended with the resignation of the chancellor, Theobald von Bethmann Hollweg. But conditions got worse, especially for the farmers – who had earlier done reasonably well, but who were now subject to food searches, regulations, and enforced slaughter of their stock – officials, who in some cases were, literally, worked to death, and the salaried middle class. Relatively speaking the upper strata of the industrial working class did better, because in official circles the industrial worker was valued more highly than any other class in the community, except the military. One bitter middle-class comment was typical: 'A family with two munitions workers normally enjoyed not only extra rations but a higher purchasing power than the family of a professor (whose war value, if he was a physiologist, was limited to the writing of articles proving the scientific adequacy of wartime standards of nutrition).'

The blockade, on both sides, brought home to the civilian populations some of the grim truths of war. From governments it brought, in a curious way, certain positive responses. Minimum wage laws and social welfare, designed to meet some of the grievances of the industrial worker were now seen to be as vital to the nation's survival as the man in the trenches. France was sorely tried. One more bloody reverse on the field of battle might well have been sufficient to let loose civil disorder. But on the whole civic loyalty in Great Britain and in France withstood the test. It was in Germany, apparently the efficient, disciplined nation, that the pressures of economic warfare exposed the selfishness of the employers, the jealousies of the different localities, the class antagonisms, and the hollow facade of the parliamentary structure.

In January 1918 Germany was hit by the third and mightiest wave of strikes. Subsiding before the priority needs of the last great German offensive, it was, nonetheless, a clear sign that while Britain and France had, by a hair's breadth, managed to survive their worst year, 1917, the existing German system was approaching collapse and revolution.

Socialism and Unrest

J. R. C. Wright

At the outbreak of war in 1914 the German trade union leadership and the German Social Democratic Party (SPD) in the Reichstag decided to support the German government and not to oppose the war. They abandoned the class struggle and joined the middle class and conservative parties to defend the German fatherland. This action marked a break with many of the principles proclaimed by the German labour movement in the past and it led to a split in its ranks which was never closed. From 1914 until 1918 the German labour movement was . not only at war for Germany against foreign enemies; it was also at war with itself. The national war was lost in 1918; the civil war between the two parties which emerged within the labour movement is still being fought. How did the division within the party come about?

The origins of this division may be traced before 1914 to the foundation of the German working-class movement in the 1860's and 1870's. The most famous German socialist, Karl Marx, had only a limited influence on the movement. His theory of the inevitable collapse of the capitalist order and the duty of the proletariat to prepare for revolution commanded great reverence in Germany, but it did not stimulate much action. Marx himself did not specify the type of revolution to be aimed at: he did not advocate a foolhardy recourse to the barricades which was certain to end in disaster, and he had no time for the isolated acts of violence practised by the anarchists; but equally he rejected the idea that the working class should be content to acquire rights within the existing system. This last policy was recommended by another famous personality in the early history of the German labour movement, Ferdinand Lassalle. His colourful career ended in a duel fought for love. Unlike Marx he believed that social revolution could be won within the Prussian state and even with its help: he was ready to co-operate with Bismarck to gain political rights for the working man.

The question of whether to prepare to overthrow the existing state or to work for reform within it remained at the centre of disputes within the German labour movement. No agreement was reached either before the war or after it. Nevertheless, the labour movement did not divide into two separate parties before the war: unity was maintained by compromise and evasion. The war led the movement to commit itself more definitely and this broke it. After the war the division became formalized in two separate parties, the old SPD and the German Communist Party (KPD).

The world of make-believe

There were good reasons why the SPD did not choose between peaceful or aggressive methods of changing society before the war. There were arguments in favour of each method and objections to each of them. Bismarck's anti-socialist legislation, enforced between 1878 and 1890, showed both the need for revolution and the danger of attempting it. At the same time his social insurance measures gave Germany a system of social welfare twenty years in advance of Great Britain. In the 1890's it did not look as though the capitalist world would collapse. Germany was experiencing a period of great industrial expansion – by 1900 Germany produced more steel than Great Britain – and the German working class benefited from the increase in national wealth brought by economic growth. Friedrich Engels, a close friend of Marx, tried to interpret Marx's theories to suit a situation in which revolution seemed a distant prospect. He believed that the development of large working class political parties like the SPD was the correct policy. Eduard Bernstein, a member of the SPD, challenged Marx's theories directly – for instance he said that the standard of living of the working class was rising not falling.

Between 1900 and 1913 there was a spectacular rise in trade union membership. This gave the trade unions great influence within the working-class movement as a whole: in 1914 about a third of the SPD parliamentary party consisted of trade union officials. Under the leadership of Carl Legien they were a conservative body favouring moderate and not revolutionary policies. They were suspicious of party 'intellectuals' like Karl Liebknecht or Rosa Luxemburg who advocated mass strikes. The trade union leaders believed that such strikes would fail and that union organization would be ruined in the process. Some of the right-wing leaders thought that the interests of the working man would be better served by the expansion of German industry and the extension of German power to other parts of the world.

The SPD, like the trade unions, grew fast. In the 1912 elections it won a great victory, receiving over four million votes (a third of the total number cast) and 110 seats in the Reichstag. Like the trade unions, the more the party grew, the more conservative its officials became. Friedrich Ebert, a man of working-class origin, later to be the first President of the German Republic established in 1918, typified this outlook. He is reported to have said that he hated social revolution like sin.

Those who favoured peaceful reform were probably right in thinking that more aggressive policies would not be successful: the power of the German state was too great. There was also much to be said for sharing in the benefits of the existing society. The weakness of this argument was that the benefits were not shared equally. Although Germany had a parliamentary system, its parliament did not have the same power as in France or Great Britain: it was not able to appoint ministers. In the greatest of the German states, Prussia, the state parliament was not elected on a democratic basis: the franchise was weighted in favour of landowners and industrialists. In this situation the SPD did not have the influence on public policy which its strength merited; in addition its members were discriminated against, for instance in appointments to the higher civil service. There were also restrictions on trade union activity: unions were not allowed in the agricultural and railway industries. Despite its parliamentary strength the SPD was unable to effect reform. This gave force to the argument that the exercise of parliamentary rights was not enough.

It is not surprising, given the difficulties facing the party, that the SPD leadership did not commit itself to either of the policies open to it. In theory it remained true to the goal of revolution; in practice it pursued policies of moderation. The party programme of 1891 allowed for both. Karl Kautsky, who undertook the unenviable task of reconciling theory and practice in a new theory, summarized the position by saying that the SPD was a revolutionary but not a revolution-making party. Although this was a natural position to take, it was also a false one. The party had failed to win power but it could not admit defeat. It lived in a world of make-believe, standing apart from the state which it had failed to conquer but which it was unwilling to join.

The impact of war

The war forced the German labour movement to choose between Germany and the international socialist movement. It could no longer simply stand aside, and its decision exposed the contradictions in its pre-war attitude. The war also made the support of the German working class much more important to the government than it had been before. Once the chance of a quick victory had faded, the continuation of the war required the mobilization of the whole of the nation's resources. This meant that the bargaining power of German labour was greatly increased. The SPD leaders could hope to win the concessions which had been denied them in peace in return for their support of the war. At last there seemed a real prospect of achieving reform through co-operation with the existing state. Yet, at the same time, the war offered new hope and opportunity to those who believed that the grievances of the German working class could be put right only by revolution. For the war put a strain on the German state and the German people which weakened the government and increased the revolutionary temper of the working class. Before the war neither the supporters of moderate policies nor those who advocated revolution had looked like succeeding; now both thought their hour had come. This made each side more determined to go its own way and increased the hostility between them.

On 3rd August 1914 the SPD parliamentary party decided at a private meeting to vote in favour of the government bill to raise money for the war. The voting was seventy-eight in favour, fourteen against. On the following day, accepting the decision of the majority of its members as binding on them all, the SPD gave its united support to the government in the Reichstag. The majority saw the war as a war of national defence against Russian Tsarism, the traditional enemy of the European Left. The decision of the party to support the war was a great relief to many of its members: Eduard David, a member of the right wing of the party, wrote in his diary on 4th August: 'After this storm I had the feeling that the world war was over, that peace had again returned'. If the party had opposed the war, David continued, its resistance would have been speedily overcome by military force but wide sections of the army and population would have been discouraged and embittered in the process. 'Now,' he concluded, 'we have won a common basis for influential activity during and after the war and we must not let ourselves be excluded again.'

The split in the Party
The victory of the SPD majority did not long go unchallenged. In December 1914 the most extreme opponent of the war policy within the parliamentary party, Karl Liebknecht, ignored the rules of party discipline and voted against war finance in the Reichstag. In 1915 he defended his action by saying that it was his loyalty to socialist principles which had led him to disobey the party line. At a meeting of the international socialist movement in Stuttgart in 1907 the SPD had agreed that if war broke out it would be their duty 'to intercede for its speedy end, and to strive with all their power to make use of the violent economic and political crisis brought about by the war to rouse the people, and thereby to hasten the abolition of capitalist rule'. This now became the programme of a small group of radicals, including Liebknecht, who were known as Spartacists (after the leader of a revolt of gladiators and slaves during the Roman Empire) and who later formed the nucleus of the KPD. Their source of inspiration was Rosa Luxemburg, a Jewess from Russian Poland, a woman of great humanity and determination. She applied to herself words

attributed to Martin Luther when he was asked to retract his heretical teaching at the Diet of Worms in 1521, 'Here I stand, I can do no other, God help me'. She was a devastating critic, feared by the SPD leaders and the government alike. She spent three of the war years in prison and was murdered together with Liebknecht by a group of soldiers in January 1919.

During 1915 more members of the SPD began to have doubts about the wisdom of supporting the government. Their opposition became focused on the question of whether the war was a war of defence. Those who believed that Germany had been encircled by hostile powers before the war thought that they must gain more by the peace settlement than a return to the pre-war frontiers: otherwise, they argued, Germany would be just as insecure in the future. This led to the demand for annexation of new territory to make Germany the dominant power in Europe. The SPD leaders were confused on this issue: they accepted the aim of national security but they could not endorse a war of conquest. There was a growing feeling within the party from 1915 that the war had become an imperialist venture and that the party should withdraw its support and press for peace without annexations. The chancellor of the Reich, Bethmann Hollweg, refused to give a clear assurance that the German government did not intend to annex new territory, and in December 1915 twenty SPD deputies went into open opposition against both the war and the Social Democratic leadership.

The action of this opposition minority led to bitter debates within the parliamentary party. Haase, a lawyer and one of the leaders of the opposition, explaining why the minority intended to challenge the party line, said that it would be different if the party were fighting the enemy but that it was not. By the 'enemy' he meant the class enemy; he was echoing a slogan of Liebknecht's, 'The chief enemy is at home'. One of the party 'intellectuals' accused the majority of hypocrisy on the issue of annexations and another member of the minority described the war finance bills as 'blood bills' and 'murder credits'; '700,000 men have already been killed in Germany', he said. 'I will not take responsibility for this any longer.' On the other hand, another lawyer argued that the majority must be allowed to decide whether it was a war of defence or not. Noske, a man of working-class background who was to earn notoriety within the socialist world by using right-wing volunteer troops against the Spartacists in 1919, said that a class war was absurd in the present situation and that the front was against the country's enemies. Legien, the trade union leader, demanded that in the interests of party unity the minority should be separated from the parliamentary party. Otherwise, he said, there would be chaos. He likened the minority to strike-breakers, adding, 'When someone has spat in my face once, I do not turn my face towards him again'.

Between 1915 and 1917 members of the SPD opposition to the war attended meetings in neutral Switzerland with other anti-war socialists including Lenin. In September 1916 a conference of the whole SPD failed to restore unity. In January 1917 the minority called a conference of their own. The SPD leadership ruled that by doing this the opposition had separated itself from the main party. This forced the minority to found a new party, which was called the Independent Social Democratic Party (USPD). This new party contained people with different aims although they all opposed the policy of co-operation with the government. The main division within the USPD was between those whose first interest was peace and the Spartacist minority who eagerly expected revolution. Rosa Luxemburg in a letter to the wife of one of the more moderate leaders dismissed them as a 'company of singing toads'.

The fruits of co-operation

The SPD leaders had little influence on the course of the war. They were unable to prevent the policy of unrestricted submarine warfare being adopted although they disagreed with it. After the American declaration of war in April 1917 and the failure of the German government to make peace with the new regime in Russia established by the February Revolution of March 1917, the SPD became critical and pessimistic. At a private meeting of the parliamentary party on 5th July 1917 one member said that no one believed that Germany could win the war; it was only a question of how long she could hold out. Another member condemned government policy as 'insane and criminal'.

The SPD tried to put pressure on the government by acting in concert with the Catholic Centre and liberal Progressive parties; together they had a majority in the Reichstag. In July 1917 these three parties succeeded in getting a peace resolution passed by the Reichstag, but the resolution did not commit the government to anything definite. In March 1918 the weakness of the SPD was revealed when it decided merely to abstain from voting on the Treaty of Brest Litovsk which proposed sweeping annexation of Russian territory. The reason for the SPD's abstention was its fear of alienating the Centre and Progressive parties which voted for the Treaty. The same fear led the SPD to continue to vote for the war finance bills.

The efforts of the SPD to force democratic reform on Prussia were also unsuccessful. Despite the support of the Centre and Progressive parties and a promise of reform from the Kaiser, the SPD was thwarted by Prussian conservatives with the backing of General Ludendorff. However, the three parties of reform (SPD, Centre, and Progressive) were successful in the last year of the war in increasing the power of the Reichstag over the chancellor.

The SPD was also able to defend the interests of the trade unions during the war. In this the party was helped by the military authorities on the home front who appreciated the importance of union co-operation. The Auxiliary Service Law of December 1916 applied the principle of conscription to labour, but it did not control wages and it allowed workers' committees in the war industries and arbitration committees on which workers and employers were equally represented.

To an increasing number of SPD voters during 1917 and 1918 the failures of the party seemed to outweigh its successes. Large sections of the German working class turned against the SPD and rejected its appeals to them to 'stick it out' in the national interest. This working-class opposition to the war was influenced by the USPD and the Spartacists but it also had its own leaders, a group of radical shop-stewards under Richard Müller, centred on the Berlin metal industry.

The workers' strikes

The main causes of unrest were economic. Germany imported a third of her food supply before the war; the war, the Allied blockade, and the failures of organization soon resulted in serious shortages. The severe 'turnip winter' of 1916-17 (so-called because during it the population had to eat turnips instead of potatoes) led to strikes for more food and higher wages (with which to buy food on the black market). As the war progressed the strain of working long hours with inadequate nutrition began to tell. To the casualties of battle were added the casualties of disease and starvation. To food shortages were added shortages of housing, clothing, and soap. The resentment of the deprived mass of the population was intensified by the scandal of war profiteers. As the conviction grew that opportunities of peace had been missed to satisfy the ambitions of those who wished to annex new territory and as it became plain that promises of democratic reform would not be fulfilled, so the sacrifices imposed by the war seemed hollow and feeling against the government hardened. The example of Liebknecht was honoured; in 1916 when he was sentenced to two and a half years hard labour for agitation against the war and the government, the radical shop-stewards organized a demonstration strike which was supported by 55,000 Berlin workers.

The groups within the German labour movement which opposed the war were no more successful than the SPD in influencing its course. The opposition was not powerful enough to threaten the government or to make it modify its war aims. The most serious strike waves (which were later to form the basis of the right-wing myth that the German army had been defeated by a 'stab in the back') occurred in April 1917 and January 1918.

The strikers demanded better food and conditions, peace without annexations, the release of political prisoners, and democratic reform. In 1917 the strikers appealed to the working class throughout Germany to set up workers' councils, on the model of the Russian soviets, to protect their interests. The most important centres in 1917 were Berlin and Leipzig, and in 1918 some 400,000 Berlin workers were involved. In 1917 the government promised economic improvement but did not meet the political demands. In Berlin, where the strike continued, it was suppressed by force: some of the munitions factories were taken over by the army and strike leaders were drafted to serve at the front. In 1918 the government refused to negotiate with the workers' council in Berlin although the Social Democrats as well as the USPD was represented on it. Again force was used and the strike collapsed.

During the great German offensive of the spring and early summer of 1918 the home front was quiet although conditions were no less severe than in the previous year: so long as there was a prospect of victory the German government was able to contain the forces of opposition. In the autumn of 1918, however, when it became clear that the war had been lost, the old regime was critically weakened. By November, in the words of Richard Müller (the leader of the radical shop-stewards), 'Germany was like a powder-barrel – a spark was enough and the explosion was there'.

The defeat of Germany gave the German labour movement the opportunity of power which had eluded it so long. This did not restore its unity. The divisions which had grown up in the search for power and which had been brought into the open by the pressure of war were perpetuated by differences which now arose over how power was to be used.

War Weariness and Peace Overtures

A. J. P. Taylor

The First World War affected the lives of ordinary men and women to a far greater degree than any war between supposedly civilized powers had ever done before. In the autumn of 1914 the hopes of a quick victory for either side faded, and from that moment the war machine clamoured for more men and more resources, a clamour which continued for almost four years. Millions of men were drafted into the armed forces. More millions, and women also, were directed into work on munitions or other industries essential for war. In most countries, profits and wages were regulated, more or less ineffectively. Prices rose as the governments poured out paper money, and supplies ran short. The free market which had brought prosperity in normal times now broke down. There was rationing of essential goods, particularly of foodstuffs. Very often there was a sharp reduction of the pre-war standard of life, and even so the rations were not supplied in full. Quite apart from the countless dead on the battlefields, the war brought hardship and sometimes starvation to the living.

There was social discontent and political unrest. The surprising thing is how slowly and how late this was translated into war weariness. For much of the period, men were demanding instead that the war should be waged more fiercely and more completely. The demagogues who called for aerial reprisals or the internment of enemy aliens evoked more response than did the few enlightened men who sought a way out. Equally surprising, the rulers of most countries, though usually of a conservative cast, showed little anxiety that the war would shake the fabric of society. On the contrary, they believed that failure to achieve a decisive victory would open the door to revolution. In the last year of the war, the prospect of revolution came to haunt Europe in the shape of Bolshevism, but even this only spurred the governments of the various belligerents to more violent efforts.

In the first two years of the war, peace overtures came from Woodrow Wilson, President of the one great neutral power, and not from any of the countries at war. Wilson strove to be 'neutral in thought and deed'. He refused to judge between the combatants, though his private sympathies were on the Allied side. His sole aim was to bring the belligerent countries to the conference table, and he therefore shrank from propounding terms of peace himself. His overtures were rebuffed by both sides. The Allies and the Central powers remained equally confident of victory, though they did not know how to achieve it. Even the few who advocated compromise were fundamentally in disagreement. Compromise, it was agreed, meant an acceptance of the *status quo,* but each side had a different *status quo* in mind. On the Allied side, the *status quo* meant a return to the frontiers of 1914 with reparation for the devastated areas particularly in Belgium and northern France. For the Germans, the *status quo* meant the actual situation as established after their first victories: Germany would retain all she had conquered or at the very least be generously compensated for any territory from which she withdrew.

A question of territory

Thus there were few peace overtures during this earlier period, because any common ground was lacking. The Germans made some cautious soundings of Russia in the hope of detaching her from the Allied side. Even here they were trapped by their own victories after the campaign of 1915. They would not surrender all the Russian territory they had overrun, and the Tsar Nicholas II was equally determined to liberate the soil of Holy Russia. In the autumn of 1916 the reactionary Russian ministers at last took alarm. They began to fear that war weariness was really beginning in Russia and were ready to respond when the Germans made overtures through Stockholm. At exactly this moment the German high command insisted on a declaration in favour of Polish independence. General Erich Ludendorff, the real director of the German high command, imagined, wrongly, that thousands of Poles would then join the German army. The Poland he proposed to recognize was entirely drawn from Russia's share of the partition. The negotiations with Russia naturally broke down. The Germans lost their chance of ending the war on the Eastern Front.

The topic of peace was first publicly aired in December 1916, though there was no serious intention behind it of ending the war. The impulse came from the renewed demand in German governing circles for unrestricted submarine warfare. The Germans had tried this earlier in 1915 and had then given it up when faced by American protests. Also they did not possess at that time enough submarines to make their threat effective. Now Ludendorff insisted once more. The German attack on Verdun had failed to produce a French collapse. The German armies had been heavily strained by the prolonged engagements on the Somme, and Ludendorff did not believe that his armies could achieve a decisive victory in 1917. On the contrary he confessed that the Germans would have to stand on the defensive when he prepared a withdrawal to the Hindenburg Line. Ludendorff accepted, however, the claim of the German naval leaders that unrestricted submarine warfare would bring about the collapse of Great Britain. It might also provoke the United States into entering the war against Germany. Ludendorff did not care. He did not imagine that the Americans could develop any effective military strength, still less that this could be deployed on the European battlefield.

Bethmann's Peace Note
Theobald Bethmann Hollweg, the German chancellor, was less confident. He had seen the brave hopes of German generals and admirals dashed time and again. He was anxious to stave off unrestricted submarine warfare, but this could be done only if he offered a firm prospect of ending the war on Germany's terms. On 12th December 1916 Bethmann therefore issued a Peace Note. This merely announced Germany's willingness to negotiate. There was no indication of the terms Germany would propose. Privately Bethmann intended that they should be those of victory: control of Belgium and north-east France for Germany. Even so, he imagined that war

weariness in the Allied countries would produce some sort of favourable response. There had in fact been some discussion behind the scenes in Great Britain whether victory was possible. The people had not been consulted and were still not disillusioned. David Lloyd George, who had just become British prime minister, rejected Bethmann's Peace Note out of hand and answered by demanding the complete defeat of Germany, or, as it was called, the 'Knock Out Blow'.

President Wilson, like Bethmann, wanted to avoid a breach between Germany and the USA. He, too, recognized that negotiations for peace were the only way of achieving this. Despite the failure of Bethmann's Note, Wilson tried much the same tack. On 20th December he invited the contending powers to formulate their war aims: perhaps these 'would not prove irreconcilable'. The Germans failed to answer. They knew that their aims, if openly stated, would outrage Wilson and be the more likely to provoke him into war. The Allies, though offended at being put on the same moral level as the Germans, devised idealistic war aims which could not be denied Wilson's approval. The interchange had not much reality. Both sides were bidding for Wilson's favour, not trying to clear the way for negotiations. The Germans did not bid at all seriously. Even Bethmann had despaired of preventing the renewal of unrestricted submarine warfare and merely kept Wilson in play until the submarines were ready. The Allies picked out the more respectable bits of their aims, but there was a great deal more which they intended to demand and which they did not reveal to Wilson.

Obstacles to peace
These first manoeuvres brought out the obstacles to a negotiated peace then or thereafter. Governments had to display a confidence of future victory in order to keep up the spirits of their peoples. If any country stated the terms which it expected would follow its victory, the opposing side was indignant and spurred to new efforts. If, on the other hand, a country tried to be moderate, the enemy regarded this as a confession that it foresaw defeat. More than this, negotiations were not needed to demonstrate that Belgium was the insuperable obstacle to a negotiated

peace. The Germans were in possession and would insist on remaining there more or less openly. They even perversely used their own invasion of Belgium as proof that her neutrality was no protection for the Ruhr. They argued that what they had done in 1914, the British and French would do next time. The British, on their side, were equally adamant that Belgium must be evacuated and fully restored by the Germans. This was the ostensible reason why Great Britain had entered the war, and the British never wavered from it. The fumbling negotiations, far from making victory unnecessary, showed that nothing could be achieved without it.

Social unrest

Even so, the idea of a compromise peace, however impractical, had been aired for the first time, and this was not without effect on the warring peoples. The early months of 1917 brought the first open signs of war weariness, though rarely in the clear form of a demand to end the war. Living conditions were at their worst during the hard winter of 1916-17. Food, clothes, and fuel ran short. There were strikes everywhere in factories and coal mines. In Germany there was a mutiny among the bored sailors who never left harbour. But there was still a margin for concession. Wages were increased. The trade unions were brought into partnership with government departments and the armed forces. Rationing did something to ensure that the reduced supplies went round more fairly.

In two great countries, the social unrest had political results. In Austria-Hungary, the Emperor Karl, who had succeeded to the throne in November 1916, tried to conciliate the nationalities of his nondescript empire. In Russia, the Tsar, Nicholas II, abdicated and a republic was proclaimed, in the belief that this would provide a government more worthy of the national confidence. It is sometimes said that the first Russian revolution of 1917 was made by the army and was against the war. On the contrary, the army was never in better spirits or better equipped. The revolution came after bread riots in Petrograd and took the army by surprise. The generals and the politicians who most favoured the war at first welcomed the overthrow of the Tsar as a preliminary to waging the war more effectively. Neverthe-

less, the people of Russia were now given a voice, at least in theory, and this voice was soon raised for peace.

The Emperor Karl and the democratic politicians in Russia both recognized that their countries would be ruined unless peace was made in the near future. Both made overtures for peace though they used different ways of doing it. Emperor Karl's way was by secret negotiations, a last splutter of old-style diplomacy. His brother-in-law, Prince Sixte of Bourbon-Parma, approached President Raymond Poincaré of France with terms which he thought the French might accept. Poincaré did not object to them, and Prince Sixte then showed them to Karl as official French demands. The most solid point in them was that France should recover Alsace and Lorraine. To this, Karl on his side made no objection. The British and French governments were now highly excited. They imagined that they were in sight of a separate peace with Austria-Hungary which would deprive Germany of a valuable ally and perhaps even open a backdoor for the invasion of Germany.

In fact the whole affair was a muddle, as usually happens when amateurs dabble in diplomacy. Karl only meant to invite terms which he could show to his German ally. The British and French supposed that he was deserting his ally. There was a further difficulty. Great Britain and France were at war with Austria-Hungary only in theory. Their forces never clashed except for an occasional naval encounter in the Adriatic. Italy was the only Allied power seriously engaged against Austria-Hungary, and the Italian statesmen had no particular interest in securing Alsace and Lorraine for France. The Italians wanted South Tyrol and Trieste. In 1915 the Austrians had accepted war rather than surrender these territories, and their resolve was still unshaken.

However Lloyd George and Alexandre Ribot, the French premier, dangled peace with Austria-Hungary before the Italian foreign minister, Baron Sonnino, though they did not reveal Emperor Karl's so-called peace offer. Sonnino was unmoved. No peace without victory was his policy as it was that of his allies, except that in his case it was victory over Austria-Hungary, not over Germany, that he wanted.

The Austrian peace offer, never very seriously made, ran into the sands. Soon in any case the French decided that they would not welcome a peace which merely benefited Italy, while they went on fighting Germany. Only Lloyd George continued to pursue the dream of a separate peace with Austria-Hungary. General Smuts, for the British war cabinet, and Count Mensdorff, the Austrian diplomat, had long meetings in Switzerland. Their discussions always broke on the same point. Lloyd George wanted to be able to attack Germany through Austrian territory. The Austrians would only abandon their German ally after a general peace had been made. The Habsburg monarchy remained shackled to the war.

Socialist efforts

The Russian search for peace was more open and created more stir in the world. Russia was now theoretically a democracy, and the Provisional Government sought to satisfy the wishes of the Russian people. They abandoned the imperialist aims of tsardom which had been enshrined in the secret treaties and announced a programme of peace without annexations or indemnities. At the same time they remained loyal to their Western allies and desired a general peace, not merely Russia's withdrawal from the war. There were many in the West, particularly among the socialist parties, who desired the same thing. For the first time, public opinion in the West took the talk of peace seriously. Even in Germany there was a pull in the same direction. The moderate Russian socialists thought that peace without annexations or indemnities would prove irresistible, if socialists from all the warring countries combined to support it. They proposed a meeting of European socialists at Stockholm. The German socialists agreed to come. British and French socialists also wished to come, though their object was to show that Germany would not agree to the programme and thus to keep Russia in the war, not to secure a real peace. The French government refused to allow their socialists to go. The British government reluctantly gave their socialists permission to attend the Stockholm conference. However, the British seamen, who were furiously anti-German because of the U-boat warfare, refused to convey the socialist delegates.

The Stockholm conference was never held.

With this, the hope for a general peace without annexations or indemnities was dead. However, its influence went on rumbling. In Germany, Matthias Erzberger, a leader of the Centre Party, began to doubt whether Germany would win the war. He put forward a peace resolution in the Reichstag, and the Social Democrats supported him. Bethmann also welcomed the peace resolution as a means of restraining the high command. Instead, the high command secured his dismissal. When the peace resolution was passed by the Reichstag, George Michaelis, the new chancellor, endorsed it 'as I understand it'. What he understood was that it would not count as annexation for Germany to keep her present conquests nor would it count as indemnities if she were paid to leave them. When later Germany made peace with Russia and Rumania, it turned out that the Centre and the Social Democrats understood the peace resolution in the same sense. The peace resolution of the Reichstag had no effect in Allied countries. In Germany it helped to stem war weariness. Many Germans believed that the Reichstag had proposed idealistic peace terms and that the Allies had rejected them.

There was another remarkable overture for peace in 1917. The pope – Benedict XV – wanted to save the old order in Europe. Especially he wanted to save the Habsburg monarchy, the last surviving Roman Catholic power. Also he felt the socialist competition for peace. On 12th August 1917 the pope proposed peace to the warring powers in much the same vague terms as Woodrow Wilson had used earlier. The papal peace note envisaged a return to the *status quo* of 1914 and even mentioned the restoration of Belgian independence – not terms likely to please the Germans. The Western powers had promised Italy that they would not accept the help of the Vatican in peace negotiations. Arthur Balfour, the British foreign secretary, rashly asked for more precision in regard to Belgium. When France and Italy protested, he withdrew his enquiry. Nevertheless, the Vatican passed the enquiry on to the German government. The Germans, who meant to hang on to Belgium, gave an empty answer. The pope had failed to break the deadlock, like the socialists before him.

The German government was not wholly

inactive. Richard von Kühlmann, who became secretary of state on 6th August, doubted whether Germany could win the war and was proud enough of his diplomatic skill to believe that he could end it. His aim was to divide the Allies by negotiating separately with one of them. There had already been some unofficial approaches from French politicians in the same direction. Joseph Caillaux, who had been prime minister before the war, gave repeated hints that he was ready for a separate peace with Germany, though it is uncertain whether he actually attempted to negotiate with German representatives in Rome, while Germany and Italy were still not at war with each other. Aristide Briand, another former prime minister, also fancied that he could make a separate peace and perhaps recover Alsace, or part of it, at the same time. None of this was more than empty talk by out-of-work politicians. The French people, after all their sacrifices, would not accept peace without regaining Alsace and Lorraine. The Germans would not surrender the two provinces unless they were defeated.

Kühlmann thought in any case that it was a waste of time to negotiate with any French politician. In his opinion, it was British resolve which kept the war going. If the British were satisfied, the war would come to an end. Kühlmann therefore approached the British government through the King of Spain. He hinted, quite without authority, that the Germans might withdraw from Belgium if the British made a separate peace. The British, far from wanting to desert their allies, were afraid that France and Italy, both in a shaky position, might desert them. The British answered Kühlmann that they were prepared to discuss peace terms only if their allies were included. Kühlmann announced that Germany would never surrender Alsace and Lorraine. Lloyd George in return pledged that Great Britain would fight by the side of France until Alsace and Lorraine were recovered. The mere attempt to start discussions over peace terms thus, far from bringing understanding, drove the belligerents farther apart.

Pressure from below

The fumblings towards negotiation, which had always been pretty futile, now came to an end and were not seriously resumed until the end of the war. There was, however, considerable pressure from below for some sort of action. Indeed 1917 was the great year of war weariness and even of revolt against war. This went farthest in Russia. Once the Provisional Government had failed to secure a peace without annexations or indemnities, its hold over the Russian people crumbled. It sought permission from its Western allies to make a separate peace. This was refused, for fear of the effect it would have on public opinion in France and Italy. For in these countries war weariness reached the level of action and resistance to war. In both countries discipline was breaking down in the armies, and order was breaking down behind the lines. In France, after the military failures under General Robert Nivelle in April 1917, most of the army refused to obey orders for any new offensive. At one time fifty-four divisions were in a state of mutiny. The more rebellious soldiers talked of marching on Paris and overthrowing the government. In Italy there was less open mutiny, but soldiers deserted their units and went home, where the police dared not arrest them and often did not want to. Thus, by the summer of 1917, the French army was incapable of fighting, and the Italian army was at little more than half its paper strength. The spirit in the factories was little better. In Turin and Milan, the workers were already planning to take over the factories for themselves as they did after the war.

Yet this discontent did not last. The war weariness gradually faded away, and there was a revival of national enthusiasm, though on a more cautious scale. General Henri-Philippe Pétain, who took command of the French armies in May 1917, assured the French soldiers that they would not be flung into more futile offensives and declared his intention of waiting for the Americans. When there was a governmental crisis in November, President Poincaré recognised that he must decide between Caillaux, the man of compromise peace, and Clemenceau, the man of more ruthless war. He chose Clemenceau as premier. From this moment, France was committed to the bitter end. Clemenceau arrested a few so-called pacifist agitators and arraigned Caillaux before the high court for correspondence with the enemy. These gestures were hardly necessary.

There was still enough national enthusiasm to sustain Clemenceau, particularly with the Americans just over the horizon.

In Italy the national spirit was actually revived by a catastrophe—the great defeat of Caporetto. As the shattered Italian armies fell back behind the Piave, politicians of all parties rallied to the national cause. Disputes stopped in the factories. Soldiers went back to their units. The war actually became popular in Italy for the first time.

Russian overtures

The Russian army, it seemed, was beyond saving. It began to break up after an unsuccessful offensive in July. The Russian people had become indifferent to the war. There was no mass movement to stop the war, but still less was there any mass support behind the Provisional Government. There was merely indifference, and this indifference enabled the Bolsheviks to seize power in November. Peace was the most urgent point in the Bolshevik programme. Lenin, the Bolshevik leader, believed that the people of every warring country would immediately respond to an appeal for peace if it were made firmly enough. The imperialist governments, as he called them, would have to conform, or they would be swept away by their angry proletariats.

On 8th November 1917 Lenin read the decree on peace to the All-Russian Soviet. It proposed immediate negotiations for 'a just and democratic peace'—with no annexations, no indemnities, and self-determination for every people, however long they had been ruled by another. An armistice of three months should be at once concluded on every front, so that negotiations should proceed. Here was certainly an overture for peace, the most practical and urgent made throughout the war. The German government responded. They welcomed an armistice on the Eastern Front, though they were not moved by the idealistic phrases.

The Western powers were more embarrassed. They wanted the Russians to go on fighting, not to make an armistice. They did not believe that the Germans would ever make peace on Lenin's principles, nor did they intend to do so themselves. Lloyd George and Clemenceau were both symbols of war to the end. If they now compromised, they would be replaced by more sincere peacemakers—Caillaux in France, Lord Lansdowne in England. The old theme was repeated that the only way of saving society and beating off socialist revolution was to carry the war to a victorious resolution. On 29th November the Allied supreme council gave a sharp and final negative to Lenin's Decree on Peace. From this moment the Bolsheviks were denounced as treacherous and disloyal, and their withdrawal was blamed for the continuance of the war. At the same time, anyone who proposed a compromise peace or even idealistic terms could be branded as a Bolshevik. This was a convenient arrangement, with rewarding results. War weariness became a symptom of Bolshevism. Most people disapproved of Bolshevism, which was supposed to maintain itself by Chinese methods of torture and to practise among other things the nationalization of women. Most people therefore did their best not to be war weary.

Peace at Brest Litovsk

Peace negotiations between Germany and Soviet Russia were duly held. The Germans interpreted no annexations in the peculiar form that they should keep what they possessed. They also interpreted self-determination to mean that the inhabitants of the Russian territories occupied by German armies did not wish to be put under Bolshevik rule. Trotsky, who led the Soviet delegation, resolved to appeal from the German rulers to the German people. On 10th February 1918 he announced to the astonished conference: 'No war—no peace' and departed. The German and Austrian workers were now supposed to come to the aid of their Russian comrades. So at first they did. There was a renewed outbreak of strikes in both countries. Once more the strikers were mollified by increased wages and more food, itself looted from the Russian land. The strikes died away. On 3rd March 1918 the Soviet government reluctantly concluded with Germany and her allies the Peace of Brest Litovsk. This peace was not based on the principles which Lenin had laid down. The confident hope that idealistic terms would automatically end the war was dispelled.

With this, overtures for peace virtually came to an end. Some vague chat drifted on between British and German spokesmen at The Hague and between British and Austrian in Switzerland. An American,

George Heron, also talked interminably to well-meaning Austrian professors who had no influence on their government. In July 1918 Kühlmann said in the Reichstag that the war would ultimately have to be ended by negotiations. For this he was dismissed from office by order of the high command. No one in the Allied countries went even as far as Kühlmann, though Lord Milner and perhaps others had the bright idea of buying Germany out of western Europe by allowing her a free hand to dominate Russia. All such ideas were mere whimsy, another aspect of the anti-Bolshevism with which many Western statesmen were driving themselves demented.

War weariness, strangely enough, also declined. Food supplies improved in both Germany and Austria-Hungary, as the occupied Russian lands were more systematically looted. In many parts of Austria-Hungary there was a collapse of public order, or something near it. Deserters formed 'Green bands' and lived by terrorizing the countryside. These disturbances did not reach the industrial areas and had little effect on the Austro-Hungarian armies. In any case, with Russia out of the war, it did not much matter what happened in Austria-Hungary. Her armies in Italy could stand against the Italian forces which were in equally bad shape.

Both Germans and Allied peoples were shored up by the prospect of decisive victory. The Germans were inspired first by Ludendorff's offensives from March to July. During this period there was no war weariness in Germany—a clear indication that it sprang far more from boredom and discouragement than from hardship. During the same period the British and French people were actually stimulated by defeat. From the middle of July onwards they were inspired by victory. After 8th August the Allied armies rolled forwards. War weariness, though still there, was replaced by a confidence that the war would soon be over.

There were now peace overtures of a different kind. The earlier overtures had been political devices with which to embarrass the enemy or sometimes to placate a powerful neutral. At the end of September 1918 both Germany and Austria-Hungary made peace overtures with a genuine intention of ending the war. The two governments imagined that they were still free to choose: if the Allied terms were unsatisfactory, Germany and Austria-Hungary would go on with the war. This was an illusion. The two governments were making peace overtures only because they had lost the war. Moreover, as soon as the peace overtures became known, war weariness burst out. Later it was alleged that the German armies had been stabbed in the back. This was the reverse of the truth. Ludendorff confessed that the war was lost when he insisted on an immediate request for an armistice. Only then did political discontent blaze at home. Similarly, in Austria-Hungary the nationalities staked out their claim to independence only when the imperial government had begged for peace terms from President Wilson.

An ignorant, though rational, observer might assume that war weariness would provoke peace overtures. But, in the First World War, peace overtures, themselves usually a political manoeuvre, provoked war weariness, and when these overtures were rejected, enthusiasm for the war was revived. No doubt the people ought to have demanded an end to the war. In fact fiercer war was from first to last the popular cause.

Ludendorff's Last Victory

Barrie Pitt

By the end of 1917, Europe was on the verge of bankruptcy–but a bankruptcy far more vitiating than one declared in some centre of commercial law, for it was of blood and spirit, of manhood and human hopes. Three and a half years of war had bled the nations white. France alone had provided the burying-ground for two million men; in the Ypres Salient and at Loos in 1915, at Verdun and on the Somme in 1916, and as a result of the Nivelle and Passchendaele Offensives of 1917.

Grim despondency was the mood which dominated the peoples of the warring nations–not yet plunged into defeatism, but unable to perceive the means of victory. All Europe–indeed the whole world–was hypnotized by that appalling spectacle known as the Western Front.

To its embittered inhabitants, the Front was known as 'The Sausage Machine'; for it was fed with live men, churned out corpses, but remained firmly screwed in place. This was its keynote–frustration and deadlock; it was a massive block to the progress of humanity, robbing it of happiness, ending so many lives in futile and inconsequential agony. From the Belgian coast near Nieuport down in a straggling curve to Beurnevisin on the Swiss border, the trench lines and the strips of shattered earth between and behind them, lay smeared across the land like the trail of a gigantic snail.

Along it, all day and every day, death was present–and at night the working parties went out to court it. From dusk until just before dawn they were out, hacking at the earth to carve connecting trenches between isolated posts or even between shell-holes which could be used by machine-gunners, driving iron screw-pickets or wooden stakes into the ground to support lines of hastily-draped wire, lying close to enemy trenches all night in order to overhear their conversation; perhaps leaping into them, and after a few minutes' nightmarish activity with bomb and bayonet, dragging back to their own lines some whimpering, blood-smeared prisoner for the sake of a few morsels of incoherent military intelligence.

Draped on the wire belts were the bodies of the men killed during those white, nerve-racked, back-breaking nights. Some were killed by rifle-bullets as they crawled over the ground carrying coils of wire, some caught by scything machine-gun fire as they stood to fix the wire, some bombed by prowling patrols as they worked, hearing above their own exertions only the last few footfalls of the oncoming enemy, or the soft thud of the grenade as it landed at their feet. The entire trench system from the Channel to the Swiss frontier was dug, fortified, and held by pain and death.

At any hour of the day or night, death or mutilation could come from the guns. In winter, the shells would burst on the ice-hard ground with devastating violence, slivers of steel sighing or screaming as they sped through the frost-laden air to clatter on the ground, or to thud dully into animate or inanimate obstruction. Each type of gun had its own noise, each type of shell its own evil. German 77-mm field artillery spat 'whiz-bangs' which arrived with the noise of giant fire-crackers; 5·9s threw out their shells with vicious barks, the shells whining and growling over the valleys and ridges before ending their lives with vicious, ill-tempered crashes. Heavy guns pounded the back areas with shells that roared overhead like express trains and smashed to earth with tremendous and awful effect: and every now and then *minenwerfers*–huge trench-mortars–would cough their black burdens into the air, to wobble uncertainly in terrifying parabolas and burst with wide obliteration in the trenches.

The infantry hated the artillery. They hated its wantonness, its random, murderous power: above all their defenceless-ness against it. It was like a primitive god, uncertain, inconsistent, and unjust.

As 1917 died, a battle was fought in a sector of the British front known as the Flesquières Salient which typified the bitterness and the fury, the bravery and the squalor, the resolution and the waste of all the trench fighting which had taken place along the Western Front since it had first been formed. From just before dawn on 30th December until the early afternoon of 31st December the men of the British 63rd Division fought to hold a derisory hillock called Welsh Ridge, under attack from two and a half divisions of the German II Army. For thirty hours, the sector was a cauldron of fire, of bursting shell and erupting bomb, of drifting smoke and creeping gas, of savage bayonet attack and counter-thrust, laced throughout with the dry rattle of machine-gun fire.

And at the end, less than a mile of trench had changed hands. One thousand four hundred and twenty British soldiers and nearly two thousand Germans had died, and four thousand men of both sides were wounded or missing; and ironically, those who had been driven back found themselves in far better and stronger positions than those which they had originally occupied, while the victors were so exposed to hostile fire and counter-attack that they quickly abandoned their gains.

There was little other fighting along the Western Front on that last day of 1917 — sporadic sniping, routine shelling, a few lengths of trench blown in by mortar fire. It is probable that the average daily 'wastage' of some two thousand men of all nationalities due to action or sickness caused by the conditions in which they lived, was maintained.

As light began to fail, the armies stood to. Flares and starshell rose into the sky with the evanescence and sinister loveliness of tropical plants; the crater-studded, moon-like waste vibrated spasmodically to the percussion of desultory shell-fire and explosion. More men were killed, more were wounded, more died. As midnight approached there were sounds of music and singing along the German and Austrian trenches, and there was a little mild celebration among the British.

Just south of the Ypres Salient a battalion of the Royal Sussex Regiment were in the line, and a group of junior officers drank healths together, and stared out across the snowy miles at the lines of casual flares, rising, floating, dropping. One of them was Edmund Blunden, the poet, who wrote of the scene: 'The writing on the night was as the earliest scribbling of children, meaningless; they answered none of the questions with which the watcher's eyes were painfully wide. Midnight; successions of coloured lights from one point, of white ones from another, bullying salutes of guns in brief bombardment, crackling of machine-guns small on the tingling air; but the sole answer to unspoken but importunate questions was the line of lights in the same relation to Flanders as at midnight a year before. All agreed that 1917 had been a sad offender. All observed that 1918 did not look promising at its birth.'

Yet, in fact, 1918 was to bring the end of the conflict, and despite the atmosphere of horror and waste which mere mention of the year 1917 evokes in European memories, two events had occurred during the twelve previous months which would dangle the golden prize of victory first before the eyes of the Central powers, then of the Allies.

In March had begun the Russian Revolution. It did not immediately release German and Austrian divisions from the Eastern Front—indeed the Russian General Brusilov was to launch yet another offensive there—but it was obvious to the German rulers that by early 1918 they should be able to concentrate their strength in the west. In order to expedite the Russian collapse, the German government even allowed the passage of Lenin across the country ('in a sealed carriage, like some dangerous bacillus' as Churchill was to describe the episode), for they knew that if they were to grasp their chance of victory, they must do it quickly. Germany's chance was *now,* for in April 1917 had occurred another event which might well serve to snatch victory from her; America had entered the war, and her vast potential of men and materials would undoubtedly tip the scales against the Central powers if given time to do so. So it became a race—*against* time for Germany, *for* time for Great Britain and France.

Race against time

To nobody was the reality of this situation more clear than to the first quartermaster-general of the German forces, Erich Ludendorff. Since August 1916, this large, rather stout, typically Teutonic soldier had been virtual dictator of Germany, for there was no doubt that although his great friend and admirer Hindenburg held the higher rank – chief of the general staff of the field army – Ludendorff's was the guiding brain and personality.

Ludendorff had realized for some time that between the end of the British 1917 offensive and the summer of 1918, Germany must win the war; otherwise the arrival of the American armies would tip the balance against the Central powers and all their hopes and ambitions would be tumbled in the dust.

The decision must be forced in the west, and on 11th November 1917, he had presided at a conference held at Mons to decide how it could be brought about. Present at the conference were the chiefs of staff of the groups of armies nominally commanded by the Crown Prince and Prince Rupprecht of Bavaria, but it is noteworthy that neither of these two exalted personages were invited, and neither were the Kaiser himself nor Hindenburg – even though both of them were in the neighbourhood. The subject of discussion was deemed of too great an importance for any but strictly professional soldiers.

The main, broad issue first to be decided was whether to launch an attack westwards against the British-held sector of the front, or southwards against the French. The disadvantage of the first was that if the British retreated, they would do so across old battlefields and the desolation and waste intentionally created by the Germans when they retreated to the Siegfried Line (known to the Allies as the Hindenburg Line). This would undoubtedly hamper the attackers, and the British were likely to prove difficult enough to dislodge from the first line of trenches, without giving them the advantage of successive lines to protect them as they fell back.

On the other hand, the French to the south had almost unlimited space into which they could retreat, thus bulging out the trench line until even Ludendorff's reinforcement from the Russian front would not provide sufficient numbers to hold the line of advance – especially with ever-lengthening lines of communication. A successful onslaught on Verdun might dislodge the eastern hinge of the French army – with enormous effects on French morale and probably on Franco-American co-operation (for the newly-arriving Americans were stationed in that area) – but as Ludendorff presciently remarked, the British might not feel themselves compelled to send assistance to the French so far away from their own areas of interest, and he would then be faced with mounting another large-scale offensive in Flanders.

He eventually summed up the conclusions of the conference in the following words: 'The situation in Russia . . . will, as far as can be seen, make it possible to deliver a blow on the Western Front in the New Year. The strength of the two sides will be approximately equal. About thirty-five divisions and one thousand heavy guns can be made available for *one* offensive: a second great simultaneous offensive, say as a diversion, will not be possible.

'Our general situation requires that we should strike at the earliest moment, if possible at the end of February or beginning of March, before the Americans can throw strong forces into the scale.

'We must beat the British.

'The operations must be based on these conditions.'

There were to be many more conferences, many more planning sessions before final directions could be issued, but eventually on 21st January, 1918, Ludendorff gave his final decisions with regard to the direction and scope of his great offensive.

Ludendorff's plans

He would greatly have liked to attack the Allied line along its northernmost fifty miles – from just south of Armentières up to the coast – in converging attacks on each side of the Ypres Salient which would meet near Hazebrouck and cut the vital north-south railway which fed the Allied armies, then turn north and drive the British into the sea. Two schemes, code-named St George 1 and St George 2, were drawn up on these lines but reluctantly Ludendorff came to the conclusion that they would be too dependent upon the weather. He had no desire to engulf his armies in virtually the same mud as that which had absorbed the force of the British attacks in 1917.

South of this area, the British held the thirty-five-mile front covering Béthune and Arras along the Vimy Ridge in great strength, and although his staff produced plans Valkyrie and Mars to push them off it, Ludendorff was well aware of the tenacity of British infantry when well dug in.

However, from Arras down past St Quentin to la Fère was a stretch of line held by the British 3rd Army in the north (down to Flesquières) and their 5th Army (down to la Fère) which seemed to promise very well indeed. Not only was it likely to be thinly manned in view of the fact that the British had only just taken over the most southern stretch from the French (thus extending existing forces) but opposite it was his own immensely strong and capaciously excavated Hindenburg Line—surely the best place in which to concentrate his force and launch his attack. Accordingly, his staff produced an overall plan under the code-name St Michael, which was then sub-divided into three sections, numbered downwards from the north.

The left flank of the St Michael 3 attack lay therefore on the banks of the Oise where it flowed through la Fère. As that river flowed on across the lines, it could conveniently continue as the left flank of the attack in that area, and then four miles on behind the British lines lay the Crozat Canal—which again would act as a line upon which his southern attack group could rest and guard its flank, while the remainder of the XVIIIth Army (the main force chosen for the opening of the offensive, under General von Hutier) broke the British front on each side of St Quentin and flooded forward until it reached the concave line of the Somme between Ham and Péronne. This would be the flank of the whole offensive, and Hutier's duty would be to see that no counter-attacks broke through to upset the balance of the attack to the north, to be borne by General von der Marwitz's II Army (St Michael 2) and General von Below's XVII Army (St Michael 1). These two armies would drive forwards until they reached, respectively, Albert and Bapaume, and on that line they would swing north and obtain a decision.

As Ludendorff knew only too well the vanity of man's proposals and the myriad accidents which can overset them, he also had plans drawn up for offensives along all the rest of the front from la Fère south and east as far as the Verdun Salient, naming them with an odd mixture of classical and religious fervour, Archangel, Achilles, Roland, Hector, Castor, and Pollux.

But the main emphasis was to be on Michael—with perhaps some assistance from Mars to the north and Archangel to the south.

The offensive opens

As early as the beginning of February, British Intelligence had garnered sufficient information for the staffs to be able to make a fairly accurate assessment of Ludendorff's plans; not that there was much they could do to protect the most immediately threatened area around St Quentin and la Fère, for there was hardly enough labour available to make good the front-line trenches just taken over from the French (who, after the Nivelle Offensive, had been so occupied with their own internal troubles that they had been content—so far as battle was concerned—merely to observe the gigantic conflicts in the Ypres Salient and do little else even to strengthen their own defences).

General Sir Hubert Gough, commanding the twelve infantry and three cavalry divisions of the British 5th Army, had thus been able only to strengthen the forward zone as far as its occupiers could manage in night working parties, the main battle zone immediately behind (varying in depth up to four thousand yards depending on the lie of the land) so far as fatigue parties from the units 'resting' could manage, and the rear zone only insofar as his labour force (consisting mostly of Chinese coolies) could construct roads along which material could be brought for the more urgent work farther forward.

Given time, Gough's men would undoubtedly have constructed defences comparable to those along Vimy Ridge, but no amount of labour—nothing short of a fairy wand—could have prepared the necessary defences in a few weeks. But the men of the 5th Army did what they could, and awaited the onslaught with that mixture of resignation and bitterness which by now typified the front-line soldier's attitude to the war, to his commanders, and to his probable fate.

Just before five o'clock on the morning of Thursday 21st March, 1918, began the most concentrated artillery barrage the world had known. Nearly 6,000 German guns opened fire almost simultaneously along the forty-mile stretch between the Sensée river and the Oise, and when 2,500

British guns answered, the additional noise was hardly noticed even by the men who fired them.

Tons of steel and high explosive fell with shattering force upon the 5th Army forward and battle zones, and as the men crouched deafened and dazed in their trenches or staggered drunkenly towards control points, the ground rocked and heaved under them and the air filled with the taint of lethal and lachrymatory gas.

In the battle zone gun positions, battery and brigade headquarters, telephone exchanges, and road junctions collapsed or split apart under the weight and volume of fire, ammunition dumps blew up in towering mushrooms of flame and destruction, laboriously-laid signal wires were ripped apart and cannon were pounded into unrecognizable lumps of metal. For forty miles the eastern horizon was a line of leaping red flame, with dulled reflection beneath a sheet of fog which covered the southernmost of the British positions near the Oise.

For four and a half hours this barrage of fire continued, sweeping back and forth across the forward and battle zones, obliterating the trenches, blasting the control organizations and tearing up what flimsy obstructions the British troops had been able to lay down. And at 9.40 am the German infantry rose to their feet and stormed forward.

The main assault troops moved fast as they had been recently trained to do, generally with rifles slung—relying for effect upon the ample supplies of stick-bombs they all carried, and upon the effect of the light machine-guns and flame-throwers which accompanied each section. Where aided by the fog, they passed quickly through the forward positions, evading the known strong-points and redoubts, leaping across the trenches, racing ahead to reach the remains of communications centres and artillery batteries in the battle zone. Behind them the second and third waves mopped up—sometimes by merely directing dazed and bleeding prisoners to the rear, sometimes completing the havoc of the guns with bayonet and rifle butt. Then they followed the first wave on into the battle zone.

Their fortunes varied inversely with their distance from the Oise, where the fog was thickest. Along the banks of the river where the fog had originated and was slowest to disperse, German infantry were right through the battle zone by early afternoon; but around St Quentin and to the north the British were able to hold on, though at a terrible price; of eight British battalions in one part of the front line only fifty men survived to reach the battle zone, and no indication of the fate of two whole battalions of the King's Royal Rifle Corps was found until months later, when the few survivors were discovered in a German prison-camp, recovering from their wounds.

Farther north still, towards the Flesquières Salient, the British infantry were proving the value of Ludendorff's forecast of their tenacity. Here the fog had not been so thick and had dispersed by 10.30 am; and the British were also fighting in trenches which had been their own responsibility for some time. The result was that by the end of the day, in the far north all positions had been held, down as far as St Quentin the battle zone had been entered but not penetrated by the Germans, and only in the extreme south had it been overrun. Here, by evening, the line was back to the Crozat Canal, and Hutier's southern flank had done all it had been asked.

That night, the Kaiser presented the Iron Cross with Golden Rays to Hindenburg (the last occasion had been to Blücher in 1814), Ludendorff and General von Kuhl (chief of staff to Rupprecht of Bavaria) coolly and dispassionately studied their maps, while on the field of battle, streams of British soldiers made their way surreptitiously back towards their own lines from positions in which they had been isolated, while the German attackers rested after their vast labours and prepared themselves for ordeals still to come.

During the days which followed, the pattern of the opening hours of the offensive was repeated, with the British positions in the north holding fast but those in the south being forced back as Hutier's advance pressed relentlessly forward against ever-weakening obstruction. By the evening of the second day, the British in the south had been flung back over the Somme almost as far up as Péronne, and positions north towards Flesquières had perforce been abandoned in order to keep some form and shape of a defensive line. It was as though a door was being forced open, hinged on Flesquières and with its outer edge swinging ominously back towards Amiens.

But this movement, of course, opened a gap in the wrong direction so far as Ludendorff was concerned. He had no wish–or perhaps more important, no plans–for a break-out to the south-west, despite the fact that it could lead towards Paris. His plans were for a break-out to the north and, with this in mind, he tried to shift the weight of his attack to the Michael 1 section, along the Cambrai-Bapaume road, in order to smash the door off its hinge. Gradually, between the Salient and the Sensée Canal, the weight of this attack forced the defences to yield until a bulge formed anchored on the Arras defences in the north and the Flesquières Salient in the south, and it seemed as though these two positions were iron spikes driven into the ground, each anchoring the end of a flexible and slightly elastic cable; but it seemed that the Michael 1 offensive could not break it.

All through Saturday 23rd March the pressures everywhere continued and under it the defences in the south crumbled, the 5th Army slowly but surely disintegrated. Reeling with weakness and fatigue, the troops fought on until they were killed, or retreated until they dropped unconscious –and inevitably contact with the forces holding to the north was lost. At 7 am the following day the six battalion commanders of the Royal Naval Division holding the tip of the Flesquières Salient, having apparently lost contact with higher command and concluding–as they watched the gaps on either flank widen–that their position was fast becoming untenable, decided that in order to avoid annihilation, they must withdraw. The Salient was evacuated and the iron spike wrenched from the ground.

The Great Retreat had begun.

Part nine · The End

After years of almost total stagnation on the Western Front the war moved with unexpected speed to its dramatic close. The momentum of the last months was in feverish contrast to the long period of inactivity that preceded it. In March 1918 Germany, her eastern anxieties allayed by the withdrawal of revolutionary Russia from the war, responded to the new American threat by launching a 'pre-emptive' strike against the British sector. The Allied armies, battered but not smashed, gave ground in orderly fashion and, under unified command at last, began the counter-attack. In making its supreme effort the German army had overreached itself. It had nothing to hope for now except a fighting retreat.

The defeat of Ludendorff marked the turn of the tide. With the Americans poised to tip the balance permanently against him Ludendorff knew the time had come to make his final bid. But as the days passed, so the St Michael offensive – after making great initial inroads – began to snarl up. Battle-weariness, heavy casualties, the confusion of the old Somme battlefields, overextended lines of communication – all the familiar factors reasserted themselves as obstacles to swift progress. In addition, many of the soldiers took with relief to the well-stocked cellars of the villages they had surprised. Drunkenness slowed the advance.

One innovation on the Allied side was the appointment of the buoyant General Foch as overall commander-in-chief. Unity of command allowed a more flexible response to the changing military situation. The passing weeks confirmed Ludendorff's territorial gains but also his inability to ram his advantage home. On 1st June a German attack was met for the first time by American troops – and firmly repulsed.

Henceforward the Allies could count on a regular intake of fresh troops, while Ludendorff's divisional strength was gradually being whittled down. For the first time since the days of Verdun and the Somme the Allied armies felt themselves victorious, and their counter-attacks were strong and confident. On 8th August, 'the Black Day of the German army' as Ludendorff later called it, the Allied advance to the Rhine began, eased by an unprecedented loss of nerve on the part of the German divisions.

The decisive blow that brought Germany to her knees was delivered from an unexpected quarter – the almost forgotten south-eastern front. Lloyd George had formed the idea that the surest way of defeating Germany was by 'knocking away the props' – knocking Germany's allies out of the war. Most military leaders in London and Paris saw Austria-Hungary, Turkey, and Bulgaria as distracting sideshows from the main theatre of war: the Western Front. It was not until September 1918 that the Allies determined to isolate Germany by striking her from the rear.

Part of the trouble stemmed from the clash of interests among the Allies. Italy, for example, saw Austria as the main enemy. To Britain Austria-Hungary and Bulgaria seemed unimportant. The French had little interest in Turkish affairs but were more concerned that the Bulgarians be kept out of Greece.

Lloyd George's particular concern was Turkey. The new regime of the 'Young Turks' had ignored the growing aspirations of the non-Turkish communities within the Ottoman Empire. The long-promised 'Arab awakening' was at hand. The liberation of Jerusalem appealed to Lloyd George's sense of the grandiose; he saw the capture of Palestine as the means to knock Turkey out of the war, thereby opening up the way to German-dominated Europe from the south-eastern tip.

While General Allenby put this plan into operation, rapid gains were made on both the Bulgarian and Austro-Hungarian fronts. General Franchet d'Esperey had been put in command of the 'Army of the Orient', a cosmopolitan force under French leadership based on Salonika whose purpose was to support the Serbs and prevent the Bulgarians invading Greece. Bulgaria herself was exhausted by the Balkan Wars. She had suffered much and gained nothing. The little industry she had was commandeered by the German war machine, and agriculture was hard hit by the absence of able-bodied peasants.

So Germany was faced with a crumbling south-eastern front. Disaffection was rife in both the Bulgarian and Turkish ranks, and — worse still — the oldest of Germany's allies, Austria-Hungary, was riddled with discontent. Here the Dual Monarchy was under mounting pressure from her nationalist minorities — Czechs, Slovaks, Poles, Rumanians — to sue for peace. The ties that held the empire together had been loosened by economic austerity. Hindenburg's slogan *Durchhalten!* ('See it through') held no appeal for the increasingly assertive subject peoples of the empire.

Relations between Berlin and Vienna had never been easy, and when the Emperor Franz Josef died in November 1916 he was replaced by his vacillating nephew, Archduke Karl. Karl's inclinations were all on the side of peace. Early in 1918 Hungary — like Germany — was 'hit by a wave of industrial strikes inspired by the success of Bolshevism in Russia. Elsewhere the Habsburg empire was threatened by the growing demand for national independence on the part of the Poles, the Czechs, the South Slavs, and the Rumanians. The Czech exiles in Paris, led by Thomas Masaryk, led the anti-Habsburg campaign. They denounced the regime as corrupt, inhuman, and ready for liquidation, and proceeded to build up Czech and Slovak military units in Russia, France, and Italy. The Allies could hardly ignore their plans for independence.

In the autumn and winter of 1918 all these developments came to a head. While the German armies fell back on the Western Front, Germany's allies folded in the south. On 30th September Bulgaria withdrew from the war. Turkey had already been defeated in Palestine and faced collapse in Mesopotamia as well. On 30th October the Turkish armistice was signed. On the same day the Austrian line on the Piave river caved in to a massive Italian offensive. The Austrian headquarters at Vittorio Veneto was overrun, and fighting ceased on 3rd November. Emperor Karl had had enough. He and his Habsburg officials had lost conviction in their right to govern. It was with relief that he signed the document of abdication on 11th November.

Ludendorff had realized since July the hopelessness of his position on the Western Front. On 11th September the Allies had broken the great defensive Hindenburg Line and were now for the first time poised to invade the sacred fatherland. Ludendorff, conceding victory, was able to persuade parliament to make the peace. In this way the myth was born that Germany had been 'stabbed in the back' by the politicians of the Left. This was to become a powerful weapon in Nazi hands. Erzberger's government — the 'November criminals' as they were later known in extreme right-wing circles — signed the armistice at Compiègne on 11th November — the same day that Karl I of Austria-Hungary had abdicated. The terms were those of unconditional surrender.

So it came about that in November 1918 the double-headed eagles of the Austrian empire were removed from official buildings and the imperial anthem ceased to be sung. The complex structure of the Dual Monarchy fell apart to leave Vienna the leading city of a now insignificant country. The Allies had sanctioned the break-up of the Habsburg empire months before it took place. So too with the Turkish Empire. No trace of Ottoman rule remained in Arabia after November 1918. Turkey's modernizing ruler, Kemal Atatürk, came to see that it was only by turning his back on Ottoman imperialism that he could hope to build up a strong centralized Turkish state. The principle of self-determination among nations, which had come to the fore in the course of the war, was duly ratified at the Treaty of Versailles in 1919.

Collapse of Germany's Allies

Alan Palmer

Throughout the First World War most military leaders in London and Paris assumed that the prime task of the British and French armies was to defeat the Germans on the Western Front. Victory, they believed, would come only after a long war of attrition, in which the German army would be bled to death by endless attacks across the shell-scarred fields of France and Flanders. To these 'Westerners' the struggle against Germany's allies–Austria-Hungary, Turkey, and Bulgaria–was at best a tiresome sideshow and at times a dangerous distraction, ravenously consuming both men and munitions. Yet, from the first, the Western strategy had its critics on either side of the Channel. 'Why', they asked in effect, 'pit thousands of men against heavily fortified positions in a theatre of operations selected by the Germans themselves for their main effort? If there is deadlock between the huge armies on the Western Front, then surely a decision should be sought elsewhere, by striking at Germany's vulnerable partners so as to isolate the principal enemy and turn the natural fortress of central Europe from the rear?' This policy was broached in the first winter of war; and yet it was not until September 1918 that the Allies managed, almost as an afterthought, to put it into practice effectively.

Not all the delay stemmed from the obduracy of the Westerners. The differing importance of Germany's partners to the various Allied governments led to confusion, and even suspicion, in their counsels. To the Italians, for example, the war remained a last chapter in the Risorgimento, with the Austrians no less an enemy than in the days of Cavour and Garibaldi; and the nationalists in Rome regarded Turkey and Bulgaria as insignificant adversaries, less of a danger to Italy's aspirations than her nominal ally, Serbia (who also aspired to win influence in Dalmatia). The French, too, could not neglect the Austrian threat in northern Italy, for there was always a possibility of a Napoleonic campaign in reverse, with a joint Austro-German army sweeping across Lombardy and making for Lyons and the heart of France (a strategic project which was actually proposed by the Austrian chief-of-staff to the German high command in 1916). Although the French had clearly defined ambitions in Syria, they had in general little interest in Turkish affairs, but there was far greater concern in Paris than in London for the 'Army of the Orient', that supremely cosmopolitan force which, under French command, had been gathered at Salonika to succour the Serbs and keep the Bulgarians out of Greece.

The British, by contrast, became increasingly convinced as the war continued that Turkey was second only to Germany among their enemies. Each successive Turkish affront rankled: the sanctuary afforded to the Goeben and Breslau in 1914; the gullies of Gallipoli, silent with the humiliation of vain endeavour; and the ominous lists of prisoners from Mesopotamia dying in Turkish camps. On the other hand, in London, Austria-Hungary and Bulgaria seemed of little account. There was a tendency to leave the Habsburg empire to the Italians, for it was assumed–at least until Caporetto–that fifty-two divisions and 5,000 guns concentrated on so small a front as the Isonzo would, sooner or later, crack the Austrian defences. And, although the London press made much of Bulgarian atrocities in Macedonia, a Gladstonian-Liberal sympathy with the Bulgarians lingered on at Westminster, where the war was notoriously slow to shatter the enchantment of lost illusions. The prospects of entering Sofia in triumph held little appeal compared with the glory of liberating Jerusalem or of humbling the Turk in his capital on the Bosporus.

The changes in the British attitude are clearly illustrated by the evolution of Lloyd George's ideas on general strategy. Even before becoming prime minister in December 1916, Lloyd George had convinced himself that the surest method of defeating Germany was by 'knocking away the props' afforded by her allies. But his priorities for destruction varied with the fluctuations of the war: thus in December 1914 he wanted an inter-Allied force from the Balkans to advance up the Danube; by January 1917 he had come to favour a joint offensive in northern Italy, with supporting attacks on the Bulgarian positions in Macedonia; but six months later he emerged as a latter-day Crusader, seek-Jerusalem as a Christmas gift for the British people, and triumphs in Turkey continued to fire his imagination until the final collapse of 1918. He maintained that, if the Turks were forced by defeat in Palestine to make a separate peace, the Allies could insist on occupying Constantinople and its hinterland and thus roll up the map of German-dominated Europe from its south-eastern tip. Few military advisers agreed with him; but Lloyd George was not to be inhibited by the disapprobation of brass-hat pundits.

The instrument chosen by Lloyd George in June 1917 to fulfil his wishes in Palestine was General Sir Edmund Allenby, who had gained a striking success for British arms at Arras that spring, but had subsequently fallen out of favour with Haig. Allenby was a soldier of personality, a physical and moral giant. His predecessor as commander of the army in Egypt, Sir Archibald Murray, had lost nearly six thousand men in the last assault on the olives and cactus-hedges of Gaza; and Allenby, weary of the wastage on the Western Front, was determined to avoid all such costly attacks on the heavily fortified positions along the Palestinian coastal plain. He had the cavalryman's instinctive liking for a war of movement. At the end of October 1917 he struck at Beersheba, in the Judaean hills, twenty miles east of Gaza, breaking through the Turkish lines and swinging round so as to take Gaza from the sand-dunes on the flank of its defences. A rapid pursuit carried the advance fifty miles up the coast to the port of Jaffa. With rain falling night after night, so that the army was forced to rely on mules and donkeys for transport along the mud-caked tracks, Allenby himself pressed forward from Beersheba north-westwards to Jerusalem. On 9th December the city, which had been in Muslim hands

for over 600 years, fell; and the victory was hailed in London as the most impressive conquest yet achieved by British troops in the war. Yet the Turkish army, bolstered by a leavening of German officers and specialist units, was still far from beaten. Heavy rain prevented any further British advance. In February 1918 Jericho was taken; but Allenby, who was forced to send sixty battalions back to France after the German spring offensive, had to mark time all that summer, improvising an army of British, Australian, New Zealand, and Indian divisions which, supplemented by Lawrence's 'Arab Legion', would be capable of striking a decisive blow in the autumn.

'Desperate Frankie'

Across the Mediterranean, the Allies in Salonika were also preparing to go over to the offensive. Maurice Sarrail, the politically ambitious general who had presided like a proconsul over the 'Army of the Orient' since its inception in October 1915, was recalled by Clemenceau in December 1917. His post was offered to General Franchet d'Esperey, an 'Easterner' by conviction and a soldier who knew from his enterprising travels before the war the Balkans and central Europe better than any other high-ranking Frenchman. But Franchet d'Esperey was reluctant to relinquish his command on the Oise and the Aisne at this crucial hour in what he regarded as a personal duel with Hindenburg. It was accordingly General Guillaumat whom Clemenceau sent to Salonika, with the hard task of reconciling the British, Serbian, Greek, and Italian commanders, long estranged from the French by Sarrail's slights and pinpricks. He restored some of the confidence of this much despised army, but before launching an offensive he was summoned back to a Paris menaced by the Germans on the Marne; and Franchet d'Esperey, whose Army Group had sustained a reverse on the Chemin des Dames, was peremptorily sent east as Guillaumat's successor.

Although totally different in appearance and physique, Franchet d'Esperey had much in common with Allenby: the same liking for independence in command, the same sudden eclipse on the Western Front, the same broad strategic sweep of the mind, the same conviction that, after years of entrenchment, the hour of the cavalry was at hand and that fast-moving squadrons could turn tactical success into final triumph. Like Allenby, he combined a volcanic temper with the personal magnetism which lifts the spirit of a downcast army; and, again like Allenby, his determination to achieve victory was hardened by the tragic loss in battle of an only son. When he landed at Salonika on 17th June 1918 he bluntly told the group of officers assembled to greet him, 'I expect from you savage vigour'. His British subordinates, struggling with the unfamiliar pentasyllabic surname, promptly dubbed their new commander 'Desperate Frankie'. It was an apt nickname; for, within nineteen days of arriving in Macedonia, his energy and drive had produced plans for an offensive to smash the Bulgarians and carry the war back to the Danube, nearly three hundred miles to the north.

The proposed Balkan offensive was discussed at a meeting of the supreme war council at Versailles on 3rd July, which was attended by the French and British prime ministers and their principal military advisers. The plan came under attack not only from the die-hard Westerners, who disliked any enterprise which might draw troops away from France, but from Lloyd George as well, primarily because he feared that it would divert men and material from Allenby in Palestine. A sub-committee of inter-Allied military representatives studied the project in detail and, on 3rd August, gave it their support, provided that it did not interfere with operations on the Western Front or require extensive re-routing of shipping in the Mediterranean. The British government was, however, still reluctant to give its consent, while the chief of the imperial general staff, Sir Henry Wilson, remained positively hostile to any operations in the Balkans. A curious situation thus developed: General Milne, the commander of the British Salonika Army, was confident of success and informed Lloyd George that 'an offensive here at the psychological moment may have more than local effect'; and he therefore made preparations for an attack which London was reluctant to authorize. In great secrecy but, in this instance, with cautious British backing, Allenby too was putting the final touches

to plans which bore some resemblance to those contemplated in Macedonia.

Franchet d'Esperey wished to attack on 15th September and Allenby on 18th September. Not until 4th September did Lloyd George, overruling General Wilson's objections, finally give his approval to the Balkan offensive. He came firmly down on the side of the Easterners after a visit to London by General Guillaumat who, drawing on his own experience of the Macedonian Front, was able to assure the prime minister that a resolute attack would sap the war-weary Bulgarians' will to resist. Characteristically, once Lloyd George had decided to give his backing to Franchet d'Esperey, he reverted to his earlier argument for a comprehensive knocking aside of all the 'props'; and he insisted that every effort should be made to induce General Diaz, the Italian commander-in-chief, to take the offensive against the Austrians along the river Piave. Marshal Foch, watching his armies in France roll the Germans slowly northwards, was also eager for a simultaneous Italian attack, but Diaz, the Italian commander-in-chief, to take the offensive against the Austrians along the river Piave. Marshal Foch, watching his armies in France roll the Germans slowly northwards, was also eager for a simultaneous Italian attack, but Diaz refused to move until he had some clear evidence that Austria-Hungary was on the verge of disintegration. As recently as the middle of June the Austrians had crossed the Piave in force and, although they had been repulsed with heavy casualties, the Italians were taking no risks. They could not afford a second Caporetto.

The cancer of defeat

The bonds binding Germany's partners to the government in Berlin were under considerable strain even before the joint Allied offensives. The sentiment for peace was probably most widespread in Bulgaria, as Guillaumat and Milne had perceived. Such industry as the country possessed was harnessed by German managers to the German war machine. A few businessmen in the towns made fat profits from German contracts, but for hundreds of workers there was nothing but hard work and low wages. With agriculture hit by the absence of able-bodied peasants, there was a threat of starvation. Moreover, the casualties suffered by the small kingdom in the combined campaigns of the Balkan Wars and the two-year struggle in Macedonia had eliminated a higher proportion of the active population than in either Germany or France. The Bulgarians had made enormous sacrifices without gaining a single tangible reward; and, with the example of their fellow-Slavs in Mother Russia in mind, it was hardly surprising that many of the younger generation were thinking in terms of revolution.

Turkish disaffection took a different form. The Germanophile leaders, Enver and Talat, were still in power in Constantinople but, since the collapse of Russia, they had been solely interested in acquiring territory in Armenia and the Caucasus. Reinforcements–often only raw recruits–were sent to the Tigris to meet the danger from General Marshall's Mesopotamian Army, toiling northwards from Baghdad with the thermometers registering 110°F. for days on end; but few Turkish levies (and even less equipment) found their way to Palestine. There the commander was General Liman von Sanders, the greatest German expert on Turkish affairs, whose flair for organization had saved Gallipoli in 1915. But Liman could do little with an army which was short of food and plagued with typhus and malaria. Morale had declined considerably during the winter and spring; and in June 1918 Liman gloomily reported to Berlin that his effective strength was less than the number of deserters who had slipped away in the previous three months. There was no threat of revolution in the Ottoman empire; but a mood of apathy and surrender pervaded almost every unit on the Palestine Front. More and more Liman was forced to rely on his German 'Asia Corps'; for, of the beys, only General Mustafa Kemal was still willing to offer spirited resistance.

The oldest of Germany's allies, Austria-Hungary, was no less tired of war than Bulgaria and no more able than Turkey to prevent desertion in large numbers among the reluctant conscripts, especially those from Czech, Slovak, or South Slav districts. The Emperor Karl (who came to the throne on Franz Josef's death in November 1916) did not conceal his desire for peace and there was a movement to break all bonds with Germany even among the more intransigent Hungarians. Everyone dreaded another winter of privation. But it is easy to exaggerate the demoralization in the Dual Monarchy. The Italians were wise to treat their adversaries along the Piave with respect; for, although the 'Imperial and Royal Army' was short of supplies, short of food, and deployed for internal security as well as for external war, the hard core of professional soldiery was steeled by two centuries of tradition and discipline. In the old battle zone at the head of the Adriatic the Army still offered strong resistance: it was among the scattered units who were in the Albanian mountains, or struggling back from the Ukraine, or policing the Serbian lands, that the cancer of defeat consumed the will to fight. And it was in this very area of south-eastern Europe that the Allies struck their first blow.

Early on 14th September five hundred guns began to pour shells on the Bulgarian positions along eighty miles of mountain and ravine in Macedonia; and on the following morning Serbian, French, and Senegalese infantry stormed the heights of a broken formless ridge known as the Dobropolje, more than 7,000 feet above sea-level. It was a dramatic start to Franchet d'Esperey's offensive; and it took both the Bulgarians and their German advisers completely by surprise, for no one anticipated an attack across such grim terrain. At first the Bulgarians resisted fanatically and the French were forced to use flame-throwers against their emplacements, but after three days of fierce fighting several Bulgarian regiments were on the verge of mutiny, and the Serbs were able to thrust an arrow-head fifteen miles into the enemy position, threatening the supply depot in the small town of Gradsko and the vital artery of the Vardar valley.

On 18th September, fifty miles to the east, the British and Greeks launched their assault on the hump of hills above Lake Doiran, where concrete casements and concrete machine-gun nests protected the frontier of the Bulgarian homeland. Twice in 1917 the British had sought to win these three miles of scrub and rock, looming over lake and trenches like some miniature Gibraltar. Now they tried once more to scale 'Pip Ridge' and the 'Grand Couronné', while a Cretan division moved round the lake to cut communications. But, though the South Wales Borderers reached the last defences, courage and enterprise could not carry the Grand Couronné. And yet, after two days' fighting, a strange silence settled on the ridges and ravines. Cautiously the British and Greeks advanced. They found the emplacements abandoned. On German orders, the Bulgarians had pulled back into the Balkan mountains rather than risk being cut off by Franchet d'Esperey's columns from the west.

There followed nine days of hectic pursuit. The French and the Serbs advanced up the Vardar valley, covering twenty-five miles in a day, with no regular rations, 'in rags and bare-footed', reported one French general. A French colonial cavalry brigade of Spahis from Morocco, led by General Jouinot-Gambetta (a hard-riding and hard-swearing nephew of the radical statesman of the 1870's), swung left from the line of advance and, by crossing some of the worst country in the Balkans, succeeded in seizing the key town of Skoplje on 28th September, while the main body of Serbs and French were still thirty miles to the south. At the same time, the British began to penetrate the valleys of Bulgaria, with the RAF obliterating the enemy columns, caught on impossible roads through the rocky ravines. The cascade of bombs turned the retreat into a rout; although barely noticed at the time, it was the first real victory of air power. With riots in four Bulgarian towns and local soviets striking Leninist attitudes, the Bulgarian high command asked for an armistice. Peace delegates waited on Franchet d'Esperey at Salonika; and on 30th September Germany's least powerful ally withdrew from the war. The British entered Sofia and a battalion of the Devonshire Regiment reached the Danube at Ruse.

The Salonika Armistice terms included the occupation of strategic points in Bulgaria and the use of Bulgarian railways. It was thus possible to isolate Turkey and march overland on Constantinople from the west and from the north. Accordingly, while Franchet d'Esperey continued to pursue German and Austro-Hungarian units through Serbia, General Milne was ordered from London to concentrate the bulk of the British Salonika army against Turkey 'with a view to helping her surrender', as Lloyd George wrote. Yet it may

be doubted if these dispositions were necessary, for the Turks had already been defeated in Palestine and were on the verge of collapse in Mesopotamia as well.

Allenby opened his offensive in Palestine on 18th September, the same day as Milne. Elaborate deception had convinced Liman von Sanders that the main British attack would come from the east, beyond Jordan. But the blow fell on the coastal plain of Megiddo, where the cavalry broke through to the hills under a fierce artillery bombardment. As in Macedonia, heavy bombing threw the Turkish rear into confusion and Liman himself narrowly avoided capture in a daring cavalry raid on his headquarters at Nazareth. With Lawrence's Arabs helping in the east, the Turks and the German 'Asia Corps' were thrown back towards Damascus and Aleppo. An impressive roll of captured cities graced the war communiqués — Haifa and Acre on 23rd September, Amman on 25th September, Damascus itself on 2nd October. The French, far more interested in Syria than in Palestine, took a hand in the operation on 7th October, when their naval forces seized Beirut; but the victory was Allenby's, and it was his divisions which pursued the Turks relentlessly northwards to Aleppo.

With General Marshall pressing along the Tigris towards Mosul (whence he, too, could have advanced on Aleppo), realization of defeat slowly penetrated the palaces of Constantinople. At last on 13th October Sultan Mahmud VI plucked up the courage to dismiss Enver and Talat, and on the following day the new grand vizier, Izzet, sought an armistice. The Turks, however, made contact, not with Allenby, but with the commander-in-chief of the British Mediterranean Fleet, Admiral Calthorpe. It was, accordingly, at Moudros — the island base in the Aegean established by the British before the Dardanelles expedition — that the Turkish armistice was duly signed on 30th October. All fighting in the Middle East officially ceased on the following day; and on 12th November an Allied naval squadron sailed up the Dardanelles, past the rusting wrecks on the Gallipoli beaches, to anchor below the Golden Horn in Constantinople.

While Turkey was seeking peace, the war against Austria-Hungary was entering its final phase. But one Allied commander, at least, was in no mood for peace. With the towns of Serbia falling into his hands throughout October, Franchet d'Esperey was confidently preparing to march on Berlin by way of Belgrade, Budapest, Vienna, and Dresden. Spurred forward by Napoleonic notions of grandeur, he reported on 19th October that French guns had been heard on the Danube for the first time in 109 years. Belgrade was liberated on 1st November and with one Serbian army following the French into southern Hungary and a second one marching on Sarajevo, the wheel of war had come full circle.

Yet the final blow against the Habsburgs came, not from the French and the Serbs, but from the enemy they had despised since Metternich's day; for the Italians, fearing that peace might break out before they had avenged Caporetto, went over to the offensive at last on 24th October. With British and French support, they launched a furious attack on the Piave, which cost them 25,000 men in sixty hours of grim fighting. On 30th October the Austrian line caved in, and squadrons of cavalry and armoured cars took the Austrian headquarters at Vittorio Veneto (the name subsequently given to the whole battle). Already the Austrians were suing for peace and fighting ceased on 3rd November. In ten days the Italians had no less than half a million dispirited prisoners.

A last tragi-comedy was played out on 7th November in Belgrade. The newly-independent Hungarian government did not consider itself bound by the Italian armistice, which was signed by representatives of the old order. The Hungarian Liberal, Count Mihaly Károlyi, accordingly travelled to Belgrade, confident that he would obtain generous treatment for his country from the spokesman of republican France. Károlyi asked that Hungary might be occupied by the French, British, Italians, and Americans and not by the east European peoples or by 'colonial troops'. But Franchet d'Esperey brusquely turned aside his requests. By the Belgrade Armistice more than half of the old Hungarian kingdom was occupied by Allied soldiery, including Serbs, Rumanians, and Czechs. The revenge of the 'subject nationalities' was complete — but it was not without significance for the future that they owed their newly found status to the favours dispensed by a French general.

The successes gained by the Allied armies from Salonika and Cairo and Baghdad were soon eclipsed in the public eye by the humbling of Germany; and only Italy among the great powers regarded a victory against one of Germany's allies as the crowning glory of the war. With the coming of peace, private disputes hardened into an open controversy which was sharpened by the publication of military and political memoirs: some writers insisted that final victory had come when it did only because German might was vanquished on the fields of France and Flanders; others argued that the rapidity with which Germany's collapse followed the fall of her partners fully vindicated Lloyd George's policy of 'knocking away the props'. In the bitterness of this debate, the achievement of the soldiers and airmen in the distant theatres of war was sometimes misrepresented or denigrated. All too frequently people forgot that Germany's allies were no less the declared enemies of Great Britain and France than the government in Berlin; and it was hardly possible for their military potential to be ignored, especially when they were already in occupation of so much Allied territory. The great merit of the offensives of Allenby and Franchet d'Esperey was that they formed part of a general strategy for enveloping Germany, while disposing of her partners with a limited use of manpower and resources. Militarily they are of particular interest, for they combined the tactical employment of both the oldest and newest instruments in a war of movement, cavalry and aircraft.

The Break-up of the Habsburg Empire

Z. A. B. Zeman

Like most important events in this century, a general European war had been discussed often enough. But when it happened, it took everyone by surprise. There were scenes of wild enthusiasm in Vienna when war was declared; they took place as well in Berlin, Paris, St Petersburg, London. It is doubtful whether anyone realized what they were in for.

The involvement of Austria-Hungary in the Balkans was one of the principal causes of the First World War; the war became, in its turn, one of the main reasons for Austria's dissolution.

The long, tremendously demanding war brought out the weaknesses of all the great powers: it helped to destroy the Habsburg empire. The empire's political and social structure was more complex than that of any other European state, and more sensitive to strains put on it by the war.

The army, which took the full brunt of it, reflected the national composition of the empire. It was multinational even among its senior ranks. The language of command was German and it consisted of some sixty words only: otherwise the troops spoke the language they found most convenient. The army offered a tempting career for young Poles and Czechs as well as Germans and Hungarians: Croatia supplied some of its most famous commanders. On the whole, it gave a good account of itself during the hostilities. When the war ended, the battle-lines manned by the Austro-Hungarian armies ran through enemy territory.

It was not on the battlefields that the army did badly. The declaration of war gave the military authorities new powers. By an imperial edict, high treason, offences against the Emperor and the members of the house of Habsburg, disturbances of public order, and acts of sabotage were withdrawn from civil and placed under military jurisdiction. In addition, the military had complete administrative control over the 'zones of war', often extending far behind the battle-lines. While exercising their new powers, the soldiers assumed that army methods could be used in regard to the civilian population, and they often exceeded the limits of good sense and sometimes of legality. But worse than that, for almost two years after the outbreak of the war, the Army high command waged a relentless struggle with the civil government and administration. The military in fact wanted to take over the running of the country. They found their match in the Hungarian prime minister, Count István Tisza, who successfully protected the Hungarian part of the monarchy. There was no politician of the same stature as Tisza in Austria, where the military came near to victory.

Though in the end the high command concentrated first on the conduct of the war, it had succeeded in further undermining the political stability of the Austrian part of the monarchy. In order to show the incompetence of the civil authorities, the military exaggerated and generalized isolated instances of treason. By treating harshly the guilty and innocent alike, they made new enemies for the Austrian state.

Hungary keeps its corn

At the same time as the struggle between the civil and the military authorities was taking place, the Austrian parliament was in recess; it had not been meeting when the war broke out, and it was not summoned again until May 1917. In spite of its many deficiencies and circumscribed powers, the Reichsrat (parliament) embodied the unity of the Austrian lands. It brought politicians of many nationalities from distant towns and regions into contact with each other, with the government, and with the court. It was a constant reminder of the diversity of the Habsburg lands and of the many difficulties involved in running them as a more or less unitary state. It had been a civilizing influence which disappeared at a crucial time.

The political life in Austria—the Hungarian parliament in Budapest continued meeting—became fragmented after the outbreak of the war more than was necessary. The lack of contact with the capital, the scarcity of reliable political information, the chicanery, especially in the case of the Slav peoples, of the military, all combined to produce an atmosphere in the provincial towns that was not really conducive to good political sense. The war did not improve relations between the two parts of the monarchy, Austria and Hungary, nor between the monarchy and her allies, Germany and Italy. Tisza, the Hungarian prime minister until June 1917, a politician as obstinate as he was shrewd, defended Hungary, usually successfully, against every attempt at interference from Vienna. Perhaps too successfully. In September and October 1916 the two meetings of the council of ministers for both Austria and Hungary dealt with no other problems but food supplies. The Austrians had become convinced that the Magyar magnates, led by István Tisza, the men who had the political power as well as the corn, were holding out on them. This was at the time when the effects of the Allied blockade were making themselves felt in the central empires; an Austrian later said that he could forgive the blockade imposed by the enemy but not by the Hungarians.

It may be that the ties of a prosperous economy were the strongest link holding together the peoples of the empire and that as the economy grew weaker and was transformed from an economy of plenty into one of scarcity those ties were loosened. The peoples of the empire found no appeal in Hindenburg's grim slogan *Durchhalten!* – see it through. They were not ready to go as far in making sacrifices as their German comrades in arms.

Indeed, from the very beginning of the war, the relations between Vienna and Berlin left a lot to be desired. Immediately after the outbreak of hostilities, when the Germans concentrated most of their forces in the west, the Austrian high command was left in charge of a larger section of the Eastern Front than it had foreseen. The Austrians complained at once and loudly: the German ambassador to Vienna, for his own part, kept on reporting on the 'spirit of Sadowa' – the Austrian desire to revenge their defeat by the Prussians almost half a century ago – in Austrian ruling circles.

Vienna's war-time association with Berlin was never smooth and sometimes stormy: the relations between Vienna and Rome ended in disaster. On the outbreak of the war Italy, a member state of the Triple Alliance, remained neutral; in May 1915 the Italians joined Great Britain, France, and Russia and attacked their former allies. Italy was finally won over by the side that had more to offer: she had been promised large chunks of Austrian territory by the Allies. The tortuous negotiations the Italians had conducted with the two sides before the outbreak of the war broke the health of an Austrian ambassador to Rome, and the temper and the career of the Austrian foreign minister. Before his resignation in January 1915, Count Berchtold said that he would rather fight the Italians than negotiate with them.

Death of an emperor

At the beginning of the third and so far bleakest winter of the war, the emperor Franz Josef died in Vienna on 21st November 1916. His death had a deeply depressing effect on the monarchy; crowned heads came to Vienna for the last time, to attend his funeral. The empire survived Franz Josef by less than two years.

His nephew, Archduke Karl, who succeeded Franz Josef as Karl I, was twenty-nine years old. He was handsome, slight, impressionable; like the German Kaiser, he had a fondness for fast changes from one splendid uniform into another. His spontaneous boyish gaiety and readiness to experiment might have become assets in more peaceful times. He entered an unenviable inheritance. After the formidable, paternal figure of Franz Josef, Emperor Karl appeared, and was, insubstantial. When he was crowned the king of Hungary in Budapest the Crown of St Stephen came down over his eyes, covering half his face.

Soon after his accession, Emperor Karl and his new foreign minister, Count Czernin, began to explore the possibilities of peace. The Emperor's good intentions did not compensate for his inexperience. He conducted the negotiations partly behind the back of his own foreign minister as well as his allies: when Karl's private negotiations were revealed his foreign minister resigned, the Emperor had to apologize to Berlin, and his country became tied to Germany more firmly than ever.

In the same reforming spirit Karl summoned the Austrian parliament in May 1917, and proclaimed an amnesty for political prisoners. Again, those good ideas went wrong. The concessions were not backed up by any comprehensive plan for political reform and, anyway, they came too late.

Throughout the war, the attention of everyone in Austria-Hungary was riveted to the events on the Eastern Front and in Russia: the Germans were taking care of the war in the west and it was therefore of much less consequence for the Austrians. In March 1917 the revolution in Russia made a profound impression on them, and on their rulers in particular. They were haunted by the threat of a revolution. When Lenin came into power on 7th November 1917, and when he started putting into practice his peace policy, the Austrians were more frightened than relieved. Some of the units released from the Eastern Front in the winter of 1917-18 were kept at home, to maintain internal order: the prisoners-of-war returning from Russia were given an elaborate screening treatment, so that they would not infect their fellow-citizens with Bolshevik doctrines.

Despite the extensive strike movement in Austria-Hungary early in 1918, the main threat to the Habsburg order did not come from a Russian-Bolshevik type of social revolution. The social unrest stimulated by the Bolshevik victory made itself felt mainly among the two top nations of the empire—the Germans and the Hungarians. With their national aspirations either satisfied or absent, the cause of national independence took second place to social reform. For the rest of the Habsburg peoples—the Poles, the Czechs, the South Slavs, the Rumanians, the Italians—national independence was the first aim.

It had not always been so. Before the war, the politicians had been fully occupied by their party and national politics: both were very absorbing and parochial pursuits. The outbreak of the war broadened their horizons while depriving them of their usual pastimes. All kinds of political plans were spun in the war-time isolation and gloom of the provincial towns.

The Italians in South Tyrol and Dalmatia and the Rumanians in Transylvania had Italy and Rumania to look to, and both countries eventually joined the ranks of Austria's enemies. The task of the Italian and the Rumanian politicians in the Habsburg monarchy was therefore comparatively simple, and most of them gradually transferred their sympathies to their own national kingdoms during the war. For those Serbs who liked the idea of being its subjects, there was the kingdom of Serbia—but there existed the alternative, properly developed only during the war, of a united kingdom of all the South Slavs: the Serbs, the Croats, the Slovenes. The position of the Poles, divided among the three powers—Austria, Germany, and Russia—was the most tragic because they were engaged in a fratricidal fight. But it had the advantage that they could not help ending up on the winning side.

The Czechs, with their powerful industry and recently developed, though very articulate, national life, had at first no assets on their side. Whether they liked it or not, they were very much a part of the fabric of the Habsburg state. If the Italians received South Tyrol and a large part of the Dalmatian coast, or if the Rumanians took away Transylvania from the Habsburgs, the monarchy could have survived without much trouble. Perhaps even the amputation of Galicia or Croatia would not have proved fatal. But without Bohemia and Moravia the Habsburgs could not have survived as the rulers of a great power.

As in every other province of the empire, the beginnings of the Czech movement for independence were small and unorganized. A few exiles abroad, a few sympathizers at home: none of the national movements possessed an organization, after the outbreak of the war, that could approach the strength and the efficiency of, say, Lenin's revolutionary organization in Russia.

The Serbs and the Croats of Dalmatia gave the anti-Habsburg movement its first, and most numerous, group of political exiles. Most of them had Italian as their second language, and all of them had the example of the unification of Italy before their eyes. Ante Trumbić and Fran Supilo (a Croat leader of the Serb and Croat coalition working for the union of the South Slavs) had left for Italy a few days before Austria-Hungary declared war on Serbia. After that they moved from one Allied capital to another, propagating the idea of South Slav unity, raising funds, recruiting volunteers. They were staggered when they got to know, by accident in Petrograd, of the Allied promise to Italy, as part of the terms of the Treaty of London which committed Italy to war, of a large part of Dalmatia. Their activities suffered from isolation from their home country.

The Czech exiles, on the other hand, were careful to keep their lines of communication with Austria-Hungary open. They claimed to represent their people at home, a claim that became true only towards the end of the war, and they developed an intensive anti-Habsburg publicity. They announced that the Habsburg empire was rotten, inhuman, and ready for liquidation; that it was dominated by the military who, in their turn, were nothing but tools of Berlin and its expansionist plans. The Czech political exiles were fortunate in having Thomas Masaryk for their leader (p. 611). Born in the Moravian-Slovak border area, he was a university professor and politician, sixty-four years old when the war started. Masaryk was the founder of one of the smallest of the Czech political parties. During the war, he mobilized the few Slovak exiles and the many Slovak immigrants in America for the fight, with the Czechs, against the Habsburg monarchy. By no means a revolutionary before the war, Masaryk maintained that the Central powers could not win against the combined forces of France, Russia and, especially, of the British empire. Masaryk disapproved of the pro-Russian sympathies of the Czechs: he tended to rely instead on the support for his plans of the Western powers.

By the end of 1917, Masaryk and his Czechoslovak National Council, based on Paris, had successfully organized Czech and Slovak military units in Russia, France, and Italy: they had made the Allied governments take note of their plans for the break-up of the Habsburg empire. They kept in touch with the secret revolutionary society in Prague, informing the Czechs at home of their successes abroad.

The end of an empire

After the failure of the attempts at separate peace with Austria towards the end of the year 1917, and under the impression of military necessity in the spring of 1918, the Allied governments started recognizing the claims of the Czechs, the South Slavs, and the Poles to independent states. They sanctioned the break-up of the Habsburg empire before it took place.

Nevertheless, inside the monarchy the anti-Habsburg national movements had been gaining support since the spring of 1917. The ties that had bound the peoples to the monarchy were gradually loosened; the plans entertained by a few visionary politicians in September 1914 received a broad political support four years later. The peoples of the Habsburg empire entered the war with one kind of 'nationalism' and left it with another. At the end of the war, nothing but completely independent states could satisfy them.

It was too late when, on 16th October 1918, the Austrian premier made a proposal for the transformation of Austria into a federal state. The previous attempts at reform by Emperor Karl had been less broadly based and they did not have the desired effect. After the re-opening of the Reichsrat in May its work was impeded by violent scenes; the pre-war *Kameraderie* of the deputies had disappeared. The amnestied political prisoners increased the ranks of the anti-Habsburg politicians. Anyway, at one point in the months after the Russian Revolution, Emperor Karl seems to have lost the little self-confidence he may have possessed. In the last months of the war, as he was growing more bewildered, his political actions were becoming more and more erratic. His loss of nerve affected every level of the official hierarchy of the Habsburg state. Sometime before the end of the war, its rulers lost conviction in their right to govern. The informal document of abdication which Karl signed on 11th November 1918 contained no trace of his desire to carry on the burden of the government: 'Since I am filled now, as before, by unchangeable love for all my nations, I will not place my person as an obstacle to their free evolution . . .'

At the time, the empire existed no more. The double-headed eagles had been taken down from official buildings; the imperial anthem was no longer sung; the whole machinery of the Habsburg state had disappeared. The Serbs, Croats, and Slovenes were busy building a united state under the Karageorgević dynasty; the Rumanians and the Italians joined their own national kingdoms; the Poles were trying to amalgamate three disparate provinces into one republic; the Czechs and the Slovaks were building their common state. The Hungarians and the Austrians had to come to terms with their new insignificance.

Break-up of the Turkish Empire

Brigadier Stephen Longrigg

An observer in the Constantinople (Istanbul) of 1914, looking back over the last ten years of Turkish history, would have reviewed a varied, disturbed, and disturbing, but not disastrous, scene. The Ottoman empire, after six centuries of unbroken continuity, was still in being. To its subjects it was a source of pride, indeed of a naïve superiority complex, however clever, rich, or self-righteous might appear the ever-criticizing Christian powers of Europe. The prestige of the Sultanate, though diminished by the fall of Abdul Hamid II in 1909, was still high and widespread, and the Caliphate, held since the 16th century by the Turkish rulers, could be a potent instrument of statecraft. The empire-wide administration conducted in the Sultan's name not only operated in accordance with semi-modernized laws and regulations, but had, since the reintroduction of the constitution in 1909, been tightened and partially purged by improved instructions and inspections, and generally superior personnel. Much of the organization was indeed archaic or ill-conceived; officialdom was excessively numerous, riddled with corruption and nepotism, and financially starved; the public services were shamefully deficient; nevertheless the tens of thousands of state-employed officials included a fair proportion who were honest, vigorous, and intelligent; and the armed forces, and the new-type politicians behind them who promised democracy and universal freedom, did in fact seem to open the doors of public life and opinion to new hopes and new standards. The impending fall of the empire was not due, therefore, to fallen or falling standards of loyalty or service to the throne, nor to a collapse of the administration; these had indeed recently and hopefully revived.

The newer spirit in public life was personified by the group of army officers and high officials to whose intrigues and military coups the 1908-9 revolution was due. Those in the highest places were Enver Pasha, clever, handsome, vain, and unstable; Jamal Pasha, keen-sighted but brutal; Talat Bey, competent administrator and economist; and Javid Bey, shrewd half-Jewish financier. The progressive, democratic régime promised by these and the other 'Young Turks' in the programme of their Committee of Union and Progress, resulted in the election of a short-lived parliament and equally short-lived popular enthusiasm; but the new régime disappointed the hopes of liberal citizens that freedom of speech, assembly, and politics was at hand. The government, instead, became more stringent and the 'freedom' turned out to be freedom only to be homogenized Turks with fewer concessions than ever being made to the aspirations of non-Turkish communities, or to the recognition of non-Turkish loyalties.

The foreign relations of the empire had not greatly changed for a century. Russia remained the menacing neighbour, persistently seeking control of the Dardanelles and gaining ground in eastern Asia Minor. Great Britain was a long-time friend and had for decades (though without complete continuity) supported the integrity of the Sultan's empire as being a lesser evil than any probable successor. British influence, however, though powerful in Victorian days had been since the 'nineties largely replaced by German, thanks to the latter's railway-building activity, trade, diplomacy, and massive military aid. Italy and France both had cultural, economic, and even territorial ambitions in Turkey, but their present influence was limited.

In recent years the empire had, in successive foreign wars—notably the Balkan Wars of 1912-13—sustained further losses to its already diminished European territory. It had lost also, to Italy, its North African province of Libya, as well as Rhodes, and the Dodecanese. Crete had already been ceded to Greece, as had Cyprus to Great Britain. The Sultan's centuries-long sovereignty over Egypt was by now nominal.

Within the area still ruled by the imperial government, our observer in 1914 would sharply differentiate between the true Turkish-feeling and Turkish-speaking provinces and those with Arab populations, which were neither. From eastern Arabia the Sultan's governors and garrisons had been expelled in 1912 by the Arab ruler of Najd, Abdul Aziz ibn Sa'ud, while elsewhere in the centre of Arabia Istanbul enjoyed only the valueless allegiance of ibn Rashid's Jabal Shammar. In the Red Sea littoral and hinterland, his *Vali* (provincial governors) barely maintained a position of dignity and minimal power against the high religious prestige of the Sharif of Mecca; in south-western Arabia, the Yemen, his forces and functionaries only by endless suppression of uprisings (the latest in 1911) maintained a precarious authority against that of the dynasty of the Zaidi Imam; and southern and south-eastern Arabia were never Ottoman-governed. The three Arab but long Turkish-ruled *vilayets* (provinces) of future Iraq, Basra, Baghdad and Mosul, and those of Syria (which included the Lebanon, Palestine, and Jordan) had equally been ruled by the Sultan's officials and cowed by his regiments, with many interruptions by local dynasties and rebels, for four centuries. The *vilayets* of Asia Minor remained, in spite of disloyal Greek, Kurdish, Armenian, and lesser minorities within it, the true Turkish homeland and the source of such wealth and capability as the empire still possessed.

An Arab awakening

The Arab-speaking provinces, altogether, easily outnumbered the Turkish in population and extent. But the always unwilling obedience of the politically conscious elements in them was, by 1914, further threatened by a growing Arab self-consciousness. This was based on the alien nature of Turkish government and on an instinctive groping towards self-determination as Arabs, or at least to special status suggested by the recent Balkan liberations. A gradual 'Arab awakening' throughout the 19th century embodied this trend, and specifically Arab movements with secret and later overt societies had grown up, first literary and local but later political and widespread, with côteries, clubs, and publications in Paris and Istanbul as well as Beirut, Cairo, Damascus, and Baghdad. The Arab Conference in Paris in June 1913 was but one such meeting, demanding a decentralization or local Arab autonomy which the Turks could not ignore but would certainly reject. The Arabs of the Fertile Crescent were thus by mid-1914 ready to launch modern-type nationalist movements, if only their Turkish masters could be persuaded to accept them — or driven out. The failure of the nationalists in Iraq and Syria during the war to collaborate with their liberators was not due to lack of conviction but to the severity of Turkish repression — and to the possibility that their old masters might after all survive the war.

The adhesion of Turkey to the Central powers in case of war had been secretly promised to the Germans by the Committee of Union and Progress leaders in August 1914, and became effective by their declaration of war on 5th November 1914. This eventuality, anticipated by Great Britain and its allies was, whatever its ultimate results, destined to bring to Turkey four years of misery, loss, and humiliation, and the end of its imperial career.

The early proclamation by the Sultan of an Islamic Holy War was almost everywhere, and notably in Arabia, ignored. Great Britain declared Turkish sovereignty over Egypt and Cyprus to be terminated; the former, with the deposition of its pro-Turkish Khedive, became a British protectorate, the latter a crown colony; and British armies in Egypt and India were made ready for immediate action. An ill-planned, ill-timed attempt by Enver Pasha to invade Transcaucasian Russia was a total failure and evoked an effective Russian counter-invasion. An incursion into north-western Egypt by the Turkish-inspired Libyan Senussi was, expectedly, a fiasco. Turkish violation of west-Persian territory served no purpose but to attract Russian counter-strokes, which lasted until the Bolshevik revolution of 1917. An attempt in 1915 by the Turkish IVth Army in Syria to breach or cross the Suez Canal — a spirited and gallant initiative — was easily repelled by British forces. The pitiless hanging by Jamal Pasha, then governor of Syria, of a score of Syrian Lebanese, and Palestinian members of a discovered anti-Turkish secret society horrified the Arab world, and led many Arab (mainly Iraqi) officers in the Turkish army to join the British when they could

The Turkish army itself, still largely under German direction, maintained much of its discipline and traditional stubbornness, but had to face daily more serious difficulties of supply, manpower, armament, and communications in face of the advances made by British armies invading Iraq and Syria. Nevertheless the sequence of Turkish losses and defeats was in part redeemed by their success in repelling the British invasion of Gallipoli, which in 1915 threatened the Dardanelles and Istanbul, by the successful siege and capture of Kut on the Tigris in 1915-16, and by other well-fought engagements in both Iraq and Syria.

While these events in 1914-16 were taking place the Foreign Offices of Europe, assuming as certain the victory of their countries' arms, were, with no little confusion and inconsistency, arranging the future map of western Asia. By the Constantinople Agreement of March 1915 Russia was promised most of the coasts of the Sea of Marmora, with Constantinople as a free port. Italy, by the Pact of London of April 1915, was awarded a generous tract of Asia Minor. The Sharif of Mecca, Husain ibn Ali, was led, after prolonged and tortuous correspondence with Sir Henry MacMahon, the British high commissioner in Egypt, to expect the formation of some sort of post-war Arab empire—with certain areas only excepted. An Anglo-French (the Sykes/Picot) agreement of May 1916 partitioned the whole Fertile Crescent into future Arab states, subject to varying degrees of French or British 'assistance' or control. Italy, in November 1917, by the Treaty of St Jean de Maurienne, was promised Smyrna. And in the same month the blessing of the British government was assured to the Zionist organization for a 'national home for the Jews in Palestine', provided strictly that this be 'without prejudice to the civil or religious rights of existing non-Jewish communities' (that is, the ninety-three per cent Arab majority then present). This undertaking was communicated at the time to the French and American governments.

None of these war-time agreements or promises was destined visibly to affect the course of the military operations, which ended with the expulsion of Ottoman forces and government from the Arab countries.

In Arabia, the fate of their Hijaz province was sealed when in June 1916 the Sharif of Mecca, encouraged by his correspondence with the British, revolted against Turkish authority, assumed the title of King and, aided by British arms, transport, supplies, and a military mission, raised tribal and military forces of his own. These with little difficulty drove the Turkish garrisons out of Mecca, Jidda, and the coastal villages, besieged (but by-passed) Medina, and pressed northwards to Aqaba and beyond. A remembered figure in these picturesque operations was that of T.E. Lawrence, a young member of the military mission. With fair Arabic, a taste for desert life, a tough physique and much courage, a keen but capricious intelligence, his contribution to the success of these very minor military operations was appreciable, while that of the Arab forces whom he accompanied is variously assessed; but in spite of his naïve egoism and not always truthful boasting, he was a striking and to some an inspiring figure.

In the Yemen, where the Turkish garrison maintained itself in complete isolation from its homeland, the Imam Yahya was content to avoid committing himself and to tolerate the status quo. After the armistice of November 1918 surviving Turkish troops were repatriated; Turkish forces had advanced into Aden territory early in 1915 and had stayed there in the close vicinity of Aden itself until the armistice, without, however, disturbing the activities of war or peace within the port or city. No vestige of Ottoman rule remained in Arabia after November 1918.

In Syria the British campaign had a slow and costly, but ultimately a victorious, course. The Suez Canal and northwestern Egypt were in 1915 successfully defended against incursion, while British forces were mustered in the Delta, and thousands of Egyptian non-combatants pressed into the service. The invasion of southern Syria (Palestine) began in 1916, secured al Arish and Gaza, and advanced slowly and not without local setbacks. The Arab forces, under the Amir Faisal, with whom Lawrence assured liaison, formed a loosely co-ordinated right flank, east of Jordan and the Dead Sea. Jerusalem was entered by General Sir Edmund Allenby in December 1917. Operations of mopping up and local advances continued, further preparation and training was carried out, and a war-time administration of the occupied territory was created; the national home promised to the Zionists was not announced. The final and massive advance of Allenby's now powerful (largely cavalry) forces began in September 1918 and swept the ill-supplied and now demoralized Turks before it. Damascus was entered on 1st October 1918. An Arab government—still subject, however, to Allenby's overriding command—was established under Faisal, the remainder of northern and western Syria was occupied, and interim arrangements were made for the country's administration. Beirut and the coastal strip were handed over to the French, a small detachment of whom had accompanied the British forces.

The last hostilities in northern Syria were carried out, on the side of the retreating Turks, by General Mustafa Kemal Pasha, defender of the Dardanelles and already a war-time hero. The armistice of Mudros, 30th October 1918, ended for ever Ottoman rule in all of Syria.

The British campaign in Iraq lasted for four full years, from the landing at Fao of a British-Indian brigade in November 1918 to the Mudros armistice. Continually reinforced, the army advanced up river, secured the oilfields in south .Persia, occupied Basra and its neighbourhood—not without sharp fighting—and in the spring of 1915 took Qurna and Amara, and reached Kut. Here General Townshend's tired troops, over-extended and ill-supported, sustained a siege of 140 days, and on 29th April 1916 were forced to surrender.

The rest of 1916 was devoted to the rehabilitation and increase of British and British-Indian forces, with improved communications and supplies. General Sir Stanley Maude took command in August. He began a powerful advance in December, retook Kut, reached and entered Baghdad in March 1917, and in the spring advanced well beyond it on both rivers. This movement was resumed into the lower Kurdish foothills after a pause early in 1918, and in the autumn British troops moved again northwards, against Turkish opposition, to take Kirkuk and Arbil and the small Euphrates towns. Mosul was reached three days after the signature of the Mudros armistice, and the Turkish commander Ali Ihsan Pasha withdrew, under protest, his forces from all parts of the Mosul *vilayet*. The British war-time 'civil administration' under Sir A.T.Wilson thereafter ruled all Iraq, under the general authority of the commander-in-chief, until an Iraq government was set up by Sir Percy Cox in November 1920; legal sovereignty over the territory remained, however, the Sultan's until its abrogation under the peace treaty.

Turkey ended the 1914-18 war in a state of general disintegration, poverty, and disunion. The correction, almost the reversal, of this distressing weakness was the achievement of the outstanding personality of Mustafa Kemal, later surnamed Atatürk and first president of the Turkish republic till his death in 1938. In the period from late 1918 to 1922, he rallied and inspired Turkish troops throughout Asia Minor, created and trained a new, loyal, and effective army, and scornfully repudiated the defeatist and semi-captive government of the Sultan and his entourage in Istanbul. He rejected, as an outrage, the occupation of wide areas of Asia Minor to which French, Italian, and Greek forces had proceeded as masters immediately after the armistice; he managed to secure the withdrawal of the French and Italian contingents by armed resistance and ultimately by agreement, while those of Venizelist Greece were attacked in a series of campaigns and finally expelled in 1922 from Turkish territory, followed by four-fifths of the Greek population of Asia Minor. A new government of Turkey was established by enthusiastic delegate conferences at Erzerum and Sivas, a National Pact was drafted, and a Grand National Assembly was elected and convened as the highest authority in Turkey. The Treaty of Sèvres of August 1920, drafted by the Allies and incorporating terms wholly destructive of Turkish integrity, was signed by the Sultan's government but repudiated by the Kemalists; nevertheless, the right of the 'non-Turkish' *vilayets* to self-determination—which meant effectively the secession of all the Arab *vilayets* from the Turkish state—had been assured by the National Pact.

This abandonment of the ex-Ottoman *vilayets* in Iraq, Syria, and Arabia was a striking act of wisdom and courage on the part of Kemal Atatürk. By reversing the Ottoman land-hungry imperialism of earlier days it immensely strengthened the Turkish state thenceforward; at no time, indeed, had the Arab provinces been a source of strength, wealth, or credit to the empire. Arabia was left to enjoy its own conceptions of indigenous rule and sovereignty, while the Arab territories of Syria and Iraq were destined after 1920 to pass first for limited periods under French and British mandates, and later into independent statehood.

Only on two occasions after the announcement of Kemal's self-denying decision and its ratification by the Treaty of Lausanne of July 1923, did Turkey press claims in seeming contradiction of it. The first of these was the Turkish claim made in 1923-26 to the Mosul *vilayet,* or large parts of it, a claim based on the quite falsely alleged majority there of Kurds and Turkomans. This was rejected by the Council of the League of Nations on the advice of its special committee of investigation on the spot. The second occasion was the demand in 1936 for the re-transfer to Turkey of the historically and actually Arab *sanjaq* (district) of Alexandrette-Antioch. This was pressed on the French mandatory — with a wealth of local intimidation, faked figures, and rigged elections — and was, to the despair of Syrians, finally successful in 1939; an outcome accepted by the French through their need to ensure Turkish goodwill in the world war then imminent.

Ludendorff's Defeat

Barrie Pitt

Ludendorff was making a bid for final victory. At the end of 1917 he had decided that he must knock the French and, above all, the British out of the war before the promised American reinforcements could arrive and turn the tide once and for all in the Allies' favour. On 21st March 1918 the greatest bombardment the world had ever seen started up on the Western Front. In heavy fog the German assault troops stormed through the British strongpoints from St Quentin to la Fère, and in the following days they pushed the British back over the old hard-fought battleground of the Somme. Ludendorff's plan, St Michael, envisaged a complete breakthrough down from Arras through the Flesquières Salient to St Quentin and la Fère. On 24th March, while the Germans pushed through to north and south, the British started to withdraw from the Flesquières Salient, the last point they held south of Arras on the old front line. But Arras, contrary to German plans, stayed firm as the British front line retreated. It was as though a door hinging on Arras was swinging open.

As a result of the mutual respect which existed between the British and French commanders-in-chief, Sir Douglas Haig and General Philippe Pétain, French divisions had been hastily flung into the gap left as the door opened, and after a conference held at Doullens, on 26th March, the Allied armies had an overall commander-in-chief in the person of General Ferdinand Foch. It was to prove a happy choice, and in the existing circumstances the British could only gain from this apparent surrender of their independence; reserves could only flow towards them—at least until this vast emergency was over.

By 29th March reserves were coming up from the south to fill the gaping holes in the British line—which now ran from Arras down through Albert, Villers Bretonneux, and Cantigny—and it was also evident that the steam was going out of the German attack. Many factors contributed to this—inevitable casualties, accumulated fatigue in the surviving assault troops, the ever-lengthening lines of communication, and the foreseen difficulties of moving men and supplies forward across the enormous confusion of the old Somme battlefields.

But there was another reason, illustrated by an entry in the diary of a German officer, Rudolf Binding: 'Today the advance of our infantry suddenly stopped near Albert. Nobody could understand why. Our airmen had reported no enemy between Albert and Amiens . . . our way seemed entirely clear. I jumped into a car to investigate.

'As soon as I got near the town I began to see curious sights. Strange figures which looked very little like soldiers . . . were making their way back out of the town. There were men driving cows before them in a line: others who carried a hen under one arm and a box of notepaper under the other. Men carrying a bottle of wine under their arm and another one open in their hand. Men who had torn a silk drawing-room curtain from its rod . . . more men with writing paper and notebooks. Evidently they had found it desirable to sack a stationer's shop. Men dressed up in comic disguise. Men with top hats on their heads. Men staggering.'

Ludendorff's dream vanishes

Three and a half years of grim austerity had led to this. As the front of the German advance crept out of the battle area into the line of villages which had until a few days before been inhabited by civilians—grown rich on commerce with the British troops—it seemed to the Germans that they had stumbled into Aladdin's cave. All were affected, officers and men, rich and poor alike, for the wealth of Prussia had been unable to buy during the last years the booty which now lay around them for plunder. Binding himself writes, almost with hysteria, of 'smearing our boots with lovely English boot-polish . . .'

And together with this understandable

but uncontrollable lust for trivial comforts and luxuries which had been for so long denied them, drunkenness now joined to check the German armies. Fear and battle had dried the moisture from the soldiers' bodies quicker than the desert sun — and after a week living on scummy water from the bottom of shell-holes foul with cordite and decomposition, the troops found themselves in deserted villages whose houses still held wine-stocked cellars. To those few who could remember, the scenes stirred memories of the great sweep to the Marne in 1914.

And so the March offensive petered out. In all, it won from the Allies some 1,200 square miles of territory, vast quantities of stores, over 90,000 prisoners, and 1,000 guns; it had also presented the victors with nearly fifty extra miles of front to hold, none of which could possibly be as strongly fortified, as defensible, or even as comfortable as the Hindenburg Line from which it had started.

With the halting of St Michael (and also the failure of a brief attack aimed at smashing away the door-hinge at Arras) Ludendorff realized that his dream of a break-through in the southern half of the British front was fast vanishing — but there were still other schemes produced by his staffs, notably the St George attacks, which had attracted him when they had first been presented to him in December. These plans proposed attacking the Allied line along its northernmost fifty miles — from south of Armentieres to the coast — in offensives on each side of the Ypres Salient, which would meet near Haze-brouck and then turn north and drive the British into the sea. Ludendorff had originally rejected them because of the uncertainty of the weather—he had no desire to engulf his armies in the Flanders mud as the British had done in 1917. March 1918, however, had proved an exceptionally dry month and the ground was likely to be firm–so as many men as could be spared from the coalescing fronts between Albert and Cantigny were withdrawn, the German artillery train hurriedly transferred north, and the plans examined for converging attacks on the Ypres Salient.

However, it soon became evident that insufficient numerical strength was available for so grand a project, and only the southern

half of the blow could be launched. Even this was limited to a twelve- instead of a thirty-mile front, and at the suggestion of one of Ludendorff's more sardonic staff officers the code-name was changed from St George to Georgette.

While the German general staff busied itself with the organization of this second act of their offensive, the Allies — severely shaken but thankfully aware of the passing of their most immediate peril — held a series of rapid and salutary post-mortems, which resulted firstly in the dismissal of the unfortunate Sir Hubert Gough, and secondly in the further strengthening of General Foch's position. The agreement reached at Doullens was superseded by the following announcement: 'General Foch is charged by the British, French, and American governments with the co-ordination of the action of the Allied armies on the Western Front. To this end all powers necessary to secure effective realization are conferred on him. The British, French, and American governments for this purpose entrust to General Foch the strategic direction of military operations.'

There were certain reservations with regard to tactical direction in the final passages of the agreement, but the Allies were at last obtaining for themselves the immense advantage of a single supreme commander — which the Central powers had enjoyed for many months. Another most hopeful factor was the presence of two American generals at the conference, Generals Pershing and Bliss.

It was tacitly admitted that in the circumstances the sooner American troops were in action the better; and that General Pershing's natural desire for the American army to fight solely as a national army under his own command might in days of such emergency be modified to allow separate American divisions to be fed piecemeal into the front wherever the Allied requirements were greatest.

According to legend, General Pershing made a high-flown speech ending 'I come to tell you that the American people will esteem it a great honour that our troops should take part in the present battle. . . . There is at the moment no other question than that of fighting. Infantry, artillery, aeroplanes, tanks, all that we have is yours. Dispose of us as you wish. . . . The American people will be proud to take part in the greatest and finest battle in history.'

Apart from the fact that no American aeroplanes, artillery, or tanks had as yet arrived in Europe (in the event, none arrived before the Armistice), a study of Pershing's character reveals that it is most unlikely that he would ever indulge in such verbal histrionics. It is far more likely that whatever he said approximated far more closely to General Bliss's remark.

He had said: 'We've come over here to get ourselves killed; if you want to use us, what are you waiting for?'

Despite its mordant note, few speeches have ever afforded greater relief. Munitions for the front were ready and to hand, but only America could replace the lost legions—and within a week American engineers were working on the defence lines and taking part in repelling German attacks on British positions.

It was, of course, problems of manpower which most deeply worried Sir Douglas Haig, the British commander-in-chief during the days immediately following the last spasms of the St Michael offensive— and the condition of some of the divisions which had been involved in it. Five of these divisions he removed from the line and replaced by rested divisions from the northern sector—transferring the battered remnants of the 9th, 19th, 25th, 34th, and 40th Divisions to a quiet section between the Ypres-Comines Canal and la Bassée; as neighbours on their right flank, they should have had the 1st and 2nd Portuguese Divisions, but as it happened, shortly after the arrival of the British divisions from the south, the 1st Portuguese left the line and as no replacements seemed to be forthcoming the 2nd Portuguese thinned themselves out to occupy the spaces left vacant by their compatriots.

On 7th and 8th April, Armentières to the north and the area around Lens to the south were deluged in mustard gas, and at 3 am on the 9th the opening of Georgette was signalled by an intense bombardment from Ludendorff's 'battering train', followed shortly after 8 am by a violent onslaught by the infantry of nine full-strength German divisions. The main weight of the attack fell upon the Portuguese sector, and pausing only long enough to remove their boots, the troops fled to the rear, several of them assisting their passage by commandeering the bicycles of the British 11th Cyclist Battalion who had been rushed up to hold the gap.

The remainder of the morning was a wild confusion of attack and counter-attack, as every available British unit was hastily flung into the breach, but by evening the Germans had stormed forward for six miles as far as the banks of the River Lawe, behind which the Highlanders of the 51st Division waited in grim anticipation of the next morning's battle.

As it happened, the main weight of the next day's attack was directed by Ludendorff farther to the north than the Highlanders' positions. In the first onslaught, only half of Georgette had been delivered (against the northern flank of the British 1st Army, commanded by Sir Henry Horne) and now it was time for the southern flank of Sir Herbert Plumer's 2nd Army to take the brunt of the attack. As the Ypres Salient was a part of the 2nd Army's responsibility, both the men and their beloved commander were well used to the horrors and vicissitudes of battle.

All day long the battle raged (again the attackers were aided at first by thick fog in the Lys valley) but unlike the previous day—and unlike the previous weeks of the March offensive—the British line remained unbroken as it went slowly back; it was yielding ground quite methodically, and just as methodically exacting an enormous price in German blood for every inch it gave. Armentières and Erquinhem, Messines and Ploegsteert, all fell into German hands that day—to the dismay and astonishment of many armchair strategists weaned on the belief that to lose ground was to lose the battle—but already Plumer sensed his command of the situation was secure, and this was confirmed on 12th April when Sir Douglas Haig extended his sector southwards so that the whole British defence would be directed by one man.

Plumer's sector thus resembled a gigantic reversed S from the right bank of the Coverbeek stream north of Ypres, right around the Ypres Salient through Poelcapelle to the Passchendaele Ridge of fearful memory; back across the Wytschaete Ridge, and around in the first twelve miles of the bottom curve of the S as far as Merville. It was a line won at dreadful cost during three and a half years of slaughter and agony, and every yard of the northern sector in the Salient itself had been the site of deeds recorded in some British regimental history – and with a refreshing realism Plumer decided to withdraw from it in order to shorten his line and accumulate reserves for the defence of Béthune and Hazebrouck.

As a result, when Ludendorff again shifted his attack north to probe for a weak spot, his opening bombardment fell on empty trenches, and to attack the new British line his infantry had to advance down the open face of the deserted ridge, while their support artillery tried to heave its way over two miles of churned mud.

Georgette bogged down. A week after that first storming success against the Portuguese, the battle of the Lys began to show the same signs of stagnation as those which had heralded the halting of the St Michael offensive. Although the attacking troops still made progress – and Baillieul fell into their hands a smoking ruin on 15th April – they were tired, their supplies were arriving late and were inadequate, while all the time the defences against which they battered, grew stronger. The defensive crust, in fact, had been given time to harden, and Ludendorff's chance of a break-through was vanishing. On 16th April, violent but unsuccessful German attacks were launched to the south against the left flank of Sir Henry Horne's army, but on 19th April a lull descended on the entire front.

French divisions now came up to take over the line from Méteren to Wytschaete, and the five British divisions most severely mauled on the Lys – including the 19th and 25th which had been brought up from Flesquières after their battering during St Michael – were transferred south to a quiet section of the French front along the Chemin-des-Dames, where it was confidently believed that they would enjoy ample facilities for rest and recovery.

The British hold fast

During the whole of the recent crises, the new Allied commander-in-chief General Foch had been indomitably and sometimes infuriatingly optimistic whatever happened. His invariable reaction to every piece of news, however alarming, had been *'Bon!'* until on one occasion Haig's patience had worn thin and he slapped the table and retorted *'Ce n'est pas bon du tout!'* – but nonetheless Foch's attitude

of supreme confidence and energy played some considerable part in the battle.

But Ludendorff, on the other side of the line, had been growing increasingly depressed. Despite the gains in territory, booty, and prisoners – vast in comparison with those of any Allied offensive on the Western Front – he had nevertheless failed to attain the type of sweeping victory which had attended his efforts on the Eastern Front, and which he knew would be necessary if the Central Powers were to win the war. However loudly the German press might proclaim his genius as a military commander and however striking the gains might look on the maps and in the balance sheets of the stores depots, the cold fact remained that a large number of his finest soldiers had been killed and those that were left had to hold fifty more miles of line than when St Michael began.

He had, he began to feel, been mistaken in attacking the British section of the front, however sound his reasoning had appeared when the decisions were made, and on 17th April he instructed his staff to prepare plans for yet another large-scale offensive, this time against the French, in the area adjacent to the southern edge of the now moribund St Quentin attack. It was here that the original line of the Western Front had curved around from roughly north-south to west-east, before beginning its sixty-mile straight run to Verdun.

There were still two battles to be fought against the British, however, the last spasms of Georgette and St Michael. On 24th April thirteen German tanks led an attack which finally succeeded in taking Villers Bretonneux though the town only remained in German hands a matter of hours, a combined British and Australian attack retaking it during the following night. And on 25th April a violent German attack captured Mont Kemmel from the French troops who had just taken it over from the exhausted British.

But again, gaps torn in the Allied lines were not exploited. Plumer poured his accumulated reserves like cement into the line, the line hardened and set, and nothing Ludendorff could do could break it; in any case, his attentive and slightly bulbous gaze was now fixed on the scene of his next offensive which, abjuring both religion and the classics and placing his trust in history, he had now christened 'Blücher'. Perhaps he hoped for an Iron Cross with Golden Rays for himself.

When the men of the British divisions transferred south for a well-earned period of rest and recuperation first arrived in the delightful Champagne country, blossoming now in the warm spring sunshine, the contrasts from the drab mists and mud of the Flanders plain had been to them a blissful revelation. The verdant countryside was broken by hills among which nestled charming villages untouched by war, and if the trenches were shallow and insanitary to a degree which only French troops could have tolerated, they were nevertheless so screened in foliage as to resemble more the brambled hideouts of childhood games than the fortifications of more adult pursuits. Not that this mattered, for this was a cushy front.

At first.

But after a week the men began to wonder, for in addition to glorious weather May brought an increasing feeling of tension coupled with an almost imperceptible daily increase in the amount of German shell-fire. And if the troops felt uneasy, the battalion commanders were soon horrified to discover the manner in which their men were disposed along so shallow a defensive line.

Unfortunately, there was nothing which could be done about this, for these British divisions were now in the command area of the French 6th Army, under the command of General Duchesne, whose choleric disposition was such that he fiercely resented criticism even from superior officers of his own nationality. When suggestions for changes in disposition came from subordinates, and when the subordinates were British—and those moreover who had recently and disgracefully retired in front of German attacks—then they met with flat rejection, worded in the most insulting terms. When the British staff remonstrated further, he dismissed them with a basilisk stare and breathed a curt *'J'ai dit!'*

All troops in Duchesne's sector, British and French alike, were thus herded compactly up into front lines of dubious protective value, and when, despite Duchesne's repeated announcements that no German attack was imminent, the opening bombardment of Blücher fell upon them at 1 am on the morning of 27th May, it trod them into the ground with an obliterative effect even greater than the opening barrage of St Michael. At 3.40 am German Storm Troops began to move forward behind the wall of their own bursting shells, through scenes of carnage and destruction beyond the imagination of Hieronymus Bosch.

By mid-day they were across the Aisne —Duchesne had delayed blowing the bridges until too late—and by evening German spearheads had reached the Vesle on both sides of Fismes. The following morning they crossed the river and surged onwards towards the Marne, at the same time broadening the base of their advance to threaten the rail centre of Soissons—thus advancing twelve miles in one day, a feat long considered impossible upon the Western Front.

An attack launched in conditions which applied in France between 1914 and 1918 has been aptly compared to the overturning of a bucket of water on a flat surface. Unless action is taken with extraordinary rapidity and decision in the first vital seconds, attempts to dam or channel the floods are of no avail, and there is nothing to do but wait until the waters lose their impetus and reach the limit of their dispersion.

This happened with Blücher. Day after day the German tide flooded southwards, until on 30th May troops of General von Böhn's VII Army reached the Marne, with Paris lying fifty miles away straight up the corridor between the Marne and the Ourcq. But however entrancing this view may have been to the Kaiser and the Crown Prince (both following their armies some fifty miles to the rear), to Ludendorff and his staff two ominous facts were emerging which thoroughly dampened their spirits. Firstly, the map now showed a huge bulge depressingly similar to those lately and abortively formed by their own efforts to the north; and secondly, their troops were now passing through the Champagne country and the reports coming back from the front indicated that all ranks were appreciating the contents of French cellars far more than the need to press forward; and *Feldpolizei* dispatched to restore order far too often succumbed to temptation themselves.

Thus Blücher, too, lost impetus and died – and one of the most significant facts about the halting of the tide occurred on 1st June at Château-Thierry, when for the first time a German attack was met and firmly repulsed by American troops. It had taken rather longer than had been expected for General Pershing to augment his promises made at Doullens, but now the 2nd American Division was in action and American troops were to take part in all the battles still to come.

The Black Day of the German army

It was now that the essential book-keeping behind warfare began to reveal the true state of affairs. There was no denial of the fact that, so far as possession of real estate in France was concerned, Germany had made vast gains during the past few weeks, to the direct loss of the Allies – but the cost had been excessive. Ludendorff's strength in divisions on paper was little less than it had been at the beginning of St Michael, but the average battalion strengths had been reduced by this time from 807 to 692 – despite the arrival of 23,000 recruits of the 1899 class, and some 60,000 men withdrawn from rail, transport, and other supply services. Moreover, the quality of the battalions was distinctly lower than at the beginning of the year, for the simple reason that Ludendorff had creamed off the best men to form his Storm Troop units; these had inevitably suffered the highest casualties, as they had both led every attack and then been flung in to hold any gaps.

Now, therefore, his best men were gone and in their place were the unfit, the very young and the middle-aged, and that irreducible proportion of men in every army which normally manages to occupy the safest and most lucrative positions, and who are therefore most aggrieved when circumstance forcibly exchanges their comfort for danger. This undesirable faction had already been responsible for some ugly incidents; desertion had increased, troops had failed to return from leave, and many of those who did return as far as the railheads behind the lines, now joined up with others as sullen and mutinous as themselves to roam the back areas, defying the *Feldpolizei,* raiding stores and dumps, and generally spreading confusion and dismay.

On the Allied side, however, once American troops joined the line, the man-power problem was solved. Not only did Pershing's command form an apparently inexhaustible supply of young, fit, eager – and, most important of all – inexperienced and therefore confident soldiers, but their very presence in such visible abundance spread optimism through the Allied armies, who, despite the vast bulges on the maps, regained during the early summer of 1918 that feeling of certain victory which had been missing since the days of Verdun and the Somme.

There were to be two more attempts by Ludendorff to break out of the net in which his armies seemed to be caught – one at Noyon, between the St Michael and Blücher bulges, and the second on the eastern flank of the Chemin-des-Dames bulge – a double-pronged attack aimed at isolating Rheims; but the Allies were now in growing strength and well able to absorb and counter Ludendorff's ever-weakening blows.

On the morning of 18th July, after a violent cloudburst, the first stage of the Allied counter-attack opened under command of General Mangin on the western flank of the Chemin-des-Dames bulge, aimed at cutting the German supply route down to Château-Thierry. Three hundred and forty-six Renault tanks took part in the opening phase, and although these broke down within a matter of hours, they gave essential aid during the first break-through – and the menace of the flank attack was enough to bring Ludendorff hurrying back from a conference in the north.

The following day, American divisions attacked in the south of the bulge, and Ludendorff – acutely conscious of the exposed position of his troops at the bottom of the sack – authorized, and indeed organized, a retreat; that he was still a competent soldier is shown by the fact that despite another Allied flank attack, this time from the east, he managed to wedge open the jaws of the trap west of Soissons and west of Rheims, until by 4th August most of his men were back behind the line of the Aisne and the Vesle, and the sack formed by Blücher had vanished.

But on 8th August, British, Canadian, and Australian divisions, supported by almost the whole of the British Tank

Corps – 604 tanks in all – struck at Ludendorff's line in front of Amiens, in an attack stretching from the Ancre in the north, down across the Somme and past Villers Bretonneux to the Luce. The blow had been elaborately and most efficiently prepared and was, almost ironically, aided on this occasion by nature who provided the Allies with fog – almost the first time an Allied attack had been so favoured.

All the way along the attack front, the first thrusts were successful and the tanks proved an immense success in supporting the infantry, who whenever a machine-gun post gave trouble lay down and waited for one of the mastodon shapes of their armoured protection to lumber forward and crush the opposition. By that evening, fifteen miles of the German front had been stove in and British Whippet tanks and infantry, with their Dominion comrades, were seven miles in advance of their startline.

Ludendorff was shocked when, on the following day, he appraised the results of the fighting on 8th August – but not so much by the loss of territory, of material, or even of men; the Allies had lost far more in all these categories every day for over a week during the March offensive, but they had not lost the war. It was an entirely different loss which spelled out to him the presage of doom. It was the loss of spirit.

According to the reports on his desk, six German divisions had collapsed that day in scenes unprecedented in German military legend. Companies had surrendered to single tanks, platoons to single infantrymen, and on one occasion retreating troops had hurled abuse at a division going forward resolutely to buttress the sagging line, accusing them of blacklegging and 'toadying to the Junkers'.

'8th August was the Black Day of the German army . . .' he wrote afterwards, and history has justified the comment.

On 8th August began the Allied advance to the Rhine.

From then on, the front was never quiet. Whatever shortcomings may have in the past blemished Foch's planning, in the summer of 1918 his doctrine of the continual offensive brought success – so long as attacks were switched as soon as the defensive crust in front hardened.

On 11th August the battle of Amiens was called off after an advance of ten miles, but two days before, the French army under General Debeney had attacked and taken Montdidier, while the following day General Humbert's French 3rd Army – one stage farther south – advanced towards Noyon and liberated Lassigny in fighting which lasted until the 16th. And on the 18th, Mangin's army struck on Humbert's right, and took the Aisne heights on the 20th.

Each attack was broken off as soon as it lost its initial impetus, by which time another attack had been launched near enough to the previous one to profit from its success – and again continued only until resistance stiffened to such a point that further attacks would be unprofitable.

So it was to continue. On 21st August the British 3rd Army, under General Sir Julian Byng, attacked north of Albert (an attack buttressed by 200 tanks salvaged from the battle of Amiens), and the following day Rawlinson's 4th Army struck a few miles to the south, between Albert and the Somme. By that evening the front was back running along the edge of the old Somme battlefields across which the flower of British manhood had gone to its death two years before, and twenty-four hours later both Byng's and Rawlinson's troops were three miles farther forward!

23rd August was thus an even blacker day for the German army than had been 8th August and there was to be no respite for them until an armistice was signed. Throughout the remaining days of August and the opening week of September, the Allies beat a continual tattoo on the German line, and by 9th September almost the entire territorial gains of the Ludendorff spring offensive had been lost, a hundred thousand German soldiers had entered Allied prison-camps, many more had been killed or wounded, and – most ominously of all – had deserted.

Two days later the American attack on the St Mihiel Salient opened and within two days this perpetual thorn in French flesh had vanished, 14,500 German prisoners and 443 German guns lay behind American lines, and Pershing was regrouping his forces for a vast offensive northwards through the Argonne.

But there was still one slender hope in Ludendorff's mind – that the concrete fastnesses of the Hindenburg Line might give him some respite; he thus watched the opening moves of the attack on it with great anxiety. It began with a fifty-six-hour bombardment, launched on a five-division front by British, American, and Australian divisions. Again, fog aided the attackers, allowing the British to cross the St Quentin Canal almost unseen, then to turn and lever away the defensive positions on each flank as these came under frontal attack. With admirable organization, reserve divisions came up through the gaps created, leap-frogged through the remnants of the assault divisions and drove even deeper into the complex of trenches and dug-outs, wire belts and tunnels which all Germany had confidently expected to withstand any onslaught.

All day long German troops had fought from the defences of their famous line with much of the skill and ardour which had distinguished them in the past — their defeat was due mainly to fog, to the offensive spirit of the Americans and the Australians, and the spirit of victory which animated the British; and possibly to German luck, which had changed.

For although no one realized it then, that afternoon Germany had lost the war.

Under the accumulating strain, Ludendorff's nerve had cracked, and at four o'clock that afternoon he had suffered a minor stroke while staying — appropriately — at the Hôtel Britannique, in Spa. He had gone there to attend another of the eternal conferences to which he was of late always being summoned, in order to convince politicians from home that his plans for victory were developing well.

That evening, pale and shaken, he visited his superior and constant ally Hindenburg in the suite below his own, and admitted that he could see no way out of the impasse into which Germany had been manoeuvred; and sadly, Hindenburg — as ever — agreed with his chief subordinate. An armistice must be asked for, and the staff must immediately commence drawing up movement orders for a planned withdrawal of the army, together with as much of the heavy materials of war as could be moved, back to the western frontier of Germany. There they would present to the world a spectacle of an unbeaten force still capable of defending their honour and the fatherland.

That two men in such high position in the world could be so divorced from reality that they could believe their position was such that the Allies would agree to this, merely exemplifies the lack of political common sense which permeated the entire military conduct of the war, on both sides. In the event, the Allied powers exacted a surrender as unconditional as the one they were to exact twenty-seven years later, though the actual terms agreed to were less demonstrative of Allied victory.

The conditions of the Versailles Treaty may well have been harsh and ungenerous, but German memories might not have been so short if their own country had been subjected to some of the physical damage which had been inflicted upon France, and affected future French attitudes to war.

The Road to Armistice

Imanuel Geiss

Germany's unlimited submarine warfare had been a military as well as a political gamble. In the short run, the military gamble seemed to come off, for the results of the first four months were far above expectations. It was only later in 1917 that Allied counter-measures made the number of German submarine successes decline sharply.

Politically, however, submarine warfare was one unmitigated failure from the outset. It brought the USA into war, and with its entry, the defeat of Germany. American participation in the war infused the war-weary Western nations with new hopes, while it discouraged correspondingly the Central powers who were no less sick of the war, in particular the Slav nationalities in Austria-Hungary. Their hearts had never been in a war which had started as a 'punitive action' against an independent Slav nation–Serbia.

By the spring of 1917 the situation in the Dual Monarchy had become so desperate for the ruling German and Hungarian groups that the new Emperor Karl took to heart a deeply pessimistic memorandum by his chief minister, Count Czernin, on the urgent necessity to make peace very soon, and passed it on to Matthias Erzberger, a leading member of the German Catholic Centre Party. Erzberger was deeply impressed. In Germany disillusionment about submarine warfare, and political unrest under the stress of the war reached a new intensity in the summer of 1917. Even the SPD (the Social Democratic Party), smarting under the sharp attacks by the USPD (the Independent Social Democratic Party), their left-wing breakaway, was becoming restive and threatened for the first time to vote against the war credits. It was in

this situation that Erzberger and the SPD took the parliamentary initiative to relieve somehow the domestic pressure by attacking Chancellor Bethmann Hollweg. Philipp Scheidemann and Friedrich Ebert, the two outstanding leaders of the loyal Socialists, criticized both the overoptimistic assessment of submarine warfare and the chancellor's refusal to come out for a peace of moderation, and demanded political reform in Prussia. On 4th and 6th July Erzberger joined the fray in the central committee of the Reichstag. Erzberger declared the submarine warfare a failure and suggested that the Reichstag should pass a resolution declaring itself in favour of a peace without annexations.

The result was shattering, and Erzberger initiated one of the most extraordinarily muddled political affairs in Germany, the so-called crisis of July 1917. In it aspects of foreign and domestic policy were inextricably mixed – submarine warfare, war aims, war credits, reform of the franchise in Prussia and of the political structure in the Reich, the fear of the Majority Socialists that they would be outmanoeuvred by the left-wing USPD. The main results of the crisis were a vote of the Prussian ministry for equal franchise in Prussia (11th July), Bethmann Hollweg's fall (12th July), the Peace Resolution of the Reichstag (19th July), and the uncertain beginnings of parliamentary government in the Reich.

The fall of Bethmann Hollweg
Since spring 1917 Bethmann Hollweg had been in favour of reforming the Prussian franchise in order to appease the working class and to strengthen the majority leaders of the SPD against the USPD. His success in carrying a reluctant Prussian ministry with him on 11th July was, however, only a Pyrrhic victory for it incensed the high command against him even more. Ludendorff and Hindenburg hurried to Berlin and threatened to resign, if equal franchise and the Peace Resolution, as drafted by an informal committee of the three new majority parties (Centre, Progressive Party, and Majority Socialists), were accepted. The Kaiser, on the other hand, did not want to come to a decision without consulting the Crown Prince, whose views were con-

sistently reactionary and Pan-German. The Crown Prince took the unusual step of consulting the leaders of the political parties. To his surprise, he found that all of them, except the Progressives, were against the chancellor: the Conservatives and National Liberals thought he made too many concessions to the Left and was too weak in pursuing vigorous war aims; the Centre Party and the SPD felt he had become a liability because of his ambiguity over war aims and because it was in any case he who had led Germany into war.

The Crown Prince presented his father triumphantly with the result of his soundings. In a hectic atmosphere of confusion the Kaiser dismissed the chancellor, before Ludendorff and Hindenburg had time to storm in and confront their sovereign with their resignation. When they arrived, the Kaiser merely told the surprised generals: 'He is gone.' Thus Bethmann Hollweg was felled by a strange alliance. That he had incurred the enmity of the conservative and military element could not astonish anybody. But the Centre Party and the SPD turned against him at the very moment when he had adopted their programme of domestic reform and relatively moderate war aims. On the other hand, if Bethmann Hollweg had gained the support of a Centre-Left coalition in the Reichstag and had fought for his new moderate line, defying the will of his sovereign, it would have amounted to revolution by German standards.

Some German historians recently make out Bethmann Hollweg's fall as the beginning of parliamentary democracy in Germany. But it was a very curious beginning, for the 'victory' of parliament had been achieved in a most haphazard and unexpected way, over a chancellor who was about to collaborate with the new majority. Bethmann Hollweg's fall solved nothing. The parliamentary parties were unable even to nominate any successor, let alone one who would suit them. Out of continuing malaise and confusion emerged the new chancellor, Georg Michaelis, a non-political non-entity, who only ushered in the dictatorship, barely veiled, of Ludendorff and the army high command. On 19th July the Reichstag did vote the Peace Resolution, after it had been modified and accepted by Ludendorff and Michaelis.

But even the Peace Resolution, if looked at in the light of the general concept of German war aims in the First World War, was far from being a straightforward and honest declaration of the intention to return to the *status quo*. Whatever propaganda value it may have had was destroyed by the new Chancellor's notorious rider that he accepted it, 'as I understand it', and by the violent reaction of the Right against the 'weaklings' in Parliament.

The immediate effects on the constitution of Bethmann Hollweg's fall were negligible. The committee of the majority parties, which had drafted the Peace Resolution, did keep together during sessions of the Reichstag. But their tortuous debates on reforms only demonstrated painfully their utter inability to reach any positive conclusions at all, except for the pious wish for some modification of the constitution which would create the impression that a peaceful parliament had come to power. Far from being revolutionaries, they wanted neither the republic nor genuine democracy, nor a peace on the basis of the *status quo*, so long as Germany was powerful. In the days following the signing of the Treaty of Brest Litovsk and the apparently successful German offensive in the west, even the outwardly moderate appearance of the new majority faded away. The Treaty of Brest Litovsk was carried in the Reichstag by a huge majority. Only the USPD voted against it; the Majority Socialists meekly abstained.

The only perceptible result of the whole crisis of July 1917 in political terms was the appointment of one Prussian minister, two secretaries and two under-secretaries of state in the central government of the Reich, who were representatives of the political parties in favour of domestic reforms. Even these modest gains, however, were more than offset by the fact that most of the freshly appointed party politicians stood on the conservative wing of their respective parties, and by Ludendorff's unproclaimed yet effective dictatorship. If parliamentary government started in Germany in July 1917, it did so only in outward appearance; more than ever before parliament served as a fig leaf for a regime which remained autocratic and undemocratic.

Fear of the Socialists

The progress of the Russian Revolution and its repercussions on Germany made that delicate and artificial structure less and less tenable. The influence of radical groups on the left, in particular of the USPD and, to a lesser extent, of the Spartacists (the followers of the Socialist Karl Liebknecht), increased amongst Berlin workers and sailors of the fleet, whereas the Pan-German element rallied in the 'Vaterlandspartei' (Fatherland's Party), a combination of various right-wing organisations. Under the leadership of Tirpitz, the proto-Fascist element in Germany thus found its first powerful organizational form.

While war went on without hope of peace, the increasing polarization of political forces in Germany weakened the empire from within. The extreme Right was dissatisfied with the formal concessions to the moderate Left, and mistrusted them as a halfway-house to revolution and Socialism. The extreme Left rightly feared that small political changes were only made in order to forestall genuine reform and to patch up the regime, which remained intrinsically undemocratic.

In autumn 1917 these tensions came into the open for the first time when they brought about the downfall of Michaelis. For all his political inexperience, the new chancellor was intelligent and open-minded enough to realize that Germany would never be able to conclude peace on the basis of German war aims. This is why he demanded, at a crown council on 11th September, that Germany give up claims on Belgium in order to facilitate peace. His act of political independence and relative shrewdness did not endear him to the generals or the Kaiser, who dropped him at the first opportunity.

During the days of the Peace Resolution there had been an agitation among sailors of the German battle fleet in favour of a peace without annexations, which they found most strongly championed by the USPD. There were arrests and courts-martial among the sailors; five were sentenced to death, two of them actually executed. When he was attacked in the Reichstag by leaders of the USPD on 9th October, the chancellor created the impression that he wanted the USPD banned. The majority parties, no friends of the USPD, baulked, because they feared the chancellor would turn next against them. In a turbulent session of the Reichstag the parties clearly expressed their lack of confidence in the chancellor. The high command did nothing to keep Michaelis, and the Kaiser did not want to antagonize the parties who once again had to vote the war credits. Less than three weeks later, Michaelis was dismissed.

His successor was Count Hertling, seventy-three years old and half-blind. He had been one of the leaders of the Centre Party in the Reichstag before the war, and Bavarian prime minister since 1912. Although he was a party politician, he had not been nominated by the majority parties, nor was he their representative. Hertling, a staunch Conservative throughout his political life, was willing enough to appease the majority parties by agreeing to their political demands, especially the reform of the franchise in Prussia, but he definitely felt himself to be the servant of the crown, not dependent on parliament. The reform of the Prussian franchise made, indeed, no progress under Hertling. As for German war aims, the high command succeeded in committing the new chancellor to their programme. The Germans decided to pin down the Austrians, with whom they were at that time conferring, to staying in the war until all the German war aims had been accomplished. The conference with the Austrians took place on 6th November.

One day later the Bolsheviks seized power from the Provisional Government in Russia.

From now on the domestic situation in Germany became hopeless. While internal polarization continued, the parliamentary façade disguising Ludendorff's dictatorship had been strengthened a little by appointing Payer, a south German Progressive, vice-chancellor under Hertling. The south German, non-Prussian element apparently was destined to save the Reich from its impending catastrophe. But following developments showed that the ostentatious prominence of south German Liberals and Catholics at the top of the government did not alter the policy of the Reich. When President Wilson announced his Fourteen Points in January 1918, Hertling rejected them out of hand, whenever they affected Germany. During the great strike of the metal workers in Berlin, which spread to other German cities in the last days of the same month, the goverment did not budge an inch to meet the political demands of the striking workers. In spring 1918 even the pretence had gone that parliament ruled Germany, when Erzberger, during the debate on the Treaty of Brest Litovsk, declared it perfectly compatible with the demands of the Peace Resolution, following in fact the guidance of Ludendorff.

Thus, the German Reich drifted unreformed into its next political crisis in the autumn of 1918. Now Germany was even more exhausted, her people even more embittered than in summer 1917. The last illusions about submarine warfare, the miracle in the east and German offensives in the west were definitely gone. The Allied counter-offensives of July and August 1918 had, at last, destroyed even Ludendorff's hopes of winning the war.

In autumn 1918 the end of the war came, where it had started—in the Balkans. At the end of September the Allied Army of the Orient smashed the Macedonian front and Bulgaria sued for peace. Turkey was tottering, Austria-Hungary was on the brink of political decomposition. It was only a matter of weeks before Turkey and the Dual Monarchy would leave the war. However firm the German front might keep in the west, Allied troops would be able to invade Germany from the south and south-east within a few months.

On 28th September, when Ludendorff learned of Bulgaria's collapse, it was not difficult for him to foresee the chain of future events. It was only now that he admitted military defeat.

Yet, typically, Ludendorff, the military dictator at the end of his tether, blamed chiefly the forces of the Left for the coming débâcle. On 1st October he explained to his closest collaborators in the army high command, why it had become necessary to have a parliamentary government. He had asked the Kaiser, 'to include also those circles in the government to whom we owe chiefly our present situation. . . . Let them now make that peace, which has to be made. Let them now bear the consequences of what they have done to us'. The famous 'stab-in-the-back' legend was invented as a face-saving device by Ludendorff even before Germany laid down her arms.

In a desperate effort to save what could be saved Ludendorff ordered parliamentary government into existence in Germany and coupled it with the demand for an immediate armistice, before the German Western Front broke as well. Hertling, honest Conservative to the last minute, refused to become chancellor of a parliamentary government and resigned. After a few days of hurried search, the last imperial chancellor was found. Again, he was not chosen by the now 'victorious' parliamentary forces. He was not even a party politician or a member of any parliament, but the member of a south German dynasty, Prince Max von Baden, who had a reputation for liberal leanings. There was a certain historic logic and justice in this choice: Baden and her Grand Duke had been Bismarck's most important agent and ally in 1870-71 when he was founding the Second Empire. Now, in its dying days, a member of the same dynasty was called to save the Reich and the monarchy. Prince Max was half successful. It was beyond his power to keep the monarchy, because the Kaiser stubbornly clung to his throne, when hardly any one, even in Germany, wanted him there any more. But he managed to preserve the Reich and its social order by a most liberal interpretation of the Constitution and by ingeniously handing over power on 9th November to another south German, Friedrich Ebert, the conservative SPD leader from Heidelberg.

On 3rd October Prince Max was appointed chancellor. Payer remained vice-chancellor, while several members of the Reichstag joined the cabinet, among them Scheidemann for the SPD and Erzberger for the Centre Party. The political changes were institutionalized on 26th October, when the Reichstag voted an amendment to the constitution, which made the chancellor dependent on the confidence of parliament. Parliamentary government had been formally introduced for the first time in the Reich. Germany, by a simple vote in parliament, had become a *'Volksstaat'*, although for the time being the monarchy remained.

Yet political progress had not been spontaneous. It had only been effected with one eye to threatening unrest from inside and another to certain military defeat from outside. Wilson had made it clear in his note of 23rd October that he did not want to conclude a negotiated peace with the old autocratic regime in Germany. The constitutional changes of 26th October were the German response. With disturbing flexibility Germany had suddenly donned parliamentary democracy in the hope of some tactical advantage; less than fifteen years later she was to divest herself of this alien political structure, the adoption of which, after all, had not apparently brought the advantages Germany had hoped for.

Once Ludendorff had made up his mind that the war was lost, he was in a hurry. He got his way without serious trouble on the domestic front by hastily installing the Prince Max-Scheidemann-Erzberger government on 3rd October. But it was more difficult to convince the political leadership of the urgent need for an armistice. Their reluctance was understandable, because the majority parties did not want the responsibility for having surrendered. It was only after hard pleading on the part of Ludendorff and a special session of leading members of the Reichstag on 2nd October to whom an officer of the general staff explained the catastrophic military situation, that the political leadership gave in once more to the pressure of the generals. On 3rd October 1918 the new government under Prince Max officially asked for an armistice.

'November criminals'

Even in the hour of defeat Germany tried to make the best of a bad situation. The note asking for an armistice also indicated Germany's willingness to conclude peace on the basis of Wilson's Fourteen Points, and it was addressed not to the Allies, Great Britain and France, but to the United States. Wilson's Fourteen Points, scorned only nine months ago, now became the saving plank for the Reich. The choice of the American President as addressee of the German note was a very clever move, because it appealed to his ambition to bring peace to the world.

Meanwhile, fighting went on, submarine warfare as well as the battles on land. The German armies, retreating under pressure on the Western Front, practised the policy of 'scorched earth'– systematic destruction–on French and Belgian soil. At Wilson's demand Germany made an end to submarine warfare, but

protested that she had done nothing contrary to international law on her Western Front. At the last minute, the armistice demanded by Germany seemed to be in danger. In his third note to Germany of 23rd October, Wilson had pointed out that the only form of armistice acceptable to the United States and the Allied powers was one which would make it impossible for Germany to renew hostilities. Now Ludendorff brusquely reversed his position again. He suddenly found that Germany's military position turned out not to be so gloomy as he had first thought, and it would be better for Germany to perish than conclude peace on dishonourable terms: Ludendorff spoke for a certain segment of Germany's political leaders, who toyed with the idea of a last-minute *levée en masse* for the defence of the Fatherland to the last ditch. Even Walter Rathenau joined the chorus in demand for an end worthy of *Götterdämmerung*. A phrase went round, which Goebbels was to take up one generation later in a similar situation: 'Better an end in terror than terror without end!'

This time it was the civilian government that resisted the temptation of a heroic-demagogic gesture. Collective suicide was not practical policy for a nation of sixty-five million people, as one minister put it. Ludendorff was relieved of his post on 26th October and thus happily escaped the formal responsibility for concluding the armistice. He fled abroad incognito to hibernate in neutral Sweden, in wait for better times, in which he could stage his comeback. Ludendorff's successor was yet another south German, General Groener. Hindenburg remained as formal head of the German army.

Whatever doubts may have lingered in German minds about the necessity of laying down arms, they were definitely destroyed by events inside and outside Germany. On 27th October Emperor Karl of Austria-Hungary threw up the sponge and announced to the German Kaiser his intention to sue for peace. Austria-Hungary fell apart, and so did her army. On 3rd November Austria signed an armistice which put her roads and railways at the disposal of the Allies. Germany lay practically open to invasion through Bohemia and Tyrol into Silesia, Saxony, and Bavaria. To wage war on foreign soil was one thing, to have the destructions of modern warfare on sacred German soil was another.

This explains why the spontaneous, quasi-revolutionary movement of soldiers and workers to end the war started at the periphery of the Reich, in Bavaria and Saxony. It became even more urgent for the ruling groups to avoid a crushing defeat in the west and to effect an orderly retreat into the Reich. This alone could prevent a genuine social revolution.

But some kind of revolution was already in the offing when on 29th and 30th October sailors of the battle fleet refused to join in a last naval battle. From then on there existed in Germany two competing movements for ending the war quickly, an official one from above and a popular one from below. The official one sought an early armistice in the hope of preserving the political and social *status quo*. It was supported by approximately the same kind of alliance that had supported the war: the army high command, the bureaucracy, industrialists, and the majority of the Reichstag. The popular one hoped, by ending war through revolutionary pres-sure, for the establishment of democracy and–very vaguely–of some kind of socialism. Although the movement from above had started earlier, on 28th September, Wilson's delaying tactics resulted in the movement from below overtaking the official one. The revolutionary upsurge reached Berlin and its culminating point on 9th November, the armistice was concluded near Compiègne only two days later.

The victory of the German revolution was more apparent than real. Even the democratic wing of the parliamentary establishment was not rewarded for its self-effacing loyalty to the Reich. After Erzberger had played Ludendorff's game and signed the armistice on 11th November 1918, he and his friends were denounced 'November criminals' by the extreme Right. Erzberger himself was murdered in 1921, less than twelve years before the Weimar Republic was strangled by the same political forces who had dreamed first of Germany's bid to become a world power and then to stage national suicide when they saw they had miserably failed.

Part ten · The Settlement

When peace came in 1918 the Allies had achieved their one agreed aim. For the moment anyway the threat of German militarism had been removed and German hegemony of Central Europe diminished. But the war had had consequences far beyond the checking of German ambitions and ones which the Allies had neither foreseen nor intended. The three great empires of eastern Europe had collapsed; new national states had sprung up; and a communist revolution had taken place in Russia. The train of events unleashed by the 20th-century total war had proved far beyond the control of any statesman or nation and, although Germany was defeated and the Allies had thereby done what they had set out to do, the face of Europe was so changed in 1918 from what it had been in 1914 that many felt a deep unease about the future victory would bring.

Not only had old political boundaries vanished overnight but economically Europe was in a terrible state. Millions of her men had been killed and countless maimed; factories, mines, and houses had been destroyed; fertile land torn up; shipping sunk. No arrangement made about reparations would undo the great material losses. The unprecedented scale of the slaughter and damage provoked in some the feeling that at any price such a war must never be allowed to break out again and in others the longing to pin the blame for their four years' suffering on Germany and to make her pay.

So when the peace conference met at Versailles it faced two supreme tasks. A settlement of some kind had to be made with Germany which would prevent her resurgence as an aggressive military state and the map of central and eastern Europe had to be redrawn and old dynastic empires

replaced by new frontiers based on realities of national groupings, economic viability, and national security. But these tasks had to be undertaken amid an atmosphere of exhaustion and war-weariness. For four years Europe had been fighting and when the peace conference met at Paris the guns had not been silent very long. Four years of such a war could not be forgotten overnight. The Allied leaders, Clemenceau, Lloyd George, Woodrow Wilson, and Orlando, were all leaders of democratic states and each had to take account of the opinion of their electorate. From the start the conference was torn by the conflict of those who saw their victory as a chance to create a more orderly world in which international disputes would not lead to war and the human emotions of vindictiveness and vengeance. France, which had suffered German occupation twice during the past fifty years, was obsessed with the problem of the security of her eastern frontier. To her Woodrow Wilson's dream of a League of Nations was the idealistic fancy of a man whose country had never been directly threatened by Germany. To France demilitarizing the Rhine was far more practical and necessary for securing a lasting peace than collective security could ever be.

In Eastern Europe too Woodrow Wilson's hopes for a peace firmly based on the principles of absolute justice and national self-determination also proved out of touch with reality. The complete mixture of nationalities in this area made the clear cut drawing of boundaries on ethnic lines impossible. The rival claims of Italy and Yugoslavia in the Adriatic, for example, could be solved neither by applying principles of self-determination nor by doctrines of absolute justice, but only by some give and take compromise which very probably would not really satisfy either of them. Then the decision that countries should be economically viable as well as nationally homogeneous led to complications. The need to give Poland access to the sea meant depriving Germany of some of her territory which was inhabited by Germans.

The settlement of Eastern Europe was coloured by a further very important consideration: fear of the spread of Bolshevism into Europe. The lurking idea that Germany might be used as a bulwark was already present and there was a strong inclination to make the eastern states from Finland down to Rumania as large and as strong as possible in order to serve as a quarantine zone to keep back the tide of communism.

But the fundamental fault of the settlement was that it was imposed by the victors on their enemies. The conference was a meeting solely of the winning powers and the exclusion of enemy states, especially Germany, turned the peace it produced into an imposed settlement for which the Germans felt no kind of responsibility since they had not been consulted. In the atmosphere of the time no other course seemed possible but in the long run it was a major weakness. The famous 'war guilt' clause, which pinned responsibility for the war firmly on Germany's aggression, gave the whole settlement an aura of moral judgement. It ensured that the conference was not concerned simply with the political realities of the present but that the conditions imposed on Germany were in some measure a punishment for past behaviour. Not surprisingly German resentment grew and German national pride was given an immediate stake in overthrowing the settlement.

It was very easy to end by having the worst of all worlds and to frame a settlement which alienated the vanquished from any true acceptance of the new order while leaving them free and powerful enough to lay immediate plans to destroy it. Germany's military forces might be momentarily eliminated but she still had the largest population in Central Europe. She was not physically dismembered; and she was soon to prove her industrial resilience. In such a situation there would be little guarantee that her military power would not be restored. Had the settlement been either more lenient or more severe the chances of a renewed outbreak of Germany's ambitions would surely have been less.

In so far as the aim of the conference was to solve the German question then it must be counted a failure but as an attempt to refashion the world to avoid future wars, and by putting this aim above national interests, it stands as an important landmark in international peace-making. The League of Nations was in one sense simply an improved and wider version of the series of congresses which the great powers of Europe had held from time to time throughout the century before 1914. But in another light it was something quite new and quite different. It was a multilateral treaty by which each participant bound itself not only to seek peaceful means of settling any dispute in which it became involved, but also to shoulder some share of responsibility for defending every other signatory against aggression. There was no means provided of enforcing this obligation. But the ultimate failure of the League in preventing another war was simply the outcome of those who attached inordinate hopes to it without giving it any means of fulfilling them. But in less dramatic ways the League did do much to promote international understanding and its work here is perhaps the most durable and original achievement of the peacemakers at Versailles.

The Problems of Peace

J. M. Roberts

The First World War was, above all, a war against Germany. Some historians have even called it 'the first German War' and this is why it was 11th November, more than any of the other armistice days, which released across the world a torrent of pent-up emotion. It became a carnival for millions of people. Everywhere, wives, mothers, sisters, children suddenly felt released from a great shadow; husbands, sons, brothers, fathers were free at last from the terror of a scourge which had flailed across Europe for fifty-two months. The worst war in history was over.

For the Allies there was victory to celebrate. Few were untouched by the emotions of the time. The aged Empress Eugénie, in exile from France since 1870, told an English journalist that she could kiss Clemenceau for what he had done for France (she hastily added that he was not to pass the message on). The 'Tiger' himself had special grounds for happiness, for he was, as he reminded the Chamber of Deputies when giving them the news of the Austrian armistice, the last survivor of the small band of deputies who had protested in 1871 against the surrender of Alsace and Lorraine. A few weeks later, he went to the newly liberated Strasbourg and there the leather-nerved old warrior was seen to weep with emotion.

Even the defeated could rejoice that the war was over, and some of them could find something more positive to celebrate. Two days before the end of the fighting, for example, many German Social Democrats saw the culmination of a lifetime of hope in the proclamation of a socialist republic from the steps of the Reichstag. That it was only there because of the defeat of their country and that there was another contender for power a little way away (the Spartacists had proclaimed their republic from the Imperial Palace) did not seem to most of them very important at first. The Allies' efforts, as the pronouncements of President Wilson seemed to make clear, had been directed against Germany's wicked and undemocratic rulers and not against the German people. Only some of the soldiers felt disgruntled and they, too, were glad to stop fighting and were to be welcomed back as conquering heroes. And even the most patriotic citizen, socialist or not, had had enough of blockade, and the mark it left in the pinched, pale faces of his children or the chill of his unheated home.

'Everyone suddenly burst out singing,' if only for relief. And there were other reasons to celebrate, when men thought about the future. The very horrors of the war had encouraged men to dream of making a new world in which the seeds of such a tragedy could never again take root. Liberals everywhere had debated the opportunities of a peace made on new principles, and they knew President Wilson sympathized with them; old imperial rivalries would be ended, the oppressed nations of Europe would be freed to govern themselves, and the old diplomacy which had brought the war would be swept away. It was a noble moment, as well as a happy one. Yet it rested on illusion. Even the bloodshed was not yet over.

Europe's wounds
It was too easy, in the euphoria of the moment, to overlook the damage Europe had done herself, above all in the last year of the war. Whether men looked forward or back, whether they wanted to build a new world on new principles or restore what some of them now looked back to as a golden age of peace and security, there was a terrible burden of material destruction, disruption, and privation which would have to be borne for years to come. It had to be removed before any real recovery could come to Europe. The most visible evidence of this was the devastation in the battle zones; a great tract of France had been blighted and ravaged by the fighting, and more had been deliberately damaged as much as possible by the Germans in their retreat. Mines had been flooded, machinery taken from factories, railways torn up— even the fruit-trees had been ringed and left to die. The French were confident that

the Germans would pay for the repair of the damage (the magical effect that reparations would have was one of the earliest illusions to take root), but even if they did, the destruction was a diminution of Europe's wealth. In eastern Europe, devastation was less intense because fighting had swung back and forth over a bigger area, but there had in some places been less to destroy in the first place. Over huge areas cultivation had been interrupted time and time again. The railways, on which the movement of food depended, were in ruins; they would have to be put right before Europe's granaries could again feed her peoples. Until they did, central and eastern Europe would be condemned to hunger and privation.

Nor was this all. Even those countries where little had been destroyed by fighting were much poorer. Capital had been used up to fight the war; labour had been dragged from factories and farms to serve in the armies. All the European states were producing less to satisfy their basic needs in 1918 than in 1914. Between 1913 and 1920 European manufacturing output went down by nearly a quarter; the war cost Europe eight years of normal pre-war economic growth. The cost could be seen in 1918 in the railways lacking locomotives, the factories lacking machines, and the shops with empty shelves.

The central need of the European economy was to get the German industrial machine to work again, producing the goods to re-equip depleted stocks and providing the markets and capital for Germany's southern and eastern neighbours. But not only were there immense political difficulties in the way of doing this, there were also big practical obstacles to overcome. The war had terribly disrupted Europe's complicated and highly-integrated pre-war economy. In 1914 Germany and Great Britain had been one another's best customers; four years of economic warfare and frantic searching for alternative suppliers had put paid to that. Russia had been both a great market for capital from the industrial nations and the biggest of the European food exporters; now her economy was in ruins and she was cut off from her neighbours by the revolution and the fears it engendered. Austria-Hungary, for all its political inadequacies, had provided a framework of economic unity for much of the Danube valley; now this economic entity had fallen apart into new rational units already so conscious of their weakness that they would not even allow the little rolling-stock they possessed to cross their frontiers for fear that it would not return.

Life among these economic ruins was bound to be very hard for at least another winter. For many, moreover, hardship meant a real threat to existence. German death-rates—especially those of children and old people, the most susceptible sections of the community—had already shown the effects of the blockade. In Russia the story was even more horrible, but no reliable figures were available for a long time. And on such weakened and starved populations as survived in eastern and central Europe—and, indeed, on those of Great Britain and France too—there now fell the blow of the great influenza epidemic which swept across the world.

Destruction, dislocation, starvation, disease; these were the immediate and most striking perils. Unfortunately, they did not exhaust the list of those which faced a Europe which suddenly found itself at peace. There were others which arose from a breakdown of old institutions and administrative structures; they were both dangerous in themselves and an additional handicap to nations striving to deal with economic collapse and near-starvation.

Ever since the Russian revolution in March 1917, the governments which had for centuries ruled most of central and eastern Europe had slowly been giving way. The emergence of new regimes demanding independence in the borderlands of old Russia had been the first result. Then after the Dual Monarchy had collapsed during September and October 1918, the representatives of the nations who had made it up assumed power. This, whatever western liberals might think, was a far from simple change of authority. Given the economic chaos and deprivation amid which it took place, it was bound to be accompanied by turmoil and upheaval. Worse still, national rivalries held in check by the old imperial structures could suddenly burst out violently. The first fighting between the successors of the old empires, between Poles and Ruthenes, began even before Germany had been defeated. Soon the

Hungarians found themselves hemmed in by menacing new states with old scores to pay off and a taste for territorial expansion at Hungary's expense.

Above all, there was the problem of political change in Germany. Germany was the key to any satisfactory European reconstruction, yet, days before the armistice, she too seemed to be disintegrating into revolution. Workers' councils ruled her main seaports. A republic was declared in Bavaria. Germans everywhere swept away the institutions under which they had lived since 1871 — or seemed to do so to those who did not look too closely. 'We lived through scenes that no Prussian had thought possible since 1806,' wrote Ludendorff of those days. (1806 had been the blackest year in Prussia's history, when she had been overthrown by Napoleon.)

The climax was the disappearance of the monarchy itself. Early on the cold and foggy morning of 9th November, further news of crumbling discipline in the army and of a general strike at Berlin had finally convinced Hindenburg that the Emperor would have to go. Overcome by emotion and the distress proper to a Prussian officer forced to admit that Wilhelm could no longer rely on soldiers bound to him by oath, the Field-Marshal took the Württemberger General Groener along to deliver the verdict. The interview which followed was painful. It was interrupted by more bad tidings: that none of the troops in Berlin were any longer reliable and that a conference of thirty-nine senior officers could produce only eight willing to guarantee that their men would march against the Bolshevists in Germany. While Wilhelm hesitated, his last chancellor, Prince Max of Baden, announced on the same day in Berlin, without waiting for a royal decision, that the Emperor had abdicated both the throne of the Empire and that of Prussia. So ended a historic European ruling house and the last of the three empires which had between them ruled eastern Europe in 1914. 'Such a spectacle' (wrote Winston Churchill later) 'appals mankind; and a knell rang in the ears of the victors, even in their hour of triumph.'

The abdication only dramatized a fear which had for weeks been crystallizing in the Allied councils. If this could happen in disciplined, authoritarian Germany, where could it not? On the very day of his announcement, Prince Max handed his powers to Ebert, the socialist leader who was desperately anxious to get control of the situation before the German revolution broke out in earnest. Ebert just managed to do so in the coming weeks. For months the fate of the new regime seemed to hang in the balance. It was only by relying on the army (whose discipline rapidly recovered when the fighting ended and the ranks were purged of unreliable troops) that the socialist founders of the German Republic held on to power.

That they did this was often to be held against them later. Yet they felt obliged to do so because of the danger of revolution which they felt threatened Germany. This was not merely one more of the paradoxes of German socialism, so often accused by its critics of talking revolution while becoming a part of the establishment. The threat felt by men like Ebert was not just a personal one. It was a threat to the whole nation, not only because it would mean an end to the hopes of parliamentary democracy liberal-minded Germans had long cherished, but because a Bolshevik revolution would inevitably lead to an Allied invasion, the occupation of Germany, and its disappearance for an unforeseeable time as an independent nation. What men believe is as important historically as what is true. They were not, perhaps, right in thinking that there really was a danger of revolution in Germany; they were certainly right in thinking that already the Allies feared one and were determined to prevent it.

This fear had troubled the Allied leaders weeks before the armistice. Together with a general over-estimation of German strength and of the German will to fight it was a powerful incentive to come to terms quickly rather than to fight on and impose a peace — as Lloyd George had briefly suggested — in Germany itself. It was a fear reinforced by what was known of economic and social conditions in central and eastern Europe. The day after Wilhelm's abdication an American official in Europe reported that 'there was running through the minds of all the high political men the fear of revolution and Bolshevism in Germany and their belief that the only barrier against the spread of it would be to leave the German army sufficiently armed to put down such a revolution'. It was to prove a terrible handicap to making a European settlement and it crippled relations with the new Russia from the start.

This fear had two main sources. One was the revolutionary potential of the economic and political chaos of much of Europe. The turmoil was already great in October, and it was all the more alarming because social and national revolution had not been clearly distinguished in the Allies' support for the minorities of the Dual Monarchy. Into this volatile situation had flooded back prisoners from Russia who had been exposed to Bolshevik propaganda and had sympathized with it. The German workers' and soldiers' councils seemed to the Allies repetitions of the Russian soviets, and when they proclaimed the abolition of bourgeois law-courts or forbade the wearing of insignia of rank in the army their words seemed all too familiar. That the capitalist system in Germany had not collapsed and showed no sign of doing so, and that a revolutionary programme did not have the support of the German workers was not yet clear.

The other source of fear was the behaviour and language of the Russian government itself. It was hampered in its own understanding of the outside world by two things, the Marxist dogmas on which it claimed to base its actions, and the Civil War. By November 1918 White Russians were already inextricably tangled up with Allied operations in Russia whose origins had lain in quite different purposes from theirs. This made the regime deeply suspicious. It was fighting for its life and for the control of its borderlands. In these circumstances it was bound to use all weapons which came to hand, and a revolutionary appeal was the obvious one. The result was a barrage of propaganda, beginning long before November, encouraging the expected workers' revolution in the west. Unfortunately, by Armistice Day the Russians were mis-reading the European situation as much through over-optimism as the Allies were through fear; on both sides it was assumed that the danger of proletarian revolution was real and imminent. In retrospect this seems a misjudgement. But the result was an assiduous fanning of revolutionary

flames by Russian propaganda which convinced men far from reactionary that the danger was real.

And of real reactionaries there were enough. The war had everywhere shaken traditional authority and traditional institutions. In the victor nations labour had won great gains because its services had been bought by concessions long resisted in peace-time. Allied propaganda had made much of the prospects of reform in the post-war world; now the returning soldiers were going to ask for the postdated cheques to be cashed. There was a stirring on the left everywhere, and it alarmed conservatives. They were only too anxious to blame it on Bolshevism and to see it as one more manifestation of a great international threat.

The psychological legacy of the war
By itself an atmosphere tense with the terror of Bolshevism would have been a serious handicap to the construction of a healthy post-war order, for it ruled out several possible approaches to European recovery and the reintegration of Russia into Europe's affairs. Yet it was not the only psychological barrier to successful peace-making. There were also the legacies of wartime hatred and bitterness. 'Suspicions, resentments, misunderstandings and fear,' wrote Lloyd George, 'had poisoned the mind of mankind.'

For every idealist in 1918, there were ten men demanding a punitive peace. The casualty lists had been immense; almost no French or British family had been spared. There were many Frenchmen and Englishmen who believed that Germany should both pay for what she had done and then be crippled so that she could never do it again. In part the bitterness was the result of war-time propaganda, a weapon used more effectively than ever before. All the great victor powers were democratic nations and all would soon have elections in which their peoples would pass judgement on their leaders. Great Britain had hers in December 1918, and the result was taken as clear evidence of the electorate's desire for a punitive peace. The rulers of democracies cannot afford to take up enlightened positions if this is going to mean that they lose office and cease to be able to influence events; only a Lloyd George could have retained as much freedom of manoeuvre as he did in these circumstances. Already, there were signs that President Wilson was out of step with the sympathies and aspirations of great numbers of his countrymen; his party lost control of Congress in November. Ironically, in the end even Clemenceau was to be rejected as President by Frenchmen who felt he had not fought hard enough against his allies for a more punitive peace than was in fact imposed. Argument had continued about the terms which were settled at Versailles: the psychological atmosphere must not be overlooked when judging them.

It was also too easily forgotten that the Allies were, after all, different nations with different interests and would approach the peace with different aims. British fears of German naval power had been removed by the armistice itself; the French had still to find a way of preventing a resurgence of German land power. Both, in any case, had doubts about the practical consequences of Wilsonian idealism, the bill for which would have to be paid not by Americans but by Europeans. Already in October the British foreign secretary had warned his colleagues of the troubles that might be expected if Poland was given (as Wilson wished) access to the Baltic by a corridor which would divide East Prussia from Germany. General Smuts pointed to the inevitable dangers which would follow a Balkanization of Austria-Hungary. Here were future disputes in embryo.

Another problem was whether the Allies had the means to impose a satisfactory settlement even if they could agree on one. Because it was virtually inconceivable that the armies could be remobilized for a new struggle, the Allies had rapidly dwindling powers once the armistice was signed. Any strategy for the future resumption of war against Germany if successful peace terms were not agreed, or for intervention to prevent the collapse of rickety new states, had to be made in very awkward conditions. It was extremely unlikely that the British and French armies could be kept up to strength to carry out major operations. Certainly the Americans would not be there; they would have gone home. The implications of this were many and unpleasant. Soon, almost the only coercive instrument left available to the Allies would be blockade. Another

implication was that Germany had better be enabled to police itself and defend itself in the east; that meant the retention of the nucleus of a German army. It also meant that the Allies could not control the new nations still fighting to settle their borders with Russia; soon a French general would save Warsaw from the Red Army and German soldiers would be defending the Baltic states. Other Allies who had forces on the spot would be free to pursue their own aims if western soldiers were not available and this would mean further rancour and bitterness. It would be the Rumanians, with long memories of oppressive Magyar landlords in Transylvania, who eagerly attacked the communist regime set up in Hungary by Béla Kun, to the eventual embarrassment of the Big Four. As Balfour bitterly remarked in July 1919, only eight months after having fifteen million men under arms, the great powers could hardly raise one battalion.

When the Paris Peace Conference finally opened, on 18th January, not all these handicaps and troubles were yet fully apparent. Europe's economic weakness was obvious enough and some people already suspected that there were greater political difficulties ahead than had been realized on the delirious morning of 11th November, but there was still optimism in the air. A few thought that Paris was the wrong place for so colossal a task as faced the Peace Conference, that the atmosphere was too thick with rancour and hatred for the practice of true statesmanship in the difficult months to come. Perhaps still fewer realized the complexity of the problems which would reveal themselves. We should remember this with humility and not judge too hardly the men of Versailles; by the time they had finished, they had at least — some of them — seen more deeply into Europe's predicament after her suicidal struggles, and striven harder to grapple with it rationally, than many of their later critics were to do. One critic, gifted with one of the finest minds of his age, who himself joined in the work of the Peace Conference, looked back after his disillusionment and, while not sparing the men he blamed, yet recognized something of the deep helplessness in which they stood. Towards the end of his book, *The Economic Consequences of the Peace,* Maynard Keynes passed a grim verdict on what the war had cost Europe: 'We have been moved already beyond endurance, and need rest. Never in the lifetime of men now living has the universal element in the soul of man burnt so dimly.' The cost of the war had gone far beyond the statistics of casualty lists and economic balance-sheets.

The Treaty of Versailles

Martin Gilbert

The Germans surrendered to the Allies on 11th November 1918. Seven months later they signed the Treaty of Versailles, accepting new frontiers and stern penalties. During those seven months the victorious powers debated, both openly and secretly, every aspect of the future of Germany. Was it to be split up into small, separate states? Was it to be crippled economically? Was it to be deprived of territory? Was it to lose its empire in Africa and the Pacific? Was it to be prevented from ever having a powerful army, navy, or air force again? These were some of the questions on which every public figure, and most private people, held strong opinions, and argued over during the seven months between the military cease-fire and the signature of the treaty.

Yet the peace conference did not decide all of these issues. Many had been determined beforehand. During the war itself each side had worried continuously over the post-war settlement. Every nation had its dreams, its hopes, its secret agreements and its publicly proclaimed aspirations. France was pledged to take back the provinces of Alsace and Lorraine which Germany had annexed in 1870. Great Britain was determined to absorb as much of the German colonial empire as possible. As early as 1915 Italy had been promised Austrian, Turkish, and German territory in return for entering the war on the Allied side. Serbia was promised parts of Bosnia and Albania; Russia was promised Constantinople; the Jews were promised a 'National Home' in Palestine; the Arabs were promised independence from the Turks; and the Poles were offered the restoration of an independent Poland.

Woodrow Wilson, the President of the United States, had, in January 1918, offered *all* subject peoples the right of 'self-determination'. This gave an impetus to many ambitious nationalists, to Czechs and Slovaks, to Serbs, Slovenes, and Croats, to Ukrainians, to the Baltic peoples, to the Rumanians inside Austria, to the Armenians inside Turkey, indeed, to a hundred groups, however small, who saw in 'self-determination' a chance, however slim, of statehood. Even the young Vietnamese Communist, Ho Chi-Minh, asked the Paris Peace Conference to liberate his people from the 'curse' of French imperial rule. But most of the small nationalities, like Ho Chi-Minh's, were doomed to be disappointed. Wilson's idealism shone like a beacon to the dispossessed; but to the French and the British, with their large empires and many subject peoples, and with their own hopes of territorial gain, 'self-determination' was a theme to be dampened down wherever it conflicted with their own ambitions.

The 'war for human liberty'

Wilson believed that the war was the 'final war for human liberty'. He therefore wished to infuse the peace treaties with his own concept of liberty. For him, the central issue was that of national dignity: the right of people to be independent, with secure frontiers and unavaricious neighbours. When he spoke to Congress in February 1918 Wilson made it clear that, in his and the American view: 'Peoples are not to be handed about from one sovereignty to another by an international conference or an understanding between rivals and antagonists. National aspirations must be respected; peoples may now be dominated and governed only by their own consent. "Self-determination" is not a mere phrase. It is an imperative principle of action, which statesmen will henceforth ignore at their peril.'

Great Britain and France had little faith in self-determination. As a vague, idealistic liberal concept, they approved it in their public utterances; but during the heat of battle they had to consider other pressures besides liberal sentiment. At various moments in the war the Allied position was precarious. New allies had to be found. But neutrals do not easily agree to join in a war which they see to be one of terrible carnage, both on land and sea, involving the suspension of peaceful trade and industry, hardships in daily life, and, above all, the ever-present risk of defeat, occupation, humiliation, and national ruin.

The pledges made during the war had thus one dominating purpose, to persuade the uncommitted and the uncertain that it was in their full interest to support the Allied cause. Once that support had been forthcoming, the Allies could hardly go back on their promises. Where they did so, as in the case of Italy, they created a sense of grievance which had widespread repercussions. Italy had been promised, by Great Britain, France, and Russia, a share in any partitions of Turkish or German territory in Africa and the Near East. She was promised also the Austrian provinces of the Trentino, the South Tyrol, Gorizia, and Istria, the Dalmatian coast and control over Albania. But most of these promises were unfulfilled. Albania became fully independent. The Dalmatian coast went to Yugoslavia. Great Britain and France kept all Germany's African colonies for themselves, and gained all the benefits of the Turkish collapse. At the peace conference all Italy's protestations were in vain. Although she emerged from the peace treaties with her territory enlarged, she had become an unsatisfied nation, anxious to see a further revision of the treaty frontiers. Within a few years Mussolini was exploiting this sense of deprivation. He demanded the fulfilment of what Italy had been promised. But immediately the peace conference ended the world sought only to be done with alarms and crises, wars and arguments. At Paris, from January to June 1919, any claim could be made with impunity, for the six months of the conference was essentially a period when every nation pressed for as much as it dared to claim, and urged its claims with passion. But once the treaties were signed, any call for revision was made to seem an incitement to aggression, and the word 'revisionist' quickly became synonymous with 'troublemaker', even when the power demanding revision was a former ally.

In one case the war-time pledges could be easily ignored. For in 1917 the Russian Bolsheviks renounced the secret treaties and declared that they would not accept any of the territorial gains promised to Russia. As a result, the Anglo-French promise of Constantinople to the Tsar could lapse. But even so, the strategic waterway from the Black Sea to the Mediterranean was not to return easily into Turkish hands. From 1918 to 1924 the 'Zone of the Straits' was occupied by an Allied force, and for six years a British High Commissioner was the effective ruler of the former Turkish capital. Only the military successes of Kemal Ataturk made it possible for Turkey to retain Anatolia intact, and, although deprived of all her Arabian, Syrian, and Mesopotamian territory, to survive as a robust national state.

The spoils of war

The secret treaties were not the only complications confronting the peace-makers when they reached Paris. Territory had changed hands at every stage of the war, and it proved difficult to dislodge claimants who were already in possession of what they claimed. During the conference Woodrow Wilson criticized the Australian Prime Minister, William Hughes, for insisting that Australia should keep control of German New Guinea, which Australian troops had occupied as early as 1914, within a month of the outbreak of war. Did Hughes really intend, questioned Wilson, to flout the opinion of the civilized world by annexing territory? Would she let it be said that she took part of the German empire as the spoils of war? Was Australia proposing to make a profit out of Germany's defeat, to impose her rule on aborigines, to take over valuable mineral rights, to extend her sovereignty as far north as the equator? To all of which Hughes replied acidly: 'That's about it, Mr President.'

The Australians were not alone in insisting upon the maxim of 'what we have, we hold'. Japan pressed vigorously for control over the Chinese port of Tsingtao, a German possession which the Japanese had occupied in 1914, after a month's hard fighting. To the chagrin of the Japanese, the peace-makers forced them to return Tsingtao to China. As a result, the Japanese, like the Italians, felt cheated of a 'fruit' of victory, and looked for a chance to redress the balance. The Japanese invasion of China in 1937, like the Italian invasion of Albania in 1939, was in part a legacy of the frustrations of the peace conference. Other victor nations were less frustrated. No one dislodged the New Zealanders from German Samoa, the South Africans from German South West Africa, the British from German East Africa, or the Australians from New Guinea. Even the Japanese were allowed to retain control of most of Germany's vast Pacific island empire, which included over two thousand islands and covered three million square miles. Great Britain and France partitioned the German territories of Togoland and the Cameroons between them; the Italian occupation of the former Turkish Dodecanese Islands was made more secure; Cyprus, occupied by Great Britain under nominal Turkish suzerainty for forty years, was transformed into a permanent British possession. The areas of Turkey conquered in October 1918 remained firmly under the controlling hands of their conquerors – the British in Palestine, Transjordan, and Iraq, the French in Syria and Alexandretta, the Arabs in the Yemen and the Hejaz.

Such were the many territorial gains which were made during the course of the war. Most were criticized at the peace conference, particularly by Woodrow Wilson. But all survived the peace-making, and became a part of the new world order. Some even survived the Second World War; South Africa still rules German South West Africa; Australia still controls German New Guinea; New Zealand still occupies Samoa. Japanese control over Germany's Pacific Islands north of the equator passed, in 1945, not back to Germany, but on to the United States, the third imperial power to come into possession of the islands and atolls which stretch in a broad band out from the coast of China across three thousand miles of ocean.

The new map of Europe

When the victor powers met in Paris they had to consider more than the promises which each ally had made, and the existence of new possessions which particular Allies had every intention of making permanent. They had also to take into account the people who, even before the war was ended, had proclaimed themselves independent. There were many such people, each determined to keep the territory which they claimed as the basis of permanent national frontiers. Thus the Czechs and Slovaks had declared their complete severance from Austria-Hungary before the Austro-Hungarian surrender; and they were insisting upon a new state which would include the historic frontiers of Bohemia, thereby placing over two million German-speaking people within their proposed territory. The South Slavs had also declared themselves an independent state, ruling over territory in which were to be found Hungarian, Italian, and Austrian minorities. These frontiers were of course still open to negotiation and change. But the Allies had for most of the war given support to all enemies of Austria-Hungary. In April 1915 they promised the future Serb state a part of the Adriatic coast and the Austro-Hungarian provinces of Bosnia and Dalmatia. They might strive to create 'ideal' frontiers, excluding minorities and satisfying conflicting claims and promises, but since the same territories were often occupied by different nationalities this was no easy matter, even from the point of view of abstract national geography.

As a result the frontiers in existence before the conference met tended to become the permanent ones. The pre-conference frontiers had been established by the subject peoples of Germany, Austria-Hungary, and Turkey. As the conference was made up of those who had fought these three empires in the war, the likelihood was that the pre-conference frontiers would, in the main, be allowed to survive – as indeed they were. When the Paris Peace Conference met a new map of Europe had already come into existence, drawn by new nations upon the ruins of the German, Austrian, and Turkish empires. The victor nations did not redraw the old map of Europe; instead, they fussed and argued over the new one. The conference obtained many marginal modifications; but the map which they saw in January was in most respects the same one which they were to agree upon in June.

Woodrow Wilson obtained some verbal changes in the war-time decisions. Instead of Germany's colonies being described as integral parts of the empires which conquered them, they were given the name of 'Mandates'. The new owners were in theory responsible to the League of Nations, a world organization designed by Wilson to secure permanent peace and the just settlement of all international disputes, and which was transformed in 1945 into the United Nations. But the 'Mandates' remained securely under the powers who obtained them. The new

League of Nations was also to safeguard the rights of minorities: and, this being so, minorities were allowed to remain in Poland, Czechoslovakia, Rumania, and Yugoslavia. Yet when persecution and discrimination began, the League was powerless to intervene.

Conditions of armistice

The main barrier to a well-balanced treaty was built before the peace conference. When Germany, Austria, Bulgaria, and Turkey each surrendered, they did so by signing armistice agreements with the Allies. These agreements contained sets of conditions, on the acceptance of which the Allies agreed to stop the fighting. The armistice conditions were severe, and had to be carried out immediately. As a result of this, long before the Paris Peace Conference began, they had irrevocably altered the map, and the mood of Europe. Much of what politicians later denounced and historians criticized in the peace treaties was in fact created by the armistices.

The atmosphere at the time of the drafting of the armistice agreements was an atmosphere of war: the guns still roared, the fighting was still savage, the outcome was still uncertain. The terms were therefore harsh. It was necessary for the Allies to ensure that the armistice agreements were not tricks, brief halts engineered to obtain the breathing space necessary for recuperation and renewed fighting. Each armistice agreement was intended to make absolutely certain that the fighting capacity of the enemy was utterly broken. This they did. As a result, when the Paris Peace Conference opened, Germany, Austria, Bulgaria, and Turkey had already been treated with a severity which was both intentional, effective, and by its nature largely irrevocable.

The first armistice to be signed was with Bulgaria, on 29th September 1918. The Bulgarians were desperate for peace: their armies in Greece and Serbia were in retreat, while a large corps of Bulgarian mutineers was marching on Sofia, the capital. They therefore agreed to evacuate all Serbian and Greek territory which their troops still occupied, and which they had hitherto claimed for themselves. A month later, on 30th October, the Turks, two-thirds of whose Palestinian army had been taken prisoner, the remnant of which was

in retreat, signed their armistice. They were obliged to accept the use of their capital, Constantinople, as an Allied naval base; to surrender the Black Sea port of Batum and the oilfields of Baku, both of which they were occupying; and to surrender all garrisons in Arabia, the Yemen, Syria, Mesopotamia, and Cilicia. The surrender of these garrisons was to be followed by immediate French and British occupation; the obvious prelude to political control.

On 3rd November the Austrians, beaten back on the Italian front, signed an armistice which was similarly decisive. Italian troops were allowed to occupy the territory which they claimed, and the Allies obtained the right to move at will along every line of communication throughout the Austro-Hungarian empire. The new nations had already proclaimed themselves. The Allied presence provided them with a firm guarantee that they would survive. They were thus two months old before the peace conference met.

'Reparation for damage done'

But it was towards Germany that the armistice was most severe. The total collapse of Bulgaria, Turkey, and Austria was taken for granted once the Allied military advances had begun. But Germany was believed to be stronger and more resilient than her allies. On 12th September, speaking at Manchester, Lloyd George, the British prime minister, insisted that 'Prussian military power must not only be beaten, but Germany herself must know that'. With the Allied armies reinforced by fresh, enthusiastic troops from the United States, and the German trench fortifications in Flanders broken, such a double aim seemed feasible. But a month later Sir Douglas Haig, the commander-in-chief of the British forces in France, sounded a warning note. On 19th October he returned to London from France to tell the war cabinet that all was not well. The American army, he claimed, 'is disorganized, ill-equipped, and ill-trained. . . . It has suffered severely through ignorance of modern war'. As for the French army, it seemed 'greatly worn out'. The British army, he concluded, 'is not sufficiently fresh or strong to force a decision by itself' and the war would go on, in Haig's view, well into 1919. All this pointed to the need for a severe armistice, which would deprive the Germans of any opportunity of hitting back once they had agreed to surrender. The war cabinet felt that if the armistice terms were comprehensive, they would serve as 'pledges for the fulfilment of our peace terms'.

On 11th November the fourth and last armistice of the war was signed. Germany accepted total defeat. Lloyd George's conditions were fulfilled: all military power was broken, and the German people were presented with a document both comprehensive and severe. Of the thirty-four clauses, the following give a picture of how much Germany had to agree to, not to make peace, but merely to bring an end to war.

Immediate evacuation of the invaded countries – Belgium, France, Luxemburg, *as well as Alsace-Lorraine.*

Surrender in good condition by the German Armies of the following equipment –

5,000 guns
25,000 machine guns
3,000 trench mortars
1,700 aeroplanes
5,000 locomotives and 150,000 wagons, in good working order, with all necessary spare parts and fittings, shall be delivered to the Associated Powers. . . . 5,000 motor lorries are also to be delivered in good condition.

To surrender . . . all submarines at present in existence . . . and

6 battle-cruisers
10 battleships
8 light cruisers
50 destroyers of the most modern types

Evacuation by the German Armies of the districts on the left bank of the Rhine. These districts . . . shall be administered . . . under the control of the Allied and United States Armies of Occupation.

By signing this armistice, Germany abandoned all hopes of territorial gain; even of retaining Alsace-Lorraine. She also agreed to accept a four-word financial condition: 'Reparation for damage done.' The interpretation of what was meant by these four words proved a major point of argument during the treaty negotiations, and poisoned the international atmosphere for twenty years, giving Adolf Hitler a powerful lever against the western democracies. The four words that the Germans, at the moment of defeat, accepted without discussion, provoked the most bitter discussion of the inter-war years.

The idea of 'reparation for damage done' was not a new one. Germany had imposed such reparations on France in 1870, even though the fighting took place on French soil. Nor was there any doubt that the 'damage done' by Germany in France and Belgium was severe. Some small damage was done by Allied aeroplanes dropping bombs on Germany, but this was offset by the many more German air-raids, particularly on London, and by the German naval bombardment of undefended seaside towns on the east coast of Great Britain. The amount of damage done by Germany was immense, and little of it was made necessary by the dictates of war. In German-occupied France nearly 300,000 houses were completely destroyed. Six thousand factories were stripped of their machinery, which was sent to Germany. The textile mills of Lille and Sedan were smashed. Nearly 2,000 breweries were destroyed. In the coal mines around Roubaix and Tourcoing 112 mineshafts were blown in, and over 1,000 miles of underground galleries flooded or blocked. During their retreat, the Germans burned and looted on a massive scale, destroying over 1,000 miles of railway line, blowing up 1,000 bridges, looting thousands of houses, and stripping churches. During the four years of occupation the Germans took away half a million cows, half a million sheep, and over 300,000 horses and donkeys. These were the acts of vandals. And in the military sphere too it was France and Belgium, not Germany, that suffered most. After the war the French had to pull up over 300,000,000 metres of barbed wire, and fill in over 250,000,000 cubic metres of trenches. Much agricultural land was rendered useless because so many shells had fallen on it; some remained dangerous for many years because of unexploded shells and the leakage of poison gas from unused canisters.

The British were equally determined to secure reparation. The Germans had torpedoed five hospital ships during the war; an action which inflamed the public and created an atmosphere in which the demand for high reparations flourished. The German U-boats had taken a cruel toll of merchant shipping. They had sunk thousands of unarmed ships mostly without warning. The British lost nearly 8,000,000 tons of commercial shipping; and many of the crews had been left to drown. Among the Allied nations, France, Italy, and the United States lost between them 2,000,000 tons of shipping; among neutrals Norway lost over 1,000,000 tons, Denmark, Holland, and Sweden over 200,000 tons each. No nation had been spared the deliberate terror of submarine war. The Allies had not, of course, sat idly by to watch these losses. The blockade of Germany was rigorously enforced, and as a result as many as 500,000 German civilians probably died of starvation. But in the moment of victory these victims of war's all-pervading cruelty did not seem to compensate for what the Allies had suffered. Nations use victory to settle the debt which they feel is owed to them; the other side of the account is ignored. The demand for reparations combined the physical damage that had been done with the psychological need to have tangible evidences in the form of gold, that the 'enemy' would make amends. Rudyard Kipling, who had lost a son in the fighting, expressed this feeling in a bitter poem (he wrote it in 1917 when the reparations issue was being discussed in public):

These were our children who died for our
  lands: they were dear in our sight.
We have only the memory left of their home-
  treasured sayings and laughter.
The price of our loss shall be paid to our
  hands, not another's hereafter.
Neither the Alien nor Priest shall decide on
  it. That is our right.
But who shall return us the children?

That flesh we had nursed from the first in
  all clearness was given
To corruption unveiled and assailed by the
  malice of heaven
By the heart-shaking jests of Decay where it
  lolled on the wires—
To be blanched or gay-painted by fumes—
  to be cindered by fires—
To be senselessly tossed and retossed in
  stale mutilation
From crater to crater. For this we shall
  take expiation.
But who shall return us the children?

'Squeeze the German lemon'

During the British general election held before the treaty negotiations began, the public cried out for heavy reparations. Almost every responsible politician tried to soften the public mood. But one, Sir Auckland Geddes, told an eager audience in London that 'we would squeeze the German lemon till the pips squeaked' and even Lloyd George, tired out by the strains of electioneering, told a large meeting at Bristol that the Germans 'must pay to the uttermost farthing, and we shall search their pockets for it'. These were not his true views. He had begun, from the day the war ended, to adopt a moderate stance. He feared most of all that if Germany were humiliated too much by the treaty it would go Bolshevik, and not a single clause would be fulfilled, nor a penny of reparations paid.

In secret Lloyd George pressed his colleagues to adopt a certain leniency towards Germany, to send food to the starving millions in Germany and Austria, to think in terms of a peace free from vindictive clauses. But the public did not approve of such liberal sentiments. As Winston Churchill, who was then minister of munitions, recorded: 'The Prime Minister and his principal colleagues were astonished and to some extent overborne by the passions they encountered in the constituencies. The brave people whom nothing had daunted had suffered too much. Their unpent feelings were lashed by the popular press into fury. The crippled and mutilated soldiers darkened the streets. The returned prisoners told the hard tale of bonds and privation. Every cottage had its empty chair. Hatred of the beaten foe, thirst for his just punishment, rushed up from the heart of deeply injured millions. All who had done the least in the conflict were as might be expected the foremost in detailing the penalties of the vanquished. . . . In my own constituency of Dundee, respectable, orthodox, life-long Liberals demanded the sternest punishment for the broken enemy. All over the country the most bitter were the women, of whom seven millions were for the first time to vote. In this uprush and turmoil state policy and national dignity were speedily engulfed.'

Like Lloyd George, Churchill urged a moderate treaty. He too feared that harsh terms would force Germany into the Bolshevik embrace. But when Lloyd George reached Paris in January 1919, he found the French determined to obtain maximum reparations, and the sternest possible treaty.

At the peace conference Lloyd George was handicapped by the moods and utterances of the general election: the anti-German moods, continuing fierce, meant that in any moderation he urged he had to keep one eye on his own public opinion, which, when it felt that he was exercising undue leniency, could, and did, protest; while the bravado of the election speeches, vivid in French minds, meant that when Clemenceau, the French prime minister, urged severity he could always refer to Lloyd George's public statements as support for his own contentions. Although Lloyd George tried, throughout the negotiations, to control the evolution of the treaty, he began from a position of weakness from which he was unable fully to recover, and which obstructed many of his efforts to obtain a viable peace.

At Paris Lloyd George was the leading advocate of moderation. He sought to act as if he were above national antagonisms. He tried to be the arbiter of conflicting passions. But the House of Commons would not let him forget in what tone the election had been fought. When it became clear the reparations were being calculated on the basis of what Germany 'could' pay, rather than on what she 'ought' to pay, 370 Coalition Conservatives sent a petulant telegram, reminding him of what they and the electorate expected, and ending: 'Although we have the utmost confidence in your intention to fulfil your pledges to the country, may we, as we have to meet innumerable inquiries from our constituents, have your renewed assurance that you have in no way departed from your original intention?'

Within a week of receiving this challenge Lloyd George returned to London, and on 16th April 1919 rebuked the House of Commons for its impatience. He reminded MPs that he was having to settle the fate of five continents in Paris; that ten new states had to be brought into existence; that territorial, military, and economic questions had all to be decided upon, and that 'you are not going to solve these problems by telegram'. He reminded them that, even if mistakes were made, the League of Nations, which was being set up as part of the treaties, would be able to make the necessary adjustments later. He made it clear to his critics that if they insisted upon terms which the League were ultimately to judge unduly severe, those terms would be modified. For an hour Lloyd George cajoled, threatened, appealed to, and won over his listeners: '. . . and when enormous issues are dependent upon it, you require calm deliberation. I ask for it for the rest of the journey. The journey is not at an end. It is full of perils, perils for this country, perils for all lands, perils for the people throughout the world. I beg, at any rate, that the men who are doing their best should be left in peace to do it, or that other men should be sent there. . . .

'We want a stern peace, because the occasion demands it. But its severity must be designed, not to gratify vengeance, but to vindicate justice. . . .

'[It is the duty of] statesmen in every land, of the Parliaments upon whose will those statesmen depend, of those who guide and direct the public opinion which is the making of all — not to soil this triumph of right by indulging in the angry passions of the moment, but to consecrate the sacrifice of millions to the permanent redemption of the human race from the scourge and agony of war.'

Lloyd George as moderator

Lloyd George returned to Paris. But although he appeared to have convinced the House of Commons that leniency was needed, he was unable to convince the French. They made some concessions, abandoning their hopes for the creation of a separate Rhineland State, and for a Polish annexation of Danzig, but in general French desires were met. The treaty as finally published had a vindictive tone about it.

In a memorandum which Lloyd George wrote while at the peace conference, he declared that his concern was to create a peace for all time, not for a mere thirty years. A short peace might be possible if punitive measures were taken against Germany. But unless the Germans were placated, they would go Bolshevik, and Russian Bolshevism would then have the advantage, according to Lloyd George, 'of the organizing gift of the most successful organizers of national resources in the world'. The initial shock of war would pass, and then, wrote Lloyd George: 'The maintenance of peace will depend upon there being no causes of exasperation constantly stirring up either the spirit of patriotism, of justice, or of fairplay to achieve redress. . . . Our Peace ought to be dictated by men who act in the spirit of judges sitting in a cause which does not personally engage their emotion or interests, and not in a spirit of a savage vendetta, which is not satisfied without mutilation and the infliction of pain and humiliation.'

This was utopian. Yet Lloyd George was convinced that he was right. He went on to criticize all clauses which might prove 'a constant source of irritation', and suggested that the sooner reparations disappeared the better. He deprecated putting Germany under alien rule, fearing that by doing so 'we shall strew Europe with Alsace-Lorraines'. He emphasized that the Germans were 'proud, intelligent, with great traditions', but that those under whose rule they would be placed by the treaty were 'races whom they regard as their inferiors, and some of whom, undoubtedly for the time being, merit that designation'. These arguments fell upon stony ground: the French could not understand Lloyd George's sudden conversion to what they could only describe as imbecilic pro-Germanism. Clemenceau replied icily to Lloyd George's memorandum that 'if the British are so anxious to appease Germany they should look . . . overseas . . . and make colonial, naval, or commercial concessions'. Lloyd George was particularly angered by Clemenceau's remark that the British were 'a maritime people who have not known invasion', and countered angrily that 'what France really cares for is that the Danzig Germans should be handed over to the Poles'.

These bitter exchanges were symptomatic of a growing rift in Anglo-French relations. For Clemenceau, the treaty was perhaps the best chance that France would have of designing effective protection against a Germany that was already almost twice as populous as France, and must therefore be shown by deliberate, harsh action that it would not pay to think of revenge. For Lloyd George, the treaty was an opportunity to arbitrate for Europe without rancour, and to create a continent whose future problems could be adjusted without malice. Great Britain, by supporting the League of Nations, would be willing to help in the process of adjustment. Clearly it was the treaty that would first need to be altered: Lloyd George did not fear that. For him the treaty was not a sacred instrument but a pliable one. It was obvious from his comments while it was being drafted that he would not be content to see it become the fixed rule of the new Europe.

At Paris Lloyd George opposed strenuously, but in vain, the transfer to Poland of areas predominantly German. His protest was a forceful one, yet it was not forceful enough to break the French desire for the reduction of German territory.

'I am strongly averse,' Lloyd George wrote, 'to transferring more Germans from German rule to the rule of some other nation than can possibly be helped. I cannot conceive any greater cause of future war than that the German people, who have certainly proved themselves one of the most vigorous and powerful nations in the world, should be surrounded by a number of small states, many of them consisting of people who have never previously set up a stable government for themselves, but each of them containing large masses of Germans clamouring for reunion with their native land. . . . [These proposals] must, in my judgement, lead sooner or later to a new war in Eastern Europe.'

The Treaty of Versailles was not as vindictive as France had hoped; nor was it as moderate as Lloyd George desired. It was certainly not as utopian as Woodrow Wilson envisaged. A study of its clauses reveals great concern for detail, an often punitive attitude, and very little account taken of the personal hardships and political discontent which the clauses might arouse. Thus Austria and Germany were forbidden, by Article 80, to unite, a future possibility which the British foreign secretary, A.J.Balfour, had regarded as a sensible solution which might soften the blow of defeat. Article 100 took away from Germany the entirely German city of Danzig, turning it into an isolated 'Free City' within the 'customs frontiers' of Poland, and depriving all its citizens of German nationality. Under Article 118 Germany renounced all her 'rights, titles and privileges . . . whatever their origin' outside Europe. This meant that even purely commercial concessions, freely negotiated before 1914, were lost. All Germany's colonies were taken from her, together with 'all movable and immovable property in such territories'; even the property of the German school at Shanghai was given to the French and Chinese governments. All pre-war German trading agreements were declared null and void, and the patient, innocent, costly efforts of German businessmen in China, Siam, Liberia, Egypt, and Morocco were entirely undone. Article 153 laid down that 'All property and possessions in Egypt of the German empire and the German states pass to the Egyptian government without payment'; and Article 156 transferred to Japan all German state submarine cables in China 'with all rights, privileges, and properties attaching thereto'.

The military clauses were as one would expect. The size of the German army was limited to 100,000 men. Germany was forbidden to import any arms or munitions. Compulsory military training was abolished. Universities and sporting clubs were forbidden to 'occupy themselves with any military matters'. They were specifically forbidden to instruct or exercise their members 'in the profession or use of arms'. All fortresses in the Rhineland were to be dismantled. At sea, Germany was restricted to six battleships, six light cruisers, twelve destroyers, and twelve torpedo boats. She was allowed not a single submarine. Her naval personnel were limited to 15,000 men. All warships under construction were to be broken up.

One clause was a dead letter from the moment it was signed. Under Article 227 the Allies announced the trial of the Kaiser 'for a supreme offence against international morality and the sanctity of treaties'. He was to be tried by five judges, an American, an Englishman, a Frenchman, an Italian, and a Japanese. It was their duty 'to fix the punishment which it considers should be imposed'. Despite the British public's keenness to 'hang the Kaiser', Lloyd George felt that such a solution was a mistake. When, therefore, the French began to demand the return of the Kaiser from Holland, Great Britain refused to give France any support. The Kaiser remained safely in exile, cultivating his garden.

'War guilt'

The most controversial clause in the Treaty of Versailles was Article 231, the notorious 'War Guilt' clause against which successive German governments argued in vain, and which even many British politicians thought too extreme. The Article read: 'The Allied and Associated Governments affirm and Germany accepts the responsibility of Germany and her allies for causing all the loss and damage to which the Allied and Associated Governments and their nationals have been subjected as a consequence of the war imposed upon them by the aggression of Germany and her allies.'

How had this clause come into being? What made the Allies so anxious to get Germany to accept responsibility for 'all the loss and damage'? Why was 'the aggression of Germany' referred to so bluntly?

The War Guilt clause originated before the end of the war. The Supreme War Council, meeting under the leadership of Clemenceau and Lloyd George at Versailles on 4th November 1918, had drafted a note to President Wilson, explaining to him the need for reparations from Germany. The note began: 'They (the Allied governments) understand that compensation will be made by Germany for all damage caused to the civilian population of the Allies by the invasion by Germany of Allied territory. . . .'

As Germany had never denied invading Belgium, Luxembourg, or France, this clause was a fair one: a statement of acknowledged fact. But someone at the meeting pointed out that as the clause stood, while Germany would have to pay for damage done from the Channel to the Vosges, there was nothing in this wording to enable any economic compensation to go to the non-continental allies, the USA, India, Australia, Canada, or even Great Britain, and that certainly the Dominions, who had played such a large part, not only in providing men but also materials, would resent their exclusion from money payments. The clause would therefore need redrafting. The new draft cut out 'the invasion by Germany of Allied territory' and replaced it by 'the aggression of Germany'. Aggression was a word that could cover a much wider sphere: it could be claimed that every aspect of war costs was involved. But it was also a condemnatory word. Invasion had been admitted; aggression had not. The justification in German eyes for the invasion was self-defence; aggression was a word pregnant with moral disapproval, allowing of no subtle interpretation; spelling, all too clearly, guilt.

Lloyd George's personal assistant recalled in 1931: 'I remember very distinctly discussing with L.G. the interpretation to be put upon the question of "restoration" or "reparations". His view was—"We must make it clear that we cannot charge Germany with the costs of the war. . . . She could not possibly pay it. But she must pay ample compensation for damage and that compensation must be equitably distributed among the Allies and not given entirely to France and Belgium. Devastated areas is only one item in war loss. Great Britain has probably spent more money on the war and incurred greater indirect losses in, for instance, shipping and trade, than France. She must have her fair share of the compensation."

'He then instructed me to prepare a form of words. . . . I did so. . . . I remember thinking, after the draft had been taken by L.G., that it did not cover adequately the point that compensation was due to all the Allies. . . . I therefore revised it to read "damage to the civilian population of the allies by the aggression of Germany by land, air and sea".'

Thus was written the clause which most aggravated Anglo-German relations between the wars, made the task of appeasement with Germany so difficult, and made the Germans feel that, whatever concessions Great Britain made, whatever gestures of friendship she volunteered, in reality her policy was dictated by an explicit belief in German guilt.

The reparations clauses were the most often criticized part of the treaty. Yet the total demand of £24,000,000,000 was whittled away at a series of international conferences, until finally, at Lausanne in 1932, reparations were brought to an end. To this day, Great Britain is paying off her war debts to the United States; Germany stopped paying for the war thirty-six years ago.

The new frontiers

The treaty's most lasting clauses were those which created new frontiers. They were also the most defensible. Many were established, not by Allied insistence, but as a result of plebiscites, in which the in-

habitants were asked where they wanted to go. The plebiscites in East Prussia resulted in the province remaining entirely German. In two border areas of Austria the inhabitants voted to remain Austrian. The people of the Saar, after fifteen years of League of Nations supervision, voted to return to Germany, and were reincorporated into Hitler's Reich– this, his first territorial acquisition, was a positive gain made possible only because of the treaty which he was always denouncing. In Silesia the plebiscite results were indecisive, and this rich industrial region was therefore divided between Germany and Poland. The Danes of Schleswig voted to leave Germany: the sole plebiscite to go wholly against the German interest.

The lands which Germany lost outright were Alsace-Lorraine, a German war gain of 1871, and territory in the east which went to Poland. Germany had helped destroy Polish independence at the end of the 18th century, and had annexed Polish territory during the three partitions: now that territory was returned to the recreated Polish state, and with it a corridor which gave Poland an outlet on the Baltic Sea. The Germans later made a great fuss about this corridor. But its inhabitants were mostly Poles, and Poland, after over a hundred years of subjugation, was entitled to a measure of security.

The greatest frontier changes arose from the disintegration, in the last weeks of the war, of the Austro-Hungarian empire. Czechoslovakia had proclaimed itself an independent state; the treaties gave it a generous frontier. Yugoslavia did likewise, fulfilling the Slav dream of a new South Slav kingdom; and the Allies were again generous, though not allowing the port of Fiume to go to the new state. The Poles obtained territory from both Germany and Austria, and the Allies, eager to see Poland as a bastion between Bolshevik Russia and the west, encouraged an eastern frontier drawn very much at Russia's expense. Yet even here, Lloyd George was reluctant to see Poland push too far east or west, and it was left to Polish military action, not any Allied treaty, to secure parts of the Ukraine, Belorussia, and Lithuania for the new Poland. To Rumania the Allies allotted the primarily Rumanian districts of Austria-Hungary, principally Transsylvania. Bulgaria, an 'enemy' power, lost her outlet on the Aegean Sea, which went to Greece; but her full independence, secured from Turkey not ten years before the war began, was not tampered with. Austria lost only one basically Austrian province, the South Tyrol, which went to Italy. The nation with the most convincing grievance was Hungary; large communities of Hungarians found themselves inside Czechoslovakia, Rumania, and Yugoslavia. But once again, Hungarian independence was secured, and although Hungary extended her frontiers when in alliance with Hitler, she returned to her 1919 borders in 1945; and they survive to this day.

What was the balance sheet of the peace treaties? Out of the collapse of the Austro-Hungarian empire emerged three independent states — Czechoslovakia, Hungary, and Austria; and three states gained from the old empire territory filled mostly with their fellow-countrymen — Poland, Yugoslavia, and Rumania. Two states, Austria and Hungary, felt deprived of territory; the other four were well satisfied.

Out of the collapse of the Ottoman empire emerged, after a brief period of British control, four independent states — Iraq, Transjordan, Saudi Arabia, and the Yemen. A fifth state, the Jewish national home in Palestine, remained under British rule for nearly thirty years, but was then partitioned between Arabs and Jews. The Armenians, too, were given a state of their own: but when the Turks destroyed it in 1922 the Allies did nothing to intervene. Over a million Armenians were murdered by the Turks during the war; but the Allies made no efforts to protect them after the war. Soviet Russia provided a haven for some, in the Soviet Republic of Armenia. Others fled to Europe as refugees, stateless, without a national patron.

Out of the collapse and Bolshevization of Russia emerged four new independent states — Finland, Latvia, Lithuania, and Estonia. The Caucasian states also declared their independence; and the Allies encouraged Georgia to maintain its sovereignty. But when Stalin sent Soviet troops into the land of his birth, the Allies accepted the fall of Georgian independence.

The German problem

Of the four empires shaken by the war only the German empire survived; it had lost one eastern province and restored Alsace-Lorraine to France, but its sovereignty was secure. As the Kaiser had abdicated before the end of the war, Germany became a republic; but alone of the defeated nations it preserved its territorial unity. The treaty restrictions were irksome, but made no serious inroads on national sovereignty, and, if anything, provided a powerful stimulus to German nationalism. The Treaty of Versailles may have created Hitler; it also preserved as a state the country in which he was to make his mark.

Neither the defeat of Germany nor the Treaty of Versailles solved the German problem. Germany was still the country with the largest population in Europe. The day after the treaty was signed Austen Chamberlain, the chancellor of the exchequer, wrote to his sister: 'So Peace is signed at last . . . Will the world have rest? . . .

'Even the old Germany would not, I think, rashly challenge a new war in the West, but the chaos on their Eastern frontier, and their hatred and contempt for the Poles, must be a dangerous temptation. . . .

'But if Germany remains or becomes really democratic, they cannot repeat the folly of Frederick the Great and Bismarck and his later followers. No democracy can or will make aggressive war its year-long study and business, though it may easily enough flare up in sudden passion. But think of Germany with its 60 or 70 millions of people and France with its dwindling 40! I shudder!'

The League of Nations

Francis Paul Walters

The foundation of the League of Nations was a direct consequence of war, so much so that the whole process of its conception, elaboration, and establishment, was contained within the five years which divided the outbreak of the First World War from the adoption of the Covenant by the Peace Conference of Paris. No previous peacetime effort had any direct relationship of parentage with the new foundation. The century from Waterloo till 1914, so rich in progress and reform in almost every field, saw little or no advance in the conduct of international affairs. Every country, however peace-loving its people and its government might be, continued to claim for itself, and to admit for others, the right to be the unquestioned judge of its own decisions. The Hague Conferences of 1899 and 1907, in their efforts to provide an acceptable alternative to war, could make no attempt to modify the established practice of sovereignty. Indeed, strange as this may now appear, even those who were radical reformers in home politics seemed to find it natural that foreign policy should be treated as a mysterious function, not to be understood or judged by the ordinary citizen.

The shock of war forced men to think seriously for the first time of the creation of a new system by which such disasters might be averted in the future. In countries whose total energies had to be concentrated on the war, these ideas could only be a matter of unofficial and unpublicized discussion. Nothing approaching a detailed plan could as yet be formulated. However, the phrase 'League of Nations', unknown a few months before, began to be used. A League of Nations Society was founded in London in May 1915. Other similar bodies arose in the neutral countries of Europe,

in France, and even one in Germany, where it was promptly suppressed. In Great Britain alone among the belligerents, men in high office – Asquith, Grey, Robert Cecil – openly supported the movement, though it remained completely unofficial. But in the United States, on neutral ground, men could speak freely, with no fear of encouraging the enemy; and there it spread so fast that by May 1916 the leaders of both great parties stood together on the same public platform, each declaring that a new international system must be set up, that peace must be ensured, if necessary, by the armed forces of the peace-loving powers, and that the United States must take its full part in this new creation.

A year later, the United States entered the war. And in January 1918 President Wilson, in formally setting forth the war aims of his government, concluded by declaring: 'A general association of nations must be formed under specific covenants for the purpose of affording mutual guarantees of political independence and territorial integrity to great and small States alike.' This formed the climax of his famous Fourteen Points, which were in due course accepted, with one reservation, by all the Allies, and taken by Austria and Germany as the basis on which they sued for peace. Thus in barely three years an unknown name, and an undefined plan, had been adopted as one of the main war aims of the belligerents. The neutral countries also, which felt no direct concern with the other purposes of either side, gave their support to the proposed association, expecting indeed to be consulted as to the form it should take and invited to join it on equal terms with the rest. Still more important was the growing popular sentiment – ill-informed, perhaps, but none the less passionate – that some new way must be found to save future generations from the miseries of the past four years.

In these circumstances it was quickly agreed, when the Conference of Paris met in January 1919, that the discussion of plans for the League of Nations should be taken up without delay. This was an important decision, since Allied unity was soon to be subjected to serious strain by conflicting territorial claims. For the time, however, and particularly in the special committee set up under Wilson's chairmanship to draft the constitution of the new organization, the work went forward with such harmony and speed that in only eleven days after its first meeting, a unanimous committee was able to present to the conference and the world a draft Covenant of the League. This draft, polished up and improved in various minor points, was approved by a plenary session of the conference on 28th April 1919, and was destined to endure, practically without change, until the demise of the League in 1946.

That the representatives of the many states represented in Paris could reach conclusions of such importance in so short a time, was due in great part to certain intensive preparatory studies carried out during the last two years of the war. Officially appointed groups in Great Britain, France, and the United States had worked on that part of the general plan to which the name of collective security was later attached, laying down in careful language the obligations to be accepted by all members for peaceful settlement of their own disputes and for common action against any aggressor. At the same time, unofficial bodies were formulating their ideas on subjects which the diplomats preferred to leave aside, but which many believed to be a necessary part of an effective peace-keeping system—open diplomacy, the elimination of all secret treaties, the reduction and control of armaments, and organized co-operation in social and economic affairs. This last was the only part of the new system on which some positive action had already been taken before 1914.

These ideas were brought together, luminously explained, and developed into a truly magnificent political whole, by Field-Marshal Smuts in his pamphlet 'The League of Nations: A Practical Suggestion', published in December 1918.

The Covenant itself, brief and concise as it was, included in its twenty-six articles all the essential substance of these preparatory schemes; it went, indeed, surprisingly farther than all previous proposals except those of Smuts. It presented a complete system for the peaceful settlement of disputes and for joint resistance to aggression; a provision for the reduction and control of armaments, and for eliminating the evil effects arising from their private manufacture; an engagement to the effect that all future treaties should be registered with, and published by, the League Secre-

tariat; a pledge to join in promoting social and economic progress in every field where international co-operation was essential; and a duty of supervision over the various colonies and territories from which their German or Turkish rulers had been evicted. This last provision, handed over ready-made by the Supreme Council to the drafters of the Covenant, was less clearly and concisely worded than the rest, but it worked well enough in the League's lifetime.

And finally, the Covenant created an Assembly of all League members, a Council consisting of five great powers as permanent members and four lesser ones to be elected by the Assembly, and a permanent Secretariat. It also decided, not without fierce argument by a minority in favour of Brussels, that the seat of the League should be on the neutral ground of Geneva.

The Covenant was an integral part of the peace treaties, and therefore had no legal effect until one of these had been ratified. But it was expected that ratification would soon take place, and that the first meetings of the Council and Assembly would be held in the autumn of 1919. In this belief, the conference, when adopting the final text of the Covenant, took the first steps to set the new machine in motion. It nominated Belgium, Brazil, China, and Spain as temporary members of the Council; set up an organizing committee; and appointed a British official, Sir Eric Drummond, as the first secretary general.

Drummond promptly left Paris for London, and began to recruit his staff, on the basis of what was then the bold and indeed unprecedented decision, to make the whole organization an international one from top to bottom. His funds were short, and the future was beginning to look uncertain. But the desire to serve the new institution was strong, he had no difficulty in securing the men he needed, and by the late summer of 1919 a fairly complete embryo of the future Secretariat was assembled.

American defection
Meanwhile, in Washington, disaster was building up. In the face of the united will of most of the nation, and by the use of partisan manoeuvres disgraceful in the context of such an important decision, a minority in the Senate was able to prevent

American membership. The vote of 19th November 1919, confirmed by that of 19th March 1920, was a stunning blow to the twin hopes of lasting peace and of a rational organization of international life. The military and economic power on which the planning of the Covenant was based, were drastically reduced; its moral power also, since the United States had seemed to be the natural leader in reconciliation and peaceful reconstruction.

The American defection was of course an immense encouragement to all those military and diplomatic influences which opposed, and indeed despised, the idea of collective security, believing that a country's safety lies in the strength of its armed forces and the firmness of its alliances. However, no government showed any sign of following the American example; and popular support for the League suffered less of a setback than might have been expected, partly because it was still hoped that the Senate's decision might be reversed in the years to come. When, in January 1920, the Treaty of Versailles was at last ratified, all the neutral countries invited to do so had accepted membership of the League. Nor was there any serious suggestion that the plan should be abandoned. For the leading Allied powers, indeed, it would have been almost impossible to do so, since many articles of the peace treaties depended for their fulfilment on action by the Council.

Throughout its existence, the League presented a double aspect, on the one hand as the centre of action in which all members could share, and from which all could benefit, on the other hand as supervisor of various provisions of the peace treaties which were a matter of indifference to most members and of resentment to some. This latter function was one of the elements which now ensured its stability in spite of the absence of the United States. In the long run, it was a source of weakness and irritation which most members would have been glad to shake off.

During its first year, the Council was dominated by two statesmen, Arthur Balfour and Léon Bourgeois, whose wisdom and courage kept it free from the quarrels of their own and other governments. It worked quietly on the special tasks arising from the Treaty of Versailles; on setting up the various institutions foreseen by the Covenant; and on dealing with a few minor disputes. It also authorized the secretary general to establish the permanent headquarters at Geneva, agreed that the first Assembly should meet there in November 1920, and ordered that a full report of its own work should be drawn up and submitted for the Assembly's information.

If there was still any doubt about the capacity of the League to develop a life of its own, to become at least in part what Smuts had said it must be, 'an ever visible, living, working organ of the polity of civilization', this was decisively resolved by the first Assembly. In Paris it had been laid down that the Council should meet 'at least once a year', and the Assembly 'at stated intervals' — this latter rule being regarded as a precaution lest a body which it was then thought would meet every third or fourth year, might tend to fall into disuse. In fact, the Council held an average of five meetings a year throughout the existence of the League; while the Assembly not only decided to meet in September of every year, but established itself from the first moment as the most original, lively, energetic, and enterprising of all the new institutions. Meanwhile, the Secretariat had become an efficient international civil service, and the chief subsidiary organs of the League were either already at work, or at least in various stages of gestation. In the first group were the International Labour Office, the Communications and Transit Organization, the economic and financial committees, and those dealing with social problems; in the second, the Permanent Court of International Justice, the Health Organization, the Mandates Commission. These bodies included top-ranking experts from many countries, who in almost every case served without payment.

No such progress was to be seen on the political front. The great powers were not yet ready to refer to the Council their own disputes or those of other countries which they felt capable of handling; still less to discuss with the rest of the world their difficult relations with Germany, or to open the great debate on armaments, which the Assembly and public opinion in general considered to be the acid test of the new dispensation. All this was still to come.

So here we must break the story, leaving the League almost fully grown and ready for action, yet forced to wait for another three years before becoming, at least for a time, the main centre of world politics. Most of its supporters at this moment would have expressed bitter disappointment, when they compared present results with the hopes of only two years before. And yet, in that brief space, the existence and the practice of the League had in fact revolutionized the whole conception of international relations as it stood before 1914. No power could any longer claim in the name of sovereignty to be exempt from public debate on its external actions, and in this debate the smallest state had the same rights as the greatest. In every field, international co-operation was at work, organized and ready to be called on for help and advice by all members, as a matter of right and not of favour. New world-wide institutions, the Assembly, Council, Secretariat, were firmly established, and the Court on the way to be so. These creative achievements, hardly foreseen by the peacemakers in Paris, yet destined to stand until the Second World War and indeed, in all essentials until the present day, are surely something real and great to set against the failure of those greater and grander hopes with which the League was founded.

The Post-War Slump

Trevor Lloyd

During the 1918 election, held immediately after the armistice with Germany that ended the fighting, Lloyd George spoke of making Great Britain into 'a fit country for heroes to live in'. When he proclaimed this objective it must have seemed a natural and attainable goal. Pre-war Great Britain had not been perfect, but improvement looked a fairly simple task on which all men of goodwill could agree.

It was particularly easy for men of goodwill to agree because it was taken for granted by practically everybody that the Germans were going to pay for it all. Sir Eric Geddes spoke of 'squeezing Germany till the pips squeaked'; Lloyd George was a little more cautious, but when he spoke of accepting the principle that Germany must pay, and said 'we shall search their pockets', he did nothing to warn his listeners that the Germans' pockets might be empty. The opposition parties did not plunge into the subject of 'making Germany pay' with the same gusto, though they certainly did not warn their listeners of the difficulties of extracting reparations.

The electorate was optimistic, unreasonable, and xenophobic: what it wanted to hear was 'Hang the Kaiser', 'Make Germany Pay', and 'Britain for the British'. Lloyd George began the campaign in a liberal frame of mind; but by the end he had adopted the popular slogans with a few verbal amendments which completely failed to warn the electorate that it was asking for too much.

In the election Lloyd George and his Conservative partners from the wartime coalition could draw on popular approval of their work in winning the war, a reaction against the Liberal government which had done badly in the opening years of the war, and a belief that a strong government was needed for the negotiations that were about to begin at Versailles. The coalition gained an enormous majority in the House of Commons (Coalition Unionists 339, Coalition Liberals 136 against Independent Liberals 26, and Labour Party 59). But in a way the most surprising thing about the election was that the Liberals who followed Asquith out of office and the newly reorganized Labour Party polled almost half the votes cast.

The hard-faced men

Despite this, Lloyd George's majority was too large for his own comfort. Before the election he had been comfortably balanced in the middle: if his Conservative allies had turned on him, there was always the possibility that he might have turned to the left and made an alliance with the Labour Party and the Asquithian Liberals. After the election the Conservatives had a majority; Bonar Law might say that Lloyd George could be prime minister for as long as he liked, but in fact he could only be prime minister as long as the Conservatives liked. He had as many Liberal supporters in the Commons as in the previous House, but they had been elected mainly because they had received the 'coupon' – a letter of approval from Lloyd George and Bonar Law – which freed them from the fear of Conservative opposition. If there were another election, they could expect to be opposed. Their prospects were dim.

The House of Commons elected in 1918 has never been very well thought of. Baldwin called the members 'hard-faced men who looked as if they had done well out of the war' and Lloyd George said that when he spoke he felt as though he had the Associated Chambers of Commerce behind him and the Trades Union Congress in front of him. This was natural enough: there were a couple of dozen more trade unionists than in the previous Parliament, and there were perhaps a hundred more businessmen than previously. One of Lloyd George's contributions to the war effort was to bring businessmen into the work of running the administration of government, and it was natural that they now moved on to take a larger place in political life than before.

Lloyd George had probably struck a deadlier blow at the Liberal Party than he could possibly have realized when he brought the businessmen so firmly into the work of governing the country. Before the war businessmen had made up a good deal of the strength of the Liberal Party, and because they wanted to see things changed they had been allies of other groups that wanted change. The pre-war Liberal Party had looked rather like the Democratic Party in the United States, firmly attached to the capitalist system, but always ready to consider ways of making it less harsh if this could be managed without overthrowing the system. After 1918 the Liberal Party was much less ready to contemplate change, and the Labour Party was much more committed to changing the structure of society, by means of extensive nationalization.

The newly elected Conservative MPs were in a false position. Lloyd George had been elected on a platform that included a good deal of social reform; they were pledged to follow him, and they tended to see him as the great vote-winner responsible for their own success, but if it came to a choice between social reform and lower taxes they were going to choose lower taxes. During the election the question had been avoided by hoping for large reparations; as it became clearer and clearer that there were not going to be large reparations for a long time to come, the problem became harder to avoid.

Demobilization was carried out fairly successfully; at first the government tried an immensely complicated scheme which let skilled workers out first; as they were usually men who had been kept at work in factories as long as possible, the scheme looked rather like 'last in, first out'. The result was that mutinies broke out, and the government had to reconsider its approach. When a simpler 'first in, first out' scheme was tried, the soldiers accepted it peacefully, and the bulk of demobilization was over by the summer of 1919. The government was afraid that the soldiers might have difficulty finding jobs, and it provided a system of unemployment benefit to cushion the shock. This was a foundation of universal unemployment benefit, but at the time it was not needed.

Post-war boom
After a few months of pause and demobilization, the economy launched itself into a post-war reconstruction boom. Soldiers found jobs easily, factories were sold, and new companies were floated at capital values which suggested that manufacturers expected a happy combination of wartime full order books and pre-war absence of controls, and prices resumed the steady upward course they had followed since 1914. In these conditions trade unions could get pay increases, often without going on strike, and the country's difficulties appeared to be the pleasant difficulties that sometimes accompany a sudden rush of prosperity to the head.

The government did very little to hold this expansion in check. The budget continued the war-time deficits, and this was natural because Great Britain was still maintaining a large army, part of which was occupying Germany. The housing problem which had been forcing itself on the attention of politicians before the war was now acute; Dr Christopher Addison, at the newly created Ministry of Health, was given responsibility for building more houses. But while it was a generous and humane step for the government to commit itself to providing houses, not much could be done immediately; the whole economy was going ahead so fast that the effect of Addison's attempt to build more houses was to drive up prices for everybody because the government was bidding against the private contractors. But although the Addison scheme came to an undistinguished end, the principle had been accepted and future governments had to work out better schemes.

Two million unemployed
The period of explosive post-war prosperity lasted for a little over a year. When the war ended the government had refused to allow any further exports of gold to the United States. The result was that the pound, which had been worth $4.76 in 1918, fell in price to about $3.75. This fall was entirely natural and reasonable at the end of a war which had reduced Great Britain's foreign investments and had turned the United States into a leading creditor nation, but the Bank of England and most of the City of London were determined to bring the pound back to its pre-war level. When Montagu Norman became governor of the Bank of England in 1920, he moved decisively to put this programme into effect. In April the bank rate was

raised to seven per cent, and was kept at this level for a year.

If any twelve-month period decided the pattern of British life between the wars, it was the year of Norman's seven per cent bank rate. The boom slowed down and came to a stop, the foreign exchange value of the pound went up, and unemployment rose to over 2,000,000. This crushing level of unemployment fell a little in the next few years, but throughout the 'twenties and 'thirties men were looking for work and not finding it.

The problem was two-fold. Markets for traditional British products, such as coal, cotton textiles, and ships, had disappeared during the war; other countries had built up industries of their own and no longer wanted British exports, and coal was beginning to be replaced by oil. According to the laws of economic theory the men who had lost their jobs should have gone off and found new ones. But the second part of the problem was that not many new jobs were appearing. High interest rates and the attempt to force the exchange rate up to the pre-war level had a discouraging effect on people who wanted to start new businesses; when new factories opened, they were often in London and south-east England, and the bulk of the post-war unemployed lived in Wales, Scotland, and the north of England.

London had its own difficulties. When the Poplar borough council tried to give poor relief to the unemployed in the borough at a more generous rate than the government thought proper, the councillors were told to make it up out of their own pockets. When they did not do so, they were sent to prison and for some weeks in the autumn of 1921 the government considered what to do. Eventually, the councillors were released, and expenses of poor relief were shared more evenly over London.

But although this cleared up a local difficulty, the prospects for finding a job by moving continued to be bad: a man out of work in Wales knew that he had a better chance of getting work if he went to London, but he also knew that there was a considerable risk of finding himself out of work a long way from his home and friends. In these conditions it was natural for him to stay at home and hope that one day the mines would get back to pre-war prosperity. This was never very likely to happen: for one thing, so many more people were trying to find work in the mines in 1924 than before, and for another, other countries in Europe were developing their coal-mines more efficiently.

Once the post-war reconstruction boom was over, there seemed to be about a million men to spare in England. The government expanded the 1911 Unemployment Insurance scheme to include more people during the war, gave unemployment benefit for some months to all ex-servicemen, and in 1920 insurance was extended to almost everybody. Even so, this was insurance for only fifteen weeks of unemployment in a year—the underlying idea was that people were out of work for a short time when moving from one job to another. The 1920 act was not designed for the long-term unemployment of the inter-war world, and perhaps no insurance scheme could be devised to deal with it. Variations were invented in the years to come, but the basic principle remained: insurance payments as a matter of right for a limited period of time, and then an appeal to the authorities for poor relief.

The modern economic theory is that, in circumstances like this, a government should spend generously and pump demand back into the economy. But in 1920 this idea was unheard-of; its inventor, John Maynard Keynes, had left the civil service, protesting violently at the Treaty of Versailles in his *Economic Consequences of the Peace,* but he had not yet worked out his new approach. The field was open to the budget-cutters, because the orthodox view was that a balanced budget would restore the health of the economy.

The Geddes Axe

The government's economic policy consistently made matters worse. During the rapid expansion of 1919 and 1920 it had had a deficit on the budget, which meant that inflation went ahead all the faster. When the economy slowed down to a crawl in 1921 the government appointed a committee under Sir Eric Geddes, who had recently retired from office, to investigate ways of cutting down expenditure. This was the first of many attempts in the next fifty years to reduce spending, and the government's approach was a little naïve. The Geddes Committee was asked to recommend steps to be taken, and when its report — so sweeping that it became known as the Geddes Axe — came out, the government declined to accept all its suggestions. Less was taken out of the education programme and the naval estimates than had been proposed, because the government could not give the committee complete control over its policy. But the Conservative backbenchers felt the government had let them down. Candidates had been elected at by-elections on an 'anti-waste' platform, which was intended to reduce government spending, and in the House of Commons they were led by Horatio Bottomley; before the war he had been on the left, asking for a 'businessman's government' as a way to push the old ruling class out of office, but after the war he was on the right, asking for a 'businessman's government' as a way to cut spending and taxation.

Lloyd George suggested from time to time between 1919 and 1922 that it would be a good idea to create a Centre Party. He was thinking of uniting his own Liberals with the main body of the Conservative Party to resist the Labour Party, who were more or less seriously called Bolsheviks by some people, and also to resist the Bottomley men as 'die-hards'. But the Conservative Party never really accepted this distinction between die-hards and the rest, and certainly did not intend to allow Lloyd George to create one. By 1921 a large number of Conservatives blamed the prime minister for some of the things they disliked about the post-war world.

Fisher's 1918 Education Act, which raised the school-leaving age to fourteen and gave teachers higher pay, looked progressive to most people; the higher Tories disliked it because it meant more taxes, and because education would make the servant problem worse by giving children ideas above their station. The relaxation of British rule in India expressed in the Montagu-Chelmsford reforms, and made explicit when General Dyer was censured for killing off 300-400 Indians while suppressing a riot at Amritsar, also infuriated them. And Ireland was even worse.

At the end of the war the government had to face the fact that Home Rule had been put on the Statute Book at the beginning of the war. Lloyd George's coalition certainly was not going to allow Home Rule in the pre-war sense, which meant placing Ulster under Dublin, even for the relatively limited number of areas of government activity being transferred to an Irish parliament. So Northern Ireland got Home Rule for itself, and acquired the limited powers which it enjoys to this day.

There was no such quiet ending in the rest of Ireland. Almost all the seats outside Ulster had been won by Sinn Feiners in 1918, and instead of going to Westminster they set up a parliament of their own in Dublin. They wanted much more than Home Rule; they tried to ask for self-determination and the right to independence at Versailles, and when this failed Ireland began to drift to civil war. By modern standards it was a normal, even fairly civilized guerilla war; by late 19th-century standards it was a shocking reversion to barbarism. Civilians were shot for helping the rebels, and for cooperating with the government; Irish prisoners were shot while attempting to escape, and British officers were shot in front of their families. There were other familiar symptoms. Lloyd George said confidently: 'We have got murder by the throat'; the Irish looked for outside help, which they thought would come from the United States; and the people of Ireland suffered more than the people fighting on either side. Eventually, Lloyd George decided to make peace, and he moved cautiously in 1921, first winning Conservatives like Birkenhead to accept his point of view, and then getting the Irish to agree to remain inside the Commonwealth with Dominion status, as the Irish Free State, rather than insisting on independence.

This was perhaps the best settlement that could have been managed, but it infuriated the die-hards. At the 1921 party conference they were restrained from denouncing negotiations with the Irish only by appeals for loyalty to the leadership; this appeal could not be used again. The Conservatives were also annoyed by the way in which Lloyd George sold titles and honours. Selling honours was far from unheard-of; the Liberal and Conservative parties had been helping their finances for some years in this way. But they were selling on behalf of recognized party organizations, and were selling in relatively restricted quantities. When Lloyd George's agents went out, they looked for men with no particular political allegiance who would give money for a fund under his personal control.

But although there was a good case against some of the people Lloyd George ennobled, and although he gave more titles than any previous government had done in a comparable period of time, the real Conservative objection to the sale of honours was that it represented the triumph of businessmen who had done well during the war–the *nouveaux riches*. The 'new poor', as the people who felt less well-off after the war rather ostentatiously called themselves, resented the way that businessmen had taken charge during the war, and were now being accepted into the ruling class. The protests at the sale of honours concentrated on undesirable people getting titles in return for money (though the Conservative Party funds shared the proceeds); there would have been irritation even if every peerage had gone to a businessman who had worked hard all through the war and had never given a penny to the Lloyd George political fund. The rich as a class did not lose much ground to the poor, but the old landed class lost ground to the new businessmen. In 1919 and 1920 there were enormous land sales as the old owners finally accepted that there was not going to be a return to the days before the war; a good many of Lloyd George's peers bought country houses at the time, though they did not try to keep up great estates and usually sold the farms off to the tenants.

'A great dynamic force'

After Ireland and the argument about honours, Lloyd George could survive only by convincing the Conservatives that without him they would be unable to resist the Labour Party. This argument was wearing thin, and in any case the Conservative backbenchers were no longer sure they cared to pay this price for resisting the Labour Party. In the summer of 1922 the government came very close to war with Turkey over the Middle East settlement. The cabinet might find this satisfactory, but the backbenchers had no desire for any more adventures or worse. In any case, they were rather pro-Turkish.

The cabinet might still have held its position, but only if no leading Conservative would oppose it. The day before the Conservative MPs were to meet and discuss the situation, Lord Beaverbrook persuaded Bonar Law to come out of retirement and lead the discontented backbenchers. On 19th October the Conservatives decided they no longer wanted Lloyd George, who was condemned at the meeting for being 'a great dynamic force'. There was no danger that his successors would be described in such terms.

The Fall of Lloyd George

Colin Cross

David Lloyd George was perhaps the most brilliant politician 20th-century Great Britain has so far produced. He was a short, tense man with a big head and long hair. He had energy, drive, and imagination. His oratory could sway a public audience. His cajoling charm could coax men and women in private. He lived for the moment but often had an uncanny prevision of the future. 'Always,' said Winston Churchill of him, 'he seemed to be looking into the next field.'

In 1918 Lloyd George was aged fifty-five and stood at the height of his power. No politician had ever had such prestige. He had led Great Britain to victory in the war and in the 1918 general election he won a majority of 229 seats over all his opponents combined, the greatest vote of confidence ever given by the British electorate. The Conservative leader, Andrew Bonar Law, remarked that Lloyd George could be prime minister for life.

Just four years later he was ejected from office, never to return. It was the greatest fall in British political history.

What went wrong?

Vanity had something to do with it. He was rightly convinced that he was cleverer than other politicians, but he failed to see that mediocrity can sometimes be a political advantage. Moreover, although his skill could command respect, admiration, and affection, it failed to command trust. Lloyd George was unpredictable. He 'shed his friends like an ermine sheds its winter coat', wrote Beaverbrook. He was not the man to produce the sense of stability sought by many after the excitements of war.

And his political backing was unsatisfactory. His power was personal and he had no proper party to support him.

'A son of the people'

By background and instinct Lloyd George was a radical and he loved to proclaim that he was 'a son of the people' (which was true). Yet in assuming office in 1916, at the worst stage of the war, Lloyd George had split his own party, the Liberals. His supporters in the House of Commons, after the 1918 election, consisted of 374 Conservatives and only 133 Coalition Liberals. (There were also ten 'Coalition Labour'.) This contradiction produced obvious strains. Conservative Party workers in the country and many backbench Conservative MPs failed to understand why they should support a Liberal in power when they had enough seats to set up a prime minister of their own. Lloyd George felt frustrated at being in the power of his old enemies. He believed he had been elected by the people and that many of the Conservatives had won their seats not for their own merits but because of the Lloyd George name.

Lloyd George devoted a disproportionate share of his attention to foreign affairs. His aim was to be the pacifier of Europe; he negotiated the Versailles Treaty on behalf of Great Britain as a personal plenipotentiary, and he took part in twenty-four international conferences in four years.

Yet the electorate was more interested in home affairs and here the Lloyd George administration dissatisfied the radicals who were the prime minister's natural allies. In the general election, Lloyd George had promised 'homes for heroes', but in fact the housing programme was extravagant in money and produced too few houses. Proposals for nationalizing the mines and the railways and for a capital levy on inflated war fortunes all had powerful radical support but were turned down. The steam went out of the economy and by 1922 there were rising prices and rising unemployment; ex-servicemen were drawing the dole instead of being petted as heroes. The government's most constructive act had been to widen Lloyd George's own pre-war creation of unemployment insurance to cover the whole working class.

The mess of Ireland, with Great Britain attempting to suppress nationalism by force, further antagonized the radicals. Lloyd George did, in fact, show political deftness in negotiating a treaty acceptable both to the Irish and to his own Unionist colleagues. He was praised for having 'solved the insoluble', but his more natural place would have been on the opposition front bench using his oratory to denounce the black-and-tans.

Conservative outrage

He received little Conservative gratitude. Strait-laced Conservatives professed to be shocked at his selling of peerages and baronetcies to raise political funds. His sex life outraged the conventions. There was an element of hypocrisy in this, but the feeling grew that getting rid of Lloyd George would 'clean up' public life.

As his troubles deepened, Lloyd George cast about for methods of strengthening his position. He started by proposing a merger between the Conservatives and the Coalition Liberals under his leadership. This got nowhere and so he turned to the opposition Liberals under the former prime minister H.H.Asquith, but they still distrusted him as the man who had run the 1918 election against them. He toyed with the idea of a Centre Party, to be formed by individuals from all parties under his leadership. For a moment he thought of giving up altogether and becoming editor of *The Times*.

His weakness was his attachment to office and a belief that he was indispensable. Had he quit at a moment of his own choosing and set himself up as focal point of a radical opposition he might have swept back to power in the next general election. But instead he hung on, his position getting ever weaker, until his enemies overwhelmed him.

Crisis over Greece

The crisis came over a foreign matter. Lloyd George admired Greece and thought it would be a good thing if she became the dominant power in south-east Europe. The Greeks thought so too and aspired even to conquer Constantinople. The Turks, under vigorous new national leadership, struck at Greek forces occupying part of their territory and won. Lloyd George proposed to support the Greeks to the point of going to war with Turkey.

Almost nobody in Great Britain wanted such a war and the rank and file Conservatives rebelled. It was a rebellion not so much against Lloyd George as against their own Conservative leaders—especially Austen Chamberlain and Birkenhead—who were serving with him in the cabinet. The Conservative leadership had decided to fight a general election in continued coalition with Lloyd George but, on 19th October 1922, the Conservative parliamentary party met at the Carlton Club and by 187 votes to 87 decided that the coalition must be broken. The speeches which most effectively swayed the majority were by Andrew Bonar Law, who had emerged from retirement for the occasion, and the rising Stanley Baldwin, president of the Board of Trade.

The same day Lloyd George resigned. Bonar Law replaced him, formed a solely Conservative administration, and won the ensuing general election. The Labour Party increased its representation from 63 to 142 seats and thus became the official opposition and alternative government.

Never again were Lloyd George's talents to be at the service of the nation. His was the first and greatest example of the characteristically 20th-century pattern of British politics: that of allowing excessive adulation to a leader at one moment and at the next discarding him entirely.

The First Labour Government

Colin Cross

'As we stood waiting for His Majesty, amid the gold and crimson magnificence of the Palace, I could not help marvelling at the strange turn of Fortune's wheel, which had brought MacDonald the starveling clerk, Thomas the engine driver, Henderson the foundry labourer, and Clynes the mill-hand, to this pinnacle beside the man whose forebears had been kings for so many splendid generations. We were making history.'

Thus J.R.Clynes recorded in his *Memoirs* the start of the first Labour government in January 1924. It was an event doubly unique. Not only had the old Conservative-Liberal alternation in office, which had seemed to be the fixed system of British politics, been broken, but also actual members of the manual working class were taking over some of the highest positions in the state. No subsequent cabinet has contained so many ministers of strictly proletarian origin as that formed by James Ramsay MacDonald in 1924.

It had come about suddenly and almost accidentally.

The Labour Party in its modern shape had been formed as recently as 1917, only seven years earlier. Before that the tiny group of Labour MPs had been a loose alliance of trade unionists with socialist propagandists; they had been more a pressure group than a party. It was less than two years earlier, in 1922, that Labour had for the first time become a major national party and the official opposition. The party leader, MacDonald, had never held any kind of office and was not even a privy councillor.

Nor had the electorate deliberately chosen a Labour administration.

The Conservative prime minister, Stanley Baldwin, had dissolved parliament three years before he needed to do so in order to appeal to the electorate to return him to power with a mandate to place duties on goods into Great Britain. He claimed that this was the only way in which the leading problem of the moment, mass unemployment, could be solved. The two opposition parties, Liberal and Labour, both believed in free trade and so fought Baldwin on this issue. The election results gave the Conservatives 258 seats, the Liberals 159, and Labour 191. Thus no party commanded a clear majority in the House of Commons. Moreover, since they had just fought each other over free trade it was difficult for Conservatives and Liberals to join forces against Labour. The only rational outcome was for the stronger free trade party, Labour, to form a government and for the second free trade party, the Liberals, to support it.

There was six weeks' interval between the election and the assembly of Parliament and the King insisted that Baldwin should stay in office until the House of Commons had formally expressed its wishes. It was a time of great public perturbation, many traditionalists believing that Labour in office would inaugurate a wholesale red revolution similar to that which Lenin had conducted in Russia. A countess telephoned the Labour MP Philip Snowden to ask if her throat would be cut. Baldwin and the Liberal leader, H.H.Asquith, were flooded with appeals to combine to 'save the nation'. A proposal was floated to set up a 'caretaker government' under the banker Reginald McKenna, who was not even a member of the House of Commons.

However, the King, Baldwin, and Asquith agreed that Labour should be given a fair chance. The balance of the parties gave Labour leaders an opportunity of acquiring ministerial experience in safe conditions. If they misbehaved, the old parties could always eject them.

Labour takes over
Labour leaders in the past had expressed distaste at the possibility of taking office while lacking a parliamentary majority. It would mean accepting responsibility without the power of carrying out the fundamental remedies they had advocated. Snowden, in particular, had only eighteen months earlier laid it down that in such circumstances Labour should refuse office

and force Liberals and Conservatives into coalition.

In the circumstances of the moment, however, Labour took it for granted that it should accept office. The possibility of refusing was not raised by any leading Labour figure; it would have looked too much like running away. Moreover, the Labour leaders decided they should act moderately. The alternative possibility of their taking office, courting defeat in the House of Commons on radical proposals to redistribute wealth and then appealing to the country was not raised in any of the preparatory discussions.

On 21st January the Conservatives were defeated in the House of Commons. The following day the King sent for Mac-Donald, swore him into the Privy Council and appointed him prime minister. The King made a little speech referring to his own experience in the navy which, he said, had brought him into contact with many kinds of people and offering the prime minister the benefit of his advice. Mac-Donald, for his part, said he and his colleagues would do their best to serve the country.

To the annoyance of his colleagues, Mac-Donald insisted on the full prerogatives of prime minister by appointing the whole government himself, without consultation. He took the office of foreign secretary himself. From the leading Labour personalities he appointed Snowden to the Exchequer, Arthur Henderson to the Home Office, J.H.Thomas to the Colonial Office, and J.R.Clynes to the leadership of the House of Commons.

It was difficult for so new and prole-tarian a party to fill all the traditional offices, especially those attached to the House of Lords. The only peer who belonged to the Labour Party was Lord Parmoor and he became Lord President of the Council. MacDonald, anyway dissatisfied with what he regarded as the 'paucity' of the talent at his disposal, took in outsiders to make up weight. The experienced Liberal, Lord Haldane, became Lord Chancellor and Lord Chelmsford, a former viceroy of India, became first lord of the Admiralty.

Of the twenty members of the cabinet, eleven were of definitely working-class origin. The remainder mostly belonged to the old ruling class. The only middle-class 'intellectual', of the kind which in the next generation was to become charac-teristic of Labour leadership, was Sidney Webb, president of the Board of Trade. In the junior ranks, the administration in-cluded the first woman ever to attain office, Margaret Bondfield, parliamentary secre-tary to the Ministry of Labour, and a future prime minister, Clement Attlee, who was made under-secretary for war.

Cloth cap to silk 'at

It was a piquant situation in a country in which by tradition only 'gentlemen' were fit to rule. A co-op van drove up to deliver groceries at 10 Downing Street. J.H.Thomas, who made a point of contin-uing to drop his 'h's, alleged that when he first appeared at the Colonial Office and claimed to be colonial secretary the door-man turned to a colleague, tapped his head and remarked: 'Another case of shell-shock, poor chap.' The little former miner, Stephen Walsh, secretary for war, stupefied the generals at his first meeting of the army council by opening the proceedings with the remark: 'Gentlemen, always re-member that we must all be loyal to the King.' John Wheatley, the left-wing minis-ter of health, cheerfully chatted to the King that of course when socialism was estab-lished the monarchy would have to go.

The King was worried about clothes. He tried, unsuccessfully, to get the ministers all to wear silk hats and frock coats for Buckingham Palace audiences. He insisted that for court functions they should wear ceremonial dress of embroidered tail coat with white knee-breeches and sword and got his secretary to send Ramsay Mac-Donald details of second-hand outfits avail-able at Moss Bros., Ltd. Ministers, fearing the ridicule of their supporters, co-operated as little as possible: Webb and the minister of agriculture, Noel Buxton, were embar-rassed when the Glasgow Independent Labour Party circulated a picture of them in knee-breeches with the caption: 'Is this what you voted for?' The handsome Mac-Donald minded less than most; in May 1924 he stood by the throne in full uniform, while wives of his ministers were presented to His Majesty.

Haldane advised on the procedure for cabinet meetings, telling the ministers that they must refer to each other by their departments and not by name. Smoking was for the first time introduced at cabinet meetings, a lasting innovation. On the whole, the government worked at least as efficiently as its predecessors; the main complaint was that MacDonald, grossly overworked by combining the offices of foreign secretary and prime minister, was too busy to keep in close touch with his colleagues. However, the main achievement of the government was in foreign affairs; MacDonald managed to reconcile France and Germany and to settle for a while the problem of German reparations for war damage.

In home affairs the most lasting achievement was a housing act brought in by Wheatley. This inaugurated what is still the basic system of council houses with subsidized rents built by local authorities. Wheatley showed skill and persistence in getting it through.

Longer-term plans, in which Snowden was prominent, included a scheme for rationalizing the electricity supply which had grown up haphazard with hundreds of independent power stations operating on different frequencies. Snowden also attached importance to 'sound finance', which he believed would lead ultimately to the reduction of unemployment; he brought in moderate tax reductions and set in train the policy which two years later led to the restoration of the gold standard.

Collaboration with the trade unions was minimal. The Labour ministers made no attempt to communicate to the union leaders the secret plans which had been prepared in Whitehall to deal with a general strike. Hardly had the government assumed office than there were strikes of engine drivers, dockers, and London tram drivers, which the minister of labour, Tom Shaw, dealt with on the same principles as those of past administrations.

Because of its parliamentary weakness, it was unlikely that the government would last for long. The Liberals, although supporting it with their votes, were spiteful, resenting their position. The Conservatives were eager to get back into power.

Breaking point

The probable breaking point came in August, eight months after the government had taken office, with a proposal to make a commercial treaty with the Soviet Union with a loan from Great Britain as one of its terms. Neither Conservatives nor Liberals liked it and the downfall of the government appeared certain when parliament reassembled in the autumn.

However, before the Russian crisis came properly to a head there arose a subsidiary scandal over a Communist journalist, R.J. Campbell, who had written an article inciting soldiers to disobey their officers if ordered to act against strikers. The director of public prosecutions ordered Campbell to be prosecuted for sedition, but later withdrew the case.

The government was accused, not entirely without foundation, of having interfered with the ordinary course of justice. The Liberals demanded a select committee of the House of Commons to inquire into the incident. MacDonald refused and the government was defeated by 364 votes to 198. The King allowed MacDonald to appeal to a general election, but this returned the Conservatives to power with a majority of 213 over all other parties. One factor in the Conservative success was a scare over the 'Zinovyev Letter', a forged document which, published during the campaign, purported to set out plans by the Comintern in Moscow to subvert Great Britain.

On 4th November MacDonald resigned. 'I like him and have always found him quite straight,' the King wrote in his diary.

It had been a brief, interesting adventure. It had settled the Labour Party within the framework of ordinary British politics. The real losers of the general election had not been Labour, which had lost only forty seats, but the Liberals whose strength had fallen catastrophically from 159 to 40. It was the end of the old Liberal Party and the start of a new political pattern: from now on Conservatives and Labour would alternate in office.

Part eleven · Survival of Bolshevik Russia

The First World War had a shattering impact on every European country that fought in it, but none was more affected than Russia. The losses and defeats of her armies were more catastrophic, the collapse of her government more complete, and the breakdown of her social and economic structure more disastrous, than in any other European country. It was this chaos which gave the Bolsheviks their chance to seize power. Later Soviet historians have tended to underestimate the opposition the party subsequently encountered and to attribute their difficulties to Allied intervention. But the Bolsheviks were only a small minority of the Russian people; they had to resort to ruthless improvisation in order to crush opposition. For nearly four years the fate of the Revolution hung in the balance and Russia was the scene of a massive civil war.

Russia's vastness and diversity have always made her difficult to control. Although the definite programme and firm discipline of the Bolshevik party enabled them to seize power from the vacillating Provisional Government which had replaced the Tsarist regime, the problem of establishing their authority over the more remote regions was not easy. The non-Russian nationalities who had made up the Tsarist Empire, particularly in Finland and the Ukraine, now saw their opportunity to establish their independence. The old supporters of the Tsarist regime, the dispossessed landlords, those peasants who had achieved some measure of prosperity and who had got something to lose, and others who were alarmed by the ruthlessness of the Bolsheviks were also opposed to their take-over and saw in the uprisings of repressed nationalities a chance to thwart any further extension of their power.

The intervention of foreign powers was decisive in embittering relations with the Communist government once the Civil War was over. It also determined much of Russia's future relations with the West. When the Bolsheviks first seized power in 1917 the Allies' first thought was not to save Russia from the revolutionaries but to safeguard themselves from losing an ally in the war against Germany. But Lenin's view of the war as a capitalist and imperialist struggle combined with the war-weariness of the Russian peasants who had borne the brunt of the fighting made Russia's withdrawal from the war only a matter of time. It was not until the end of the First World War in 1918 that the Allies could really spare attention to what was going on within Russia. Even then though their attitude towards the new regime was hesitant. They varied in aims and policies. Britain's half-hearted policy of sending supplies and money but not soldiers to the White Russians achieved nothing because the aim was not clear. But Britain, like Russia, was exhausted by war and while British soldiers had been prepared to fight the authoritarian Germans for four years, many feared they would not be so willing to turn against the revolutionaries in Russia. Few shared Churchill's vision of the momentous consequences for the world of a Bolshevik victory.

But Britain was not an immediate neighbour of Russia's. Other countries were and their attitudes to the new regime were coloured by traditional prejudices. Poland and Russia were age-old enemies and their hostility towards the Bolsheviks was in one sense just another phase in their attempt to restore the boundaries of 18th-century Poland. Far away on the other side of Asia Japan and Russia had been eyeing each other warily long before the assassination of Nicholas II, and now the Japanese took advantage of a young and insecure government to occupy vast tracts of Asiatic Russia.

But the same factors which made it difficult for the Bolsheviks to establish their rule throughout Russia also made it difficult for their enemies to unite and this in the long run saved them. Pockets or sometimes huge areas of Russian soil were gained by their opponents but these were nearly all on the peripheries of the Russian Empire. The Bolsheviks clung on to the heartlands and it was this which enabled them, against heavy odds, to establish themselves. They had another advantage too. They had a definite political programme to offer while their opponents re-lied purely on military force which can never be more than a short-term weapon.

The Bolsheviks had to pay a heavy price for their triumph. The demands of such a struggle were only met by ruthlessness, by sacrificing everything to the war effort and by silencing all opposition. The Kronstadt rising of the Baltic Fleet – traditionally the 'conscience of the revolution' – exposed a deep-seated discontent with the Bolsheviks among those on whom they depended most – the ordinary industrial workers and the sailors. The Bolsheviks had won their freedom from outside intervention but at a heavy cost, the full effects of which were only realised in the next fifty years.

The Civil War (1)

S. V. Lipitsky

The three years of strife within Russia after the Bolshevik Revolution was the most massive civil war the world has ever seen. Well after the First World War was over in the west, there were some two million troops under arms in Russia, ranged along an uncertain and wavering front over 6,000 miles long.

But the Bolsheviks had to meet more than the four major challenges from within Russia. At an Allied conference in Paris towards the end of 1917, an agreement for dismembering Russia was worked out. The Caucasus, Kuban, and other regions were declared 'spheres of special interest' to Great Britain; the Ukraine and the Crimea were earmarked by France; Siberia and the Russian Far East were 'placed at the disposal' of the United States of America and Japan.

In Paris and London, in Washington and Tokyo, the hide of the 'Russian Bear' was eagerly divided, with no doubt that he would soon die—at his own hand. To the political and military leaders of the Allied powers, the Bolshevik state then seemed extremely unstable, and they reckoned on eliminating it by means of conspiracies, terrorist acts, and anti-Soviet risings. The Russian counter-revolutionaries willingly accepted the proposal that it should participate in these opportunist activities.

At first, events looked like proving the Allies right. There was an immediate challenge from Kerensky, the former prime minister of the overthrown Provisional Government. With General Krasnov, he ordered a Cossack corps to march on Petrograd. The rebels had no doubts of their ultimate success, for the newly-formed Soviet government had no regular military forces. But while the Cossacks were advancing on the capital the entire working population was placed at the defence of the town. The Cossacks were halted and defeated on Pulkovsky Heights. But force was not the only weapon—an even more effective one was the simple message addressed to the Cossacks by the defenders of Petrograd. The sailor, Pavel Dybenko, a minister in the newly-formed Soviet government, made his way at night into the Cossack camp; he organized a meeting there and convinced his unusual audience that it was necessary not merely to stop this revolt against the Soviets, but to arrest the organizers of the rising—Kerensky and Krasnov.

This fearless Soviet minister, only twenty-eight years old, acted absolutely correctly: the Cossacks arrested Krasnov and handed him over to the Soviet authorities. The victors acted magnanimously by freeing the rebel general after he had given his word not to take further part in anti-Soviet activities. General Krasnov, however, soon broke his word of honour to lead a White army of Don Cossacks in the south. Kerensky learned of Dybenko's visit in time, and escaped abroad.

Scarcely had the Red Guards dealt with the next risings–by Cossacks on the Don and the Orenburg steppes–than Germany attacked along the entire Russo-German front. The Soviet government turned to the nation with an impassioned and stern appeal to come to the defence of the socialist motherland. The response was immediate, and the February days of mass mobilization of volunteers proved the true birth of the Red Army. On 3rd March 1918 a Soviet delegation signed the extremely harsh peace terms dictated by the Germans at Brest Litovsk.

Allied intervention

The events of the winter of 1917-18 revealed that the power of the Soviets was considerably more stable than had been believed by their enemies inside and outside Russia. As early as 15th March at the conference in London of the prime ministers and foreign ministers of France, Italy, and Great Britain, the 'Russian Question' was debated afresh. The conclusions were communicated to the United States on the following day by Arthur Balfour, the British foreign secretary. Balfour stated that in order to prevent the German occupation of Russia 'there is only one means – Allied intervention'.

There was no delay: in March 1918 the first units of foreign troops disembarked on Soviet soil at Murmansk, from the British cruiser *Glory*. Large reinforcements were later landed near. Murmansk from the French cruiser *Admiral Aube,* the American cruiser *Olympia,* and other war vessels.

At the beginning of April, the first Japanese landings began in Vladivostok, and were followed in August by British, American, and other foreign troops. Thus, under the false pretext of defending the interests of the Allied countries from the 'German threat', intervention began in Russia. But in spring 1918, with the First World War still continuing, the Western powers were unable to spare many troops for the struggle against the Soviet Republic. They therefore decided to make use of the Czechoslovak Legion, which had been formed in Russia in 1917 from prisoners-of-war – former officers and men of the Austro-Hungarian army who had expressed their desire to fight to free Slav territories from Habsburg rule. By the summer of 1918, the Legion had some 50,000 troops and constituted a strong military force.

The Czechoslovak revolt

The Soviet government had given permission for the Czechoslovak Legion to travel to France by way of Siberia and Vladivostok. At the end of May 1918 the Legion's open revolt began when echelons of Czechoslovak soldiers, moving towards Vladivostok, were spread out along the entire length of the Trans-Siberian Railway.

Beyond the Volga and the Urals there were only small local detachments of Soviet troops, who were unable to oppose the well-organized and well-armed Czechoslovaks.

The revolt quickly assumed huge proportions as large forces of local counter-revolutionaries and foreign troops backed the rebels.

Breaking the terms of the Treaty of Brest Litovsk, the Germans occupied the Crimea and advanced into the Caucasus. They helped General Krasnov to defeat the Soviet forces in the Don area, and

there raised a large army of White Cossacks.

British troops moved into Transcaucasia and the Kazakhstan region and captured Baku and other important economic centres. With the support of British and French troops, Generals Alexeyev and Denikin formed the counter-revolutionary 'Volunteer Army' in the northern Caucasus.

In the north, the interventionists occupied the whole White Sea coast and the important harbour of Archangel.

Thus ended Soviet Russia's peaceful respite. The Soviet government had soon lost control of three-quarters of Russia and faced a challenge on a 6,000-mile front. Its army of 300,000 men opposed enemies numbering 700,000.

In the spring of 1918, the Soviet Republic introduced compulsory military service. A broad network of courses to train military leaders was created, and thousands of ex-Tsarist officers were invited to join the Red Army.

Within three months, the number of troops almost doubled, in time to meet a renewed challenge. Czech and White Guard troops appeared on the Middle Volga, threatening the central regions of the Soviet Republic. Areas producing metal, oil, coal, and cotton were seized. Factories and mills ground to a halt for want of fuel and raw materials. Food shortages became more severe.

The high command of the Red Army was ordered to concentrate on the eastern front. 'Now the whole fate of the Revolution is staked on a single card: a swift victory over the Czechoslovaks on the Kazan-Urals-Samara front. Everything depends on this,' Lenin wrote.

The struggle against the Czechs saw the formation of the Revolutionary War Council for the central direction of the armed forces. The concentration of forces on the chosen front, the transition from semi-partisan methods of waging war to regular forms of military organization, stiff discipline, and centralized command soon brought important military successes. There was even support from the first Soviet aviation units. The Czechoslovak rebels and Russian White Guards were driven out of Kazan and Simbirsk in September 1918. The Red Army on the eastern front went over from defence to attack, cleared the middle Volga area of enemy troops, and advanced determinedly to the Urals.

An armed camp

The development of events in summer 1918 finally convinced the Soviet leaders that it was only possible to obtain victory in the Civil War through the total utilization of all reserves. On 2nd September 1918, the supreme legislative organ of the Soviet Republic issued a decree in which it stated:

'The Soviet Republic has become an armed camp.

At the head of every front and all military establishments stands the Revolutionary War Council with a single commander-in-chief.

All the forces and means of the socialist republic are placed at the service of the sacred task of armed struggle against the aggressor.'

The Red Army was gradually transformed into a fighting force, able to withstand the assaults of numerous enemies and even deliver powerful counterblows.

In the autumn of 1918 events took place on the world stage and in Russia itself which changed the balance of forces and seriously affected the course of the Civil War. The end of the First World War permitted the Soviet people to annul the unjust conditions which the Germans had imposed on them when they signed the Treaty of Brest Litovsk.

In addition, the Allied leaders could now send newly released military forces and arms to resolve the 'Russian Question'. Local and (naturally) 'democratic' governments were created in the summer of 1918, in Siberia, the Urals, and the Volga area under the aegis of the interventionists and with the participation of the Mensheviks and the Socialist Revolutionary Party.

The east: 'Supreme ruler of Russia'

But when the early successes by counter-revolutionaries on the eastern front turned into defeats, the mask of democracy in Siberia was flung aside. Brought by the Allies to Siberia and appointed war minister of the Siberian 'government', the former Tsarist admiral, Alexander Kolchak, staged a *coup d'état* in November 1918, established a strict military dictatorship, and was proclaimed the 'supreme ruler of Russia' with the task of creating a large and powerful army, capable of crush-

ing the Bolsheviks with Allied aid. Kolchak enforced mobilization in the vast territories under his control, with supplies donated in unlimited quantities by the western powers. In a short period the United States supplied 200,000 rifles, 220,000 shells, many guns and machine-guns, and 350,000 pairs of boots. According to the evidence of Winston Churchill, Kolchak's army at that time received from British sources alone about 100,000 fire-arms.

At the same time the Allies swiftly increased the numbers of their own troops in eastern Russia: in December 1918 there were nearly 200,000 foreign soldiers there, more than 100,000 of them Japanese.

The decisive military operations of the Civil War began in March 1919 when Kolchak made his bid for victory. His army, now numbering between 130,000 and 145,000, with 1,300 machine-guns and 211 field guns, faced a Soviet force over 100,000 strong, deploying 1,882 machine-guns and 374 field guns.

Kolchak's first main blow fell on the northern section of the 1,200-mile eastern front, but he failed in his aim to join up with anti-Bolsheviks on the coast of the White Sea. But further south, in the direction of Ufa, where the Whites outnumbered the Reds four to one, they broke through, and began a swift advance towards the Volga.

The Bolsheviks rallied, urging newly mobilized communists to the front along the boggy roads and across rivers swollen by the melting ice. A counter-attack on Kolchak's flank, planned by Mikhail Frunze, commander of the southern wing, flung the White armies back to their original positions. The counter-attack turned into a general advance across the Urals and into the vast Siberian plains.

As the Red Army went forward, the Siberian peasants turned partisan, and took up arms against the terrorist dictatorship of Kolchak and the White armies they had been forced to serve. With no social base, Kolchak's army melted away, its remnants fleeing eastward with interventionists and 'Allied missions'.

When the insurgent workers of Irkutsk seized the town and barred the only escape route, the Allied representatives gained permission to withdraw by handing over Russian gold reserves captured the previous year — and by betraying Kolchak. The 'supreme ruler of Russia' was shot in February 1920 after the Bolsheviks took over the town.

The north, west, and south

Meanwhile, the bitterness and the scale of the armed conflict elsewhere had grown. In the north, round Murmansk and Archangel, the Allies increased the number of their troops to 22,000 and were joined by nearly 7,000 Whites. Even so, encountering fierce resistance from numerically small but extremely stubborn Red Army units, these forces had no success.

In the south, the 50,000-strong army of General Krasnov seized the whole of the Don region, threatened Voronezh, and attempted to take Tsaritsyn.

In the northern Caucasus, the White 'Volunteer Army', many battalions of which consisted almost wholly of former officers, seized vital rich areas.

In November 1918 Allied squadrons appeared in the Black Sea, captured the most important Russian Black Sea ports — Novorossiysk, Sevastopol, Odessa — and landed large expeditionary forces. The southern attack promised the interventionists rich prizes. There lay the main areas of oil, coal, iron ore, and manganese. The northern Caucasus, the Crimea, and the Ukraine were the granaries of the nation. There, the Allied troops could immediately rely on the sizeable armed forces of the local counter-revolution. The roads to Moscow were much better and comparatively short.

But the Bolsheviks had also learned the art of war. The All-Russian Central Executive Committee of Soviets decided on 30th November 1918: 'To set up a Council of Workers' and Peasants' Defence under the chairmanship of comrade Lenin as chairman of the Council of People's Commissars (prime minister).'

At one of the very first sessions of the Council of Defence, a decree was issued: 'The Council of Defence approves the plan of forming an army with a total strength of 1,500,000 men and 300,000 horses.'

War Communism

It is today difficult even to imagine the poverty and ruin confronting Lenin and his comrades-in-arms in their task of building a mass army and organizing its supply of weapons, clothing, equipment, and food.

To achieve this, the policy of 'war Communism' was strictly applied. Transport and industry were wholly turned over to the needs of the front. Every pound of metal, coal, oil, cotton, and bread was carefully accounted for and utilized by a centralized system in accordance with prime necessities. The peasants were compelled to hand over to the state their grain surplus, which ordinarily went to market.

The Red Army grew swiftly. By the beginning of 1919 more than a million men were mustered under its banners.

The spring of 1919 saw a further important strengthening of the Bolshevik position. The Eighth Congress of the Communist Party announced a policy of firm union with the middle peasantry. These were the peasants of average means who comprised some sixty per cent of the rural population. They had been neutral at the start of the Civil War, the basic support for Soviet power coming from the working class of the industrial areas and, in the countryside, from the hired labourers and poorest peasants. The union with the middle peasants thus widened the social base of Soviet power and the superiority of the revolutionary forces became overwhelming.

In the south, the newly-strengthened Red Army was able to throw Krasnov back from Voronezh and Tsaritsyn and drive him far to the south.

For a short time the Soviet troops held almost the whole of the Ukraine and found themselves facing the Allied forces. In the regions held by the interventionists, Bolshevik underground agents risked their lives to demonstrate to many of the Allied soldiers and sailors the true aims of Soviet military action.

'Hands off Soviet Russia'

In their own countries, the Allied populations demanded more and more clearly: 'Hands off Soviet Russia'. Under the influence of these ideas and opinions, the interventionist army, which had so recently seemed such a threat, went to pieces. Ships and regiments alike refused to give battle. The Allied High Command was forced to surrender Kherson, Nikolayev, and Odessa almost without a struggle and hastened to evacuate its troops from Ukrainian soil.

When the Red Army advanced into the Crimea the French seamen hoisted red flags and demanded an immediate return home.

British troops, too, firmly refused to fight the Russian people. As the British prime minister, Lloyd George, told the House of Commons on 16th April 1919: 'Russia . . . has never been conquered by a foreign foe, although it has been successfully invaded many times. It is a country which it is easy to get into, but very difficult to get out of.'

Denikin's army

Meanwhile, from the counter-revolutionary cadres concentrated in the south, there had been formed three armies under the general command of Denikin. The Allied powers supplied them with money, weapons, equipment, and everything they needed for their struggle with the Bolsheviks. In May 1919 the counter-revolution in the south had about 100,000 officers and men, powerful cavalry forces, armoured trains, tanks, and aircraft.

At a time when all the attention and strength of the Soviet Republic was directed towards the struggle with Kolchak, Denikin's army marched out from the northern Caucasus onto the expanses of steppe between the Volga and the lower reaches of the Dnieper, seized the broad districts of the Lower Volga, the Don region and the eastern Ukraine, and captured Tsaritsyn, the Donets basin, and Kharkov. In its advance, the White army swelled its ranks with Don Cossacks and the kulaks—the rich peasants—of the southern Ukraine. In the summer of 1919 Denikin had more than 150,000 officers and men under his command. He made up his mind that with such forces it would be possible to deal a death blow to the Bolsheviks, and on 3rd July issued the order to attack Moscow.

'All against Denikin!'

The centre of gravity of the armed struggle once again swung south. 'All against Denikin!' became the nation's slogan as Denikin moved towards Moscow during the summer months. Kursk was taken on 20th September. In a concentrated attack, specially selected divisions of the 'Volunteer Army' reached Orel. From here it was no distance to Tula, the chief arsenal of Soviet Russia. And beyond Tula lay Moscow. For the first time in the whole course of the war, White Guards had broken into the central regions of the country.

All possible reserves were thrown into the southern front. The fighting reached unprecedented fierceness as powerful shock forces, concentrated by the Soviet command in the region of Orel and Voronezh, went over to the counter-attack. The White Guards broke into Orel on 13th October, but after a few days they were driven out. Denikin's crack divisions were bloodied and smashed.

Near Voronezh, Soviet cavalry inflicted a crushing defeat on the best cavalry corps in Denikin's army. The southern front's counter-attack soon developed into a general offensive against Denikin throughout the whole southern theatre of the Civil War.

At the beginning of 1920, having cleared the area between Orel and Rostov, the Red Army came out onto the shores of the Sea of Azov and the Black Sea, and in February and March succeeded in routing Denikin's army from the northern Caucasus. A small portion of it managed to retain a stronghold in the Crimea, to be dealt with later.

During the struggle against Kolchak in the east and Denikin in the south, White Guards in the Baltic began an advance on Petrograd under General Yudenich. They were halted, defeated and thrown back into Estonia in November 1919.

In all, the Soviet people had brought about the utter rout of the main forces of the counter-revolution in a single year, between March 1919 and March 1920.

During the spring of 1920 the Soviet people tried to use every peaceful day for work on reconstruction. Armies were converted into labour units, laying aside their rifles for a time to rebuild railways, bridges, factories, and mines.

Russo-Polish War

But at this time, embittered by their recent defeats, the forces of reaction were feverishly preparing new military adventures. Urged on by the rulers of the Allied countries, Poland declared war, and at the beginning of May her armies seized Kiev and part of the Ukraine. But this was a temporary and illusory triumph. The Soviet people sent to the defence of their western frontiers the divisions of a Red Army hardened by many battles.

The Polish invaders were swept out of Soviet territory in the summer of 1920, and the fighting moved into Poland. Soviet troops reached the suburbs of Warsaw and Lwow, but they were obliged to retreat to the frontiers of White Russia and the Ukraine.

Not having the strength to continue the war, the Polish government agreed to conclude peace on terms considerably less advantageous than those proposed by the Soviet government before the war started.

Only then could the Red Army seriously proceed with the liquidation of the last opposition stronghold. General Wrangel – Denikin's successor – still held a considerable part of the southern Ukraine and constituted a serious threat to the Donbass.

Soviet victory

On the night of the third anniversary of the October Revolution, troops of the southern front began the storming of Wrangel's Crimean stronghold. The enemy's defences were destroyed and the Red Army poured into the Crimea in a wide flood. The rout of Wrangel and the final liquidation of Wrangel's forces was accomplished within a few days. On 16th November, the Soviet commander, Frunze, sent Lenin news of the final victory: 'Today our cavalry took Kerch. The southern front is liquidated.'

Thus the Civil War in Russia came to an end. The Socialist revolution had proved that it knew how to defend itself against aggression. The new social and political system had endured the most severe trials and had demonstrated its strength. Now it had to build a new society. (*Translation*)

The Civil War (2)

J. F. N. Bradley

The situation in the Russian empire after the collapse of the Tsarist regime in March 1917 was chaotic. Any disciplined group, military or civilian, could have seized power and several tried to do so. But no one seemed capable of maintaining control for long. In November 1917 it was Lenin's turn and his Bolsheviks' 'armed uprising' proved immediately successful. It was the Bolsheviks who really began the Russian Civil War when, on 9th September 1917, their central committee voted for Lenin's proposal to stage a *coup d'état* in Petrograd and overthrow the socialist-dominated Provisional Government.

Although the faction's name, the *Bolsheviki*, signified the majority, they were in fact a minority faction of the Russian Social Democratic Workers' Party, and it was obvious that in order to keep power they would have to fight for it. Almost immediately after the coup, the Bolsheviks were challenged by one single, demoralized Cossack division and only political shrewdness helped them beat it off. After some inconclusive fighting near Petrograd, the Cossacks were persuaded to go home peacefully when the Bolshevik leaders promised to do the same. The opposing groups promised to exchange their leaders as an expression of peaceful intentions. The Cossacks handed over their General, Peter Krasnov, but Lenin never arrived in return; neither was he dismissed as prime minister, although this was one of the conditions for peaceful withdrawal.

However, this was only the first engagement in the Civil War and real fighting broke out as soon as the Bolsheviks began to extend their power to the provinces. In fact their progress was very slow and it took them almost a month to take over the supreme army headquarters and over three months to control the armies themselves. Nonetheless, by February 1918, the Bolsheviks had succeeded in crushing even the two chief provincial protagonists, the Ukrainian nationalists and the Cossack Don Union. Though the two regimes were militarily defeated and their territories occupied, they were far from destroyed. Their armed forces simply withdrew, the Ukrainians under German protection, the Cossacks into the steppes, and after regrouping they were back within two months claiming their territories from the Bolsheviks.

To this day, Soviet historians disagree among themselves as to when the Civil War actually started. Opponents and enemies were cropping up, disappearing and emerging again from 1917 to 1920, and only one thing seemed assured: the Bolsheviks could deal with them all, one by one. Military victories gave them confidence enough to try their hand at more peaceful pursuits. In December 1917, when already in power, they permitted the first and last free general election in the country. But the results proved disappointing: they did manage to get some ten million votes, but the Socialist Revolutionaries amassed some sixteen million and even the persecuted liberals got almost two million. Lenin simply chose to ignore the election and opted for the 'military' solution. Success seemed assured: he was a purposeful leader, and a strict party disciplinarian with single-minded ruthlessness – qualities which none of his opponents could boast. Above all, the rank and file Bolsheviks had a particular, Russian brand of the messianic Communist faith; they firmly believed that they were bringing progress and a superior social order to the backward Russian empire. Initially, they put this faith into practice: their first two acts were to pull Russia out of the war and give the peasants all the land they had taken from the landlords. Thereafter, they concentrated on the Civil War.

The Bolsheviks' enemies

There was the possibility of a political solution to the crisis. After all, the Bolsheviks had had, since late November 1917, a coalition partner, though a reluctant and uncertain one, the left-wing faction of the Socialist Revolutionaries. But from the start, the partners mistrusted each other.

In March 1918 the Left Socialist Revolutionaries were kicked out of the coalition. An attempted uprising four months later was easily suppressed. Lenin and his party could proceed with the Civil War.

By concluding a separate peace with the Central Powers, the Bolsheviks incurred the hostility of the Allies, which complicated the Civil War and considerably delayed Bolshevik victory. Until November 1918 the Allies could do nothing against the Bolsheviks except issue empty threats and moral condemnations. It is true that in March 1918 the Allies managed to land token forces at Murmansk, Vladivostok, and then at Archangel, but ostensibly only to protect Allied war materials.

Lenin quickly used these pinpricks to justify the Civil War and to enforce party discipline. His argument was that the Allies first bled Russia white in the war and then proceeded to interfere in her domestic affairs.

In May 1918 the Czechoslovak Legion, an army corps composed mainly of Czech and Slovak prisoners-of-war destined for the Western Front via the Trans-Siberian Railway and Vladivostok, rebelled against the Bolsheviks, and Lenin could again appeal to Russian patriotism against this 'foreign' interference.

The Czechs had been unwilling conscripts into the Austro-Hungarian army, and now welcomed the chance to fight for the Allies, who had promised to free Czechoslovakia from Austro-Hungarian rule. But there was mutual distrust between the Legion and the Bolsheviks, who had just concluded peace with Germany. The Czechs increasingly feared action against them and the Bolsheviks suspected them of being used by the Allies.

The balance of trust finally broke over an incident in Chelyabinsk. The Czechs in revolt became masters of the central Volga region and Siberia overnight. Their success was the signal for a general civil war. Every opponent of the Bolsheviks anywhere in Russia began to make his bid. The Socialist Revolutionaries immediately staged a series of uprisings in central Russia — in Vladimir, Rybinsk, Kazan, Simbirsk, and of course also in Moscow. After bloody fighting, they were all crushed and the Bolsheviks remained masters of central Russia for the duration of the Civil War.

In the Volga region, the Socialist Revolutionaries proved more successful, under the protective umbrella of the Czech Corps. They were able to form a small army, but, more important, they convened the Constituent Assembly whose members were elected in December 1917 and in which they were the majority party. The Assembly was to elect a new Russian government which would gradually take over from the Bolsheviks. Ultimately, a broadly-based Directory emerged from this rump Assembly, but its army proved weak. In September 1918 the Bolsheviks counter-attacked, the Czech Corps gave way and retired behind the Urals to Siberia, the Volga region was reoccupied by the Bolsheviks, and the Assembly, the Directory, and its little army were swept away, or retreated to join the Siberians.

In November 1918 the Bolsheviks had three main opponents: the Siberian Whites, who had a regional government and were building up an army while the Czechoslovak Corps still protected them; the Ukrainian nationalists, who had reestablished their separate state in March 1918 with German aid; and the Don Cossacks and southern Whites who re-established their Union in May 1918 after the Germans had dealt the Bolshevik armies a severe blow just before the Peace of Brest Litovsk. In comparison with the engagements that had followed Lenin's November coup, these new opponents promised a real fight, and the Bolsheviks were forced to build up a new army to deal with the situation. Trotsky became war commissar and soon proved successful.

When large-scale fighting began in May, the Bolsheviks controlled only a few Red Guard (workers' militia) detachments, several units of Baltic sailors, and a sprinkling of army formations which were not demobilized or did not desert. But Trotsky was fortunate to have under his control a whole rifle division. They were the Latvian Rifle Regiments whose country was occupied by the Germans. They refused to disband and threw in their lot with the Bolsheviks shortly after the November coup. Round this nucleus Trotsky built up his new Red Army into which he forced the unwilling peasants and former Tsarist officers. He stiffened it with Bolshevik workers and political commissars. This haphazard army then took on all their opponents, and eliminated them;

but it took over two years to do so, and the issue was often in the balance.

In the meantime, the First World War came to an end and the German and Austro-Hungarian armies began to withdraw from Russia. The Bolsheviks made great efforts to seize as much territory left empty by the Germans as possible, but did not succeed in putting out of action Germany's 'allies', the Don Union and the Ukrainians. The Ukrainians staged an internal coup, a left-wing government took over from the German-protected Hetman Skoropadsky and the Bolsheviks were kept in check for the time being. The Don now subordinated itself to the Volunteer White movement and declared itself pro-Allied. Mercifully the winter put a stop to large-scale fighting, and both sides prepared for the next round in the spring.

With the end of the war, the threats of the western Allies seemed more realistic. But, exhausted by the war, they made no decisive intervention against the Bolsheviks. Instead, they offered the Bolsheviks' opponents moral and material aid. The French landed a colonial division at Odessa in southern Russia which was later joined by two Greek divisions. These forces were to create a protective shield behind which the Volunteer armies of General Denikin would form. In Siberia the situation was similar: under the protective shield of the Czech Corps, the Whites were building up their armies with the aid of Allied experts. In the north-west, General Yudenich was trying to build an army without a protective shield. The newly independent Poles and Ukrainians were constructing their own defences.

But this concentration on military problems ultimately proved fatal. Soon it was clear that Allied military aid would be insufficient and events would prove that the Czech and French 'shields' were completely demoralized and unable to help the Whites. Moreover, the Whites were incapable of creating political movements to back up their new armies, nor were they capable of administering territories under their control. Disunity paralysed all the White efforts and Allied half-measures only sapped White morale still further. The problem in Russia was either to help the Whites defeat the Bolsheviks decisively or not help at all. As it was, the Whites were given surplus war equipment and told that their moral superiority would carry the day.

Spring — the Bolsheviks advance

After the winter lull the first to strike were the Siberians. In March 1919 Admiral Kolchak, who had come to power in Siberia after a *coup d'état* in November 1918, launched his offensive and was surprisingly successful. His armies advanced a considerable distance from the Urals to the Volga, but when the Bolsheviks counter-attacked they panicked and general rout followed. The relatively small Bolshevik army then advanced into Siberia proper, sweeping up all the White armies as it went. Admiral Kolchak was shot by the Bolsheviks at Irkutsk after his erstwhile allies, the Czechoslovak Corps, handed him over. The Corps itself was forced to conclude an armistice with the Bolsheviks and the latter were only stopped when in 1920 they reached the maritime province occupied by the Japanese army. Only two years later did the Japanese withdraw, leaving the Whites to their Bolshevik opponents.

In southern Russia, General Denikin succeeded in building up considerable armies which he launched in July 1919 with orders to capture Moscow. But once again political weakness robbed the Volunteers of their military victory. General Denikin's regime was purely military. The armies were backed by a political council which contained representatives from all the Russian political parties, but they were bent on neutralizing each other, not winning a war nor supporting their armies. Thus, after initial military victories, the politicians refused to follow their armies to install civilian administrations in the conquered territories, and explain their policies to the population. Instead, the 'liberated' learned that the White military masters were as bad as the Bolsheviks. Their rule would probably mean the return of former landlords whose land the peasants were tilling. This lack of civilian support slowed down the White advance and military incompetence led to final collapse. By January 1920 General Denikin was back where he started, in southern Russia. A *coup* removed him from the leadership, but his successor, General Wrangel, lingered on only until the Bolsheviks could concentrate sufficient forces against him to finish him off. In November 1920 the Red Army broke into the Crimea. Some two million Whites were evacuated and the Volunteer and Cossack movements in the south eliminated.

While fighting Denikin and Wrangel, the Bolsheviks had to deal with several other purely military threats. Perhaps the most dangerous one was that of General Yudenich who collected a motley army in the Baltic provinces and struck twice against Petrograd. At his second attempt, in November 1919, his armies reached the suburbs of Petrograd. The offensive was halted, a panicky retreat ensued and Yudenich's army ended in complete dissolution.

The other blow the Bolsheviks had to parry was a combined Polish-Ukrainian drive with the object of restoring the Ukraine to the nationalists. Previously Ukrainian nationalists had been defeated by the combined onslaught of the Bolsheviks, Volunteers, and the very Poles who were now their allies. The Ukrainian left-wing leaders called on the peasantry to support the Polish armies which invaded under Marshal Piłsudski and took the capital, Kiev, within three weeks. But few Ukrainians joined the Poles. They were easily outmanoeuvred by the Bolsheviks, who forced them to retreat to Poland and even threatened the Polish capital, until Piłsudski drove the Bolsheviks back to Russia. The peace he concluded with them in 1921 marked the end of the Civil War.

The Intervention

Martin Gilbert

For the first four years of Bolshevik rule in Russia Great Britain did its utmost to destroy Lenin's regime. British troops and guns were pitted against the Bolshevik armies on every frontier of Russia. By March 1919 the Bolsheviks had been thrown out of vast areas of Russia, including the fertile grainlands of the Ukraine. British money poured into the coffers of the White forces, Russian troops raised under the banner of counter-revolution. On all fronts, the anti-Bolshevik armies were sustained by British moral encouragement and financial support. It was only the grim determination of the Bolshevik leaders which enabled Bolshevism to survive.

Such is the story which every Russian and most Englishmen believe. They also believe that the policy of intervention was planned and carried out by 'the warmonger' Winston Churchill. But the opening of the vast British government archives of this period paints quite a different picture. The disagreements in the cabinet, the proposals made privately by ministers, the secret telegrams, the War Office orders, the Foreign Office discussions are now all open to the public gaze.

When Bolshevism came to Russia in November 1917 Great Britain was at war with Germany. For Lloyd George, the Prime Minister, the only danger Lenin presented was that he would take Russia out of the war. Since 1914 Great Britain had depended upon Russian support, if only to tie down millions of German soldiers on the Eastern Front. Lloyd George feared that if Lenin made peace, these Germans could be sent to the west, and might well turn the tide against Great Britain by the spring of 1918. The first War Cabinet meeting to discuss the Russian revolution was held on 10th December 1917. The minutes of the cabinet discussion show that ministers were agreed that every effort should be made to keep Russia in the war. 'It was difficult,' said one minister, 'to foretell how strong the Bolsheviks might become or how long their power might last; but if, as seemed likely, they maintained an ascendancy for the next few months only, these months were critical, and to antagonize them needlessly would be to throw them into the arms of Germany.'

For the next few months every effort was made by Lloyd George's agents in Russia to reach some agreement with Lenin. But Lenin was determined to make peace with Germany and not to fight on as Great Britain's ally. He denounced the war as an 'imperialist war' which working people the world over should oppose, and indeed much of the support which the Bolshevik government received came directly from Lenin's promise to end the war as soon as possible.

Although Lloyd George continued to seek negotiations with Lenin, at the same time, in order to protect the vast military stores which Great Britain had sent to Russia before the revolution, he sent British troops to the ports of Archangel, Murmansk, and Vladivostok. They were ordered to prevent the stores from falling into German hands.

The War Cabinet also decided to support any group of Russians who would agree to go on fighting against the Germans. Many of these groups were also anti-Bolshevik; but Lloyd George made it clear to the War Cabinet that he personally had no intention of using these Russian groups to fight Bolshevism. His aim was to defeat the Germans. One minister pointed out: 'We must either support the Ukrainians, Cossacks, Georgians, and Armenians, or the Bolsheviks: we could not do both. It would be impossible to go on any longer running two horses.' Lloyd George, however, continued both to negotiate with Lenin and to support his enemies.

From January to November 1918 the anti-Bolshevik armies received British guns and ammunition, military advisers, tanks, and even planes. In theory, all this help was for fighting Germany; but in practice it went increasingly to fight Bolshevism. The policy of helping Russians who would fight against Lenin was tacitly approved by the War Cabinet. Most ministers hoped that, somehow or another, Bolshevism would be defeated, and a strong, anti-German government would return to Russia. But War Cabinets which watched intervention grow in this way did not include the man always thought of as the principal activist in all anti-Bolshevik activity — Winston Churchill. He took no part in their discussions and made no effort to influence them from outside.

In March 1918 the Bolsheviks finally made peace with Germany. There was great bitterness in British government and military circles that Russia had pulled out of the war. The Bolsheviks suddenly appeared, not as cranks or mere revolutionaries, but as traitors. They had sabotaged the Allied cause. As a result a feeling arose, particularly in the War Office, that Great Britain should now help the anti-Bolshevik Russians, not only to halt the Germans, but also to destroy Lenin and his regime. This was the beginning of the open policy of intervention. Churchill was still not a member of the War Cabinet and played no part in this decision.

By the autumn of 1918 the Bolsheviks were showing an increasing capacity for violence. They had suppressed the Constituent Assembly which had been elected just after the October Revolution. They imprisoned or shot their opponents, even those on the left. As the war in the west drew to a close, the British government became alarmed that to the east, in Russia, a regime of terror was being created.

Murder in the embassy

On 31st August 1918 Bolshevik troops broke into the British embassy in Petrograd. The British naval attaché, Captain Cromie, tried to prevent them from searching the building. Shooting began, and after killing three Bolshevik soldiers, Cromie was killed. A Foreign Office telegram reached London on 3rd September, sending a shudder of anger and apprehension through the whole government: *'The archives were sacked and everything was destroyed. Captain Cromie's corpse was treated in a horrible manner. The cross of St George was taken from the body and subsequently worn by one of the murderers. English clergyman was refused permission to repeat prayers over the body ... Bolsheviks in the Press openly incite to murder British and French. It is urgently necessary that prompt and energetic steps be taken.'*

The War Cabinet met on 4th September. The First Lord of the Admiralty paid a tribute to Cromie, who had 'apparently died in a very gallent manner, remaining behind on duty at the Embassy . . . the only man left and defending himself to the end'. The War Cabinet discussed what was to be done. It was feared that all British representatives in Russia might now be in grave danger. Indeed the Foreign Secretary went so far as to say that he thought 'that the British representatives had all been killed'. They therefore decided to send a severe telegram to the Soviet government 'threatening reprisals against Trotsky, Lenin, and the leaders of that government if the lives of British subjects were not safeguarded'.

Cromie's death created a new mood within the government. The War Cabinet agreed with General Smuts, the South African leader, when he told them that 'Bolshevism was a danger to the whole world' and that definite steps should be taken to defeat it. But it was easier to argue such a policy than to carry it out. Scattered about the periphery of Russia were a host of anti-Bolshevik groups, Russians, Ukrainians, Czechs, Italians, French, Japanese, Americans, and British. But the geography of Russia made it almost impossible for them to link up with each other, while each group thought the other should be doing more for the common cause. The War Cabinet often discussed what they considered to be the failure of the French and Americans to pull their weight effectively. They resented the fact that the principal 'burden' of intervention fell on British shoulders.

The strongest argument in favour of massive intervention was put before the War Cabinet in November 1918. It came from the man whom Lloyd George has sent to negotiate with Lenin in the early days of the revolution, Bruce Lockhart. He, too, had suffered personally as the regime grew more savage. From being a respected emissary of the British government he had ended in a Russian prison. In a long memorandum written immediately after his release he informed the War Cabinet of the wide extent of Bolshevik terror. He wrote vividly of 'executions on a wholesale scale', of a policy of 'depriving all opponents of Bolshevism of everything they possess', of the widespread 'confiscation of their treasures, furniture and jewellery and even clothes', and of prison conditions so foul 'that they can only fitly be compared with the horrors of India and China'. Bruce Lockhart warned the War Cabinet that 'the Bolshevik leaders are not working-men. They are a band of intellectuals, some of them of great intelligence, who have been studying international revolution for years, and who have a dangerous knowledge of the best means of exploiting class hatred'.

Bruce Lockhart urged the government to intervene with British troops in force. 'We should do more by proceeding openly against the "Bolsheviks",' he urged, 'than by trying to suppress them surreptitiously.' Not only would the destruction of Bolshevism save the Russians from tyranny, it would also 'give the Allies a predominant economic position in Russia. It will be more than paid for by economic concessions . . . by restoring order in Russia at once not only are we preventing the spread of Bolshevism as a political danger, but we are also saving for the rest of Europe the rich and fertile grain districts of the Ukraine, which in the event of half measures, or no measures at all, will be rendered sterile by anarchy and revolution'.

The War Cabinet considered Bruce Lockhart's recommendations. The war with Germany was at that very moment coming to an end. Many ministers realized that the British people had had enough of war and might not support a government which told them they must fight on, this time against Russia. A special conference was held at the Foreign Office on 13th November, of which Balfour, the Foreign Secretary, was chairman. It concluded that the British government could not embark on an anti-Bolshevik crusade in Russia: 'It was natural that our advisers on the spot should take a direct line as they were obsessed with the external and visible violence of Bolshevism. On the other hand, the people of this country would not consent to such a crusade.' At the same time the conference felt that Great Britain 'must continue to support all the anti-Bolshevik forces already relying heavily upon us'. These resolutions were contradictory. If we had no intention of trying to destroy Bolshevism, it was clear that our support for the anti-Bolshevik forces could only be half-hearted.

With the ending of the German war, a new figure suddenly emerged as a champion of intervention: Winston Churchill. During the last year of the war he had been too busy as Minister of Munitions to become involved in the discussions of action against Bolshevism. He was not even a member of the War Cabinet. But when the war ended Lloyd George made him Secretary of State for War and brought him into the War Cabinet. Churchill immediately took a strong anti-Soviet view. He was convinced, he told the Imperial War Cabinet on 31st December, that 'Bolshevism in Russia represented a mere fraction of the population and would be exposed and swept away by a general election held under Allied auspices'.

Churchill, champion of intervention
Churchill now stood forward as the strongest opponent of Bolshevism in the government. But he knew that the British army would mutiny rather than fight against the Russians, for they were weary of war and pressing increasingly for demobilization. He realized that if Bolshevism was to be overthrown by force, all the Allied armies must play a part: Great Britain could not do it alone. Churchill even told the Imperial War Cabinet that he would prefer a settlement without fighting; but he considered 'that there was no chance of securing such a settlement unless it was known that we had the power and the will to enforce our views. What we should say to the Russians was that if they were ready to come together we would help them: and that if they refused we would use force to . . . set up a democratic government'. Churchill was opposed to the restoration of Tsarism, and was also against the return of land to the landlords.

Lloyd George opposed Churchill's suggestion to use force. He had made up his mind that nothing Great Britain could do would destroy the Bolshevik regime. For over a year Great Britain had antagonized and castigated Lenin and his regime. That regime had survived. It was far stronger than anyone could have forecast a year before. There was no doubt that it was ruthless; but it was also successful. Lloyd

George knew the dangers of an anti-Soviet policy: in Russia, he told the Imperial War Cabinet, 'we were, in fact, never dealing with ascertained, or, perhaps, even ascertainable, facts. Russia was a jungle in which no one could say what was within a few yards of him . . .' Lloyd George stressed that he was 'definitely opposed to military intervention in any shape'.

Lloyd George then turned to the representatives of Australia, New Zealand, Canada, and South Africa. He asked them 'what contributions Australia, Canada, New Zealand or South Africa were prepared to furnish to the task of conquering and keeping down Russia'. He warned them that 'no British troops could be found for the purpose without conscription, and if Parliament endorsed conscription for that purpose he doubted whether the troops would go'. Finally Lloyd George impressed upon them that Great Britain was unable to launch an anti-Bolshevik crusade: 'Our citizen army were prepared to go anywhere for liberty but they could not be convinced that the suppression of Bolshevism was a war for liberty . . . for Russia to emancipate herself from Bolshevism would be a blessing but the attempt to emancipate her by foreign armies might prove a disaster to Europe as well as to Russia. The one thing to spread Bolshevism was to attempt to suppress it. To send our soldiers to shoot down the Bolsheviks would be to create Bolshevism here'.

Although Churchill was Secretary of State for War, he could not pursue an independent policy. Like all War Cabinet ministers, he was bound by the policy which the War Cabinet as a whole laid down, and he had at all times to accept its ruling. Throughout January and February 1919 the War Cabinet discussed what to do about Russia, but would not commit itself to sending further British troops. Churchill was anxious for more active intervention. He pressed his cause as strongly as possible. Many of the cabinet agreed with him that Bolshevism was a danger to world peace. All of them had read the reports of Bolshevik atrocities which appeared in the press. All had seen the telegrams in which Bolshevik violence was detailed.

A particularly lurid report was received in the Foreign Office on 11th February and immediately circulated by Lord Curzon. The report, which was marked secret, described the Estonian victims of a Russian attack:

'All the bodies showed signs of the rage and revenge of the Bolsheviks. The victims were all robbed of everything except their linen, their boots also having been taken. The Bolsheviks had shattered the skulls of thirty-three of the bodies, so that the heads hung like bits of wood on the trunks. As well as being shot, most of the murdered had been pierced with bayonets, the entrails torn out, and the bones of the arm and leg broken.'

The effect of Bolshevik terror was overwhelming. But so, also, was the realization that British soldiers would not relish war against Russia. When, on 12th February, Churchill urged the War Cabinet to intervene on a massive scale, Lloyd George countered by pointing out that 'if we were going to do any good we should need a million men at least'. Churchill bowed to Lloyd George's argument, to which he had no answer, and was forced to agree, rather lamely, 'that intervention on a large scale was not possible'. He accepted the view of the War Cabinet that all the government could do was to help the anti-Bolshevik forces already fighting around the perimeter of Russia. For all his pugnacity, Churchill was a realist. While he hated all that Bolshevism stood for, he knew that there was almost nothing that Great Britain could do without a vast army to support its action. In public he continually spoke and wrote with vigour, and even venom, against Lenin and his regime. But less than a month after he became Secretary of State for War, he had to accept a policy of non-intervention.

Let Russia save herself

The final decision rested with Lloyd George, for he had the power to persuade the vacillating War Cabinet to whatever courses he chose. Despairingly, Churchill pressed for a lead either way: 'If we were going to withdraw our troops,' he said, 'it should be done at once. If we were going to intervene we should send large forces.' In mid-February Lloyd George made up his mind, and in two telegrams to Churchill in Paris on 16th February he laid down what was soon to become official British policy:

'The main idea ought to be to enable Russia to save herself if she desires to do so and *if she does not take advantage of opportunity then it means either that she does not wish to be saved from Bolshevism or that she is beyond saving.*

'There is only one justification for interfering in Russia, that Russia wants it. If she does then Kolchak, Yudenitch and Denikin [the leaders of the anti-Bolshevik armies] ought to be able to raise more forces than Bolsheviks. These forces we could equip and a well equipped force of willing men would soon overthrow Bolshevik armies of unwilling conscripts especially if the whole population is against them.

'If on the other hand Russia is not behind Kolchak, Yudenitch and Denikin, it is an outrage on every British principle of freedom that we should use foreign armies to force upon Russia a government which is repugnant to its people.'

In the second telegram to Churchill Lloyd George argued even more forcefully:

'If Russia is really anti-Bolshevik then a supply of equipment would enable it to redeem itself. If Russia is pro-Bolshevik, not merely is it none of our business to interfere with its internal forces, it would be positively mischievous. It would strengthen and consolidate Bolshevik opinion.

'An expensive war of aggression against Russia is a way of strengthening Bolshevism in Russia and creating it at home. We cannot afford the burden . . . if we are committed to a war against a continent like Russia, it is the road to bankruptcy and Bolshevism in these islands.'

Confronted by Lloyd George's determination, there was nothing that Churchill could do other than reiterate his opinions. Lloyd George ignored them. By the end of February Churchill had, with great reluctance, to bow to Lloyd George's pressure. He continued to state his own arguments. But he knew that he could not prevail against the Prime Minister. In a series of private letters to Lloyd George, in speeches in the House of Commons, in statements to the War Cabinet, Churchill continued to warn his colleagues and the country about what he considered the real danger to the world if Bolshevism triumphed in Russia. He did his utmost to support the anti-Bolshevik forces. But once the decision went against him in the War Cabinet his was a voice crying in the wilderness, angry but impotent – and he knew it.

At the end of February the War Cabinet, pressed by Lloyd George, decided definitely against British intervention in Russia. All British troops then on Russian soil were to be withdrawn. Churchill could do no more than concur in these decisions, which he had no power to alter in any way. During the whole of Churchill's period as Secretary of State for War he was not responsible for sending a single British soldier to fight in Russia. All the British troops on Russian soil had been sent there before he went to the War Office. Publicly, Churchill made himself the spokesman for an anti-Bolshevik crusade. But there was no such crusade. Instead, for the nine months following the decision of the War Cabinet, he supervised the withdrawal of British troops from Russia.

Nevertheless, throughout 1919 Churchill bombarded Lloyd George with letters and memoranda, urging stronger British military support for the anti-Bolshevik armies. On 14th March he wrote to Lloyd George: 'I apprehend that after numerous possibilities and opportunities have been lost and great potential resources have been dissipated, we shall nevertheless be drawn, in spite of all your intentions, into the clutches of the Russian problem.' He was convinced that 'when the whole of the Caucasus and Trans Caspia have fallen into Bolshevik power, when their armies are menacing Persia and Afghanistan and their missionaries are at the gates of India, when one after another the Border states in the West have been undermined by want and propaganda, or overborne by criminal violence, not only the League of Nations but the British Empire, with which we are particularly concerned, will wake up to the fact that Russia is not a negligible factor in world politics'.

On 9th April he wrote bitterly that if Germany followed Russia's example and went Bolshevik she might escape all the consequences of the war: 'Once you are a Bolshevist you are apparently immune. All past crimes are forgiven and forgotten; all past sentences are remitted and all debts are forgiven; all territory that you want to have is restored to you. You may fight anybody you like and nobody may fight against you. The armies of the victorious Allies are impotent against you.' On 5th May he warned that: 'The overthrow of Bolshevism in Russia is indispensable to anything in the nature of a lasting peace and will cut off from Germany every refuge from Bolshevism which she may seek in her despair.'

These letters continued throughout the year. To most of them Lloyd George gave no reply, and when he did reply it was only to rebuke.

Churchill reprimanded

By September Lloyd George was sufficiently provoked by Churchill's constant harping on Russia to write what is surely one of the strongest letters ever sent from a Prime Minister to a cabinet colleague. For many weeks Lloyd George had been urging Churchill to make proposals for cutting down general military expenditure over the whole field of War Office activity. But for Churchill the Russian problem still dominated all else.

Lloyd George was exasperated. His patience was now at an end. He wrote to Churchill on 22nd September 1919: 'You know that I have been doing my best for the last few weeks to comply with the legitimate demand which comes from all classes of the country to cut down the enormous expenditure which is devouring the resources of the country at a prodigious rate. I have repeatedly begged you to apply your mind to the problem. I made this appeal to all departments, but I urged it specially upon you for three reasons. The first is that the highest expenditure is still military; the second that the largest immediate reductions which could be effected without damage to the public welfare are foreseeable in the activities controlled by your Department. The third is that I have found your mind so obsessed by Russia that I felt I had good ground for the apprehension that your great abilities, energy, and courage were not devoted to the reduction of expenditure.

'I regret that all my appeals have been in vain. At each interview you promised me to give your mind to this very important problem. Nevertheless the first communication I have always received from you after these interviews related to Russia. I invited you to Paris to help me to reduce our commitments in the East. You then produce a lengthy and carefully prepared memorandum on Russia. I entreated you on Friday to let Russia be for at least 48 hours; and to devote your weekend to preparing for the Finance Committee this afternoon. You promised faithfully to do so. Your reply is to send me a four-page letter on Russia, and a closely printed memorandum of several pages – all on Russia. I am frankly in despair.

'. . . The various Russian enterprises have cost us this year between £100 and £150 millions, when Army, Navy and Shipping are taken into account. Neither this Government nor any other Government that this country is likely to see will do more. We cannot afford it. The French have talked a good deal about Anti-Bolshevism, but they have left it to us to carry out the Allied policy.

'. . . I wonder whether it is any use my making one last effort to induce you to throw off this obsession which, if you will forgive me for saying so, is upsetting your balance. I again ask you to let Russia be, at any rate for a few days, and to concentrate your mind on the quite unjustifiable expenditure in France, at home and in the East, incurred by both the War Office and the Air Department. Some of the items could not possibly have been tolerated by you if you had given one-fifth of the thought to these matters which you devoted to Russia.

'. . . you won't find another responsible person in the whole land who will take your view, why waste your energy and your usefulness on this vain fretting which completely paralyses you for other work?

'I have worked with you now for longer than I have probably co-operated with any other man in public life: and I think I have given you tangible proof that I wish you well. It is for that reason that I write frankly to you.'

White atrocities

By January 1920 the anti-Bolshevik forces, of whose victory Churchill was confident, were decisively defeated by the Red Army. During the previous year the British government had authorized over £150,000,000 to support them. Churchill had supervised the distribution of this money in arms and equipment. This was the only positive action in support of the anti-Bolsheviks.

During 1919 the anti-Bolsheviks had resorted to atrocities of their own. These had disgusted British opinion. Churchill himself frequently protested with great vigour to Denikin of the anti-Semitic atrocities which White forces committed wherever they advanced. By the end of 1919 over 100,000 Jews had been butchered in south Russia. The Whites had also tried to restore to landlords their estates and hinted also at the restoration of the Russian monarchy. Churchill and Lloyd George both agreed that such actions were intolerable. White Russian stupidity and savagery drew many Russians to support Lenin's regime. They also alienated most of those in Great Britain who wished to continue an anti-Bolshevik crusade, including Churchill himself. He still hated all that Bolshevism stood for – suppression of individual liberty, terror, and the call for world revolution. But he could not wax enthusiastic about the existing alternative. He was willing to go on fighting Bolshevism until a democratic, parliamentarian Russia emerged; but he knew that such a solution was becoming increasingly remote.

Lloyd George respected Churchill's opinions. But he was now determined, not only to stop all intervention, but even to come to some agreement with the Bolshevik regime. He persuaded his cabinet that intervention was too costly and too unpopular to be worthwhile. Of the anti-Bolshevik rulers only General Wrangel survived, but in a battered state. The cabinet therefore agreed to negotiate with Lenin, and warned Wrangel not to provoke further hostilities. Wrangel decided to advance, and the cabinet at once cut off all support for him: on 3rd June 1920 he received a blunt telegram from the admiral commanding the British Black Sea Fleet: *'Sir, I beg to inform you that I have received a message from the British High Commissioner at Constantinople directing me to inform you that His Majesty's Government are a good deal disquieted by rumours of your intention to take the offensive against the bolchevik forces. I am also directed to inform you that if you attack, His Majesty's Government's plans for negotiating with the Soviet Government will inevitably fall through and His Majesty's Government will be unable to concern themselves any further with the fate of your army.*

I have the honour to be, Sir,
Your obedient servant,
(Signed) G. Hope Rear-Admiral'
Churchill did not like this policy, but he

had no political power to reverse it. He depended upon Lloyd George's friendship for his place in the cabinet. If he resigned, there was nowhere he could turn for a base to influence events. During 1920 he continued to write ferociously against Lenin and his regime. But in terms of positive action he knew that he was powerless. When the Red Army advanced into Poland he shared, with Lloyd George, the belief that the Poles had provoked the Bolshevik attack. Whereas, in public, he defended the Poles, in cabinet he could do nothing but accept Lloyd George's policy. In a final effort to rouse public opinion, he wrote on 28th July 1920 a strong article, 'The Poison Peril From the East', in the *Evening News*. But its theme was not a call for British action; instead, Churchill appealed to the Germans to take up the cudgels of democracy: 'It will be open to the Germans either to sink their own social structure in the general Bolshevist welter and spread the reign of chaos far and wide throughout the Continent; or, on the other hand, by a supreme effort of sobriety, of firmness, of self-restraint and of courage – undertaken, as most great exploits have to be, under conditions of peculiar difficulty and discouragement – to build a dyke of peaceful, lawful, patient strength and virtue against the flood of red barbarism flowing from the East, and thus safeguard their own interests and the interests of their principal antagonists in the West.

'If the Germans were able to render such a service, not by vainglorious military adventure or with ulterior motives, they would unquestionably have taken a giant step upon that path of self-redemption which would lead them surely and swiftly as the years pass by back to their own great place in the councils of Christendom, and would have rendered easier that sincere co-operation between Britain, France and Germany on which the very salvation of Europe depends.'

The public did not like this theme. Hatred of Germany was still too strong. Churchill had a new warcry: 'Kill the Bolshie, Kiss the Hun'; but there was no one willing to echo it. His desire for reconciliation with the new, democratic Germany, like his implacable hostility towards Bolshevik tyranny, found few supporters. To the public it smacked of adventurism and irresponsibility; proof of Churchill's lack of balance and desire for notoriety. Yet Churchill was sincere and serious: he saw the twin dangers to Europe of Bolshevism rampant and Germany isolated.

In November 1920 Lloyd George took the final initiative: he urged his colleagues to accept a trade treaty with the Bolsheviks. He used all his powers of persuasion to achieve his objective. The verbatim record of the cabinet meeting on 12th November shows him in action, and triumphant. Such a detailed account, in the first person, is rare even among cabinet records: 'I have deferred a good deal,' Lloyd George told the cabinet, 'to the feelings of some of my colleagues and I must now make up my mind. It is a decision of the first magnitude. If we take a wrong turning it will be a responsibility which we shall regret. If we allow our judgment to be deflected by natural repugnance the people of this country will visit it on us. There has been too much considering all this as conferring a boon on Bolshevik Russia. Our hatred leads us to say we would rather hurt ourselves than do them good.

'But we have primarily got to consider our interests for we are in for a bad time. I have seen a good many business men and they have rather frightened me about the next 18 months. Bonar Law and I met Rylands, the Chairman of the Federation of British Industries, and he was not in a position to challenge the view taken by business men. There are no orders coming in. Customers won't buy. We may have the worst period of unemployment any of us have known.

'The Russians are prepared to pay in gold and you won't buy. We trade with cannibals in the Solomon Islands. Within the last few days an offer has been made to the British Government for £10 million worth on condition that the order shall be put in this country but I must not give details. I am appalled by the accuracy of the information in the newspapers today about this meeting. In the case of this offer payment will be made by British firms. If we refuse it, it will leak out that we turned it down because . . . we hate the Bolsheviks at a time when we are voting £4 or 5 millions for the unemployed. Of the

£10 million, half of it would be wages. This will be said over and over again and will add to the public discontent.

'. . . In spite of a lot of newspaper propaganda here there has been no response to the campaign to prevent trade with Russia. It was tried in the House of Commons but with no success. When I mentioned the possibility of our going to war to support Poland a shudder passed through the House and those who were clamouring against Bolshevism immediately shewed the white feather. I hope you will allow Horne to negotiate on the basis of the draft agreement of July 1st. If we try to enlarge it we are departing from it. It was circulated at the time. If we make conditions *precedent* it will mean that we are not prepared to trade while there is a Soviet government.

'I have heard predictions about the fall of the Soviet government for the last two years. Denikin, Judenitch, Wrangel, all have collapsed but I cannot see any immediate prospect of the collapse of the Soviet government.'

Lloyd George's argument prevailed. It was only left to Churchill to protest passionately, but ineffectually, against the decision to trade with Russia. 'I object,' he said, 'to helping them out of the difficulties which they have made for themselves by their communism.' But Lloyd George was determined to start trading. He saw no sense, economic or political, in continuing the half-hearted ideological conflict. Churchill's last words to his colleagues were: 'Signing this agreement in no way alters the general position we have taken up as to the Bolsheviks, namely, that Ministers shall be free to point out the odious character of their regime. It seems to me you are on the high road to embrace Bolshevism. I am going to keep off that and denounce them on all possible occasions.'

This he did. But the government of which he was a member signed the trade agreement with Russia and thus opened the first European door to the Bolsheviks. All Churchill's mental anguish, all his forebodings, all his hatred of tyranny counted for nothing when faced with the nimble political skills of David Lloyd George.

The Russo-Polish War

Elizabeth Wiskemann

Towards the end of 1919 circumstances had induced a fairly conciliatory mood – in the short run – in the leaders of Soviet Russia. This state of mind brought about negotiations with the Polish chief of state, Piłsudski, for the exchange of prisoners and the cession of further territory to the Polish forces. Piłsudski was less afraid of the Bolsheviks than of the Tsarist generals who were trying to drive them out because he thought the Tsarists would be more inimical to Poland and the other former nationalities of Russia. By now the Soviet leaders had recognized the independence of the Baltic states and, of course, of Finland. It was Piłsudski who had in the spring of 1919 taken Vilna (Wilno) from Lithuania, although the Russians had recognized it as Lithuanian. By July 1919 the Poles had occupied formerly Austrian Eastern Galicia which the Ukrainians and the Russians regarded as the western Ukraine.

In November 1919 the British prime minister, Lloyd George, made clear that he intended to abandon intervention in Russia, and, on the contrary, to work towards the resumption of trade relations with USSR. Early in 1920 the Tsarist generals, Kolchak and Denikin, were finally defeated by the Bolsheviks. A little later, in the spring of that year, however, Piłsudski decided to use Russia's difficulties to make a bid for the restoration of the Greater Poland of the 18th century. He thought in terms of a Polish 'federation' to include the Ukraine and of course his native Lithuania. On 28th April 1920 he issued a proclamation to all the inhabitants of the Ukraine in this sense, and by 6th May the Poles had occupied the Ukrainian capital, Kiev; they remained there for about five weeks.

The Ukraine, sometimes called Little Russia, was an ill-defined area most of which had belonged to the Tsarist empire. The Ukrainians (or Ruthenes) belonged to the Orthodox Church and their language was close to Russian. Before the partitions of Poland, however, the Poles had exerted a good deal of influence in the Ukraine where the big landowners were often Polish. Parts of old Austria-Hungary had also been Ukrainian, notably Eastern Galicia, and the Ukrainians, after the Habsburg collapse, hoped for an independent Ukrainian state of about 40,000,000 inhabitants. They were divided from the Catholic Poles by religion.

The newly independent Poland, composed of former Russian, Austrian, and German territories, had been brought into existence by the Treaty of Versailles with the Germans in June 1919 and by the Treaty of Saint Germain with Austria a little later. Article 87 of the Treaty of Versailles stated that the Allies would settle Poland's eastern frontier in due course. In December 1919 the British Foreign Office put forward as the solution a line which guessed at the ethnographic and religious frontier between the Catholic Poles and the various near-Russian Slavs of the Orthodox or Uniate faith (the Uniate Church practised Orthodox rites but accepted the religious suzerainty of the Pope, which had been imposed on it by the former Polish masters of the Ukraine). It was fairly accurate, perhaps as accurate as possible. This line was named the Curzon Line after the then British secretary of state for foreign affairs.

It seemed incredible that the armies of the new, apparently polyglot Poland, whose territory had been savagely fought over and wrecked during the war years, could achieve the audacity of advancing far beyond the Curzon Line, to seize Kiev and remain there for five weeks.

The Polish army in the Ukraine consisted of formerly Russian or Austrian or German Polish soldiers who were willing to go on fighting in the east far away from the new Polish-German frontiers which were also being fought over.

The Polish army in the Ukraine included a few younger volunteers. It was ill-equipped, but in consequence relatively mobile. How Piłsudski fed his troops at that time of year, even in the corn-rich

Ukraine, is difficult to explain. In spite of Western hostility to the Soviet government the Polish advance had been undertaken against forcible warnings from the British. It is all the more remarkable to find that a British naval officer, Lieutenant-Commander Rawlings, reported by the British minister in Warsaw to have been in Kiev while the Poles were in occupation, 'was evidently much impressed by the excellent behaviour of the Polish troops in and about Kieff, and with the manner in which order was maintained': this is particularly interesting because this sort of person was often scornful of the Poles, not understanding their problems. When, however, the Red Army took the offensive it is not surprising that the Poles were quickly driven out, evacuating Kiev on 11th June 1920.

German hostility

It should be made clear that although the Treaty of Versailles had in theory established Poland's frontiers with Germany these were still fluid, since plebiscites were to be held in Allenstein, Marienwerder, and Upper Silesia: the first two were indeed held on 11th July 1920, but the Upper Silesia one was postponed to March 1921.

Germans felt bitterly anti-Polish, and with Piłsudski's invasion of the Ukraine anti-Polish feeling in Germany reached wild extremes, and jubilation set in when the Poles were obliged to withdraw. On the one hand the old German ruling-class and former officers regarded Russia, whether Red or not, as a natural military ally, and the Ukraine as Germany's legitimate grain-reserve. The advance of the Red Army offered chances of handing over German arms in East Prussia to the Russians, rather than destroying these weapons, as part of Germany's disarmament — anything rather than surrender to the Allies. On the other hand much of the German industrial working class still felt a good deal of sympathy with Soviet Russia; it was also hostile to the Poles as traditionally providing competitive cheap labour. Throughout the Russo-Polish War the German dockers of the newly 'free city' of Danzig tried to prevent arms from passing through the port of Danzig for the Poles. This was a big Polish grievance, but the Allied authorities were naturally loath to use their troops as strike-breakers in Danzig. Czech Communist workers also tried to boycott supplies for Poland.

In July 1920 the Russo-Polish War assumed dimensions of world importance. The Soviet armies continued to advance and the Poles seemed demoralized. Early in July Allied representatives met for the first time with German ones at a conference at Spa in Belgium to consider the distribution of German reparations. The new Polish prime minister, Grabski, appeared at the conference and spoke almost apologetically on his country's behalf. He was repeatedly told (on 9th and 10th July) that the Poles must retire west of the Curzon Line, and that, if they did so and the Russians failed to accept a settlement based on this frontier, the Allied supreme council would do all it could to help Poland. On 11th July a British note — the French agreed, but for technical reasons did not participate — was sent to Chicherin, the Soviet commissar for foreign affairs, demanding an immediate armistice with Poland on the basis of the ethnic frontier. The Spa Conference was also the occasion of the settling of the frontier between the Poles and the Czechs of Teschen; the Poles always felt that their preoccupation with the Russian war brought them a bad deal over this.

'Over the corpse of Poland'

Shortly after the British note was despatched to Chicherin the Second Congress of the Third International (the Comintern) assembled in Moscow. The Russian advance against the Poles was greeted euphorically as the advance of the world revolution. 'Our way towards world-wide conflagration', Tukhachevsky, the Russian commander-in-chief, proclaimed, 'passes over the corpse of Poland.' At the end of July, in spite of Allied protests and those of Trotsky and Stalin, Tukhachevsky led his armies across the Curzon Line into ethnic Poland; he was encouraged to do so by Lenin who still regarded Germany as the goal and the prize of the Communist world revolution, now only fenced off by a fetid Poland. At the end of July, also, senior Allied officers arrived in Warsaw to advise and assist the Poles; the most outstanding of these was General Weygand who had been Marshal Foch's right hand. Weygand placed his services and those of his French subordinates at the disposal of the Polish chief of staff.

Between 4th and 6th August Anglo-Russian conversations took place in London over the possibilities of a Russian-Polish truce. Lloyd George reproached the Russians with their insincerity in invading ethnic Poland and he ordered the British navy to re-impose the blockade against them. Kamenev, the chief Russian representative, complained to Lloyd George about his one-time tutor in Paris, Millerand, now the French prime minister; the latter, Kamenev claimed, was lending support to another anti-Bolshevik general, Wrangel, who was going into action against the Soviet authorities. On 8th August the French arrived to confer with the British at Hythe, and Millerand expressed the much stronger pro-Polish and anti-Soviet feeling in France compared with that in Great Britain. At last on the night of 9th-10th August terms for a Russo-Polish truce were agreed, and the Russian and Polish peace delegations met at Minsk on 11th August. Although the Russians agreed to rectify the Curzon Line in Poland's favour in two places, they demanded the limitation of the Polish professional army and the construction of a workers' militia, the latter a Communist device which Pilsudski and his generals would never have accepted. They need not have feared it, however, for there was next to no Communism in Poland in spite of great social inequality. Most Polish industrial workers were patriotic socialists, while the big majority of Poles were peasants who were devoted patriots. But in any case Piłsudski was thinking in other terms by the middle of August.

Russians driven back

Meanwhile, on 8th August at Hythe the French and British considered the likelihood of the destruction of Poland. On 13th August, with the Russian armies only twelve miles away, the British minister, Sir Horace Rumbold, was ordered to leave Warsaw for Posen or, in Polish, Poznán. On 6th August, however, Weygand and the Polish generals had decided to counter-attack. The Polish troops, traditionally inured to defeat as they were, according to Rumbold, became aware that 'a master mind' was behind them and recovered their morale. Suddenly on 16th August

they counter-attacked the now greatly extended Soviet lines and drove the Russians back, taking thousands of prisoners.

On 24th August Rumbold wrote to Curzon, 'It is a repetition of the defeat of the Turks under the walls of Vienna in 1683. On this occasion a French General played the part of Sobieski.' By that day the Poles had taken 60,000 to 70,000 prisoners and were within sight of clearing the Soviet armies out of ethnic Poland up to the Curzon Line. 'They [the Poles],' Rumbold wrote with engaging naïveté, 'have, I think, been cured of unreasonable and far-reaching ambitions.' On the contrary the British now had the thankless task of begging the victorious Poles, who felt themselves to be the saviours of western Europe, to be moderate. The French government was less eager for Polish moderation and less parental about the Curzon Line; it was also supporting Wrangel. The British, however, saw clearly that an independent non-Communist Poland was a keystone of the peace settlement: indeed thanks to the Russian advance into Poland Lloyd George had abandoned all his efforts to restore British trade with the USSR.

Now the Polish armies swept eastwards and north-eastwards again, and at the beginning of October they were once more ominously near Vilna. Vilna, or Wilno in Polish, was a town with a Polish veneer though the province was much less Polish. In the far past Lithuania and Poland had been united and no problem had arisen about it. Now independent Lithuania wanted Vilna as its capital city, and the Russians had agreed to this. But the new League of Nations was considering Poland's claims. Since the majority of the intellectuals in Vilna probably spoke Polish (the Lithuanian language was completely different), the League would certainly have adjudicated language rights to the Poles in Vilna which the Lithuanians had hitherto not considered. On 10th October, however, General Zeligowski, one of the Polish generals who had taken part in the battle of Warsaw under Sikorski's command, seized Vilna for Poland. After this there were no diplomatic relations between Lithuania and Poland until early in 1938, each side vying with the other in intransigence. That autumn of 1920 the question of Vilna exasperated everyone, particularly Piłsudski, who threatened to resign as head of the Polish state and to enflame the situation by going to Vilna himself.

By the end of August 1920, it has been seen, the Soviet troops had been pushed back to the east of the Curzon Line, and during September the Poles had established positions a good deal farther to the east, although not quite so far as the Russians had been willing to concede in the — for them — unfavourable period at the end of 1919. At Riga in Latvia on 12th October 1920, two days after Zeligowski had seized Vilna, an armistice and preliminary peace treaty was signed between the Poles and the Russians. By the end of the year the Soviet authorities defeated Wrangel, but early in 1921 they had trouble with the Kronstadt Rising. During the winter Poland's economic circumstances seemed desperate. On 18th March 1921 both parties were willing enough to confirm their armistice in the Treaty of Riga. Lenin was still optimistic about world revolution, and regarded the frontiers agreed by this treaty as little more permanent than those agreed by the Treaty of Brest Litovsk.

World revolution halted

Lord D'Abernon, first British ambassador to Germany after the First World War, was in Warsaw in August 1920: he called the Polish victory initiated on 16th August with advice from Weygand the eighteenth decisive battle of the world. Germany at the time was still felt to be politically unstable, and the Soviet threat to stride over the 'corpse of Poland' and touch off Marxist revolution in Germany was taken seriously by the Bolsheviks and also by their enemies. The battle of Warsaw came five months after the Kapp Putsch when the predominantly Social Democratic trade unions had beaten Kapp by striking. But power in the Weimar Republic was already partly in the hands of General von Seeckt and his colleagues who were only pro-Russian abroad; it is not clear whether the trade unions would have preferred the Soviets to Seeckt: judging by Ebert and Noske they would not have done so. What is certain is that Russian mastery of Poland was postponed for twenty-four years. It is clear, too, that the defeat at Warsaw helped to transform the attitudes and policy of the Soviet leaders: the way was prepared for 'socialism in one country' and the New Economic Policy to replace plans for world revolution after the German Communists had failed to assert themselves and Lenin was dead.

The Russo-Polish war of 1920 was not in reality what the Bolsheviks envisaged, not, except in the minds of men like Lenin and Zinovyev, an international crusade. The Russo-Polish feud for the Russian or Polish peasants was an instance of ferocious nationalism garnished with rival religious creeds. The *élan* of the Russian advance in July 1920 was primarily due to Russian patriotic indignation against the Polish occupation of Russia's 'western territories' which were not quite Russian. Then in August the Polish riposte and the Polish advance nearly as far as Minsk were impelled by traditional contempt for the Russians as barbarians, which was tremendously reinforced by the Catholic zeal of nearly all Poles against the atheism of the Communists. There was also enthusiasm for the recapture of Poland's 'eastern territories', which, although they had sometimes belonged to Poland, were scarcely Polish at all, because they were scarcely Catholic at all; where the peasants of Eastern Galicia or White Russia were not Orthodox, they were Uniate. The Treaty of Riga left Poland with some 6,000,000 Ukrainians and White Russians in territories which the Russians regarded as Russian. The German minority in Poland seemed a minor problem by comparison.

The Kronstadt Rising

J. N. Westwood

At the Tenth Congress of the Russian Communist Party in 1921 Lenin intended to introduce radically new policies so as to gain a breathing space and to show that 'proletarian democracy' had not really been abandoned during the ruthless years of 'war Communism'. Among these changes the New Economic Policy would be the most important. That changes were urgently needed was proved by the Kronstadt Rising, which took place while the Congress was in session and, in Lenin's words, 'illuminated reality like a flash of lightning'. For the rebellion of the Baltic Fleet showed that the masses had been pushed too far, that moderation was called for. In rising against the government the rebels made it easier for Lenin to persuade Party members to accept his new line.

Trotsky once described the sailors of the Baltic Fleet as 'the pride and glory of the Revolution'. It had been in the ships and bases of the Baltic Fleet that most blood had been shed in the otherwise relatively peaceful March Revolution; the Tsar's abdication had been a signal for old scores to be settled with ships' officers. In the Bolshevik Revolution of November it was the sailors of the Baltic Fleet who brought the guns of the cruiser *Aurora* to within point-blank range of the Winter Palace in Petrograd. When Lenin decided to dissolve forcibly the Constituent Assembly — freely elected by Russians on 25th November 1917 and lacking a Bolshevik majority — it was the Baltic sailors who were there with their rifles and bayonets. In the drawn-out and bitter fighting of the Civil War, the only Red units which could be relied upon not to dissolve into retreat were the sailors. They were an unruly collection of men, embittered by years of hardship and disciplinarianism suffered in the claustrophobic confines of iron-clads. They often showed contempt for others — especially peasants — fighting in the Red ranks. But they had an underlying sense of what popular democracy meant, and they were willing to fight hard for it. By 1921 many of the sailors of 1917 had disappeared and been replaced by new recruits, but the Baltic sailors still preserved their belief that they were the first rank of the Revolution. The public, too, accepted this, and so did the Bolshevik leaders in their speeches and writings.

The headquarters of the Baltic Fleet was Kronstadt, situated on Kotlin Island, fortified and commanding the sea approach to Petrograd. From December to March the sea is frozen and there is thus good access either to the nearest shore (Russia, five miles distant), or to the more distant northern coastline (Finland). In the town itself there were, apart from soldiers and sailors, many workers and their families. The trade unions had a strong membership there, but of Kronstadt's total population of around 50,000 less than two per cent were Communist Party members.

A second 'pride and glory' of the revolution were the workers of Petrograd, but it was these who in fact set off the Kronstadt Rising. In February 1921 thousands of Petrograd workers came out on strike, and the Red Army cadets sent to prevent their demonstrations took no strong action. The workers' demands were mainly economic, although there were political overtones. In particular, the workers protested against Trotsky's so-called Labour Army, which was simply an organization of strike-breakers selected from the Red Army. They also demanded the freedom to choose and change their jobs, and to elect genuinely chosen representatives to trade union and governmental (soviet) bodies. The presence of armed Communist detachments in the factories and the arrests and executions by the Cheka were also resented, especially now that the Civil War was over.

It was a tradition of the Revolution that the Kronstadt sailors took a fraternal interest in the affairs of the Petrograd workers, and they had the unwritten right to send their delegates to the workers' meetings. These delegates came almost daily, and returned to their ships and barracks to report. At this disturbed time a glaring difference appeared between what the delegates reported and what the Party reported. In particular, the sailors soon noticed that the Party and government were misrepresenting the demands of the workers, were minimizing the seriousness of the strikes and demonstrations, and concealing the repressive measures which the government was beginning to take.

The meetings held in Kronstadt were quite unofficial, but nevertheless, by tradition, influential. Officially Kronstadt was administered by the Kronstadt Soviet of Workers', Sailors', and Soldiers' Deputies. In this body the Communist Party was dominant, largely, the sailors thought, because the Communists rigged the elections. Thus the Party organization in the Baltic Fleet was the power behind the scenes, and the commissars which it appointed to the various ships and barracks were both its ears and its voice.

The sailors' protest

At the end of February a sailors' mass meeting held in the battleship *Petropavlovsk* to discuss the disturbances in Petrograd passed a long resolution which in essence was a list of political demands. These demands had a striking resemblance to what the revolutionaries of 1917 had believed they were fighting for, and reflected the sailors' belief that the Bolsheviks were, for ideological reasons, betraying the very people who had made the revolution.

The first item in the resolution attempted to deal with a fundamental grievance: it stated that, since the existing soviets did not genuinely reflect the wishes of the Russian workers and peasants, new elections should be held, and by secret ballot. Then followed other demands: for freedom of the press and of speech for the workers and peasants and all left-wing groups; for freedom of assembly, especially for trade unionists; for the liberation of all left-wing political prisoners and imprisoned trade unionists, and a review of the cases of all other prisoners; for the freedom of individuals to bring food into the towns from the countryside without fear of confiscation; for peasants and craftsmen to organize their own production provided they did not use hired labour; for the abolition of extra rations for privileged persons; for the withdrawal of armed Communist guards from factories; and for the abolition of the Propaganda Departments (because they were financed by state funds but propagandized only the Communist Party).

At its face value, this resolution was not anti-Bolshevik because for the most part it only repeated the aspirations of 1917, which had never been formally repudiated by the Party. But it did draw attention to the differences between the Party's promises and its performance. It was especially menacing because the Kronstadt sailors had always been considered the guardians of the 'conscience of the Revolution'. Moreover, the Baltic sailors had access to the outside world, and their activities and demands could less easily be concealed than the peasant and urban disturbances which at this time were occurring in the Russian interior.

However, the Party leaders realized that although the demands did not seem too inconsistent with the stated goals of the Party, this resolution and its upholders were perhaps the most dangerous threat they had ever faced. The resolutions plainly implied that the Bolsheviks had too much power in proportion to their numbers, that they had captured this power by arresting rivals and by rigging elections to the soviets, and that it was high time the other left-wing groups had a say in policy. The sailors, soldiers, and workers of Kronstadt at no time demanded concessions for surviving right-wingers or moderates; they were in no way interested in moderating the anti-bourgeois ideals of 1917. They certainly wanted to keep the Soviet state, but they did not want one party to have the monopoly of power. However, a monopoly of power was precisely what that one party did want, and that is why the men of Kronstadt found themselves treated not as just a pressure group, but as enemies.

On 1st March, Kalinin, the popular and earthy Party stalwart, was sent to Kronstadt to calm the sailors at a mass meeting. But he was ineffective, while his supporting speaker, the Baltic Fleet's commissar, made things worse by threatening the sailors. Especially menacing for the regime was that many Party members of Kronstadt were on the sailors' side, and some even resigned from the Party. But until 2nd March there was nothing which could be termed a rising; there was just a mass of servicemen no longer ready to obey the Party without question. But on 2nd March a start was to be made on arranging new elections to the Kronstadt Soviet, and the men were adopting procedures which would allow them to vote secretly for candidates of their own choice: the Communists were no longer to have undue influence in the electoral process.

On 2nd March, the local commissars, who had continued to threaten the sailors, were arrested by the latter — although they were never ill-treated. The rebels published their own *Izvestiya* in which, unlike the official newspapers, both sides of the argument were presented (in fact, since the Party's statements on the Kronstadt situation were already denouncing the whole issue as a plot hatched by White officers, their publication in Kronstadt only strengthened anti-Party feeling).

On 3rd March the government arrested and shot naval airmen at a mainland base south of Kronstadt, who were preparing to support the rebels. On 5th March an ultimatum from Trotsky was delivered, composed in menacing terms. On 7th March Tukhachevsky, the hero of the Red Army's Polish campaign, acting on Trotsky's orders, launched an infantry assault across the ice. This failed, because the troops sympathized with the rebels.

Tukhachevsky realized that Kronstadt had to be taken before the thaw, while infantry could still attack across the ice and before the rebels could move their ships to Petrograd, where mutinous workers were ready to rise at the slightest sign of armed support. Accordingly, during the next two weeks more reliable troops were brought up, arrangements were made to feed them better, and they were stiffened with a sprinkling of Red cadets and delegates from the Party Congress. On 16th March the preliminary bombardment began and at dawn on the 17th the assault troops, dressed in white, advanced across the ice in two columns.

One column was almost totally destroyed or drowned when it marched in close formation into a minefield laid on the ice. However, the other column, after hours of bitter fighting, entered the streets of Kronstadt. By this time the rebels were disorganized and the street fighting assumed the character of a massacre. On the 18th the battleships were captured and the Kronstadt Rising was over.

The lies about Kronstadt

From the rebel prisoners a handful were carefully selected by pedigree and shot as alleged ringleaders. This enabled the announcement of the execution to denounce the leaders as former landowners or priests. Those of the genuine leaders who had not escaped over the ice to Finland, together with other participants, were imprisoned and shot quietly in batches during the succeeding months.

Soviet history books still cloud the facts of the Kronstadt Rising, even though an objective account would surely reveal how much damage Trotsky was doing to the Party at this time. Many of the policies against which the sailors revolted were Trotsky's policies: the army strike-breakers, the arrest of trusted trade union officials, the appointment of unpopular commissars with a thirst for regimentation. It was Trotsky who composed the ultimatum which left the rebels no room for compromise. It was Trotsky who supervised the assault on Kronstadt. And no doubt it was Trotsky whose fertile imagination invented many of the lies about Kronstadt which were put out for public consumption and are still in circulation.

The Rising was not a White conspiracy aiming at the restoration of the monarchy. Nor was it an anarchist or Menshevik or Socialist Revolutionary conspiracy. It was a protest made by simple men with simple aims, and it is always easy to accuse the simple, honest, and outspoken of all kinds of complex machinations. The case of Petrichenko exemplifies this. He was a leader of the Kronstadt sailors and fled to Finland. In enforced exile there he remained pro-Soviet and attracted the attention of the Finnish police. Then in 1945 Finland sent him back to Russia, where he was immediately gaoled. In gaol he lasted only a few months.

Lenin: October and After

A. J. P. Taylor

The outbreak of the First World War found Lenin in Galicia, close to the Russian border. With industrial unrest sweeping Russia, he had expected a revolution at any moment and was preparing to direct it. Instead the war ended unrest and Socialist discontent in every country. The Socialist International collapsed. Revolutionary Socialists, including even some of Lenin's followers, became patriots overnight. Lenin himself was briefly interned by the Austrian authorities and transferred, a solitary and disregarded figure, to Switzerland.

Lenin and his wife Krupskaya settled in Zurich, where they lived on exiguous remittances from his family. Lenin worked in the public library, researching into the economic causes for the war. The result was a highly-charged book on *Imperialism, The Highest Stage of Capitalism,* which blamed the war on foreign investments. Alternate days Lenin did the housework, while Krupskaya read in the library, less productively. Occasionally they went for short holidays in the mountains. They had no Swiss friends and few friends even among the Russian exiles. In 1915, opponents of the war from many European countries gathered at Zimmerwald. Lenin attended, to small effect. Most of the Socialists at Zimmerwald were pacifists and wished to end the war for humanitarian reasons. Only Lenin proposed the slogan: 'Turn the imperialist war into a civil war.' Lenin called himself 'the Zimmerwald Left', by which he meant that he stood alone.

In Russia, Lenin's followers, the Bolsheviks, had dwindled to a handful. The more prominent were in exile like Lenin himself—in France, in the United States, or elsewhere. The second-rank leaders, such as Stalin, were in Siberia. Only the unknown remained, and Lenin had little contact with them. He sent only brief messages that they should prepare for a revolution. But he had little hope for it. In January 1917 he told a gathering of Zurich students: 'We older men (he was then 46) will not live to see the international Socialist revolution. But you youngsters, you will see it.'

In March 1917, out of the blue, there was revolution in Russia. The Tsar abdicated. A provisional government was set up. In Petrograd the Soviet of Workers' and Soldiers' Deputies really exercised such authority as existed. The revolution had not been made by the Bolsheviks nor indeed by any other Socialists. It has been a spontaneous uprising by the masses. Far from ending the war, the revolution produced the cry that the war should be run better and more energetically. Even the first Bolsheviks who returned from exile took up this slogan. Lenin was in impotent frenzy: it seemed that the opportunity for upheaval and civil war was being thrown away. Somehow he must get back to Russia and bring his followers to their senses.

Lenin returns to Russia

The French government would not allow Lenin to travel through France. A Swiss Socialist, negotiating on his behalf, secured approval from the German High Command that he could go through Germany. Some thirty Russians, not all of them Bolsheviks, had a slow and uncomfortable train journey. There was little food, and smoking was possible only when locked in the lavatory. Finally Lenin arrived in Petrograd at the Finland Station. He expected to be arrested. Instead there was an official deputation from the Soviet waiting with flowers and greetings. Lenin brushed the deputation aside and pushed out of the station. He climbed on to an armoured car and shouted to the crowd: 'The revolution is being betrayed by its leaders.'

Lenin at once met the Bolshevik Central Committee and told them they must prepare for a new revolution. All, including Stalin, thought he was crazy, and it was resolved to destroy all records of his speech — one survived by chance. Lenin was undismayed. He said: 'The masses are a hundred times more revolutionary than we are', and he went on preaching revolution.

In July there was another outbreak of mass demonstrations. Lenin, worn out by the unaccustomed strain of practical activity, was away in the country. The Bolsheviks could not decide whether to encourage the demonstrations or to damp them down. *Pravda,* their organ, came out with a blank front page. By the time Lenin returned, the demonstrations were dying down. The Provisional Government now arrested many Bolsheviks. They accused Lenin of being a German agent. Lenin was sure that, if he fell into their hands, they would kill him without trial. He went into hiding and escaped over the border into Finland, disguised as an engine driver. There he took refuge in the house of the Helsinki chief of police, himself a Bolshevik. From afar he still urged his followers to prepare the revolution. Meanwhile he occupied his leisure writing an academic tract entitled *The State and Revolution.*

The Provisional Government was threatened by a military counter-attack. It turned to the Bolsheviks for aid. Their leaders were released from prison. Trotsky became chairman of the Petrograd Soviet. Under his authority, the Soviet set up a Military Revolutionary Committee for the defence of the revolution. The Bolsheviks ordered Lenin to remain in Helsinki. He ignored their ban and returned to a suburb of Petrograd, where his hiding place was known only to Stalin. From there he instructed his followers to seize power. They trembled and failed to obey him. A secret meeting of the Bolshevik Central Committee was called. Lenin appeared, clean-shaven and disguised. The argument lasted all night. Its conclusion: the seizure of power would take place on 15th October. That day came and went with no seizure of power. Lenin summoned another meeting. Again the seizure of power was determined. Again the fixed day passed without action.

The action came instead from Kerensky, head of the Provisional Government. He closed down the presses of *Pravda.* Trotsky gave the order that they should be re-opened. Thus, casually, the Bolshevik revolution began.

Revolution and peace with Germany

The Provisional Government was overthrown virtually without combat. On 25th October (7th November by our calendar), six Red Guards were killed – four by stray shots from their own side. The seizure of power was not planned by Lenin. It was not directed by him. He arrived at Smolny, the Soviet headquarters, only when everything was on the move. Trotsky, not Lenin, made the Bolshevik Revolution.

The All-Russian Congress of Soviets was about to meet. Theoretically power had been seized in its name. When the delegates met, they were told that a Soviet government had been formed. They duly approved without being given the chance to do anything else. Lenin had proposed that Trotsky should head the new government. Trotsky replied: 'First, I am a Jew. Second, you will stay outside and criticize.' Reluctantly Lenin became chairman of the Council of People's Commissars. He held this post until his death.

Lenin had no experience of administration and tired easily. He laid down broad principles and left others to apply them. He was older than the other Bolsheviks, who called him always 'the old 'un'. They respected and feared him, but he often had to fight to get his own way. He was always far from being the unquestioned dictator. Within twenty-four hours Lenin announced his programme: the land for the peasants, Socialism for industry, and immediate peace. The Soviet Congress applauded. The old officials refused to conform. Chaos spread across Russia.

Lenin believed that if one of the warring powers made peace, all the others would follow. If not, revolution would sweep across Europe. At his behest, Trotsky invited all the countries at war to attend a peace conference. The Entente powers refused. Germany agreed to an armistice, and the Bolsheviks negotiated with them at Brest Litovsk. The Bolshevik proposal was a peace with no annexations and no indemnities. The Germans answered by demanding the surrender of a third of Russia's territory. Many of the Bolsheviks wished to proclaim a revolutionary patriotic war. Lenin replied: 'The soldiers have voted against the war. They have voted with their feet by running away.'

Trotsky proposed a compromise. He would refuse to sign the German terms and would merely declare that the war was over. The Germans, he argued, would not dare to resume hostilities. Lenin was unconvinced. He waited in vain for any signs of revolution in Germany or Austria-Hungary. Trotsky made his declaration. The Germans broke off the armistice and advanced farther into Russia. The great problem was posed: should the Bolsheviks perish heroically or should they sacrifice Russian territory in order to survive? Lenin had no doubt: the Bolshevik regime must survive at all costs. After bitter debate he carried the day. In sullen silence Bolshevik delegates signed the Treaty of Brest Litovsk.

Communism in practice

This was the turning point in Lenin's life. Until this moment he had been an idealist, believing that a perfect Socialist society could be established without delay by those who had sufficient faith. Now he realized that faith was not enough. He transformed himself into a practical statesman, who postponed Utopia to a distant future. His original object in October 1917 had been immediate peace and immediate Socialism. In March 1918 he aimed only to hang on: somehow Bolshevik rule must survive until international revolution broke out – and that would take much longer than he had originally expected. Lenin not only made sacrifices of territory. He was equally ready to sacrifice principles or human beings, so long as the Bolsheviks, now called Communists, remained in power.

In March 1918 the Soviet government moved to Moscow. Lenin took up residence in the Kremlin. He lived humbly and shared a bathroom with the Trotsky children, who delighted in him as a welcome playmate. He also acquired a country cottage where he spent much time duck-shooting. No one could be less like the conventional dictator. Lenin dressed simply, with a cloth-cap stuck at an angle. He refused to exceed the normal, and very inadequate, food rations until ordered to do so by the Central Committee. He went around a good deal in streets and factories, addressing meetings in a rather academic way. He always welcomed visitors and had an engaging twinkle in his eye, which some people found sinister.

Lenin had never supposed that Socialism could be established in a single country, particularly one so backward as Russia. He agreed with Trotsky that either revolution would become universal or the capitalists would unite against the one Socialist state. Hence the aim of Soviet foreign policy, so far as it existed, was to keep the capitalist powers divided. Once the Treaty of Brest Litovsk had been signed, Lenin gave every appearance of co-operating with the German imperialists and was even ready to enlist their aid when the Allies, in answer, began to intervene in Russia against the Bolsheviks.

Intervention hardened the Bolshevik dictatorship and also provoked terror. Lenin was not sorry. After being harassed ineffectively himself by the Tsarist police, he was glad to turn the tables and got particular pleasure from the protests of more moderate Socialists, who were shocked at this departure from democracy. Lenin maintained that proletarian democracy still existed so long as there was freedom of discussion within the Communist Party, and this he still tolerated. Though violent in speech, he was not yet violent in acts against his own comrades. On 30th August Lenin addressed a factory meeting. As he was leaving, a woman called Dora Kaplan fired a revolver at him. Two bullets were lodged in his body and not removed. Lenin had never been strong and from this time became frailer than before.

Lenin, though clearly the most powerful man in the Soviet government, did little of the practical work himself. He remained in Moscow, while Trotsky, Stalin, and others directed the war of defence against the Whites and the Allies. Lenin had time on his hands. He listened to individual grievances and sometimes redressed them. He read all the foreign newspapers and sought to establish contact with revolutionaries in other countries. His most considerable activity in 1919 was the writing of a pedantic tract, which instructed British Communists to support the Labour leaders 'as a rope supports a hanged man'.

Civil war

After the defeat of Germany, Lenin feared Allied intervention more than ever. He offered to leave most of Russia in White hands if only the Bolsheviks were allowed to survive in Moscow. When the peace conference assembled in Paris, Lenin answered by founding the Third or Communist International, as the general staff of the coming revolution. He knew that the few foreign delegates represented nobody but themselves and yet insisted on the pretence of large-scale support. Angelica Balabanoff, an idealistic Italian Socialist, expostulated with Lenin against the crookedness of his agents, such as Zinovyev. As she talked, she realized that Lenin knew this already. When she finished, Lenin screwed up his eyes and said to her: 'Comrade Balabanoff, what use can life make of you?' Then characteristically he gave her a passport and smuggled her out of Russia despite the protests of the secret police. There was nothing Lenin liked better than conspiring against his own associates.

Gradually the Red Army, under Trotsky's leadership, won the Civil War. By 1920 the White generals had been defeated. The Poles attempted to invade Russia. They were defeated, and the Red Army invaded Poland. Trotsky opposed this. He declared that the revolution could not be extended by bayonets and that the Polish workers would respond to the call of patriotism. Lenin could not resist the temptation of success. He claimed that the Red Army would be welcomed in Poland and that when it reached the German frontier, the German Communists would rise also. Instead the Red Army was defeated at the gates of Warsaw. Lenin swung round and was now as insistent on peace as he had been on war. With his approval, the Treaty of Riga surrendered to Poland great areas of ethnic Russian territory.

Lenin had justified the Communist dictatorship by the needs of civil war. Now the war was over, but Lenin had no intention of weakening Communist control. On the other hand, he recognized the exhaustion and poverty of Russia. In his new crisis he showed once more the ruthless realism with which he had promoted the peace of Brest Litovsk. The New Economic Policy which he introduced in 1921 abandoned most of the Socialist measures which were now dismissed as 'war Communism'. Private trading was restored. The peasants were encouraged to produce food for profit. The merchant, previously persecuted, became an honoured citizen. If Lenin had had his way, the industries and resources of Russia would have been distributed as concessions to foreign investors. Only the refusal of the foreign capitalists spared Russia from becoming an imperialist colony.

Lenin was still waiting for the international revolution, and began to think that he would have to wait for a long time. He saw also a tiny chink of hope even if the international revolution did not come. Perhaps in time Russia would become an advanced industrial country, and then Socialism would be a workable system. He announced over and over again: 'Communism equals Soviet power plus electrification.' Being entirely ignorant in scientific matters, he imagined that with electricity everything would work itself. Lenin had now stood Marxism on its head. According to orthodox Marxism, the political order grew out of the economic system. In Soviet Russia, a political dictatorship was preparing to force Socialism on an almost precapitalist country. Implicit in Lenin's policy was 'Socialism in one country' and the long period of Stalin's dictatorship.

Lenin was becoming physically weaker. He spent long stretches at his country cottage. When he presided over the Council of People's Commissars, smoking was forbidden and each item limited to ten minutes. The growth of bureaucracy exasperated him. His correspondence was full of complaints against red tape. For Lenin still had a fantasy that, since he was supreme in Russia, the workers ruled. He did not appreciate that the Communist dictatorship had lost whatever working-class character it once possessed. Even within the party, democracy was finishing, and Lenin helped to finish it. In his enfeebled state, he could no longer tolerate disagreement.

In May 1922 he had a stroke. He recovered somewhat during the summer and began to prepare his succession. He nominated Stalin as general secretary, then rebelled against Stalin's control and almost in his last act urged the Party to throw Stalin out. Lenin had another stroke in December 1922 and a third, even more severe, in March 1923. He still tried to take a political line. Despite Stalin's supervision, he managed to slip out to Trotsky a plan of rebellion by which the two of them should overthrow the Party dictatorship and restore democracy. Thus at the end Lenin sensed that somehow everything had gone wrong and stretched out his hand to Trotsky as his only personal friend and near equal among the Bolshevik leaders.

Lenin fought against death. With his wife's help, he re-learned to speak a few words and to walk a few steps. One day in

October he insisted on being driven to the Kremlin. He went into his old office and leafed through the papers on his desk. On 20th January 1924 he complained of his eyes. A specialist came out to see him. Lenin's main anxiety was that the doctor should not have to return to Moscow late at night. This little kindness was his last recorded act. Lenin died on the evening of 21st January 1924.

Lenin did more than any other political leader to change the face of the 20th-century world. The creation of Soviet Russia and its survival were due to him. He was a very great man and even, despite his faults, a very good man.

Part twelve · Left and Right in Germany and Italy

The fear of Bolshevism spreading into Europe from Russia preyed heavily on the minds of western statesmen just after the war. The destruction and dislocation the war had brought to eastern and central Europe had created an explosive situation which might well be exploited by the revolutionary left, and events in Russia had shown only too clearly that revolutionaries could no longer be dismissed as cranks.

It was Germany which seemed to stand in the greatest danger. The old structure of government and society had been shaken by defeat and by the harsh terms imposed at Versailles. Defeat itself had been brought about by internal collapse — destruction and shortage had sapped Germany's economy and had exhausted her people. Yet in retrospect the changes of a revolution from the left seem far slighter here than either reactionaries or the revolutionaries themselves believed at the time. The old-pre-war unity of the German socialists had never recovered from the blow of 1914, and now the left had disintegrated into a series of constantly shifting groups. The number of genuine committed revolutionaries was very small and they had nothing like the Russian Bolsheviks' rigid discipline or conspiratorial experience. For a moment in 1918 the discontent of the armed forces and industrial workers seemed to be leading Germany along the same path as that taken by Russia, but only for a moment. The revolutionaries were too weak to give an effective lead and national habits of respect for order and traditions of discipline rallied all save the extremists to the prospect of constitutional government. The only lasting result of the 'revolution' was the disappearance of the Hohenzollern dynasty and the German monarchy from the Euro-

pean scene. It rested on no genuinely revolutionary sentiment or movement in the country. It was the outcome of national defeat and corresponded to 1871 in France — not to 1789, or even 1848. The forces which were later to amalgamate to destroy German democracy were there but they were not forces of the left. Militarism and aggressive nationalism had been inflamed by the terms of the peace and were then encouraged by the reliance placed on them as a bulwark against the left.

Italy was another country where democracy was in danger but not only from the left. Italy gave the words 'Fascist' and 'Fascism' to the world and, as the first Fascist state, was an important example and influence. For more than half a century the Italians had striven to build a liberal, progressive state from a struggling economy and a backward society. And they had had considerable success. Whatever her shortcomings, Italy in 1914 had been a constitutional state with a free press, universal male suffrage, and an executive dependent on an elected Parliament. Yet in 1918 Italian democracy was on the defensive and by 1924 it had been swept away by Mussolini's dictatorship.

Although she had been on the winning side during the war, post-war Italy had more in common with Germany than with her wartime allies. Like Germany Italy was disillusioned and frustrated by the peace settlement. She felt she should have reaped far more territorial gains from the collapse of her old enemy the Austro-Hungarian Empire. Many of those who had fought in the war believed the politicians had betrayed them in the peace and the desire for revision could easily take a truculent form, as D'Annunzio's attempt to gain the port of Fiume showed. Economically the war had been disastrous for Italy. Weaker than her allies, Italy had in comparison with them undergone a much heavier financial and economic strain and she was hard hit by the post-war slump. For a moment the strains of the war seemed likely to throw Italy into a left-wing revolution. In 1920 rural poverty combined with industrial unrest to create a situation which appeared ominously like that in Russia in 1917. But Italian Socialists were unprepared and were too disorganized to convert it into a genuine revolution. Here again, there was a great difference between them and the Russian Bolshevik party. But as in Germany, the spectre of revolution combined with social and economic turmoils and bitterness at the peace created a dangerous situation.

The roots of Italian fascism go back further than 1914. Its extreme nationalism was partly a product of the unification; the violent social struggles after unification help explain the strength of anti-parliamentarianism in Italy; and the divorce between patriotism and the left was foreshadowed by the teachings of pre-war socialists which, in turn, gave nationalist feelings an anti-socialist tinge. The importance of the war was that it had precipitated a crisis in Italian politics and society which made these facts more important. Bitterness at the peace, the alarm of middle class people who saw nationalism

derided at home and thwarted abroad and whose standard of living was being eaten into by inflation, the fears of the clericalists and the Right, and the number of ex-service rough-necks with nothing to do, gave Mussolini his chance. And he was helped by the ineptitude of the Italian politicians.

Mussolini gained power in Italy over a decade before Hitler became Chancellor of Germany but the year after Mussolini's March on Rome saw Hitler's first abortive coup—the Munich Putsch. In one way the significant thing about this coup was that it failed. Democracy in Germany proved tougher than in Italy and in the 1920's, while Mussolini was building his Fascist state, hopes for the Weimar Republic in Germany were still flourishing. It was not until the economic crisis of 1929 with its concomitant political disorders that Hitler was able to gain power. Despite enormous handicaps laid on the young German republic by an authoritarian, anti-democratic culture and society the Weimar Republic did survive the widespread violence of its early years. But although the Munich Putsch landed Hitler in prison, the foundations of German democracy were never free from the menacing forces of the radical right and Hitler, a relatively obscure agitator in 1923, was able to use the Munich episode to build up his reputation for another attempt later on.

The New Germany

Imanuel Geiss

According to text-book history, a revolution is said to have taken place in Germany in November 1918. Indeed, there was turbulent change of governments in that period, there were revolutionary noises all over the place, but once the dust had settled, it soon emerged that precious little had actually changed in Germany. The so-called 'November Revolution', however was such an extraordinarily muddled and confused affair that it is extremely difficult to give an adequate sketch of the course of events in the space available.

Germany's collapse, formalized by the Armistice of 11th November 1918, had not been the result of the imaginary 'stab in the back', but of sheer physical exhaustion, her sudden isolation by the collapse of her allies in autumn 1918, and her exposure to foreign invasion from south and south-east. Germany's breakdown ('Zusammenbruch'), as it was significantly and justly called, did not constitute the Revolution, because the motives of the masses and most of the political leaders of the Left were apolitical or very limited in political range. The genuinely revolutionary forces were weak and largely ineffective; they were rather driven by events than actually moulding them.

Those who appeared as leading the revolution, the Majority Socialists (MSPD), had been already in the government. Thus the curious situation arose that those who wanted the revolution did not make it, while those who made it did not want it. To a certain extent, the 'revolution' of November 1918 was hardly more than a historical mishap, largely due to the stubbornness of the Kaiser who refused too long to abdicate, instead of saving the monarchy by clearing the way for an early and more tolerable peace. Until 9th November no political force in Germany save the extreme Left seriously thought of abolishing the monarchy. The Conservatives clung to it for reasons of political and social preservation – 'No king, no Junker', to modify James I's famous dictum of 1604 'No bishop no king'. The middle class had got more than they wanted by the constitutional reforms of October 1918: parliamentary government under a crown stripped of its traditional powers. Next to the Kaiser, the key to Germany's political future lay with the working class and its leaders, most of them Socialists of one kind or another. In theory, they were for the Republic, yet only the radicals among them wanted to do something about getting a Republic.

Three-fold split

In November 1918 the state of the Socialist movement in Germany was chaotic. The decision of 4th August 1914 to support the war effort and the length of the war had destroyed the SPD's famous unity, discipline, and strength of happier pre-war days. Since April 1917 the SPD was formally divided into two political parties. The majority, roughly comprising the right and the centre, under Friedrich Ebert and Philipp Scheidemann (MSPD), and the minority, roughly the old Left, under Hugo Haase, the Independent Social Democratic Party (USPD). Within the USPD there was another group, led by Karl Liebknecht and Rosa Luxemburg, the Spartacists, who formed practically a left-wing party of their own, which they formally launched on 30th December 1918 with the foundation of the Communist Party (KPD).

In spite of that three-fold division, none of the three parties was homogeneous and there was a curious overlapping between their various wings. The leadership in all of them was more or less identical with the right wing of their respective parties, while the rank-and-file stood more to the left. Thus the masses of the MSPD and the leaders of the USPD on the one hand, the masses of the USPD and the leaders of the Spartacists on the other hand were more in agreement than with their leadership and followers respectively. This state of affairs further increased the confusion and paralysed the socialist movement to an incredible extent. The leaders of the MSPD paid only lip-service to their republican ideals and were violently opposed to any revolutionary adventures. In particular, Ebert tried to save the monarchy to the last moment and was furious when his more quick-witted colleague Scheidemann proclaimed the Republic on 9th November for tactical reasons. 'I hate the revolution like sin,' Ebert is reported to have said in those days. The leaders of the MSPD were satisfied with a few limited reforms, in particular of the franchise and social legislation. They intended to develop parliamentary government as achieved in October 1918 in the direction suiting their limited objectives. The left wing of the MSPD and the right wing of the USPD stood for a parliamentary and democratic Republic with a strong socialist flavour.

The left wing of the USPD, Liebknecht and Rosa Luxemburg, were among the few political elements who seriously aimed at revolutionary action and revolutionary change of German society, if the chances offered themselves. They were prepared to act as a left-wing socialist opposition in a parliamentary democracy, if, as they were realistic enough to see, they were to fail to gain and keep power in Germany. Most of the Spartacists, in contrast, were adventurous and wild-eyed putschists, who yearned for violent revolutionary action almost for its own sake, regardless of the chances of success. Although their numbers were hardly more than a few hundred in November 1918, their disruptive influence was considerable. The quasi-revolutionary turbulence in Germany of November 1918 was triggered off by events beyond the control of the Left, whether revolutionary or not—the mutiny of the Fleet. After that events moved so quickly that the Left was taken by surprise and caught practically unprepared, both technically and intellectually. This alone is proof enough for refuting the old-fashioned theory that the 'November Revolution' had been plotted in advance and executed by a group of revolutionaries.

While parliamentary constitutionalism was introduced in October 1918, nothing much had changed in daily life, where the military element remained supreme. Thus the MSPD's participation in the Reich Government did not sink in sufficiently in the few weeks until the 'Revolution'. The first symptoms of demoralisation and dissolution became visible on the eve of defeat.

There was a fresh urgency in the public debate on the issues of war and peace. The grip of the military loosened when a amnesty for political prisoners was declared and Liebknecht was released from prison on 21st October. He arrived at Berlin two days later and was appalled by the lack of preparation for revolutionary action.

Revolutionaries overtaken

The revolutionary element was very weak indeed. The few hundred members of the Spartacists were scattered all over Germany, and their leaders had until recently been in prison. There were only two relatively local strongholds, represented by two other groups, the Bremen Left-wing Radicals and the Berlin Revolutionary Shop Stewards. Both formed officially part of the left wing of the USPD, but followed an independent line of their own. The movement in Berlin was the more important one, because it controlled large parts of the Berlin Metalworkers, workers in the armament industry, and, of course, because it was at the seat of the central government. After his return to Berlin, Liebknecht established contact. At a first meeting on 2nd November future steps were discussed. The early date of 4th November for proclaiming a general strike, out of which revolutionary action might develop, was ruled out, however, as it would have been too soon; 6th or 7th November was out of the question, because Thursdays and Fridays were pay-days for the workers. Thus, 11th November was chosen, two days, as it turned out, after the actual event. The poor revolutionaries in Berlin were completely overtaken by their 'Revolution'.

The 'Revolution' is sparked off

What became known in history text-books as the 'German Revolution of November 1918' mainly took its origin from developments which were connected with the problem of war and peace. In October 1918 the German High Command had oscillated between admitting defeat and asking for a last desperate stand to save the 'honour of the army', tactics which did nothing to increase the readiness of the common soldier to die for an openly lost cause, at a time when the end of the war was clearly in sight. When Ludendorff, covered by Hindenburg's signature, called upon the armies to stage *resistance a outrance* on 24th October, he provoked his dismissal two days later. But it was in this spirit that the Supreme Naval Command had made plans for a last naval engagement to save the honour of the German Battle Fleet as well. It was this decision which set the 'revolutionary' ball starting.

On 29th and 30th October a number of sailors refused to obey orders and sabotaged technical preparations for the sailing of the Battle Fleet from Wilhelmshaven. The Supreme Naval Command had to scrap its plans, and, thanks to crude handling of the movement and to the dispersal of the Fleet, ordered by the admirals the mutiny spread rapidly to other ports. It soon acquired political dimensions when it reached Kiel, a key port, major garrison, and industrial city, on 4th November. From there sailors on leave, returning home by railway, rapidly spread the ferment. On 7th November the monarchy collapsed in Munich, when Kurt Eisner, the leader of the local USPD, organized a huge mass demonstration through the city and a mutiny of the soldiers in the barracks. The 'revolutionaries' were supported by the liberal, anti-clerical wing of the Bavarian peasants who dreaded the prospects of an Allied invasion via Tyrol; the 'Revolution' was tolerated by the urban middle classes, because they feared the bombardment of Munich and Augsburg.

After Kiel, Munich was the decisive event, and from now on Workers' and Soldiers' Councils took over in Germany. Berlin was last to follow on 9th November. There, a curious situation had developed. The working class was by early November in a vaguely revolutionary mood, clamouring, as almost everybody, for the Kaiser's abdication in order to get a more lenient peace. The MSPD, forming part of the Imperial Government since 3rd October, was willing enough to save the monarchy, as Ebert told General Groener, Ludendorff's successor, during a meeting as late as 6th November. But Ebert felt that the desired result could be achieved only by sacrificing the Kaiser. When Groener refused, the SPD leaders demanded in an ultimatum the Kaiser's abdication by 9th November and sought contact with the rival USPD in order to regain control of the Berlin working class.

All that made the 'Revolution'

On 9th November Berlin was excited and nervous. When there was no news of the Kaiser's abdication, the ministers of the MSPD resigned from the Imperial Government, thus precipitating a cabinet crisis. On the other hand, workers started to leave their factories, milling around by tens of thousands in the city and near the Wilhelmstrasse. The last Imperial Chancellor, Prince Max von Baden, profoundly alarmed by the demonstrations and the near general strike, did two things. When the Kaiser refused to abdicate, he proclaimed on his own the Kaiser's abdication at about 11 a.m. One hour later he himself resigned and handed over his office to Ebert who had appeared in the Chancellery to present the demands of his party. Ebert accepted. At 2 p.m. the impulsive Scheidemann proclaimed the Republic, standing in a window of the Reichstag, in order to forestall a similar move by Karl Liebknecht only two hours later. Those three acts—the chancellor's unauthorized proclamation of the Kaiser's abdication (which actually forced the latter's hand), the handing over of his office to Ebert and the twofold proclamation of the Republic—were the only political acts that happened outside the existing constitution. Taken together, they were all that made the German 'Revolution' of November 1918. From then on, everything was strictly legal, even if occasionally turbulent and violent.

Originally, Ebert wanted to form a government on the old basis, that is to say with the Progressive and the Catholic Centre Parties. But the catchword of the day was 'Proletarian Unity', and, under pressure from below, talks for forming a government by the two Socialist parties, MSPD and USPD, were opened in the evening. A little later Soldiers' Councils met in the Reichstag, and they were all summoned to a meeting next day in the Circus Busch, where they were to form a central body of all the Workers' and Soldiers' Councils.

Early next day the Kaiser arrived in Holland, where he spent the rest of his life in exile. In Berlin, Ebert, still styling himself as 'chancellor', formed a new government, which consisted of three members of the MSPD and three members of the USPD: Ebert, Scheidemann, Landsberg; Haase, Dittmann, Barth. The real power

lay with Ebert, who mistrusted his unwanted colleagues from the Left and regarded all turbulence as 'Bolshevism'.
After the meeting in the Circus Busch had
formally proclaimed his government as one
issued from the 'Revolution', he concluded
late in the evening a working alliance with
the Military High Command. About 11
p.m. Groener rang up the Chancellery from
General Headquarters at Kassel, only to
find Ebert answering the telephone. Groener offered the loyal co-operation of the
army, on condition that the new government put down any kind of 'Bolshevism'.
Every day from then on Ebert and Groener
discussed late at night the political situation and measures to be adopted. Ebert had
willingly made himself prisoner of the
military.

Farce and reaction
The German 'Revolution' was, however,
already dead by about midnight on 10th
November. What followed was hardly more
than a revolutionary farce with a reactionary outcome. While Ebert, Scheidemann, and most of his colleagues from the
Majority Socialists used a revolutionary
vocabulary, they worked hand in glove
with the most powerful element in Germany interested in destroying the very
same revolution—the Army High Command. Groener wanted to preserve the
privileged position of the officer corps as
the most powerful bulwark against social
revolution. It is easy nowadays to see the
limited range of change effected in Germany in November 1918, but one has to
realize that, while the turbulent events
of early November were not yet *the* revolution, they did create a situation out of
which a genuine revolution might have
risen. And it was against such a contingency that Groener and Ebert, the
'democratic' general and the conservative
Social Democrat—both, by the way, from
southern Germany—allied themselves.
Their principal aim became not only to
defeat all the revolutionary forces, but also
to throw out of the government the moderate USPD-leaders Haase and Dittmann as
soon as possible.

The short-term aims were to strangle
the movement of the Workers' and Soldiers'
Councils, which claimed to be the source
of revolutionary legitimacy in the new
Germany, and to convene a Constituent

National Assembly, which in fact meant
the preservation of the existing social
order. All demands for nationalization of
basic industries were practically defeated
by setting up a commission which produced very meagre results indeed. On 15th
November the industrialists concluded an
agreement with the trade unions, which
gave some more power (or at least the
semblance of power) to the latter in the
industrial field, while it neutralized them
as a dynamic political force. On 19th December the Executive Council of Workers'
and Soldiers' Councils, where the MSPD
had the overwhelming majority, voted for
holding general elections as early as
possible for a Constituent National Assembly. The USPD was in favour of postponing
the elections, and the Spartacists were
against them anyway.

Meanwhile, the extreme Left tried to
exploit the fluid situation by pushing on
towards a genuine revolution. The old
society was visibly shaken, as was demonstrated by the complete absence of resistance against the political change. But
when, after a few weeks of paralysis,
nothing much happened, the middle-class
and aristocratic wing of the old establishment recovered courage and strength. They
profited from the fact that even the first
'revolutionary' government of Ebert and
Haase wanted primarily order and stability. The old bureaucracies in the Reich
as well as in the various states remained
intact, the great landowners and the great
industrialists remained unscathed. The
military power remained the monopoly of
the old classes, and very soon they wielded
the real power in Germany.

At first, however, the old army, once
they returned home, seemed to melt away.
The great retreat from Belgium and France
was carried out in an orderly fashion, but
the troops were too weary to go on fighting
after they had returned to their garrisons.
A humiliating fiasco resulted when, on
23rd December, the government ordered
returning troops to shoot down a band of
'revolutionary' sailors who had installed
themselves in the former Imperial Stables
in the centre of Berlin. The soldiers simply
refused to shoot and went home. In this
situation, the extreme Left, Spartacists and
Revolutionary Shopstewards, did no more
than proclaim their wish to overthrow the
government. The USPD did resign from

the government but their ministers were replaced by two more MSPD leaders, Wissell and Noske. Gustav Noske, who before the war was the SPD's military and colonial expert in the Reichstag, was now the real strong man in the government. He was quick in learning the lesson of the pre-Christmas days; together with the old generals and officers he hastily organized new regiments out of those soldiers and officers who had been too young before the war to learn a trade or a profession, who were single and who had taken a liking to soldiery. They formed the nucleus of the subsequent 'Free Corps' who afterwards carried on in Hitler's SA and SS. Under the pressure of massive left-wing demonstrations in Berlin, some Social Democrats had organized a few regiments of supporters to protect the government. They would have been strong enough to deal with major disturbances, but Noske preferred the more professional military groups led by military experts, the old officers and generals. By early January 1919 they had concentrated their troops around Berlin. Their day came very soon, thanks to tragic developments within the extreme Left.

Ill-prepared fighting

From 30th December 1918 to 1st January 1919 the Spartacists, reinforced by other groups, constituted the Communist Party (KPD). Against the counsels of their most outstanding leaders, Karl Liebknecht and Rosa Luxemburg, they decided to boycott the elections for the National Constituent Assembly, and to stage an uprising in Berlin. For both undertakings they were too weak. They did succeed in mobilizing a large part of the Berlin working class for demonstrations against the Ebert-Noske government, but only a few hundred were willing to fight it with arms. Ebert and Noske called for the 'Free Corps', who easily put down the desultory and ill-prepared fighting in a few streets of Berlin. Liebknecht and Rosa Luxemburg refused to flee the city for safety. They were hunted down, caught and brutally murdered on 15th January 1919, a sinister sign-post to the future.

Four days later the National Constituent Assembly was elected, for the first time on the basis of women's suffrage and proportional representation. The result of the elections came as a shock to the MSPD leadership. Although the MSPD gained 11,500,000 votes (thirty-eight per cent) and 163 seats, the USPD 2,300,000 votes (seven per cent) and 22 seats, even the two rival socialist parties combined had failed to achieve the majority. The Catholic Centre Party, with 6,000,000 votes and eighty-nine seats, remained the second largest party. Three new parties had been formed in the middle and on the right: the Democratic Party, re-grouping the old Progressive Party and the left wing of Stresemann's National Liberals, the German People's Party (Deutsche Volkspartei —DVP) under Gustav Stresemann, more or less the centre and right wing of the National Liberals plus the left wing of the more moderate Free Conservative Party; and the German National People's Party (Deutschnationale Volkspartei— DNVP), which combined the rest of the old Right. The Democrats obtained 5,600,000 votes and 74 seats, the DVP 1,600,000 and 22 seats, the DNVP 2,900,000 and 42 seats. The Left was numerically strong, the Right numerically weak, but the real power in German society lay with the conservative forces, who had quickly rallied when they found that their worst fears in November 1918 had not materialized.

The Assembly was sitting in Goethe's Weimar, at safe distance from troubled Berlin. When the USPD refused a coalition with the MSPD, the MSPD turned to the Democrats and the Centre Party, forming the Weimar Coalition under Scheidemann. Ebert was elected provisional President of the Reich on 11th February. After bitter conflicts Parliament accepted the Peace Treaty of Versailles and voted the new constitution, the Weimar Constitution, in summer 1919.

The return to political normalcy was accompanied by a long-drawn campaign of the Prussian and Reich governments, both dominated by the MSPD, against the Workers' and Soldiers' Councils, the only genuine revolutionary outgrowth of the 'revolution'. Every pretext was used to employ the 'Free Corps' against them. One city after another was 'liberated' from their 'rule', which meant that the only instrument of large masses for expressing their political will was destroyed. In their eagerness to please the reactionary military, the MSPD leaders ignored that most of the councils were formed by members of their own party and of the trade unions. The net effect of the campaign was to kill hundreds of political activists in the working class, to drive large sections of the erstwhile socialist working class into the Communist Party or into political apathy. Thus, having failed to push forward the revolutionary situation of November 1918 to a genuine revolution, at least democratic and middle class in character, the MSPD also destroyed the only mass basis for the unwanted Republic—the working class. This did not appease the conservative and extreme right-wing elements in Germany. On the contrary, they were only encouraged to press their advantage, as shown by the Kapp Putsch.

The Kapp Putsch

Taking as an excuse the continuing sitting of the National Constituent Assembly even after voting the Constitution, in March 1920 part of the 'Free Corps' and some extreme right-wing elements staged the Kapp Putsch, called after its leader, Kapp, one of the leaders of the *Vaterlandspartei* in 1917-18. Significantly enough, the *Reichswehr,* the new professional army allowed under the Treaty of Versailles, refused to shoot at the 'Free Corps' and some contingents of the *Reichswehr* who had joined them. The government had to flee Berlin, and it was only a general strike ordered by the government which brought Kapp down to his knees within four days. Nothing happened to the putschists. They were in fact quietly rehabilitated by the government, when they were used to crush a spontaneous movement in working-class districts, such as the Ruhr area, who wanted to strengthen the political and social basis of the Republic by an energetic counter-offensive against the extreme Right. The butchering of workers that followed is one of the most nauseating incidents in German history before 1933.

The Kapp Putsch did force the hands of the government. Noske was dismissed as army minister, because he was too lenient towards his generals, and general elections for the first Republican Reichstag took place in June 1920. It brought a crashing defeat for the MSPD whose popular vote was almost halved, while the USPD gained correspondingly, and the KPD polled only 400,000 votes. The right wing was, however, greatly strengthened. From then on, the Republic had only few chances left; the more so, since two of its most dynamic middle-class politicians were killed off by the extreme Right: Erzberger, from the left wing of the Catholic Centre Party in 1921, and the independent Walter Rathenau, in 1922.

The Fascist Take-over

Adrian Lyttleton

'A corpse in a state of putrefaction was found to-day in the Naviglio. It seems that it is that of Benito Mussolini.' This was the sarcastic comment of the Socialist newspaper *Avanti!* on the defeat of Mussolini in the elections of November 1919. His Fascist list, which included the famous conductor Toscanini and the Futurist artist Marinetti, had just received less than two per cent of the votes in the Milan constituency. It was the lowest point in Mussolini's career; he thought of emigrating. To his mistress Margherita Sarfatti he talked wildly of becoming an air pilot, a dramatist, or even a wandering violinist. Yet only three years later he was prime minister of Italy. How was this possible?

In the elections of 1919 Mussolini was not the only loser. They also decimated the Liberal ruling class which had governed Italy since the Risorgimento. The Socialists won 156 seats, and another 100 went to the new Catholic party, the *Partito Popolare*. Only the backward south, where personalities counted for more than programmes, remained a Liberal stronghold. But the two mass parties, which now had the majority in parliament, were not ready to take over the government. They were traditional enemies, and in any case the Socialists were pledged to a policy of absolute revolutionary intransigence. Since the Russian Revolution the influence of moderate reformist leaders, like Filippo Turati, who believed that Socialism would be the result of a process of gradual evolution, had dwindled; for the *massimalisti* (revolutionaries) the only project worth consideration was 'the violent conquest of political and economic power . . . to be entrusted to workers' and peasants' councils'. However, this revolutionary stance was more doctrinaire than practical. The *massimalisti*

lacked the conspiratorial experience of the Russian Bolsheviks, and they had no coherent strategy. During 1920 not only the industrial working class but the countryside as well was in agitation; in the south the peasants, led by their village priests, occupied the lands of the great estates. But the Socialists failed to co-ordinate industrial and rural unrest, or to profit from the spontaneous movement of the southern peasants. Their leaders had not learned from Lenin, and their insistence on collective ownership of the land, while it pleased the landless labourers, alienated many of the more prosperous peasantry.

Revolutionary agitation reached its height in September 1920, when 500,000 workers in the engineering and steel industries occupied their factories. Elected works committees took over management, and 'red guards' were posted at the factory gates. But the Socialist party was quite unprepared to take the political leadership of the movement. They abdicated responsibility to the central council of the unions, in which the moderate reformists were still strong. A majority decided against extending the occupation to other industries; as one delegate said, 'one does not put revolution to the vote'. The crisis was handled astutely by the Liberal prime minister, Giolitti, Italy's most experienced politician, who forced the industrialists to accept many of the workers' demands. The occupation of the factories in fact ended in a technical victory, but for the Socialists it was a psychological defeat. The onset of an industrial depression and severe unemployment reinforced the decline of revolutionary enthusiasm. At the same time, the industrialists, who had had a terrible fright, blamed the government's weakness for destroying business confidence.

The Fascists did not, as they later claimed, destroy the menace of red revolution in Italy. During the occupation of the factories, Mussolini, so far from heading resistance, tried to offer his services as a mediator. Once the menace was past, however, the Fascists were able to profit from the fear and indignation of bourgeois opinion.

After the armistice, the Socialists had continued to exploit the popular mood of hostility to the war. This brought them votes, but by continuing to treat the war as a senseless crime they inflamed the resentments of the returning officers and other patriots. It was a fatal mistake. For it meant that in the politics of violence the Socialists were no match for their opponents. Mussolini on his side had been quick to appreciate that the war had created the conditions for a new type of organization and tactics, which could counter the traditional left-wing techniques of the mass demonstration and the strike. On 10th November 1918, while crowds were still celebrating Italy's victory, he had leapt on to a lorry of the *Arditi*, the shock troops of the Italian army, and had made them a short speech: 'Brothers! Fellow-soldiers! I defended you when you were defamed by the cowardly philistines. I feel that there is something of mine in you, and perhaps you recognize yourselves in me. You represent the marvellous warrior youth of Italy. The flash of your daggers and the hiss of your bombs will execute judgement on all the miserable wretches who try to block Italy's path to greatness. Italy is yours! You will defend her! We will defend her together!' Soon he had formed a bodyguard of *Arditi* to defend the offices of his newspaper, the *Popolo d'Italia*. The *Arditi* were attracted by the Futurist cult of dynamism and the violent destruction of traditional values and institutions, which Mussolini had adopted and made his own.

The early Fascists

The first *Fascio di Combattimento* was founded on 23rd March 1919 in Milan. Others soon sprang up in many of the cities of north and central Italy, but the *Fascio* of Milan remained much the most important throughout 1919. *'Fascio'* means 'bundle', and *'fasces'* was the name given in Ancient Rome to the symbol of state authority, the axe and bundle of rods, which the Fascists also adopted. The atmosphere of the first *Fasci* was bohemian; besides the *Arditi* and Futurists they attracted other young officers and students who had been too young to fight and wanted to see some action. Mussolini's own personal entourage was mostly made up of former Socialists and revolutionary syndicalists who had followed him in his campaign for Italy's intervention in the war. The *Fasci* were originally conceived not as a party but as a broad patriotic coalition; Mussolini bid for the support of the Left by adopting republican and syndicalist ideas of constitutional reform and the taxation of war profits, but the *Fasci* already included a number of right-wing supporters of the monarchy. They proved at first ineffective in winning mass support, but they were able to claim the credit for one significant victory over the Socialists. On 15th April, three weeks after the foundation of the *Fascio,* during a general strike in Milan, a column of Socialist demonstrators was routed by a large group of Futurists, *Arditi,* and students, who then sacked the offices of the newspaper *Avanti!* The action was not organized by the *Fasci* or Mussolini, but two of the leaders, Marinetti, and the captain of the *Arditi,* Ferruccio Vecchi, were Fascists, and so it could be claimed as the first triumph of the new movement.

During the summer of 1920 the Fascist movement began to recover from its election debacle. It had shed many of its early members, who had taken the radical demands of the original programme seriously, and its most conspicuous activity was the formation and training of 'squads of vigilance', led by demobilized officers, to fight the Socialists in street brawls and keep order during strikes. Most of the *Fasci* were still tiny groups of students, disgruntled ex-officers and petty bourgeoisie, who would meet in the back rooms of cafés. They were drawn together by a common mood rather than a programme; they were adventurers and rebels without a cause, attracted by the novelty of the movement, scorn for the older established parties, the claim to be a heroic, combative elite, and the exaltation of violent action. All fixed rules and principles were derided: *'Me ne frego'* (I don't give a damn) was the favourite motto of the early squads, and Mussolini boasted: 'We are the heretics of all the churches.'

What happened at the end of 1920 was that the destructive potential of the Fascist movement was harnessed by conservative interests. The decisive breakthrough came in the rich, agricultural provinces of the Po Valley. Here, as the small groups of students and ex-servicemen grew bolder, they began to attract the benevolent attention of the professional classes and the *agrari* (rich landowners and farmers). The respectable middle class shared with the petty bourgeoisie of shopkeepers and employees a resentment of the rising standard of living of the workers at a time when their own incomes had been hit by inflation. Many *agrari* had suffered from the savage boycotts imposed by the Socialist unions; these could only hold together the mass of under-employed wage labourers, who were lucky if they could find work on more than one day in three, by a system of rigid discipline.

The critical event needed to set off a chain reaction of violence took place in Bologna, the capital of 'Red Emilia'. The situation in the province of Bologna was particularly explosive. A long and bitter agricultural strike, during which the harvest rotted in the fields, ended in a victory for the unions, when the government, only anxious to head off revolution, imposed a settlement on the angry *agrari*. After this they started to talk openly of organizing their own defence. On 21st November, during the inauguration of a new Socialist mayor, the Fascists fired a few shots into the crowd outside the town hall. The Socialists panicked, and inside the council chamber someone shot dead the nationalist councillor Giordani, a war hero. The 'tragedy of *Palazzo Accursio*' gave the Fascists the pretext they needed for a campaign of terror. The *agrari* and the owners of sugar-factories hastened to provide the Fascist action squads with lorries and petrol, so that they could carry their exploits into the countryside. The Socialist strongholds were terrorized into submission by 'punitive expeditions', which soon spread through the whole of the Po valley. The Fascists used their superior mobility to concentrate squads from a wide area, when local forces were insufficient to crush resistance. They soon dropped the pretence that only 'Bolsheviks' were to be attacked: in Tuscany and the Veneto the squads broke up the Catholic unions of share-croppers with equal ferocity.

Success, and new tactics

Success brought converts, and Fascism became a mass movement. In the towns recruits still came mainly from the middle classes, but in the country the squads were swollen by unemployed labourers, to whom the Fascists had promised jobs or small plots of land.

The techniques of *squadrismo* were made possible by the connivance of large sections of the army, the police, and the magistracy.

Even when the government tried to check Fascist terror, its attempts were generally sabotaged by its subordinates. Unfortunately, too, Giolitti, irritated by Socialist obstruction of his financial measures in parliament, believed that he could use the Fascist movement. He called new elections and allowed Fascist candidates to join the government bloc, and thus undermined the credibility of his instructions to his prefects – provincial governors – to prevent violence; it was a part of Italian official tradition to allow a fairly free hand to the friends of the ministry. Only thirty-five Fascist deputies were returned to parliament, including Mussolini, but in a number of provinces they headed the polls.

Mussolini had watched the astonishing progress of agrarian Fascism with mixed feelings. He was not troubled at first by his followers' methods, but he was eventually alarmed both by the dangers of political isolation, as public opinion became less concerned with the Socialist threat, and by the decentralized, almost anarchic, character which the movement had assumed. He felt that control was slipping from his hands. Many of the urban petty bourgeoisie in the ranks of the movement also resented the dominant position of the reactionary *agrari*. One of 'the Fascists of the first hour' wrote: 'We have seen the *Fasci* allow agrarians and industrialists to obtain a controlling influence . . . once we were few, now we are many but surrounded by hostility. . . . We never dreamed of denying other parties freedom of organization. . . . We never thought we had to suppress the unions . . . the branches of the Socialist party, even their party songs.'

Mussolini tried accordingly to execute a tactical retreat by accepting a 'pact of pacification' with the Socialist party, and he even made a speech prophesying the formation of a three-party alliance of Fascists, *Popolari*, and Socialists to rule Italy. The local bosses of the movement in Emilia, Tuscany, and the Veneto, however, refused flatly to accept Mussolini's policy. Led by an eloquent lawyer, Dino Grandi, and a half-educated provincial stationmaster, called Roberto Farinacci, they forced him to back down. Mussolini had tacitly to repudiate his pacification policy in return for their acknowledgement of his leadership.

The government, now led by the honest but ineffectual Bonomi, totally failed to profit from the divisions in the Fascist movement to reassert its authority. In December 1921 an attempt to secure the dissolution of the squads ended in a fiasco. The weakness of the government encouraged the Fascists to turn in 1922 to new tactics. They started to hold great mass rallies to overawe opposition; at the end of May they concentrated 20,000 or more Fascists in Bologna to force the resignation of a tough and hostile prefect. The punitive expeditions reached a new pitch of barbarity; Balbo, the leader of the Ferrara squads, wrote in his diary after a punitive expedition to Ravenna: 'We passed through the province destroying and burning all the offices of the Socialist and Communist organizations. It was a terrible night. Our passage was marked by high columns of fire and smoke.' The last strongholds of Socialist power capitulated after the disastrous general strike called at the end of July. After this, most of the Liberal leaders became convinced that the Fascist movement could only be tamed by offering Mussolini a place in the cabinet. But was this enough? Mussolini now sensed the possibility of gambling for higher stakes.

The preparation of the March on Rome was a masterpiece of deception. Mussolini's hesitation to commit himself to the dangers of an attempt to seize power by force helped to convince the Liberal leaders that he was sincere in preferring a peaceful solution. On 16th October Mussolini held a meeting with the three leaders of the Fascist squads, Balbo, De Bono and De Vecchi, the secretary of the party, Michele Bianchi, and two generals of the regular army. De Bono and De Vecchi were for caution, but not Balbo, who pointed out: 'We enjoy the advantage of surprise. No one believes seriously in our insurrectionary plans.' Bianchi convinced Mussolini of the need to act quickly. The government at this time was headed by Luigi Facta, an amiable old gentleman with few powers of decision, who owed his position to his faithful service of Giolitti. Mussolini still feared Giolitti's return to power; a man who had given orders to fire on d'Annunzio in Fiume was certainly capable of giving orders to fire on him. Ironically, the other man whom Mussolini feared at this stage was d'Annunzio himself: the poet's latest pose was that of the great pacifier, the man who would reconcile the irreconcilable and heal the wounds of national disunity. Many Fascists were still under his spell, and the news that he intended to address a great rally of ex-servicemen on 4th November, the anniversary of victory, was probably important in determining Mussolini's decision. Right up till the last minute Mussolini continued to negotiate with Giolitti for the formation of a coalition government under the latter's leadership, while simultaneously he offered to d'Annunzio the presidency of a future revolutionary triumvirate.

The final plans for the March were laid during the congress of the Fascist party at Naples, after 40,000 *squadristi* had paraded in front of Mussolini. The direction of the movement was entrusted to a quadrumvirate – Balbo, De Bono, De Vecchi and Bianchi, who were to take up their headquarters at Perugia. Mussolini himself remained at Milan. On the evening of 27th October the Fascist squads began to mobilize throughout north and central Italy. At 8 p.m. the King arrived from his country residence.

To Rome

The plan called for the occupation of public buildings throughout north and central Italy as the first stage in the seizure of power; in the second stage three columns would concentrate on the roads leading into Rome, and converge on the capital. In reality, the March on Rome was a colossal bluff. The city was defended by 12,000 men of the regular army, under a commander of undoubted loyalty, who would have been able to disperse the poorly armed Fascist bands without difficulty. Many of the Fascists failed to arrive at their points of concentration; they were travelling by train and were stopped by the simple expedient of taking up a few yards of track. Those who did arrive were poorly armed, with rifles, shotguns or just bludgeons, and they were short of food. They could do nothing except hang around miserably in the torrential autumn rain. Everything depended on the will to resist of the government, the army, and above all the King. Victor Emmanuel III had always behaved as a correct constitutional monarch: he had shown little sympathy for the Fascists. But by temperament he was a pessimist, who had little confidence in his advisers or his subjects. He was keenly conscious that he cut a poor figure in military uniform by the side of his cousin, the Duke of Aosta: the King would have been the shortest man in the army if the minimum height for recruits had not been tactfully lowered. His personal feelings of inferiority may have been decisive.

At 8 p.m. on 27th October, when the King arrived in Rome from his country residence, he told the prime minister that he was determined to resist force. Facta, with rather excessive sang-froid, then retired to bed. During the night news started to come in from all over Italy of the occupation of railway stations, telephone exchanges, post offices, and government buildings in the provinces. At last Facta was woken up, and at 6 a.m. the cabinet met and, confident of royal approval, decided to proclaim a state of emergency. But at 9 a.m., when Facta went to the King with the emergency decree, Victor Emmanuel refused his signature.

The King was an extremely taciturn man, not given to indiscretions, and the reasons for his change of mind during the night of 28th October remain one of the mysteries of history. But it is probable that he was afraid that some of the army generals wanted him to abdicate in favour of the Duke of Aosta, who was known to be in sympathy with the Fascists. Even if he had been able to resist, this would have meant the danger of civil war and the discrediting of the dynasty. Although the March on Rome itself was no real threat, the Fascist insurrection had achieved the disintegration of government authority in many of the provinces, and in this sense it was an effective means of pressure. Once the King had refused the signature of the emergency decree, the game was in the hands of Mussolini. Victor Emmanuel himself, the right-wing parties, and even some of the Fascists, still believed that it would be possible to form a government under the conservative leader Salandra, but Mussolini refused to accept any office except that of prime minister. The King had left himself no choice but to give way, and Mussolini arrived in Rome peacefully by wagonlit on the morning of 30th October. With his fine sense for propaganda, he insisted, in spite of the King's extreme reluctance, on allowing the Fascist legions a victory march through the capital. The trains were now working again, and the wet and hungry columns of marchers who now at last entered Rome were joined by thousands of Fascists from all over Italy. The occupation of Rome was thus the result and not the cause of Mussolini's seizure of power; but it served a purpose. The myth of the Fascist revolution had been born, and Italy had acquired her Duce.

The Munich Putsch

A. J. Nicholls

'On the very first day there sat next to the bed that had been allotted to me a man who had nothing on except an old torn pair of trousers—Hitler. His clothes were being cleaned of lice, since for days he had been wandering about without a roof and in a terribly neglected condition.' The year was 1909, the place Vienna, the speaker a tramp. Hitler had formed a partnership with him to sell postcards showing views of Vienna which he had painted himself and signed 'A.Hitler'. By this means he eked out a meagre living in the company of tramps and drunkards. These were the formative years, when the prejudices which were to guide his future conduct took shape in his mind: anti-Semitism, anti-republicanism, fanaticism.

In 1913 he moved to Munich where his dislike for hard work continued to keep him out of regular employment. On the outbreak of war in 1914 he joined 1st Company of XVI Bavarian Reserve Infantry and served throughout the war as a runner of messages. He was promoted to lance-corporal, twice wounded, and won the Iron Cross. The capitulation of Germany came as a profound shock to him. 'Everything went black before my eyes as I staggered back to my ward and buried my aching head between the blankets and pillow . . .' he recalled. Defeat and the establishment of a democratic republic were intolerable to him, and he resolved to save his country. The instrument by which he hoped to fulfil this mission was the German Workers' Party which he joined in September 1919 as member No. 5. In April 1920 he obtained control of the party and that same month its name was changed to the National Socialist German Workers' Party (abbreviated to 'Nazi'). He planned to build it into a mass party through which he would destroy his internal enemies, 'the November criminals', and win Germany a great empire. Violence,

armed thuggery, and mass oratory were his methods. He put them into action in the promising atmosphere of Bavarian politics, characterized by the famous reply of Pöhner, police president of Munich, who when asked if he knew whether there were political murder gangs in Bavaria said 'Yes, but not enough of them'. Action came with the Munich Putsch of 1923.

The so-called Beer Hall Putsch which took place on the night of 8th November 1923 in Munich was the event which first brought Hitler wide-spread publicity outside Bavaria. Its tragi-comic quality and its complete failure seemed at the time to mark the end of his career. In fact it was an important step towards the achievement of his political objectives. The notoriety which it brought him and the lessons he drew from it were of the greatest importance in the years which followed. Even after the Nazi movement had shifted its centre of gravity from Bavaria to the north and east of Germany, Munich still remained the 'capital of the movement' and the men who died in the Putsch were revered as martyrs to the Nazi cause.

Hitler's attempt to seize power was not the first revolutionary disturbance experienced in the Bavarian capital. Five years earlier, on the night of 7th November 1918, the old Wittelsbach monarchy had been overthrown by a Socialist government based on the authority of workers' and soldiers' councils. There had followed a period of confusion and uncertainty punctuated by acts of violence. In April 1919 a Soviet republic was proclaimed in Munich. It was organized in its later stages by the Communist Party, which looked to Lenin for advice and support. Before any effective contact with Russia could be established, however, the Soviet had been crushed with considerable brutality.

These events left a powerful psychological legacy behind them in Bavaria. The fact that it had been necessary to call in forces from north Germany to suppress a Red dictatorship in Munich was regarded by many army officers and civil servants as a stain on the nation's honour. There was also the lively fear that left-wing revolution might break out again. The official mind in Bavaria therefore tended to be obsessed with the need to strengthen counter-revolutionary elements which could protect the country against Bolshevism.

These attitudes were personified in the figure of Gustav von Kahr, a former royal civil servant who became Bavarian prime minister in March 1920. Under his leadership the country became notorious as the home of reactionary elements, some of which were engaged in violent conspiracy against the Weimar system. Para-military formations, including many successors to the Freikorps units which had helped to suppress left-wing radicalism in 1919, proliferated in Bavaria. Arms caches kept in defiance of the Versailles Treaty were carefully overlooked by the Bavarian government. It also connived at the use of intimidation and even murder to prevent informers revealing their whereabouts to the Allied Control Commission. Kahr resisted attempts from Berlin to enforce laws designed to protect the Republic against right-wing terrorism. He was forced to resign over this issue in the autumn of 1921, but he remained an important figure in the Bavarian administration, and the state itself continued to be a source of difficulty for the Reich government.

Among those enemies of the Weimar Republic who were able to benefit from the situation in Bavaria was Adolf Hitler. Hitler entered politics under the auspices of the Bavarian army, having first been trained as a military propagandist. In September 1919 he was sent to report on a political group called the German Workers' Party. He joined it and quickly became its most dynamic leader. The party, which became the NSDAP (Nazis) in 1920, profited from Hitler's contacts with the army and sympathizers in the Munich police. One of many racialist and extreme nationalist political groups in Germany at this time, it was able to build up a relatively impressive local membership. The unrestrained nature of its attacks on the republican system would hardly have been possible without the tolerance of the Bavarian authorities.

The strained relationship between Munich and Berlin reached breaking point in 1923. As a result of the Franco-Belgian occupation of the Ruhr and the cataclysmic inflation of the mark, national insecurity was at its most extreme. The policy of passive resistance in the Ruhr had encouraged the German army, the Reichswehr, to build up unofficial reserve forces which could be mobilized in the event of actual war with France. These were for the most part existing para-military formations of a right-wing character. In Bavaria the Reichswehr had always maintained contacts with such groups. Some of them were self-consciously Bavarian and looked to Kahr for political leadership. They tended to put Bavarian interests before those of Germany as a whole and were willing to contemplate a break with Berlin if the regime there developed left-wing tendencies. On the other hand, many were very hostile to any hint of separatism and wanted to establish a national dictatorship in Berlin. Several of these started to co-ordinate their activities in February 1923, and at the beginning of September a 'Fighting Association' (Kampfbund) was established, with Hitler as its political leader. General Erich Ludendorff, the quartermaster-general of Germany's armies in the Great War, was also associated with it.

On 26th September Stresemann announced that the campaign of passive resistance in the Ruhr with which the Germans had been opposing French occupation was to be abandoned. There was an immediate reaction in Munich, where the cabinet declared an emergency and appointed Kahr state commissioner with dictatorial powers. A counter-declaration of a state of emergency by the Berlin government was not very effective. The Bavarians controlled their own police, judiciary, and civil service, even though in theory they were supposed to be subordinate to the authority of the Reich. It soon became apparent that even the army in Bavaria was not prepared to obey instructions from Berlin. Its commander, General von Lossow, refused to accept a politically embarrassing order from General von Seeckt, the creator of the German Reichswehr. When he was removed from his post the Bavarian authorities simply declined to let him go. On 22nd October his troops were ordered to make a pledge of obedience to Kahr's regime, pending restoration of normal relations with Berlin.

Kahr and Lossow both wanted to see a change of political system in Germany. Their ideal would have been a return to Bismarck's Imperial Reich, with a monarchist, conservative form of government and some special rights for Bavaria. In order to attain this objective they wanted to unite all the para-military formations in the country behind them. The greatest difficulty they faced in this enterprise lay in Hitler's Kampfbund, which had no faith in Kahr's ability to lead a crusade against the government in Berlin. In fact, although Kahr was certainly more cautious than Hitler, his immediate aims were not dissimilar. His attitude was well expressed in a speech to Bavarian army officers on 19th October 1923. Referring to the conflict with Berlin over General von Lossow he said: 'This relates to the great struggle between the two philosophies which are decisive for the fate of the whole German people, the international Marxist-Jewish conception and the national-German conception. The choice is, on the one hand, German: on the other, un-German. Every officer and every German man must choose. Bavaria has been selected by fate to take over the leadership in this struggle for the great German objective, and it would be a dereliction of its duty if it allowed itself to be swayed from its task by fear of taking responsibility. . . . It is up to each man to decide if he wants to be a German or not.'

Reasons for caution

There was very little Bavarian separatism in this. Suspicions certainly existed in Berlin that the Bavarians – who had been among the least enthusiastic recruits to Bismarck's German empire in 1871 – might want to break away from the Reich. Yet General von Seeckt had every reason to avoid an open conflict with Bavaria. He himself sympathized with those who were working for a change of system in Germany, and did not wish to see divisions appear among them. Even more important to him was the unity of the Reichswehr, which he was determined to preserve in the face of all political difficulties. He knew that Kahr's attitude towards the Republic was shared by many officers throughout Germany.

There were, indeed, good objective reasons for caution. In October Germany experienced an abortive coup by clandestine reserve units at Küstrin in Prussia, a mismanaged Communist rising in central Germany and Hamburg, and growing pressure from French-inspired separatist move-

ments in the Rhineland. Of these problems the Communist threat, based on sympathetic governments in Thuringia and Saxony, was the most serious. At the end of October the German cabinet authorized Reichswehr units to occupy these states, depose their governments and establish authorities loyal to the Reich. The army obeyed with alacrity, happy to use force against rebels on the Left.

Once the threat from the Communists had been suppressed there seemed even less excuse for Bavarian insubordination. A cabinet crisis over this issue occurred in Berlin, and reactionary elements plotting against the Republic hoped that Seeckt would use his position to overthrow the Weimar system. Seeckt had no love for the Republic, but he was not prepared to use force to overthrow it. He advised his contacts in Bavaria that they should avoid dangerous adventures.

Hitler chooses force

His attitude aroused dismay among those reactionary conspirators who had been hoping for support from the Reichswehr. Kahr and Lossow shared this disappointment. On 24th October Lossow had told the leaders of para-military formations that they should expect to march on Berlin within three weeks. Now Kahr was forced to urge them to hold back until the ground had been prepared in northern Germany for what he called 'a national Reich government freed from parliamentary restraints'.

This was not good enough for the Kampfbund. Hitler did not trust the Bavarian government. He felt – probably rightly – that if action were not taken quickly the republican system might be given a chance to revive. He began to prepare for a coup. The aim was not to start a civil war in Bavaria but to spark off a general rising against Berlin. He hoped that, once the action was under way, the Bavarian authorities would not resist the 'national' cause. The news that Kahr was planning to address a meeting at the Bürgerbräukeller beer hall on the evening of 8th November caused Hitler to accelerate his plans. Many leading members of the Bavarian administration wouldbe present at the meeting. It would provide an ideal opportunity to seize them and begin the Putsch.

On the night of 8th November the Bürgerbräukeller, a large and well-appointed beer hall somewhat away from the centre of Munich, was packed to capacity to hear Kahr deliver a lecture on the moral justification of dictatorship. The audience included Lossow and Seisser and members of the Bavarian government. Also present were numerous supporters of the Nazis, who had smuggled weapons in with them. Kahr had not got very far with his exposition when Hitler appeared in the hall supported by a group of armed SA men, Nazi stormtroopers. Many hitherto peaceful onlookers now produced pistols and handgrenades. A machine-gun appeared in the main entrance covering the crowd. Hitler, who had centred attention on himself by jumping on a chair and firing a shot into the ceiling, hustled Kahr, Lossow, and Colonel von Seisser, of the Bavarian state police, into an adjoining room. There he told them that he was setting up a national government. He claimed that Ludendorff, who actually knew nothing of the whole affair, would be the commander of a 'national army'. Waving his pistol at the bewildered Bavarian leaders he offered them places in the new regime.

Hitler's captives, for such they were, did not seem very impressed. Kahr declared that Hitler could jail or kill him if he wanted to, and Seisser reproached the Nazi leader for having broken his word not to start a coup. This promise had indeed been extracted from Hitler—though with some qualifications—and he felt embarrassed enough to offer his apologies. Since the situation was not developing well Hitler dashed back into the main hall and announced that the national revolution had begun. He implied that Kahr and his colleagues had agreed to participate in it. Ludendorff, who had been fetched from his house outside Munich by one of Hitler's aides, now made his appearance. Although he was angry at Hitler's presumption in launching a coup without first notifying him, he agreed to join the rebels. His prestige and authority were of enormous importance. General von Lossow was now persuaded to drop his resistance, and Kahr himself was won over by the promise that he should act as a Bavarian regent pending the restoration of the monarchy. Tremendous scenes of enthusiasm followed, and it seemed that Hitler had obtained his first objective: official support for his 'national' cause.

Doubts arise

It is still open to question how far Kahr and Lossow were sincere in their acceptance of Nazi plans. After the Putsch had failed they naturally maintained that their promises to Hitler had been pure bluff, and a response to the threat of force. It seems possible, however, that in the heat of the moment they may have been genuinely tempted to accept Hitler's *fait accompli*. His objective, the overthrow of the Berlin government, was the same as their own. They disliked Hitler but saw him as a demagogue useful to rally support against the Republic. It was not to be imagined that he could really become dictator.

Hitler himself had been reluctant to allow the Bavarian leaders to retain their freedom, but Ludendorff was confident that his prestige would hold Lossow's loyalty. In this he was badly mistaken. The general returned to his headquarters and found that his subordinates were firmly against any collaboration with Hitler and assumed that he would act to suppress the Putsch. They had secured communications centres, and issued orders to prevent Nazi forces receiving weapons from army barracks. Whatever his original intentions had been, Lossow now set his face against the Putsch. The Bavarian state police had also been alerted against it, and after a conference with its senior officers Kahr decided to come out firmly against Hitler. At 2.55 a.m.—several hours after the events in the Bürgerbräukeller—Kahr and Lossow flashed a message to all German radio stations dissociating themselves from Hitler. Army units were ordered to Munich to protect the legal government.

Hitler had not expected that he would have to face really serious opposition in Munich. His aim had been to win the army and the police over to his side. In this he had seemed to be succeeding in the hours after the Bürgerbräukeller meeting. The Munich city police, under the guidance of Wilhelm Frick, later to be a Nazi minister under the Third Reich, had refrained from interfering as Hitler's SA mobilized and surrounded the beer hall. Individual army officers were known to be sympathetic to the Nazis and an officer cadet school at

Lichterfeld went over almost *en bloc* to Hitler's side.

However, with the open resistance of army and state police Hitler found himself facing almost certain defeat on the morning of 9th November 1923. He had made no preparations to deal with armed opposition. In despair he tried to enlist the help of Crown Prince Rupprecht of Bavaria as a mediator between his supporters and the government. Ludendorff was more adventurous. He persuaded Hitler to gamble on a political demonstration which might win the people of Munich to his side and sway the army from its allegiance to Lossow. Ludendorff hoped that his own presence would have a powerful effect on men in uniform.

Hitler's supporters formed up and marched across the River Isar into the centre of the city. They received a warm welcome from the crowds on the streets. Swastika banners and the old imperial colours of black, white, and red were to be seen everywhere. A police cordon was brushed aside as the marching column approached. It seemed as if the Putsch might yet have a chance of succeeding. But as it neared the centre of Munich – its objective was the Bavarian war ministry – it had to pass through a narrow street leading in front of the former palace of the Wittelsbachs. At the end of the street stood a cordon of state police which had hastily doubled into position when the approach of the Nazi column became known. As the column reached the cordon a shot was fired, killing a police officer. The men in the cordon answered with a volley of rifle fire. Hitler's neighbour in the march, with whom he had linked arms, fell mortally wounded and Hitler dislocated his shoulder. The demonstrators scattered and fled, leaving some dead and wounded behind.

After the shooting Ludendorff picked himself off the ground and marched haughtily on through the cordon. He was put under house arrest, but treated with great respect. Hitler fled, but was captured two days later.

Failure?

The Putsch put an end to hopes in Bavaria that the province could be used as the base for a right-wing assault on the Weimar Republic. Kahr and Lossow became absorbed in the task of explaining away their actions and demonstrating that they were really opposed to the Putsch all along. This gave Hitler a great advantage from the political point of view, for at his trial in March 1924 he was able to claim all the credit for having led the movement against the 'treasonable' Weimar system in Berlin. Moreover, the imprisonment that followed allowed him to devote his attention to writing *Mein Kampf* in which he clearly laid down the inflexible principles which were to guide him through the stormy years to come. His reputation among extreme nationalist elements was finally established throughout Germany. The years immediately after the coup were a lean period for such a movement, but Hitler was able to use the machinery he had created in Bavaria and the prestige the Putsch had given him to build up a unique position among German racialist radical opponents of the Weimar Republic. When the crisis of the Republic came in 1930, he was able to gain his reward.

Part thirteen · Towards Stability

In the early 1920's Europe struggled to rebuild the strength sapped by the long years of war. But it was also a time when the weaknesses and contradictions of the Versailles settlement began to emerge as a threat to future stability. The settlement, as we have seen, was one imposed by the victors on the vanquished. But once the armies had been demobilized and Europe started to nurse her sick economy back to health, the Allies had no way of compelling the defeated countries to accept the settlement short of renewing the fighting. And in the war-sick atmosphere of the early 'twenties this was out of the question. The exhaustion of all the participants ruled out any immediate revision of the settlement but in the long-run there was no guarantee of its lasting if the countries defeated in 1918 did not co-operate.

This underlying fact was not immediately apparent. Consequently, while the early 'twenties was a time when grievances crystallized, it was also a period when adjustments were made to the new situation and the possibilities of peaceful solutions to the grievances began to be explored. It is perhaps too easy in retrospect to see events of this period as simply the first bars of a prelude to the Second World War.

The Treaty of Rapallo signed between Russia and Germany in 1922 gave the Allies a shock which was out of all proportion to the actual content of the treaty. It demonstrated clearly that, while both countries had been defeated in war and excluded from having any voice in determining the shape of post-war Europe, the Allies could not preserve their diplomatic isolation and prevent them coming together. The victors of 1918 could not dictate the future indefinitely. At the time the Bolsheviks were

regarded as outcasts and it was therefore regarded as highly irresponsible of Germany to have concluded an alliance with her. Though later on when the Germans rather than the Russians became the main object of European disapproval the moral obliquity of Rapallo was chalked up against the Russians. In fact there was little chance of much active co-operation between the two signatories. Neither was in any position to challenge the Versailles Settlement; both wanted no more than to be left lone. But the treaty did give Germany added bargaining power in dealing with the Allies, and showed them that if Germany and Russia could negotiate the Allies would have to pay a high price for the friendship of either.

The settlement in Eastern Europe gave Russia and Germany a common grievance for they both disliked the new and powerful Polish state which it had erected. But it also alarmed the new states created out of the collapse of the Austro-Hungarian and Ottoman Empires. The new state of Hungary which emerged after Versailles was short of nearly two thirds of its pre-war territory and not surprisingly was one of the bitterest opponents of the settlement. As democracy collapsed within, Hungary's territorial ambitions alarmed her neighbours and drew them together into a new diplomatic alignment. Once again Eastern Europe was divided into two camps fighting for the remnants of the old multi-national empires.

But while Hungarian revisionism made more noise at this time than German revisionism, it was the question of absorbing a still united Germany into a peaceful Europe which was the major problem. If this were settled, everything would be settled; if it remained unsolved, Europe would not know peace. Even had there been no humiliating settlement at Versailles to arouse Germany's resentment the German problem would have remained. But the Versailles Settlement ensured Germany's dissatisfaction with the status quo and the question of reparations more than any other provoked German bitterness at her treatment. The actual effect of reparations on the German economy is a much-debated point and certainly wasn't either as catastrophic as the Germans complained or as the French hoped. The real significance of reparations lay in their psychological effect. They created resentment, suspicion, and international hostility. More than anything else they cleared the way for the Second World War.

Reparations also had a critical influence on relations between France and Great Britain. The contradiction between the two countries' attitudes towards the resettlement of Germany had been present at Versailles but it emerged even more strongly over the question of reparations. Once the German navy had been sunk and once Germany had been deprived of her colonies, Britain, now the only European power with an Empire, felt in no danger from Germany. She could afford to be magnanimous; but France could not and was obsessed with the problem of securing her north-east frontiers. Reparations were seen by many Frenchmen not simply as a chance to obtain compensation for war damage but as a weapon to keep Germany down. Britain's approach was the more practical one of restoring the economic life of Europe and she was quite willing to listen to German grievances. But once Britain had condemned reparations she soon condemned other clauses of the peace treaty too. The idea took root that Germany had just grievances which should be met and so the ill-fated policy of appeasement was born. In the early years this was a policy of strength, not weakness – the product of Britain's sense of her own security and the realization that an embittered and impoverished Germany was no aid to European stability. Few were far-sighted enough to realize, with Austin Chamberlain, that meeting German grievances would inevitably lead to German domination of Europe. French fears were dismissed as pernicious nonsense and when the Treaty of Locarno was signed it was hoped that this would end the problem of the Franco-German frontier. But the fragility of the treaty lay in its failure to rule out revision of Germany's eastern frontier. The way was left wide open for German demands on Czechoslovakia, and Poland.

Treaty of Rapallo

Elizabeth Wiskemann

The Russo-Polish war had aroused traditional Russian feeling against the Poles: in doing so it enlisted national support on a big scale for the Communist regime. At the same time it exploded the myth of the triumph of world revolution, either in political or in economic terms. Lenin and his colleagues knew that concessions must be made to their peasants at home and therefore in March 1921 introduced their New Economic Policy (NEP) which suspended the Communist programme; they had also become convinced that they must come to commercial terms with the big capitalist powers. The willingness of Lloyd George to do this had been interrupted by the Russian invasion of Poland. In March 1921, however, two days before the Treaty of Riga between Poland and Russia, an Anglo-Russian trading treaty was agreed and in fact a Russo-German one was achieved two months later in May 1921. Soon after this the general economic confusion of Russia was intensified by the disaster of famine in the Volga area and elsewhere. For the time being the trade treaties remained difficult to implement.

The attitude of post-war Germany towards Soviet Russia was a complicated one. The mass of Social Democratic trades unionists was eager to come to terms with the West and suspicious of Communism, though in certain parts of Germany, such as Saxony or Hamburg, many industrial workers were at this stage Communists or nearly so. The old ruling classes and everyone dependent upon them detested Bolshevism on principle as Socialist, godless and foreign. Nevertheless, among certain members of the officer class there was a love-hate feeling for the Soviets, a rueful admiration for the dynamics, the ruthlessness of their revolution; there was, indeed,

a certain ambition to achieve something like it in Germany in German terms, National Bolshevism. Detestation of the new Poland, which was regarded as the arch-symbol of the 'tyranny' of Versailles, created more sympathy for Soviet Russia during the Russo-Polish war. Although the defeat of Russia at Warsaw in August 1920 reduced this feeling, it did anything but destroy it.

Hans von Seeckt

Probably the most powerful single influence in Germany in this period was that of General Hans von Seeckt. His power rested on two facts, one being that the remnants of the Imperial German Army were under his control and he was responsible for their reorganization into the Reichswehr, which according to the Treaty of Versailles was to be a small professional army of 100,000 men without important weapons. Seeckt had every intention of expanding and rearming this army illicitly with up-to-date weapons. The second fact which made Seeckt powerful was that the Socialist rulers of the new Weimar Republic had appealed to Seeckt for military support. When their power was challenged from the extreme Right or Left, he had agreed to back them, so that they depended physically upon him and his embryonic army. Seeckt had agreed to this, not because he liked the Weimar Republic, but because for the time being he saw no other possibility of any political stability in Germany. A republic which depended upon him and his soldiers could be discarded when he and his soldiers felt the time was ripe to go back to a more authoritarian regime, more like that of Bismarck.

Seeckt's opinions were in fact strikingly close to those of Bismarck in almost every way, particularly with regard to Poland. Polish nationalism was nonsense; Poland could be nothing but a menace to Germany and therefore had no right to exist; its only conceivable justification was that it was equally obnoxious to Russia and hence gave any kind of Russia an interest in common with Germany. Bismarck, in being pro-Russian, had a simpler position because in siding with Russia he was siding with authoritarian monarchy, the only form of government of which he approved. But Seeckt was undaunted by the Russian Revolution. He felt no scruple about resisting its influence mercilessly within Germany and at the same time co-operating with the Soviet authorities in all sorts of ways outside Germany. The Russo-Polish war made it clearer to him that Germany could make good use of Russia in evading the implementation of the Treaty of Versailles; sooner or later he felt sure that the Poland of Versailles would be destroyed, and he hoped for the restoration of the Russo-German frontiers of 1914.

Supply and demand

The leaders of German heavy industry had long worked in alliance with the German military authorities – in a sense they had always done so. Imperial Russia had been one of their most important markets, and Krupp and Stinnes felt paralysed by the disappearance of any major outlet to the east; they would have felt this without the obligations laid on Germany by the peace treaties. After the initial shock of the Bolshevik Revolution, which represented everything inimical and repulsive to them, they began to feel, as Lenin was also beginning to feel, that they and the new Russians needed each other, as Lenin said, as 'merchants'. These feelings were at the back of the commercial agreement between the two countries in May 1921 and led to the foundation of various Russo-German mixed companies later in that year – Krupp was involved in one, and another iron and steel magnate, Otto Wolff, in a second.

When the famine came in Russia German organizations were thus in a position to provide help more practically than other countries except for the American Relief Administration organized by Hoover. German indignation against the Entente Powers rose steadily during 1921, partly with the presentation of the Allies' reparations bill on 1st May, and partly as the result of the plebiscite in Upper Silesia on 20th March. German public opinion was enraged because, in spite of a German majority, the Entente Powers in October 1921 decided upon a division of Upper Silesia between Poland and Germany while insisting upon a German-Polish agreement to preserve the economic unity of Upper Silesia for 15 years. (Agreement on this was not reached until May 1922.)

It appears that in the winter following the battle of Warsaw Seeckt had already started up a small secret department in the German War Office to concern itself with the possibilities of manufacturing in Russia the arms for Germany which the Peace Treaty forbade. In March 1921, at much the same time as the Treaty of Riga ending the Russo-Polish war, a Communist rising in Germany was attempted but easily supressed. It has been suggested that Seeckt was all the readier for military understandings with the Russians after this demonstration of the impotence of German Communists. Early in 1921 Trotsky, people's commissar for war, seems to have responded favourably to German probings. Trotsky thus became a pioneer in the Communist technique of exhorting humble Communists in other countries to resist at deadly risk a regime with which the Soviet authorities had every intention of doing business. For Trotsky of course had every interest in engaging German specialists to rebuild the Russian armaments industry and to get Russians trained by German officers in modern military techniques: there was a particularly strong common interest in training pilots. At any rate it was secretly agreed by early in April 1921 that German firms should manufacture aeroplanes, submarines, and weapons of all kinds, including poison gas, on Russian territory. A company was founded in Berlin as a cover for the Reichswehr and for German firms to organize illicit arms transactions with Soviet Russia. This was the beginning of years of close and secret collaboration between direct ideological enemies – apparently the Russians and Germans involved worked together as the happiest of colleagues until the days of Hitler.

Until October 1921 the machinations of Seeckt were known to none but the few of his military subordinates whom he chose to tell. It appears, however, that he now calculated that his financial needs might be greater than he could supply from his own secret funds. So he confided what was going on to Wirth, who was chancellor and also at that time minister of finance. Wirth made no objection. At about this time a change that was to count for much was made at the German Foreign Office; Ago von Maltzan, a brilliant and keen supporter of a pro-Russian policy, was brought back from a post in Athens to preside over the eastern division of the German Foreign Office. He was soon initiated into the affair of secret

German-Russian collaboration over armaments and training. Ebert, the President of the German Republic, was only informed later.

The Genoa Conference

Towards the end of 1921 the plan of a Consortium to help reconstruct Russia economically was discussed in Paris and London: this was to involve the co-ordinated action of international capital, and was fiercely resisted by the Russians as likely to reduce them to the economic dependence of a 'colony'. When the Supreme Allied Council met at Cannes in January 1922 Lloyd George put forward the Consortium idea in connection with the wish of the USSR to trade with the capitalist world. A German delegate at Cannes, Walther Rathenau, expressed approval of an international syndicate to assist Russia. On 6th January 1922, at the recommendation of Lloyd George, an economic and financial conference was convened to which all the European powers, including Russia and Germany, were to be invited to consider how 'to remedy the paralysis of the European system'. This conference was to meet at Genoa.

In the intervening period relations between France and Britain worsened because Briand's government fell and he was succeeded by Poincaré who took a hard line towards German non-payment of reparations. In Germany although Wirth appointed Rathenau as foreign minister in February 1922, he, who represented German light industry and its links with the West, lost influence to German heavy industry: the latter rejected the Consortium idea, wishing to deal with Russia independently. This tendency in Germany was encouraged by the arrival of the Russian delegates to Genoa in Berlin with suggestions that Germany should come to terms with the USSR before the Genoa Conference even met. The Russian foreign minister, Chicherin, joined the Russian mission after its other members had reached the German capital and he increased the pressure on the Germans. But Rathenau was determined to go to Genoa first and come to terms with the West if he could find any way of doing so. The Russians insinuated that Moscow was on the verge of coming to terms with France and of agreeing to demand reparations for Russia from Germany

in accordance with Article 116 of the Treaty of Versailles. Thus when the Genoa Conference met on 10th April the Germans were in great anxiety. This particularly applied to Rathenau, whose hypersensitive temperament exposed him to the Russian threats. At Genoa, however, Rathenau was kept in idleness while Lloyd George repeatedly received the Russian delegates in secrecy at his villa where he refused to receive Rathenau.

In the night of 15th to 16th April — 16th April was Easter Sunday — the Russian delegate, Rakovsky, telephoned from Rapallo to Maltzan who was in Genoa: the Russian conversations with Lloyd George had been concerned with old scores such as Russian pre-war debts and hence had been unsatisfactory to the Russians. Rakovsky therefore suggested that the Russian and German delegates should meet forthwith at Rapallo. In spite of the disagreeable insinuations made by the Russians in Berlin, just before the conference met at Rapallo a Russo-German agreement had been worked out in some detail, and the Russians now suggested that this should be completed. Rathenau still hoped to come to terms with Lloyd George, the more so if the Russians had been unsuccessful. But Maltzan threatened to resign if Rathenau did not immediately lead his delegation to Rapallo: Wirth supported Maltzan who laughed later over this 'rape of Rathenau'.

It was thus that on Easter Sunday, 16th April 1922, the Weimar Republic and the USSR signed at Rapallo a treaty which, according to its third article, re-established full diplomatic and consular relations between them. By Article 1 all claims to reparations from Germany, or to compensation for German property confiscated in Russia, were cancelled. Article 4 provided most-favoured nation treatment and Article 5 stipulated that 'the two governments shall co-operate in a spirit of mutual goodwill in meeting the economic needs of both countries'.

(It was the second treaty to be signed at Rapallo within two years: the first was between Italy and Yugoslavia in 1920.)

The immediate result of the Treaty of Rapallo was an increased anti-German indignation in France, and also in Britain for Lloyd George himself had been strangely unforeseeing of the Russo-German rapprochement. Indeed, relations between

Germany and the West now rushed down the slope leading to the Franco-Belgian occupation of the Ruhr in January 1923. The USSR was soon represented by Krestinski as ambassador in Berlin. After some initial difficulties, Count Brockdorff-Rantzau went to Moscow to represent Germany. He was a difficult character, imperious in his demands, who, however, got on well with Chicherin, and was not out of sympathy with Soviet Russia.

Naturally there were rumours that the Treaty of Rapallo contained secret military clauses; this was not strictly true because the secret military understanding preceded it and worked independently of it.

The longer-term results of the Treaty of Rapallo were on the one hand that it increased Germany's reputation for duplicity –Rapallo became a synonym for this in the West–but on the other hand it enhanced Germany's bargaining power, becoming an important factor in Stresemann's diplomatic success. There were, however, several severe ups and downs in Russo-German relations in the years immediately following Rapallo. In October 1923, the year of the French occupation of the Ruhr, of the complete collapse of the German currency, and of Stresemann's heroic acceptance of the chancellorship in August, Moscow ordered the Germans to instigate the 'world revolution' in Germany.

It was a total miscalculation by Russia. Moscow supposed that the catastrophe of the German currency would cause the German Social Democrats to support the German Communist Party. It seems fondly to have imagined that the military understanding with Seeckt might inhibit the Reichswehr from decisive intervention against a Communist uprising. In actual fact President Ebert on 26th September entrusted Seeckt with special powers according to that part of Article 48 of the Weimar Constitution which dealt with martial law. The German Communist leader, Brandler, finding no Socialist support, was obliged to call off insurrection in the leftist strongholds of Saxony and Thuringia, and a rising in Hamburg was attempted only through a misunderstanding. The Reichswehr had not the slightest difficulty in ousting the Socialist and Communist leaders from Saxony and Thuringia, and from Hamburg as well. Indeed it proved an advantage to

Seeckt and to Stresemann when they suppressed Hitler's putsch the following month to have appeared firm in dealing with insurgents from the other side.

The 'German October' has been described by some writers as the end of Rapallo. A never fully explained incident in the following May, when police invaded the offices of the Soviet trade delegation in Berlin, did not improve the atmosphere. Moreover, from now on Stresemann was absorbed with the diplomacy of coming to terms with the western powers without guaranteeing Germany's eastern frontiers. The fact that he could indicate that the USSR was still bound to him by the Treaty of Rapallo strengthened his hand: it implied that the Germans could choose their partner. Although the Russians by 1924 had received a fairly general diplomatic recognition they displayed an almost fantastic sensitivity about Stresemann's negotiations with the West. The reconstruction of Germany, which had really taken place according to the Dawes Plan, did of course appear to the Soviet rulers as the capture of Germany by the West. The idea of Germany as a member of the League of Nations, which the Soviet authorities persisted for years in regarding as an 'imperialist conspiracy' against them, filled them with anxiety.

Stresemann, at all events, made it clear to Moscow that he did not wish to sign a new treaty with the USSR before his treaties with the western powers – finally concluded at Locarno in 1925 – had gone through. He also guaranteed that he would only join the League of Nations on condition that Article 16 of the Covenant of the League, obliging members to use force against any aggressor, was modified. He achieved this, the obligation being reduced to being conditional upon the location and armaments of each member. In March 1926, however, when Germany was to have entered the League, there were unexpected obstacles. The Russians did have another, smaller, triumph, for in April 1926 in Berlin a Russo-German treaty, more or less prolonging Rapallo, was signed, after Locarno, certainly, but before Germany was welcomed into the Council of the League of Nations in September.

This Treaty of Berlin, however, was relatively uninteresting. It was at most a warning to Poland that only her alliance with France (originally made in February 1921), could protect her against the hostility of Russia and Germany. At Rapallo the two 'outcast' powers had come to terms in spite of the flat contradiction between their political ideologies. This had been sensational. By 1926 the trade between them had visibly expanded and their military collaboration had invisibly grown. Both states were now secure and accepted, and Germany was enjoying a remarkable prosperity.

Poincaré: Hammer of the Germans

Alistair Horne

To many Frenchmen, Poincaré symbolized not only the war of 1914-18, but also the occupation of the Ruhr and the dogged spirit of Lorraine – the one a virtual continuation of the war, the other a lost province which the war had at last won back for France. But these were over-simplifications: his background and his actions were more complex.

Poincaré, in the first place, was never a man who wanted war. In the summer of 1914, he did all he could to prevent the impending catastrophe; though, when it came, his moral leadership of France as President has linked his name lastingly with the First World War. He had been among those who, before 1914, thought that a strong France – strong in her government, her army, and her alliances – could discourage German aggression and avert war. So too, after 1919, he believed strength would prevent any recovery of German military power.

Then again, the occupation of the Ruhr basin at the beginning of 1923 was certainly Poincaré's decision, but he took it hesitatingly, while colleagues pressed for immediate action. 'If I don't undertake it myself,' he said in the end, 'someone else will be entrusted with it. And he won't do it so well.'

And Poincaré was indeed a man of Lorraine; but not of the Lorraine annexed by Germany in 1871 – he was no exile pining for a lost homeland. He was born in Bar-le-Duc in 1860, and his parents were native to the western part of Lorraine. But even so he learned to know invasion in 1870 and to fear the German aggressor at an early age.

Early contact with national disaster did much to mould the future statesman, to produce the severity, the inflexibility to-wards Germany for which Poincaré is remembered. He had seen German aggression, his school years had been shaped under its shadow.

The measured, rational outlook of his liberal middle-class background had also influenced Poincaré's thought: there would be none of the emotional optimism of a Briand in his approach to the German problem, no trust in some hidden better nature in France's enemy. Another element in Poincaré was the quality of his own considerable intellect, its logical cast, its precision. Poincaré therefore not only became a lawyer, but his political actions and outlook were concerned in the first place with legality. So, in the years after 1919, it was the legality of the Treaty of Versailles which he always emphasized.

Poincaré was not in his personality an outstanding man, he was neither colourful nor commanding. By nature he was shy, even timid, and often indecisive. His intellect, his mastery of fact and detail, his uprightness and honesty, brought him respect and gave him increasing confidence; but he was not one to sway men's hearts, to inspire them with his dreams, to stand head and shoulders above them or to be their leader: he was in no way a man of fire, a Clemenceau. Middle-class Frenchmen saw in him a man like themselves, a man they could trust in a crisis.

It was work on budgetary commissions, not any political finesse, which first brought him to office in 1893. Ten years later he entered the Senate, and by 1906 had made his name, both as a barrister and a parliamentarian. The same year he became, briefly, minister of finance; but his ambition was to become prime minister, and he did not again accept a lesser office.

Following the Agadir incident, a Senate committee of inquiry was set up into the handling of negotiations with Germany by the prime minister, Caillaux; Poincaré played a prominent part on it. The committee showed hostility to Caillaux, who was thought to be a pacifist and appeaser, and its criticism led to Caillaux's resignation. On 12th January 1912 the President, Fallières, entrusted Poincaré with the formation of his first government.

Poincaré was by now widely known for his integrity, his indifference to party manoeuvres, and his devotion to the interests of France, and his appointment received considerable public support.

At the beginning of 1913, Fallières's seven-year term of office as President came to an end, and Poincaré allowed his name to be put forward for election. He was, however, violently opposed by the Left in a ruthless campaign led by his old critic Clemenceau, and though he was elected, it was by a small majority. Nevertheless, at this time of international tension and increasing French uneasiness, Poincaré was greeted as the saviour of the country, the man above party and sectional interests, the embodiment of France itself.

France went to war in 1914 inspired with heroic patriotism. The response to Poincaré's appeal for a government of national union, a *union sacrée* of all parliamentary interests in face of the invader, was immediate and sincere. This firm coalition government was at first given full powers by parliament; but as the war dragged on, the Chamber demanded a greater say in the government, with secret sessions in which it could exercise some control over the cabinet and the army commanders.

As parliamentary participation in the war increased, governments became weaker, more partisan, and more transient. In the critical days of November 1917, Poincaré, with remarkable statesmanship, called on his persistent antagonist Clemenceau to form a government. As president of the army committee since the outbreak, Clemenceau had nagged away unceasingly at the conduct of the war, and Poincaré had not escaped his bitter criticism. Now, at the age of seventy-six, but retaining his unquenchable vigour and independence, Clemenceau was the man France needed. He dominated the Allied camp in this last year of war and drove France to victory.

Shortly after the armistice, Poincaré and Clemenceau made a triumphant tour of the newly recovered territories of Lorraine and Alsace — visiting Metz, Strasbourg, Colmar, and Mulhouse. 'Now I can die,' sighed Poincaré, echoing the lassitude of so many others. But new trials awaited him. Clemenceau a war leader had been one thing; Clemenceau negotiating peace and security for victorious France was another matter, and Poincaré was extremely uneasy. But faced by a prime minister who refused to consult him, he was helpless, so small in fact was the authority left to a President.

As negotiations resolved themselves into secret bargaining between President Wilson, Lloyd George, and Clemenceau, Poincaré's anxiety, and humiliation, increased; for he realized that Clemenceau was being induced to negotiate away France's hopes of tangible security — a frontier on the Rhine, which Poincaré as well as Foch regarded as being worth more than all the polite Anglo-American promises for the future.

It was not long after the Treaty of Versailles was signed that both Clemenceau and Poincaré left the scene of their dual leadership. The 1919 elections brought in, for the final time in decades, a right-wing Chamber, and early in 1920, Poincaré's term of office as President came to an end. At last he could leave his 'prison', he was free to speak and act. He was re-elected to his old seat in the Senate without difficulty and at once appointed chairman of the Reparations Commission.

Political fortune is perverse. Clemenceau, no longer prime minister, was defeated as a candidate for the presidency in 1920, and passed the last years of his life in straitened circumstances. Poincaré, remaining in the political arena, was honoured as France's saviour.

It is hard to see statesmanship in the narrow horizons of Poincaré, Clemenceau, and Foch in 1919. But France had been invaded, while Great Britain and the United States had no experience, and therefore little understanding, of the desperation and the lasting sense of insecurity that invasion brings. Foch, backed by Poincaré, had pleaded for an independent buffer state at least to be carved out of Germany's Rhineland: Lloyd George retorted, 'You're not going to make another Alsace-Lorraine!'

While Wilson and Lloyd George planned the new Europe, of which neither would be part, the four-years' battlefield lay, a scar of devastation, across France's northeastern provinces, over her wheat-lands and through her coalfields; and in their retreat in 1918, the Germans had deliberately flooded the French mines. It was natural that Frenchmen should be thinking of Germany as a beast to be caged, of security as a matter of physical barriers and of territory on the Rhine as compensation for her weakness in manpower.

Poincaré regretted the compromises and concessions which Clemenceau had made over the peace treaty, but the treaty was now signed and a legal fact, and Poincaré, as a lawyer, would respect and uphold its legality, its binding force, whatever its shortcomings. He saw too that in France's interests the treaty must be made to work: it was all she had.

The hope of positive security against Germany had again receded when the British and American promises of guarantees against unprovoked aggression, which Clemenceau had so joyfully accepted in place of a Rhineland barrier, proved to be a mirage. But some security, it seemed, could still lie in Germany's continued weakness, and a return to prosperity in Germany was felt by French politicians to be as much a danger as any German recovery of military power. This attitude lay at the root of France's contradictory approach to the problem of reparations from Germany: she demanded astronomical sums – 209,000 million gold francs for herself alone – and yet denied Germany all means of producing this wealth. Reparations had ceased to be just reparation for physical war damage: they had become instead a political weapon to ensure that Germany remained defeated. Reparations poisoned international relations for many years. 'More than anything else,' A.J.P. Taylor has written, 'they cleared the way for the Second World War.'

When the United States refused to ratify the Treaty of Versailles and backed out of its European obligations, it became all the more important that France should retain the support of Great Britain. But over reparations, as over France's physical security, British politicians proved increasingly unreceptive. Not only did they see in a prosperous Germany a debtor better able to foot the bill, but also a more useful market for British trade. And the overwhelming power the French army had retained after 1918, which seemed linked with symptoms of territorial acquisitiveness, worried them more than the distant threat of German militarism.

In January 1921 the liberal Briand had become prime minister and foreign minister in the right-wing Chamber. He was inclined to see some justice in the British point of view, and he and Lloyd George were not unlike in outlook and temperament. The two prime ministers met at Cannes in January 1922 to try to find ways for a common approach to the German problem on a new basis. But Briand's moves provoked extreme nervousness in Paris, and his two most powerful opponents, President Millerand and Poincaré, now chairman of the Senate Committee on Foreign Affairs, forced Briand's resignation.

Since leaving the presidency, Poincaré had devoted his energies, in parliament and in newspaper articles, to the defence of French policies and to the harassment of a recalcitrant Germany. He had been chairman of the Reparations Commission, and his background and competence in the field of political finance made the problem of reparations his natural concern. It was indeed in his character and training to regard the due payment of reparations by Germany as an immovable corner-stone of the whole legal structure of the Treaty of Versailles. For him, the security of France, imperilled by the failure to create adequate physical barriers, was now entrenched in the regular payment of reparations.

After Briand's resignation, it was evident to Millerand and the conservative deputies that Poincaré was the man the country now needed, and he was greeted as the new premier and foreign minister with general satisfaction. The declaration of policy of Poincaré's cabinet on 19th January 1922 showed that France once more had a government which would allow no nonsense: 'The problem of reparations dominates all others,' it read, 'and if Germany, in this essential question, fails in its obligations, we shall be forced to examine, after seeking advice from the Reparations Commission, the measures to be taken.'

Years of France's obstinacy

The 1920's in France were not, in fact, years hammered out by the will of one exceptional man. They were the years of all France's obstinacy, expressed through Poincaré, of a whole country's weary determination in the face of a changed and changing Europe. Despite the shades and divisions of French political outlook at this time, Poincaré's attitude towards Germany was that of France; and Briand's paths of adventure stemmed merely from the same fruitless search for security which engaged them all.

The German mark was falling rapidly,

and the already thorny path of reparations payments was reaching an impasse. In Great Britain it was thought that the excessive French demands for reparations were the cause of the German inflation; in France it was thought that Germany was deliberately causing inflation to evade the payment of reparations. There was a certain amount of truth in both views. Soon, however, the mark was getting out of hand, and the German government was asking for a moratorium on payments. Lloyd George, more flexible than Poincaré, was ready to agree, but Poincaré was obdurate, and the gulf between the outlook of the two countries, which Briand had started to bridge, now widened. Matters were made worse when the United States, now the distant creditor of all, agitated for settlement and provoked inter-Allied wrangling over debts.

The fall of Lloyd George and his replacement by the more conciliatory Bonar Law made little difference: British financial interests were still concerned with the economic revival of Germany, and Lord Curzon, as stubborn as ever, remained at the Foreign Office. An international conference to consider Germany's request for a moratorium was held in London in December 1922, at which Italy was represented for the first time by Mussolini. Poincaré agreed to nothing: if there were any moratorium on payments from Germany, it could only be allowed in exchange for guarantees; and such guarantees, 'productive pledges', must be provided by the coal mines and steel mills of the Ruhr basin, the heart of Germany's heavy industry. The deadlock was complete.

Poincaré returned to Paris convinced of the rightness of his cause and disappointed that Bonar Law had seemed unable to see his point of view; but he was uncertain what should be done next. He was by nature and training a redoubtable advocate, but faced with the need for action he could be a prey to indecision. Parliament, the President, and his cabinet colleagues, notably Maginot, minister of war, pressed him to act. To satisfy his own mind, Poincaré worked out legal justification for steps against Germany over the non-delivery of a reparation consignment of timber and telegraph poles; but still he hesitated. A renewed Allied economic conference at the beginning of January 1923 brought no

agreement. Then on 11th January a commission of French, Belgian, and Italian engineers, supported by two French divisions and a Belgian detachment, entered the Ruhr and took possession of its mines and factories. Poincaré's announcement in the Chamber was approved by a massive vote. France had come to make sure of her guarantees.

Since the end of the war, the Allies had already been occupying all the left bank of the Rhine – Cologne, Koblenz, Mainz, the Palatinate, the Eifel – and some parts of the right bank, and to occupy the Ruhr was geographically only an extension of the main occupation. There had been other temporary occupations too, or threats to occupy, to help enforce Allied demands. But the occupation of the Ruhr, an area on which the whole German economy was dependent, coming at a time when their finances were already in disruption, was the last straw to the German government, who immediately organized and subsidized passive resistance throughout the Ruhr: the area was completely strike-bound, and there was sabotage and violence. The crisis finally destroyed the German currency, and worthless bank-notes with a face value of millions of marks were swapped in English schools by the sons of officers serving on the Rhine.

By September 1923, beaten by French persistence and efficiency, the Ruhr strikes were over. French technicians had got mines, mills, and railways working despite all German opposition, and the coal and steel were flowing westward, into Belgium and France: the guarantee was being slowly made productive.

Technically, the Ruhr occupation had been a minor victory for France, and Poincaré continued to enjoy the support of parliament. But outside that conservative citadel, the French people were realizing that the cost of the operation was proving too high, particularly in precious manpower. The Allies were faced, too, with a prostrate Germany, from whom monetary reparations at least could not immediately be expected. The German industrialists who had first manipulated the mark into its decline were now ready for peace at any price, and for once the chance for economic agreement between France and Germany was there, for the marriage of Lorraine iron-ore and Ruhr coal, for the adjustment of Franco-German relations on the basis of their mutual economic needs. But to the lawyer Poincaré, the occupation of the Ruhr had served its purpose: it had made Germany see the force of France's demands. To his precise mind there was no further political advantage to look for.

The Dawes Plan

The occupation of the Ruhr lingered on into the summer of 1924. But by then the British government, especially after Ramsay MacDonald became prime minister, was putting pressure on France to withdraw. So evacuation of the Ruhr was made part of the new Dawes Plan for reparations. The plan was accepted by Poincaré, and ratified under Herriot after the elections of May 1924, when the right-wing Chamber was outvoted by a coalition of the Left.

The Dawes Plan, and later the Young Plan, emerged out of Germany's financial collapse, and the United States, still keeping its official distance from Europe, was to guide negotiations into more temperate and more practical channels in an attempt to obtain for the European Allies at least sufficient reparations from Germany to enable them to pay their American debts. The occupation of the Ruhr had had the merit of bringing back some sense and proportion into France's reparation demands. In Germany it had brought in Schacht to retrieve the currency and Stresemann to work for the return of Germany to the fold; but the Ruhr episode had also given substance to the rantings of a demagogue called Hitler.

Herriot, the new French prime minister, was no financial wizard, and he took office at a time when the Ruhr occupation and the continued default in German reparations were beginning to have a marked effect on the French economy. The reconstruction of the war-ravaged north-eastern provinces of France, for which German reparations had initially been intended, had been going on steadily and obstinately, undeterred by political uncertainties, and by 1926 it was virtually complete. It had been financed immediately by internal loans. The holders of these bonds expected to be repaid by German reparations. The failure of reparations to materialize made the bond-holders nervous. It had been planned, too, to wipe out the enormous French budget deficit with the help of

reparations. This seemed now impossible. The franc itself began to spiral downwards. Such a situation has never been food and drink to a coalition of the Left.

As confidence in the franc diminished, ministries succeeded one another and a committee of experts reported. The franc had fallen in two years from a rate of 70 to the pound to 243 when, in July 1926, the Radicals, whose instincts were conservative and orthodox where their pockets were concerned, dropped the Socialists and turned to Poincaré as their rescuer. So a new government of National Union (in fact, more of the Centre than national) was accepted by this Chamber of the Left, headed, incongruously, by 'Poincaré la guerre, Poincaré la Ruhr'.

It needed only the announcement of Poincaré's appointment to make the franc rise immediately to 220 to the pound, such was the faith, Ruhr or no Ruhr, in his integrity and competence. The measures he took were firm and unspectacular, and little different from those recommended to the previous government by the experts. It had been in many ways a crisis of confidence, and Poincaré's sure hand guided the franc back to a rate of 120-125 to the pound. In June 1928, after elections had returned a majority in favour of his policy, Poincaré stabilized the franc and based it on gold again — at a fifth of its pre-war value. Such, in the end, was the measure of the cost of the war to France.

In this Centre coalition Briand remained foreign minister throughout, with the aura of the Locarno Pact around him and a reputation for the conduct of foreign affairs as magical as Poincaré's for financial competence. It was strange to see these two in harness, Poincaré, the bitter upholder of each word in the Treaty of Versailles, and Briand, flexible, conciliatory, linked in the public mind with Germany's Stresemann. But the Poincaré-Briand years, with their new stability at home, also mark a time of constructive work by France abroad: security, that elusive goal, could perhaps be attained by a series of pacts, or even through the machinery of the League of Nations. It was not until severe illness had suddenly removed Poincaré from the scene in July 1929, however, that Briand allowed himself to make his big concession to Germany, advancing the final withdrawal of occupation troops from the Rhineland to

Occupation of the Ruhr

Maurice Baumont

When it became clear that the United States intended to take no further part in the implementation of a peace treaty so forcefully stamped with its own influence, Frenchmen saw two courses of action open to them. Some like Clemenceau's successor, Millerand, wanted to take advantage of the country's military superiority to smash German resistance and enforce the Treaty of Versailles with the utmost severity. This attitude triumphed with Poincaré's occupation of the Ruhr in 1923. But there were French politicians who did not want to apply the treaty to the letter, a liberalism which led to much-improved relations with Germany after 1923.

In the months immediately following the war the four great powers had tried to form some clear idea of what reparations should be demanded of Germany. A number of Allied experts submitted wild estimates for the financial indemnity they thought Germany should pay, and on 26th March 1919 the French industrialist and politician Loucheur told Lloyd George that France should, if necessary, occupy the Ruhr to enforce payments.

Henceforth the occupation of the Ruhr was to loom large on the horizon at many of the international reparation conferences. In fact, the French never ceased threatening occupation as long as Germany maintained her recalcitrant attitude and appeared disinclined to honour her pledges under the Treaty of Versailles.

In January 1921 Aristide Briand formed a government. He affirmed his desire to obtain for France 'her due, all her due', and on 5th April he assured the Reich that it would see a 'firm hand fall on its neck' if it tried to avoid its commitments by further obstruction and vacillation. On 12th April he threatened 'to have recourse to the police if the debtor persists in his recalcitrance'.

Poincaré, who at this time was chairman of the Senate Commission on Foreign Affairs, sharply criticized 'the singular forbearance which is being shown to Germany at a time when France has . . . the means to enforce respect for the peace treaty'.

Moreover, the President of the Republic, Millerand, together with many of Briand's ministers, was not prepared to accept a proposal that Germany be granted a moratorium on reparations payments. This suggestion had been agreed to by Lloyd George and others at the 1922 Cannes conference. The proposal provoked a furore in France and compelled Briand to resign. 'Others will do better,' he told the Chamber of Deputies on 12th January 1922 as he stepped down to make way for Poincaré. Poincaré symbolized French determination to impose a strict and rigorous interpretation of the Versailles Treaty on Germany. He had never been slow to denounce its half-hearted application in the past and had resigned as French delegate on the Reparations Commission which he thought had been neutralized when the San Remo conference decided, in April 1920, that representatives of Allied governments should meet again to enable Germany to put her point of view.

His attitude was apparently backed by events. On 10th April 1922, Wirth, the German chancellor, informed the Reparations Commission that Germany was unable to continue payments. 'First bread, then reparations!' he declared.

Poincaré gauges opinion

Poincaré had no intention of granting a moratorium without security. He was, moreover, angered by the Reich's preparations for revenge, which included the hoarding of arms, the avoidance of disarmament regulations, and increased recruiting to para-military organizations. He also denounced the total apathy of the German government in the face of inflation and expressed the conviction that the German government was to be equated with the large Ruhr industrialists.

Although Poincaré proposed to seize the Ruhr and then negotiate with the Reich, he was a careful and somewhat

1930, five years before the treaty's term, though leaving it demilitarized.

Poincaré never fully recovered health and was forced to remain outside active politics. When he died on 15th October 1934, the financial stability which he had so patiently restored to France was in serious danger; in the Germa attempted to render harmless, l and promised military glory, shortly to march back into the l and Poincaré's own France, whc helped to steer, united, through t terrors of war, was again cruell

C
t

N

indecisive man who viewed the formidable task of occupying the Ruhr with considerable anxiety.

There were after all many objections to what was essentially a financial enterprise. Czechoslovakia, a faithful ally of France, was against the operation, fearing it might lead to disastrous upheavals in Central Europe.

Marshal Foch and Clemenceau (in illtempered retirement) once again found themselves at one in expressing their instinctive apprehensions. But opinion on the whole was favourable. Millerand, President of the Republic, was a vigorous supporter of occupation, as was the war minister André Maginot. They thought it obvious that the huge Rhine-Westphalian industrial complex was the nerve centre of resistance to the Versailles Treaty and considered it necessary to strike at the very heart of the business areas which constituted the main strength of the Reich. There is no doubt that the fall of Lloyd George considerably reinforced Poincaré's position and encouraged him to strike a psychological blow at a Reich discredited by its sudden friendship with Bolshevik Russia.

Dangerous counter-moves might have originated from the imaginative Lloyd George, but not from his successors. The British statesman could have reached an understanding with Clemenceau or Briand but his amazing lack of restraint would not have permitted any fruitful exchange of views with an obstinate, legalistic, carping, and frequently argumentative Poincaré.

The Conservatives – Bonar Law and his successor, Stanley Baldwin – shared Lloyd George's view of the reparations question, but they were mentally static and fundamentally conciliatory and would never sour a difficult discussion with a sharp and vindictive francophobia as Lloyd George would have done.

At the beginning of November 1922 the Reparations Commission arrived in Berlin under the leadership of its new president, the subtle, energetic, Louis Barthou. It immediately found itself faced with a situation largely the result of war-time destruction and general economic errors incorporated in the peace treaty. The coffers were officially empty and all liquid resources had been taken abroad under Allied supervision. But Germany had done little to help itself. The large industrialists – to all intents and purposes the controllers of the Ruhr – had systematically speculated with the mark, pleading the burden of reparations as an excuse.

On 13th November, the Reich officially asked for a reparations moratorium. The threadbare Wirth government, deprived of even the semblance of authority, was replaced by a more right-wing cabinet under Wilhelm Cuno, director-general of the large Hamburg Amerika company. Since Great Britain no longer believed in the possibility of obtaining any substantial reparations from Germany, Poincaré was forced to take unilateral action.

Soon after, the Reparations Commission certified Germany's insolvency. The country had only delivered seventy-eight per cent of the coal and eighty-four per cent of the coke it had undertaken to supply. Germany had clearly failed to abide by its word. But the Cuno government certainly committed a massive error in permitting the catastrophic occupation of the Ruhr to be launched in reprisal for what were little more than minor shortcomings.

Although British and French opinions on the occupation of the Ruhr clashed, the ensuing breach between the two countries was made in an atmosphere which remained friendly. Bonar Law observed that British opinion would be shocked by the occupation of the Ruhr but Poincaré replied that whatever happened he had to go ahead with it. Both, however, expressed the conviction that Franco-British friendship would not be affected.

Belgium, although sensitive to pressure from London, associated herself with the operation and Mussolini, aware of Italy's coal shortage, sent some Italian engineers, who joined the French and Belgian engineers in making up the inter-Allied mission for the control of works and mines. This engineers' mission was shielded by Franco-Belgian forces under the command of General Degoutte.

The operation is launched

'We are going to look for coal, that's all!' Poincaré told the Chamber, 'if this search gives us the opportunity, sooner or later, of talking with a more conciliatory Germany or to less exacting industrialists, we will not shun doing so. We have no intention of strangling Germany or ruining her; we only want to obtain from her what we can reasonably expect her to provide.'

The Chamber approved the entry into the Ruhr by 452 votes to 72. It had been, after all, a legally authorized action, specifically designed to counter German default on reparations payments. The Ruhr operation, however, became unexpectedly large. It was planned with reference to the experience gained when Frankfurt was occupied in 1920 and Düsseldorf, Ruhrort, and Duisburg a year later, and no serious, certainly no obstinate, resistance was expected. In fact it sparked off nation-wide opposition in Germany. Encouraged by the vehement protests this peace-time 'invasion' provoked, notably in Great Britain, Germans were as one in feeling they had to put up opposition in the only way possible, by 'passive resistance', which amounted to a general strike.

The occupation of the Ruhr stirred up national fury in Germany the like of which neither the war nor the Versailles peace had aroused. France was made responsible for all misfortune; restaurants even stuck up signs reading: 'Dogs and Frenchmen forbidden.'

The German government came to bear an enormous responsibility, for it had to succour an immense number of people as a result of the passive resistance proclaimed in the Ruhr and extended throughout the occupied territories. Its greatest burden was the assumption of responsibility for the tens of thousands expelled from the Ruhr. It had to support the workers and railwaymen who were sacked when they refused to work, and it had to help their families. Cascades of paper money were poured into a seemingly bottomless pit, and Germany was in no state to sustain a long financial battle of this kind.

Miners and workers of every sort were sent into the occupied Ruhr from France and Belgium and the two countries took it upon themselves to keep the main railway lines open.

Almost the whole German population was ranged against the occupation troops, and reactions abroad were more serious than had been foreseen. Stanley Baldwin stated that the French, in occupying the Ruhr, were like children who had tampered with a watch and damaged its complex works with a knife. Coal, he maintained, could not be extracted by force of arms, and Pius XI observed that one cannot secure peace with bayonets.

Sabotage began to disturb the occupation authorities. Railway lines were blown up and secret organizations began to form an underground Reichswehr. 'Passive resistance' was threatening to become active resistance. Schlageter, who specialized in derailing trains, was shot and became a national hero whose portrait was shown everywhere, although his was the only death sentence to be carried out.

On 22nd May 1923 Poincaré declared: 'We are patiently waiting for Germany to see reason' – and Gustav Stresemann, the founder of the Volkspartei, the party of the industrialists, had no illusions about France's ability to tighten the screw. France, he said, had become 'the only great military force in Europe. At the height of his glory, Napoleon never held comparable power'.

On 14th August 1923 Stresemann formed a government on the resignation of Cuno and on 27th September announced the abandonment of passive resistance in the Ruhr. Poincaré had, apparently, won. Stresemann demanded negotiations but Poincaré waited, and kept on waiting. He refused to talk with an unsettled Germany, where monetary depreciation was proceeding at a fantastic rate. On 19th October, a dollar was worth 12,000 million marks; on 1st November 120,000 million and on 20th November – at its most extreme – over four billion. For foreigners, the rates were even worse than in Berlin. History had never known a monetary depreciation like it. At least the promissory notes issued during the French Revolution had preserved a four thousandth part of their face value.

Why did Poincaré shy away from talks? Was it because he was afraid of being accused of making concessions to the Germans? Was he worried about being blamed for upsetting the general peace and unleashing French imperialism? Was he perhaps just hoping that Germany would fall to pieces leaving him to exploit the Rhineland? Whatever his motive, he failed to take advantage of his victory. His incisively legalistic mind did not mix its briefs and had determined on an immediate financial solution. Poincaré did not work intuitively and gave no consideration to a possible longer-term solution. Even when the scale of his action became apparent he was unable to deviate from his original, avowed intention of making Germany pay.

On 23rd November he told the Chamber of the agreement concluded between the Ruhr industrialists and the inter-Allied control mission. After a fierce fight, heavy industry had had to submit to his conditions. But Poincaré's negative attitude soon lost him the benefits of his tenacity and Millerand did not hide the bitterness he felt over his obstinate refusal to come to a decisive understanding with Berlin.

Poincaré discredited

'However powerful the international financiers may be, I have no wish to make them arbiters of our legal rights,' Poincaré remarked. But he was already facing pressure from Great Britain and was becoming increasingly aware of his own country's financial difficulties. On the 13th November 1923 Barthou, president of the Reparations Commission, demanded that a committee of experts meet to examine Germany's capacity for payments, and at the end of the month, Poincaré was forced to accept the 'independent experts' who snatched away the complete freedom of action he had won for himself. On 14th January 1924 the experts who were to draft the Dawes Plan held their first meeting. On 9th April, the month before the French elections which saw the victory of the Left and Poincaré's defeat, they announced their recommendations. They foresaw a reflation of the German economy in preparation for an international loan coinciding with a French withdrawal from the Ruhr. Frenchmen had already come to recognize the failure of Poincaré's policy. It had brought only trouble and expense in its train and effectively demonstrated that reparations could not balance the French budget.

In the spring of 1924 Poincaré had been compelled to accept the Dawes Plan by which Germany was to meet her reparations commitments out of levies on customs, railways, and industry and on 1st September 1924 the plan began to operate with immediate success. Ironically, French occupation of the Ruhr, designed to ensure regular and maintained German reparations payments, provoked widespread passive resistance and sabotage and to French dismay, the final collapse of the mark.

Hungary and the Little Entente

Dr. Alena Gajanova

The First World War had left Hungary in a desperate situation. Military defeat and the subsequent collapse of the Austro-Hungarian monarchy had deprived the Magyars of a very large part of what had once been the Hungarian half of the empire. Hungary had suffered revolution in 1918 and the establishment of a Soviet Republic the following year had coincided with invasions from neighbouring Czechoslovakia and Rumania. When the Republic collapsed a 'trade union government' was formed, to be overthrown a few days later by Stefan Friedrich's putsch which appointed Archduke Josef, a member of the Hungarian branch of the Habsburg family, as head of state. Hungary was faced with the problem of negotiating a peace treaty, yet the Allied Supreme Council refused to recognize the archduke's government and would not treat with it. The country was in a state of economic and political chaos, exacerbated by the activities of the Rumanian army of occupation whose troops terrorized the populace, exacting revenge for the Hungarian requisitions imposed on Rumania during the war. The Allies, particularly Great Britain and the United States, urged their withdrawal in vain. Finally it was decided in Paris to send a special delegate to Hungary to settle the problem of the Rumanian troops and ensure the creation of a representative government capable of holding parliamentary elections and opening peace negotiations with the Allies. Sir George Clerk was accordingly despatched to the country and the result of his efforts was the military dictatorship of Admiral Horthy, who entered Budapest with his troops on 14th November, the day that the Rumanians withdrew.

Nothing now remained of the original Allied plan to introduce democratic rule into Hungary, a plan particularly dear to the American delegation which had cast itself as watchdog of the anti-monarchical forces in the new central Europe. One reason for the failure was the state of Hungary itself, split by Béla Kun's regime into revolutionary and counter-revolutionary camps. After Kun's defeat a right-wing conservative group came to the fore, of which Horthy's army was the most aggressive component. But another factor was Clerk himself, who in addition to the task assigned to him by the Supreme Council was concerned also with the goals of British foreign policy. It was Great Britain's object to gain influence in Hungary as a counterpoise to French influence in the central European area covering Czechoslovakia, Yugoslavia, and Rumania. Admiral Horthy represented the pro-British line in Hungary's foreign policy, and the support he received from Great Britain is quite evident from all the diplomatic correspondence of this period. Indeed it would be fair to say that diplomatic records have rarely revealed such entire confidence in a foreign politician as the British representatives in Hungary, without exception, displayed toward Admiral Horthy.

At the end of November 1919 Horthy appointed as premier Károly Huszár, whose government contained an absolute majority of members of Horthy's own party, the Christian Bloc. This cabinet never lost its aristocratic and clerical colouring. The Social Democrats were given two ministries but resigned before elections were held in view of the terrorism unleashed throughout the country against former supporters of the revolution. Ad hoc courts were set up on an emergency basis and passed sentences of death; a wave of internment and imprisonment swept the land. Such was the background to the Hungarian elections, from which the Christian Bloc emerged completely victorious. The slender democratic forces were pushed into the shadows, the majority of the democratic politicians including Count Károlyi having in any case emigrated after the revolution.

On 1st March 1920 Horthy was elected regent and with army support managed to enlarge his authority beyond generally accepted limits, particularly in respect of the right to dissolve parliament. His authority, in fact, stemmed less from his formal position, as a strong head of state in a country where the system of authoritarian democracy had been legally enshrined, than from his decisive influence over the army of which he was supreme commander.

Hungary had preserved a monarchical form of government. But it was a 'kingdom with no king', for Karl I, former Emperor of Austria and King of Hungary, had been forced by the collapse of the empire to leave the country. (His legal restoration to the Hungarian throne was for the time being out of the question, in view of the opposition of the other successor states, Yugoslavia and Czechoslovakia.)

Disputes had arisen over the choice of a future monarch and the most varied proposals had been made. There were the legitimists led by the Count Julius Andrássy, who maintained that Karl was still their legal king. Others rallied in support of Prince Otto, and many again favoured Archduke Josef or Archduke Albrecht, all young members of the House of Habsburg. A second group favouring union with Rumania included the Transylvanian potentate, Count Stephen Bethlen. Moves were even made towards a unification with Yugoslavia, but the Yugoslav government rejected this idea. Some of the Hungarian royalists thought the best plan would be to secure an English prince for the throne of Hungary, but Westminster was not anxious to be involved to that extent in central European politics. The British view was that the Hungarian throne should be occupied by a member of the Hungarian aristocracy. London s favourite for the purpose was Horthy, and around him a further group was formed which stood for 'free elections to the throne'.

As soon as the Allies had recognised Huszár's government, a Hungarian peace delegation was nominated under the leadership of Count Apponyi. When peace terms were communicated to Hungary, the government started an immediate campaign of vigorous opposition. It took several months of negotiation, accompanied by a great deal of backstairs intrigue, before the Hungarian government was prepared to sign a treaty. It finally did so in the Trianon Palace at Versailles on 4th June 1920. The treaty registered the fact that Hungary, although the successor to the former Hungarian empire, had lost 62·7 per cent of its former territory, for the most part, however, inhabited by non-Hungarian peoples and groups. The lost territory was divided up among Rumania, Czechoslovakia, Yugoslavia, and Austria. The non-Hungarian and largely Slav elements on whom pre-war Hungary had imposed a harsh denationalizing policy seized the opportunity of Austria-Hungary's defeat to transfer their loyalties to the new national states. Some of the lost areas were naturally inhabited partly or wholly by Hungarians and it was to be foreseen that sooner or later Hungary would demand rectification of the frontiers.

Hungary's political demands, however, went much further than this from the very start. Even after signing the Treaty of Trianon the government clung to its aim of 'renewing the empire of St Stephen' with its former frontiers and unleashed an unrestricted propaganda campaign of the bitterest kind against the peace terms. *Nem, nem, soha* – 'No, no, never!' – was the slogan of Hungarian revisionism. On every occasion Hungary made it clear that she would never be reconciled to the treaty.

This attitude on the part of the Horthy regime was, of course, a provocative challenge to those of Hungary's neighbours who had received portions of her former territory. The government was moreover not content with verbal protests. Before the treaty was signed and when Poland with French support was preparing to attack Soviet Russia after boundary negotiations had broken down, Hungary tried to win a revision of the peace terms in return for a promise of military assistance in the war against Russia. Simultaneously she embarked on a policy of *rapprochement* with France, seeking to achieve frontier changes in return for economic concessions to French capital in Hungary. These revisionist efforts by the Hungarians persisted even after the treaty was signed.

During the summer of 1920 the Russo-Polish war reached a critical point. Russian troops had penetrated deep into Polish territory and revolutionary tempers flared up throughout central Europe. The Polish government turned in its distress to the Allies, who sent a special Anglo-French military mission to Poland.

At the same time a search began for forces capable of coming to Poland's aid. Powerful, albeit unofficial, pressure was exerted on Czechoslovakia who, however, declared herself neutral in the Russo-Polish conflict. In actual fact Czechoslovakia was in no position to afford Poland military aid. Public opinion in the country was on the whole far more pro-Russian than pro-Polish. The domestic situation was restless, and revolutionary working-class elements had proclaimed a movement in defence of the Soviets. Nor would the new Czechoslovak army, which was still in the process of formation and inspired by feelings of pacifism rather than bellicosity, have been willing to embark on any military adventure. Austria, a similar case, likewise proclaimed her neutrality.

The Little Entente is born

Czechoslovakia's failure to permit her army be used for counter-revolutionary purposes injured her military reputation in France and alarmed the government. There was, however, greater anxiety in Prague lest Hungary range her fully equipped army alongside that of Poland. Her forces, moreover, were untainted by any pacifist or democratic persuasions, unlike most European troops of the day.

In addition to Czechoslovakia, Yugoslavia and Rumania felt threatened by Hungarian aggressiveness. The three countries accordingly decided on a defensive pact and made their first agreement for mutual aid in face of the danger of Hungarian revisionism. On 14th August 1920 a treaty of alliance was signed in Belgrade between Czechoslovakia and Yugoslavia and on 17th August a protocol with Rumania was signed in Bucharest. A new grouping in central Europe, the so-called Little Entente had taken shape.

Its aim was not only to reinforce the strength of the three states but to create a central European 'Great Power' capable of maintaining the status quo in the area against Hungarian revisionist demands.

Contrary to Allied expectations that the ending of the Russo-Polish war would bring about a period of calm in central Europe a major confrontation between Hungary and the Little Entente took place in the very next year. Czechoslovakia had in fact already begun negotiations with Hungary and the first meeting had taken place in Most nad Litavou between the Czechoslovak foreign minister, Eduard Beneš, and Hungary's prime minister, Count Teleki, and foreign minister, Gratz. But the meeting broke off with the sudden news that the former Habsburg Emperor, Karl I, had just reappeared in Hungary.

The Little Entente countries strongly opposed Karl's bid for a return to the Hungarian throne. Diplomatic relations with Hungary were severed, and Czechoslovakia and Yugoslavia showed readiness to intervene by force. Faced with this pressure, the conference of ambassadors in Paris repeated its objections to any restoration of the Habsburgs; Karl was obliged to leave Hungary and return to Switzerland. In Budapest a change of government took place, Count Teleki being ousted as premier by Count Stephen Bethlen, who was no supporter of the monarchist movement but an outstanding political personality with pro-British leanings. In protesting against Karl's attempt to recover the throne, the Little Entente countries had consistently pointed out the reactionary character of the Horthy regime, the undemocratic nature of Hungarian elections, and the harshness with which the authorities had countered political opposition. It was therefore expected that Bethlen would give at least some appearance of liberalism to the tough methods of the Budapest government. Urged on by the Western powers, Hungary asked to be admitted to the League of Nations. In Budapest this was regarded as a concession of sorts, since formally, at least, it implied some sort of compliance with the peace treaty and the status quo. Most of the legitimists, however, were opposed to it.

On 21st October 1921 Karl I appeared on Hungarian soil once again. He landed by plane at Sopron in the Burgenland, a territory under dispute between Hungary and Austria, where Hungarians had organized a rising the previous month. Rebel troops under monarchist officers were still at large to form the possible basis of a monarchist army.

The Little Entente immediately protested to Budapest, sending notes to the Allies the same day. The Czechoslovak and Yugoslav governments ordered mobilization and Rumania moved some of her troops to the Hungarian frontier.

It soon became clear, however, that

Karl's hopes of recovering the throne rested on too frail a basis even inside Hungary. The government failed to support his campaign. Horthy issued orders banning any transfer of authority to him. He did so in a formal manner under pressure from the Allies, but it was clear that he had no inclination to hand over the leading position in the country which he now occupied so firmly. The Hungarian government was more anxious to use Karl as a pawn in its political game than to see him actually restored to power.

The Western powers were satisfied with Horthy's reaction, but the Little Entente wanted more. It presented Hungary with demands for the abrogation of all claims to the throne by the entire Habsburg family; for the disarming of Hungary under joint surveillance by the Little Entente; for the complete implementation of the peace treaty; and for payment of the cost of mobilization. Czechoslovakia's foreign minister, Beneš, further requested that Karl should be temporarily interned in that country.

The purpose of these demands, drafted by Beneš as the most energetic and diplomatically skilled politician in the three countries, was to shake the Horthy regime from outside in the hope that it would then collapse internally. Beneš hoped for the replacement of that government by a more democratic, liberal, and moderate one with which it would be easier to have dealings. He was also in contact with emigré liberal politicians opposed to Horthy, and lent them his support.

But the Western powers took a different view. In France there existed fairly strong monarchist circles who would have been very pleased to see a Habsburg back on the Hungarian throne. The Little Entente received reports that Karl enjoyed the favour of Marshal Franchet d'Esperey, of the French ambassador in Budapest, Fouchet, and even of the premier and foreign minister, Aristide Briand. Of course, the French government had to fulfil its obligations as an ally of the Little Entente powers and reject Karl's claim officially. More than that, however, it did not propose to do.

Ruling circles in Britain were also opposed to Beneš's demands. They were reluctant to jeopardize the positions of Horthy and Bethlen for fear of causing new trouble in central Europe. London warned Prague against military action and demanded immediate demobilization.

Under this pressure Beneš was forced to withhold his ultimatum to the Budapest government, not daring to act independently against Allied wishes. As a compromise he decided to seek an arrangement by which the Habsburg family were banned from the throne, and this demand was approved by the conference of Allied ambassadors. On 3rd November the Hungarian parliament passed a law abolishing any claim to the throne on the part of Karl I.

The elimination of any Habsburg attempt to regain the throne, however, by no means put an end to the disagreements between Hungary and the Little Entente. Horthy's government continued to regard the peace terms as provisional and determined to use every opportunity of changing them. The revisionist campaign inside Hungary did not cease. The Little Entente, on the other hand, still sought an opportunity to weaken the Hungarian regime. The state of tension thus generated between Hungary and the countries of the Little Entente was to be the principal factor uniting the three partners in years to come.

The anxiety felt about Hungary in central Europe was also due in part to her serious economic and financial position. A currency crisis occurred in Hungary at the beginning of 1923 and the value of the crown fell rapidly. Hungary was bankrupt of foreign currency. The government debt to the central bank rose 31,000 million crowns and the price of goods rocketed. It was generally believed that the country was heading for complete financial breakdown, and that this in turn would weaken the Bethlen regime. The situation gave the Little Entente countries a fresh opportunity to attempt to change Hungary's rulers.

Budapest at this time was badly in need of an international loan, which was practicable only if the burden of reparations was reduced. The basic requirement was that Hungary should be able to use the loan to mend her economy, and at the same time to postpone reparation payments.

Great Britain was especially interested in saving the Hungarian economy in view of the amount of British capital invested in Danube shipping. France also favoured financial aid for Hungary, since she had likewise invested in the country. The Little Entente countries, by contrast, felt that their interests would be harmed by any postponement of Hungary's reparation dues. Yugloslavia and Rumania were direct beneficiaries and so refused to grant a hostile Hungary any relief at the expense of their own income. Czechoslovakia was not a direct recipient, but she sided with her central European allies in the matter. Besides, Beneš believed that the catastrophic situation in Hungary afforded a new chance to exert political pressure on the Budapcst government and perhaps to break its hold.

Great Britain obstructs the Entente
Plans for overthrowing the Horthy regime were hotly discussed in Hungarian opposition circles and, above all, among emigrés. Inside the country there was a group of some thirty to forty Social Democratic and liberal deputies opposed to Bethlen. Outside, the emigrés who still treasured hopes of returning home, saw in their homeland's tottering economy a last chance for political revision and the introduction of liberal democracy. They trusted the Little Entente countries and liberals in the West to take advantage of Hungary's plight to unseat the reactionary Horthy regime.

One group of exiled Hungarian democrats was at this time in Yugoslavia, and had established contact with the Yugoslav foreign minister, Ninčić. Czechoslovakia's foreign minister, Beneš, also assisted the emigrés with passports, personal references, and money; his country would have been happy to see these people return and replace the Bethlen government with a democratic one. A British expert on the region, Robert Seton-Watson, also interested himself in the situation, suggesting to Šeba, the Czechoslovak minister in Yugoslavia, that since Hungary was on the brink of economic collapse the Little Entente should draw up a programme of reforms to put Hungary on her feet again. He declared that he would himself support such a programme. On 1st May two Hungarian emigrés, Count Károlyi and O. Jászi, met Ninčić and asked him to support their own line in the Little Entente. A group of exiles drew up a memorandum offering, in the event of their return to power, the following guarantees: a system of secret elections based on universal franchise would be introduced; all emergency legislation would be repealed; a final decision would be made on the future form of the state, specifically excluding a return of the Habsburg monarchy; there would be complete freedom for political canvassing under the surveillance of an international commission; irregular military formations would be dissolved; and land reform would be speedily carried out.

Emendi, the Rumanian minister in Belgrade, objected to this programme. In Rumanian eyes the Károlyi group was too radical and left-wing, and it was recommended that Horthy and Bethlen should rather be replaced by conservative figures from the pre-war period.

A hard battle over the issue of Hungarian reparations now ensued in the Reparations Commission. To a certain extent France sided with her Little Entente allies. After a brisk altercation with the British delegate a Franco-Little Entente resolution was passed, expressly stating that part of the Hungarian loan must be devoted to liquidating reparation debts. The Little Entente continued to demand further political guarantees aimed at undermining the Horthy regime.

British circles close to the conflict, however, were dissatisfied with the outcome of the negotiations and decided to apply pressure on the Little Entente. Czechoslovakia was the main target. Prague was at this time negotiating for a loan from the London bankers, Barings. The firm's representative, Lord Revelstoke, informed Prague that the loan would not go through unless the Czechoslovak attitude to Hungary changed. When the Czechoslovak minister enquired of the Foreign Office whether Barings were justified in linking British official approval of a loan with the Hungarian reparations question, a message arrived from the British government of which the second part began with the words: 'I have the honour to inform you that Messrs Barings' telegram correctly represents the views of His Majesty's government, which has noted with great regret the attitude of the joint delegate to the Reparations Commission toward the latest proposal for facilitating a loan to Hungary . . .'

Beneš's position was rendered acutely difficult by the British line and once again it was clear that attempts by the Little Entente to disrupt the Horthy regime could only meet with very firm opposition on the part of Great Britain who then went on to threaten the other partner states with a closure of the money market. Negotiations ranging over the entire vexed problem persisted for several months, ending eventually in Hungary's favour. The return of a British Labour government in 1924, which looked with disfavour on the Horthy regime, did not change the situation at all. A delegation from the Hungarian Workers' Party called on the British prime minister, Ramsay MacDonald, to seek his support, but with little success: the new British government was as anxious as its predecessor to forestall further unrest in central Europe but its own position was not strong enough to allow it to interfere with the interests of British financial circles. At this point the Little Entente abandoned hope of getting rid of Horthy.

At the insistence of the Western powers the two central European groupings began negotiations with a view to cooperation, particularly in the economic field. Beneš met Bethlen on behalf of the Little Entente, but talks were never free from an atmosphere of mutual annoyance.

In 1925, a currency scandal in Hungary involving highly-placed personalities, led emigrés to clamour for the overthrow of the military dictatorship and encouraged domestic opposition. But Great Britain predictably intervened again to help Bethlen. This time Czechoslovakia, Yugoslavia, and Rumania contented themselves with a *pro forma* protest, stressing that the Little Entente had no intention of bringing about internal changes in Hungary.

Beneš also used this opportunity, coming as it did when a non-aggression pact was being signed with Germany, to propose a non-aggression pact for central Europe too. But there was little hope of such an agreement being reached. Conflicts within the area were too acute and it proved impossible to resolve them. *(Translation.)*

The Roots of Appeasement

Martin Gilbert

The word 'appeasement' has come to mean the policy of Neville Chamberlain towards Nazi Germany. As a result, much of the anger at Chamberlain's policy has been directed against the concept of appeasement itself. An 'appeaser' is regarded as little worse than a coward; a man who, while neglecting his own defences, cringes and crawls before the threats of others. But appeasement was not invented by Neville Chamberlain; it was a policy with roots deep in the traditions of British foreign relations, and with its moments of triumph which contrast favourably with the more dubious achievement of 'Munich'.

The first use that I can find in recent British history of the term itself comes in 1911, when the Liberal Party was searching for a new policy towards Ireland which would heal the wounds of many centuries of violence and conflict. Churchill, aware of the growing European dangers, feared that a discontented Ireland might lead to British weakness in the diplomatic arena, and suggested to his colleagues that they pursue *'une politique d'apaisement'* towards Ireland. He used the French phrase; and he meant the granting of Ireland's legitimate grievances—construed in a generous fashion—in return for an Irish pledge not to disrupt the internal life of Great Britain. This Irish appeasement was frustrated by the coming of war, and savaged by the repressions of the Easter Rebellion; but it did not die.

The four years of war did more than fill the cemeteries of Europe with the bodies of its young men. It embittered every nation, and inflamed national passions to fever pitch. The whole concept of diplomacy seemed threatened. No nation wanted to sit down quietly with its rivals to ponder and to discuss the issues of the moment.

At the Paris peace conference threats and hypocrisy played as large a role as compromise and conciliation. The defeated nations thought only of revenge when they had regained their strength; the victor nations thought only of repressing, for as long as possible, the aspirations of those whom they had defeated; and the new nations, their territories constructed suddenly and artificially, strove only to hold their gains and to preserve their independence by whatever means possible.

Into this cauldron of suspicion and fear was thrown a quite unexpected extra ingredient—the policy of David Lloyd George. Historians are still unable to agree about the true motives of this remarkable man. Was he a crusader or an infidel, a man of high principle or low cunning? Did he seek to heal the wounds of a shattered continent, or to impose upon it a British dominance which would be deep and lasting? Whatever his motives, there can be no doubt about his policy. He aimed at no less than the reconciliation of the former enemies—France and Germany—and the return to the councils of Europe of the revolutionary outcast—Bolshevik Russia.

It was a member of Lloyd George's government who first put in words the new policy of the prime minister. Writing from the Paris peace conference in June 1919, H.A.L.Fisher, a distinguished Oxford don who had been brought into politics during the war, wrote privately that 'passion still runs too high to get a really enduring settlement now, but that if a Treaty *tel quel* is signed there will be an appeasement, and by degrees readjustments and modifications can be introduced which will give Europe a prospect of stability'. Fisher saw clearly that the alternatives were appeasement or anarchy. But he also realized that the 'readjustments and modifications' would take a long time. Lloyd George lacked the academic temperament. He wished to accelerate the process of reconciliation by his own exertions.

Lloyd George had no hatred of Germany. He had admired, and to a certain extent copied, German social policies before 1914; and he respected the sacrifices which the Germans had made during the war. He was not a hysterical anti-German of the type that used toilet paper with the Kaiser's portrait printed on it. He was also a practical statesman who saw clearly that the alternative to a contented Germany was a Bolshevik Germany. His instinct called for reconciliation with the beaten foe; his political common sense envisaged a German democratic bastion against Bolshevism. But no pro-German policy could be effective without French support. Nor was Lloyd George able, during four years of busy and at times frantic diplomacy, to persuade the French leaders to seek German friendship. Lloyd George saw the future security of Europe in Franco-German co-operation; the French people urged their leaders to provide security by keeping Germany continually weak.

The first failure

The first appeasement was a failure. Lloyd George was unable to persuade the French to act leniently towards Germany during the Paris peace conference. When Lloyd George had urged Clemenceau to make concessions towards Germany the French leader replied caustically that 'if the British are so anxious to appease Germany they should make colonial, naval, or commercial concessions of their own'. Clemenceau thus put his finger upon the flaw in the British position. Lloyd George and his colleagues had no intention of making concessions of their own. They intended to keep all the German colonies which they had conquered during the war. They were determined to destroy Germany's naval power. And they were delighted with the advantages gained by British traders as a result of stripping Germany of all legally obtained commercial concessions in Africa and the Far East. Lloyd George did not want to embark upon an appeasement policy where imperial interests were concerned; he was quite prepared to use the British victory as a unique opportunity to increase the British empire and to enhance Great Britain's commercial interests overseas, both at Germany's expense.

Yet appeasement was not hypocritical. Lloyd George saw nothing unethical in separating Europe from imperial interests. For Great Britain, her empire was a necessity; Europe was a luxury. To preserve imperial power, money could be spent, wars fought, even — in India and Iraq — bombs dropped on recalcitrant tribesmen. But to keep Europe at peace, the reverse method was adopted. Tempers had to be soothed, conflicting interests reconciled and vindic-

tive policies overcome. Thus Lloyd George successfully opposed the high German reparations which France insisted upon. Thus Lloyd George refused to support the French demand to hang the Kaiser.

The post-war appeasement policy was more than a practical attempt to keep Europe docile while Great Britain built up her power elsewhere; it was more than a device to frustrate Bolshevik designs in Europe by bringing French and German interests into harmony. It was also an idealistic concept. It aimed at no less than the 'world without war' of the publicists and visionaries. It was for this reason that appeasement proved so attractive: it seemed to offer more than yet another diplomatic settlement — useful today and outdated tomorrow. In a world shaken by the cruel experience of war, it offered a new hope. Thus, in May 1919, while the Paris peace conference was still in session, the *Manchester Guardian* had informed its readers that 'a wise policy will treat Germany no longer as an enemy to be feared and destroyed, but as a part of the Europe of which we ourselves form an integral part, and which for many a long year will need all our help and all our care to save it from ruin. . . . For us the fundamental question is whether we desire a peace of appeasement or a peace of violence'.

There was nothing necessarily humiliating about a 'peace of appeasement'. As Edmund Burke had written during the War of American Independence: 'The superior power may offer peace with honour and with safety.' In 1920 Great Britain was the superior power. The United States had withdrawn from European affairs to seek security in isolation. Russia had withdrawn to build a new future with Communism. France was weakened by her immense physical and material exertions during the war. And the former Austrian and Turkish empires were broken into fragments. Great Britain alone of the great powers emerged from the war both strong and active. Her policy could be conciliatory without betraying weakness. She could make strong efforts to bring France and Germany together, without seeming to be cringing before any future threats. 'The aim,' Churchill told the Imperial Conference of 1921, 'is to get an appeasement of the fearful hatreds and antagonisms which exist in Europe, and to enable the world to settle down.' It was a noble aim. But it came to nought. France clung tenaciously to her belief that there would be no peace in Europe once Germany was allowed to take her place as an 'equal'. Austen Chamberlain, who became British foreign secretary in 1924, shared this view. He too feared a revived Germany. He did not believe that any gesture of appeasement, however wide, however sincere, would deter the Germans from seeking revenge for the humiliation of defeat.

Lloyd George conducted his search for appeasement at a series of European conferences. He really believed that the force of his arguments – and the power of his personality – would influence French policy. But after four years of active diplomacy he found himself without success. Germany had turned, not towards France, but towards Russia – an ominous foreshadowing of later events. Lloyd George had himself become reconciled to the Bolsheviks, and, to the alarm of those who feared a Bolshevik world-conspiracy, was busy trading with Russia – even buying Russian petrol. He had been unable to prevent France from occupying the Ruhr when Germany fell short of her reparations payments. He had been equally unable to entice the United States back as a mediator on the European scene. Yet alone, Great Britain could not prevail against the French view, or persuade Frenchmen to try the policy of reconciliation. Four years after the Armistice, European tempers were still violent and unpredictable. Nations saw their futures, not in terms of federation, co-operation, or concession, but only from the standpoint of national self-interest, narrowly defined. Such an atmosphere destroyed all Lloyd George's efforts at amelioration.

It was the first Labour government, under Ramsay MacDonald, which carried forward the appeasement policy to a certain high point. MacDonald was not only prime minister – he acted as his own foreign secretary as well. He did not share the violent anti-French feelings of many of his fellow Socialists. He understood French fears of a revived Germany. But he was equally keen to help Germany to shake off the stigma of defeat. It was six years since the Armistice; MacDonald hoped to inaugurate a new era of positive reconciliation. In 1915 he had written of his plans for a post-war policy: 'If German militarism is to be crushed so that it is no longer to be a European menace, Germany must not be given, as an inheritance from this war, the spirit of revenge.' In 1924 MacDonald worked to eliminate that spirit of revenge from European politics; but he was too late. He accelerated the French withdrawal from the Ruhr; he treated the Germans as equals at the conference table; and he spoke eloquently of a Europe freed from hatred. But neither France nor Germany were willing to make more than gestures of amity. The war hatreds had been too severe, the losses too recent, the fears for the future too deep, for fine phrases, deft diplomacy, or practical policies to overcome them.

MacDonald fell from power after nine months. But the Conservatives who followed him seemed equally intent upon reconciling France and Germany. Churchill – who had become chancellor of the exchequer – continued to advocate a British initiative in ending the war mentality in Europe. The new foreign secretary was Austen Chamberlain, who still felt uneasy at too pro-German a policy. When the British ambassador in Berlin suggested that, as a gesture of appeasement, Great Britain should open discussions aimed at guaranteeing Germany's western frontier, Chamberlain replied that 'these overtures are premature'. But in drafting a new Anglo-German commercial treaty the ambassador found an ally in Churchill, and the treaty gave Germany substantial advantages in trade with Great Britain. It was a step on the road to normalization.

By early 1925 it seemed possible that France and Germany might agree to a mutual guarantee of each other's frontiers. Great Britain was the obvious country to sponsor and facilitate such an agreement. The British ambassador in Berlin wrote directly to King George V, urging that if Germany were treated 'with a certain degree of confidence' she would respond by accepting an agreement on frontiers with France. The ambassador filled the King with enthusiasm for an active British intervention; 'Now is a unique, but perhaps only a passing, moment,' the King wrote at once to Austen Chamberlain, 'and one not to be lost to expedite the work of peace.' But Austen

Chamberlain was not the man to be hustled by royal command. Nor did he share the ambassador's belief in the German desire to seek a settlement. 'The Germans,' he replied to the King, 'seem to be singularly obtuse to their own interests and the effect of what they say and do upon French opinion.'

Austen Chamberlain was not a man for diplomatic adventures. He shared the view of his senior officials in the Foreign Office that British security rested, not upon any future rapprochement with Germany, but in a constant and close partnership with France. He did not envisage wide-scale changes in the Treaty of Versailles – as did Lloyd George and Ramsay MacDonald – in order to satisfy German aspirations. He aimed, rather, at trying to show the German people that their new position was a tolerable one. 'As they regain prosperity under it,' he replied to the King, 'they may in time become reconciled to it, and unwilling to put their fortunes again to the desperate hazard of war.' According to the foreign secretary, 'the key to the solution is to be found in allaying French fears'; not, initially, in trying to satisfy German aspirations. Chamberlain suspected that these aspirations might not be as limited as the German government was claiming.

Under Austen Chamberlain's influence British policy edged away from its appeasement enthusiasms. In February 1925 a Foreign Office memorandum was circulated to the cabinet, with Chamberlain's approval. It opposed any British initiative in trying to bring France and Germany together with frontier guarantees. It proposed instead a return to the pre-war policy of Entente Cordiale with France. The Foreign Office believed that whatever pledges Germany made now, she would not hesitate to break them as soon as she felt strong enough to do so. The only possible British policy, argued the Foreign Office, was to be willing to defend France, and to support the French desire for a weak Germany. This was a powerful argument. In both 1870 and 1914 Germany had attacked France; why should nations pretend that a third attack was impossible? Yet such an argument was a body-blow to those who still believed in the possibility of European appeasement sponsored by Great Britain.

Long-term aims

It was to re-establish appeasement as a viable policy that Churchill now entered the cabinet discussions. He disagreed with the Foreign Office view that Great Britain's security lay in supporting France against Germany. He believed that Great Britain's true interest lay in reconciling France and Germany, and being the friend of both rather than the partisan of one. In a secret memorandum – which has never been published before – he pointed out that the only danger of war lay in the quarrel between France and Germany remaining 'unappeased'. Great Britain was deeply involved in this quarrel: 'Though we do not share its hatreds, though we cannot control its occasions, though all our interests and desires are to avoid it, we may irresistibly be drawn in.' It was no use, he argued, to say that Germany was too weak to seek revenge, or France too powerful to feel threatened. The present was, in his view, little more than 'a breathing space, measured by decades'; and Great Britain's problem was 'how to use this breathing space to end the quarrel'. He feared the Chamberlain solution of alliance with France, a solution which would, in his opinion, 'bind one's self and bind one's children to the obligation of fighting a disastrous war, the outbreak of which would occur through the working of forces outside our control'.

Churchill's solution was to offer Germany the hand of reconciliation. He wanted the British government to say to France:

'These are the years in which you have the opportunity of establishing much better relations with Germany, and so rendering a renewal of war less likely. We will do everything in our power to promote these improved relations.

'If at any time you approach a real state of peace with Germany, we would be willing to come in, in order to achieve, consolidate and render unbreakable that peace. . . . We might well be partners in a genuine triple accord between England, France, and Germany. Apart from such a triple accord, we cannot enter into specific obligations towards you.'

Churchill's arguments were supported by several senior cabinet ministers. Chamberlain had to abandon his scheme for an alliance between Great Britain and France alone. He deferred to his colleagues, and accepted the wider concept. After six months of intensive diplomatic activity a treaty was ready. When the German delegates met the 'Allied' statesmen at Locarno in October 1925, it was the first time in which they did not appear as the 'enemy'. Yet the effects of wartime hatreds were not entirely cast off. When the Germans asked to be released from the 'war guilt' clause of the Treaty of Versailles, Austen Chamberlain refused. He did not have the flexibility of mind to grasp the full potentialities of the new atmosphere. When the Germans, encouraged by their new-found status as partners with the old Entente, asked for discussions on their lost colonies, Chamberlain again refused. Yet if he were unwilling to explore the avenues opened up by Locarno, what possibility was there for further appeasement?

The Locarno agreements appeared significant. By them, Germany and France gave mutual pledges not to attack each other. Both agreed not to attack Belgium. Great Britain and Italy both stood as guarantors of these multiple pledges. But these were not as important as they seemed; each signatory knew that it was the spirit, not the wording of the agreements that mattered. Newspaper comment was euphoric; and every statesman, returning home, trumpeted Locarno as a triumph. Chamberlain went so far as to overlook his initial scepticism, and to tell the Commons that the government saw Locarno, 'not as the end of the work of appeasement and reconciliation, but as its beginning'.

Such optimism was not universal. Some left-wing critics viewed the absence of Soviet Russia from the conference table as a serious omission and asked, not without some reason, whether the limitation of guarantees to the western frontier of Germany meant tacit – and indeed overt – approval of any German advances eastwards, towards Russia. Other observers realized that too much violence had fallen upon Europe, too many national hatreds had been stirred up, too fierce a desire for dominance or revenge had entered the souls of nations, for the spirit of peace to be given life through signatures on a piece of paper. Ramsay MacDonald summed up this mood in a private letter which he wrote while negotiations were in progress:

'We can make pacts and agreements . . . which . . . are of very little importance from the point of view of possible causes of war, and which on the outbreak of war would be dealt with by no nation in accordance with agreements. . . .

'The problem of security is mainly psychological . . . it is met only to a very small degree by coming to agreements of a military nature regarding it. It is in fact the dramatic form of a deep-seated suspicion that no country is really safe from the machinations of others.'

Locarno could not dispel these deep-seated suspicions. The idea of peace through treaties did not seem very real to people who had been dragooned into armies in the name of treaties; 'peace in our time' rang as a hollow cry to those whose time had been so savagely cursed by war.

As a practical policy, appeasement had too much 'to contend with to be successful. It was not easy for politicians – far less easy for the man in the street – to accept the idea of a reconciliation with the enemy of less than a decade before. It was even more difficult to think in terms of enabling that enemy to become once more, not only rich and powerful, but, by the iron laws of population, richer and more powerful than any of its neighbours. Yet, as Austen Chamberlain had warned as early as 1919, constructive appeasement, if successful, could only end in one way – with Germany the dominant power in Europe. And who could guarantee that she would then continue to regard as her friend and patron the former foe – Great Britain – who had set her on her feet again?

As a political philosophy, the appeasement of Lloyd George, Ramsay MacDonald, and Winston Churchill, supported by such idealists as the Socialist minister Arthur Henderson and indeed men of all parties, had many admirable facets. It was magnanimous to deal leniently with the fallen foe; it was good business to welcome him as a trading partner; and it was sound security to enlist a Christian state into the assembly of those who feared a Bolshevik crusade. It was common sense to seek an end to war passions, and courageous to try to build a working partnership upon the foundations of such reconciliation. Appeasement was, at its most serious, a fight against a status quo based upon greed, prejudice, and fear. But even its most ardent supporters could not guarantee that however vigorously they were able to strike out at the status quo, they could remove the traumas upon which it was based, or that they could create a new order in which new greeds, new prejudices, and new fears would not be equally active, and even more destructive.

Locarno

V. M. Turok

The Western press, in propaganda developed on a grand scale, depicted the 'spirit of Locarno' as the spirit of peace and reconciliation. One hundred and fifty highly-skilled journalists were present at Locarno. Every day they sent off to their papers enthusiastic odes in honour of the security pact which seemed to mark reconciliation with Germany. The following account, in the *Berliner Tageblatt*, which was repeated in various forms in dozens of newspapers, conveys the atmosphere created at the moment when the conference ended and the agreements were initialled: 'When the delegates arrived in their cars at the Praetorium, they passed through dense crowds . . . When the final signature had been appended . . . the Belgian lawyer Rollin went to the window, opened it and held the pact aloft. Loud cheers and prolonged applause arose from the street . . . Then came speeches of Stresemann, Briand, Chamberlain, Vandervelde, and, finally, Mussolini . . . The conference building was floodlit in red and green. Soon afterwards the delegates left the building. Vigorous shouts of approval, especially directed at the Germans . . . Chamberlain, seated in his car, held a copy of the pact in his hand and received the cheers of the crowd. His wish that this matter should be brought to a successful conclusion on his birthday had been realized.'

The British press congratulated Austen Chamberlain on his success. Officials of the Foreign Office greeted the beaming minister by singing 'For he's a jolly good fellow'. Much later, however, it was revealed that this happiness was alloyed with a considerable dose of scepticism. One of the Foreign Office men of that time recalled that behind the minister's back his colleagues passed round a rather different sort of greeting, in which occurred the lines:
'Good Sir Austen at Locarno
Fell into a heap of guano.'
The writer commented that this made 'a most abominable rhyme but a good prophecy'.

The bulk of the French press rejoiced unrestrainedly. The French journalist Geneviève Tabouis describes in her memoirs the enthusiasm with which she greeted the signing of the security pact: 'I was literally drunk with joy. It seemed too good to be true that Germany, our enemy of yesterday, had actually signed the pact with its eight clauses of reconciliation! From now on, no more fears for the future! No more war! . . . I was not alone in my blind enthusiasm. Everyone in Locarno was jubilant about the pact.'

On her way from Locarno to Paris Madame Tabouis stopped off at Geneva in order to visit her uncle, eighty-year-old Jules Cambon. The veteran diplomat poured cold water on his niece's enthusiasm: 'Can't you see,' he asked, 'that in spite of all those fools at Geneva who are congratulating themselves on Locarno, nothing has been basically altered? . . . If our safety depends on that institution (the League of Nations), then we are indeed badly off.'

The old man was right: there were no grounds for rejoicing. Stresemann's diplomacy had triumphed at Locarno, with British support. And Stresemann had defined the principle governing his foreign policy quite accurately in a speech made to a meeting of his party: 'The tragedy of our foreign policy is that it is no longer backed by the Prussian and German armies on which Frederick the Great was able in his time to rely for support.' Stresemann drew the conclusion that 'in the last resort a policy of force will always be decisive, but if no force is at hand, one can also fight by means of ideas'. Stresemann's ideas were quite simple: blackmailing Germany's Western opponents with the 'Bolshevik Menace', and exploiting the differences between Great Britain and France. Not for the first nor the last time, British and French diplomacy succumbed to these methods.

The illusion of Locarno, that Western Europe had been covered by the armour of a security pact and German expansion diverted to the East, was followed by the appeasement policy and Munich.

The origins of the pact

Among the acute problems in international relations which arose after the war was what was called the problem of security, or of guarantees.

At the same time as the Versailles Treaty was signed, President Wilson, Lloyd George, and Clemenceau signed a treaty guaranteeing military aid to France in the event of an attack by Germany. This treaty was to come into force only after ratification by the parliaments of the three powers concerned, but the American Senate refused to ratify either the Treaty of Versailles or any of the other documents produced by the peace conference. The question of guarantees against the danger from Germany remained one of the main problems of French foreign policy and was frequently the subject of Anglo-French negotiations. In 1925 the British foreign secretary, Austen Chamberlain, tried to exploit the problem of guarantees in order to ensure that future German expansion would be directed eastward. He was supported by the French foreign minister, Aristide Briand.

In February 1925, preliminary talks began between Great Britain, France, and Germany for a security pact. Formally, the initiative for these talks came from the German foreign minister, Gustav Stresemann, on whose instructions the German ambassadors proposed in London and in Paris that talks be started with a view to the conclusion of a 'Rhine Pact'.

These talks, which went on into the autumn of 1925, continued and developed the system of economic and political measures laid down in August 1924 by the Dawes Plan. The Dawes Plan virtually ended Germany's reparation payments, together with supervision of Germany's war production and the German economy as a whole. Enormous American loans made possible a rapid restoration of Germany's economic potential. American and British banks, subsidizing the economic recovery of German imperialism, at the same time facilitated the restoration of Germany as a political factor in Europe.

The conference held at Locarno, in Switzerland, lasted from 5th to 16th October 1925. The participants were the foreign ministers of Great Britain, France, Germany, Belgium, and Italy, joined at the concluding stage by those of Poland and Czechoslovakia. For the first time since Versailles, Germany took part in an international conference on the German question, not as the accused but with the same rights as her former adversaries. The conference agenda was devoted to discussion of a security pact and related questions: the entry of Germany into the League of Nations and the conclusion of arbitration treaties.

The conference proceedings showed the extreme interest taken by the participants, especially Chamberlain, in the 'Bolshevik Menace'. The German delegation made use of this to obtain concessions from the other Western powers in Germany's favour.

One of the most controversial and at the same time most secret questions discussed was the obligations under Article 16 of the League Covenant which Germany would incur by joining the League. (Under Article 16 all member nations undertook to join in common action against any member which made war in violation of the Covenant. If economic sanctions against the offending state failed, joint military action would be taken.) How this question was decided would largely determine the role to be played by Germany in the event of war against the USSR. Stresemann utilized the discussion of it to secure Chamberlain's support of German rearmament.

Stresemann's case was very simple – if Germany was to take part in direct military sanctions against the USSR she would need a large army', and the 100,000-strong Reichswehr was inadequate for this purpose. Consequently, the size of the German army must be increased.

Both during the conference and afterwards, the Western diplomats tried more than once to deny that at Locarno they were engaged in forming an anti-Soviet bloc. When two months after the conference Chicherin, the Soviet commissar for foreign affairs, visited Paris and saw Briand, the latter strove to convince him that the Locarno agreements were not aimed against the USSR.

Especially insistent were the assurances given by the members of the conference that Germany's acceptance of Article 16 of the League Covenant had nothing to do with possible participation by Germany in sanctions against the USSR. According to the Western diplomats the discussion of Article 16 at Locarno was a mere academic exchange of views about abstract hypotheses. In reality the whole discussion was concentrated around one single possibility – war against the Soviet Union. This is reflected in the conference minutes which speak of it quite straightforwardly. Thus, for example, Briand said, addressing the German delegation: 'It is necessary to choose. You cannot have one foot in the League of Nations and, at the same time, the other foot in the camp which is hostile to it . . . Herr Stresemann must know the dangers with which the war that the Soviets might unleash would be fraught, and to what it would lead. Could Germany look on with folded arms at the collapse of Western civilization?'

Freedom for German expansion

Stresemann's line of argument had undoubted success at Locarno. However, neither Great Britain nor France could at that stage consent to the restoration of the German army. This, though, was not what the German diplomats were trying to achieve, realizing as they did that the time for it had not yet come. Stresemann's aim at Locarno consisted in opening the way to revival of Germany's war potential in the immediate future. And this he largely achieved. Regarding the application of Article 16, a compromise was arrived at which fully satisfied the German diplomats. The obligations under Article 16 of each member of the League, and so of Germany, were interpreted as follows: 'to oppose any act of aggression to the extent compatible with its military situation and taking into account its geographical position.'

Thus, the further definition of Germany's military obligations depended in practice on that state's own discretion, having regard to circumstances. German diplomacy retained the possibility of blackmailing the Western powers, while at the same time not renouncing its freedom to continue pursuing the Rapallo policy in relation to the USSR.

On the central issue of the conference, security, a treaty was initialled which provided for reciprocal guarantees by Germany, Belgium, France, Great Britain, and Italy. In addition, arbitration agreements were initialled between Germany and France and between Germany and Belgium, and also treaties of arbitration between Germany and Poland, and Germany and Czechoslovakia. At the same time, Briand signed two further agreements on behalf of France, with Poland and Czechoslovakia, but these were connected with the Locarno Conference only insofar as they were signed at the same place where it was held and were accorded a vague mention in the final communiqué of the conference. Thus, these two French treaties imposed no obligations on the other participants in the conference.

Article 1 of the security pact declared: 'The high contracting parties collectively and severally guarantee, in the manner provided in the following articles, the maintenance of the territorial status quo resulting from the frontiers between Germany and Belgium, and between Germany and France, and the inviolability of the said frontiers as fixed by or in pursuance of the Treaty of Peace signed at Versailles.

Article 2 stated that 'Germany and Belgium, and also Germany and France, mutually undertake that they will in no case attack or invade each other or resort to war against each other.' The only exceptions allowed were 'the exercise of the right of legitimate defence', and 'action in pursuance of Article 16 of the Covenant of the League of Nations'.

Thus the security pact merely confirmed existing frontiers established six years before at Versailles. It laid no new obligations upon Germany.

In this sense, German chancellor Luther was quite realistic in making this comment on the pact when ratification of the Locarno agreements first came up for discussion by the Reichstag: 'Rights and duties under the Versailles Treaty remain unaltered. This does not mean that Germany has made a new formal and solemn reaffirmation of the Versailles Treaty. Nor does it mean that a fresh juridical basis has been created for the operation and continuation of Versailles . . . Nothing has changed in Germany's attitude towards individual clauses of Versailles, either morally, politically or juridically. The Western pact has made only one change: the exercise of rights under the Treaty, themselves unchanged, has been put on a different basis, with the subordination of these rights to a compulsory arbitration procedure. Thereby the ground has been taken away from the policy of sanctions and ultimatums based upon a unilateral interpretation of the Treaty.'

France's international position was undoubtedly worsened as a result of Locarno. The reciprocal undertaking to refrain from invasions meant in practice that France renounced applying military sanctions against Germany in the event of her violating the Versailles Treaty. German diplomacy had achieved that end which Stresemann had in mind when, during the preliminary talks on the convening of the conference, he explained, in a speech to the Reichstag, that 'one of the most important tasks of German foreign policy is to put an end, through a clearly defined settlement, to the unstable condition of Germany's western frontier'. By 'unstable condition' Stresemann meant those provisions of the Versailles Treaty whereby German territory could be occupied in connection with the enforcement of sanctions against a violation of this treaty.

The security pact protected Germany against implementation by France of these provisions of Versailles. Henceforth, anything like the occupation of the Ruhr in 1923 was impossible. Only a concentration of German armed forces in the demilitarized Rhineland zone was equated by Article 2 of the security pact with an attack on France that would give the latter the right to 'legitimate defence'.

In the circumstances of autumn 1925 Germany did not, of course, envisage an attack on France as a task for the immediate future. This was why German diplomacy agreed so easily to the inviolability of French territory. In a letter to the former Crown Prince, dated 7th September 1925 – the eve of Locarno – Stresemann noted: 'The pact also rules out the possibility of any military conflict with France for the recovery of Alsace-Lorraine; this is a renunciation on the part of Germany, but a renunciation of a merely theoretical character, insofar as there is no possibility of a war against France.' Consequently, from the practical standpoint, in this period the British guarantee had no real value for France, and did not hinder the steady strengthening of Germany. In practice, Great Britain was giving a guarantee to Germany against France, depriving the latter of the possibility of independent action against Germany. The Locarno guarantees were bilateral, and it depended on Great Britain's discretion which side would be regarded as the aggressor and so would receive Great Britain's support.

But the most dangerous feature was the situation established by Locarno on Germany's eastern frontiers. Briand did not succeed in obtaining even an appearance of a guarantee of the German-Polish and German-Czechoslovakian frontiers. France's allies, Poland and Czechoslovakia, were allowed no share in the discussion of the security pact, and were not present at the conference meetings. Only after the conference, on the morning of 15th October, had finally approved the text of the security pact, were the representatives of Poland and Czechoslovakia (Skrzyński and Beneš) invited in. When they appeared, Chamberlain told them the conference was now proceeding to examine the texts of the treaties of arbitration between France and Germany and also between Belgium and Germany. The conference, he said, considered it appropriate to invite them to be present at this meeting because they also were to conclude treaties with Germany and the discussion which was to take place that day might be to some extent useful to them.

Thus, even at this penultimate meeting of the conference, the presence of Beneš and Skrzyński was restricted to the purpose of obtaining information. The German delegation had made a point of trying to prevent the foreign ministers of Poland and Czechoslovakia at Locarno, from being invited at all.

Briand's attempts to obtain some sort of guarantee for France's allies proved fruitless. Germany's signature of arbitration treaties with Poland and Czechoslovakia constituted only a formal concession to Briand. Procedure for the settlement of conflicts was laid down on the same lines as in the German-French and German-Belgian arbitration treaties, but an important change was made in the preamble – in Germany's treaties with Poland and Czechoslovakia, unlike those with France and Belgium, there was no reference to the security pact, by which the parties undertook the obligation to maintain the status quo. The German government refused to assume such an obligation as regards Eastern Europe. In this way, Germany fully retained her freedom to put forward territorial claims against Poland and Czechoslovakia. Nor did the British government assume any additional obligations in the event of conflicts between Germany on the one hand and Poland or Czechoslovakia on the other. There was a glaring difference between the way the territorial status quo in the West and that in the East were dealt with —through the guaranteeing of the frontiers between Germany, France, and Belgium, the centre of gravity of future conflicts was shifted to Eastern Europe.

The position of Poland and Czechoslovakia was worsened because France, bound by the security pact, could henceforth intervene in a conflict between Germany and France's allies only within the limits laid down by the League Covenant. The French diplomat and minister Georges Bonnet tells in his memoirs how, on his return from Locarno, Briand explained to the French cabinet his understanding of France's obligations as an ally of Poland and Czechoslovakia: 'It is not at all a question of an alliance like those of former times. We shall not be required to render assistance except within the framework of the Geneva Pact, that is to say, our intervention will never take place in isolation; it will be put into effect only by an action taken jointly by *all* the members of the League.' Munich was already present in embryo in the agreements initialled at Locarno. German diplomacy was victorious. It shook the Versailles system and prepared the conditions for Germany's subsequent expansion, which, ten years later, enabled Hitler to cancel the Locarno agreements, and in violation of both them and the Treaty of Versailles made it possible for him to send his troops into the Rhineland. The French and British reactionaries reaped the bitter fruits of their optimism and their anti-Soviet policy.

A Note on Using these Readings

These two volumes do not provide a comprehensive history of Europe in the years they cover. They do not tell the whole story. Other books exist to do that. Almost all these readings appeared first in the *History of the 20th Century,* a presentation in weekly parts of world history, and they were designed therefore to fit into its overall scheme rather than to say all that might be said about Europe. They were also accompanied there by supporting material both in the form of illustrations and of maps and diagrams covering geographic and statistical material which not only enlarged upon but supplemented the material in these articles. Even without this additional material, though, it is obvious that these articles can be of great use to students and teachers, particularly to students interesting themselves for the first time in recent history. They are deliberately introductory, assuming virtually no previous information. They were written for a large audience willing to be interested in modern history if it was well presented, but not if it was produced in conventional academic trappings, and almost all of them were written by acknowledged experts — sometimes by the world authority — in their fields. All that has been added to this reprinting is the series of brief introductions to each group of articles. These have been written especially for these volumes by members of the BPC editorial staff. They aim to provide a brief sketch of the way in which each section fits into the overall picture of European history in this century. Two further volumes are planned; the fourth will contain an index to the whole set.

To make it easier to move on from these readings, the bibliographical notes which follow have been compiled. They are grouped to correspond to the sections of readings in these two volumes. The student will need also to have access to some general works of reference and atlases, and a section devoted to these comes before the more specialized recommendations. On the whole, it is nearly always the best policy to read specialized books. You may find it convenient to equip yourself with a general account from those in the first section below, to read it once straight through, and then to concentrate on a topic which particularly interests you, following it through the books suggested, some of which will give further suggestions for reading, and referring back to your general account for information about matters alluded to in the more specialized books.

J.M.Roberts

Select Bibliography for Volumes 1 and 2

GENERAL HISTORIES

Derry, T.K. and Knapton, E.J.D., *Europe and the World Since 1914* (Murray, 1967).

Gilbert, Martin, *British History Atlas* (Weidenfeld & Nicolson, 1968).

—*Recent History Atlas* (Weidenfeld & Nicolson, 1966).

Mowat, C.L. (Ed.), *New Cambridge Modern History, Volume 12: The Shifting Balance of World Forces, 1898-1945* (Cambridge University Press, 1968).

Roberts, J.M., *Europe, 1880-1945* (Longmans, 1967).

Thomson, David, *Europe Since Napoleon* (Penguin, 1966).

VOLUME 1

Europe: the world's overlord

Ascherson, N., *The King Incorporated; Leopold II in the Age of Trusts* (Allen & Unwin, 1963).

Bury, J.P.Y., 'International Relations', in *New Cambridge Modern History, Volume 12: The Shifting Balance of World Forces, 1898-1945* (Cambridge University Press, 1968).

Elgood, P.G., *The Transit of Egypt* (Arnold, 1928).

Ensor, R.C.K., *England, 1870-1914* (Oxford University Press, 1936).

Fieldhouse, D.K., *Colonial Empires* (Weidenfeld & Nicolson, 1966).

—*The Theory of Capitalist Imperialism* (Longmans, 1967).

Fraser, L., *India Under Curzon and After* (Heinemann, 1911).

Gifford, P. and Louis, W.R. (Ed.), *Britain and Germany in Africa* (Yale University Press, 1968).

Henderson, W.O., *Studies in German Colonial History* (Frank Cass, 1962).

Hobson, J.A., *Imperialism* (Allen & Unwin, 1938).

Langer, W.L., *The Diplomacy of Imperialism 1890-1902*, 2 volumes (Knopf, 1951).

Magnus, Sir Philip, *Kitchener: Portrait of an Imperialist* (Penguin, 1968).

Seton-Watson, C., *Italy from Liberalism to Fascism, 1870-1928* (Methuen, 1967).

Slade, R., *King Leopold's Congo* (Oxford University Press, 1962).

Russia: defeat and revolution

Fuller, J.F.C., *The Decisive Battles of the Western World, Volume III* (Eyre, 1956).

Harcave, S., *First Blood: the Russian Revolution of 1905* (Bodley Head, 1965).

Pares, B., *The Fall of the Russian Monarchy* (Cape, 1939).

Seton-Watson, H., *Decline of Imperial Russia* (Methuen, 1964).

Wolfe, B.D., *Three Who Made a Revolution* (Penguin, 1966).

Germany stirs

Anderson, E., *First Moroccan Crisis* (University of Chicago Press, 1930).

Holborn, H., *A History of Modern Germany, Volume III* (Eyre & Spottiswoode, 1965).

Ramm, Agatha, *Germany 1789-1918: A Political History* (Methuen, 1967).

Schorske, C., *German Social Democracy 1905-17* (Wiley, 1965).

Stolper, G., *German Economy 1870 to the Present* (Weidenfeld & Nicolson, 1967).

Woodward, E.L., *Great Britain and the German Navy* (Frank Cass, 1964).

Britain and France

Beloff, Max, *Imperial Sunset* (Methuen, 1969).

Chapman, G., *The Dreyfus Case: a Reassessment* (Rupert Hart-Davis, 1955).

Cross, C., *The Liberals in Power, 1905-14* (Barrie & Rockliff & Pall Mall, 1963).

Dangerfield, George, *The Strange Death of Liberal England* (MacGibbon & Kee, 1966).

Fergusson, Sir James, *The Curragh Incident* (Faber, 1964).

Fulford, R., *Votes for Women* (Faber, 1957).

Jenkins, R., *Asquith* (Fontana, 1967).

Johnson, D., *France and the Dreyfus Affair* (Blandford, 1968).

Monger, G.W., *The End of Isolation: British Foreign Policy, 1900-07* (Eds. Hinsley, F.H. & Clark, G.K.) (Nelson, 1963).

Pankhurst, E., *My Own Story* (Nash, 1914).

Thomas, D., *Democracy in France since 1870* (Oxford University Press, 1964).

New forces in society
Braunthal, J., *History of the International, 1914-43* (Nelson, 1967).
Caute, D., *The Left in Europe* (Weidenfeld & Nicolson, 1966).
Cole, G.D.H., *A History of Socialist Thought*, 5 volumes (Macmillan, 1953-60).
Curie, E., *Marie Curie* (Heinemann, 1938).
Friedlaender, H.E. and Oser, J., *Economic History of Modern Europe* (Prentice-Hall, 1953).
Goldberg, H., *The Life of Jean Jaurès* (University of Wisconsin Press, 1962).
Joll, J., *The Anarchists* (Eyre, 1964).
— *The Second International 1889-1915* (Weidenfeld & Nicolson, 1955).
Jones, E., *The Life and Work of Sigmund Freud* (Pelican, 1967).
Nettl, J.P., *Rosa Luxemburg* (Oxford University Press, 1966).
Nevins, A., *Ford: the Times, the Man, the Company* (Scribner's, 1954).
Rostow, W.W., *The Stages of Economic Growth* (Cambridge University Press, 1960).
Shub, D., *Lenin: A Biography* (Penguin, 1966).
Woodcock, George, *Anarchism* (Pelican, 1963).

Shadow over the Balkans
Dakin, D., *The Greek Struggle in Macedonia, 1897-1913* (Zeno, 1968).
Macartney, C.A., *The Habsburg Empire, 1790-1918* (Weidenfeld & Nicolson, 1969).
May, A.J., *The Habsburg Monarchy, 1867-1914* (Oxford University Press, 1951).
Ramsaur, E.E., *The Young Turks* (Princeton University Press, 1957).
Schmitt, B.E., *The Annexation of Bosnia 1908-1909* (Cambridge University Press, 1937).
Taylor, A.J.P., *The Habsburg Monarchy 1809-1918* (Peregrine, 1964).
West, R., *Black Lamb, Grey Falcon* (Macmillan, 1968).
Wickham Steed, H., *The Habsburg Monarchy* (Constable, 1913).

Europe before the storm
Barlow, I.C., *The Agadir Crisis* (University of North Carolina Press, 1940).
Brenan, G., *The Spanish Labyrinth* (Cambridge University Press, 1950).
Carr, Raymond, *Spain, 1808-1939* (Oxford University Press, 1966).
Derry, T.K., *A Short History of Norway* (Allen & Unwin, 1957).
Fergusson, Sir James, *The Curragh Incident* (Faber, 1964).
Salomone, A.W., *Italian Democracy in the Making. The Political Scene in the Giolittian Era* (University of Pennsylvania Press, 1945).
Stewart, A.T.Q., *The Ulster Crisis* (Faber, 1967).

The outbreak of war
Albertini, L., *The Origins of the War of 1914*, 3 volumes, ed. and trs. by Massey, I. (Oxford University Press, 1967).
Churchill, W.S., *The World Crisis 1911-18* (Thornton Butterworth, 1923).
Clarke, I.F., *Voices Prophesying War, 1763-1984* (Oxford University Press, 1966).
Fischer, F., *Germany's Aims in the First World War* (Chatto & Windus, 1967).
Geiss, I. (Ed.), *July 1914: The Outbreak of the First World War: Selected Documents* (Batsford, 1967).
Schmitt, B.E., *Origins of the First World War* (Historical Association, 1958).
— *Triple Alliance and Triple Entente* (H. Holt & Co., 1934).
Steiner, Z., *The Foreign Office and Foreign Policy, 1898-1914* (Cambridge University Press, 1970).
Wolff, T., *The Eve of 1914* (Gollancz, 1935).

VOLUME 2

The opening moves
Adams, J.C., *Flight in Winter* (Princeton University Press, 1942).
Blond, G., *The Marne*, trs. Hart, H.E. (Macdonald, 1965).
Golovin, N.N., *The Russian Army in the World War* (Yale University Press, 1931).
Horne, Alistair, *The Price of Glory* (Macmillan, 1962).
Palmer, Alan, *The Gardeners of Salonika* (Deutsch, 1965).
Ritter, G., *The Schlieffen Plan* (Riband, 1966).
Thayer, J.A., *Italy and the Great War* (University of Wisconsin Press, 1964).

Central Powers ascendant
Churchill, W.S., *The World Crisis, 1911-18* (Thornton Butterworth, 1923).
Clark, Alan, *The Donkeys* (Mayflower, 1967).
Falls, C., *Military Operations: Macedonia, Volume I* (Macmillan, 1933).
James, R. Rhodes, *Gallipoli* (Batsford, 1965).
Liddell Hart, Sir Basil, *The War in Outline, 1914-18* (Faber, 1936).

Attrition
Farrar-Hockley, A.H., *The Somme* (Pan, 1966).
Golovin, N.N., *The Russian Army in the World War* (Yale University Press, 1931).
Horne, Alistair, *The Price of Glory* (Macmillan, 1962).
— *Death of a Generation* (Macdonald Unit 75, 1971).
Marwick, Arthur, *The Deluge* (Bodley Head, 1965).
Cambridge History of the British Empire (Cambridge University Press, 1929).

The war at sea

Birnbaum, K.E., *Peace Moves and U-Boat Warfare* (Almqvist & Wiksell, 1958).

Consett, M.W.W.P., *The Triumph of Unarmed Forces* (Williams & Norgate, 1923).

Gibson, R.H. and Prendergast, M., *The German Submarine War 1914-1918* (Constable, 1931).

Hase, G.O., *Kiel and Jutland* (Skeffington, 1921).

Hurd, Sir A., *The Merchant Navy* (Murray, 1924).

Jellicoe, Earl, *The Submarine Peril* (Cassell, 1934).

Macintyre, D., *Jutland* (Evans Bros., 1957).

Russia's collapse

Chamberlin, W.H., *The Russian Revolution* (Macmillan, 1935).

Deutscher, I., *The Prophet Armed* (Oxford University Press, 1954).

Florinsky, M., *The End of the Russian Empire* (Yale University Press, 1931).

Fueloep-Miller, R., *Rasputin, the Holy Devil* (G.P.Putnam's Sons, 1928).

Katkov, George, *Russia 1917, the February Revolution* (Longmans, 1967).

Kerensky, A.F. and Browder, R.P. (Eds.), *The Russian Provisional Government 1917* (Oxford University Press, 1961).

1917: The Allies' worst year

Blake, Robert (Ed.), *The Private Papers of Douglas Haig 1914-1919* (1952).

Hemingway, Ernest, *A Farewell to Arms* (Cape, 1929).

Seth, Ronald, *Caporetto – The Scapegoat Battle* (Macdonald, 1965).

Watt, Richard M., *Dare Call It Treason* (Chatto & Windus, 1964).

Williams, John H., *Mutiny 1917* (Heinemann, 1962).

Bolshevik Revolution

Carr, E.H., *The Bolshevik Revolution* (Pelican, 1966).

Kennan, G., *Russia Leaves the War* (Faber, 1956).

Trotsky, Leon, *The Russian Revolution* (Labour Literature Department, 1933).

Warth, R.D., *The Allies and the Russian Revolution* (Duke University Press, 1954).

Wheeler-Bennett, J.W., *Brest-Litovsk. The Forgotten Peace, March 1918* (Macmillan, 1938).

Wolfe, B., *Three Who Made a Revolution* (Penguin, 1966).

The beginning of the end

Chambers, F.P., *The War Behind the War, 1914-1918* (Faber, 1939).

Clemenceau, G.E.B., *Grandeur and Misery of Victory* (Harrap, 1930).

Fontaine, Arthur, *French Industry During the War* (New Haven, 1926).

Grebler, L. and Winkler, W., *The Cost of the War to Germany and Austria-Hungary* (Yale University Press, 1940).

Link, C., *Wilson* (Princeton University Press, 1947).

Marwick, A., *The Deluge* (Bodley Head, 1965).

Nicolson, H., *Peacemaking 1919* (Methuen, 1965).

Ryder, A.J., *The German Revolution, 1918-1919* (Routledge & Kegan Paul, 1959).

Schorske, C.E., *German Social Democracy 1905-1917* (Wiley, 1965).

Spears, Sir Edward, *Prelude to Victory* (Cape, 1939).

Tschuppik, Karl, *Ludendorff: the Tragedy of a Specialist* (Allen & Unwin, 1932).

The end

Burdick, C.B. and Lutz, R.H., *The Political Institutions of the German Revolution, 1918-1919* (Praeger, 1963).

Falls, Cyril, *Armageddon 1918* (Weidenfeld & Nicolson, 1964).

Liddell Hart, Sir Basil, *Foch, the Man of Orleans* (Eyre & Spottiswoode, 1931).

Palmer, Alan, *The Gardeners of Salonika* (Deutsch, 1965).

Ryder, A.J., *The German Revolution, 1918-1919* (Routledge & Kegan Paul, 1959).

Wheeler-Bennett, Sir John, *Hindenburg, the Wooden Titan* (Macmillan, 1967).

Zeman, Z.A.B., *The Break-up of the Habsburg Empire 1914-1918* (Oxford University Press, 1961).

The settlement

Cross, Colin, *Philip Snowden* (Barrie & Rockliff, 1966).

Mayer, A.J., *The Politics and Diplomacy of Peacemaking* (Weidenfeld & Nicolson, 1968).

Walters, F.P., *A History of the League of Nations* (Oxford University Press, 1960).

Survival of Bolshevik Russia

Carr, E.H., *The Bolshevik Revolution, 1917-1923* (Macmillan, 1950-53).

Deutscher, Isaac, *The Prophet Armed: Trotsky, 1879-1921* (Oxford University Press, 1954).

Serge, V., *Memoirs of a Revolutionary* (Oxford University Press, 1967).

Left and Right in Germany and Italy

Carsten, F.L., *The Reichswehr and Politics, 1918-33* (Oxford University Press, 1966).

Eyck, Erich, *A History of the Weimar Republic* (Harvard University Press, 1962).

Finer, Hermann, *Mussolini's Italy* (Cassell, 1964).

Towards stability

Gilbert, Martin, *The Roots of Appeasement* (Weidenfeld & Nicolson, 1967).

Kochan, Lionel, *Russia and the Weimar Republic* (Bowes, 1954).

Macartney, C.A. and Palmer, A., *Independent Eastern Europe* (Macmillan, 1961).

Biographical Notes on Contributors to Volumes 1 and 2

Roger Anstey is Professor of Modern History at the University of Kent. His books include *Britain and the Congo in the 19th Century*, and *King Leopold's Legacy: the Congo Under Belgian Rule, 1908-60*.

Glen Barclay, Reader in History at Queensland University, is the author of books on the British Commonwealth and Latin American diplomacy.

Maurice Baumont is Honorary Professor of Contemporary History at the Sorbonne. He is the author of *La fallité de la paix*.

Brian Bond is Lecturer in War Studies at King's College, University of London, and author of *Victorian Military Campaigns*.

K.D.Bracher, Professor of Political Science and Contemporary History at Bonn University, is President of the German Political Science Association. His books *Conscience in Revolt* (with A.Leber and W.Brandt) and *The Foreign Policy of the Federal Republic of Germany* have been published in English.

J.F.N.Bradley is Lecturer in International Politics at the University of Manchester. He is the author of *Allied Intervention in Russia* and *La Légion tchécoslovaque en Russie*, and co-author of *Czechoslovakia, Past and Present*.

Hugh Brogan is a Fellow of St John's College, Cambridge, and Assistant Lecturer in American History at Cambridge University.

Raymond Carr is Warden of St Antony's College, Oxford, and Professor of Latin American History at Oxford University. He is the author of *Spain 1808-1937*.

Alan Clark is a military historian. His publications include *The Fall of Crete, Barbarossa: the Russian-German Conflict 1941-45*, and *Suicide of the Empires*.

Colin Cross, a member of the staff of the London *Observer*, has written widely on 20th-century political history. His books include *The Fascists in Britain, The Liberals in Power 1905-14*, and *Philip Snowden*.

Douglas Dakin, Professor of History at Birkbeck College, University of London, is Editor of the first series of *Documents of British Foreign Policy, 1919-1939*. Among his publications are *British and American Philhellenes during the Greek War of Independence 1831-1833*, and *The Greek Struggle in Macedonia*.

Vladimir Dedijer is an Honorary Fellow of Manchester University and a full member of the Serbian Academy of Sciences. Among his publications are *Yugoslav-Albanian Relations, Tito*, and *The Road to Sarajevo*.

T.K.Derry is the author of the official history of the Second World War campaign in Norway, and joint author of *The European World* and *The World since 1914*.

John Erickson is Professor of Politics at the University of Edinburgh. His works include *The Soviet High Command, 1918-1941* and *Pan-slavism*.

Christopher Falkus was Editor of *The History of the 20th Century* and of *The History of the English Speaking Peoples* until 1970. He is now Director of the Art and Illustrated Book Division of Weidenfeld and Nicolson.

Malcolm Falkus is Lecturer in Economic History at the London School of Economics, University of London.

David Floyd is the special correspondent on Communist affairs for the London *Daily Telegraph*. He is the author of *Russia in Revolt*.

Alena Gajanova is a member of the Historical Institute of the Czechoslovak Academy of Sciences where she specializes in the history of Central Europe.

Imanuel Geiss is a Research Fellow of the

Deutsche Forschungsgemeinschaft. His publications include *Der polnische Grenzstreifen 1914-1918* and *July 1914, the Outbreak of the First World War*.

Martin Gilbert is a Fellow of Merton College, Oxford. He is author of *The Roots of Appeasement, Recent History Atlas*, and *The European Powers 1900-45*, and has been appointed official biographer of Sir·Winston Churchill.

Y.N.Gorodetsky is an authority on the Soviet period of Russian history. Among his publications are *The Development of the Revolutionary Crisis in Russia* and *The Birth of the Soviet State*.

Alexander Grunt is a senior member of the staff of the Institute of History in Moscow. His chief works are a two-volume *History of Russia in the Epoch of Imperialism* (written in conjunction with V.N.Firstova) and *The Victory of the October Revolution in Moscow*.

Alistair Horne is a foreign correspondent for the London *Daily Telegraph*. He is the author of *The Fall of Paris, The Price of Glory*, and *Death of a Generation*.

Robert Rhodes James, a Fellow of All Souls College, Oxford, is Director of the Institute for the Study of International Organization at the University of Sussex. Among his publications are *Lord Randolph Churchill* and *Rosebery*.

Douglas Johnson is Professor of French History at the University of London. He is the author of *Guizot* and *France and the Dreyfus Affair*.

James Joll is Stevenson Professor of International History at the London School of Economics, University of London. His published works include *The Second International, Intellectuals in Politics*, and *The Anarchists*.

George Katkov is a Fellow of St Antony's College, Oxford, and Lecturer in Soviet Economy and Institutions at Oxford University. He is the author of *Russia 1917: the February Revolution*.

R.Kedward is Lecturer in European History at the University of Sussex. He is the author of *The Dreyfus Affair, Fascism in Western Europe*, and *The Anarchists*.

Georges Lefranc was formally a Professor at the École Internationale in Geneva. In 1932 he became Director of the Institut Supérieur Ouvrier. His works include *Une histoire du travail et des travailleurs* and *Une histoire des doctrines sociales dans l'Europe contemporaine*.

G.H.Le May was elected Senior Research Fellow of Worcester College, Oxford, in 1967 and is now Tutor in Politics. He has published *British Supremacy in South Africa, 1899-1907* and *Black and White in South Africa*.

S.V.Lipitsky, a Colonel in the Russian army, is an Assistant Professor at the M.V. Frunze Military Academy.

Michael Llewellyn-Smith, a member of St Antony's College, Oxford, is an authority on modern Greek politics. He is the author of *The Great Island—A Study of Crete*.

Trevor Lloyd is an Associate Professor of History at the University of Toronto. His publications include *The General Election of 1880, England 1906-1965, Canada in World Affairs 1957-59*, and *Suffragettes International*.

Brigadier Stephen Longrigg, who was Visiting Professor at Columbia University in 1966, is a specialist in Middle Eastern politics and history. His books include *Four Centuries of Modern Iraq, Oil in the Middle East*, and *Syria and Lebanon under French Mandate*.

Adrian Lyttleton, an authority on the Fascist regime in Italy, is a Fellow of St Antony's College, Oxford.

Captain Donald Macintyre specializes in naval history and is the author of *Jutland*.

John Man was Deputy-Editor of *The History of the 20th Century* until 1969 and is now on the staff of Time-Life International.

John Marlowe is an authority on the modern history of the Middle East. His publications include *Arab Nationalism and British Imperialism* and *The Persian Gulf in the Twentieth Century*.

Arthur Marwick is Professor of History at the Open University. Among his publications are *The Deluge: British Society and the First World War* and *Britain in the Century of Total War*.

R.B.McCallum was Master of Pembroke College, Oxford, until 1967. His publications include *The Life of Asquith, The British General Election of 1945*, and *The Liberal Party from Earl Grey to Asquith*.

W.N.Medlicott, who is now retired, was Stevenson Professor of International History at the London School of Economics, University of London. His books include *Bismarck and Modern Germany* and *Contemporary England*.

Roger Morgan holds a senior research appointment at the Royal Institute of International

Affairs. Among his publications are *The German Social Democrats and the First International* and *Modern Germany*.

Major-General J.L.Moulton was Chief of Amphibious Warfare during the Second World War. He is the author of *Haste to the Battle, Defence in a Changing World* and *The Norwegian Campaign of 1940*.

The late C.L.Mowat was Professor of History at the University College of North Wales, Bangor, and Editor of the revised edition of the *New Cambridge Modern History*, Volume XII. He is the author of *Britain Between the Wars, 1918-1940*.

The late J.P.Nettl was Reader in Politics at the University of Leeds and Professor of Sociology and Political Science at the University of Pennsylvania. His works include *Rosa Luxemburg, Political Mobilization*, and *The Soviet Achievement, 1917-1967*.

A.J.Nicholls is a Fellow of St Antony's College, Oxford. He is the author of *The Weimar Republic* and *The Rise of Hitler*.

Alan Palmer, Senior History Master at Highgate School, London, is the author of *Napoleon in Russia, The Gardeners of Salonica, Dictionary of Modern History 1789-1945*, and (with C.A. Macartney) *Independent Eastern Europe: A History*.

Barrie Pitt, who was Editor of *The History of the First World War* and *The History of the Second World War,* is an authority on military history. His publications include *Revenge at Sea* and *1918 — The Last Act*.

Hartmut Pogge von Strandmann is a Lecturer in History at the University of Sussex. He is the author of a study of Germany before the First World War and edited the Rathenau Diaries.

J.M.Roberts, the General Editor of this series, is a Fellow and Tutor in Modern History at Merton College, Oxford. He is the author of *Europe, 1880-1945* and Joint-Editor of the *English Historical Review*.

Captain S.W.Roskill is a Fellow of Churchill College, Cambridge. His publications include *The War at Sea* (official history), *The Navy at War,* and *The Art of Leadership*.

Vice-Admiral Friedrich Ruge, who served in the German navy in both world wars, is a Professor at the University of Tubingen. Among his books are *Der Seekrieg, 1939-45* and *Seemacht und Sicherheit*.

Louis Saurel is a specialist in French colonial history. His publications include *Robespierre, La guerre d'Indochine*, and *Les camps de la mort*.

The late Bernadotte Schmitt was an Honorary Fellow of Merton College, Oxford, and Andrew MacLeish Distinguished Professor Emeritus of Modern History at the University of Chicago. Among his best-known works are *The Coming of the War, Triple Alliance and Triple Entente,* and *The Origins of the First World War*.

Ronald Seth is an authority on naval and military history. His publications include *Stalingrad — Point of No Return* and *Caporetto — The Scapegoat Battle*.

Hugh Seton-Watson is Professor of Russian History at the School of Slavonic and East European Studies, University of London. Among his works are *Eastern Europe Between the Wars, The Decline of Imperial Russia,* and *Neither War Nor Peace*.

Maurice Shock, Fellow and Tutor in Politics at University College, Oxford, is an authority on modern British political history.

Wolfgang Steglich is a Lecturer in Modern and Contemporary History in the Philosophy Faculty of the University of Freiburg.

A.J.P.Taylor is a Fellow of Magdalen College, Oxford, and Director of the Beaverbrook Library. His books include *Bismarck, The Origins of the Second World War, English History, 1914-1945* (Volume XV of *The Oxford History of England)*, and *War by Time-Table*.

Marcel Thomas is Keeper of Manuscripts at the Bibliothèque Nationale in Paris. He is the author of *Le procès de Marie Stuart, L'affaire du 'Bounty',* and *L'affaire sans Dreyfus*.

V.V.Turok is a Senior' Research Fellow of the Institute of Slavonic Studies, part of the Soviet Academy of Sciences.

Jaroslav Valenta is head of research in the inter-war period at the Czechoslovak Academy of Sciences, Prague.

Brunello Vigezzi, Professor of Political Studies at Milan University, is the editor of *Conversazione della guerra* and author of *L'Italia di fronte alla Prima Guerra Mondiale* (1°Volume, *L'Italia neutrale)*.

Francis Paul Waters is an Honorary Fellow of University College, Oxford.

C.J.H.Watson is a Research Fellow at Merton

College, Oxford, and has published numerous papers on the history of science and technology.

D.C.Watt is Reader in International History at the London School of Economics, University of London. In 1962 he was appointed Editor of the *Survey of International Affairs*.

J.N.Westwood is Senior Lecturer in Russian History at Sydney University. He is the author of *Russia, 1917-1964*.

Elizabeth Wiskemann is an authority on modern international affairs. Her publications include *The Rome-Berlin Axis* and *Europe of the Dictators*.

S.J. Woolf is Reader in Italian History at the University of Reading and Director of the university's Centre for the Advanced Study of Italian Society. He is the author of *Studi sulla nobilita piemontese* and *Italian Public Enterprise*.

J.R.C.Wright is Tutor in Politics at Christ Church, Oxford.

Brigadier Peter Young is Head of the History Department at the Royal Military Academy, Sandhurst. His books include *The British Army, 1642-1970* and *The Israeli Campaign, 1967*.

Z.A.B.Zeman is Lecturer in History at the University of St Andrews. His publications include *The Breakup of the Habsburg Empire, 1914-1918, The Revolution in Russia, 1915-1918*, and *Twilight of the Habsburgs*.